Forms of marketing evolve and change. The dry-goods vendor of the 1870s becomes the Fuller Brush man or Avon lady of the twentieth century. Product identification—whether it be the zoot suiter of the 1940s projecting his irresistible image or the architectural reconstitution of a coffee pot—is an ever present facet of marketing. The anthropomorphised loaf of bread on the billboard becomes today's Pillsbury Doughboy.

The Stockmarket

United Press International

Culver Pictures

DRAMATIC EDSEL STYLING is here to stay
—bringing new distinction to American motoring

In one short year, the fresh and original individuality of Edsel styling has become a familiar part of everyday American life. Today, everyone recognizes the distinctive Edsel. And everyone who's driven an Edsel knows that Edsel *features* are out in front, too. Exclusive Teletouch Drive that lets you shift by a touch at the steering-wheel hub, Edsel's high-economy engines, new self-adjusting brakes and comfort-shaped contour seats are the biggest advances in years. Why not enjoy all these wonderful features—and drive the car with the advanced design—right now? Especially since there's less than fifty dollars difference between the magnificent new Edsel and V-8's in the Low-Priced Three!* See your Edsel Dealer about it this week.

E D S E L   D I V I S I O N   •   F O R D   M O T O R   C O M P A N Y

Less than fifty dollars difference between Edsel and V-8's in the Low-Priced Three *Based on comparison of manufacturers' suggested retail delivered prices.*

USED CARS

BUICK Roadmaster '56 PS, brks, windows, seats, air, Auto. 27,000 mi. $1,900 firm 276-8527.

EDSEL '59, My Mistake, Your Gain. Edsel Ranger. Very solid, only 11,000 miles. Will sell very cheap. Make offer over $700.00. Call after 5 p.m. 271-1318.

FORD '51 Club Cpe, 6 cyl. w/overdrive $800. 484-2379.

FORD '56 Pickup, low mi, P./pty. 281-5681.

CHEVY. '49 Coupe, good cond. Lots of extras $795.00. 826-4454.

CHEVY '55, Cameo Carrier PU, xlnt, see to appreciate $1200. Pr/pty. 528-66

'52 MG TD . . . .
'55 MG TS . . . .
These are restored classics & represent an excel. investment.
GARTON BRITISH - 743-6601

SMITH & MARSEE
Vintage Motor Car Sales
'36 MGPB xlnt (KXS156)
'55 MGTF, restored (526JWS)
'55 MGTF (basket) (842)
'30 Mod A cpe restored xlnt (234NLE)
'36 Ford 4-dr dlx unrest (HVE880)
'66 Mustang GT loaded (WBU114)
EDSELS—Villager '59 $2,500 (PDG457)

1927 BUGATTI boat tail speedster replica. VW powered, canary yellow $4900 firm (13382) 223-8182.

Our Classic car paint div is now
Ye Olde Exec. Motorcar Co.
Open

United Pictures International

The sheer staying power of a bottle of pop through decades of repetitious product identification contrasts with the automotive giant that produced a quaint antique and with nature's orange, which remains for an eternity.

Projection of the personal image, whether positive or negative, enters the marketplace in the form of philosophical renditions of themes ranging from spiritual recovery to consumer fraud. Which of these, one might ask, does a necktie on a German Shepherd represent?

United Press International

Black Star

From personalized service to
impersonal display, from corner
grocery to sprawling supermarket
—marketing extremes are admirably adapted to the nature of the
times and of the consumer. Even
body and soul are marketed, advertisements for them sometimes
sharing the same streets, the
same billboards.

arketing by the government—to the people, by the people, for the people—may be little noted, largely ignored. Consumer appeals range from the fatherly demands of our historical Uncle Sam to the inspiring image of human-kind standing utterly alone on an extra-terrestrial surface.

Chiat/Day
vs.
Politics

Since things are now quiet in political advertising, it's a good time to slip in a public announcement of what has been a private policy: Chiat/Day won't work on political advertising accounts.

It's been our observation that on the polar extremes, political advertising can either tell the truth and lose or lie and win. And there's not much satisfaction to be gleaned anywhere in between.

In line with our viewpoint, we've sent a letter to the Federal Trade Commission suggesting that they keep careful record of all advertised political campaign promises for comparison against performance in office. It seems to us that if the FTC is really intent on punishing false and misleading advertisers, they ought to go after the worst offenders first.

For our money, a liar in elective office is one hell of a lot more dangerous to the public than Wonder Bread's nutritional claims.

U.S. Navy

Our College of Nuclear Engineering.
The Navy

FIND YOURSELF IN THE AIR FORCE.

SCOTT, IRWIN & WORDEN DID.

Now the Air Force guarantees you a choice of jobs before you enlist. For more information, call 800-631-1972 toll free. (*In New Jersey call 800-962-2803.)

Chiat/Day

U.S. Air Force

From the bazaar to the bizarre, the marketplace attracts the consumer through the simple display of goods or through the powerful magnetism of sophisticated shopping centers. The consumer's attention, once gained, may be maintained by constant messages of marketing issuing forth from the skies above or the earth below. On billboards and on blimps, the messages of marketing range from well-known trademarks to pet rocks to golden locks.

TRADE   MARK ®

MARKET

ING PRINCIPLES

The Management Process
Second Edition

Ben M. Enis
University of Houston

Black Star

Goodyear Publishing Company, Inc.
Santa Monica, California 90401

Library of Congress Cataloging in Publication Data

Enis, Ben M
  Marketing principles: the management process.

  Includes bibliographies and indexes.
  1. Marketing management. I. Title.
HF5415.13.E54   1977   658.8   76-19703
ISBN 0-87620-567-8

Library of Congress Catalog Card Number: 76-19703
ISBN: 0-87620-567-8
Y: 5678-1

Current Printing (last number): 10 9 8 7 6 5 4 3

Printed in the United States of America

Design: Don McQuiston

To my son, Trey

Contents

Preface

Marketing activities are engaged in by everyone, every day. This book focuses on the management of these activities. Its purpose is to introduce, organize, and summarize the fundamentals of marketing management.

This is a basic book. It is neither a scholarly tome nor a manual for marketing practitioners. The scholar may deplore the minimal use of footnotes, the combining and simplifying of ideas, and so on; the practitioner may say the book is too abstract—"I bet this guy never made a cold sales call." Well, I have written a couple of scholarly tomes, and have made many sales calls (sold a few, too). But the purpose of this book is more fundamental. In its organization, selection of material, and illustrations, I believe that it can provide the foundation for understanding marketing management and for assimilating and organizing on-the-job training.

The following events have occurred since the first edition of this book was written in 1973:

A functioning monopoly cartel has caused the world's price of oil to quadruple,

The oil depletion allowance was repealed,

The Alaskan pipeline was started,

Commercial supersonic transport plane flights are a reality,

The Suez Canal has re-opened,

For the first time, an American President and Vice President have resigned.

Prices of many products have risen dramatically, but prices of electronic calculators and quartz watches have fallen, and many more.

The point is that the marketing manager no longer operates in a relatively friendly environment, in which the major task is to stimulate demand and satisfy customers. Now environmental constraints, raw materials and components shortages, stringent government regulation, and a more hostile public—in addition to more sophisticated consumers—mean that the tasks of marketing management are more difficult today. And perhaps they are more interesting and more necessary than ever before.

This book was written to introduce the basic principles of marketing.

The concept of the book has basically three aspects:

1. *Managerial* (decision-making) philosophy—this book focuses on the question: How can marketing activities be performed more effectively and efficiently? rather than such questions as: Isn't it interesting how these marketing activities are performed? or shouldn't there really be a law against that? We include some scholarly aspects and public policy implications of marketing activities, but the perspective of the book is managerial decision making.

2. *A comprehensive perspective*—The marketing manager has relationships with customers, with society in general, and with suppliers, both vendors and organizational functions. The manager must design and coordinate marketing programs in light of all of these relationships.

Consequently, he/she must have a basic understanding of these three areas.

3. *A conceptual/analytical orientation*—This does not mean a heavy dose of mathematics, economics, or accounting. But it does mean content designed to help the reader to structure his thinking, to see how facts fit together, and to provide insight into real-world marketing activities. This is accomplished through careful organization, numerous headings, many diagrams, and varied presentations of ideas.

The book is designed to implement these concepts. The material is organized in parts, chapters, and sections. Since understanding marketing management requires integration of various points into a coherent whole, key points are repeated throughout the text for emphasis and to demonstrate pertinence to other points. However, topics are not confined to any one organizational division. International marketing, for example, is not treated in a separate chapter, but is introduced throughout the book to illustrate appropriate points. Similarly, channels of distribution are treated as economic institutions (a macro perspective) and then later from a micro—channel management—viewpoint. The isolated treatment of wholesaling in one chapter and retailing in the next is avoided. For the same reason social responsibility, industrial marketing, and marketing serv-ices—freestanding chapters in most books—are discussed throughout this text.

In reading this book, no particular background is required. It is helpful to recall basics from sociology, psychology, economics, and accounting. It does no harm to have had a bit of statistics, computer science, and organization theory. And it is helpful to be interested in current events—war and diplo-macy, racism and poverty, inflation and recession, and so on. Marketing is related to all of these disciplines and events. The basic prerequisite for effectively studying this book, therefore, is an interest in human activity, and in how marketing aspects of those activities can be better performed.

A textbook is never really finished. I have labored diligently on this one, and I have had consider-able help (which I am pleased to acknowledge on the next page). But errors, ambiguities and omissions no doubt remain. I apologize for them, and would very much appreciate having them called to my attention.

Ben Enis

Acknowledgments

A basic textbook is the product of many, many people. Although the author is responsible in law and in fact for the finished book, I would like to acknowledge the fine efforts of the people who helped.

From my teachers, colleagues, and students, and from scholars, writers, executives, and practitioners, I have learned so much as to render individual acknowledgment virtually impossible. I have tried to reference specific ideas and examples, but much that is considered common knowledge in a discipline appears without attribution in a basic book. I hope that those who originated such concepts find my discussions and adaptations of them acceptable.

The first edition of this book was carefully and fully reviewed by marketing professors James L. Wiek, Betsy D. Gelb, Mark I. Alpert, and Keith K. Cox. In addition, professors Norman Kangun, Harold H. Kassarjian, Max Lupul, marketing consultant Gabriel M. Gelb, and Ph.D. candidates Francis Britton, Michael Mokwa, Patrick Murphy, William Staples. Thomas Tucker,

and E. M. (Pete) Wolf read and commented upon portions of the manuscript. Several classes of undergraduates and graduate students were also exposed to much of this material.

This edition profited from unsolicited comments by a number of marketing professors. Particularly helpful were Professors Walter Woods, Jeanne Hill, Lester Neidell, Dale Wilson, William Browne. Many others sent insightful comments and useful critiques. I very much appreciate this assistance and hope it will continue. The second edition was critically reviewed by Professors Keith Cox, William Locander, William George, Barbara Pletcher, and Gerald Albaum. Doctoral candidates Lawrence Chonko and Thomas Weymann competently handled much of the routine leg work needed to write this revision. My colleagues at Houston, in addition to Professors Locander and Cox, who have been most supportive of my efforts are: Edgar Crane, Benton Cocanougher, Betsy Gelb, Norman Kangun, William Sargent, and Sam V. Smith. My heartfelt thanks to all. I did not always enjoy their criticisms, but their efforts considerably

strengthened the book. Since I did not always accept their advice, I cannot blame them for any remaining imperfections.

The task of converting second edition ideas into manuscript was handled by Jelka Woodard, with help from Randy Enis and Becky Sepolio. Anyone unfamiliar with my dictating style and my handwriting cannot appreciate the magnitude of their labors.

Although I have written several other books, this is the first one in which I became sufficiently involved with production to really appreciate the efforts of the people at Goodyear. The acquisitions editor and my advisor throughout the project was Goodyear's Steve Lock. The book's production supervisor was Gerald Rafferty, the production editor was Ms. Sally Kostal, Jane Hellesoe-Henon handled the permissions tasks and Arlene Castiglioni prepared the indexes. I appreciate the guidance of Goodyear production director, Gene Schwartz and manufacturing manager, Bob Hollander. The entire project has been managed beautifully. A great job, folks.

To the Reader

I took my first undergraduate marketing course in the summer of 1960. I had a popular and respected instructor, we used the leading textbook at that time, and I earned an A. I was planning to be married and, among other practical and financial preparations that summer, I was attempting to sell my automobile, a black 1958 Chevrolet convertible. Although selling an automobile is a marketing activity in the most traditional sense of the word, *it never once occurred to me to apply any concept, principle, technique, or fact from the course to the problem of selling the automobile.* Marketing, to me, at that time, was what one studied in school—it bore no relationship to my world outside school.

The most fundamental objective of this book is to see that your initial experience with a marketing course is not like mine was. Marketing is intimately related to everyday life. I try to never underestimate your intelligence, but not to overestimate your knowledge. I endeavored to link the book together into a coherent presentation of marketing principles. Key terms and concepts are repeated for emphasis at various points.

The subject matter has been carefully planned to maximize your understanding of an involvement with marketing management. Consider the following brief list of the book's features:

1. The primary structure is based on a model of marketing activities. The model provides a logical sequence for the material in the book, and a framework for relating topics to each other.

2. Each part begins with a short list of basic information and/or skills that can be acquired from studying that part. This list can be used to guide your reading. Each part closes with three or four cases that illustrate a variety of marketing situations. These are followed by questions for case analysis.

3. Each chapter begins with a summary. You may wish to read the summary twice—once as a preview, and again after studying the chapter, to appraise your knowledge and understanding of the material.

4. Within each chapter are these significant features:

(1) Extensive headings and captions structure and organize the material.

(2) A number of exhibits (tables and figures) illustrate the text. Summary exhibits, set apart from the text, provide background information and examples for the text material.

5. At the end of each chapter, three types of comprehension aids are provided:

(1) A list of key terms and concepts for quick review.

(2) Several questions to aid in understanding, applying, and extending the text material; these questions can provide the basis for fruitful discussions of the material.

(3) Annotated bibliography— suggestions for further reading, carefully selected for breadth and depth of coverage and for readability.

6. At the end of the book are two separate indexes. Exhibits are referenced in the subject index,

names and terms in the general name index.

7. This book is part of a complete package for learning marketing management. Other items in the package are:

(1) *Insights for Marketing Management,* by Gabriel M. and Besty D. Gelb—scholarly articles on marketing management to extend your knowledge and to provide a variety of viewpoints.

(2) *Marketing Is Everybody's Business,* by Betsy D. Gelb and Ben M. Enis—cases, descriptions, and examples of contemporary marketing situations to connect text principles to specific marketing activities.

(3) *A Student Involvement Guide,* by Dev S. Pathak; additional material and exercises to aid you in learning by actively involving you in marketing principles.

Each of these elements is designed to aid you in studying marketing. They are for your guidance and assistance. Use them, ignore them, or modify them as you deem appropriate. Good luck!

PART 1 OVERVIEW OF MARKETING

After reading Part 1, you should be ready to:

1. Describe the nature of marketing activities in contemporary society.

2. See marketing implications in the actions of individuals and organizations.

3. Explain the basic relationships between marketing management and (a) customers, (b) suppliers, and (c) society.

4. Look forward to more detailed discussions of these topics in succeeding chapters (or at least to resist the desire to set fire to this book).

Stock, Boston

1/MARKETING TODAY

The purposes of Chapter 1 are to illustrate the pervasiveness and diversity of marketing activities, to demonstrate the significance of these activities in your life and work, and to encourage you to read thoughtfully and inquisitively. Key points include:

1. Marketing activities are a vital part of life.

2. Marketing is a field worthy of serious study because (1) it is a fundamental human activity, (2) it plays a significant role in society, and (3) effective management of marketing activities is essential to the success of any organization.

3. The essence of marketing is exchange—trading value for value—for the purpose of satisfying human wants.

4. Exchange is a fundamental human activity; it develops whenever and wherever people exist. Exchange activities are one of the major driving forces in the economic development of societies.

5. Our society, an *industrial* society, is characterized by a business-oriented culture, mass production, sophisticated marketing effort, and consumer affluence. Industrial society enjoys a high standard of economic want-satisfaction, but is criticized (not always justly) for its materialistic values, inequitable income distribution, resource waste, and concentration of power. The affluent society will not disappear— but it will change.

6. *Marketing* can be defined as exchange activities conducted by individuals and organizations for the purpose of satisfying human wants. The prerequisites for marketing activities include two or more parties with (1) unsatisfied wants, (2) products they are willing to give up, and (3) some means of communication.

WHY STUDY MARKETING?

Marketing is a diverse, complex, and rapidly changing field. In many ways, the marketing activities depicted in the photo essay are very dissimilar, but they do have certain elements in common. They are all, to some extent, marketing situations. Studying marketing will increase your knowledge of the individual, of society, and of organizations.

First, marketing should be studied because it is a fundamental human activity. Everyone engages in marketing. People, therefore, need to know and understand marketing—just as they need knowledge of poetry and literature, physics and biology, psychology and political science. The scholarly search for greater awareness of the human condition provides one rationale for a course in marketing.

Second, the societal impact of marketing activities is great. As we shall see, exchange is a means of increasing the total satisfaction of a society. Business-oriented values and attitudes—and reactions to these values and attitudes—tend to permeate an industrial society. Many social institutions, e.g., religion, government, education, and recreation and leisure activities, are affected by marketing. Moreover, marketing activities provide employment for a significant proportion of the work force of an industrial society.

The third reason for studying marketing, and perhaps the most significant from your point of view, is that the effective management of marketing activities is absolutely essential to the success of almost any organization. Note that we said *organization.* Not only business firms, but also hospitals and schools, political parties and labor unions, museums and churches, and even the Mafia, perform marketing activities. As a citizen and consumer, you have been, and will continue to be, influenced by the marketing activities of many, many organizations. Someday you may hold a managerial position—perhaps even in marketing.

In my opinion, any of these reasons alone is sufficient motivation for the college-level study of the field of marketing. Of course, I admit to a certain degree of bias in this regard. But I am confident that you will find marketing a necessary, vital, and exciting subject.

THE EXCHANGE NOTION

The basis of marketing is the *exchange notion.* Let us see how this notion arises from the basic human motivation to satisfy wants, how exchange is differentiated from other means of want satisfaction, and how exchange activities become more numerous and complex as a society matures.

Motivation for Want Satisfaction

Marketing begins with the fundamental idea that most, if not all, human behavior is a purposeful quest for want satisfaction. People act so as to satisfy their wants and desires. Physiologists say that the body has the

Exhibit 1-1 Examples of Products

Goods	Services	Ideas
candy bars	pulling a tooth	see America first
locomotives	curing the flu	legalize abortion
typewriters	preparing a tax return	stop smoking
pencils	cutting hair	join a union
buildings	curing worms in puppies	drive defensively
iron ore	writing papers for a student	impeach the president
diamonds	serving a meal	reelect the president
potatoes	shining shoes	peace now
potable water	counseling a neurotic	prevent forest fires
oil derricks	repairing automobiles	join the Peace Corps
sandpaper	designing computer systems	eat more beef
staples	acting in a movie	consult an architect
pins	directing a movie	exercise regularly
thumbtacks	filming a movie	do not shoplift
automobiles	editing a movie	support your local police
tires	designing a building	do not drink and drive
books	cleaning a building	have a vasectomy
.	.	.
.	.	.
.	.	.

tendency to maintain internal stability by coordinated responses that compensate for environmental changes—a phenomenon called home-ostasis. In simple words, people seek things they think will satisfy them.

These things are called *products*. A product is anything that might satisfy some human want. Products are often divided into three categories: goods, services, and ideas. A good is a product that has tangible physical properties that satisfy wants; a service is the application of human skills and abilities to the satisfaction of want; and an idea is a new concept or different way of thinking about a situation that may lead to the satisfaction of want. Exhibit 1-1 provides a number of examples of each of these three types of products. But these are only examples—it would be impossible to list all products that humans might want. [Pedantic aside: some authorities distinguish between *needs* and *wants*. This distinction is not always clear—as we note in Exhibit 6-12. *Want* is used in this book since it is the more inclusive term.]

Note carefully that how the product is used, rather than the fact of its existence, is the basis of want satisfaction. Women seek hope and beauty—not cosmetics and liquid diet food; men seek virility and masculinity—not toupees or after-shave lotion. The product is a means to an end; the end is want satisfaction.

Definition of Exchange

Marketing requires the existence of two or more individuals or groups, each having certain wants, and each possessing certain products. Each

Exhibit 1-2   The Exchange Process

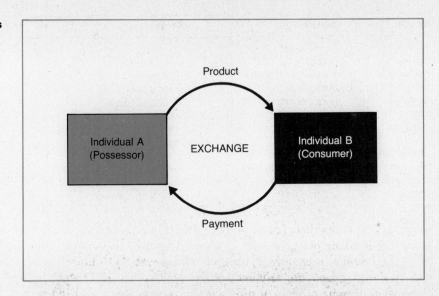

believes that his total satisfaction will be increased if he or she exchanges some of the products possessed for some of the products of the other party. Exchange is, therefore, the process of satisfying human wants via *trade* (barter, swap, purchase, lease, etc.). More precisely, exchange involves the offering of a product in the expectation of receiving payment—something having utility—in return. Exhibit 1-2 illustrates the exchange process.

Thus, exchange is differentiated from other methods of want satisfaction: origination, force, and transfer. *Origination* is the creation of form utility (change in the physical shape or composition of a product)—by discovering, harvesting, mining, manufacturing—products. *Force* is the taking of a product without offering payment. Examples of force include burglary, war, extortion, conquest, etc. Human wants can also be satisfied via *transfer*—the conferring of utility without the expectation of payment; most of the wants of children are satisfied in this way, and all members of society receive satisfaction from "public goods" such as highways and police protection. Public goods are paid for by general taxes rather than direct payments.

All societies practice all four of these means of satisfying wants. The quest for want satisfaction is a universal human characteristic, but the specific means may differ widely. Consequently, when examining actual behavior, it is often difficult to separate meaningfully the different kinds of want satisfaction. For example, products must be originated before they can be exchanged, taken by force, or transferred. Some origination activities, e.g., manufacturing, require inputs of raw materials and supplies which are often purchased—exchanged for money. Preparations for war (force) quite often involve numerous exchanges.

In addition, exchange activities are often inextricably intertwined with other human activities. For example, housewives go to the supermarket not only to buy groceries, but to converse with friends, to get little Johnny out of the house, to learn about new products, and perhaps to show off stylish clothes or a new car. Behavior rarely satisfies just one motive.

How Exchange Develops

Suppose that a small group of families has settled in a particular place—chosen for its abundant game or fertile soil, or perhaps they have been driven there by a natural disaster such as an earthquake or a flood. Each family is satisfying its own needs through origination (hunting, trapping, or growing food) or perhaps through force, e.g., one family is taking food or clothes from another. Each family is satisfying its own wants, and no exchange is taking place.

The essential prerequisites for exchange do exist: (1) motivation to satisfy wants—people are assumed to behave so as to satisfy wants, (2) possession of some product or products—in some cases want satisfaction can be realized more fully by exchanging a product which the individual already possesses for a product which some other individual or group possesses, and (3) some means of communication—the two groups must have some means of negotiating, of communicating the terms under which they are willing to exchange their products. This last prerequisite is not so restrictive as it may at first appear. Many groups—including American Indians, participants in auctions, brokers on the floor of the stock exchange—use sign language, and some groups have managed exchange activities without any direct contact, as illustrated in Exhibit 1-3. Given these prerequisites, exchange activities develop primarily as a result of four basic factors: a market, specialization, a medium of exchange, and marketing management.

Market. Although individuals may come together for some purpose other than exchange, once they assemble in one place and possess the three prerequisites for exchange, a market develops. A market is a place recognized as a setting for trade.

To illustrate the development of the exchange process let us imagine that there are four families whose heads are named Og, Guh, Thugee, and Rik. Guh admires Og's hunting prowess. Og always seems to have plenty of meat for his family to eat. Guh believes this is because Og is an expert spearmaker, but Og too is unhappy. Although he kills much game, he frequently eats it raw because the pots in which he cooks the game often break in the fire. Now it happens that Guh is a great pot-maker. His pots hold large amounts and can be used to roast game at length on a hot fire. He has noticed Og's predicament and approaches him with a deal: Guh

Exhibit 1-3   Silent Trade

One tribe takes the products it wishes to exchange to a certain spot, arranges them in piles, and retires. Another tribe then brings its products to the "market." It places its goods in proximity to the first tribe's piles, arranging the amount in each of its piles according to what it is willing to exchange for the corresponding pile of the first tribe. Then the second tribe retires.

The first tribe now returns, and studies the second tribe's offerings. If satisfied with the particular trade, it makes no change in those piles. If an offering is unsatisfactory, the first tribe redistributes its products among the remaining offerings of the second tribe, and again retires. The second tribe returns, rearranges unsatisfactory piles, and retires. This continues until no rearrangements are made. Then each tribe takes the other's products, leaving its own in exchange.

Adapted from George W. Robbins, "Some Notes on the Origins of Trade," *Journal of Marketing*, January 1947, pp. 661–72, with permission of the publisher, the American Marketing Association.

will give Og two nice pots in return for one of Og's fine spears, and perhaps a lesson or two in the art of spearing game. Og accepts and a market is born. Through exchange, the net satisfaction of both parties is increased. Guh becomes a more proficient hunter and Og has cooked meat to eat.

Specialization. The community has discovered the principle of specialization: origination coupled with exchange can increase the total satisfaction of each member of the community. Other members of the community soon join in. Thugee's forte is hut-building, and Rik seems to be able to ward off evil spirits with her chants and incantations. Soon Og is making spears (or perhaps doing the hunting) for the entire community; everyone uses Guh's fine pots and sleeps in Thugee's well-made huts; Rik causes the gods to smile upon the community.

The benefits of specialization can be extended. Suppose that Thugee's son, George, who has no interest in building huts, notices that the exchange activities of the community are not being performed very efficiently. Guh's hut once needed repairs, but at the time he had no extra pots to exchange with Thugee for the work. By the time Guh had produced the four pots that Thugee demanded, Thugee was at work on another project for Rik. Guh then sought to exchange the pots with Og, but Og was away on a hunting trip.

George decides to specialize in facilitating exchange. He informs the community that he will set up shop under the big oak tree in the clearing and remain at this post from dawn until dusk, six days a week. He offers to trade with anyone for anything. Thus, a member of the community could exchange his products for products that George had in stock, at any time, at that one central place. George becomes the community's *middleman*— his activities increase the total satisfaction to be derived from a product by adding time and/or place utility to it.

Medium of Exchange. Although the introduction of a middleman into this marketing system increases the efficiency of exchange activities, it also generates new problems. George can take game killed by Og and pay Og in pots that George has received from Guh. But Og's game spoils quickly. Rik has plenty of corn to trade to George in the fall and some vegetables to offer in the spring, but Rik needs pots and meat year-round. Thugee needs pots, meat, corn, and vegetables, but his specialty is the service of hut-building. His working time is limited by his energy and by climatic conditions. He can promise to repair or build a hut at some future time, but he has nothing tangible to give George in return for the products George has obtained from the other members of the community.

George realizes that he needs a medium of exchange—some common basis for valuing each of the products traded to him. He begins to use the glittering stones that sometimes appear in the creek bed; they are small, durable, and coveted by all members of the community. George learns not to give too many stones to Rik in exchange for Rik's corn in the fall, and to collect a few extra stones when he trades the corn to other members of the community in the winter. In short, George learns to set prices for his merchandise, and to speculate on what the merchandise might bring at some future time.

Marketing Management. As George's prowess as a trader grows, he is able, in cooperation with the originators of the various products, to satisfy the wants of the community more fully. A time comes when all members of the community have sufficient meat and vegetables, enough pots to cook them in, and warm huts. George's business is limited to replacement sales and to satisfying the wants of the occasional new family in the community. To continue to earn the means to satisfy his own wants, George becomes a more active trader. He travels to surrounding communities, extols the virtues of the products that he has on hand, reduces his prices on some items, and asks various members of the communities what types of products they would like him to stock.

In short, George begins to *market* his merchandise. As the market for various products expands, George takes orders and tries to schedule origination of those products to meet demand. The originators of the goods become even more specialized in their functions. Guh, for example, is now spending most of his days making pots of various shapes and sizes. He no longer deals directly with the consumers of his product—he depends more and more upon George's knowledge of the market to guide him in making the kind of pottery that George's customers want to buy.

George's activities have been emulated by men in other communities. George now has competitors, and this development prompts the community to erect trade barriers, such as imposing taxes upon goods imported into the community.

Exhibit 1-4 How Exchange Increases Satisfaction

Exchange Prerequisites	facilitated by	Basic Exchange Concepts	result in	Increased Satisfaction
Two or more Individuals who have:		1. a market		1. form utility: improvement in shape, function, or style of product for consumption
1. unsatisfied wants		2. specialization of labor		
2. product(s) to exchange		3. a medium of exchange		2. time utility: moving product closer to time of consumption
3. some means of communication		4. marketing management		3. place utility: moving product closer to place of consumption
				4. possession utility: conferring of right to consume the product

This hypothetical example could be extended in many ways, but the foregoing discussion is perhaps sufficient to demonstrate the general development of the exchange notion. Exhibit 1-4 summarizes the discussion, and emphasizes the key point—that exchange activity should result in increased satisfaction. As we explore in more detail in Chapter 9, economists view satisfaction as being derived from four types of utility: form, time, place, and possession. As a society grows and develops, the exchange process becomes more complex. Product originator and consumer are more widely separated, middlemen proliferate, and exchange transactions become more formalized and routinized.

Exhibit 1-5 expands Exhibit 1-2 to illustrate this development. Exhibit 1-2 shows direct interaction between originator and consumer, but exchange in a modern economy usually follows the more elaborate path of Exhibit 1-5. Resources are procured via farming, mining, importing from other places, etc. The vast majority of resources are then transformed, through manufacturing and construction processes, into more useful products. (An economist would say that the form utility of the resources had been increased.) In the terminology of our earlier discussion, both of these stages in the product flow are concerned primarily with origination, although exchange activities frequently occur between resource-procuring organizations and those engaged in manufacturing and construction. The third stage, intermediate exchange, consists of all organizations engaged

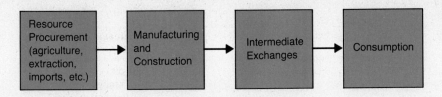

in delivering the products of the first two stages to consumers. These organizations are the wholesalers, agents, shippers, retailers, and facilitating agents, such as banks and advertising agencies, that are popularly identified with marketing activities. These organizations provide time, place and possession utilities. Exhibit 1-5 depicts the basic stages of product flow in the exchange process. Of course, flows of payment must also occur. There are countless variations of these basic stages in the real world.

MARKETING IN CONTEMPORARY SOCIETY

We can most easily comprehend the development of real world exchange relationships within the broader perspective of the stages of economic development. This perspective leads to a description of the contemporary marketing system in industrialized nations—the affluent society. The marketing activities of such a society are subject to a number of criticisms.

Stages of Economic Development

The exchange notion plays a key role in the development of an economic system. Generally, economic development can be divided into four stages: preindustrial, developing, industrial, and postindustrial. Exhibit 1-6 describes each of these four stages, identifies the primary economic problem faced by economies in each stage, and summarizes the nature of exchange activities in each stage.

Preindustrial. Our little scenario starring Og, Thugee, Guh, Rik, and George essentially describes the preindustrial stage. There are relatively few remaining societies in the preindustrial stage today, but some do exist in Africa, Australia, and Southeast Asia. The major economic problem faced by society in this phase is simple survival. Most of the waking hours of all members of the society are devoted to a constant search for sufficient food, clothing, and shelter. Exchange activities in such a society are very primitive: intrafamily or tribe bartering, possibly some trade activity with neighboring tribes.

Developing. In the developing stage, emphasis is placed upon agriculture and the extraction of natural resources. Paraguay, Indonesia, and Nigeria are examples of countries that have recently entered this stage. Countries more advanced in this phase include Mexico, Brazil, Argentina, Spain,

Exhibit 1-6   Stages of Economic Development

Stage	Description	Economic Problem	Nature of Exchange Activity
Preindustrial	Hunting, herding, gathering of products to satisfy basic wants of life by family or tribe; primitive division of labor	Securing sufficient food, clothing and shelter to survive	Intrafamily or tribe bartering; perhaps some bartering activities with neighboring groups
Developing	Emphasis upon agriculture and extraction of natural resources; towns and villages; travel along waterways and primitive roads specialization; primary emphasis upon economic growth	Reducing current consumption to provide capital for development of economic institutions and relationships	Extensive barter contacts among groups; monetary system begins; merchant class develops; trading places and channels appear
Industrial	Emphasis upon mass production; separation of production and consumption; specialization of work activities; rational accounting procedures and decision rules	Generating sufficient demand to operate the industrial system at near capacity in a stable manner	Extensive use of mass promotion; standardized products; impersonal routinized exchange activities
Postindustrial	Economic system provides basics for all members of society; increased leisure time; less emphasis on economic growth	Equitable distribution of products; minimization of resource expenditures to maintain desired living standards; setting of priorities on types of wants to be satisfied	Increasingly oriented to exchange of ideas; less competition for goods and services

and China. Economic growth is a primary goal in the developing stage. There is considerable societal pressure to abstain from current consumption in order to generate capital needed for the development of economic institutions and relationships. Extensive barter contacts develop among groups in the society, monetary systems begin, a merchant class develops, and trading places and channels of distribution begin to appear.

Industrial. The industrial stage of development has recently begun in the U.S.S.R. and in most eastern European nations. Countries having greater industrial development are the United States, Canada, western Europe, and Japan. In such societies, the economic system is well developed and is characterized by mass production; increasing separation of the origination of a product and its consumption; specialization of work activities; and rational accounting procedures and decision rules. The primary economic problem for societies in the industrial phase is generating sufficient demand to operate the industrial system in a stable manner at near capacity. Exchange activities contributing to the solution of this problem include the extensive use of mass promotion, standardized products, and impersonal, routinized exchange transactions. It is generally the goal of developing societies to reach the industrial category.

Postindustrial. The postindustrial stage is at this time an abstraction. No societies today are generally acknowledged to provide the basics for all their members. However, pockets of postindustrial societies are emerging in various industrial nations, e.g., some parts of Sweden and other Scandinavian countries and, some social observers say, in parts of the United States. Such a society is characterized by less emphasis on economic growth, increased leisure time, and an interest in individual dignity and humanism. The major economic problem of such a society would be an equitable distribution of products while minimizing the resource expenditures necessary to maintain desired living standards. Exchange activities in such a society would be increasingly oriented toward the exchange of ideas. There would be less competition for goods and services.

THE INDUSTRIAL STAGE

The economies of primary interest to most readers (the United States, Canada, Japan and western Europe) are generally classified as industrial economies. Marketing activities in these countries are significant. We should, therefore, examine the nature, criticisms, and status of this stage in some detail.

The Affluent Society

A synonym often used for *industrially mature* is *affluent*. In an affluent society, a substantial proportion of the population has relatively few worries about the biological necessities of life. Proportionately few are undernourished, ill-housed, or inadequately clothed. They do not need to spend most of their waking hours seeking satisfaction of these basic wants. Most have considerable disposable income and leisure time. For example, Exhibit 1-7 shows that U.S. citizens spent $155 million eating out in 1974, an increase of 51 percent over 1971 expenditures. Other indicators were also selected to round out the picture of affluence.

Criticisms of the Affluent Society

Inevitably, and somewhat ironically, affluence eventually results in some degree of disinterest in the consumption of material goods and services. As their basic wants become satisfied, people begin to look to the satisfaction of higher-order wants and desires. They become concerned with the price that society pays for materialism. Criticisms of marketing activities, and of other aspects of a business-oriented society, begin to emerge. We discuss some of the major criticisms, under three headings: consumer welfare, the market mechanism, and marketing's impact on society.

Consumer Welfare. In examining the well-being of consumers in any society, sovereignty is desirable. That is, the consumer should decide

Exhibit 1-7   Selected Indicators of the Affluent Society

Type of Consumption	Annual U.S. Total of Expenditure (Millions of Dollars) 1971	1974
1. Food purchased for off-premises consumption	103,128	155,174
2. Alcoholic beverages	19,122	24,681
3. Jewelry and watches	4,278	6,293
4. Funeral and burial expenses	2,263	2,621
5. Purchases of new and used cars	40,244	40,265
6. Books and maps	3,710	4,401
7. Toys and sport supplies	6,121	8,615
8. Radio and television receivers, records, and musical instruments	9,743	14,550
9. Motion picture admissions	1,214	2,274
10. Parimutuel betting receipts	1,044	1,740

Survey of Current Business (U.S. Department of Commerce, July 1975), p. 42

which wants to satisfy and what products to purchase in order to satisfy those wants. However, as an economic system grows—becomes more complex and depersonalized—it becomes increasingly difficult for the consumer to obtain the product information that he or she needs to make informed choices. Products are more complex, packaging prevents examination before purchase, advertisements contain little useful information. And society deems it to be in the public interest to restrict consumers' rights to purchase certain products, e.g., some types of firearms, hard drugs, pornography.

Closely related to sovereignty is the issue of fraud and deception in marketing activities. Questions of deceptive advertising, misleading warranties, and confusing information about price and credit are raised with increasing frequency. The safety and/or reliability of many products is thought to be inadequate by a growing number of consumers. Some social critics think that the affluent society is damaging the quality of life; pollution (high powered automobiles, throwaway drink containers, disposal of sewage into waterways) is a typical example. The affluent society has been dubbed, not entirely in jest, the effluent society.

The Market Mechanism. The interaction of supply and demand sets prices for a bewildering number of products. This interaction, called the *market mechanism,* is one means of solving the economic problem, that of allocating scarce resources among competing ends. The objective of any economic system that depends upon the market mechanism is to maintain acceptable levels of growth, price stability, and full employment. The market mechanism faces increasing criticism for being unable to hold down inflation, grow at a satisfactory rate, and keep most of the work force and other resources of the society reasonably fully employed. These are complex issues; answers are hard to find, and marketing is not the cause of all problems. But no one denies that marketing activities play a key role in the operation of the market mechanism.

Another complaint directed at the market mechanism is that it does not provide for "equitable" distribution of the products of a society. Many consumers have two or three automobiles, own closets full of clothes, and enjoy numerous types of services. But some people do not share in this affluence. In general, these are people with low incomes, who are, for the most part, undereducated and may be members of minority groups. There is substantial evidence to support the contention that the market mechanism does not allocate to them a "fair share" of the products of the society. A related complaint is that the market mechansim tends to undervalue public goods—schools, roads, hospitals, police protection, public recreation facilities, clear air and water—in favor of private goods. Exhibit 1-8 presents Galbraith's classic description of this problem. The market mechanism is said to lead, in many cases, to "unfair competition": an industry dominated by a few firms, predatory marketing practices, and anticompetitive acquisitions and mergers.

Impact on Society. In addition to criticisms about consumer welfare and the market mechanisms, marketing activities are said to adversely affect various areas of the total society. Mass promotion and distribution activities, it is said, result in an emphasis upon materialism, to the detriment of spiritual and/or aesthetic facets of life. Since promotion and distribution are of necessity geared to large numbers of people, they tend to promote homogeneity of taste—at the lowest common denominator, according to many critics. These critics contend that the emphasis on competition and materialism tends to promote discriminatory attitudes and practices toward minority groups.

Critics also charge that a marketing-oriented society tends to be dominated by business interests. For example, various business groups are often charged with possessing excessive political power; court decisions and regulatory agencies designed to restrict such power may constrain individual freedom of choice. Also, the rise of powerful labor unions is attributed to excessive power in the business sector. With big companies, big unions, and big government all jockeying for power, some social critics feel that the voice of the consumer is lost in the din.

Of course, not all of these criticisms are valid; some are only partially true, and others can be rebutted. On the other hand, additional criticisms could be leveled against marketing activities. The purpose of this brief review was not to catalog all such charges, but to acquaint the reader with the scope and diversity of criticisms of marketing activities in contemporary society.

The End of Affluence?

In marked contrast to the affluence of the booming 1960s, the early 1970s saw profound and disturbing changes in the economic environment. Inflation hit—hard. The quadrupling of crude petroleum prices in 1973 heralded rapidly rising prices of almost all products. The most severe recession since the 1930s was manifest in widespread unemployment. For the first time since World War II, there were shortages—not only of petroleum-related products (gasoline, plastics and petrochemicals)—but of steel, newsprint, and agricultural products. Consumers waited in long lines for some products (gasoline), and did without others, e.g., sugar.

Critics contended that the market-oriented economic system had failed, and called for extensive government regulation, even nationalization in some cases, of business. The term *de-marketing* was added to many executives' vocabularies, as organizational effort devoted to marketing was drastically curtailed. The costs of environmental protection were re-evaluated by some citizens, while others damned company profits as obscene. As the economic system's most visible function, marketing faced its share—perhaps more than its share—of blame for these conditions.

The situation is better in the mid 1970s. Prices are higher, and fewer types of some goods are available. But the economic system did not collapse (as some feared) nor is it radically different from the booming 1960s, though many predicted it would be.

Marketing, however, has changed. There is increased demand for smaller cars and better insulated buildings, for oil drilling rigs and alternative fuel sources. There are few first class air travelers, and almost no demand for new jet aircraft. Fewer families can afford single-family dwellings, and university enrollments are down.

No, the affluent society is not ending. But it is changing. That means new opportunities, and new threats, for all who engage in marketing. And that includes everybody. So, we explore the role of marketing in society, the economy, organizations, and the lives of individuals throughout this book.

MARKETING DEFINED

We have discussed the nature of marketing in rather general terms. Now we endeavor to add a certain amount of precision to your conception of the nature of marketing. We examine several definitions of marketing, explain more fully the one used in this book, and then relate this definition to marketing management.

Definitions of Marketing

As you might expect of a broad, diverse field, there are a number of definitions of marketing. Exhibit 1-9 presents several commonly quoted ones.

Two points about these definitions are significant. First, note that several restrict marketing to exchange activities involving economic goods and services. Second, observe that some definitions relate marketing to society (a macro viewpoint), while others define marketing as a business activity (a micro conception).

Our Definition of Marketing

Marketing is a fundamental human activity. Consequently, a broad definition of the nature and purpose of this activity is required:

> *marketing* encompasses exchange activities conducted by individuals and organizations for the purpose of satisfying human wants.

Let us examine this definition closely. It assumes two or more parties (individuals or organizations) each of whom has three characteristics: (1) ability to communicate, (2) a product or products, and (3) some desire for the other's product. Each of these characteristics is broadly interpreted.

Communication, for example, can take many forms in addition to verbal interaction. American Indians and participants in auctions use sign language; stocks and commodities are exchanged impersonally and, as we note in Exhibit 1-1, some primitive societies practice "silent trade."

Second, marketing is concerned with satisfying wants through exchange—purchase, bartering, swap, lease, trade—of one product (anything that has potential want-satisfying ability) for another. Of course, the exchange need not be completed in every case; "marketing" refers to any part of exchange activities.

Note also that the nature of the exchange is not specified. The exchange of money for goods and services is perhaps the most common form of marketing activity, but there are a large number of other types of possible exchanges. For example, goods can be exchanged directly for goods (barter), services for votes (political elections), knowledge for knowledge (scientists pooling their talents), and people for money (slavery, professional sports). In short, anything that has potential utility to any individual or organization is a product in the sense of this definition, and is, therefore, a candidate for exchange.

This broad interpretation of the meaning of marketing is a rather recent development in the marketing discipline. Some marketing scholars refuse to concede that the field of marketing has such broad scope (see Exhibit 1-10). To avoid controversy, some of the more innovative thinkers in the discipline have coined new terms for this broadening of the concept of marketing activities. For example, *metamarketing* (a five-syllable word), *furthering* (which sounds vaguely obscene), and *unselling* (e.g., nonsmoking campaigns, boycotts) have been used to describe aspects of marketing. My own opinion is that the general term *marketing* as defined here can be used quite adequately with appropriate modifiers to denote all such activities.

Third, it is difficult, and perhaps not meaningful, to distinguish clearly between marketing and other fundamental human activities.

Marketing is not synonymous with such activities as love, worship, learning, or eating and sleeping—but there are often marketing aspects of loving, religion, education, and obtaining food and shelter. And conversely, such activities frequently occur in conjunction with exchange activities.

Fourth, we view marketing as an activity engaged in by all people. The term can be applied to the actions of two or more individuals, an individual and an organization, or two or more organizations. Thus marketing, as defined here, has both micro and macro dimensions. In contrast to the first definition in Exhibit 1-9, however, marketing activities need not specify the direction of the exchange. Labeling one party to the exchange the *producer* and the other the *consumer* is not required to understand exchange activity, and may be somewhat confusing in some cases.

Thus, for scholarly purposes, it is entirely possible to study exchange activities without labeling the participants. This is in fact what anthropologists do in their studies of various societies. Our major purpose in studying marketing, however, is managerial. Marketing management focuses upon one party to the exchange—for the purpose of improving that party's performance. In the following chapter the tasks of managing marketing activities are discussed.

CONCLUDING NOTE

You are embarking on a challenging, and I hope rewarding, course of study. Marketing can seem fascinating in its diversity, frustrating in its complexity, inspired in its successes, asinine in its failures, revolutionary in its promulgation of change, reactionary in its resistance to change, wonderful in its delivery of a standard of living, and callous in its disregard for the welfare of certain segments of society. In short, marketing is a complex discipline—thoroughly deserving of serious study.

But it is not always easy. Keep the following points in mind as you study this material:

The Abstract Principle. A textbook must focus upon general principles, common—almost stereotyped—examples, and basic fundamentals. If the material is to be meaningful to you personally, therefore, you must make the effort to relate it to your own knowledge and experiences, to other courses, and to current events. Use the end-of-chapter study aids, other books (e.g., the involvement manual and readings books), and texts from other courses to relate marketing principles to the world as you know it.

The Instant Expert Syndrome. Recall the fable of the six blind men examining the elephant—each touched a different part of the ele-

Exhibit 1-10   The "Broadening" Controversy

In their classic article, Kotler and Levy assert that the principles of good marketing in traditional product areas can be transferred to the marketing of services, persons, and ideas. ". . . whether marketing is viewed in the old sense of pushing products or in the new sense of customer satisfaction engineering, it is almost always viewed and discussed as a business activity." The authors contend that marketing is "a pervasive social activity that goes considerably beyond the selling of toothpaste, soap, and steel."

For example, the authors note that the police department of a major U.S. city developed a campaign to win friends and influence people. And the junta of Greek colonels who seized power in 1967 found the international publicity surrounding their cause unfavorable, and hired a major New York public relations firm to explain why the takeover was necessary for the stability of Greece and the world—the headline was "Greece Was Saved From Communism."

Kotler and Levy define marketing as "that function of the organization that can keep in constant touch with the organization's consumers, read their needs, develop products that meet these needs, and build a program of communication to express the organization's purposes." They point out that organizations such as the United Auto Workers, Defense Department, Ford Foundation, World Bank, Catholic Church, and University of California perform this function just as do Procter & Gamble, General Motors, and General Electric. They maintain that "the choice facing those who manage nonbusiness organizations is not whether to market or not to market, for no organization can afford to avoid marketing. The choice is whether to do it well or poorly. . . ."[1]

In a critique of this position, Luck argues that "If a definition were framed to meet the authors' contentions, marketing no longer would be bounded in terms of either institutions or the ultimate purpose of its activities. If a task is performed, anywhere by anybody, that has some resemblance to a task performed in marketing, that would be marketing . . . marketers' self-image may be pleasurably inflated by claiming that political campaigns are just another part of marketing, but what progress is to be gained by such reasoning? . . . attenuate marketing's definition to make it almost universal, and it will wholly lose its identity."

Luck contends that "a manageable, intelligible and logical definition of marketing can be fashioned when its scope is bounded within those processes or activities whose ultimate result is a *market transaction*. . . . The Heart Fund does not sell donations: there is no established price or terms of sales, and the donor is given no specific quid pro quo." Luck also asks how an activity that is performed by some three million business firms can be termed "narrowly defined"?[2]

In their rejoinder, Kotler and Levy point out that the current boundary of marketing is determined more by tradition than anything else and that the concept of a market transaction is not as unambiguous or acceptable as it might at first glance appear. ". . . the fact that spiritual and educational services are usually paid for in other ways than outright purchase reflects convenience and tradition. Is anyone to see that there is not a quid pro quo? . . . nor is the aim of profit a definitive characteristic of marketing . . . for marketing activity goes on in primitive and socialist societies where the drive for private profit is not an issue. . . . The crux of marketing lies in a general idea of exchange rather than the narrowed idea of market transactions."[3]

1. Philip Kotler and Sidney J. Levy, "Broadening the Concept of Marketing," *Journal of Marketing*, January 1967, pp. 10–15; 2. David J. Luck, "Broadening the Concept of Marketing—Too Far"; and 3. Philip Kotler and Sidney J. Levy, "A New Form of Marketing Myopia: Rejoinder to Professor Luck," *Journal of Marketing*, July 1969, pp. 53–7.

phant and each therefore got a different perception of what an elephant was. And each insisted that his interpretation of the elephant was the correct one. The point is that marketing is complex.

Hopefully, the text principles will be clear and meaningful to you. Implementation of ideas you know to be right, however, is difficult, particularly since so many other people have ideas about marketing that they know to be correct—and their ideas so often differ from yours. Keep a sense of perspective. Do not take for granted that you know all the answers, e.g., how to write a better advertisement, or what laws should be passed.

The Text as Gospel. It is not. Of necessity, a basic book omits, ignores, and simplifies some material it might present. Any book reflects its author's knowledge and biases. I have endeavored to present the mainstream of fundamental marketing concepts and techniques, and have tried to keep the facts straight. But valid interpretations of the marketing discipline vary. Therefore, treat the text material as a foundation for your own thoughts and evaluations— question, compare, analyze, criticize.

If you keep these points in mind—if you question, if you relate, if you keep an open mind—I sincerely believe you will find the study of marketing interesting, useful, and perhaps even enjoyable.

KEY TERMS AND CONCEPTS

Study of Marketing
  scholarly aspects
  societal view
  managerial perspective
Wants
  motivation
  homeostasis
Product
  good
  service
  idea
Utility
  form
  time
  place
  possession
Exchange
  quid pro quo (payment)
  origination
  force
  transfer

Development of Exchange
  market
  specialization
  medium of exchange
  marketing management
Stages of Economic Development
  preindustrial
  developing
  industrial
  postindustrial
The Affluent Society
  philosophy
  consumer sovereignty
  the market mechanism
  societal impact
  inflation
  shortages
Definition(s) of Marketing
  exchange basis
  macro and micro aspects
  marketing management

QUESTIONS FOR DISCUSSION

1. List activities, in addition to those in the opening photographs of the book, that you would classify as marketing activities. Why do you consider them marketing activities? How would a psychologist, or a politician, or an engineer classify these activities?

2. Identify activities that would be classified as marketing activities for the following individuals and organizations: General Motors, a corner grocery store, a barber shop, a CPA firm, a candidate for U.S. Senator, the United Fund, the Catholic Church, your university, a dope pusher, the Federal Trade Commission, your spouse, and the local Chamber of Commerce. What products are offered by each organization?

3. List some of your wants. How could these wants be satisfied through exchange? via origination? by force? by transfer? What are some of the advantages and limitations of want satisfaction by each method?

4. Consider a recent purchase that you have made. What wants did you expect the product to satisfy? What activities were involved in delivering that product to you?

5. Exhibit 1-8 contains Galbraith's classic description of the tendency of the market mechanism to undervalue public goods. Why does Galbraith view this as a social problem? Do you agree—why or why not? What would you suggest be done about this problem?

6. After considering the text material, formulate your own definition of marketing. Do not worry about conciseness—explain marketing to your own satisfaction. Now compare your definition with those given in the text.

7. Why study marketing? Evaluate the arguments presented in the chapter. Do you agree—why or why not? What other arguments, for or against the study of marketing, can you think of?

SUGGESTED READING

1. Reavis Cox and others.
Distribution in a High Level Economy. Englewood Cliffs, N.J.: Prentice-Hall, 1965. Very scholarly, yet readable, survey of the development and appraisal of marketing activities in an industrial society.

2. John Kenneth Galbraith.
The Affluent Society, rev. ed., 1969, *The New Industrial State,* rev. ed., 1970, and *Economics and the Public Purpose,* 1973, all published by Houghton Mifflin. Perhaps the best known works by this noted economist and social critic; perceptive insights into and provocative questions concerning industrial society—negative, on the whole, toward marketing activities: Chapter 18 of *The New Industrial State,* "The Management of

Specific Demand," is reprinted in Gelb and Gelb, *Insights for Marketing Management.*

3. Alex Groner and others.
The American Heritage History of American Business and Industry. New York: American Heritage Publishing Co., 1972. An excellent summary of American economic history—comprehensive, yet brief; written in journalistic style, beautifully illustrated; a pleasant way to recall significant events in the history of industrial society in America.

4. Philip Kotler.
"The Generic Concept of Marketing," *Journal of Marketing,* April 1972. Definitive essay on the fundamental nature of marketing activities; reprinted in Gelb and Gelb, *Insights for Marketing Management.*

5. Sidney J. Levy and Gerald Zaltzman.
Marketing, Society and Conflict. Prentice-Hall, 1975. Thoughtful essay on contemporary marketing thought; insightful, provocative, and scholarly; not always easy reading.

6. Ayn Rand.
Capitalism: The Unknown Ideal. New York: The New American Library, 1967. Vigorous and uncompromising philosophical defense of the market mechanism; comparison with Galbraith's work is highly instructive.

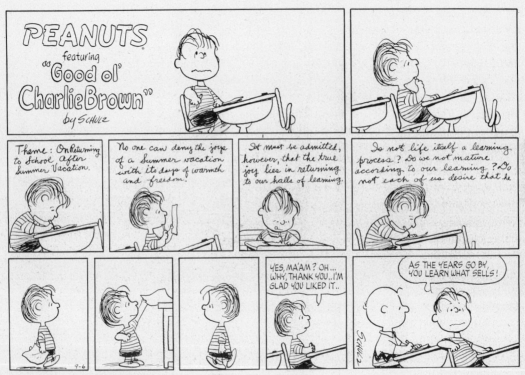

2/MANAGING MARKETING ACTIVITIES

In Chapter 1, we surveyed the discipline of marketing. Now we focus on the fundamentals of managing marketing activities. Basic points include:

1. Marketing management is the process of increasing the effectiveness and/or efficiency by which marketing activities are performed by individuals or organizations.

2. Marketing managers perform four functions: (1) seeking customers, (2) matching customers' desires and organizational products, (3) programming marketing strategies, and (4) consummating sales.

3. The ultimate purpose of performing marketing functions in an organization is to complete mutually satisfying exchange transactions with customers, within the constraints imposed by society. Thus, the marketing manager must relate to three groups of constituents: customers, suppliers, and citizens.

4. The *marketing concept* (determine the customer's desires, then provide products that satisfy those desires) can apply to all three constituent groups. This generic interpretation provides a philosophical rationale for marketing management.

5. Basic qualities associated with successful marketing management include empathy, capacity for rational analysis, tolerance for ambiguity, adaptability to change, a broad and optimistic outlook, and ethical sensitivity. While no one individual will always rate high in all these areas, the rewards (both financial and psychic) to be gained from the management of marketing activities are usually associated with these qualities.

Consider any organization—General Motors, the Defense Department, a corner grocery store, a political party, a CPA firm, a university, even the Mafia. Each has objectives, and each engages in some form of marketing activity as it strives to achieve these objectives. In this chapter we introduce the fundamental concepts and terminology needed to understand the role of marketing activities in an organization.

MANAGEMENT OF MARKETING ACTIVITIES

A definition of marketing management is a logical starting point for a discussion of the tasks of marketing management. This definition facilitates viewing marketing activities as flows between product originator and consumer, and highlights the four managerial functions necessary to accomplish these activities.

Definition of Marketing Management

It is not unusual for descriptions of marketing management to be offered as definitions of marketing. Recall from Exhibit 1-9, for example, the emphasis upon performance in the micro definition of marketing given by McCarthy. A number of introductory marketing books define marketing in terms of accomplishing organizational objectives. But proficient performance is the result of management—it is definitely not inherent in marketing activities.

When an individual or an organization desires to improve the performance of its marketing activities, then it should focus on the management of those activities. Specifically, our definition is:

> marketing management is the process of increasing the effectiveness and/or efficiency by which marketing activities are performed by individuals or organizations.

Note the following three implications of this definition. First, the definition embraces both effectiveness (maximization of stated objectives) and efficiency (minimization of resource expenditures necessary to achieve objectives). These are the fundamental dimensions of any managerial task. Second, marketing management can be practiced by buyers (as traditionally defined) as well as by sellers. Third, marketing management is a process (a series or flow of activities designed to bring about a desired result). An extremely useful tool for understanding the nature and operations of any process is the systems approach, which is reviewed in Exhibit 2-1. This tool is used rather frequently in this book.

Exchange Flows

The marketing activities to be managed can best be visualized as a set of flows between exchange participants. There are four types of flows: (1) the actual product, (2) use rights to the product (e.g., legal title), (3) payment for the product, and (4) information about the product. Exhibit 2-2

One model that we will employ frequently in studying marketing is the systems concept.

The basic systems concept includes five elements: an objective, inputs, processing, outputs, and feedback. These elements are interrelated in the following way. Given some objective, various inputs are processed, producing outputs to meet the objective. Outputs are measured against the objective; results of the measurement are fed back in the form of adjustments to the inputs. The figure depicts this concept.

The classic example of a system is the thermostatically controlled heating system. The objective is to maintain a comfortable temperature level. In operational terms, comfort is usually taken to mean between 70° and 74° Fahrenheit. Inputs include information concerning the temperature of the building (as measured by a thermometer) and fuel (oil, natural gas, or electric current), plus the initial installation of heating machinery. Processing by the heating system consists of burning fuel to produce heated air that is then circulated in the building. A thermostat measures the temperature of air in the building, compares the measurement with the objective, and feeds back instructions which are inputs into the processing operation. That is, when the building temperature falls below 70°F, the thermostat activates the heating unit. After the unit has heated the building to 74°F, the thermostat switches the unit off.

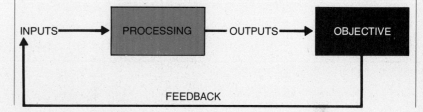

summarizes the flows and their objectives and relates them to activities required to achieve the objectives.

The physical product flows toward the consumer. The basic objective of this flow is to deliver the product to the consumer. Activities involved vary according to the product. In general, such activities include transporting the product, storing it, assembling product assortments (aggregating stocks of the product or breaking down shipments of the product into smaller units), grading, and packaging to protect the contents. In addition to the physical product, use rights to that product must also flow to the consumer. The basic objective here is to be sure that the consumer has the right to own, possess and/or use the products to satisfy his or her wants. Major activities involved in the flow of use rights include pricing, securing the product from the originator or middleman, insuring the physical product during its flow, verifying title, granting use rights to the consumer, and perhaps offering some type of guarantee or warranty.

The concept of securing and granting use rights requires a bit of additional explanation. Marketing scholars used to think in terms of buying and selling the product—the flow of legal title to the goods. We now recognize that this is inadequate in at least two respects. First, it is possible to lease many products and enjoy full use rights to them without ownership. Second, certain types of products—particularly ideas—can be used without ownership. For example, the marketing of the ideas that

Exhibit 2-2   Exchange Flows, Objectives and Activities

Flow:	Physical Product	Use Rights	Payment	Information
Primary Direction	Toward consumer	Toward consumer	Toward originator	Both ways: toward consumer toward originator
Basic Objective	Deliver the product to the consumer	Provide unquestioned right to own, possess, and/or use the product	Compensate originator and distributors for physical product and/or use rights	Promote product benefits to consumer Provide market knowledge to originator
Major Activities	Transporting, storing, aggregating or breaking bulk, grading, packaging	Pricing, securing (purchase, lease, etc.) rights from originator, insuring, verifying title, granting (sale, lease, rent, etc.) rights to consumer, guaranteeing performance	Granting credit, collection of receivables, financial advice	Advertising, personal selling, publicity, sales promotion, labeling or grading Marketing research and intelligence, sales and cost analysis, credit checks

marijuana should be legalized, or that one should join the volunteer army, is not fundamentally different from marketing goods and services—with this exception: if someone markets an idea to you, then you both possess it; he/she does not need to give up anything in order for you to enjoy its use. (This is why product ideas are often protected by society—patented.)

The third type of channel flow is payment, which moves from consumer to originator. The basic purpose of this flow is to compensate originator and distributors for delivering the product and conferring use rights. Major activities here are granting credit (which may range from 30-day billing arrangements to the financing of inventories), collection of receivables, and in some cases financial advice. The final flow is information, which moves both ways. The purpose of information flowing toward the consumer is to communicate and promote product benefits. Activities here include advertising, personal selling, publicity, sales promotion, labeling or grading, etc. The purpose of information flowing from the consumer to the originator is to provide market knowledge; representative activities include marketing research and intelligence, sales and cost analysis, credit checks, etc.

The fundamental point to be emphasized about these objectives is that *all four must be accomplished every time an exchange is consummated.* The physical product and its use rights must flow to the consumer if the product is to satisfy his wants. Payment must flow from the consumer to balance the exchange transaction. And information must flow in both directions so that marketers know what type of products consumers want, and consumers know what types of products are available and on what

Exhibit 2-3 Typical Lists of Marketing Functions

erhaps the classic statement of marketing functions is that given by McGarry:

1. Contactual—the searching out of buyers and sellers.
2. Merchandising—the fitting of the goods to market requirements.
3. Pricing—the selection of a price high enough to make production possible and low enough to induce users to accept the goods.
4. Propaganda—the conditioning of the buyers or of the sellers to a favorable attitude toward the product or its sponsor.

5. Physical distribution—the transporting and storing of the goods.
6. Termination—the consummation of the market process (agreement on at least three essentials: the quality, the quantity, and the price of the services to be exchanged).

Other lists of marketing functions are basically similar:

McGarry:	Staudt and Taylor:	McCarthy:
Contactual	Market delineation Purchase behavior Motivation	Buying
Merchandising	Product-service adjustment	Selling
Pricing	Pricing	
Propaganda	Communication	
Physical Distribution	Physical distribution Channel selection	Grading Transporting Storing
Termination	Organization	Financing Risk taking
	Administration	Market information

Adapted from Edmund D. McGarry, "Some Functions of Marketing Reconsidered," reprinted in *Theory in Marketing*, ed. Reavis Cox and Wroe Alderson (Homewood, Ill.: Richard D. Irwin, 1950), pp. 263–279; Thomas A. Staudt and Donald A. Taylor, *A Managerial Introduction to Marketing*, 3rd ed. (Englewood Cliffs, N.J.: Prentice-Hall, 1976,) pp. 34–54, and E. Jerome McCarthy, *Basic Marketing: A Managerial Approach*, 5th ed. (Homewood, Ill.: Richard D. Irwin, 1975), pp. 10–11, with permission of the publishers.

terms. From the standpoint of efficiency and effectiveness, therefore, the question is not whether these objectives shall be attained, but how to accomplish them best. To repeat, all four flows must be completed to consummate an exchange. The flows must be managed.

The Functions of Marketing Management

Marketing management can be viewed as a set of managerial functions. Because these functions comprise the essential core of marketing management, marketing scholars frequently list and examine the functions of marketing. Exhibit 2-3 presents several of the most widely recognized lists of marketing functions.

Note the similarities among the three statements, and the emphasis upon activities under the control of management, e.g., pricing, physical distribution, propaganda, and selling. These lists are useful in understanding marketing management. At the risk of tampering with tradition, however, we offer a different—somewhat broader—version of marketing functions: seeking, matching, programming, and consummating.

Seeking. The seeking function is the search for and identification of wants that the organization might satisfy. In accordance with the marketing concept, the purpose of seeking is to discover what the customer wants. This function encompasses McGarry's contactual function and Staudt and Taylor's market delineation. Performance of this function requires extensive analysis to identify customers, i.e., those with the Money (buying power), Authority (control of use rights) and Desire for the organization's products. Thus, we shall from time to time use the acronym MAD when referring to customers.

Matching. An organization cannot offer products that satisfy all desires of all consumers. In order to achieve organizational objectives, marketing managers must match the wants identified in the seeking function with organizational resources, taking environmental constraints into account. Matching involves assessment of the organization's ability to produce a product for the market or markets identified—given their nature and size, in light of such external factors as competitors' actions, general economic conditions, laws and governmental regulations, consumers' tastes and fashions, and so on. Thus, matching is the marshalling of organizational resources to serve the desires of designated customer groups in such a way as to satisfy organizational objectives.

The matching function, while implied in other lists of marketing functions, tends to be neglected in studies of marketing management—and in practice. An entrepreneur contemplating building a 400-room resort hotel, for example, might multiply $30 per room times 360 nights and conclude that no time should be wasted in breaking ground at the construction site. But it is usually not quite that simple. Matching involves considerable analysis and evaluation of demand estimates, resource costs, consequences of various degrees of success or failure, and so on.

Programming. Once consumer wants have been identified and matched with organizational capabilities, the marketing program can be devised. This function is universally recognized. In fact, most lists of marketing functions consider several separate aspects of programming. McGarry, for example, lists merchandising, pricing, propaganda, and physical distribution. Perhaps the standard set of elements of the marketing program, often called the marketing mix, is as follows: *(1) product*—the thing possessing utility, *(2) promotion*—persuasive communication about the product by the offerer to potential consumers, *(3) distribution*—the delivery of the product and right to consume it, *(4) price*—the valuation placed upon the product by the offerer. (McCarthy has suggested a helpful mnemonic for this list: the four P's—product, promotion, "place," and price.) Thus, programming is the conception, development, integration and testing of marketing mix elements.

Consummating. If the first three functions have been adequately performed for any given consumer, the organization and that consumer can consummate an exchange. The consummation function involves settling all the details necessary to finalize the exchange, and attempting to insure that the product subsequently gives satisfactory use. Finalizing the exchange—the termination or transaction function—involves buyer/seller agreement on such factors as delivery schedules and method and timing of payment, as well as filing appropriate internal records (e.g., sales invoice) and legal documents (e.g., a bill of sale). Postsale activities are also important. Showing concern for customer satisfaction—by carrying out warranty provisions, making service adjustments, maintaining spare parts inventories, and providing operating instructions and assistance—often leads to repeat sales and favorable customer comments.

The basic responsibility of marketing management is to effectively and efficiently process four types of flows (physical product, use rights, payment, and information) among exchange participants. This responsibility is met by performing the functions of seeking, matching, programming, and consummating, but these functions are not performed in a vacuum.

THE MARKETING MANAGER'S RELATIONSHIPS

In performing his or her functions, the marketing manager must relate to three broad groups of constituents. Ideally, relationships with various members of each group result in mutually satisfying exchanges. The three groups are customers, suppliers, and citizens.

Customers

The most common exchange relationship is that between producer and consumer of a product. The producer offers to the consumer a product having form, time, place, and/or possession utilities. The consumer offers payment to the producer in return for the right to use or consume the product's utilities.

But producer and consumer rarely conduct transactions directly in a mature industrial society. Most products move through a channel of distribution, i.e., are sold to middlemen who, in turn, add time, place and/or possession utilities to the product. As we discuss in more detail in Chapter 3, middlemen are generally classified as wholesalers (those who sell to other middlemen) or retailers (those who sell to ultimate consumers).

There is a third member of the customer group: the agent. Agents do not purchase products for resale, but they do facilitate the flow of products through the channel of distribution to the ultimate consumer. Agents generally facilitate only one of the four essential channel flows.

Because there are so many different products, there are many types of agents. Physical distribution agents include freight carriers (trucks, railroads, ships and barges, airlines) and warehousers (public warehouses, loading docks, grain elevators). Agents who facilitate payment flows include brokers, banks, factors who purchase accounts receivable at a discount, loan financers, mortgage companies, and savings and loan associations. Agents that assist in securing use rights include title search companies, leasing agencies, and insurance agents. Agents that deal with communication flows include advertising agencies and public relations firms, marketing research firms and management consultants, and syndicated services such as the Neilsen store audits and surveys of television viewing.

Suppliers

Products are not manufactured from thin air. Requirements for production are of three broad types: capital, human resources, and physical resources. Capital is supplied in two basic forms. The first is debt; money is lent to the organization in return for interest paid at a fixed rate. In contrast to debt, equity capital is provided by those who want an ownership position with the organization. These people are generally called stockholders, and their return is in two forms: dividends (cash or additional stock paid to them) and appreciation (increase in value of the stock that they hold). Human resources is a broader term than the traditional economic concept of labor. Human resources include all of the human talents and skills made available to the organization in return for wages and salaries. These include unskilled laborers, clerks, skilled craftsmen, technicians, professions, supervisors, executives, etc.

The third necessary group of product inputs is physical assets, a broader interpretation of the traditional economic concept of land. Production of various products requires supplies not only of land, but of buildings and installations of equipment; accessory equipment such as typewriters, desks, and wheelbarrows; component parts and raw materials used in the final product; supplies used in the production process that do not become part of the final product, and sources of energy. Each of these resources is supplied by organizations producing them as products in return for monetary payment.

In short, the marketer who wants to satisfy customers must have products to offer them. So product suppliers are essential to marketing success. Some suppliers are outside the organization, and even those inside usually do not respond favorably to direct orders from marketing managers. In fact, in many cases the most difficult task the marketing manager faces is to persuade production personnel or raw materials vendors to supply what the customer has been promised. The marketing (exchange-to-mutual-advantage) orientation can be very helpful here.

Society

It is easy to see that exchange relationships exist between marketers and

Exhibit 2-4 Examples of Competition Levels for Various Products

Competition Level	Nature of Competition	Product		
		General Motors Automobile	McDonald's Hamburger	State University Education
Brand	Other organizations offering similar products	Ford, Datsun	Burger Chef H. Salt Fish 'n Chips	Junior college Private university
Product	Other products performing similar functions	Auto repair Mass transit	Vending machine Fine restaurant	Educational television Technical school
Generic	Other ways of satisfying similar desires	Long distance telephone Planned community	Supermarket Home garden	Apprenticeship Library
Total desires	Other desires to be satisfied	Hamburgers Education	Automobile Education	Automobile Hamburgers

customers, and between marketers and suppliers of the resources necessary to produce the products that customers demand. It is perhaps less clear, but certainly no less important, to recognize that these exchanges take place within the context of a larger society. Citizens of the society are affected by every purchase of products and supplies. Citizens therefore exert constraints upon marketing activities. So marketing managers must understand and relate to citizens. It is convenient to group citizens into four categories: competitors, regulators, influencers, and the general public.

Competitors. The most direct constraint upon the activities of most marketing managers is what their competitors do. The essence of competition is the fact that customers can satisfy their desires in many ways other than consuming the marketer's product. It is important, therefore, for the marketer to view competition from the perspective of the customer. Four levels of competition should be studied: brand, product, generic, and total want satisfaction. Exhibit 2-4 provides examples.

At the brand level, the marketer competes with other organizations offering similar products. General Motors competes with Ford, McDonald's competes with Burger Chef, and the state university competes with junior colleges. At the product level, General Motors today finds itself competing not only with the Bay Area Rapid Transit system, but with Sears—now the world's largest automobile repairer. Similarly at this level, a potential customer might weigh a visit to McDonald's against dropping coins in a vending machine, and a prospective student might consider a vocational or technical school.

At the generic level, the potential customer is considering alternative ways of satisfying similar desires. Instead of traveling by automobile, for example, the customer may consider making more long distance telephone calls or moving to a totally planned community in which he or she could live, work, and spend leisure hours without extensive traveling. Similarly, the prospective McDonald's customer might satisfy a desire for food by visiting a supermarket or starting a home garden, and the potential student might consider apprenticeship to an experienced plumber or electrician, or perhaps a visit to the local library.

Finally, unless the consumer's resources for payment are unlimited, he or she must make choices among alternative ways of satisfying all of his or her desires. Economists say that wants are insatiable, but the budget is finite. Thus, the individual contemplating purchase of a new car may have to weigh its value in terms of hamburgers and/or educational benefits.

The point for the marketing manager to keep in mind is that competition is viable at all four levels. In my opinion, too many marketing managers spend too much time focusing too narrowly on brand competition. General Motors is the world's largest manufacturer of new automobiles, but fewer such automobiles have been demanded in the last few years, as consumers look for alternative ways of satisfying the desire for transportation, or even for ways to reduce the amount of transportation they need. To be specific, General Motors has handled Ford pretty well, but it may find the competition tougher as established marketers such as Sears persuade motorists to repair their automobiles and keep them longer, or as AT&T convinces people to travel less and communicate more via telephone.

Regulators. The second category of citizen groups is regulators. These are the various governmental agencies whom citizens have charged with the responsibility of being sure the marketers' actions conform to the public interest. This, of course, is a broad statement about a complex topic. Government regulators exist at federal, state, and local levels, and may be attached to executive, legislative, or judicial branches at each level. Thus, the number of potential regulators with whom a given marketing manager must relate is potentially very large. Societal regulation of marketing is explored in considerable detail in Chapter 4.

Influencers. Regulation generally results from the activities of a third group: influencers. Influencers are citizens who are not competitors of the organization and do not hold governmental positions, but who nevertheless shape social policy toward marketers. Four broad categories can be distinguished: social critics, lobbyists, community leaders, and the news media.

Social critics are citizens who, by virtue of their abilities and skills, command public attention. Two broad groups are intellectuals (including professors, editorial columnists, religious leaders, and artists and entertainers) and activists such as Common Cause and Ralph Nader and his Raiders, and lobbyists, e.g., political parties, the National Association of Manufacturers, the National Rifle Association, and the Committee on Political Effort of the AFL-CIO. The stated purpose of such groups is to influence regulators. Community leaders command influence by virtue of their position. Bankers, merchants, university presidents, political bosses, and the wealthy are among this group, often called "the establishment."

The news media can be divided into two broad classes: print and broadcast. Print media encompass newspaper, magazines, books, etc. Broadcast media include radio and television. The news media often provide a forum for the views of social critics, lobbyists and community leaders. In addition, the media themselves, by the way they choose and interpret the news that they report, influence citizens in their views about marketing and other topics.

Finally, there is everybody else. This category is difficult to define precisely. But there is no doubt that there is a phenomenon called "public opinion." Public opinion is molded by influencers, regulators, and the various competitors who comprise the market system. And public opinion can be a very powerful constraining force upon marketing activities. In 1975, for example, the automobile seatbelt ignition interlock requirement was dropped by Congress, under enormous pressure from the motoring public.

Thus, the marketing manager performs the functions of seeking, matching, programming, and consummating as these functions relate to customers, suppliers and citizens. In summary of this section, and as a guide to thinking throughout the book, we offer a framework that synthesizes our discussion of the marketing manager's relationships.

Marketing Management Model
Exhibit 2-5 presents the model. Note that it focuses upon the marketing function of an organization. In accordance with the systems concept, the organization is viewed as a processor of resources. The outputs of the system are products which flow through the channel of distribution to consumers. The model highlights marketing's relationships with three constituents: customers, suppliers, and society.

As discussed above, customers consist of final consumers and in some cases of middlemen in the channel of distribution. Some channels also make use of facilitating agents such as marketing research firms, banks and other lending institutions, and storage and shipping firms.

Suppliers of human, capital, physical, and information resources may be either external vendors such as consulting firms, stockholders and lenders, sellers of raw materials and component parts, and syndicated

Exhibit 2-5 The Marketing Management Model

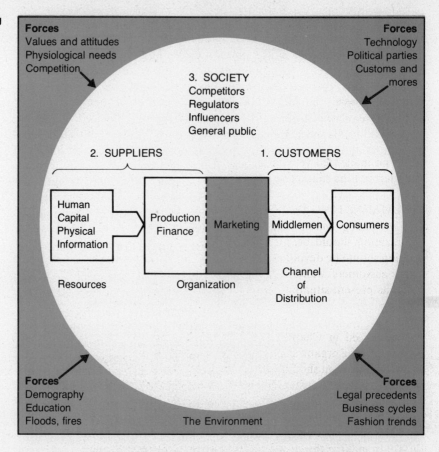

information services such as the Neilsen store audits. Suppliers of more immediate concern to marketing managers are the managers of other organizational functions, such as production and finance.

The organization processes inputs and markets product outputs to customers within the larger society, including competitors, regulators, influencers, and the general public. Society, in turn, is part of the total environment which includes not only people and institutions, but also physical characteristics. The environment is depicted as complex, with a great propensity to change when acted upon by environmental forces. Exhibit 2-6 presents examples of forces categorized according to the three marketing relationships as well as physical forces.

Managing marketing activities is not an easy task. The marketing management model is useful in structuring thinking about marketing situations. But marketing thinking requires more than structure. It re-

Exhibit 2-6 Examples of Environmental Forces

Customers	Citizens	Suppliers	Physical
Income levels	Demographics	Economic conditions	Weather and climate
Fashion trends	Education levels	Science and technology	Geography and terrain
Values	Customs and mores	Competition	Physical events (fire, flood, etc.)
Physiological needs	Political parties	Public policy	Ecology

quires an integrated viewpoint, a guiding philosophy. This philosophy is often termed the marketing concept.

THE MARKETING CONCEPT

The *marketing concept* states that the fundamental objective of the organization should be customer satisfaction. All activities of the organization should be devoted to identifying, and then producing, products to satisfy customers' wants. Let us see how this concept evolved in the past, assess its present situation, and comment upon its future role.

Past . . .

As introduced in Chapter 1, this concept states that the fundamental objective of the organization should be customer satisfaction: all activities of the organization should be devoted to identifying, and then producing, products to satisfy customers' wants. This concept can be considered a basic philosophy for organizational management. J. B. McKitterick, former president of General Electric Company, commented in 1957 that ". . . the principal task of the marketing function . . . is not so much to be skillful in making the customer do what suits the interests of the business as to be skillful in making the business do what suits the interests of the customer." Exhibit 2-7 presents a classic application of the concept.

The marketing concept has two key benefits. First, the emphasis on customer satisfaction implies that all organizational activities should be focused upon this fundamental objective. With such unity of purpose and focus, organizational activities can be coordinated and conflicts minimized. Second, the emphasis on the customer should keep the organization alert to changing environmental conditions, new markets, and shifts in customers' tastes and demands. Thus, the marketing concept can be a powerful management philosophy. This concept generally has evolved in three stages, as depicted in Exhibit 2-8.

At first, the company is production oriented. At this stage, the only activity recognized specifically as a marketing activity is actual selling work. As Pillsbury's chief executive officer once put it, "Our basic function (was) to mill high quality flour, and of course we hired salespersons to sell it, just as we hired accountants to keep our books." In this phase, the functions of production and finance assume major responsibilities, as shown in Exhibit 2-8(a). In this stage, the sales manager (responsible for sales quotas, hiring and training of salespersons, and their field supervision) would be considered on the same organizational level as the accounting manager and perhaps the legal counsel.

As the company grows and the market expands, top management begins to realize that salespersons could be profitably supported by certain types of staff assistance. Some of the hiring and training duties are given to a personnel manager, a publicity man is hired, someone is placed in charge of advertising, and rudimentary marketing research (sales and cost analysis and some simple consumer surveys) are conducted. In addition, management recognizes the need for closer coordination of sales effort with activities performed by other functions—e.g., product design, pricing, budgeting and forecasting, physical distribution. Marketing scholars generally call this development in managerial thinking a shift from production orientation to sales orientation as shown in Exhibit 2-8(b).

The third stage is described as marketing-oriented or consumer-oriented–Exhibit 2-8(c). Here the philosophy of the marketing concept is recognized, and attempts are made to systematically determine customers' wants and to integrate organizational operations for producing products that satisfy these wants. In terms of organizational structure, a vice president for marketing is often created, on an equal organizational level with the vice president of production and finance. Reporting to the vice president of marketing are the sales manager and the managers of other marketing activities deemed necessary by the firm—advertising, marketing information, forecasting, and physical distribution. As a part of this movement toward integration of operations, the personnel function also is often elevated to vice presidential status at this time.

Of course, smaller and/or newer organizations may not yet have

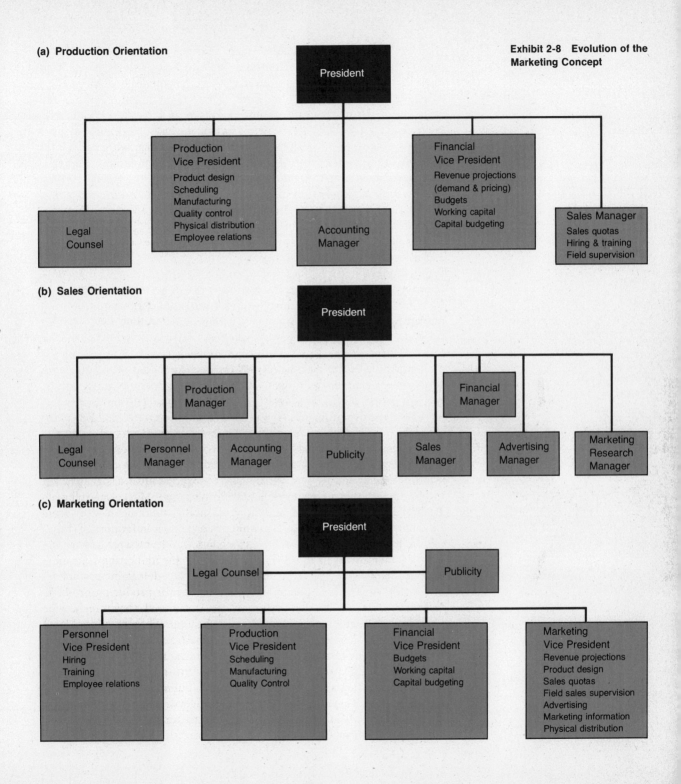

(a) Production Orientation

Exhibit 2-8 Evolution of the Marketing Concept

President

Legal Counsel

Production Vice President
Product design
Scheduling
Manufacturing
Quality control
Physical distribution
Employee relations

Accounting Manager

Financial Vice President
Revenue projections
(demand & pricing)
Budgets
Working capital
Capital budgeting

Sales Manager
Sales quotas
Hiring & training
Field supervision

(b) Sales Orientation

President

Production Manager

Financial Manager

Legal Counsel

Personnel Manager

Accounting Manager

Publicity

Sales Manager

Advertising Manager

Marketing Research Manager

(c) Marketing Orientation

President

Legal Counsel

Publicity

Personnel Vice President
Hiring
Training
Employee relations

Production Vice President
Scheduling
Manufacturing
Quality Control

Financial Vice President
Budgets
Working capital
Capital budgeting

Marketing Vice President
Revenue projections
Product design
Sales quotas
Field sales supervision
Advertising
Marketing information
Physical distribution

reached the marketing-oriented stage, and the actual strength of the marketing function varies from company to company as a result of historical development, organization politics, personalities of the various managers in the organization, and so on. Generalization about the structure of the marketing function, therefore, is somewhat speculative. Nevertheless, I believe it is fairly realistic to characterize most large business organizations in the United States and other mature economies as being in the marketing-oriented stage. And, as we noted in Chapter 1, this view of customer/organization relationships is increasingly being extended to not-for-profit organizations (such as universities, museums, charity fund drives) and to the marketing of ideas (stop smoking, do not litter) and political candidates.

. . . Present . . .

While impressive success has been claimed for the marketing concept in the past, it is not without its critics. At the present time, shortcomings can be noted in applying the concept to each of the three constituencies of marketing management: customers, citizens, and supplies.

Consumerism. Not every organization practices the philosophy of the marketing concept, not if consumer dissatisfaction is used as an index of its adoption. Consumers complain loudly about products that are unsafe, that are poorly made, that do not perform as advertised—and consumers feel powerless in getting these faults corrected. This has become a problem of such major proportions that premier management scholar Peter Drucker has labeled it the "shame of marketing."

In response, consumers—organized and encouraged by activists such as Ralph Nader and Robert Choate—have moved to ensure and augment the benefits that the consumer gets from participating in an exchange. Their methods range from mutilating computer-printed bills to direct contact with the president of the company producing offending products to boycotting products or stores to writing letters to newspaper editors and Congressmen and even, in a few instances, to looting and burning business establishments.

While consumer expectations may at times be too high and some responses excessive, the thrust of many consumer complaints seems to be justified. Some products are unsafe, and the operating instructions and warranty provisions are often difficult to understand. Many products look and perform too much like many other products, and things do seem to wear out too quickly. Salespersons may be uninformed or rude, and it is almost impossible to penetrate the computer system to find a person with the knowledge, authority and interest to attend to the consumer's grievance. Exhibit 2-9 summarizes the debate between consumerism and marketing management.

Exhibit 2-9 Consumerism and Marketing Management

Bell and Emory suggest that the marketing concept is under attack by consumerists because product originators and consumers have different assumptions about the nature of the marketing concept and its responsibility to consumers. These differences are as follows:

THE ORGANIZATION'S VIEW
The marketing concept has three basic elements:
1. *Customer Orientation.* Knowledge of the customer, which requires a thorough understanding of his needs, wants, and behavior should be the focal point of all marketing action. It implies the development of products and services to meet these needs. It does not exclude the possibility that these needs may be "stimulated" by business or that aggressive selling may be needed to persuade consumers to buy goods and services which have been created for them.
2. *Integrated Effort.* Ultimately, the entire firm must be in tune with the market by placing emphasis on the integration of the marketing function with research, product management, sales, and advertising to enhance the firm's total effectiveness.
3. *Profit Direction.* The marketing concept is intended to make money for the company by focusing attention on profit rather than upon sales volume.

THE CONSUMERISTS' VIEW
These elements should be redefined:
1. *Consumer Concern.* A positive effort by the marketer to make the consumer the focus of all marketing decisions through service that delivers a high level of satisfaction per consumer dollar spent.
2. *Integrated Operations.* A view that the entire business is a total operational system with consumer and social problems taking precedence over operational considerations in all functional areas.
3. *Profit Reward.* Profit must be viewed as the residual that results from efficiently supplying consumer satisfactions in the marketplace.
Thus, the purpose of the consumerism movement is to adjust the balance of the exchange process to be more in line with the consumer's assumptions. A careful study of the consumerism movement led Kotler to five pertinent conclusions about it:
1. *Consumerism was inevitable.* It was not a plot by Ralph Nader and a handful of consumerists but an inevitable phase in the development of our economic system.
2. *Consumerism will be enduring.* Just as the labor movement started as a protest uprising and became institutionalized in the form of unions, government boards, and labor legislation, the consumer movement, too, will become an increasingly institutionalized force in U.S. society.
3. *Consumerism will be beneficial.* On the whole, it promises to make the U.S. economic system more responsive to new and emerging societal needs.
4. *Consumerism is promarketing.* The consumer movement suggests an important refinement in the marketing concept to take into account societal concerns.
5. *Consumerism can be profitable.* The societal marketing concept suggests areas of new opportunity and profit for alert business firms.

Adapted from Martin L. Bell and C. William Emory, "The Faltering Marketing Concept," *Journal of Marketing,* October 1971, pp. 37–42, with permission of the publisher, the American Marketing Association; and from Philip Kotler, "What Consumerism Means for Marketers," *Harvard Business Review,* May–June 1972, pp. 48–57, with permission of the publisher.

It can be said in defense of marketing, that products are more complex today, that competent help is hard to find, and that people seem to complain more loudly and more often than in the past. But the fact remains that many organizations are simply not as consumer-oriented as they should be. The production orientation and the sales orientation have not disappeared from the scene.

Moreover, relationships with customers are not as straightforward as

does provide a consistent management philosophy to guide marketing decisions. It would not be easy to implement such a viewpoint in all cases. Implementation would require (1) a broader perspective, to accommodate the views of stockholders, employees, government regulators, social critics, as well as customers; (2) a longer timespan in which to recognize and evaluate less obvious or more long-range consequences of exchange relationships (such as environmental pollution or undesirable side effects of pharmaceuticals); and (3) more careful integration of all organizational activities. One version of this update of the original marketing concept is the *societal marketing* concept [Kotler; see Exhibit 2-9]:

> The societal marketing concept calls for a customer orientation backed by integrated marketing aimed at generating customer satisfaction and long-run consumer welfare as the key to attaining long-run profitable volume. The addition of long-run consumer welfare asks the businessman to include social and ecological considerations in his product and marketing planning. He is asked to do this not only to meet his social responsibilities but also because failure to do this may hurt his long-run interests as a producer.

This statement can be interpreted generically: the marketer can view all constituent relationships as potential exchange situations. This would require a careful balancing of the perspectives and goals of the various constituencies and the marketer's own objectives. The responsibility of marketing management is to effectively and efficiently perform the marketing functions of seeking, matching, programming, and consummating in a way that maintains this balance.

THE MARKETING MANAGER'S JOB

It is easier to discuss marketing management than it is to do it competently. Your appreciation of the material throughout the book will be enhanced if, at this point, we discuss the qualities of the marketing manager and the rewards of marketing management.

Qualities of the Marketing Manager

After we have said so much about the myriad problems and responsibilities of marketing management, it may appear difficult—perhaps even a bit naive—to summarize basic qualities that a marketing manager should possess. Certainly any such list could cover only the most general qualities. Nevertheless, I find it helpful in understanding the job of the marketing manager to consider duties and responsibilities in light of the following six characteristics:

1. Empathy—the ability to understand the motivations and desires of others. Since marketing management involves close and crucial relationships with other organizational managers and other suppliers, customers, and various representatives of society (e.g., social critics and public policymakers), the marketing manager must attempt to understand why members of each of these groups think and behave as they do.

2. The Capacity for Rational Analysis—the ability to absorb and integrate many different kinds of information. The marketing manager must continually develop and upgrade abilities and skills in rational analysis.

3. Tolerance for Ambiguity—the ability to act decisively even when optimum courses of action cannot be determined. This statement may seem to contradict the previous call for increased skill in rational analysis, but it does not. Although it is true that rational analysis is playing an increasingly significant part in marketing decision making, uncertainty can seldom be eliminated from marketing situations. And yet, the manager must act. He/she must, therefore, be capable of assuming the responsibility for risk taking as judgment dictates.

4. Adaptability to Change—the capacity to recognize new opportunities and modify current thinking in light of new developments. Marketing activities are very complex, and the rate of change is accelerating. The marketing manager must have the capability to keep pace with change.

5. A Broad and Optimistic Outlook—the confidence and resilience to face each new situation with a positive attitude. Management is difficult, and no managerial action is always correct. The manager must learn from past mistakes, but must not allow them to shake his or her confidence in future decisions.

6. Ethical Sensitivity—heightened awareness of ideal or appropriate decisions or actions. Issues in ethics are difficult to address, and are very personal. There is little question, however, that marketing managers in the future will be held to stricter accountability for the impact of their actions and decisions upon the welfare of individual consumers and society as a whole.

We could discuss each of these qualities in more detail, but the major issues in the first five are relatively self-explanatory. The matter of marketing ethics, however, deserves further elaboration. An individual's ethics are essentially a set of moral principles that guide his/her thoughts and behavior. Such principles are derived from many sources, e.g., parental values, religious training, education and experience, personal introspection, group norms and customs, organizational policies, industry trade practices, law, and other formal governmental policies. The ethical standards which guide the decisions of marketing managers are under close scrutiny in contemporary society. There is, therefore, a crucial need for guidelines in marketing ethics. And yet, the area of marketing ethics is relatively undefined. Consider, for example, how you as a marketing manager might react to such questions as those in Exhibit 2-10.

Absolute moral guidelines for answering such questions might be approached from two directions. On the one hand, a manager might argue that laws and other formal public policies provide adequate guidance for resolving such issues: if an action is not illegal, then it is morally sanctioned. On the other hand, religious teachings seem to prohibit certain actions under all circumstances. Neither of these extremes is likely to be particularly appealing or useful to the marketing manager who faces such questions in concrete situations. Company policies may offer some guidance, but may lead to conflicts between, say, a moral obligation to remedy defective workmanship and profit objectives. Trade and professional associations also publish ethical codes. Such statements do provide useful general guidelines for members of the association, but usually lack the specificity to be particularly helpful in concrete situations. In the last analysis, each individual manager alone must determine whether a given decision or action is within the scope of morality as he/she defines it.

The area of ethics, therefore, is a fertile one for research by marketing scholars. Much of the work to date has not been particularly impressive. Models or theories of marketing ethics have been offered, but these have usually been couched in terms so abstract that their consequences cannot be tested in the real world. Another approach has been simply to tabulate the responses of marketing managers to questions such as those raised in Exhibit 2-10. A tabulation is generally in terms of some scale extending from high ethics to low ethics. Such a tabulation produces a range of empirical responses to ethical situations, but the responses are very difficult to relate to any theoretical framework that might be used to guide future decision making. As professors are wont to say, "Further research in this area is necessary."

In summary, it is not difficult to prepare a list of qualities that an ideal marketing manager should possess. Of course, the individual who could be rated high on all of these qualities is indeed a paragon—perhaps even a superman. These are, however, the fundamental attributes that do lead to successful performance of the marketing manager's job. Generally speaking, the more of such qualities that a marketing manager has, the greater his/her rewards.

Rewards of Marketing Management

Reward for the performance of any task can be divided into two components: financial and psychic. The financial rewards of competent managerial performance in marketing are considerable. The usual trend, illustrated in Exhibit 2-11, is for beginning salaries in sales and other marketing positions to be somewhat higher than those in general business, but lower than in more technical fields such as accounting or engineering.

Exhibit 2-10   Some Morally Difficult Situations in Marketing

You work for a cigarette company and up to now have not been convinced that cigarettes cause cancer. A recent report has come across your desk that clearly establishes the connection between cigarette smoking and cancer. What would you do?

2. Your R&D department has modernized one of your products. It is not really "new and improved," but you know that putting this statement on the package and in the advertising will increase sales. What would you do?

3. You have been asked to add a stripped-down model to the low end of your line that could be advertised to attract customers. The product won't be very good, but the salespersons could be depended upon to persuade people to buy a better higher-priced unit. You are asked to give the green light for developing this stripped-down version. What would you do?

4. You are interviewing a former product manager who just left a competitor's company. You are thinking of hiring him. He would be more than happy to tell you all the competitor's plans for the coming year. What would you do?

5. One of your dealers in an important territory has had family troubles recently and is not producing the sales he used to. He was one of the company's top producers in the past. It is not clear how long it will take before

his family trouble straightens out. In the meantime, many sales are being lost. There is a legal way to remove the dealer's franchise and replace him. What would you do?

6. You have a chance to win a big account that will mean a lot to you and your company. The purchasing agent hinted that he would be influenced by a "gift." Your assistant recommends sending a fine color television set to his home. What would you do?

7. You have heard that a competitor has a new product feature that will make a big difference in sales. He will have a hospitality suite at the annual trade show and unveil this feature at a party thrown for his dealers. You can easily send a snooper to this meeting to learn what the new feature is. What would you do?

8. You are eager to win a big contract, and during sales negotiations you learn that the buyer is looking for a better job. You have no intention of hiring him, but if you hinted that you might, he would probably give you the order. What would you do?

9. You have to make a choice between three ad campaigns outlined by your agency for your new product. The first (A) is a soft-sell, honest informational campaign. The second (B) uses sex-loaded emotional appeals and exaggerates the product's benefits. The third (C) involves a noisy, irritating commercial that is sure to gain audience attention. Preliminary tests show that the commercials are effective in the following order: C, B, and A. What would you do?

10. You are a marketing vice-president working for a beer

company, and you have learned that a particularly lucrative state is planning to raise the minimum legal drinking age from 18 to 21. You have been asked to join other breweries in lobbying against this bill and to make contributions. What would you do?

11. You want to interview a sample of customers about their reactions to a competitive product. It has been suggested that you invent an innocuous name like the Marketing Research Institute and interview people. What would you do?

12. You produce an antidandruff shampoo that is effective with one application. Your assistant says that the product would turn over faster if the instructions on the label recommended two applications. What would you do?

13. You are interviewing a capable, personable black applicant for a job as a salesperson. He is better qualified than the other men just interviewed. At the same time, you suspect that some of your current salespersons will react negatively to his hiring, and you also know that some important customers will be ruffled. What would you do?

14. You are a sales manager in an encyclopedia company. A common way for company salespersons to get into homes is to pretend they are taking a survey. After they finish the survey, they switch to their sales pitch. This technique seems to be very effective and is used by most of your competitors. What would you do?

Excerpted from Philip Kotler, *Marketing Management: Analysis, Planning and Control*, 2nd ed. (Englewood Cliffs: Prentice-Hall, Inc., 1972), p. 839, with permission of the publisher.

Exhibit 2-11   Average Monthly
Salaries in Selected Fields

Field	Salary After 10 Years Class of 1964	Salary After 5 Years Class of 1969	Starting Salary Class of 1974
Sales-Marketing	$1760	$1290	$840
Accounting	1718	1322	956
General Business	1645	1271	777
Engineering	1674	1362	995

Adapted from Frank S. Endicott, "Trends in Employment of College and University Graduates in Business and Industry," 29th ed. (Evanston, Ill.: Northwestern University, 1975), pp. 4, 7, with permission of the publisher.

The marketing manager usually closes the gap rather quickly, however; remuneration from within five to ten years is on a par with the more technical fields, and considerably above salaries in general business. And marketing management is perhaps the best preparation for top management. Exhibit 2-12 presents the results of one study in this area.

Fortune surveyed the chief executive officers of the nation's largest corporations. Questionnaires were sent to the heads of the *Fortune* 500 companies, the top 50 industrial corporations, and to the 300 men who run the 50 biggest commercial-banking companies, life insurance firms, diversified financial enterprises, retailers, transportation companies and utilities—altogether, a community of 800 executives. The chart indicates that a larger proportion of these men have backgrounds in marketing than in any other field. Of course, many factors contribute to top management success, but marketing men generally are well represented. [Pedantic aside: the word "men" is not a slip of the pen, nor am I being deliberately chauvinistic. The fact is that the *Fortune* study did not report any women in chief executive positions among the largest corporations. No doubt this will change in the future.]

The greatest attraction of marketing management, at least for me, is in the area of psychic satisfaction. My biases may be showing just a bit here, but I really do believe that marketing is where the action is—nothing moves until the sale is made. Marketing enhances a society's standard of living, provides many jobs directly and contributes indirectly to almost all types of employment, motivates individual consumers to improve the quality of their lives, and is the prime generator of profits that fuel the capitalistic system.

Of course, marketing activities are not without their problems. The fascinating thing is that those who desire to change the marketing system and modify marketing activities must themselves become proficient in the use of marketing concepts and techniques. Ralph Nader is a consummate marketing manager; John Kenneth Galbraith promotes his ideas for social reform most persuasively, and many other social critics and public policy makers also display considerable skill at various marketing man-

Exhibit 2-12   Main Career Emphasis of CEO's in *Fortune* Survey

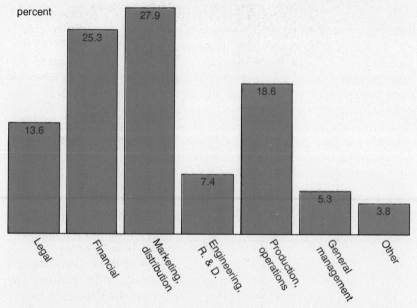

percent

13.6	25.3	27.9	7.4	18.6	5.3	3.8
Legal	Financial	Marketing, distribution	Engineering, R. & D.	Production, operations	General management	Other

Joe Argenziano for *Fortune* Magazine. Adapted from *Fortune,* May 1976, p. 316, with permission of *Fortune* Magazine.

agement tasks. Marketing management is pervasive, necessary, challenging, and rewarding.

CONCLUDING NOTE

Marketing-oriented thinking should guide all managerial decisions. Executives must understand relationships with customers, society, and suppliers of resources for products. As society grows more complex, marketing-oriented thinking will play an increasingly important role in most organizations and in society generally.

This is the textbook point of view. I think it is essentially correct, but perhaps it is also a bit idealistic. The situation in which a particular manager finds himself or herself at a given time is a unique blend of history, the manager's personality and talents, and the wants and desires of customers, citizens, and suppliers. Recognition and implementation of the changing role and scope of the marketing function takes time, and is not without cost. It is easy to criticize the decisions of marketing managers, but it definitely is not easy to make such decisions successfully. And the difficulties will be more numerous and more severe in the future. That is why I have argued in this chapter for a more comprehensive and systematic approach to the study, and the practice, of marketing management. Few marketing managers have adopted the broad perspective suggested in this chapter, but I am convinced that most will need it in the

1970s and 1980s. Of course, they will adapt it to particular situations, as their experience and judgment dictates.

To develop your own marketing management skills, you should become involved with marketing situations. That is, you must apply the concepts and processes developed in this chapter to situations that you know personally, to textbook examples and cases, to articles in *Marketing Is Everybody's Business,* and periodicals such as the *Wall Street Journal, Business Week,* and *Fortune.* Marketing management is an art based on marketing science and related disciplines. Learning the fundamentals of this art and science requires active participation and conscious effort on your part. Reach out for marketing knowledge.

KEY TERMS AND CONCEPTS
Marketing Management
   effectiveness
   efficiency
   process (systems concept)
Exchange Flows
   physical product
   use rights
   payment
   information
Marketing Management Functions
   seeking
   matching
   programming
   consummating
Marketing Mix
   product
   promotion
   distribution
   pricing
Marketing Manager's Relationships
   customers
      (consumers, middlemen, facilitating agents)
   suppliers
      (capital, human resources, physical resources)
   citizens
      (competitors, regulators, influencers, news media)
Competition Levels
   brand
   product
   generic
   total

Marketing Concept
  stages of evolution
  consumerism, social responsibility and supply problems
  the generic marketing concept
  the societal marketing concept
Ideal Marketing Manager's Qualities
  empathy
  capacity for rational analysis
  tolerance for ambiguity
  adaptability to change
  broad and optimistic outlook
  ethical sensitivity
Marketing Ethics
  difficult issues
  lack of theoretical framework
Rewards of Marketing Management
  financial
  psychic

QUESTIONS FOR DISCUSSION

1. The chapter introduction asserts that such organizations as General Motors, the Department of Defense, a corner grocery store, a political party, a CPA firm, a university, and the Mafia perform marketing activities. Examine this assertion. Give examples of each of the four types of exchange flows for each organization.

2. For each organization in question 1, provide examples of constituents in each of the three groups (customers, suppliers, and citizens).

3. Apply the four levels of competition to the product of each organization in question 1.

4. Examine performance of each of the four marketing management functions for each organization.

5. How would the (traditional) *marketing concept* guide the performance of marketing management functions for each organization? What adjustments would have to be made in managerial thinking to apply the generic marketing concept?

6. On the basis of your work with questions 1 through 5, outline the marketing strategies followed by each organization. What difficulties do you encounter? What recommendations would you make?

SUGGESTED READING

1. Wroe Alderson.

Marketing Behavior and Executive Action. Homewood, Ill.: Richard D. Irwin, 1957. Brilliant conceptual overview of the field of marketing management; not easy reading because many topics are tightly integrated; a classic.

2. Peter F. Drucker.

Managing for Results. New York: Harper and Row, 1964. A masterful statement of the role and scope of the manager's job, emphasizing the importance of the marketing function. *Management.* New York: Harper and Row, 1973. Encyclopedic expansion of 1964 statement; excellent reference.

3. Warren J. Keegan.

"Multi-National Marketing Strategy and Organization: An Overview." *Changing Marketing Systems.* American Marketing Association, 1967, pp. 203–209. Overview of the management of marketing activities using international examples; reprinted in Gabriel M. Gelb and Betsy D. Gelb, *Insights for Marketing Management,* 2nd ed., Goodyear Publishing Company, 1977.

4. Philip Kotler.

Marketing Management: Analysis, Planning and Control. 3rd ed. Englewood Cliffs, N.J.: Prentice-Hall, 1976. An excellent, rather more advanced treatment of marketing management than this text; contains numerous references.

5. Theodore Levitt.

"Marketing Myopia," *Harvard Business Review,* July–August 1960, pp. 45–56. Perhaps the single most significant article a marketing student or manager could read; reprinted in Gelb and Gelb, *Insights for Marketing Management. Marketing for Business Growth.* New York: McGraw-Hill, 1974. Updated and expanded version of 1960 classic; fast, easy reading; action-oriented; thought-provoking.

6. Philip Kotler.

"A Generic Concept of Marketing," *Journal of Marketing,* April 1972, pp. 46–54. An excellent discussion of the generic interpretation and the three stages of marketing consciousness; reprinted in Gelb and Gelb, *Insights for Marketing Management.*

CASE 1 / THE MARKETING V-P GETS A HEADACHE!

On a recent Monday morning the vice-president/marketing of Revelation Products, Inc., was studying the quarterly sales report forwarded to her by the manager/sales. The v-p was quite proud of the computer printouts before her for she had developed the sales report format when she was manager/sales three years earlier. The sales report collected dollar and unit sales data, categorized by the company's 6 geographic market areas, 10 product lines, 80 product models, 25 salespersons, 60 wholesalers, and 305 retailers. Additionally it included gross margin, cost, profit, and share of market data by product line. The report had taken the v-p and the director/systems analysis & planning almost 18 months and $30,000 to develop, but the v-p felt it was well worth the effort.

The Problem Unfolds

The v-p's joy was short-lived, however, because the data she saw was disturbing. The 5-year sales trend analysis showed that the last quarter's dollar sales were down 20 percent from the previous year and the current projection showed a decrease of 10 percent from the previous year. If this trend kept up, the v-p estimated that profit for the year would decrease almost 40 percent and the company might actually show a loss for the coming year. The v-p concluded that something just had to be done. As she was deliberating, the vice-president/finance called. The marketer answered with a heartiness she did not entirely feel, "Jim! What's up?"

"Jean, my people are worried about the latest sales data. They tell me that if this trend keeps up, our cash flow is going to be adversely affected and you know that bank loan comes due in 6 months. R. B. and the Board have already decided to pay it out instead of going for a renewal because the projected interest rate will be up 3 points. What are you people planning to do?"

"Well, Jim, we've got a couple of irons in the fire. I have just decided to call a meeting of the new product steering committee for tomorrow afternoon. Could I get back to you Wednesday?"

"O. K., Jean, but this thing needs to get moving.

We've got to generate a new cash flow projection on this loan business. By the way, have you heard that United Products has a new model coming out next month? Our banker got wind of this at the Banker's Convention last week. He says it's really creating some excitement."

"Yes, our marketing research director picked up on it when they were running a test market down in Dallas a few months back, but we didn't think they would have it ready to market this early. Get back to you on Wednesday."

The v-p called her secretary in. "Get this memo out by noon, please. Let's see. 'To the New Product Steering Committee.' Oh, where's that list! Here it is. Controller (background: accountant and tax specialist), manager/manufacturing (engineer), manager/sales (B.B.A. and 15 years in the field), manager/advertising (English literature), manager/finance (Harvard M.B.A.), Director/R&D (physicist), Director/marketing research (psychologist), Director/economic analysis (economist), Director/systems analysis & planning (computer scientist), Director/public relations (journalism), Director/legal affairs (law). 'Gentlemen, I am calling a meeting for tomorrow at 1:00 p.m. in the Conference Room. We need to explore the feasibility of moving some of our new products out of R & D into the market at the earliest possible time. Please study the attached report.' Attach that report we got from R&D a couple of weeks back."

The v-p wondered if she was doing the right thing. While the R&D report showed favorable progress on two of the three products under development, performance testing was incomplete, no market tests had been conducted, no consumer response had been obtained, and no staff work had been done on development of a marketing plan for bringing any of these products to market. Maybe the committee would come up with something.

At lunch the v-p got another jolt. The Director/public relations told her that their latest consumer awareness poll showed a drop in the corporate image of Revelation. The feeling was that the publicity associated with the product safety lawsuits pending against the company was unfavorable and that consumers were reacting to it.

After lunch the v-p called the Director/legal affairs. "Tom, this is Jean. I suppose you've already seen the

Source: Written by Francis M. Britton under the supervision of Ben M. Enis.

poll from public relations. Where do we stand on this lawsuit business? For the life of me, I can't see why consumers get so worked up over a couple of crackpot lawsuits!''

"Jean, negative consumer reaction is only the tip of the iceberg on this thing. The Product Safety Commission of the Federal Trade Commission has just informed me that they are going to look into our entire Blue Bird line and you know what that could lead to.

"It's what we feared when these lawsuits were filed,'' the lawyer continued. ''The Board wanted to settle fast to decrease the negative publicity but my people felt that move would be an admission of guilt and only intensify consumer reaction. That's why we decided to fight, but it could take a couple of years in the courts. I suppose now the Board will want to reevaluate our position. You know how the FTC worries them!''

"I wish I hadn't called,'' the v-p moaned. ''See you tomorrow at the meeting.''

At 3:00 that afternoon the Controller called. ''Jean, I just got the word from R.B. on the union negotiations. It looks like we will settle without a strike. The cost is high, however—12 percent across the board. The projections show that this will push up our unit costs approximately 5 percent. We've got to go with the cost reduction program or try for a price increase. I know the economics boys say the market won't sit still for another price hike this quickly, but the union is really putting the squeeze on our margin. Just thought you should know about this development before the meeting tomorrow.''

The Problem from Various Viewpoints

The New Product Steering Committee meeting started late, as usual. The v-p opened the meeting. ''Folks, we've got a problem and we have precious little time to solve it. You have the latest sales report and I don't have to tell you, it spells trouble. What do you think?''

After a protracted silence, the discussion went something like the following:

Manager/sales: Jean, I don't think my people should take the rap for this sales report. We have really been working with the retailers, but they say customers just are not buying as much this year. Maybe some special deals would help things along. You know, our retailers have been very cooperative in the past and shaving a few cents off our high volume models should juice up sales volume and reverse the downtrend.

Manager/advertising: We need a longer-run push than running a special on our best lines. We've got to get more media exposure, especially T.V. Both United and Surrealco spend almost twice as much as we do on T.V. exposure. If we don't match them, they're going to chew into our share of market even more heavily. Our agency says a new T.V. campaign can be ready in three months.

Director/marketing research: I think we ought to find out why our sales are slumping. Give me budget approval and I can get a consumer study going and have some answers in a couple of weeks.

Director/economic analysis: Why spend money on another consumer survey? The causal factors are rather clear. Inflation is still running at 10 percent per year and consumer incomes just aren't keeping up. As a result of this squeeze on real incomes, consumers are reducing their spending and demand is decreasing.

Director/systems planning: But if excessive inflation is the cause for our decreasing sales, why are we also losing share of market? Looks to me like our competitors would be hit just as hard as we are. This isn't happening. We're losing sales to our competitors.

Controller: And don't forget that United is coming out with their new blockbuster next month. What's that going to do to our competitive position?

Manager/sales: My salespersons tell me that the retailers they have been talking to are still leery about United's new entry. The samples going to retailers aren't very snappy and their projected price looks to be 20 percent higher than our closest line.

Director/marketing research: Still, we've got to recognize that United will have something new out and these days consumers will buy new, even if money is tight. I read a *Journal of Marketing Research* article last week that supported what I have been thinking for some time. The pace of change in consumer life styles is quickening. People are experimenting more. They grab new products that fit their life style perceptions. New is what's in demand.

Director/public relations: Our latest consumer poll shows our corporate image is not good. We think it's due to the lawsuits. Adverse consumer reaction may be what's causing consumers to switch to our competitors.

Director/legal affairs: That may be true, but it's too early to gauge the impact of the lawsuits. And remember United has been rapped by the FTC three times this year on ad substantiation. They haven't won one yet.

Controller: Actually, we shouldn't be so concerned with sales volume. If we just cut our costs, we can hold up our profit margin on the reduced volume. Seems to me cost reduction is what we should be discussing.

Manager/manufacturing: I recommended almost two months ago that we reduce the number of models we make. That would cut our manufacturing costs, lower our inventory, and release the funds we are now tying up in slow moving products. Some of these models are just gimmicks anyway.

Manager/finance: Anything that would improve our funds position would be a big help in meeting our bank loan when it comes due and that's a must!

Manager/sales: But, if we reduce the number of models, we're going to lose some buyers and they're sure to switch to our competitors. That's just going to push sales volume down even further.

Director/research and development: I seem to have missed the point somewhere. I thought this meeting was called to discuss bringing to market some of the new products we have been working on. As I indicated in my report, we think two of the three new items can be pushed to market in 6–9 months.

From what I have heard of United's new entry, one of our new products will be positioned against it. It's too bad they have a lead on us, but at least they will have developed market interest by the time we come out. That could work in our favor. Also, our product will probably have a higher performance rating than theirs since they usually use cheaper materials than we do. And as far as we know, no one now has anything like the TX-25.

If we go ahead now, we can match United rather quickly and get a lead on everyone else with the TX series. My people estimate it will take 18 months for anyone to come up with anything close to the TX-25.

Director/legal affairs: That TX-25 is going to cause some problems. First, my staff tells me that we may have some trouble getting our patent approved. Seems that some garage inventor got a patent on a device which uses the TX principle almost eight years ago. We're trying to research this but can't locate her. Secondly, the FTC is likely to want to see the results on our performance testing on the TX-25 before we can utilize performance claims in our advertising. This will probably be critical to its market success since I recall your report stressed the TX's performance advantages. Also TX might be subjected to the new guidelines being worked up by the Environmental Quality Board, but their position is somewhat uncertain at this point.

Director/systems planning: The last time R & D projected a long lead time before a competitor could match us, we got taken in half the time. By the time we got our marketing program really going, Rex-Ann was ready with an almost exact duplicate. We never did recoup our market development costs on that one.

Director/economic analysis: The next twelve months may not be a good time to introduce anything new to the consumer market. Our latest economic forecast indicates a gradual slowing in the GNP growth rate and a possible recession in nine months. If it comes, consumer disposable income is likely to dip sharply and this is going to put a lot of downward pressure on demand.

Director/public relations: I am getting confused. How can we have a 10 percent inflation rate, rapidly increasing interest rates and a recession? These seem to contradict economic principles, at least what I studied in school.

Controller: It's the new economics being practiced by Washington. I said when these price controls were put on that we were going to be taken for a ride and here we are, sputtering along. The unions are pushing costs up, costs push prices up, increasing prices spell inflation, inflation is chewing up real income and driving demand down, interest rates are so high that we can't afford to invest in new plant and equipment to hold costs down, decreasing demand and increasing costs are squeezing our margins. Now the FTC and the Environmental Quality Board are trying to interfere with our new product introductions. How can we fight our competitors and Washington at the same time?

Manager/finance: What kind of capital outlay is the TX-25 going to require and how much are the market development costs for it going to run?

Manager/manufacturing: R & D work on the TX-25 has not gotten far enough along to allow us to run a production simulation. Without the simulation, we can't project machine/man-hour standard volume. So we don't know how much equipment will be needed. But one thing is for sure; more plant space will be required. We can't manufacture what we are making now and the TX in our current plant. There's not enough room.

Director/legal affairs: Let's assume the TX-25 is pushed as fast as possible. What will the marketing program look like?

Director/marketing research: We have been testing

consumer reaction to possible brand names and the favorite thus far is 'Snowbird.'

Manager/sales: Where in the (expletive deleted) did that come from?

Director/marketing research: We explained the concept of the TX-25 to a consumer panel of average housewives and asked them to tell us what images the TX-25 projected to them. 'Snow' was mentioned 35 percent of the time and 'Bird,' 15 percent. Since these were the two highest single mentions, we combined them. Then we introduced the TX-25 to another consumer panel as the 'Snowbird' and examined their image/connotation reaction. We got a 75 percent favorable response.

Manager/advertising: My people have also worked on some copy and T.V. layouts using the Snowbird theme. We think we can come up with some catchy visuals and jingles. None of these has been tested yet, but I'm betting they will get a high Starch score.

Director/legal affairs: But Snowbird is close to Blue Bird and we're really under fire from the FTC on the Blue Bird line. Won't this similarity be a problem with image building? Also, has anyone checked to see that Snowbird is not already copyrighted?

Director/marketing research: We'll have to look into that. The polyurethane package tests are highly favorable. Consumers like to see what they're buying. Also we've checked out the sizes; the packages will stack on a standard retailer display shelf, so that's no problem.

Manager/sales: Speaking of retailers brings up a critical point. We don't think that our wholesaler/retailer network is going to be satisfactory for distributing the TX-25. It just doesn't fit very well with our current product mix. Our salespersons may need some retraining to be able to handle the TX-25 satisfactorily. Also, we will have to increase the size of the sales force. My people are overloaded now and can't take on anything new—particularly the major push required by a new product introduction.

Controller: Has anyone thought about the price we will put on TX-25?

Director/marketing research: We haven't tested consumer reaction to price yet.

Manager/manufacturing: We can't set the price until we know more about the costs.

Director/economic analysis: We need to project future competitor pricing also.

At this point the v-p, who had developed a splitting headache, interrupted. "Since it's getting close to 5:00, let's adjourn for today. You've all given me a lot to think about. We'll probably have another meeting next week."

The manager/manufacturing stayed behind to talk to the v-p for a minute. "Thought I should be the one to tell you. Our number 4 assembly line went down last night. The maintenance people project three days to replace some spent gear work. There's no way we can make the scheduled monthly shipment of Rev-C next Monday. You probably will want to let the retailers know there will be a week's delay."

CASE 2 / MARKETING A CITY OF THE FUTURE

In 1973, a city called The Woodlands, Texas, began competing with all other U.S. cities as a site for residential, commercial, and manufacturing development. The Woodlands had one unique thing going for it: the city did not yet exist.

The Woodlands Development Corp., a subsidiary of the Houston-based Mitchell Energy and Development Corp., is marketing a city from scratch. Beginning with 18,000 acres of woods about 28 miles north of downtown Houston, the development corporation has one element in its marketing mix that no other city can boast: the product—the city itself—can truly be tailored to the desires of potential customers.

The Woodlands will, in fact, be what the U.S. Department of Housing and Urban Development (HUD) calls a "new town." By definition, it starts from raw land. Projected to hold 150,000 residents, The Woodlands was in 1973 the largest new town planned in this country. Financing for the basic construction of sewers, streets, utilities, etc., would be guaranteed by HUD up to $50 million. But the marketing was strictly up to the Mitchell subsidiary.

Their strategy, as described by marketing executives, became the selling of a life style. Visitors to Woodland Development Corp. offices were offered, as suggested reading, Vance Packard's *A Nation of Strangers,* which concludes its chronicle of alienation in American life with the glowing account of a contrast: the "new town" of Columbia, Maryland. In Columbia, readers are advised, such features as hike-bike paths and "village" clusters of residences lead to a feeling of community which is absent in other cities. In other Woodlands literature, traffic, commuting, and suburban clannishness give way to a leisurely life among lakes, tennis courts, bridle paths, and a small-town atmosphere. And to top it off, readers are told, the University of Houston plans a campus at The Woodlands—guaranteeing that the city will have intellectual as well as recreational amenities.

The life style marketing is directed to Houston's residential "move-up" market, to companies nationwide who might seek to move their headquarters, and to

manufacturers seeking sites for light industry. In addition, The Woodlands had at the outset at least two other targets for its marketing efforts: HUD officials, for the guarantee of financing, and University of Houston officials who were seeking a site for a branch campus.

Marketing to HUD involved preparation of a book-length proposal matching plans for The Woodlands to the legislation which had authorized HUD to guarantee loans involved in the building of new towns. Since one objective of the federal legislation had been to develop communities that would be economically and racially mixed, The Woodlands promised to offer housing for five different economic groups in roughly equal proportions. From rich to poor, all could find suitable housing here, the proposal implied; a design that was perhaps sound marketing strategy for selling HUD on the project, but may complicate the job of marketing to future residents. "It's possible, of course, that our competitors will point to our design and use scare tactics about black neighbors to keep away whites," a Mitchell executive noted.

Marketing to the University of Houston consisted of meeting state requirements that land for the campus be donated, complete with utilities at the site and roads for access. The Woodlands was happy to meet the requirements, but so was a subdivision closer to Houston.

The U of H Board of Trustees made the final decision, and the members of its site-selection committee were the target market for the competing sites. The Woodlands' marketing effort consisted of a presentation by George Mitchell, president of Mitchell Energy & Development, and a tour of the proposed site arranged for committee members. The university official responsible for physical planning recalls that trustees were interested in a campus that would be "in the path of growth," and thus attract students. Consequently, he notes, the Mitchell presentation charted real estate transactions and development activity north from Houston toward the proposed site. The factual presentation, together with the emotional impact of the tree-covered site, carried the day.

Once The Woodlands had been selected as the University site, the last piece of the life style picture was in place. But, realizing it was still only a picture and not reality, marketers of The Woodlands decided they had to construct and populate one village of the city before

From Betsy D. Gelb and Ben M. Enis, *Marketing Is Everybody's Business,* Goodyear Publishing Company.

they could hope to attract the office tenants and industries they expected the life style to bring in. Consequently, construction began in 1973 on the village of "Grogan's Mill," which would have homes and a multipurpose center for getaway-from-it-all management seminars, among other activities. Obviously, businessmen who visited for a few days at their companies' expense to attend a seminar could not only make the facility self-supporting, but would at the same time be exposed to the attractions of The Woodlands.

Those planning the marketing program believed, however, that they would not be successful in bringing in businesses at first. Their hope was to first attract Houstonians, particularly those who did a lot of traveling and would be pleased by the 15-minute trip from The Woodlands to the Houston airport. This first group of buyers, it was felt, would form the living example of the life style, which would then attract industries whose biggest problem was keeping their employees, such as computer firms and consulting engineering firms. Such industries might be afraid to move their headquarters to a large city because of the risk that valuable employees would quit rather than move. But offered a chance to move to The Woodlands, the valuable employees would be delighted—so ran the reasoning of planners for the new city.

The first to hear this story were brokers of office space: The Woodlands executives assembled them in mid-1973 to see models of proposed office buildings and to hear the life style story. "They give us more than 300 'salesmen,'" an official of The Woodlands commented. "They know we have something that nobody else is offering."

Meanwhile, the advertising agency for The Woodlands had been preparing a marketing plan. Discussing its product first, the plan noted that the design for The Woodlands included extensive ecological planning to preserve the natural beauty; and also considerable social planning so that residents would find that the community meets their needs in education, religion, health care, recreation, and shopping.

Turning to marketing objectives, the plan listed three areas:

1. Economic
To sell improved land at a profit.
To lease space at a profit.
To develop alone and through joint ventures residential, retail, and related community service operations for profit.
To enhance the image of Mitchell Energy and Development Corporation.

2. Environmental
To develop a totally planned, ecologically balanced community with a better atmosphere for living and working.

3. Social
To develop a socially planned community that incorporates the greatest number of people from a variety of social, economic, and ethnic backgrounds, within the guidelines set down by the . . . contract between The Woodlands and the U.S. Department of Housing and Urban Development.

Listed as sales promotion ideas for The Woodlands were 21 events, including the following:

An Angler's Contest: Invite people interested in fishing to come to The Woodlands and fish in their specially stocked ponds. The one who catches the most fish in a specified period of time wins a brand new rod and reel.

A Marathon Race in The Woodlands: Invite people to come jog through The Woodlands . . . Racers would run along specified trails.

Birdwatching in The Woodlands: Open up The Woodlands for a weekend of birdwatching. Have an expert on hand to answer any questions.

Leaf Collecting Contest: Invite school children out to spend a day in The Woodlands collecting leaves. Give a prize to the child who collects the widest variety of leaves.

A Kite-Flying Contest: Invite youngsters out to fly their kites in an open area in The Woodlands and give prizes for the biggest kite, the most unusual kite, and the child who keeps his kite in the air the longest.

Free Helicopter or Goodyear Blimp Rides Over The Woodlands . . . And so forth.

Turning to the industrial marketing challenge, the plan proposed that real estate brokers be regarded as the primary target. The planners included as secondary targets banks and Chambers of Commerce in the area of The Woodlands. The plan suggested as a strategy selling the "new town" concept. Specific tactics included:

1. Giving tours of The Woodlands Business Park locations and present facilities.

2. Allowing present tenants to convey to prospects why *they* came to The Woodlands.

3. Giving helicopter tours, when possible, to locate The Woodlands within the Houston market.

To make sure there would be some "present tenants" of office space, The Woodlands Development Corp. signed up two right away. One was itself; the corporation moved its employees into the first completed office building. The second was a builder of prefabricated homes, who, of course, happened to be building many of the homes in the first village under construction in The Woodlands.

Only time will tell whether The Woodlands will meet its timetable for growing from a forest into a city of 150,000. Future marketing challenges include: persuading the Texas legislature to finance construction of the University of Houston campus buildings; and persuading HUD that every effort is being made to attract a wide economic range of residents although, for example, it may in fact be extremely difficult to sell to working-class blacks. But the personnel of The Woodlands Development Corp. are optimistic. With an 18,000-acre product, they had expected all along that their marketing job would be a big one.

CASE 3 / THE MARKET MECHANISM IN MICROCOSM

Exchange is a universal human activity. It develops in all societies—even the artificial society of a prisoner of war camp. The particular society described in the report below existed in Germany during World War II, but this is not a war story, nor an examination of prison conditions. It is, rather, a very clear illustration of the pervasive nature of exchange activity.

Economic activity is to be found in any P.O.W. camp. True a prisoner is not dependent on his exertions for the provision of the necessaries, or even the luxuries of life. But through his economic activity, the exchange of goods and services, his standard of material comfort is considerably enhanced.

Everyone received a roughly equal share of essentials; it is by trade that individual preferences are given expression and comfort increased. All at some time, and most people regularly, make exchanges of one sort or another. Between individuals there was active trading in all consumer goods and in some services. Most trading was for food against cigarettes or other foodstuffs, but cigarettes rose from the status of a normal commodity to that of currency. RMk.s [Reich Marks—German currency] existed but had no circulation save for gambling debts, as few articles could be purchased with them from the canteen.

Our supplies consisted of rations provided by the detaining power and (principally) the contents of Red Cross food parcels—tinned milk, jam, butter, biscuits, bully [beef], chocolate, sugar, etc., and cigarettes. So far the supplies to each person were equal and regular. Private parcels of clothing, toilet requisites and cigarettes were also received, and here equality ceased owing to the different numbers dispatched and the vagaries of the post. All these articles were the subject of trade and exchange.

The Development and Organization of the Market

Very soon after capture people realised that it was both undesirable and unnecessary, in view of the limited size and the equality of supplies, to give away or to accept gifts of cigarettes or food. "Goodwill" developed into trading as a more equitable means of maximising individual satisfaction. Starting with simple direct barter, such as a non-smoker giving a smoker friend his cigarette issue in exchange for a chocolate ration, more complex exchanges soon became an accepted custom. Stories circulated of an [Italian] padre who started off round the camp with a tin of cheese and five cigarettes and returned to his bed with a complete parcel in addition to his original cheese and cigarettes; the market was not yet perfect. Within a week or two, as the volume of trade grew, rough scales of exchange values came into existence. It was realised that a tin of jam was worth ½ lb. of margarine plus something else; that a cigarette issue was worth several chocolate issues, and a tin of diced carrots was worth practically nothing.

By the end of a month, when we reached our permanent camp, there was a lively trade in all commodities and their relative values were well known, and expressed not in terms of one another—one didn't quote bully in terms of sugar—but in terms of cigarettes. The cigarette became the standard of value. In the permanent camp people started by wandering through the bungalows calling their offers—"cheese for seven" (cigarettes)—and the hours after parcel issue were bedlam. The inconveniences of this system soon led to its replacement by an Exchange and Mart notice board in every bungalow, where under the headings "name," "room number," "wanted" and "offered" sales and wants were advertised. When a deal went through, it was crossed off the board. The public and semi-permanent records of transactions led to cigarette prices being well known and thus tending to equality throughout the camp, although there were always opportunities for an astute trader to make a profit from arbitrage. With this development everyone, including non-smokers, was willing to sell for cigarettes, using them to buy at another time and place. Cigarettes became the normal currency, though, of course, barter was never extinguished.

The Cigarette Currency

Although cigarettes as currency exhibited certain peculiarities, they performed all the functions of a metallic currency: as a unit of account, as a measure of value

Abridged from R.A. Radford, "The Economic Organization of a P.O.W. Camp," *Economica* (November, 1945), pp. 189–201.

and as a store of value, and shared most of its characteristics. They were homogeneous, reasonably durable, and of convenient size for the smallest or, in packets, for the largest transactions. Incidentally, they could be clipped or sweated by rolling them between the fingers so that tobacco fell out.

Cigarettes were also subject to the working of Gresham's Law, "bad money drives out good money." Certain brands were more popular than others as smokes, but for currency purposes a cigarette was a cigarette. Consequently buyers used the poorer qualities and the Shop rarely saw the more popular brands; cigarettes such as Churchman's No. 1 were rarely used for trading. At one time cigarettes hand-rolled from pipe tobacco began to circulate. Pipe tobacco was issued in lieu of cigarettes by the Red Cross at a rate of 25 cigarettes to the ounce and this rate was standard in exchanges, but an ounce would produce 30 home-made cigarettes. Naturally, people with machine-made cigarettes broke them down and re-rolled the tobacco, and the real cigarette virtually disappeared from the market. Hand-rolled cigarettes were not homogeneous and prices could no longer be quoted in them with safety; each cigarette was examined before it was accepted and thin ones were rejected, or extra demanded as a make-weight. For a time we suffered all the inconveniences of a debased currency.

Machine-made cigarettes were always universally acceptable, both for what they would buy and for themselves. It was this intrinsic value which gave rise to their principal disadvantage as currency, a disadvantage which exists, but to a far smaller extent, in the case of metallic currency—that is, a strong demand for non-monetary purposes. Consequently our economy was repeatedly subject to deflation and to periods of monetary stringency. While the Red Cross issue of 50 or 25 cigarettes per man per week came in regularly, and while there were fair stocks held, the cigarette currency suited its purpose admirably. But when the issue was interrupted, stocks soon ran out, prices fell, trading declined in volume and became increasingly a matter of barter. This deflationary tendency was periodically offset by the sudden injection of new currency. Private cigarette parcels arrived in a trickle throughout the year, but the big numbers came in quarterly when the Red Cross received its allocation of transport. Several hundred thousand cigarettes might arrive in the space of a fortnight. Prices soared, and then began to fall, slowly at first but with increasing rapidity as stocks ran out, until the next big delivery. Most of our economic troubles could be attributed to this fundamental instability.

Price Movements

Many factors affected prices, the strongest and most noticeable being the periodical currency inflation and deflation described in the last paragraphs. The periodicity of this price cycle depended on cigarette and, to a far lesser extent, on food deliveries. At one time in the early days, before any private parcels had arrived and when there were no individual stocks, the weekly issue of cigarettes and food parcels occurred on a Monday. The non-monetary demand for cigarettes was great, and less elastic than the demand for food: consequently prices fluctuated weekly, falling towards Sunday night and rising sharply on Monday morning. Later, when many people held reserves, the weekly issue had no such effect, being too small a proportion of the total available. Credit allowed people with no reserves to meet their non-monetary demand over the week-end.

The general price level was affected by other factors. An influx of new prisoners, proverbially hungry, raised it. Heavy air raids in the vicinity of the camp probably increased the non-monetary demand for cigarettes and accentuated deflation. Good and bad war news certainly had its effect, and the general waves of optimism and pessimism which swept the camp were reflected in prices. Before breakfast one morning in March of this year, a rumour of the arrival of parcels and cigarettes was circulated. Within ten minutes I sold a treacle ration, for four cigarettes (hitherto offered in vain for three), and many similar deals went through. By 10 o'clock the rumour was denied, and treacle that day found no more buyers even at two cigarettes.

The Market in Operation

The permanent camps in Germany saw the highest level of commercial organization. In addition to the Exchange and Mart notice boards, a shop was organised as a public utility, controlled by representatives of the Senior British Officer, on a no profit basis. People left their surplus clothing, toilet requisites and food there until they were sold at a fixed price in cigarettes. Only sales in cigarettes were accepted—there was no barter—and there was no higgling. For food at least there were standard prices: clothing is less homogeneous and the price was decided around a norm by the seller and the shop manager in agreement; shirts would average say 80 (cigarettes), ranging from 60 to 120 according to quality and age. Of food, the shop carried small stocks for convenience; the capital was provided by a loan from the bulk store of Red Cross cigarettes and repaid by a small commission taken on the first transactions. Thus the cigarette attained its fullest currency status, and the market was almost completely unified.

Coffee extract—relatively cheap among the tea-drinking English—commanded a fancy price in biscuits or cigarettes, and some enterprising people made small fortunes that way. (Incidentally we found out later that much of the coffee went "over the wire" and sold for phenomenal prices at black market cafés in Munich: some of the French prisoners were said to have made substantial sums in RMk.s. This was one of the few occasions on which our normally closed economy came into contact with other economic worlds.)

Eventually public opinion grew hostile to these monopoly profits—not everyone could make contact with the French—and trading with them was put on a regulated basis. Each group of beds was given a quota of articles to offer and the transaction was carried out by accredited representatives from the British compound, with monopoly rights.

There was an embryo labour market. Even when cigarettes were not scarce, there was usually some unlucky person willing to perform services for them. Laundrymen advertised at two cigarettes a garment. Battle-dress was scrubbed and pressed and a pair of trousers lent for the interim period for twelve. A good pastel portrait cost thirty or a tin of "Kam" (potted meat). Odd tailoring and other jobs similarly had their prices.

There were also entrepreneurial services. There was a coffee stall owner who sold tea, coffee or cocoa at two cigarettes a cup, buying his raw materials at market prices and hiring labour to gather fuel and to stoke; he actually enjoyed the services of a chartered accountant at one stage. After a period of great prosperity he overreached himself and failed disastrously for several hundred cigarettes.

One trader in food and cigarettes, operating in a period of dearth, enjoyed a high reputation. His capital, carefully saved, was originally about 50 cigarettes, with which he bought rations on issue days and held them until the price rose just before the next issue. He also

picked up a little by arbitrage; several times a day he visited every Exchange or Mart notice board and took advantage of every discrepancy between prices of goods offered and wanted. His knowledge of prices, markets and names of those who had received cigarette parcels was phenomenal. By these means he kept himself smoking steadily—his profits—while his capital remained intact.

Credit entered into many, perhaps into most, transactions, in one form or another. Naturally prices varied according to the terms of sale. A treacle ration might be advertised for four cigarettes now or five next week. And in future market "bread now" was a vastly different thing from "bread Thursday." Bread was issued on Thursday and Monday, four and three days' rations respectively, and by Wednesday and Sunday night it had risen at least one cigarette per ration, from seven to eight, by supper time. One man always saved a ration to sell then at the peak price: his offer of "bread now" stood out on the board among a number of "bread Monday's" fetching one or two less, or not selling at all—and he always smoked on Sunday night.

More interesting than changes in the general price level were changes in the price structure. Changes in the supply of a commodity, in the German ration scale or in the make-up of Red Cross parcels, would raise the price of one commodity relative to others. Tins of oatmeal, once a rare and much sought after luxury in the parcels, became a commonplace in 1943, and the price fell. In hot weather the demand for cocoa fell, and that for soap rose. A new recipe would be reflected in the price level: the discovery that raisins and sugar could be turned into an alcoholic liquor of remarkable potency reacted permanently on the dried fruit market. The invention of electric immersion heaters run off the power points made tea, a drug on the market in Italy, a certain seller in Germany.

In August, 1944, the supplies of parcels and cigarettes were both halved. Since both sides of the equation were changed in the same degree, changes in prices were not anticipated. But this was not the case. the non-monetary demand for cigarettes was less elastic than the demand for food, and food prices fell a little. More important however, were the changes in the price structure. German margarine and jam, hitherto value-less owing to adequate supplies of Canadian butter and marmalade, acquired a new value. Chocolate, popular and certain seller, and sugar, fell. Bread rose;

several standing contracts of bread for cigarettes were broken, especially when the bread ration was reduced a few weeks later.

In February, 1945, the German soldier who drove the ration wagon was found to be willing to exchange loaves of bread at the rate of one loaf for a bar of chocolate. Those in the know began selling bread and buying chocolate, by then almost unsaleable in a period of serious deflation. Bread, at about 40, fell slightly; chocolate rose from 15; the supply of bread was not enough for the two commodities to reach parity, but the tendency was unmistakable.

The substitution of German margarine for Canadian butter when parcels were halved naturally affected their relative values, margarine appreciating at the expense of butter. Similarly, two brands of dried milk, hitherto differing in quality and therefore in price by five cigarettes a tin, came together in price as the wider substitution of the cheaper raised its relative value.

Public Opinion

Public opinion on the subject of trading was vocal if confused and changeable, and generalisations as to its direction are difficult and dangerous. A tiny minority held that all trading was undesirable as it engendered an unsavoury atmosphere; occasional frauds and sharp practices were cited as proof. Certain forms of trading were more generally condemned; trade with the Germans was criticised by many. Red Cross toilet articles, which were in short supply and only issued in cases of actual need, were excluded from trade by law and opinion working in unshakable harmony. At one time, when there had been several cases of malnutrition reported among the more devoted smokers, no trade in German rations was permitted, as the victims became an additional burden on the depleted food reserves of the Hospital. But while certain activities were condemned as antisocial, trade itself was practised, and its utility appreciated, by almost everyone in the camp.

More interesting was opinion on middlemen and prices. Taken as a whole, opinion was hostile to the middleman. His function, and his hard work in bringing buyer and seller together, were ignored; profits were not regarded as a reward for labour, but as the result of sharp practices. The padre in Italy, or the men at Moosburg who opened trading relations with the French, are examples: the more subdivided the market, the less perfect the advertisement of prices, and the less

stable the prices, the greater was the scope for these operators. One man capitalised his knowledge of Urdu by buying meat from the Sikhs and selling butter and jam in return: as his operations became better known more and more people entered this trade, prices in the Indian Wing approximated more nearly to those elsewhere, though to the end a "contact" among the Indians was valuable, as linguistic difficulties prevented the trade from being quite free. Some were specialists in the Indian trade, the food, clothing or even the watch trade. Middlemen traded on their own account or on commission. Price rings and agreements were suspected and the traders certainly co-operated.

Despite the fact that his very existence was proof to the contrary, the middleman was held to be redundant in view of the existence of an official Shop and the Exchange and Mart. Appreciation only came his way when he was willing to advance the price of a sugar ration, or to buy goods spot and carry them against a future sale. In these cases the element of risk was obvious to all, and the convenience of the service was felt to merit some reward. Particularly unpopular was the middleman with an element of monopoly, the man who contacted the ration wagon driver, or the man who utilised his knowledge of Urdu. And middlemen as a group were blamed for reducing prices. Opinion notwithstanding, most people dealt with a middleman, whether consciously or unconsciously, at some time or another.

There was a strong feeling that everything had its "just price" in cigarettes. While the assessment of the just price, which incidentally varied between camps, was impossible of explanation, this price was nevertheless pretty closely known. It can best be defined as the price usually fetched by an article in good times when cigarettes were plentiful. The "just price" changed slowly; it was unaffected by short-term variations in supply, and while opinion might be resigned to departures from the "just price," a strong feeling of resentment persisted. A more satisfactory definition of the "just price" is impossible. Everyone knew what it was, though no one could explain why it should be so.

As soon as prices began to fall with a cigarette shortage, a clamour arose, particularly against those who held reserves and who bought at reduced prices. Sellers at cut prices were criticised and their activities referred to as the black market. In every period of dearth the explosive question of "should non-smokers receive a cigarette ration?'' was discussed to profitless length. Unfortunately, it was the non-smoker, or the light smoker with his reserves, along with the hated middleman, who weathered the storm most easily.

Opinion was always overruled by the hard facts of the market . . . prices moved with the supply of cigarettes, and refused to stay fixed in accordance with a theory of ethics. It is thus to be seen that a market came into existence without labour or production, and prices were fixed by the operation of supply and demand.

QUESTIONS FOR ANALYSIS OF CASES

1. Define ''marketing'' in your own words. Compare your definition with that given in the text, and with other definitions given in Exhibit 1- 9 Cite examples of marketing activity according to your definition in the case.

2. For each of the two examples you gave in Question 1, identify the product, i.e., what is being exchanged? Identify the customer in each exchange transaction. What product benefits does the customer receive, and what costs must the customer bear?

3. Cite examples of the effects of suppliers upon this exchange. Differentiate external from organizational suppliers of resources. Categorize each supplier by type of resource (capital, human resources, physical resources, information). Categorize the organizational suppliers by function (production, finance, legal, personnel, etc.).

4. Note the effects of society upon the exchange transactions you identified. Specify the societal group (competitor, regulator, influencer). What is the nature of each effect? How should the marketer handle these effects?

5. Cite examples of environmental forces which affect the marketing activities you have identified. Specify the nature of each force, and comment upon the opportunities and/or threats it presents to the marketing managers involved.

PART 2 MARKETING'S KEY RELATIONSHIPS

After studying this part, you should be able to:

1. Relate marketing to other social institutions and to other organizational functions.

2. Discuss major environmental and organizational factors that influence marketing decisions.

3. Identify significant trends in contemporary society and foresee possible marketing opportunities and threats that could result.

4. Begin to evaluate the role of marketing activities in an industrialized society, and in contemporary organizations.

Stockmarket

"ONE GATORADE!"

3/CUSTOMERS: CONSUMERS, MIDDLEMEN, AND OTHER MARKETS

Marketing begins with customers. This chapter provides an overview of the types of customers that the marketing manager seeks to satisfy. Major points include:

1. Potential consumer markets are first identified by demographic and income characteristics. That is, potential customers must have the ability to buy (money), the right to buy (authority), and the willingness to buy (desire).

2. The originator of a product and its ultimate consumer rarely conduct transactions with each other. Most products in a developed society reach consumers via a comprehensive distribution system.

3. The middlemen who constitute the distribution system create time, place, and possession utilities. This fact is not always recognized by producers or by consumers.

4. Customers may be found not only in the United States, but throughout the world. There are no really different principles in international marketing, but application of these principles requires specific understanding of local cultures, economies, and governments.

5. Exchange does not take place in a vacuum. Every exchange transaction affects members of society in addition to producers and consumers. Marketing managers must understand the impact of marketing activities upon non-customers.

I'm going to the store.
The polls close at 7:00 p.m.
The market for residential housing is soft this quarter.
This new machine capacity will be useful when business picks up.

These are statements about markets and customers. This chapter explores concepts and examples of the nature and composition of the customer side of the exchange transition. We begin with a look at consumers.

CONSUMERS: ULTIMATE CUSTOMERS

In Exhibit 1-2, the basic exchange model, a producer offered a product to a consumer in exchange for payment. In Chapter 2, we noted that use rights must also flow to the consumer, and information must flow both ways for exchange to be consummated. From the consumer's viewpoint, payment is given up in return for knowledge about and the right to use a product's utility. A consumer expects that benefits derived from consuming the product will exceed the payment. Consequently, not everyone demands the products of a given organization. This section first discusses the criteria for effective demand for a given organization's products, and then examines two broad groups of consumers.

Effective Demand

The marketing manager seeks customers for his or her products, and then matches customers' desires with the organization's capability to provide products that satisfy those desires. Potential customers are said to possess effective demand when they have (1) the ability to buy, (2) the right to buy and, (3) the desire to buy. To be specific, effective demand requires:

Money
Authority
Desire

Using the acronym, we may say that consumers are MAD.

Money—buying power—is the ability to buy. Three basic components of buying power can be distinguished: income, assets, and credit worthiness. The consumer who has no cash on hand, but who has a source of income, or who possesses assets which can be bartered or converted to cash, or who can borrow by virtue of reputation, skills, or connections, is said to have buying power.

Authority—the right to buy—is the power to consummate the exchange transaction. Authority in many cases is straightforward. Individuals purchase many products for their own use. In some family, and many organizational, situations, however, authority to buy can be difficult to determine. Purchase of a new home may be an involved decision for a family, and the leasing or purchase of a new fleet of automobiles for the sales force can involve a number of organizational personnel.

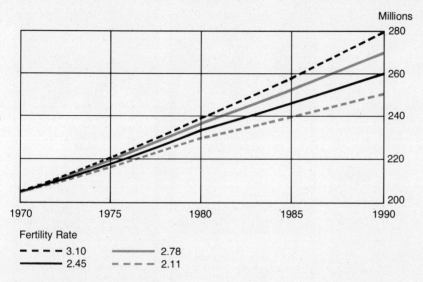

Millions

Exhibit 3-1   U. S. Population Projections

Fertility Rate
- – – – 3.10   ———— 2.78
———— 2.45   – – – – 2.11

Adapted from U. S. Census Bureau data.

The desire component is a clear necessity in effective demand. Marketing can stimulate demand, it can influence, it can persuade; but no amount of marketing effort, no matter how sophisticated or intense, can make people buy things that they do not want. We explore this topic more fully in Chapter 6.

Consumption by Households and Individuals

Effective demand is ultimately represented by people and their purchasing power. In the United States, and in other developed countries, the number of people continues to grow, but at a decreasing rate. Exhibit 3-1 indicates that the total population of the U. S. will grow from slightly over 200 million in 1975 to between 240 and 280 million by 1980. Most demographers believe that the low end of the range is more likely. Better information on consumption patterns is usually obtained by decomposing the total into categories of interest. For marketing management, the major demographic breakdowns are generally age, region of the country, and life cycle stage.

Demographic Profiles. Exhibit 3-2 presents age breakdowns and some comments upon their significance. Note that there will be higher proportions of young adults, the younger middle-age group, and people 65 and over. Implications for consumption, and therefore for marketing, are evident.

Related to the changing age mix is the state in the family life cycle. As a family develops, it goes through several identifiable stages: marriage,

Exhibit 3-2 Americans: The Changing Age Mix

Reprinted from *U.S. News & World Report.*

SPECIAL SECTION
HOW AMERICA IS CHANGING

AMERICANS: THE CHANGING AGE MIX

U.S. population is in a slow rise—from 212 million today to an estimated 233 million in 1984. But major shifts are ahead among various age groups, with broad significance for business and government.

CHILDREN AND TEEN-AGERS

NOW	75.7 million
1979	73.4 million
1984	73.6 million

CHANGE, 1974-84: DOWN 2.1 million, or 3%

Baby crop is expanding again, promising growth ahead in numbers of elementary-school children. But youths of secondary-school and college age will decrease all through the decade.

YOUNG ADULTS, 20-34

NOW	48.9 million
1979	56.5 million
1984	61.0 million

CHANGE, 1974-84: UP 12.1 million, or 25%

More than half of the growth in U.S. population will come in the young-adult group—the age bracket in which people start earning good incomes, get married, set up households, start families and spend in a big way.

YOUNGER MIDDLE-AGE GROUP, 35-49

NOW	34.5 million
1979	35.9 million
1984	41.1 million

CHANGE, 1974-84: UP 6.6 million, or 19%

Growth in this age group will come faster and faster in years ahead. These are the people that, climbing up the income ladder, move into bigger houses, become multicar families, and, in general, upgrade living standards.

OLDER MIDDLE-AGE GROUP, 50-64

NOW	31.4 million
1979	32.4 million
1984	32.2 million

CHANGE, 1974-84: UP 0.8 million, or 3%

This group, with highest average incomes, will grow slowly, then diminish in number. Result: Less lift for spending on services, leisure activities, expensive homes and luxury goods.

PEOPLE 65 AND OLDER

NOW	21.7 million
1979	23.7 million
1984	25.5 million

CHANGE, 1974-84: UP 3.8 million, or 17%

Rapid rise in number of older people promises greater demand for apartments, medical care—and broader Social Security benefits. Older people also offer an expanding market for luxuries—such as fashionable clothing, books, recreation.

Basic data: U.S. Census Bureau

Source: *U.S. News & World Report,* (February 25, 1974). Copyright © 1974 *U.S. News & World Report, Inc.*

Exhibit 3-3　An Overview of the Life Cycle and Buying Behavior

Stage in Life Cycle	Buying or Behavioral Pattern
1. Bachelor stage: Young, single people not living at home	Few financial burdens. Fashion opinion leaders. Recreation-oriented. Buy basic kitchen equipment, basic furniture, cars, equipment for the mating game, vacations.
2. Newly married couples: Young, no children	Better off financially than they will be in near future. Highest purchase rate and highest average purchase of durables. Buy cars, refrigerators, stoves, sensible and durable furniture, vacations.
3. Full nest I: Youngest child under six	Home purchasing at peak. Liquid assets low. Dissatisfied with financial position and amount of money saved. Interested in new products. Buy washers, dryers, TV, baby food, chest rubs and cough medicines, vitamins, dolls, wagons, sleds, skates.
4. Full nest II: Youngest child six or over six	Financial position better. Some wives work. Less influenced by advertising. Buy larger-sized packages, multiple-unit deals. Buy many foods, cleaning materials, bicycles, music lessons, pianos.
5. Full nest III: Older couples with dependent children	Financial position still better. More wives work. Some children get jobs. Hard to influence with advertising. High average purchase of durables. Buy new, more tasteful furniture, auto travel, nonnecessary appliances, boats, dental services, magazines.
6. Empty nest I: Older couples, no children living with them, head in labor force	Home ownership at peak. Most satisfied with financial position and money saved. Interested in travel, recreation, self-education. Make gifts and contributions. Not interested in new products. Buy vacations, luxuries, home improvements.
7. Empty nest II: Older couples, no children living at home, head retired	Drastic cut in income. Keep home. Buy medical appliances, medical-care products that aid health, sleep, and digestion.
8. Solitary survivor, in labor force	Income still good, but likely to sell home.
9. Solitary survivor, retired	Same medical and product needs as other retired group. Drastic cut in income. Special need for attention, affection, and security.

Excerpted from W. D. Wells and G. Gubar, "Life Cycle Concept in Marketing Research," *Journal of Marketing Research,* November 1966, pp. 335–363, with permission of the publisher, the American Marketing Association.

birth of children, maturation of children, children leave home, and so on. At the same time, the family's income generally rises with the age of the family head. Consequently, buying behavior is quite likely to change as the family progresses through stages in the life cycle. Exhibit 3-3 provides an overview of the various stages with examples of typical purchasing patterns in each stage. For example, the percentage of a family's budget spent for food and clothing generally increases when children arrive. On the other hand, expenditures for transportation and household furnishings decline relatively.

The life cycle concept is a useful tool for analyzing markets. But it ignores another characteristic of the population: single-person households. In the U. S. today, for example, we find that some 40 million people

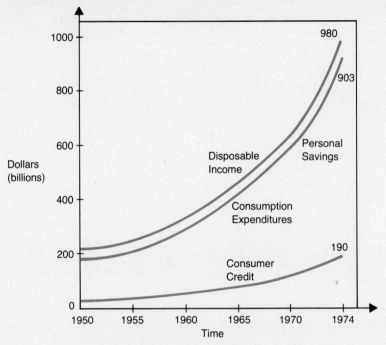

Based on *1975 Statistical Abstract of The U.S.*, pp. 380, 475.

are not married; almost half of these people are under 30, and 60 percent of them are female. Redefining the family life cycle to account for singles and for one-parent households represents a significant challenge to marketing scholars.

In addition to age and life cycle, population also varies geographically. Over the last twenty years or so, the distribution of U. S. population has tended to shift from the northeast to the southwest and far west, and most urban growth has occurred in the suburbs surrounding the central city. As the United States becomes more urbanized, some demographers project a new kind of urban-suburban strip called interurbia or megalopolis. The best known of such super cities is a 600-mile-long stretch along the east coast joining the cities of Boston, New York, Baltimore, Philadelphia, and Washington and their suburbs into one giant community—Boswash. Others include Chicago-to-Pittsburgh (Chipitts) and San Francisco-to-San Diego (Sansan). If present trends continue, most regions of the U. S. will have at least one megalopolis by the year 2000.

Buying Power. As interesting as people are, all are not necessarily consumers. They must have the ability to buy. In the 1970s there was considerable growth in monetary buying power, as indicated in Exhibit 3-4. The trend in personal disposable income, the major component of buying power, is sharply upward. Trends of personal saving and consumer credit show similar patterns.

But in the mid-1970s, these gains in monetary buying power were almost totally wiped out by inflation—rising prices. Measured in terms of the base year 1967, one dollar was worth 86 cents in 1970, 75 cents in 1973, and only 68 cents by 1974. The purchasing power of the dollar shrank by $\frac{1}{3}$ in the early 1970s. To put it another way, the average loaf of white bread retailed for 24 cents in 1970 and 35 cents in 1974; sirloin steak was $1.35 per pound in 1970 and $1.80 in 1974. Exhibit 3-5 starkly portrays the effect of inflation upon the typical middle-income family in the U. S. Moreover, the rate of inflation was generally higher in most other developed countries. "Double-digit" inflation (an inflation rate of 10 percent or greater) was experienced by Great Britain, France, Italy, and Japan during parts of the mid-1970s.

As this is written, it appears that buying power in the developed countries may be beginning to rise again—slowly. So the general outlook for ultimate consumption is cautiously optimistic. The trick, for the marketing manager, is to translate these general demographic trends into demand for specific products. For example, the percentage of babies born in the 1970s has been declining, and long term trends indicate that it will continue to do so. Makers of products for babies, therefore, have some reason to be concerned. The Gerber Company, one of the world's largest makers of baby food and other products, used to say "Babies are our business, our only business." The latter part of that slogan has been dropped from recent advertisements. Similarly, the makers of Johnson's Baby Shampoo have recently been extolling the virtues of their product for adults—"it's gentle enough to use everyday." There are various tools and techniques to assist the marketing manager in identifying specific opportunities in general demographic trends. We examine these in Part III. But not all products are consumed by individuals or households.

Consumption by Organizations

Organizations, as well as individuals and households, consume products. Organizations, therefore, are potential customers, and can be viewed in terms of markets.

Exhibit 3-6 presents categories of organizations, according to standard Census Bureau definitions. Note that the total number of organizations was nearly 13 million in 1974. This large aggregate number contains multi-billion dollar manufacturing firms such as Exxon and General Motors, small Mom-and-Pop grocery stores, the omnipotent McDonald's Hamburger franchise chain and the individual curbside hotdog vendor, the U. S. Department of Defense, and numerous other businesses, universities, hotels, prisons, barbershops, and museums.

In general, organizational consumers are more geographically con-

A Closer Look at the Middle Class—

PROFILE OF 28 MILLION FAMILIES

Though there is no official definition of "middle class," a general picture of such a group can be drawn by studying the characteristics of families that earned from $10,000 to $25,000 of income in 1973. Based on facts and figures issued by the Government, the Economic Unit of "U. S. News & World Report" sketched this profile of America's middle-income families—

NUMBER: *Just Over Half of All Families in U. S.*
Of all U. S. families—
- 28.4 million, or 52 per cent, had incomes of $10,000 to $25,000
- 39 per cent had incomes of less than $10,000
- 9 per cent had incomes of more than $25,000

INCOME: *An Average of $16,300 a Year*
Among middle-class families, those headed by self-employed professionals had the highest average income, $17,600 in 1973, followed by managers and administrators and salaried professionals, with $17,000 for each group.

WAGE EARNERS: *Two Per Family*
Wives in more than half—55 per cent—of all middle-class families are at work. Counting children, there are 2 wage earners in the average middle-class family, compared with 1.6 for all families.

RACE: *Proportionately More Whites*
93 per cent of all middle-class families are white, compared with 89 per cent for the U. S. population as a whole.

AGE: *Relatively Young*
54 per cent of the heads of middle-class families are under 45. Median age: About 43, compared with 45 for all families.

FAMILY SIZE: *Bigger Than Average*
The average size of middle-class families is 3.7 persons, compared with 3.5 for all families.

EDUCATION: *Better Than Average*
Heads of middle-class families comprise 58 per cent of all families headed by college graduates. More than two thirds—70 per cent—of all middle-class families are headed by someone with at least four years of high school.

DWELLING PLACE: *Heavily Urbanized*
96 per cent of all middle-class families live in cities or suburbs, compared with 95 per cent for all families.

STOCKHOLDERS: *Three Out of Every Five*
Of America's 31 million stockholders, 18 million are in the $10,000-to-$25,000 income bracket, holding stocks worth 150 billion dollars at the end of 1973.

TAXPAYERS: *Half the Income-Tax Load*
More than 26 million middle-income families filed federal income-tax returns in 1972, declaring 390 billion dollars in income and paying 46.6 billion in taxes—or 50 per cent of all individual income taxes paid.

Source: U. S. Commerce and Treasury Depts., Securities & Exchange Commission

THE RAVAGES OF INFLATION

For families of four in $10,000-to-$25,000 income bracket—

	IN 1970	IN 1973
AVERAGE INCOME	$15,500	$16,300
Federal Taxes	$ 2,392	$ 2,640
LEFT AFTER TAXES	$13,108	$13,660
"Inflation Tax" Since 1970	–	$ 3,079
REAL INCOME, in 1970 dollars	$13,108	$10,581

THUS: Average middle-income family in 1973 had 19 per cent less buying power than the comparable family three years earlier.

NOTE: "Inflation tax" is based on 29.1 per cent hike in consumer price index from 1970 to 1973.

Basic data: U. S. Commerce Dept., Commerce Clearing House

THE RISING COST OF MIDDLE-CLASS LIVING

Based on annual average budgets for an urban family of four needed to provide a relatively comfortable standard of living—toward the upper levels of the middle class:

$20,000
$18,201
$16,558
$15,905
$15,511
$14,571
$13,050

1967 1969 1970 1971 1972 1973 NOW (est.)

CHANGE IN 7 YEARS: UP 53%

HOW PEOPLE SPEND THEIR MONEY

Breakdown of the annual average budget —$18,201 in 1973:

	Spending	Share of Budget
Housing	$4,386	24 per cent
Food	$4,020	22 per cent
Clothing	$1,456	8 per cent
Transportation	$1,315	7 per cent
Medical care	$692	4 per cent
Personal care	$390	2 per cent
Education, recreation, tobacco, other family consumption	$1,191	7 per cent
Life insurance, gifts, other items	$1,024	6 per cent
Taxes	$3,727	20 per cent

Source: U. S. Dept. of Labor; 1974 estimate by USN&WR Economic Unit

Source: *U.S. News & World Report* (October 1974). Copyright © 1974 *U.S. News & World Report, Inc.*

Category	Number
Agriculture, forestry and fisheries	3,362,000
Mining	79,000
Construction	1,020,000
Manufacturing	436,000
Transportation, communication and public utilities	431,000
Wholesale and retail trade	2,937,000
Finance, insurance and real estate	1,467,000
Services	3,181,000
Governmental units	78,000
Total	12,990,000

Exhibit 3-6 Categories of Organizations

Source: *1975 Statistical Abstract of the U.S.*, pp. 490, 251.

centrated than their household counterparts. Seven states, California, Illinois, Michigan, New Jersey, New York, Ohio, and Pennsylvania, contain over half of the nation's manufacturing firms. One third of all retail sales are made in the 250 largest cities; the top ten cities alone account for 10 percent of all retail sales. And the bulk of sales to government are concentrated in Washington, D.C. and the 50 state capitals.

These organizations purchase an incredibly wide range of products. Exhibit 3-7 provides examples of each of the standard six categories of organizational products: installations, equipment, raw materials, components, supplies, and services. Of course, every organization does not necessarily purchase from all six categories, and differences in demand vary within organizations and over time.

It is often stated that consumption behavior by representatives of organizations is very different from the consumption behavior of individuals or households. We will argue at some length in Chapter 6 that the process of buying behavior is similar in concept, although differences of degree do occur. There is no question, however, that the purpose of organizational buying is fundamentally different from that of household demand. For the household, consumption leads directly to satisfaction. For the organization, products are purchased and consumed as a means to the end of achieving other organizational objectives. In the jargon of economists, organizational demand is *derived* from household demand, and satisfied through middlemen.

MIDDLEMEN

The majority of exchange transactions are not consummated for the purpose of ultimate consumption. In fact, for every product that reaches its ultimate consumer, a number of transactions have been completed by organizations. Collectively, the institutions constitute the distribution system. The major types of middlemen in the distribution system are wholesalers and retailers.

1. Installations
   examples: land, mineral rights, buildings, generators, kilns
2. Equipment
   examples: automobiles, tractors, typewriters, power tools
3. Raw Materials
   examples: steel, cement, wheat, livestock, timber, wrapping paper
4. Components
   examples: engines, nuts and bolts, tires, transistors
5. Supplies
   examples: lubricants, coal, pencils, brooms, paint
6. Services
   examples: typewriter repair, legal advice, management consulting

The Distribution System

Consider Exhibit 3-8 which summarizes some of the transactions necessary to get a loaf of bread to its ultimate consumer. The chain of transactions begins with a farmer. He or she buys seed, fertilizer, tractors, fuel and electrical energy, insurance, the assistance of farm hands, and so on. The farmer processes (plows, plants, harvest.) these inputs, thereby adding form utility to them. The process ends when the farmer sells wheat to the miller. In addition to wheat, the miller also buys trucks, building equipment, office supplies, etc. His or her processing involves shipping, storing, milling, packing, and transporting. The miller, therefore, adds form, time and place utility to the wheat and sells flour to the baker. The baker also buys yeast, mixing machines, ovens, bread wrapping material, etc. He or she adds form, time, and place utility to the flour and sells bread to the grocer. The grocer also buys canned goods, meat, display cases, etc. He or she therefore endows the wheat with additional time and place utility, and also confers possession utility upon the ultimate consumer when the consumer buys the loaf of bread from the grocer for food. Demand at each stage is derived from demand for the more complete consumer product at the succeeding stage.

Other products follow a generally similar distribution pattern. Consider education as a product. Students purchase education from the originator, a university. But students are "middlemen" in the distribution of education. Very few purchase education to consume it (the sheer joy of learning); most combine their college education with other skills and talents and resell them to organizations. Thus, the demand for education is largely derived from the demand for capable employees.

In an industrial economy, the distribution system consists of a large, sophisticated, and dynamic set of institutions which link product origination and product consumption. Exhibit 3-9 provides an overview. [Pedantic aside: the diagram shows that the distribution system links product origination and product consumption. To be technically correct, we should show origination occurring wherever product form is changed, i.e.,

Exhibit 3-8 Transactions Required to Get Product to Consumer

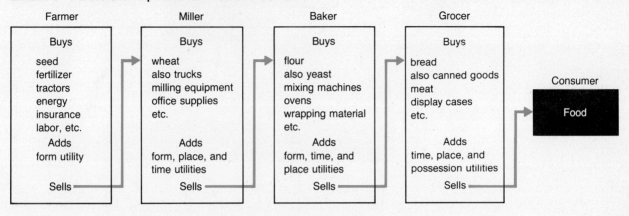

at the raw material producer stage, and at the manufacturer stage. But that technicality might obscure the point of the diagram: that the distribution system links product origination and product consumption.] Now let us look more closely at the wholesaling and retailing organizations which comprise the distribution system.

Wholesaling. Middlemen classified as wholesalers are integral components of all distribution systems. For several reasons, wholesaling requires precisely defined terms. Basically, a wholesaler performs exchange activities that link the product originator to the middleman who sells to the ultimate consumer. Note carefully three aspects of this definition. First, there are many types of middlemen engaged in wholesaling. As Exhibit 3-10 shows, there are merchant wholesalers who buy and sell goods, agents who represent buyers and sellers without taking title to the goods, specialized distributors such as mail-order houses and jobbers, and so on. Wholesaling, therefore, is a term broadly descriptive of many types of marketing activities that go on in the distribution system. Second, the wholesaler, by definition, does not originate the product that he or she markets. A new channel begins when the form utility of the product is altered. For example, the channel for automobiles begins at the plant where the automobiles are finally assembled, not with the manufacturer of engines or tires, the steel fabricator, or the organization that mines the iron ore. Third, a distributor who sells to ultimate consumers is defined to be a retailer—not a wholesaler.

Exhibit 3-11 presents the five major categories of wholesaling activity as defined by the U. S. Census Bureau, and provides some indication of the magnitude of these activities in the American economy. The definitions and the magnitudes of the various components have remained relatively stable since World War II. For this reason, the Census Bureau is

Exhibit 3-9   Distribution Channels in a Modern Economic System

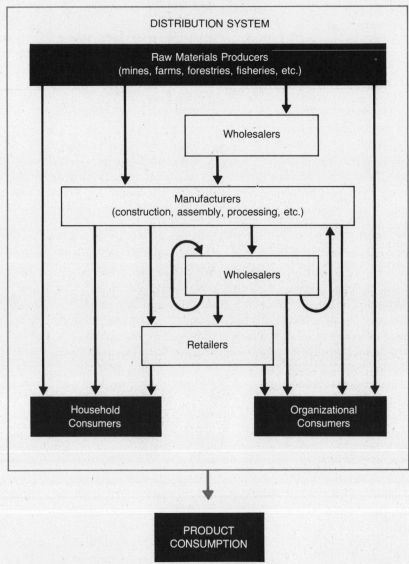

Adapted from John B. Matthews and others, *Marketing: An Introductory Analysis* (New York: McGraw-Hill, 1964), p. 18, with permission of the publisher.

Exhibit 3-10 Types of Middlemen

Agent. A business unit which negotiates purchases or sales or both but does not take title to the goods in which it deals. The agent usually performs fewer marketing functions than does the merchant. He commonly receives his remuneration in the form of a commission or fee. He usually does not represent both buyer and seller in the same transaction. Examples are: broker, commission merchant, manufacturers agent, selling agent, and resident buyer.

Branch house (manufacturer's). An establishment maintained by a manufacturer, detached from the headquarters establishment and used primarily for the purpose of stocking, selling, delivering, and servicing his product. A branch office is similar, although it is limited to the last two functions.

Branch store. A subsidiary retailing business owned and operated at a separate location by an established store.

Broker. An agent who does not have direct physical control of the goods in which he deals but represents either buyer or seller in negotiating purchases or sales for his principal. The broker's powers as to prices and terms of sale are usually limited by his principal.

Commission house (sometimes called commission merchant). An agent who usually exercises physical control over and negotiates the sale of the goods he handles. The commission house usually enjoys broader powers as to prices, methods, and terms of sale than does the broker, although it must obey instructions issued by the principal. It generally arranges delivery, extends necessary credit, collects, deducts its fees, and remits the balance to the principal.

Consumers' cooperative. A retail business owned and operated by ultimate consumers to purchase and distribute goods and services primarily to the membership; sometimes called purchasing co-operatives.

Discount house. A retailing business unit featuring consumer durable items, competing on a basis of price appeal, and operating on a relatively low mark-up and with a minimum of customer service.

Facilitating agencies in marketing. Those agencies which perform or assist in the performance of one or a number of the marketing functions, but which neither take title to goods nor negotiate purchases or sales. Common types are banks, railroads, storage warehouses, commodity exchanges, stock yards, insurance companies, graders and inspectors, advertising agencies, firms engaged in marketing research, cattle loan companies, furniture marts, and packers and shippers.

Jobber. This term is widely used as a synonym of "wholesaler" or "distributor." The term is sometimes used in certain trades and localities to designate special types of wholesalers.

Mail-order house (retail). A retailing business that receives its orders primarily by mail or telephone, and generally offers its goods and services for sale from a catalog or other printed material.

Manufacturer's agent. An agent who generally operates on an extended contractual basis; often sells within an exclusive territory; handles noncompeting but related lines of goods; and possesses limited authority with regard to prices and terms of sale. He may be authorized to sell a definite portion of his principal's output.

Merchant. A business unit that buys, takes title to, and resells merchandise. The distinctive feature of this middleman lies in the fact that he takes title to the goods he handles. Wholesalers and retailers are the chief types of merchants.

Middleman. A business concern that specializes in performing operations or rendering services directly involved in the purchase and/or sale of goods in the process of their flow from producer to consumer. Middlemen are of two types, merchants and agents. The essence of the middleman's operation lies in the fact that he plays an active and prominent part in the negotiations leading up to transactions of purchase and sale. This is what distinguishes him from a marketing facilitating agent who, while he performs certain marketing functions, participates only incidentally in negotiations of purchase and sale.

Rack jobber. A wholesaling business unit that markets specialized lines of merchandise to certain types of retail stores and also provides the special services of selective brand and item merchandising and arrangement, maintenance, and stocking of display racks. The rack jobber usually, but not always, puts his merchandise in the store of the retailer on consignment. Rack jobbers are most prevalent in the food business.

Selling agent. An agent who operates on an extended contractual basis, sells all of a specified line of merchandise or the entire output of his principal, and usually has full authority with regard to prices, terms, and other conditions of sale. He occasionally renders financial aid to his principal. This functionary is often called a "sales agent."

Voluntary group. A group of retailers, each of whom owns and operates his own store and is associated with a wholesale organization or manufacturer to carry on joint merchandising activities, and who are characterized by some degree of group identity and uniformity of operation. Such joint activities have been largely of two kinds: cooperative advertising and group control of store operation.

Excerpted from *Marketing Definitions: A Glossary of Marketing Terms,* compiled by the Committee on Definitions of the American Marketing Association, Ralph S. Alexander, Chairman (Chicago: American Marketing Association, 1960), with the permission of the publisher, the American Marketing Association.

a major source of quantitative data for marketing planning and control of the activities of wholesalers. The major change in the relationships during the postwar period has been that manufacturers' sales offices and branches have gained in sales relative to agents and brokers, perhaps because the growth of markets in various areas have led manufacturers to establish their own branches in areas once served by agents.

Retailing. Retailers are a type of middleman, in that they function in the channel by securing products and use rights to those products from originators and middlemen and granting them to final consumers. But students of marketing separate retailing from other types of middlemen for three reasons. First, there are differences in the buying behavior of ultimate consumers and those who buy for further exchange. Second, there are legal distinctions between wholesaling and retailing. For example, there are laws governing the amount and types of discounts granted to wholesalers; some cities and states have retail sales taxes that do not apply to wholesalers; conversely, retailers but not wholesalers are generally exempt from federal minimum-wage legislation. Third, retailing is often treated separately because there are so many retail establishments in our economic system, and they are so visible, that it is useful to study them separately.

The evolution of retailing institutions in American history is a most interesting one. From the fur trapper and trading post of the frontier, to the Yankee peddler and small shops of colonial days, the American retailing system has grown to almost two million establishments with an aggregate sales volume in 1972 of over 450 billion dollars—as shown in Exhibit 3-12. This table tells an interesting story: it shows that there are a great number of organizations engaged in retailing, and yet only three percent of these establishments have annual sales of one million dollars or more. This relatively small percentage of all retailing establishments accounts for almost half the total retail sales volume.

Type of Operation	Number of Establishments (1,000)		Sales (Billions of Dollars)	
	1972	1967	1972	1967
United States, total	370	311	353.9	459.5
Merchant wholesalers	244	213	255.2	206.1
Manufacturers' sales branches and offices	47	31	255.7	157.1
Merchandise agents and brokers	33	26	85.6	61.3
Selling agents	2	2	6.5	6.9
Manufacturer's agents	16	12	23.3	15.3
Brokers	5	4	20.4	14.0
Commission men	7	5	19.0	14.1
Others	3	1	16.4	10.0
Petroleum bulk plants and terminals	31	30	46.3	24.8
Assemblers of farm products	15	11	52.4	10.2

Exhibit 3-11 Types and Sales of Wholesalers

U. S. Census of Business: 1972, 1967.

The figures highlight some very interesting trends. Modern retailing began in the middle of the nineteenth century when department stores first began to appear in Europe and later in America. The growth of large multiproduct stores reflected the rising population and more efficient transportation systems of cities. The rural counterpart to the department store was the mail-order house, which appeared in the 1890s. Sears, Roebuck and Company and Montgomery Ward are prominent names in this field. Mail-order houses reflect the development of an increasingly extensive system of roadways and the rise of the modern postal service. During the early 1900s, retailers began to heed the teachings of economists with respect to economies of scale, and chain stores developed. That is, retailers began to see the economic advantages of buying in large quantities, and distributing these quantities through a number of outlets. Economies of scale could therefore be achieved in such costs as inventory, in shipping and storage, and working capital. Moreover, chains could provide better management through increased opportunities for training and promotion, and improved accounting systems. The economies of scale could then be passed on to the consumer in the form of lower prices, which further contributed to the growth of chain-store retailing organizations.

The next development in retailing occurred in the 1930s, when grocery stores adopted the chain-store concept: the supermarket was born.

Exhibit 3-12   Retail trade, 1972—United States, Sales by Size of Establishment

Sales Size of Establishments	Establishments			Sales Volume		
	Number (000)	Percent	Cumulative Percent	Sales ($000,000)	Percent	Cumulative Percent
Total, all establishments	1,913			459,040		
Establishments operated entire year, total	1,710	100.0		427,640	100.0	
With annual sales of:						
$1,000,000 or more	74	4.3	4.3	224,597	52.5	52.5
$500,000–999,999	71	4.2	8.5	48,823	11.4	63.9
$300,000–499,999	106	6.2	14.7	40,497	9.5	73.4
$100,000–299,999	450	26.3	41.0	77,724	18.2	91.6
$50,000–99,999	304	17.8	58.8	21,972	5.0	96.7
$30,000–49,999	188	11.0	69.8	7,354	1.7	98.4
$29,999 or less	516	30.2	100.0	6,671	1.6	100.0

Source: *U.S. Census of Retail Trade,* 1972, Table 1a.

Fueled by consumers' insistent demand for lower prices during the great depression, and their willingness to forego such services as personal service in selecting items, credit, and delivery, the principle of self-service was born. Grocery store operators then began to realize that they could carry a much broader assortment of items. That is, supermarkets now sell many products that are not groceries in the usual sense, e.g., health and beauty aids, drugs, automobile accessories, clothes, and garden tools. This trend has become so prevalent today that it has its own special name—scrambled merchandisimg.

The immediate post-World-War-II era in retailing is marked by the growth of suburban shopping centers. These centers reflect the rapid growth of the suburbs, increasing automobile ownership, and the congestion and decay of the central city. The purpose of a shopping center is to satisfy all of the consumer's wants in one place. The usual pattern is to have one or more large, traffic-generator stores, e.g., department store and/or supermarket, surrounded by smaller shops and specialty stores.

In the 1950s, the major retailing innovation was the discount house. Although some warehouse outlets located "out of the high-rent district" had opened in the 1930s and a few more appeared after World War II, it was when discount houses began merchandising nationally known brands and products in the 1950s that these stores became a significant factor in the American retailing structure. These lower prices were made possible through considerable economies of scale in purchasing, low-cost suburban locations, and minimum service. In effect, this is the supermarket concept extended from groceries to major appliances, home furnishings, and clothing.

The major innovation of the sixties was the franchise system. This system is characterized by retail outlets organized around a central theme that share centralized buying and management services, advertising, and so on. Major fast food franchisers include McDonald's Hamburgers, Kentucky Fried Chicken, and Howard Johnson restaurants. Holiday Inn is perhaps the best known motel franchise. Of course, petroleum companies have been using service station franchising for some time. Other major retailing trends in recent years include the rise of automatic vending, trading stamps, night and Sunday store hours, and modern door-to-door selling by companies such as Avon (cosmetics) and Fuller Brush. Some of the changes in retailing, but not all, can be plausibly explained by the wheel of retailing hypothesis presented in Exhibit 3-13.

The dominant trend in the 1970s seems to be the demise of the small retailer. Many reasons are contributing factors to this trend. Discount stores are growing rapidly—in number, size, and variety of merchandise. Consumer mobility vitiates consumer loyalty to a particular store. Indeed, nationwide franchises guarantee that the consumer knows what to expect wherever he or she goes. The recession of the mid-1970s revealed two serious weaknesses of many smaller retailers: under-capitalization (lack of working capital to finance accounts receivable and cover cost increases), and insufficient managerial competence in such areas as inventory control, bad debt losses, and product offerings. The trend to late night and Sunday shopping requires more managerial talent, or that the sole proprietor work longer hours. And, as we discuss in the next chapter, changes in certain laws and regulations have affected the small business persons adversely: fair trade laws have been repealed, consumers are more likely to sue if products fail or harm them, health and safety regulations are more stringent, and minority hiring quotas have been increased.

In summary, we have demonstrated that the economic system of an industrial economy requires a large, sophisticated, and dynamic set of institutions to link product origination and product consumption. All such societies have distribution systems. But not all members of those societies agree that such complex systems are justified.

Justifying the Middleman

We have remarked on several occasions that product originators and consumers rarely exchange directly. Middlemen link most exchange transactions in developed societies. This fact is not disputed, but it is bemoaned.

Resentment of the middleman is not new. From Plato to the French physiocrats to Karl Marx, philosophers have considered marketing to be nonproductive. Note that the very word "producer" connotes useful activity. Time after time we hear that distribution costs too much, that middlemen ripoff both producers and consumers. But middlemen continue to exist, even to flourish, because they contribute to product utility. It is just that their contribution—time, place, and possession utilities—are largely intangible and therefore easily overlooked.

Demonstration of the value of middlemen in the distribution system usually begins with a simple exposition of channel efficiency as shown in Exhibit 3-14. Suppose that an economy consists of just 4 originators of products and only 6 consumers. If all 6 consumers desired to exchange products with all 4 producers, a total of 24 (4 × 6) contacts would be required. Introducing just 1 middleman into this system would reduce the number of contacts from 24 to 10 (4 + 6). The gain in efficiency increases as the size of the economy expands. This exhibit shows clearly that middlemen do contribute to distribution system efficiency and therefore to product utility. But this is only the beginning.

As we noted in Chapter 2, exchange transactions are characterized by four flows: (1) the physical product, (2) use rights to the product, (3) payment for the product, and (4) information about the product. We reemphasize the point that all four flows must link product originator and ultimate consumer if the product is to satisfy the consumer's desires. From the standpoint of utility and efficiency, therefore, the question is not whether these flows occur, but which members of the distribution system can best accomplish them.

Predictions of (or longing for) the demise of the middleman indicate a misunderstanding of the nature of distribution systems. Middlemen exist because they perform activities necessary to complete the four flows, and they perform better than originators or consumers do. For example, the middleman may grant credit, hold inventories, ship in small lots, provide advertising allowances, or marketing research for his customers. Or he may provide expert knowledge of the local markets, financing, or storage

(a) No middlemen: 4 × 6 = 24 contacts

Exhibit 3-14 The Middleman Improves Distribution System Efficiency

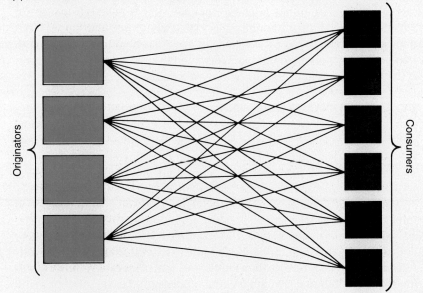

(b) One middleman: 4 + 6 = 10 contacts

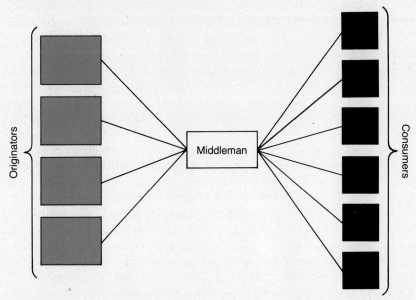

and transportation. If he did not perform these activities more effectively and/or efficiently than the originator or consumer, they simply would not include him in the distribution system. They would perform the activities themselves. This is not to say that all products should move through middlemen, or that distribution efficiency cannot be improved. The point is that these are managerial questions. We address them in Chapter 11.

INTERNATIONAL MARKETING

Our discussion to this point has focused primarily on U. S. markets. These domestic markets are the major concern of most American firms. However, the U. S. is the world's largest exporter of grain, aircraft, computers, and other products. Conversely, the more than two million automobiles imported annually to this country represent 20 percent of all automobiles sold here. Forty percent of the petroleum consumed in the U. S. is imported, and this percentage is rising.

We use international marketing examples throughout the text. There are no really different principles in international marketing, but differences in application are often subtle and sometimes substantial. Let us look at international customers, then international distribution, and finally the rise of the multinational firm.

International Consumers

There are more than four billion people in the world today. All but a few seek a better standard of living, so marketers can count on vast potential marketing opportunities. As we noted in discussing the U. S. population, however, aggregate figures often provide inadequate guidelines for marketing decisions. Population figures must be analyzed in more detail.

Geography is a convenient starting point. In the first place, population is not evenly dispersed over the earth. Population density is heaviest in northern Europe, in India, in eastern China, and in the upper eastern seaboard region of the United States. Vast areas of Australia, Africa, Asia, and North America are only sparsely populated. In addition, people in the different regions speak different languages, have different perceptions of space and time, and follow different customs and traditions in exchange activities. In its search for a new brandname, for example, EXXON corporation rejected ENCO (one of its more successful regional brands in the U. S.) because that word is part of a phrase that means "stalled car" in Japanese. A washing machine manufacturer, realizing the low literacy rate in one Asian country, developed a three-panel picture to advertise its machine. The left panel showed dirty clothes, the middle panel showed the washing machine in action, and the right panel showed sparkling clean clothes. In many countries this could have been a good idea, but the language of the people in this potential market is read from right to left. Company salespersons had a difficult time explaining how its machines converted clean clothes into dirty ones!

In the United States, delay in answering a communication, after normal reasons for delay have been eliminated, indicates that the matter is of low priority to the other person. In the Middle East, however, the time required for a decision is often directly proportional to its importance. Americans in that part of the world are innocently prone to downgrade their work by trying to speed things up. The Japanese have a saying that Americans will agree to anything if they are made to wait long enough. On the other hand, Japanese become quite offended if one is tardy for a social event. An American company was quite successful in advertising its coffee as "roasted in the American tradition" in Germany, but found that campaign unacceptable in Holland, where brewing coffee has been considered a specialized art for more than 300 years.

In the United States, the "appropriate" distance between persons engaged in business negotiations is two to three feet. South Americans and Arabs prefer less distance. It is not uncommon to find Yankees retreating, pursued by their Arab or Latin counterparts as negotiations proceed. On the other hand, Japanese and British people are accustomed to greater distances than is the American. Americans also tend to come directly to the point of negotiations quickly; this may offend Japanese, Chinese, or British negotiators. Most countries outside of the United States use metric measurements, and there are numerous other differences that can affect marketing.

People's buying power varies in different parts of the world. Income per capita in the United States is roughly one and one-half times larger than that of the countries of Western Europe, and ten to twenty times larger than that of some countries in Asia and Africa.

Incomes vary within nations too. For example, in South Africa, the average family income for whites is more than double that for Asians and about ten times that of Blacks. Many other examples could be offered, but perhaps these are sufficient to establish the point that while the principles of marketing are probably universal, specific applications of these principles vary greatly among different types of customers. These differences are accentuated by the distribution systems of various countries.

International Distribution Systems

International distribution systems vary greatly from ours. Two interrelated factors account for many of a system's differences: the country's stage of economic development, and the policies of its government.

Recall Exhibit 1-6, which classifies countries according to four stages of economic development: pre-industrial, developing, industrial, and post-industrial. Obviously, opportunities for marketing products vary considerably among countries in different stages. Pre-industrial societies, for example, are good prospects for simple tools that improve productivity, e.g., iron plowshares, scrubbing boards for washing clothes, bicycles, wheelbarrows, and hand-cranked or pedal-powered electric generators. These and other products are generally paid for by bartering agricultural products and raw materials.

Developing countries are potential customers for heavier machinery such as tractors, dams, railroads, and earth-moving equipment. The wants and desires of foreign supervisors and technical personnel aiding the development must be met. These factors spur domestic demand. Economic growth is a time of potential opportunity for developing markets and customers. Exhibit 3-15 is one of my favorites.

Developed countries—those with extensive production facilities and distribution systems—appear to be similar to the U. S. market. There is a large middle class, with consumption patterns similar to that of the American middle class. But similarities can be deceiving, as differences in languages and customs can cause unexpected problems. Take food, for example. The favorite meat dish of Americans is beef. Although cows are plentiful in India, they are regarded as sacred; eating beef is taboo. (I have an Indian friend who ate cheese sandwiches for the first six weeks he lived in this country, and then he began consuming American hamburgers and steaks. His reasoning was that American cows are not sacred.) Americans do not eat horseflesh or whalemeat, but these foods are considered delicacies in France and Japan, respectively.

Trade practices are also diverse. In a preindustrial society, barter is the rule since money is almost nonexistent. Exchange transactions are characterized by haggling, with both sides taking extreme initial positions, and each taking care that the other does not cheat.

In developing economies, exchange of many products is likely to be controlled by a rather small group of educated individuals who have good connections with the country's ruler. The naive American public during the last few years was surprised that in such situations a little judicious bribery lubricates the wheels of commerce. To be sure, some American-based companies such as Lockheed, Gulf Oil, and United Brands appear to have gone somewhat further along these lines than custom dictates. But the practice is widespread (indeed, it is not unknown in the United States). Of course, I do not condone such practices, but do wish to point out that they are a factor that marketing managers desiring to operate in international markets must frequently take into account.

In developed countries, economic issues become even more complex. Every nation wishes to export more than it imports, i.e., to have a net money income from other nations. In addition, each nation would like to protect the security and viability of its own economic system, e.g., the jobs of its workers and the capital invested by its citizens. Also, it must give some attention to national security matters. For example, the United States has only in recent years permitted trade with Communist-bloc countries. Certain strategic products, e.g., armaments and raw materials such as uranium and plutonium, are still forbidden. Thus, marketing managers face complex problems in such markets, but the opportunities are great. The nations of western Europe and Japan constitute markets of potential almost equal to that of the United States. And certain parts of the world, particularly the Middle East and Southern Africa, are rapidly becoming important markets as their exports of petroleum and other resources generate vast buying power and the desire for many types of products. Perhaps the market of greatest potential is mainland China. Exhibit 3-16 illustrates the role of the middleman in reaching this market.

In the international arena, marketing activities inevitably become intertwined with governmental policies. Thus, international marketing multiplies the challenge to marketing management. One clear example is that each nation issues its own money. Consequently, the value of one currency relative to all others has to be established. Currency exchange rates are set by processes too complex to be explored here, but from marketing management's point of view, the differing rates increases the difficulty of consummating exchanges. Moreover, since governments create money, government policy is largely responsible for inflation, which harms buying power.

In seeking their objectives, governments also restrict trade with other nations—in basically two ways. First, there are tariffs and taxes on virtually all products by almost all nations. Second, there are a variety of non-tariff barriers called NTBs. Exhibit 3-17 presents examples.

Exhibit 3-16   The Chinese Connection

If you are a marketer interested in making sales in China, there are some things you should know:

Do not treat the Chinese who is pouring the tea like an underling; he may turn out to be the overling.

Do not expound on how good your company is at making money; it will only make the Chinese suspicious. Talk, instead, about the good your products do for the people who buy them.

Watch for the jiggling of the Chinese foot under the table; if it starts you may be in trouble.

If you are male, do not make a pass at a Chinese woman. If you do, you are in trouble.

That is the sort of advice being handed out by Harned Pettus Hoose, a self-styled expert in the little known field of doing business in China. Marketing in the Peoples Republic of China is an intricate, complex, and highly ritualistic affair. Mr. Hoose is a prominent member of the "Gang at the Fang," an exclusive group of some twenty China traders who congregate at the Tung Fang Hotel in Canton on business visits to the Chinese trade center. The purpose of the Gang at the Fang is to smooth the way for trade relationships between clients back home and the world's most populous country.

Mr. Hoose is not Chinese himself, but he claims special clout in his business dealings there. For one thing, he was born in China of missionary parents, spoke Chinese before English, and lived there before he came to the United States. His income from his unique role in the China trade is in six figures.

A big part of Mr. Hoose's work is keeping up with what the Chinese want to buy or sell by reading transcripts of broadcasts and reams of public materials.

When a project does seem feasible, Mr. Hoose sends a formal query to nine Chinese government trading companies—and waits. "Perhaps my biggest job is holding the hand of company representatives," says Mr. Hoose. "By U. S. standards they have to wait incredible amounts of time."

While waiting for reaction from China, Mr. Hoose turns to tasks such as sanitizing corporate literature, by doing away with offensive phrases such as "Red China" and "Free World." Quotes about profit are also censored. Once the sanitized packet of literature has been sent, phase two of establishing the Chinese connection begins. Lesson one of phase two begins with a leisurely, exhaustive tour of the house that Mr. Hoose owns in Brentwood, a suburb of Los Angeles. Clients are shown in minute detail such highlights as the Hoose collection of pigeon flutes, tiny, piped instruments that Chinese dynasties of the past would attach to a captured bird; when the bird was released the pipes made music as the bird flew. This tour, Mr. Hoose insists, is invaluable training in the patience it requires to cope with Chinese decision processes. Such training also involves some pretty mundane manners, such as how to use chopsticks and the taboo against taking pictures without permission.

All in all, American marketers find the Chinese approach to exchange activities different, and confusing. Mr. Hoose and others like him perform a potentially valuable service in acting as middlemen for such exchanges.

Source: Roy J. Harris, Jr. "Chinese Connection: Missionary's Son Helps Smooth a Way for Trade in Mainland China," *The Wall Street Journal,* Nov. 7, 1975, p. 14.

Multinational Marketing

Because international marketing opportunities are so great, in the years since World War II we have witnessed the growth of multinational companies. A multinational company differs from a company engaged in international marketing in that the multinational firm is not based in one country and merely extended into others. Rather, the multinational takes a global perspective, i.e., its marketing managers perform the functions of seeking, matching, programming, and consummating on a worldwide basis. Exhibit 3-18 indicates that many, but by no means all, of the largest

You can sell Kentucky-fried chicken in Japan, but not if the chickens come from Kentucky. Or anywhere else in the world. ''All foreign chickens have skin diseases,'' the Japanese customs inspector explains politely. About the only thing you can do is Kentucky-fry Japanese chickens that cost more than imported ones.

In France, you cannot sell a tractor that runs faster than 17 miles an hour. In Germany, 13 miles an hour. In the Netherlands, 10 miles an hour. In each country the domestic manufacturer has the advantage: he does not have to spend money modifying his product.

You can ship fresh fruit from America to the European Common Market, but don't be surprised if it is never unloaded. The inspector may be ill or off duty when your cargo arrives. You can sell a big U. S.-made computer in Japan, but you will have to pay a special tax which adds to your price. The tax goes into a fund to develop bigger and better Japanese computers.

The number and variety of NTBs seem almost without limit. Four categories appear popular:
1. Government purchases—American sellers of heavy electrical equipment complain they cannot get their bids considered in England, France, or Japan. The governments are the customers and in effect parcel out contracts to their own companies. They give U. S. firms no notice of bidding in their countries. The same foreign countries, however, have companies that frequently underbid American firms for contracts from U. S. federal agencies. At home, they charge their own governments twice as much or more, and the governments swallow these costs to protect their industries.
2. Customs practices—Many developing countries deliberately set out to harass importers and make imports hard to buy. Farmers complain most frequently about the American selling price system applied to certain chemicals and other products. In computing the duties, U. S. customs officers apply the tariff rates to the American retailing selling price, rather than the foreign wholesale price, as is the usual practice.
3. Standards—Setting standards and specifications which foreigners cannot meet is a common device. For example, imports of pharmaceuticals can be curtailed by setting standards for the testing of drugs during the process of manufacturing them. In 1955, one basic Volkswagen model could be sold anywhere in Europe. Now nine to ten variations are needed.
4. Health requirements—Exporters have long complained that health regulations are used as protectionist devices. The French prohibit the advertising of spirits distilled from grain, but not from fruit, on health grounds. British and American producers of whiskey and gin complain that the law protects the health only of the French cognac industry.

Adapted from Sterling F. Green, Associated Press Staff Writer, ''Non-Tariff Barriers to World Trade,'' *Houston Chronicle*, 2 April 1972, p. 12, section 1, with permission of Associated Press Newsfeatures.

multinational companies originated in the United States.

From the viewpoint of marketing managers, multinational marketing presents particular complexities and challenges. We pointed out that cultural differences, e.g., language, perception of time and distance, and local ethical norms can be quite confusing. And the marketing managers must understand the peculiarities of each country's distribution system. Moreover, multinational marketing is of necessity closely interrelated with governmental policy making. We explore this topic in more detail in the following chapter. Now, let us discuss the impact of marketing on people other than customers.

IMPACT ON NON-CUSTOMERS

Our discussion to this point has focused upon the customer, the user of the

Exhibit 3-18 The 25 Largest Industrial Companies in the World (ranked by sales)

Rank	Company	Headquarters	Sales ($000)	Net Income ($000)
1	Exxon	New York	44,864,824	2,503,013
2	General Motors	Detroit	35,724,911	1,253,092
3	Royal Dutch/Shell Group	London/The Hague	32,105,096	2,110,927
4	Texaco	New York	24,507,454	830,583
5	Ford Motor	Dearborn, Mich.	24,009,100	322,700
6	Mobil Oil	New York	20,620,392	809,877
7	National Iranian Oil	Teheran	18,854,547	16,947,071
8	British Petroleum	London	17,285,854	369,202
9	Standard Oil of California	San Francisco	16,822,077	772,509
10	Unilever	London	15,015,994	322,108
11	International Business Machines	Armonk, N.Y.	14,436,541	1,989,877
12	Gulf Oil	Pittsburgh	14,268,000	700,000
13	General Electric	Fairfield, Conn.	13,399,100	580,800
14	Chrysler	Highland Park, Mich.	11,699,305	(259,535)
15	International Tel. & Tel.	New York	11,367,647	398,171
16	Philips' Gloeilampenfabrieken	Eindhoven (Netherlands)	10,746,485	152,190
17	Standard Oil (Ind.)	Chicago	9,955,248	786,987
18	Cie Française des Pétroles	Paris	9,145,778	168,472
19	Nippon Steel	Tokyo	8,796,902	111,935
20	August Thyssen-Hütte	Duisburg (Germany)	8,764,899	99,926
21	Hoechst	Frankfurt on Main	8,462,322	100,972
22	ENI	Rome	8,334,432	(134,869)
23	Daimler-Benz	Stuttgart	8,194,271	125,768
24	U.S. Steel	Pittsburgh	8,167,269	559,614
25	BASF	Ludwigshafen on Rhine	8,152,318	152,831

Adapted from "The Fifty Largest Industrial Companies in the World," *Fortune* (August 1976), p. 243. Reprinted with permission of *Fortune*.

product marketed by the organization. The basic process could be depicted, indeed, often has been depicted, by only the shaded portion of Exhibit 3-19. The underlying rationale for exchange is that if both originator and consumer believe that their net satisfaction will be increased by completing the exchange, then they do so. If such is not their expectation, then no exchange is made. However, exchange really is not that simple, nor is the explanation adequate when the distribution system is added to the diagram, as we did in the first part of this chapter.

As the total figure shows, there is a third participant in all exchange activity, the society which producer and consumer are members of. The nonshaded portion of Exhibit 3-19 is an integral component of the exchange process. Into the producer's side, society inputs education, training of workers, transportation facilities, rules and regulations, etc. Outputs of the producer include jobs for members of society, payments of taxes, waste products including pollutants, and so on. On the consumer's side, society inputs values and attitudes, styles and fashion trends, money to purchase products, and so on. Consumer outputs include labor,

Exhibit 3-19 Participants in the Exchange Process

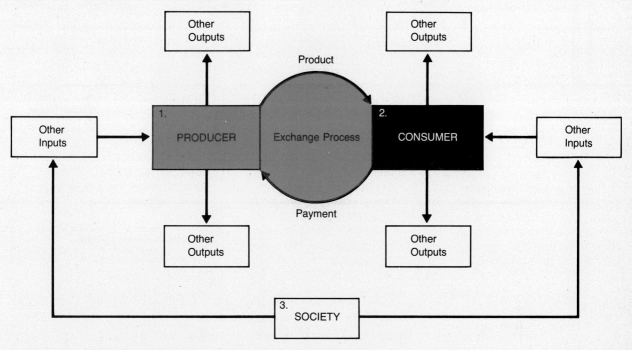

purchases of complementary products, garbage and other waste, etc.
Further elaboration of the impact of exchange activities upon society is
required in two cases: the disadvantaged consumer and externalities.

The Disadvantaged Consumer

A substantial minority of citizens in contemporary society do not share in
the general affluence. This group is the poor, the undereducated, the
unskilled, often the members of a minority race or creed. Studies have
shown that such people pay more for groceries because they are forced by
lack of transportation, limited amounts of money, and in some cases
language barriers to shop at small, inefficient "mom and pop" stores
rather than modern supermarkets. They pay more for major appliances,
because they are unable to obtain credit through the usual channels, and
because they are not skilled at comparison shopping. As a result, they pay
excessive prices even for good merchandise, and often the merchandise
that they do receive is of less than superior quality. Moreover, when they
fall behind in their payments they face wage garnishment and/or court
action that they may not understand.

Consumer education programs can help here, as can laws which protect
against fraudulent and deceptive operations, but the problem lies deeper.
The distribution system does not work well in these areas. Some social

One of the cruelest ironies of our economic system is that the disadvantaged are generally served by the least efficient segments of the business community. The spacious, well-stocked, and efficiently managed stores characteristic of America's highly advanced distribution system are rarely present in the ghetto. The marvels of mass merchandising and its benefits for consumers normally are not shared with the low-income family. Instead their shopping districts are dotted with small, inefficient *mom and pop* establishments more closely related to stores in underdeveloped countries than to the most sophisticated network of retail institutions dominant in most of the U. S. economy."

[This] crucial point seems to have been largely ignored by the critics . . . the difficulty of improvement [is great] so long as the retailing segments of depressed areas are dominated by uneconomically small stores . . . indeed, many legislators seem eager to perpetuate the system by calling for expanded activities by the Small Business Administration in offering assistance to more firms that do business in the ghettos. Another common suggestion is for the federal government to offer low-cost insurance protection to these firms. This proposal, too, may do more to aggravate than to relieve. If the plight of the ghetto consumer is to be dramatically relieved, this will not come about through measures designed to multiply the number of inefficient retailers serving these people."

Adapted from Frederick D. Sturdivant, "Better Deal for Ghetto Shoppers," *Harvard Business Review,* March-April 1968, pp. 130–39, with permission of the publisher.

critics have criticized this failure of the distribution system. The challenge to marketing here is obvious and important. Sturdivant's suggestions for improvement, excerpted in Exhibit 3-20, are classic.

Externalities

In the terminology of economic theory, *externalities* are those costs and benefits that are not accounted for in the direct product-exchange transaction. Examples include the beekeeper whose bees pollinate his neighbor's apple trees in their natural search for nectar, although he is not compensated for this service by the neighbor; and the factory smoke that damages house paint and curtains.

In marketing, examples of external costs are easy to find. Garish billboards and neon lights mar the beauty of the landscape, junk mail (advertising flyers addressed to resident or occupant) clog mailboxes, products consume an increasing amount of scarce energy (most electric utility companies give quantity discounts to users of electricity), phosphate detergents pollute waters, and more powerful airplanes raise the decibel level of urban living. These things are often cited as external costs of marketing activities. There are also external benefits of such activities. For example, research has shown that the roles portrayed by minority groups in advertisements have changed from the stereotyped cook, butler, and foreign-island inhabitant to the busy young housewife, dewy-eyed lovers, and rising young executive portrayed by members of all races. It is thought that this relaxation of stereotyping has contributed in some part to greater racial tolerance. And the role of marketing activities in raising a society's

standard of living is a social benefit acknowledged even by marketing's most ardent critics.

The dominant thrust of the recognition of externalities has been a more searching examination of the standard American bromide that economic growth—any growth—is economic progress. Members of contemporary society increasingly insist that externalities be taken into account. Exhibit 3-21 presents several examples of actions taken to block certain types of economic growth on the grounds that external costs would be excessive. Of course, the issues here are very complex, and the trade-offs involved in different views of progress are not always clear. It may be that certain elements of the society are overvaluing possible external effects (for example, air and water pollution) relative to costs of correction and benefits foregone. Marketing concepts and techniques will play an important role here.

It might be feasible to demonstrate to customers that higher prices might be required to meet anti-pollution goals or that products could be modified (e.g., catalytic converters for automobile exhaust systems, better insulation of homes and business) to reduce negative external effects. And there is increasing recognition of waste products' potential value. Consumers "produce" garbage that can be burned as fuel, scrap aluminum and steel that can be recycled, and used articles of many types that might have value for other consumers. Houses and automobiles are resold, and used clothing shops exist in many cities; distribution centers for used articles could be expanded.

The point is that society is increasingly expecting organizations to consider the external effects of their actions. Since marketing is the function most closely related to the organization's external environment, and is often its most visible function, marketing managers will inevitably bear a major share of the responsibility for this accounting.

CONCLUDING NOTE

Marketing management begins with the search for customers. In this chapter we have no more than outlined the areas in which this search takes place. Later chapters provide the tools for more complete analyses of customers and markets.

I hope that this chapter has demonstrated the fundamental importance of customers to marketing management, and the difficulties involved in precise identification of target markets. The risks, and the rewards, that result from translating potential customers into satisfied consumers of the organization's products are great because the job is complex and difficult.

It is particularly important for marketing managers to recognize the impact of their decisions upon society as a whole. There is no doubt that marketing activities increase individual satisfaction and promote material progress. These material gains also produce both the stock of necessary capital and the leisure time to enjoy cultural pursuits and other activities of a non-economic nature. Exchange activities reinforce values of individual rationality, dignity, and self-respect.

But as we noted in Chapter 1, these very successes of exchange activity also have negative impacts. Critics of marketing argue that it promotes an unhealthy interest in material goods, imposes the lowest common denominator of taste and discretion upon society, and systematically discriminates against and psychologically demeans those who do not have the economic capacity to participate in exchange activity. Moreover, the incessant drive for economic growth may not be rational social policy. In short, marketing activities must be circumscribed by the larger interests of society. The role and scope of marketing in society is discussed in the next chapter.

KEY TERMS AND CONCEPTS

Effective Demand
  money
  authority
  desire
Demographic Characteristics
  population
  age
  family life cycle

Buying Power
  monetary income
  inflation
Organizational Consumers
  categories
  product types
Middlemen
  utilities

distribution system
justification
Wholesalers
  merchants
  manufacturer's branches
  brokers
  petroleum plants and terminals
  farm product assemblers
Retailers
  department stores
  mail order houses
  supermarkets
  shopping centers
  franchising
  concentration
  wheel of retailing

International Marketing
  consumers
  economic system
  multinational marketing
Marketing in Society
  resentment of middlemen
  the disadvantaged consumer
  externalities

QUESTIONS FOR DISCUSSION

1. Exhibit 3-2 presents a breakdown of the U. S. population by age groups. What implications could the trends in population growth for each age group have for the marketing of such products as: school buildings, books and supplies; houses in the $50,000–$75,000 price range; equipment for leisure time activity; charitable causes; luxury goods such as expensive automobiles and around-the-world trips?

2. Consider the family life cycle as presented in Exhibit 3-3. Give examples of products likely to be purchased by a family in each stage. How would consumption patterns at each stage change if the family were broken up by divorce or death? Can you develop an analogous "life cycle" for individuals who do not marry? Give examples of products likely to be consumed at each stage of such a cycle.

3. How does inflation affect buying power? For example, given families in each stage of the family life cycle of question 2, how would the consumption patterns you described be changed in a period of rapid inflation, such as occurred in developed societies in the early 1970s?

4. How do the consumption patterns of families and individuals differ from those of organizations? How are they alike?

5. Do all four channel flows for a given product follow the same pattern? Why or why not? Consider for purposes of illustration the following products: an installation of heavy machinery, a carload of wheat, a haircut, automotive parts, legal services.

6. Give examples of societies that seem at the present time to be in each stage of economic development. Note pertinent demographic and income

characteristics of each country. Give examples of products likely to be consumed by each society.

7. How would marketing a product such as Coca-Cola in eastern Europe be similar to marketing such a product in the U. S.? How would it differ?

8. Examine the exchange process (use Exhibit 3-19) for such products as the following: an ice cream cone, a new winter suit, an automobile, and a house. Identify inputs and outputs for each of the three participants in the exchange process. Can such a process be applied to casting a vote for a political candidate, or donating money to charity or blood to a blood bank? Why or why not?

9. What are some externalities (social costs and benefits) of the following products and marketing activities: cigarettes, pornography, drugs, shipment by diesel truck, outdoor advertising billboards, direct mail circulars, and high-performance automobiles?

SUGGESTED READING

1. Reavis Cox.
Distribution in a High-Level Economy. Englewood Cliffs, N.J.: Prentice-Hall, 1965. Comprehensive, readable review and synthesis of empirical work.

2. Richard T. Gill.
Economics and the Public Interest. Pacific Palisades, Calif.: Goodyear Publishing Company, 1968. Concise summary of basic principles.

3. Norman Kangun, ed.
Marketing and Society: An Unconventional View. New York: Harper and Row, 1972. Thoroughly researched, broadly based anthology of papers on the role of marketing in society; convenient starting point for the serious student.

4. *Statistical Abstract of the United States.*
U. S. Government Printing Office, current year. This authoritative compilation of statistics on American life is published annually; every student of marketing should be familiar with this invaluable reference; it is interesting to simply browse through the various tables and charts—and think of marketing implications of the data.

The Declaration, lawyers' version

Edward A. McCabe, vp-copy director, Scali, McCabe, Sloves, displayed this copy of the Declaration of Independence to a Cornell U. Graduate School of Business seminar on ethics in management. "Today it's no longer enough to be in possession of the facts and communicate them honestly," Mr. McCabe said, "because everything we try to communicate is questioned and has to be proven. It hasn't always been that way. A few years ago, in a simpler time, a small group of communicators in Philadelphia turned out this piece of copy. There was no problem because the people who collaborated on this copy were, themselves, lawyers, and so received their own legal approval. But today lawyers have stopped being writers, they're editors. If the writers presented this copy for approval today, the lawyers would have a field day. I'm sorry to have to tell you that this isn't a joke. I submitted this to our agency's lawyers. These are their comments, considering the climate that exists in advertising today. These words were good enough to start a country with. But today you couldn't run them in an ad."

Jefferson, Hancock & Wythe, Inc.
INDEPENDENCE HALL, PHILA., PENNSYLVANIA

Client: House   Date: 7/4/76

Job No.: 1   Space: _____

Medium: Parchment   Publ. Date: ASAP

Copy

A DECLARATION
By the Representatives of the United States of America
In General Congress Assembled.

When in the Course of human of Events, it becomes necessary for one People to dissolve the Political Bands which have connected them with another, and to assume among the Powers of the Earth, the separate and equal Station to which the Laws of Nature and of Nature's God entitle them, a decent Respect to the Opinions of Mankind requires that they should declare the causes which impel them to the Separation.

We hold these Truths to be self-evident, that all Men are created equal, that they are endowed by their Creator with certain unalienable Rights, that among these are Life, Liberty and the Pursuit of Happiness--That to secure these Rights, Governments are instituted among Men, deriving their just Powers from the Consent of the Governed, that whenever any Form of Government becomes destructive of these Ends, it is the Right of the People to alter or to abolish it, and to institute new Government, laying its Foundation on such Principles, and organizing its Powers in such Form, as to them shall seem most likely to effect their Safety and Happiness. Prudence, indeed, will dictate that Governments long established should not be changed for light and transient Causes; and accordingly all Experience hath shewn, that Mankind are more disposed to suffer, while Evils are sufferable, than to right themselves by abolishing the Forms to which they are accustomed. But when a long Train of Abuses and Usurpations, pursuing invariably the same Object, evinces a Design to reduce them under absolute Despotism, it is their Right, it is their Duty, to throw off such Government, and to provide new Guards for their future Security. Such has been the patient Sufferance of these Colonies; and such is now the Necessity which constrains them to alter their former Systems of Government. The History of the present King of Great Britain is a History of repeated Injuries and Usurpations, all having in direct Object the Establishment of an absolute Tyranny over these States. To prove this, let Facts be submitted to a candid World.

He has refused his Assent to Laws, the most wholesome and necessary for the public Good.

Continued....

(Handwritten marginal notes:) OK only if everybody showed up / must prove existence of such laws No copies on file! / No! Must be substantiated / This is an implied guarantee! Copy must state that we don't guarantee it. / Are we prepared to disclose others? / Can't say 'all.' Qualify! / Someone may challenge this!! / Can't substantiate / Need a signed release. / Since when are your opinions facts? / Disparaging! Do we have adequate research to back up?

Reprinted from *Advertising Age* (December 1974) by permission of Edward A. McCabe.

4/MARKETING, SOCIETY, AND PUBLIC POLICY

The role of marketing in society is one of today's most vigorously debated topics. We examine it from the viewpoint of the marketer striving to understand, cope with, and possibly change it. Major aspects of this role include:

1. The purpose of an economic system is to allocate scarce resources to satisfy unlimited wants and desires. The two fundamental approaches to this allocation are planning (command) and the market mechanism (demand).

2. If pure monopoly or pure competition characterized a market, there would be little need for marketing activities. In the imperfect markets of the real world, marketing adds time, place, and possession utilities to products.

3. Every society develops a set of institutions to organize and regulate the behavior of its members. Economic activities receive particular attention in an industrial society. In general, the criteria for public policy in the economic sphere include full employment, efficiency, stability, progress, equity, consumer sovereignty, morality, and quality of life.

4. Public policy development is a complex process which can be conceptualized using a systems model. A chronological view of landmark antitrust policy developments within the context of the model is instructive. The pluralistic nature of public policy development is illustrated.

5. Public policy toward marketing generally takes three forms: intervention, protection, and market structure and conduct guides.

6. Contemporary issues result from the relationship between the economic and governmental dimensions of society. These issues are translated into public policy in a political climate characterized today by rising social expectations, and an advocacy approach that sometimes fails to understand the actual functioning of an economic system.

Exhibit 4-1   Resource Allocation: The Production-Possibility Curve

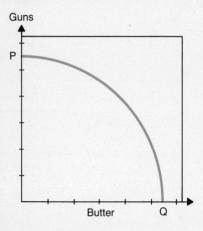

The fundamental economic problem faced by any society is to determine how it will allocate its resources to satisfy human wants. This fundamental problem arises because wants are infinite, but resources—capital, materials, people's talents and energies, and information—are limited.

APPROACHES TO THE ECONOMIC PROBLEM

Basically, there are two possible approaches to the problem of how best to deliver utility to members of the society. The command economy seeks to control the origination and exchange of products through conscious decisions by members of the society. The alternative approach is the market mechanism, in which prices and other market mix tools control the supply of and demand for various products that members of a society might desire.

The Command Economy

In concept, the most efficient way to operate an economic system is for the members of society—through their leaders—to decide what products will best satisfy the wants of the members of the society, and then direct origination and exchange activities to produce those products. Since inputs into the origination/exchange process are limited, direction of an economic system involves trade-offs. Exhibit 4-1 presents the classic explanation of this type of decision. Given available resources at a certain period of time, this society could, if it devoted all of these resources to the production of guns, produce the amount of guns indicated by the point P. Alternatively, if all resources were channeled in the direction of butter, Q amount of butter could be produced. Thus the curve PQ shows the amounts of guns and butter that could be produced with various combinations of the resources available to the society. Since the leaders of the society—in theory at least—know which products will best satisfy the desires of the members of the society, competent decision making on the part of the leaders should therefore produce the maximum amount of utility from these products for members of this society. Conceptually, this example could be extended to any number of products.

Of course, when it gets right down to operating an actual economic system, it is not quite so simple. A command economy experiences two types of problems. First is the fundamental question of who decides what products the economic system will deliver. Each individual's desires are different, and everyone has strong feelings about how best to satisfy his or her own wants. When one member or group in society claims that it should make such decisions for the whole society, conflict is inevitable—no matter how noble the group's motives or how powerful its capabilities. In fact, this type of argument is a major source of political conflict in all societies.

The second type of difficulty that a command economy faces is in operating the system according to the plan developed by the leaders. This question may be less potentially destructive of the fabric of the society, but it is more complex. Consider the problems inherent in deciding the number of doctors, factory workers, farmers, plumbers, managers, peanut vendors, baseball players, and trapeze artists that a society should have; inducing people to take each of these types of jobs, determining how much each job should be paid, and how their products should be valued. Problems of organization, coordination, and motivation become exceedingly complex. Moreover, the economic environment is dynamic: individual wants change; technology makes possible new products; floods, freezes, and droughts occur. These changes require continuous major and minor adjustments in the economic system.

While the idea of a command economy is an appealing one, it is clear that implementing such a concept would be fraught with difficulty. This has generally been the experience of command economies. Exhibit 4-2 describes one example.

Exhibit 4-2 Consumption in a Command Economy

In spite of various reforms, the Soviet economy still operates by a plan from above rather than in response to consumer demand. Goods are produced to fill the plan, not to sell. Leningrad can be overstocked with cross-country skis, yet go several months without soap for washing dishes. The list of scarce items is practically endless. They are not permanently out of stock, but their appearance is unpredictable. Quality is another nightmare for the Russian consumer. Russians turn up their noses at many goods as *shtampny*—literally, poured from the mold, the epitome of the cheapest output of mass-production industry, or *brack,* junk that does not work or that comes apart.

Soviet shopping is like a year-round Christmas rush. The accepted norm is that the Soviet woman daily spends two hours in line, seven days a week. This means that Russians stand in line 33 billion person-hours annually just to make purchases. So all women carry a string bag, *voska,* which comes from the Russian word for maybe. Likewise, almost every man carries a briefcase wherever he goes. Another precaution is to carry plenty of cash at all times; the Soviet system is devoid of credit cards, charge accounts, checkbooks, or easy loans.

Soviet officials never tire of telling the West that Russians are protected from financial disaster because they have free medical care and low-cost housing. It is true that the state provides health care, but many Russians complain that their health system, like the rest of the consumer section, is plagued by overworked doctors, shortages of medicine, poor equipment, and generally low quality service. The cheapness of medicines—often under a dollar for prescriptions—is one of the great pluses of the system, but it is frequently cancelled out by shortages.

Similarly, the Russian "sanitary housing norm," established back in 1920 at nine square meters of living space (equal to a ten-by-ten-foot room) is the minimum for each person. Yet more than half a century later, the great majority of Soviet people in urban areas have not reached the 1920 minimal level. A Leningrad playwright, in a moving drama, captured the pathetic agonies of a couple who go through divorce but are forced to continue living together afterwards because they cannot find other housing. Smith was told of specific cases in which this happened in real life.

Corruption and illegal private enterprises in Russia, "creeping capitalism," as some Russians call it, grow out of the very nature of the Soviet economy and its inefficiencies. Practically any good or service can be arranged *na levo*—literally "on the left," but idiomatically, "under the table."

The Soviet counter-economy has its own lore and lingo, its channels and conventions. The most common innocent variety is what the Russians call *blat*—influence, connections, pulling strings. In an economy of chronic shortages and carefully parceled out privileges, *blat* is an essential lubricant of life. But *blat* is only the tip of the iceberg. Bribery is just as widespread. What the Arabs call *baksheesh*, Mexicans call *mordida* and Americans call "greasing the palm"—Russians call *vzyatka*, literally, "the take." In Odessa, they have a saying that if you really get mad at another person, you put a curse on him—"Let him live on his salary."

Of course, the Soviet economy is much more complex than these excerpts suggest, and it certainly has many positive features. But I think these excerpts amply demonstrate that the command system does not work nearly so well as its proponents claim that it will, or as well as the market system works.

Source: Hedrick Smith, *The Russians*, Quadrangle/The New York Times Book Co., 1976, pp. 60–2, 64–5, 69–70, 72–4, 75, 78, 86–9.

Exhibit 4-3   The Market Mechanism Equates Supply and Demand at a Given Price

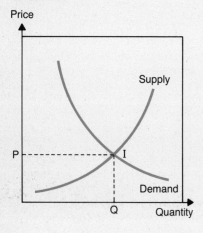

Price

P

Supply

I

Demand

Q   Quantity

The Market Mechanism

The other approach to guiding an economic system toward the satisfaction of human wants is the market mechanism. This concept is that wants are satisfied by purchasing products—at a price determined by the market mechanism (interaction of supply and demand). Exhibit 4-3, the familiar supply/demand intersection, illustrates the operation of the market mechanism. The demand curve shows the quantity of a given product that consumers would be willing to buy over a period of time at all possible prices, *ceteris paribus* (other things being equal). It slopes downward and to the right—indicating that as the price of the product falls, more of it will be demanded, if other things are equal—specifically, the prices of other products and consumers' buying power. The supply curve indicates the quantity of the product that producers would be willing to supply to consumers at all possible prices, ceteris paribus.

The crucial point is the intersection of the two curves, labeled I. This point shows that Q units of this product will be demanded by the society, at a price P. Operation of the market mechanism in actual situations is considerably more complex than this short explanation, but the principle of price adjustments to equate supply and demand is clear. Despite some imperfections and problems, the market mechanism operates in all societies to set a price on any product for which any consumer feels has utility. When one considers the myriad of possible products, and the millions of potential consumers in a contemporary industrial society, the fact that the market mechanism operates more or less successfully is little short of astounding.

Adam Smith, in his classic treatment of the market mechanism, *The Wealth of Nations,* characterized the operation of market mechanism as an *invisible hand*—as each individual seeks to satisfy his or her own wants, the economy is led as if by an invisible hand to maximum satisfaction of the wants of all members of society. This explanation is something less than completely satisfying; the truth is that the operation of the market mechanism is only imperfectly understood. As Professor P. T. Bauer of the London School of Economics once remarked:

> The market system delivers the goods people want, but its supporters cannot explain why. The socialist [command] system does not deliver the goods, but its supporters readily explain why it does not, cannot, or should not do so. The one system is long on desired goods and short on effective arguments. The other system is short on desired goods, but long on successful arguments.

This is not to say that the market mechanism functions so well in actual situations as it does in ideal conception. Let us look at the pure competition ideal and at the continuum of actual types of market structure.

MARKET STRUCTURE

Markets are analyzed by economists in terms of the ideal of pure competition. Actual structures range from (almost) pure competition to total monopoly. Economists believe that the performance of marketing activities of organizations is governed to a large extent by the structures of the market in which it competes. Marketing scholars do not necessarily agree.

Pure Competition

The foundation for the study of market structure is the theory of pure competition. As we noted in our discussion of supply/demand relationships, this theory assumes that supply and demand are equalized by price changes, ceteris paribus. Let us examine the meaning of this phrase. The assumptions underlying pure competition are as follows [pedantic aside: some economists distinguish between *pure* and *perfect* competition; we use the terms synonymously]:

1. *Product homogeneity*—products offered to the market by all suppliers are exactly alike.
2. *Rational consumers*—consumers act so as to maximize their total satisfaction, given their desires and buying power, which are stable.
3. *Rational suppliers*—producers act so as to maximize their profits; they do this by making price changes since their products are exactly like the products of every other supplier. No other type of marketing effort (advertising, personal selling, etc.) is necessary.
4. *Perfect knowledge*—both suppliers and consumers have full, complete, and accurate knowledge of all prices and market conditions; they obtain this knowledge instantaneously at no cost.

5. *Perfect mobility of resources*—there are no barriers to entry into a market; no scale economies, government licenses, costs or time lapses.

Of course, there are no such markets in the real world. Yet, the bulk of the structure of price theory in economics rests upon these assumptions. Every student of economics spends considerable time studying this type of market. Three reasons are often advanced for this emphasis upon pure competition. First, progress in many fields of study has resulted from making simple assumptions at elementary levels, and then relaxing these assumptions to permit greater realism. The classic example is the study of moving bodies in physics. The elementary formulas for speed and velocity ignore friction coefficients; once the student has mastered these formulas, factors for friction can be added. Second, the model of pure competition provides insight into real-world behavior, particularly in the markets of certain types of products, e.g., farm produce and stock and bond exchanges. Third, and particularly significant to the discussion of marketing and public policy, pure competition is often held to be an ideal against which actual market performance can be measured. As we discuss later in this chapter, this last argument is open to some question. At any rate, it is instructive to view pure competition as one end of a continuum of possible states of competition in a market.

Competition/Monopoly Continuum

If pure competition is the economist's ideal market structure, the zenith of market structure types, then the worst type of market structure, the nadir, is pure monopoly. In contrast to pure competition, a monopoly market structure is characterized by a situation in which there is only one seller, who possesses a product which consumers must accept because it has no substitutes. The monopolist enjoys this position by virtue of some type of control over resources necessary to produce the product—a patent, exclusive license by government to market in an area, sole access to raw materials, or large economies of scale. The monopolist undertakes marketing effort not as a competitive device, but to expand consumer demand for the product. But monopoly profits make this market attractive to other suppliers—if they can overcome barriers to entry into the market. In point of fact, total monopoly is no more likely to exist naturally in the real world than is pure competition. The classic examples of the feudal baron who controls the only source of drinking water, or the only accessible roadway through the valley, simply do not exist in a modern economy. Consumers in an industrial society can find substitutes for almost any product; aluminum for steel, detergents for soap, drilling a water well instead of patronizing the local utility, and private carriers rather than the U.S. Post Office.

Between the idealized end points on the continuum, an infinite

Exhibit 4-4 The Monopoly/Competition Continuum of Market Structure

	Type of Structure			
	Monopoly	Oligopoly	Monopolistic Competition	Pure Competition
Market Continuum				
Definition (Number of Suppliers):	One	Few	Many	Infinite
Characteristics:				
1. Product homogeneity	Unique (no substitutes)	Considerable differentiation (few substitutes)	Some differentiation (many substitutes)	Complete (infinite substitutes)
2. Consumer behavior	Accepts product offering	Responds to oligopolist's offers	Responds to price and nonprice variables	Responds only to price
3. Supplier market effort	Used, if at all, to expand demand	Generally eschews price competition	Markets aggressively using all elements of marketing mix	None—offers products at market price
4. Market knowledge	Perfect	Imperfect	Imperfect	Perfect
5. Resource mobility	Blocked	Some barriers	Relatively free	Complete

number of possible markets structures exist. For convenience, economists generally segment the continuum into two rather broad states: monopolistic (atomistic) competition, and oligopoly. Exhibit 4-4 illustrates this conception.

Under monopolistic competition there are many sellers of relatively homogeneous products. However, there are some product differences, so it is worthwhile to engage in marketing effort (e.g., advertising and sales promotion, branding), since the consumer may respond to these nonprice competitive tactics as well as to changes in price. Moreover, knowledge on the part of both consumers and suppliers is less than perfect in this market; consequently, the intelligent, innovative, fast-moving supplier or consumer can improve his or her satisfaction at the expense of other sellers, suppliers or competitors in the market.

Oligopoly, in contrast, describes a market structure in which there are few sellers whose products are rather different from other products that might be used as substitutes. Economists distinguish between two types of oligopolies, differentiated and undifferentiated, on the basis of degree of similarity of products within the oligopolistic structure. The U.S. automobile industry is the classic example of a differentiated oligopoly—the "big three" manufactures most U.S. cars (for which no really close

T he oligopolist offers to the market a product that is similar to that offered by a few other rivals. Consequently, if he contemplates changing his price, he will be very interested in how his rivals might respond to that change. If they do not respond, then demand for his product would be greatly affected by a small change in his price, and his demand curve would resemble Line DD in the figure. (Recall that a demand curve with this shape is called *elastic* by economists.) On the other hand, if his rivals change their prices in

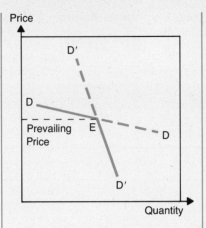

proportion to his change, then demand for his product will probably not change too much—Line D'D' in the figure.

The hypothesis about an oligopolist's price behavior is that if he were to raise his price, his rivals would not follow; therefore, demand for his product would be greatly decreased. Conversely, if he were to lower his price, his rivals would match that decrease—and his demand would not expand very much. In that case, his demand curve would be indicated by the solid line DED' Faced with this type of demand curve, the oligopolist might be expected to change his price only on those rare occasions when changing market conditions clearly call for a price increase or decrease. Consequently, according to this hypothesis oligopolists generally do not engage in price competition; they compete on the basis of other types of marketing effort, i.e., *nonprice competition*.

substitutes are recognized by consumers, mass-transit advocates notwithstanding), but each of the three makes many different types of cars. An undifferentiated oligopoly, in contrast, is an industry offering similar products which do not have close substitutes. Examples include steel making, bread baking, and network television programming.

Consequently, consumers respond to the differing offers of the various oligopolists, but find themselves dependent upon the group of oligopolists as a whole to supply the product wanted. The oligopolists, for their part, generally eschew price competition. Price changes are highly visible and quickly countered.

One rationale for the lack of price competition in oligopolistic markets is the hypothesis of the kinked demand curve, explained in Exhibit 4-5. This concept is useful in understanding the behavior of oligopolists; it underscores the interdependence of organizations in an oligopoly. However, price changes do occur. Frequently, such changes result from the actions of industry leaders, e.g., General Motors and United States Steel. When the leader changes price, other firms in the industry do likewise. Of course, there may be some "shading" of the leader-established price, but most marketing effort is focused upon elements of the marketing mix other than price.

The continuum concept and the terminology explained above are the usual economist's tools for studying market structure. The problem, of course, lies in defining the boundaries between markets, so that a given market structure can be categorized according to this continuum. The marketing student, in accordance with the marketing concept, would like to define markets in terms of products that serve similar wants and desires of consumers. Even though the products may be quite dissimilar in physical appearance, materials used, manufacturing processes, or distribution methods, they should ideally be classified in the same market or industry if the consumer sees them as substitutes. For example, although cane and beet sugar are harvested in very different ways, both become granulated sugar, so cane and sugar beet producers are generally considered to be in the same industry. That classic example causes no difficulty, but consider some others.

If, for example, some consumers perceive both narcotics and alcohol to be different ways of "turning on," then these products should be considered to be in the same market—but they usually are not. Also, consider the individual who must decide whether to spend his/her leisure time mowing his lawn or playing golf. In effect, lawn mowers and golf clubs are alternative ways of providing satisfaction, but are rarely considered to be in the same market. The problem is that the industry data used in defining markets generally comes from the U.S. Census Bureau, and that body's definitions are supplier- rather than buyer-oriented. That is, markets are defined in terms of tangible product characteristics rather than want-satisfying capabilities.

If these generally accepted definitions of a market or industry are somewhat imprecise, they are nevertheless very real to the marketing manager interested in his/her market share, or to the public policy maker worried about monopoly control of the market. The reason for their interest in market structure is simply that structure is widely believed to be related to the conduct of firms in the market.

Structure and Market Conduct
According to orthodox economic doctrine, a market structure characterized as pure competition is good—because there are so many sellers that none can influence the price of the product, discriminate against a group of consumers, or differentiate his/her product from those of any others. For this reason it can be shown mathematically that, given the assumptions of pure competition, market prices will be minimized, ceteris paribus. By the same token, a monopoly market structure is bad, since the monopolist can charge whatever price he/she desires for a unique product. Although we have emphasized the fact that this theory is an inadequate explanation of real-world market behavior, many economists, public policy makers, students, and even some businessmen look to market structure as a measure of market performance.

The usual way of determining market structure in a market is to measure the degree of concentration in that market. Market concentration

Exhibit 4-6 The OPEC Cartel

The Organization of Petroleum Exporting Countries is a cartel. By definition, a cartel is an association of producers of a particular product who organize to monopolize the market for that product. The basic purpose is to eliminate the competition which reduces the price of the product.

OPEC has done this with spectacular success. In 1974, the price of a barrel of crude oil was raised from $2.50 to over $10 per barrel, a fourfold increase. Provided that its members act in concert, OPEC can maintain prices at this high level because its members control more than two-thirds of all known world reserves of petroleum, and they provide more than 85 percent of oil for export. While some countries such as the United States and the Soviet Union produce large amounts of oil, they consume all they produce, and more. The OPEC countries, in contrast, use only a small part of their production themselves.

Oil is a vital commodity to developed societies, and it has no close substitutes. Therefore, economists say that demand for oil is inelastic. Their calculations indicate that, in the short run, a 100 percent increase in the price of crude oil leads to only a 15 percent reduction in consumption (an elasticity coefficient of -.15).

In the longer run, e.g., five to ten years, however, profits derived from the monopoly position spur development of alternative sources of supply or substitute products. There has been a tremendous expansion of exploration and production of crude oil. In a few years, the oil fields in Alaska and the North Sea will begin to contribute to worldwide supply. In addition, there is greatly increased interest in petroleum substitutes: coal, shale, nuclear power, solar energy, and direct conversion of hydrogen to power.

Overproduction and cheating by one member usually cracks a cartel. The winters of 1974 and 1975 were unusually mild. In addition, developed countries began practicing conservation (the 55 mile-per-hour speed limit in the U.S. for example). Price increases by the cartel were modest in 1975, and were held steady through June 1976. The result is that worldwide inflation has tended to reduce the real price of crude oil.

The OPEC is a loose coalition of nations of varying size, culture, crude oil reserves, and plans for economic development. Given these political and economic pressures, there is some question as to how long a cartel can remain viable.

As of 1976, the cartel is eminently successful, and this success is prompting other nations rich in other raw materials to consider cartelization. Bauxite, nickel, tin, and coffee beans are likely candidates, according to those nations which produce large quantities of these products.

They are not likely to be as successful as OPEC, which has amassed huge trade surpluses in the past three years. But the world petroleum market has adjusted, and is recycling these "petrodollars" into investments in the developed countries. In short, the market mechanism appears to be coping with a modern monopoly.

Source: Adapted by the author from "OPEC: The Economics of the Oil Cartel," *Business Week* (Jan. 13, 1975), pp. 77–81; Louis Kraar, "OPEC is Starting to Feel the Pressure," *Fortune* (May 1975), p. 186 ff.; Gary Shilling, "Lessons From History for OPEC," *The Wall Street Journal* (March 10, 1975), p. 16; and other news reports.

OPEC Country	Reserves (billions bbl.)	Production in 1973 (millions bbl./day)	Years of Reserves (at 1973 production rate)	Population (millions)
Saudi Arabia	140.8	7.7	51	8.1
Kuwait	72.7	3.1	66	0.9
Iran	60.2	5.9	28	31.9
Iraq	31.2	2.0	44	10.4
Libya	25.6	2.2	32	2.1
United Arab Emirates	25.5	1.5	45	0.1
Nigeria	19.9	2.0	27	73.4
Venezuela	14.2	3.5	11	11.3
Indonesia	10.8	1.3	22	125.0
Algeria	7.4	1.0	20	14.7
Qatar	6.5	0.5	31	0.2
Ecuador	5.7	0.2	78	6.7

Reprinted from the January 13, 1975 issue of *Business Week* by special permission. © 1975 by McGraw-Hill, Inc.

is defined as the share of sales in an industry or market accounted for by the various organizations in the industry producing and selling the product. Note that an organization may be relatively large in absolute size (assets, sales volume, etc.), but account for a relatively small share of its industry's output, e.g., Chrysler Corporation or Inland Steel Corporation. Conversely, a firm could be small by any absolute measure and yet be a "big fish in a small pond." It is relative size that is important in measuring concentration.

Concentration ratios are very carefully studied because, as noted above, the notion is widely held in our society that pure competition is desirable and monopoly is to be avoided. The actions of the Standard Oil Company during the latter half of the nineteenth century constitute the classic case of monopoly exploitation in American economic history. Today, OPEC is behaving very much like a monopolist (see Exhibit 4-6). In general, the argument is that monopolists are able to exploit markets, i.e., charge prices higher than would be allowed by pure competition, because they erect barriers to entry into those markets. For our purposes, these barriers can be divided into two types: cost barriers and marketing effort barriers.

There are two types of cost barriers, economies of scale and absolute cost. A firm which has a larger scale of operations can, ceteris paribus, produce products at a lower cost per unit. This is merely the economic penalty for starting and/or staying small. Absolute cost barriers, on the other hand, hold for all levels of production. The firm may achieve an absolute cost advantage in a number of ways. First, it may simply have access to a cheaper source of raw materials than do competitors. (Companies in the mining and extraction fields sometimes achieve this happy position.) The firm may control some type of exclusive knowledge—through a patent or, in the case of Coca-Cola, by retaining the secret formula for its ingredients in the hands of only a few company executives. Or the firm may be granted some sort of license by government, e.g., public utilities.

The other major type of barrier to entry that economists cite is product differentiation. Product differentiation is the strategy of separating the firm's products from other homogeneous products offered to the market. The idea is to convince consumers that the differentiated product will better serve their wants and desires than do other products in the market. The differentiation may be physical. The product may be shown to be more durable, easier to use, more conveniently available, more stylish, easier to repair—in short, better. Note that if this strategy is to be effective, the consumer must have some means of identifying the product that is differentiated from other products; consequently, branding plays an important role in product differentiation. If the consumer cannot identify the product he wants, he certainly cannot buy it—and no benefits from differentiation would accrue to the producer. We examine product differentiation and branding in Chapter 9.

A second type of product differentiation barrier to entry is promotional activity. It is argued that firms that can afford to spend significant amounts upon advertising and personal selling effort can achieve the same effect in the consumer's mind as physical differentiation—even when no physical differences in products exist. Classic examples are cigarettes, beer, coffee, household detergents, gasoline, liquor—products that are relatively homogeneous in a physical sense. But if via promotional activity the producer can convince the consumer that his particular brand will better serve the consumer, then he can charge a higher price for it, and the consumer's decision will not be based upon "rational" calculations of price/utility considerations. (Hence the term nonprice competition.)

Very briefly, these are the theoretical arguments against nonprice competition usually advanced by economists. From the point of view of marketing management, however, these competitive devices are necessary and legitimate components of marketing strategy. Managers see them not as imperfections but as decision alternatives for achieving the organization's objectives. Considerable attention is devoted to this viewpoint in succeeding chapters.

The reason for studying market structure is that structure is said to affect performance—specifically, that monopoly is considered bad and pure competition is good. To the extent, then, that barriers exist that prevent evolution of a market structure toward pure competition, then most economists and many public policy makers feel that the economic system is not working properly. This position is not particularly sound, for two reasons. First, as we noted above, pure competition is a theoretical ideal; it is not, however, a particularly realistic model. For example, economists would see the market for raw agricultural products as approximating the pure competition ideal, but farmers whose incomes are low and subject to forces beyond their control might not agree that this ideal was particularly pleasant. Our society is sympathetic to the farmers' position—the market for agricultural products has been distorted by price supports and acreage allotments which are definitely not in concert with the pure competition model. The theory upon which the hypothesis linking market structure and market conduct rests is not a strong one.

Second, there appears to be little empirical support for the conclusion that market conduct depends upon market structure, or that purely competitive markets are better from a social perspective than are markets that tend to be monopolistic. The general conclusion of empirical study in this area is that evidence of the link between market structure and market conduct is inconclusive. Nevertheless, we have devoted some time to explaining these issues because they loom large in the eyes of public policy makers, i.e., the government.

THE ROLE OF GOVERNMENT

The function of government in a society is to organize and enforce certain behavior patterns that society deems necessary. In preindustrial societies, government results from traditional, often unwritten, customs. But in a modern society, government can become a very complex institution. One important aspect of governmental activities is social administration of the economic system. Government limits the realm of marketing transactions—according to certain criteria by which society evaluates solutions to the economic problem.

Criteria for Public Policy Toward Economic Activities

The question, in essence, is—how does society evaluate the performance of its economic system? Answers given by economists and other students of social systems vary, but eight themes appear frequently in their answers. These themes can be grouped in two categories—essentially technical criteria and essentially humanistic criteria, as highlighted in Exhibit 4-7.

1. Full Employment. The complete utilization of all the resources available to a society at a given time has always been one of the fundamental criteria by which an economic system is measured. Systems that let resources stand idle, or underutilize them (e.g., forbidding minority group members from holding jobs for which they are capable because of religious or racial prejudice), systems that allocate resources to frivolous purposes (e.g., the Circus Maximus in ancient Rome) are not utilizing resources to full capacity. Ideally, inputs of resources of all types should move freely from product to product until the marginal product output per unit of resource is equal for all products.

2. Efficiency. In addition to full employment, the society should use resources efficiently. That is, the ratio of output effectiveness to resource input should be maximized. Economists and engineers generally recognize three types of efficiency: allocative, technical, and marketing. Allocative efficiency refers to the distribution of resources among possible uses—ideally, resources should be allocated to their most productive use, e.g., aluminum to aircraft engines rather than beer cans. Second, resources put to a given use should take maximum advantage of known techniques and skills. For example, modern machinery should be used, economies of scale should be achieved, and so on. The third type of efficiency is efficiency in marketing effort. Economists, as discussed earlier in the chapter, consider marketing (nonprice) competitive devices to be largely wasted since in a purely competitive economy there would be no need for marketing effort. However, marketing effort has a definite role to play in an economic system—it may, for example, direct the allocation of resources to products that consumers desire, and it may permit the achievement of economies of scale in production costs. Consequently, marketing decision makers should strive for maximum efficiency in the use of product, promotion, distribution and pricing concepts and techniques.

3. Price Stability. Inflation—increases in prices without corresponding increases in product quality—is universally recognized as a indicator of less than optimal economic performance. A constant, nonfluctuating general price level is taken (ceteris paribus) to be a sign of economic health.

4. Progress. Members of a society expect improvements in their lives over time. Industrial societies often equate improvements in social life with gains in Gross National Product. Postindustrial societies, it is said, would focus increasing attention upon increases in the quality of life, which may be very different from gains in the quantity of material goods. For example, indicators might include measures of living conditions, individual status, health, education and welfare, and governmental effectiveness. By whatever definition, progress is one of the key criteria by which the performance of an economic system is evaluated.

5. Equity. The way a society distributes its wealth among its members has always been a key determinant of the way that the society's economic system is evaluated. This criterion is perhaps destined to play the major role in the evaluation of the economic systems of postindustrial societies. That is, if a society reaches the point at which the basic needs of all members of a society can be satisfied, there will be increasing pressure to do so.

One measure of equity in a society's economic system is the percentage of income received by each fifth of the population. For example, in 1974 the poorest fifth of families in the United States received only 5.4 percent of the total aggregate income while the highest-paid fifth of the people received 41 percent of the total. This measure is instructive, since it shows a considerable degree of deviation from absolute income equality. On the other hand, absolute equality of incomes is probably impossible to obtain—and may not be desirable. The capabilities and efforts of some people are worth more than those of other people, and one can make a good argument that some degree of differential reward is appropriate. Moreover, income, as discussed in Chapter 3, is not the total measure of wealth (assets and borrowing power must also be considered). Nor is material wealth necessarily an adequate measure of human well-being. However it is measured, every economic system pays some attention to the criterion of equity.

6. *Sovereignty.* Another dimension of the performance of an economic system is the degree of choice it permits each individual consumer in the style and manner in which he/she may satisfy wants and desires. The market mechanism generally allows the individual more latitude than do command decisions in meeting this criterion of economic performance.

7. *Morality.* The conduct of economic activity within "socially approved" bounds is a topic of considerable discussion these days. Television programs and movies that emphasize violent or immoral themes are being censored. There is considerable pressure upon individuals and organizations to conduct themselves in ways condoned by society. Companies that resorted to bribing government officials, for example, were headline news in early 1976. Payment of such "commissions" is fairly common practice in some countries, but the public in the United States, Japan, and the Netherlands was outraged. Similarly, many companies are under considerable pressure (public opinion, law suits, directives from federal agencies) to make their products less dangerous to health and safety. The criterion of morality seems to be growing more important today than it was in the recent past and in my opinion, its importance will not diminish. Morality will play an increasingly significant role in the evaluation of economic activities.

8. *Quality of Life.* As we discussed in Chapter 3, economic activities have external effects. Developed societies are increasingly taking steps to maximize the positive, and minimize the negative, aspects of these externalities. Airplane flights over, and truck movements through, residential areas are being curtailed if exhaust noise is excessive. Vigorous steps are being taken to reduce or eliminate discrimination on the basis of race, creed, or sex. Attention is devoted to means of mediating conflicts, e.g., between economic growth and preservation of the environment, and among classes in various societies.

Of course, societies vary in the significance they attach to these (and other) criteria. And the criteria themselves are not mutually exclusive. The classic example is the trade-off between full employment and inflation: as an economy nears maximum capacity, prices of all resources are bid up. On the humanistic side, equity and sovereignty often clash: raising income taxes improves equity (if such taxes result in transfer payments to lower-income people), but decreases individual sovereignty (since personal discretionary income is reduced). And there are conflicts between technical and humanistic criteria. For example, in developing countries, economic growth often necessitates investments in capital goods at the expense of consumer goods—a blow to sovereignty. Similarly, economic progress requires that factories be built and resources mined; belching smokestacks and stripmined land despoil the environment, lowering the quality of life.

Thus, each society must attempt to determine the optimum combination of objectives for its economic system. The problem is that there is no generally accepted method of ranking these criteria. In business organizations, as we discuss in the following chapter, the overall objective of profit maximization provides a hierarchical structure for various objectives. Similarly, as we discuss in Chapter 6, individuals rank motivating factors in some fashion, e.g., Maslow's hierarchy of needs. But there is no comparable method of ranking factors associated with each of the eight social criteria for assessing economic performance. Societies generally approach the economic problem in terms of public policy toward marketing.

PUBLIC POLICY TOWARD MARKETING

Public policy toward marketing activities in contemporary society is manifest in a bewildering number of laws, regulations, court decisions, and administrative arrangements between government agencies, business firms, and other organizations. To gain a perspective on this area, we first develop a model for the formulation of public policy toward marketing and then examine the evolution of public policy toward marketing in this country in light of this model.

Model of Public Policy Formulation

The development of public policy is a process. Consequently, the systems concept can be effectively utilized to develop a model for understanding the process of public policy develpment. Exhibit 4-8 presents this model.

Note that the inputs into the public policy formulation process are various environmental forces—those dynamic factors within the environment that influence environmental change. Among the most important of these influences are population growth, rising educational levels, changes in the customs and mores of the society, shifts in the ethical standards of a

Exhibit 4-8   Formulation of Public Policy Toward Marketing

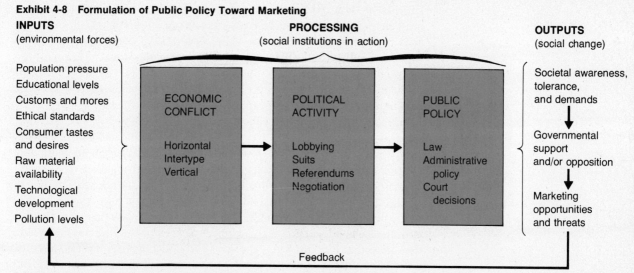

Developed from a diagram in Sturdivant, "Mores and the Legal Context of Behavior," which in turn was based on Joseph C. Palamountain, *The Politics of Distribution* (Cambridge: Harvard University Press, 1955). pp. 5–57.

people, changes in consumers' tastes and desires, shifts in raw material availability (for example, the discovery of new resources, or increased depletion rates), technological developments and rising pollution levels. These forces interact in complex fashion, causing the environment for marketing activities to change.

Specifically, environmental forces cause economic conflict—economic activity outside of the socially accepted boundaries of economic competition. There are three basic types of economic conflict: *horizontal, intertype,* and *vertical.* Horizontal conflict is the competition among organizations selling to the same market (the type of economic competition taught in elementary economics courses). For example, grocery stores compete with each other for patronage of consumers in a given market. Sometimes such competition approaches the limits of legality—perhaps by pricing below cost or even by physical damage to competitors' stores, or on the other hand by collusive pricing-fixing or customer-sharing agreements. A great many, perhaps the majority of, laws and court decisions in the area of public policy toward marketing have the underlying purpose of restraining horizontal competition within the limits of legality.

Intertype competition occurs when a different type of economic organization offers a similar product in competition with established organizations in a given market. The classic example is the "invasion" of rural America by mail-order houses such as Sears, Montgomery Ward, and Spiegel. The large mail-order companies offered a wide variety of products and services at a price that local merchants were often unable to match. This type of dynamic competition—sometimes called *creative destruction*—is not included in the static treatment of competition found in most elementary textbooks on economics. Yet it is a hallmark of economic activity in an industrial society. If the new type of competitor can offer superior products to the market, and/or can provide comparable products at lower prices—as the mail-order houses could, and as the supermarkets could in relation to mom-and-pop grocery stores—then the threatened competitors can either accept the situation, or fight back.

Naturally, they often choose to fight, since therein lies possible survival. If they are not able to compete with the established boundaries of competition, however, they resort to the political process to fight the interloper. For example, local merchants may band together to support Sunday closing laws, or chain-store tax laws, or minimum markup laws. Thus, intertype competition tends to promote group action—the hallmark of the political process. Sometimes these actions are less than completely ethical, as when local merchants battling Sears stores in the South spread the rumor that Richard Sears and Alvah Roebuck were Negroes. And the allies in conflicts are sometimes strange and even amusing. In the hard-fought and finally successful campaign in Texas to legalize the serving of liquor by the drink, in the early 1970s, two of the strongest groups of opponents of this measure were the beer brewers and the Southern Baptists.

Vertical conflict is the result of differing objectives of different channel members. A manufacturer, for example, would like to receive a steady flow of orders for his products from wholesalers and retailers—without expending too much marketing effort on advertising and personal selling. The wholesaler, in turn, would like to receive products from the manufacturer as he needs them, and to quickly return unsold items to minimize his inventory and storage costs. The retailer would like the manufacturer's advertising to draw people into his store to purchase products.

To be sure, each of the channel members shares the common interest of delivering products to the consumer, but the relative rewards and costs of this delivery are often perceived differently by various channel members. When such differences cannot be resolved within the bounds of competition, economic conflict develops. As we discuss in detail in Chapter 11, one important objective of channel management is to obtain a favorable bargaining position with respect to other members of the channel. For example, large manufacturers such as General Electric and Campbell Soup have considerable bargaining strength with wholesalers and retailers—because consumers are loyal to their products. Similarly, retailers such as Sears, A & P, and Penney's purchase such large quantities of products from wholesalers and manufacturers that they have considerable strength in negotiating prices, payment terms, styles and models of products, and so on. Often these conflicts are resolved by negotiation and contract. Consequently, the major role of public policy in vertical economic conflict is to provide a legal framework for effective negotiation, and to prescribe limits on the uses of vertical power by channel members.

As the diagram shows, the result of these types of economic conflict is political activity. Various groups will lobby with Congress, state legislatures, or county legislative bodies, to influence legislation related to their area of interest. Also, economic conflict often leads to court suits and not infrequently to appeals to higher courts.

The most direct method of political activity is the referendum. Many of the issues upon which politicians campaign for election to office are economic in character. Citizens frequently are asked to vote directly upon economic issues, e.g., bond elections. Finally, the parties involved in economic conflict may attempt to settle their differences through direct negotiation—which often culminates in contractual arrangements enforceable in the courts. The result of political activity, then, is public policy— laws, directives for administrative agencies, and court decisions.

Outputs of the public-policy process are of three types. First, changes in societal awareness, tolerance levels, and even demands for resolution of the economic conflict occur. Second, these desires on the part of members of society become translated into governmental support or opposition for certain types of marketing activities. (Because modern government is large and complex, it is not unusual to find different governmental bodies holding conflicting positions about marketing activities. The classic example here is the Surgeon General's opposition to cigarette smoking, while the Department of Agriculture provides research grants to tobacco growers to improve their products.) As a third result, therefore, public policy provides both opportunities and threats for marketing decision making. The rising societal concern over pollution levels, for example, is a definite threat to the operators of many types of businesses, but it is a real boon to marketers of pollution-control equipment.

These outputs of the political process generate societal, governmental, and marketing actions that are forces for environmental change; this is illustrated by the feedback loop in Exhibit 4-8. We will use this model to illuminate our discussion of the development of public policy toward marketing in this country. The evolution of antitrust policy is perhaps the best example.

Evolution of Public Policy: Antitrust Legislation

The traditional approach to examining the political environment for marketing activities is to chronologically list the significant legislation affecting marketing activity. This approach is instructive, particularly when structured by the political-process framework model. Exhibit 4-9 summarizes our discussion

Sherman Antitrust Act. This 1890 act was the first federal legislation to

Exhibit 4-9 Significant Public-Policy Developments in Antitrust

Legislation	Description	Pertinent Court Cases and Other Events
Sherman Antitrust Act (1890)	Prohibited (1) "every contract combination or conspiracy in restraint of trade" and (2) monopolies or attempts to monopolize.	*U.S. v. Standard Oil Co.* (1911) *U.S. v. American Tobacco Co.* (1911) *U.S. v. U.S. Steel Corp.* (1920) *U.S. v. Aluminium Co. of America* (1945)
Clayton Act (1914)	Supplemented the Sherman Act by outlawing specific practices (price discrimination, tying arrangements and exclusive dealing, merger of company stock) "when the effect . . . may be to substantially lessen competition or create a monopoly."	Many court cases, particularly in retail sector of the economy; Robinson-Patman and Celler-Kefauver Acts
Federal Trade Commission Act (1914)	Established a body of specialists to investigate under the "rule of reason" doctrine; Section 5 of the Act declared "unfair methods of competition to be illegal." Wheeler-Lea Amendment added phrase "and unfair or deceptive acts and practices."	*FTC v. Raladam Co.* (1931) Wheeler-Lea Amendment (1938) 1969 American Bar Association report
Robinson-Patman Act (1936)	Amended the Clayton Act to outlaw actions that would "injure, destroy, or prevent competition." Specifically price discrimination was defined to be unlawful; the FTC was empowered to set limits on brokerage allowances, quantity discounts, etc., and to prohibit "promotional allowances and services not made available to all buyers on proportionately equal terms."	Many court cases, with varying interpretations of the rather vague wording of the Act. Borden Company decision perhaps is landmark case.
Miller-Tydings Act (1936)	Exempted vertical price-fixing—fair trade— agreements from prosecution under the Sherman Act, in states having fair-trade laws.	California statutes Schwegmann Bros. case McGuire Act (1952) Repealed 1976
Celler-Kefauver Act (1950)	Amended Clayton Act to declare merger by assets as well as merger by stock, to be illegal "where the effect may be to substantially lessen competition or to tend to create a monopoly."	Brown Shoe Co. Von's Grocery Co. Thesis of the *New Industrial State*

Prepared by the author from Howard, *Legal Aspects of Marketing*; Caves, *American Industry: Structure, Conduct and Performance*, third edition; Kinter, *An Antitrust Primer*, second edition; and various other sources.

provide a general statement of public policy in the matter of preserving freedom of entry into markets and the maintenance of competition. Its two sections prohibit "every contract, combination . . . or conspiracy, in restraint of trade" and state that "every person who shall monopolize or attempt to monopolize, or combine or conspire . . . to monopolize any part of the trade or commerce among the several states . . . shall be deemed guilty of a misdemeanor." Both sections apply to interstate and foreign commerce, and are enforced by the Justice Department. This act is a landmark in United States legislation, because it establishes the principle that "competition is the law of the land." In terms of economic conflict, it arose from the activities of the robber barons—the oil, sugar, tobacco, and beef trusts of the late nineteenth century, who were without doubt monopolizing those markets and damaging competition.

The output of the process in this case, however, was hardly revolutionary. The law is vague, and court interpretations were generally sympathetic to big business. It was not until 1911 that two significant court cases were tried under the Sherman Act. Two giant trusts of that time, Standard Oil Company and American Tobacco Company, came as close to true monopoly of their industries as is likely to occur in the real world. Moreover, both companies used questionable tactics to force competitors to abandon markets or sell out to the trusts. If these firms were not guilty under the Sherman Act, then that act had little practical effect.

The Supreme Court did indeed find both firms guilty under the Sherman Act and ordered their dissolution. However, the court took the position that Congress did not mean to outlaw every combination in restraint of trade, but only "unreasonable" combinations. The Court emphasized that unreasonableness was determined by questionable competitive practices, and not by a high level of seller concentration in the markets. This rule was quickly confirmed by later decisions, including the United States Steel Company case in 1920. Like the oil and tobacco trusts, U. S. Steel was formed by combining several formerly independent companies into a giant conglomerate which produced at that time approximately 60 percent of the country's iron and steel. U.S. Steel, however, did not coerce or restrain its remaining rivals. Indeed, it even avoided competition with these firms. Consequently, the Supreme Court found it not in violation of the Sherman Act—"the law does not make mere size an offense or the existence of unexerted power an offense." It was not until 1945, in the Aluminum Company of America (Alcoa) case, that the court took the view that a high level of seller concentration alone would constitute a violation of Section 2 of the Sherman Act. The position, stated by famous Appellate Court Judge Learned Hand, speaking for the Supreme Court, was that the 90 percent of the United States virgin aluminum production which Alcoa controlled "is enough to constitute a monopoly; it is doubtful whether 60 or 64 percent would be enough; and certainly 33 percent is not."

Clayton Act. In 1914, Congress supplemented the Sherman Act by identifying certain actions deemed to be unlawful restraints and monopolies. Specifically, price discrimination, *tying* arrangements (forcing a seller to buy complementary products) and *exclusive-dealing* arrangements (requiring that a buyer handle no competitors' products) were prohibited "where the effect . . . may be to substantially lessen competition or create a monopoly." Thus, the government did not actually have to prove that a monopoly existed, as it did under the rule of reason, or that there was a conspiracy to restrain trade. However, the regulatory agencies—the Department of Justice, the newly created Federal Trade Commission, and the courts—were still required to interpret the meaning of substantially lessened competition. The Clayton Act has led to a large number of court cases, particularly in the retailing sector of the economy. Moreover, its major sections, those dealing with price discrimination and with mergers, have been supplemented by various amendments examined in the following paragraphs.

Federal Trade Commission Act. This act established a body of specialists to investigate economic conflict under the *rule of reason* doctrine. Thus, the new commission was expected to enforce both the Sherman Act and the Clayton Act. However, the commission was not particularly effective in its early work in antitrust cases. Also, some of its early efforts were directed toward exposing false advertising and branding, but in the Raladam Company case, the court held that the commission's power was limited to exposing *injury to competition* and not injury to consumers. This interpretation was reversed in 1938 by the Wheeler-Lea amendment, which added the phrase "an unfair or deceptive acts and practices" to Section 5 of the Federal Trade Commission Act. Nevertheless, the Federal Trade Commission was frequently accused of being weak and ineffective. The criticisms culminated in a 1969 American Bar Association report that concluded ". . . notwithstanding the great potential of the FTC in the field of antitrust and consumer protection, if change does not occur, then there will be no substantial purpose to be served by its continued existence."

The Federal Trade Commission and Clayton Acts make sense when viewed in light of the public policy formulation model. After the passage of the Sherman Act, it was soon apparent that enforcement of the provisions of this act by the courts was not effective in curbing the destructive vertical and horizontal conflicts of the major trusts. Consequently, both acts were passed to strengthen public policy in this area. The Clayton Act spelled out in more detail some of the practices that Congress felt should be prohibited, and the Federal Trade Commission was created to provide a means of investigating and enforcing both the Sherman Act and the Clayton Act.

Robinson-Patman Act. In 1936, Section 2 of the Clayton Act, which dealt with price discrimination, was thoroughly revised by passage of the Robinson-Patman Act. In terms of the public-policy formulation model, the origins of this act stem from the depression of the 1930s: consumers demanded low prices and were willing to serve themselves to get them. As noted in Chapter 3, the response to these environmental forces was the modern supermarket, largely spearheaded by the Great Atlantic and Pacific Tea Company. A & P and other chains were able to achieve economies of scale in buying, and other savings from customer self-service and low-rent warehouse locations. The chains passed these savings along to their customers—to the anguish of the independent grocery stores. In addition, the chains often managed to obtain special prices or brokerage concessions from food processors by implying that they would take their considerable business elsewhere, or perhaps do their own processing. A & P, for example, through its wholly owned subsidiary, the Atlantic Commission Company, collected a brokerage commission on all produce handled, but delivered 70 percent of that produce to A & P's retail stores. Many independent grocery stores could not survive this sort of competition.

This type of competitive behavior by the chains inevitably led to public-policy restrictions on such intertype conflicts. Since there were many independent grocers, public policy tended to take the position that these small economic units should be saved and given an essentially equal chance to compete with the chains. Consequently, in 1936, the Robinson-Patman Act was passed to regulate price discrimination.

The wording of this act is vague. As the U.S. Supreme Court once observed, "precision of expression is not an outstanding characteristic of the Robinson-Patman Act." Various courts have interpreted its provisions in different ways, but the predominant thrust has been that the act protects competitors—as opposed to protecting competition itself. That is, regulatory action will be taken against a firm that is shown to injure another competitor, even if the total performance of all firms in the market is improved, and consumer satisfaction increased. The act recognizes cost justifications for price discrimination. As we illustrate in Chapter 13, however, such justifications are difficult to formulate even for managerial purposes, much less for the more difficult task of convincing a regulatory agency or court. Consequently, the fundamental result of the act has been to make the marketing manager extremely wary of competition on a price basis at wholesale levels.

Miller-Tydings Act. Another feature of the intertype competition of the 1930s was price-cutting of branded products by some retailers. Their purpose was to increase the volume of sales on these items even though the percentage of profit per item was reduced. Inevitably, other retailers objected to this potential loss of revenue; their reaction was to ask the manufacturers of the branded items to see that retail price levels were maintained. But this would amount to vertical price fixing—a direct violation of the Sherman Act.

In 1931, therefore, the California State Legislature enacted a statute permitting manufacturers or wholesalers to set retail prices by requiring retailers to sign a contract agreeing to the price. This statute, however, did not bind nonsigners—an omission which the California legislature remedied in 1933. This was a very popular measure among small retailers in California and elsewhere. Since there are many small retailers in almost every state, 35 states eventually passed similar laws. (Thanks to skillful public relations—a type of marketing effort—these statutes were generally known as *fair trade laws.*)

In 1937, Congress removed any lingering doubts that such legislation could be in violation of the Sherman Act by passing the Miller-Tydings Act. This act was essentially enabling legislation; it permitted the states to pass resale-price maintenance laws. The act, however, did not specifically address the problem of retailers who did not sign the resale-price maintenance agreements. Schwegmann Brothers, a Louisiana supermarket chain, tested the legality of the nonsigners clause by cutting prices on, among other things, its liquor products. Schwegmann's was sued by Calvert Distillers Corporation. The result of this suit was a 1951 Supreme Court ruling that the Miller-Tydings Act was not binding upon those who did not sign resale-price maintenance agreements. Congress remedied this loophole in 1952 by passing the McGuire Act, which established the legality of the nonsigners clause. It said that all dealers in a fair-trade state had to agree to resale-price maintenance as long as one dealer did.

These laws, however, have not been all that helpful to small retailers. Resale-price maintenance is extremely difficult to enforce, since the burden rests with the manufacturer of the product which is to be fair-traded. Consequently, resale-price maintenance declined in importance. Although it was of economic significance to small retailers, it inhibited effective economic performance by large retailers, was a nuisance to manufacturers, and probably raised prices to consumers. The number of states with fair-trade laws dropped from 45 to 13 by 1976. In that year, Congress repealed the Miller-Tydings and McGuire Acts, thus ending a colorful, if uneconomic, chapter in the history of U.S. public policy toward marketing.

Celler-Kefauver Act. Section 7 of the Clayton Act, forbidding mergers which tend to create a monopoly, was relatively impotent until Congress passed the Celler-Kefauver Act. This act declared merger by assets, as well as merger by stock, to be illegal "when the effect may be to substantially lessen competition or to tend to create a monopoly." The objective of the act is to check monopoly in its incipiency—to block mergers that the regulators expect might have significant adverse economic effects on the market. In the Brown Shoe case, the first of the new cases to come before the Supreme Court under Section 7, the acquisition of the twelfth largest shoe manufacturer, G. R. Kinney Company, by Brown (the fourth largest), was denied, even though the merged firm would account for less than 5 percent of the total national output of shoes. The wording of the act specified "any line of commerce in any section of the country"—a clear indication that Congress felt the government should act to prevent any case of incipient monopoly, however local. This was illustrated in the Vons Grocery Company case in 1966, in which the Court blocked a merger between grocery chains accounting for a total of about 7½ percent of grocery sales in the Los Angeles area.

The effect of this interpretation of the act has been to substantially increase governmental activity in this area. For example, during the years 1951 to 1963, the average number of cases per year brought by the Department of Justice and the Federal Trade Commission was ten. In 1964 alone, however, twenty-one new cases were started. Consequently, firms which might consider merging—even those that could argue persuasively that such mergers would enhance competition in their markets—have tended to look for other means of improving their competitive positions. This has led John Kenneth Galbraith to argue in *The New Industrial State* that the antitrust laws protect the existing giants of industry—General Motors, Sears, Standard Oil of New Jersey (now Exxon)—but prevent other companies from growing very large. In his words, "Antitrust laws legitimatize the real exercise of market power on the part of large firms by a rather diligent harassment of those who have less of it." This argument is not supported by available empirical evidence, but it is provocative.

The Pluralistic Bases of Public Policy

The influence of government upon marketing decisions is growing, and I think will continue to do so. There are many laws in addition to those discussed here, and the laws generally are being enforced more vigorously by administrative agencies and interpreted more broadly by the courts. Perhaps the increasing influence of public policy on the economic system in general and marketing decision making in particular should not be too surprising. As Petit (*Freedom in the American Economy,* p. 251) observes:

> There is a basic rule followed by men the world over in their relationships: when you cannot obtain your objective at one level of operations move to a more fundamental level and try again . . . in economic matters, there is always the more inclusive level of the political system. Political power is superior to economic power . . . the economy is concerned with allocating scarce resources among unlimited ends, but it has nothing to say about what those ends are to be. This is the matter of value judgments. It is in the political arena that ends are decided upon because it is there that determination is made between conflicting values.

The superiority of political power over economic power has two consequences for our study of public policy influence in marketing. First, as Galbraith articulated in his *American Capitalism: The Theory of Countervailing Power,* the growth of power in one set of social institutions produces pressures for offsetting or countervailing power in other social institutions. Therefore, as economic organizations grow and markets become concentrated, we can expect government to expand as well.

Second, the superiority of political power over economic power explains to some extent why political tactics have been adopted by individuals with economic objectives but little economic power. Thus, individual merchants can band together into trade associations and significantly influence public policy, particularly at the state and local levels. Consumers whose individual claims are small can in some instances band together to sue manufacturers. Class-action suits will probably increase in the future; several states have recently streamlined their class-action procedures. Farm blocs, composed in the main of small farmers, have long dominated state legislatures. Recently, however, their influence is declining relative to that of surburbanites. Finally, the rise of organized labor as a powerful economic force clearly illustrates this tendency in contemporary society.

In short, a modern society is *pluralistic.* Different groups, having different sociocultural and economic interests, influence public policy in a variety of ways. The result is a public policy—laws, administrative regulations and guidelines, and legal precedents—that is complex, dynamic, and sometimes inconsistent. Some laws are clearly designed to encourage competition, while others, particularly at the state and local levels, are clearly anticompetitive in nature. Court interpretations of these laws also can vary, e.g., interpretation of the phrase *injury to competition* to mean *injury to competitors.* And the administrative agencies that investigate and enforce the laws do so with degrees of resources, skill and vigor that vary over time and from place to place. The decision-making difficulties here are obvious; they are perhaps best summarized by Earl Kitner, former Chairman of the Federal Trade Commission, who dedicated his book, *An Antitrust Primer,* "to the perplexed businessman—who must always obey the law without knowing what the law is."

OBJECTIVES OF PUBLIC POLICY TOWARD MARKETING

Since the marketing manager, of all managers in the organization, must be particularly sensitive to, and capable of functioning within, the political environment, he needs some sort of framework for understanding present public policy toward business and marketing. At the risk of oversimplifying the complexities of public policy/marketing relationships, we organize public policy into three categories. Recall that when we introduced the concept of exchange, we noted that exchange occurs only if both parties

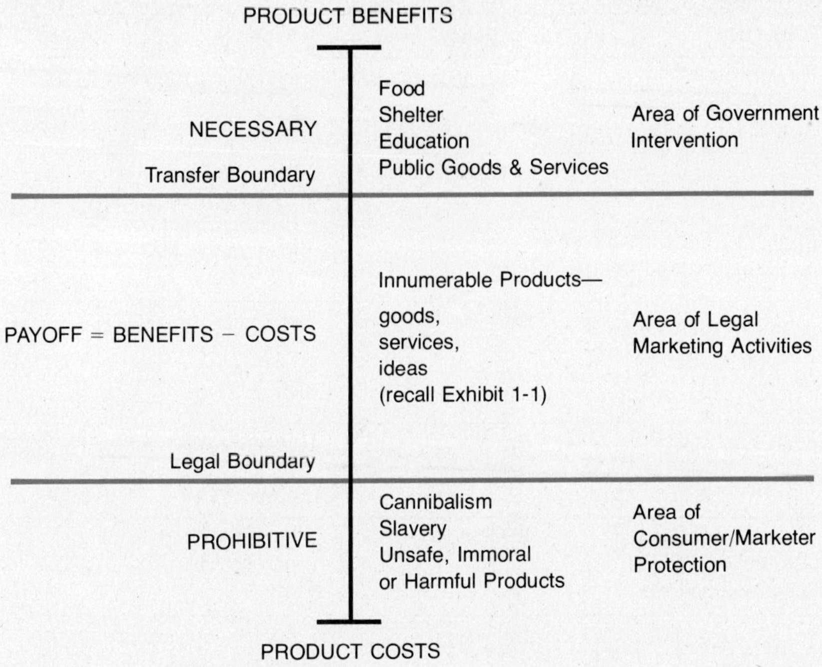

Exhibit 4-10   Social Perspective on Product Utility

PRODUCT BENEFITS

NECESSARY	Food Shelter Education Public Goods & Services	Area of Government Intervention
Transfer Boundary		
PAYOFF = BENEFITS − COSTS	Innumerable Products— goods, services, ideas (recall Exhibit 1-1)	Area of Legal Marketing Activities
Legal Boundary		
PROHIBITIVE	Cannibalism Slavery Unsafe, Immoral or Harmful Products	Area of Consumer/Marketer Protection

PRODUCT COSTS

expect the payoff (benefits minus cost) of the exchange to be positive. At that time, we stated rather dogmatically that unless this condition holds, there will be no exchange. Viewed from the perspective of social policy toward marketing, we must elaborate on this statement just a bit. Exhibit 4-10 guides the discussion.

Social Perspective on Product Utility

In every society, there are certain products that are deemed to be necessities—their benefits are available to all members of society, no matter what the cost. Examples in modern industrial societies include at least minimal levels of food, shelter, educational opportunities and "public goods" such as police and fire protection. Consumption of such products is taken to be the right of members of the society. It does not depend upon possession of buying power required to consummate exchange transactions in the usual way.

On the other hand, every society also prohibits the consumption of certain products. The cost of these products is considered excessive, no matter what benefits might accrue from their consumption. Clear examples in industrial economies include prohibitions against cannibalism and slavery; products potentially injurious to consumers and products considered immoral are also prohibited.

Between these extremes, exchange activities are allowed by society.

Exhibit 4-11 Framework for Understanding Public Policy Toward Marketing

Objective	Type of Policy	Example
Government Intervention (transfer boundary)	1. Taxes and tariffs	Income and sales taxes, import duties, product taxes
	2. Subsidies and loans	Farm price supports, Lockheed guarantee, highway construction, food stamps, Medicare, tuition loans
	3. Controls	Minimum mark up laws, rent controls, wage-price controls, utility rates
	4. Rationing	Import/export quotas, wartime rationing boards, gasoline (?)
Consumer/Marketer Protection (legal boundary)	1. Standards	Food and drugs, lending, pollution levels, safety
	2. Licenses	Doctors, lawyers, barbers, teachers, realtors, etc.
	3. Deceptive practice bans	Fraud statutes, lending, labeling advertising guidelines, "cooling-off" periods
	4. Prohibitions	Vice-laws, import bans, blue laws
Market Structure and Conduct Guides	1. Antitrust statutes	Sherman, Clayton, FTC, Robinson-Patman, Celler-Kefauver
	2. Antitrust exemptions	Labor Unions, agricultural cooperatives, professional sports, patents, trademarks
	3. Specific product/ industry regulations	Interstate Commerce, Federal Aviation, Federal Communication, etc.

Consumers enter into exchange transactions if they expect the payoff from a given exchange to be positive. Innumerable products are exchanged in this way.

Public policy toward marketing takes three different forms: government intervention in markets for necessary products; consumer/marketer protection for prohibited products; and policies that facilitate and strengthen marketing activities within the area of legal exchange. Exhibit 4-11 outlines the types of policies.

Government Intervention

Since society has determined that certain products are necessary, public policy intervenes directly with the market mechanism to assist marketers and consumers in consummating exchanges of these products. Public policies which have this objective are of four types: taxes and tariffs, subsidies and loans, controls, and rationing procedures.

Taxes and Tariffs. Taxes and tariffs encourage or inhibit production and consumption of certain products. Perhaps the most significant example here is the income tax system of the United States. Originally designed simply to raise revenues to operate the government, the income tax system has become a complex labyrinth of rules, regulations, and interpretations of the tax laws to influence various markets in certain ways. For example, businesses are given an investment tax credit which essentially lowers the price of capital equipment, and home owners are allowed to deduct from their taxes a portion of the interest on home loans—which encourages home ownership relative to renting.

Moreover, certain products that society thinks should be consumed are taxed lightly or not at all, e.g., food, prescription drugs, sales of homesteads, etc. On the other hand, certain products are heavily taxed, perhaps because society feels that these should not be consumed; prominent examples are cigarettes and liquor. Almost all products imported into a country are taxed. The rate of the import duty varies with the strength of various economic groups within the country. For example, agricultural products imported into the European Common Market face a very high duty, because the Common Market bloc is attempting to become self-sufficient in agricultural production. In this country, imports of textiles and shoes are relatively highly taxed.

Subsidies and Loans. Another form of government intervention is direct subsidies and loans to various producers. The classic example is the farm price-support system. Despite the fact that farming is the prototype of a competitive industry, farmers have long wielded political influence in this country, indeed in most industrial societies, disproportionate to their number in the population. This is because in a preindustrial society, the great majority of the population must engage in agricultural pursuits if the society is to feed itself and survive. As the economy develops, proportionately fewer resources are needed to sustain food production at a level comparable to demand, which is relatively inelastic (people simply do not eat that much more food as their degree of affluence increases). Also, the shift of population concentrations from rural to urban often is not reflected in state legislatures for several decades—because of the nature of reapportionment procedures in the various states. The result has been public policy which decrees that farming incomes should be comparable to incomes in the nonfarm sectors of the economy.

The market mechanism, however, will not generate farm incomes at this level for three reasons: the instability of market prices, excess resources devoted to the farm sector, and the low productivity and inefficiency of many farms because of their small size. Consequently, public policy has dictated that farmers should receive higher-than-market prices for their products. The difference between the market price and the policy price is a government subsidy to the farm sector. As a result of the policy, the U.S. government accumulated large stocks of certain types of food products, and reduced these stocks by "dumping" them on world markets at bargain prices. The worldwide shortage of food in recent years has enabled the United States to reduce its stockpiles of food. Nevertheless, the practice of subsidizing farm prices remains firmly imbedded in public policy.

Other recent examples of government subsidy to improve market performance of certain products and industries include the 250-million-dollar loan guarantee to Lockheed Corporation, and extensive loan guarantees to the Penn Central Railroad system. In addition to these individual examples, one of the major activities of the Small Business Administration is to provide loan guarantees to small businesses. There are any number of other subsidies to various economic activities, from federally financed highway and airport construction to the widespread and inexpensive availability of census data as aid in decision making, to new-construction financing through municipal bonds and exemptions from property taxes.

Controls. The third type of government intervention in the marketplace is controls upon the market mechanism. Many states have minimum markup percentage laws, designed to insure the existence of the independent wholesaler and retailer whose influence bulks so large in state legislatures and county legislative councils. In addition, there are quotas upon the production and sale of many products. Prominent among these are standards for crude oil and natural gas extraction, quotas on imports of products such as steel, textiles, rubber, and others which compete directly against strong economic groups in this country.

The most prominent form of control on the market mechanism in recent memory is the 1971 imposition of wage and price controls upon the economy by President Nixon. The president established a Price Board which had a general policy guideline of holding price increases to approximately 3 percent per year. This guideline was to control prices of all products with the exception of raw agricultural products. Experience

Exhibit 4-12 Some Experiences with Price Controls

hase-2 price controls produced some interesting results, called "unforeseen disturbances" by administration officials. A big part of the problem was that Phase-2 controllers are dealing even-handedly and uniformly with all segments of the economy when in fact the economy itself does not operate that way.

One example is the rule that companies that have raised prices cannot increase their profit margins above the rate they were earning during a specified base period. This rule was applied to Piggly Wiggly Southern Incorporated, a Georgia-based food chain. The chain was ordered to roll back prices to bring profit margins within the specified limits. The chain complied by sharply cutting prices on some food items, making them *loss leaders.* The move was eminently successful—at the expense of the chain's smaller local competitors. They complained that they were not able to match Piggly Wiggly's price cut, were losing customers fast, and may be driven out of business.

Companies that are not in a position to turn a price rollback to competitive advantage are quietly raising costs to offset increased profits. Many of the added costs are legitimate, but some companies are understood to be relaxing their recession-tight purse strings for such expenses as advertising and research—partly to avoid becoming "too profitable."

Second, consider the case of the yeast industry. This market is dominated by two large companies: Standard Brands Incorporated, a diversified food processor, and Anheuser-Busch, Inc., the well-known brewer; together they sell about two-thirds of the nation's yeast. The rest of the highly competitive market is shared by several small companies. Labor and operating costs have been increasing for all yeast makers; in normal times most of the manufacturers would simply pass along such increases by raising prices. But the combination of Phase-2 profit-margin controls and normal competitive pressures has effectively frozen the price of yeast. This is because Standard Brands and Anheuser-Busch are big yeast makers, but yeast plays a minor role in the sales and profits of the two companies. Profitability of their major lines—which are also in the government's broad category of food products—is so good that a boost in yeast prices would probably push their profit margins too high. The other companies could raise prices without violating the profit margin ceiling—but if they do, their prices will be higher than those of the two industry leaders.

These are illustrations of the basic problem with wage-price controls: if they are applied rigidly and uniformly, serious disruptions will soon occur; but if they are flexible enough to accommodate different situations in the economy, then they are no longer effective as controls. Alternatively, control procedures could be made more complicated—and probably more burdensome. A high-ranking controller was quoted as saying that the price commission is considering requiring companies ordered to make price rollbacks to submit, in advance, plans for reducing the impact of price reductions on small businesses and avoiding market disruptions. This suggested solution, the author notes, "comes, amazingly, from the same folks now confessing the appearance of unforeseen consequences."

Adapted from "Phase Two's Yeasty New Problem," *Wall Street Journal,* 27 June 1972, p. 14. Reprinted by permission of The Wall Street Journal © 1972 Dow Jones & Company, Inc. All Rights Reserved. For more detail, see C. Jackson Greyson, Jr., *Confessions of a Price Controller* (Dow-Jones-Irwin, 1974).

gained from the operation of command economies has indicated that such controls lead to deviations from prices that might be set by the market mechanism. An assessment of the political pluses and minuses of the president's action is probably beyond the scope of a textbook on marketing management. There is little doubt, however, that price controls have a significant impact upon the decisions of marketing management. Exhibit 4-12 presents several examples of this impact.

Rationing. When supplies of certain products are limited, they are rationed. This was done, for example, during World War II. In 1973, there was speculation that rationing supplies of energy would be imposed. Such factors as population growth; rising per capita consumption of energy in industrial societies; opposition to domestic petroleum extraction and refining by environmentalists; the growing nationalism and political sophistication of Middle Eastern petroleum-exporting countries; and governmental import restrictions and price controls have generated a potentially severe shortage of gasoline and fuel oil.

Consumer/Marketer Protection

At the other end of the spectrum, society decrees that certain products should not be available for consumption. In 1906, Congress passed two laws which mark the beginning of explicit public policy toward consumer protection. These were the Pure Food and Drug Act, and the Meat Inspection Act.

The former act is largely due to the efforts of Dr. Harvey W. Wylie, first head of the Chemistry Division of the United States Department of Agriculture. Beginning in 1883, Dr. Wylie battled almost singlehandedly against the misbranding and adulteration of foods and drugs. *The Washington Post* ran a series of articles and two important publications of the time, *McClure's* and *Colliers Weekly*, ran editorials supporting Wylie. But not until Upton Sinclair published *The Jungle,* a novel depicting in grisly detail the conditions in America's meatpacking plants (see Exhibit 4-13), was public opinion sufficiently aroused to compel passage of these laws.

The need for Pure Food and Drug laws can be traced to both horizontal and vertical types of competition. In the late nineteenth century, increasingly urban populations and improved transportation facilities lengthened the channel of distribution for food products. No longer was the farmer growing and selling food in his local market. Often raw agricultural products would be processed and preserved, handled by two or three middlemen, and finally sold to ultimate consumers a thousand miles away. Since food forms a basic part of the budget of all consumers, there has always been heavy pressure on every organization in the food industry to hold down food prices and therefore costs. Thus, as the channel lengthened, vertical competition among distributors led inevitably to such transgressions of normal industry practices as the adding of artificial preservatives to food and drugs. Formaldehyde (embalming fluid) was a favorite preservative for meat. Peas and other green vegetables, which lost their farm-fresh color during processing, were given a dose of copper sulphate. Wherever needed, artificial coloring or flavoring—often in the form of coaltar dyes—was added to restore produce to its original appearance. At the same time, sales of nostrums at the corner apothecary (forerunner of the modern drugstore) paralleled the rise of questionably preserved foodstuffs. Many of these drugs contained high percentages of alcohol, and others used various kinds of narcotics in unlabeled compounds.

Thus, the sheer development of the economic system fostered economic conflict among channel members. A middleman could not risk losing the profits from a carload of meat due to spoilage. A cannery owner might be responsible for the livelihood of dozens or hundreds of employees—and besides there was no evidence at that time that the preservatives did any real harm. In addition to the vertical conflict, there was horizontal conflict at every stage in the channel. If one firm refused to handle such products, it was certain that several competitors would be only too happy

Ralph Nader published *Unsafe at Any Speed* in 1965. This book was a scathing indictment of the General Motors Corporation Corvair, a well-documented and often hair-raising chronicle of safety faults and problems with the car. Supported by President Kennedy's concern for the consumer (expressed in his 1962 declaration of consumers' rights), *Unsafe* prompted a series of Congressional hearings on a number of matters relating to consumer protection in general and automobile safety in particular.

The hearings were lively and often informative. Witnesses had many complaints—not infrequently legitimate and well-substantiated complaints. Still, the highway safety bill might not have passed; it clearly meant vastly increased government influence over the automobile industry. At that time, the automobile industry was unique in the transportation system of the United States in that, unlike airlines, railroads, and trucks, it was virtually free from federal regulation.

But someone at General Motors made a serious mistake: Nader was placed under surveillance by a team of private detectives. They watched him 'round-the-clock in Washington, visited his home town to talk with his friends and neighbors, and generally conducted a most thorough and harassing investigation of the man's professional and even his personal life. General Motors president, James Roche, was summoned to Congress to explain the incident. All that Roche could say was that had he known about the surveillance he would have ordered it stopped.

Now perhaps this incident had no bearing on the passage of the highway safety bill. However, a remark widely repeated in Washington at the time and attributed to several senators was, "All of us were outraged that a great corporation was out to muzzle a guy because he wrote critically of it. If there were nothing wrong with their products, why did they tail him? At that point, most of us said the hell with General Motors." The bill passed.

Adapted from Bishop and Hubbard, *Let the Seller Beware* (Washington National Press, 1969), Chapter 5.

to take up the slack. In such an environment, public policy changes were necessary.

As Exhibit 4-15 indicates, the breadth and scope of consumer protection have increased significantly over the years. In 1938, the Federal Food, Drug, and Cosmetic Act supplanted the 1906 Act and added stronger enforcement procedures. Consumer protection legislation received increasing attention in the sixties. In terms of the public-policy formulation model, pressure for consumer-protection legislation had been building for several years. As we have noted, the increasing size and impersonality of large corporations, the awesome technological achievements in space exploration and in military hardware, and the rising educational levels of consumers have combined to generate an awareness of the need for legislation in this area. Perhaps the most significant was the National Traffic and Motor Vehicle Safety Act.

Many marketing students feel that a major catalyst for this type of legislation was Ralph Nader, whose initial impact upon marketing and public policy is chronicled in Exhibit 4-14.

Public policies designed to further this social objective can also be grouped in four categories: standards, licenses, deceptive practice bans, and outright prohibitions.

Exhibit 4-15 Selected Consumer Protection Laws

1906   Food and Drug Act
Meat Inspection Act

1914   Federal Trade Commission Act: declared "unfair methods of competition" to be illegal

1938   Food, Drug and Cosmetics Act: expanded 1906 act
Wheeler-Lea Act: expanded 1914 act to include "unfair or deceptive acts or practices"

1939   Wool Products Labeling Act

1951   Fur Products Labeling Act

1953   Flammable Fabrics Act

1958   Textile Fiber Products Identification Act
Food Additives (Delaney) Amendment: outlawed carcinogenic substances in food

1960   Hazardous Substances Labeling Act

1962   Kefauver-Harris Amendment: amended 1938 FDC Act to require testing of all drugs

1966   Fair Packaging and Labeling Act
National Traffic and Motor Vehicle Safety Act
Child Protection Act: banned harmful toys and other children's articles
Cigarette Labeling Act: required health warnings on cigarette packages

1967   Flammable Fabrics Act Amendments
Wholesale Meat Act: upgraded state inspection to federal standards

1968   Consumer Credit Protection Act: required full disclosure of terms and conditions
Wholesome Poultry Products Act

1969   Child Protection and Toy Safety Act: broadened 1966 Hazardous Substances Act

1970   Fair Credit Reporting Act: broadened 1968 act to include consumer credit records
Poison Prevention Packaging Act: required child-resistant packaging

1972   Consumer Product Safety Act: established Consumer Product Safety Commission

1975   Warranty/Federal Trade Commission Improvement Act: empowered FTC to regulate product warranties; expanded FTC powers with respect to unfair or deceptive acts or practices

There are a great many examples of standards which products must meet. Health and safety codes constitute one form: buildings, automobiles, some equipment installations, working areas in manufacturing plants, and traffic regulations. Standards of health and cleanliness are applied to restaurants, cabarets, theatres, hotels and motels, certain manufacturing operations and plants, and hospitals. Sometimes such standards are quite complex and detailed. Exhibit 4-16 provides a darkly humorous example.

Marketers must have a license to offer certain types of products to the public. This is particularly true of services, where an occupational license is often required. Medical doctors, lawyers, barbers, beauticians, plumbers, realtors, public school teachers, dentists, electricians, truck and bus drivers, and airline pilots are among the groups in our society who must be licensed, usually by a state examining board. One must also have a license to dispense alcoholic beverages, to peddle products door-to-door, and to erect a house or building.

Bars to deceptive practice derive from English common law and have been supplemented by an extensive and growing list of legislation and

Exhibit 4-16   Cowboy After OSHA

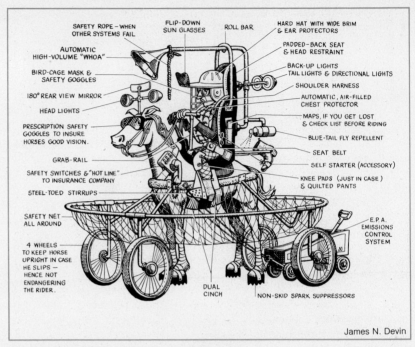

SAFETY ROPE – WHEN OTHER SYSTEMS FAIL

FLIP-DOWN SUN GLASSES

ROLL BAR

HARD HAT WITH WIDE BRIM & EAR PROTECTORS

AUTOMATIC HIGH-VOLUME "WHOA"

PADDED – BACK SEAT & HEAD RESTRAINT

BIRD-CAGE MASK & SAFETY GOGGLES

BACK-UP LIGHTS TAIL LIGHTS & DIRECTIONAL LIGHTS

180° REAR VIEW MIRROR

SHOULDER HARNESS

HEAD LIGHTS

AUTOMATIC, AIR-FILLED CHEST PROTECTOR

PRESCRIPTION SAFETY GOGGLES TO INSURE HORSES GOOD VISION.

MAPS, IF YOU GET LOST & CHECK LIST BEFORE RIDING

BLUE-TAIL FLY REPELLENT

GRAB-RAIL

SEAT BELT

SAFETY SWITCHES & "HOT LINE" TO INSURANCE COMPANY

SELF STARTER (ACCESSORY)

KNEE PADS (JUST IN CASE) & QUILTED PANTS

STEEL-TOED STIRRUPS

SAFETY NET ALL AROUND

E.P.A. EMISSIONS CONTROL SYSTEM

4 WHEELS TO KEEP HORSE UPRIGHT IN CASE HE SLIPS — HENCE NOT ENDANGERING THE RIDER.

DUAL CINCH

NON-SKID SPARK SUPPRESSORS

James N. Devin

court decisions. Areas covered include fraud, labeling, advertising, "cooling-off" periods for certain types of sales, and many others. Marketers certainly recognize the necessity for such policies. However, as Exhibit 4-16 shows, such policies are not always clear. Moreover, they sometimes impede such transactions. Regulations with respect to home mortgage procurement, embodied in the Real Estate Settlement Procedures Act of 1975, were so complex that sales of houses slowed markedly. Consumer groups and realtors together petitioned the government for relaxation of such stringent requirements.

Finally, the consumption of certain types of products is flatly prohibited. The variety of products prohibited is wide, and the origins of such prohibitions are diverse. For example, certain products are considered damaging to the moral fiber of the community. Selling another person into slavery or consuming human flesh are crude but clear examples of prohibitions of this type. Less than unanimous agreement is reached when society bans such products as drugs (particularly marijuana), prostitution, and pornography. No doubt the classic example of societal prohibition of a specific product was the National Prohibition Act of 1919—which prohibited sales of liquor in this country. This act was repealed in 1935.

Another type of prohibition attempts to protect a particular market from outside competition. At the national level, many countries have import bans on many types of products. Conversely, countries often have export prohibitions as well. For example, the United States until recently prohibited exports of strategic raw materials and armaments to Communist-bloc countries. And a number of countries, particularly those with developing economies, prohibit conversion of revenues earned in their country to foreign exchange dollars or other currencies. At the local level, such prohibitions commonly take the form of *blue laws*—laws prohibiting sales of certain products on Sunday—or *Green River ordinances* (prohibitions against door-to-door selling).

This is not to say that there is not exchange activity involving such products. It is just that marketers and consumers of such products are not protected by the laws of society. All states, for example, have maximum interests ceilings. There is a legal maximum interest rate set by law; rates in excess of the legal maximum confront the biblical injunction against usury. If a consumer borrows money from a friendly finance company and defaults, the friendly finance company may do a number of unpleasant things, including threatening letters, lawsuits, and garnishment of wages. If our potential loan consumer cannot qualify for the services of the friendly finance company, he may deal with a loan shark and "five for six on payday," that is, he/she may borrow five dollars and agree to pay back six dollars at the end of the month, an interest rate of at least 480 percent. If that loan is defaulted, the loan shark might resort to sending goons with ball bats to break the legs of the debtor. Levy and Zaltman provide another example of "shadow marketing" in Exhibit 4-17.

Market Structure and Conduct Guides
Within the area of legal exchange, public policy seeks to structure markets and constrain conduct by outlawing some types of market structures and marketing practices, and regulating others. This type of public policy can be visualized as shown in Exhibit 4-18: the monopoly/competition continuum from a public policy perspective. The left end of the continuum is seen in roughly the same way by economists and public policy makers—monopoly in ineffective competition. As we discussed earlier in the chapter, a monopolist with no competition has no incentive to serve customers effectively or efficiently. The individual monopolist dominates the market by setting whatever price he deems appropriate, controlling the rate of product innovation, organizing distribution of his products as he sees fit, and so on. In some cases, a group of producers may band together to form a cartel. As long as the cartel functions viably, as OPEC does, the effect of this *collusion* on the market is the same as that of the individual monopolist.

Consequently, we would expect public policy to be directed toward correcting a monopoly situation. Correction may take the form of

Exhibit 4-17   Illegal Marketing: The "Shadow System"

The following example depicts a typical "hijacking" operation where a truckload of goods is stolen and ultimately sold to consumers. Such thefts are estimated to total $1.5 billion per year. The example was gleaned from testimony of a convicted safecracker-hijacker before the United States Senate.

The classic theft begins with the existence of a valuable cargo—a load of liquor, meats, clothes, or pharmaceuticals often worth more than $100,000 at retail. The key man in the hijacking is the trucking company dispatcher or other knowledgeable employee (see figure). The dispatcher knows the value of the cargo shipments as well as the time, place, and route of delivery. Typically, the dishonest dispatcher will meet with a contact man in the local tavern or restaurant and inform him of the cargo. The contact man (who may or may not work directly for the underworld) will relay the information to his connections in organized crime. If these individuals deem the opportunity suitable, they will supply the dispatcher with "front money"—often up to $10,000—to fix the contract. The dispatcher, in turn, will make arrangements with a truck driver to deliver the truck to a prearranged "drop."

Why would the driver cooperate with the dispatcher? Invariably, the dispatcher or another party would coerce or bribe the driver. For example, the driver might owe a gambling debt to a loan shark (who may also work for the dispatcher, contact man, or underworld), or he might be blackmailed for some indiscretion conveniently set up by those who desire his cooperation. The possibilities for manipulation are many. In any case, the driver may be willing to assist in the crime and when cross-examined will claim that he was "robbed by armed bandits." For his part, the driver is usually paid by the dispatcher from the front money. After they receive the goods, the underworld managers dispose of them through the established fences. The fences, in turn, sell the goods to retailers or to other fences who ultimately sell to the consumer.

Source: Sidney J. Levy and Gerald Zaltman, *Marketing, Society and Conflict* (Prentice-Hall, 1975), pp. 90–1. Data excerpted by Levy and Zaltman from U.S. Congress, Senate, Select Committee on Small Business, *An Analysis of Criminal Redistribution Systems and Their Impact on Small Business*, Staff Report, October 26, 1972.

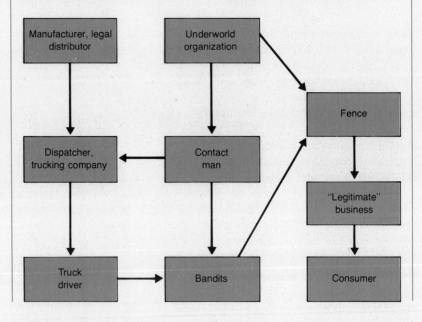

breaking up the individual monopolist (as in the case of the Standard Oil Company in 1911 and Alcoa Aluminum after World War II). Divestiture is another antitrust device. In the 1950s, Procter & Gamble, the giant packaged goods marketer, acquired Clorox Company in order to enter the liquid bleach market. After prolonged litigation, P & G was required to divest itself of Clorox, i.e., to sell its Clorox stock. The Supreme Court

Exhibit 4-18 Public Policy Perspective on Market Structure and Conduct

Market Structure	Monopoly	Oligopoly	Monopolistic Competition	Pure Competition	
Probable Conduct	Dominance and/or collusion	Tacit cooperation	Healthy competition	Cutthroat competition	Economic warfare
Public Policy	Antitrust prosecution	Market structure regulation	Contract enforcement; Competition encouragement	Market conduct regulation	Antitrust exemptions ("natural monopolies")
Examples	Standard Oil Alcoa break-ups; P & G Clorox divestiture; Price-fixing litigation	IBM case; Oil industry divestiture; "Hart Proposal"	Resale price maintenance repeal; Professional fee schedules questioned	Federal Communications Commission; Interstate Commerce Commission; Civil Aeronautics Board	Labor unions; Agricultural cooperatives; Patents; Public utilities; U.S. Post Office

indicated that if P & G wanted to enter the liquid bleach market, it should bring out its own brand. When monopoly is the result of collusion among firms, antitrust action generally involves prosecution of the firm and its senior executives. Such collusion may take the form of price fixing, as illustrated in Exhibit 4-19.

The other end of the competition/monopoly continuum is seen quite differently by economists and public policy makers. In contrast to the smoothly functioning impersonal markets envisioned by economists, real-world experience has shown that when there are a number of competitors in a market, the resulting situation is often akin to open warfare. In the late 1800s and early 1900s, for example, workers seeking to sell their services to industrial concerns, and farmers seeking to sell their product to packers and stockyards frequently engaged in acts of violence and sabotage upon one another, and offered bribes and rebates to buyers. In the early days of telephone service, it was not uncommon for an individual subscriber to have two, and sometimes three, different instruments in the same home, with separate wires connecting the subscribers of each company. Work crews for the various companies often engaged in verbal jousts and sometimes traded physical blows.

Public policy to alleviate these conditions has generally taken the form of exemptions from antitrust policies. These exemptions reflect public policy that, for several reasons, the antitrust and restraint of trade

In 1975, the nation's six largest gypsum makers and ten of their highest executives or former executives have pleaded *no contest* to federal criminal charges or have pleaded innocent and been found guilty of price-fixing. During the alleged conspiracy, the companies together sold more than $4 billion worth of gypsum—over 90 percent of the industry's total volume.

Price-fixing in gypsum, the government says, began before 1951. In that year, a federal court in the District of Columbia enjoined several companies against it. Later in the 1950s, the government charged that top executives of the company knew that prices were still being rigged as were other sales terms that affected the company's revenues and earnings. For example, the government charged that credit managers of the firms met in 1957 and agreed to raise the interest rate charged customers who bought on credit to 6 percent from 5 percent.

In 1965, the companies followed the industry leader, Georgia-Pacific, in announcing a price increase. In addition, companies decided to eliminate kickbacks and cancel industry-wide discounts from list prices. And on March 1, 1966, they agreed to tighten and make more uniform the credit terms extended to customers. The 1965 and 1966 price and credit agreements, the Justice Department alleged, set a pattern for illegal arrangements that were conspiratorially achieved and maintained into the 1970s. The government also charged that some of the companies later tried to conceal their price-fixing contracts from the courts handling civil suits against them and from the federal grand jury investigating them. The companies and individuals convicted still protest their innocence; they are appealing their convictions. Among other things, they point out that some gypsum prices were actually lower at the end of 1973 when the government brought its suit than in earlier years. The government does not deny that, but argues that without price-fixing, prices would have been even lower. The defendants also argued that if they seemed to violate the Sherman Antitrust Act, it was only because they were trying to comply with the Robinson-Patman Act. This rationale, the government alleged, was cooked up after charges were brought. The jury apparently accepted the government's view.

Despite criminal prosecution and civil lawsuits, price-fixing is considered widespread in some industries. This is partly because the potential rewards are high, and partly because it is difficult to prove overt collusion. In this case, however, the big gypsum makers still face trouble even if the convictions are overturned. It is likely that the Justice Department will soon file a civil antitrust suit to force them to divest themselves of certain manufacturing facilities and to end joint operating agreements.

Source: David McClitick, "Busting a Trust: Gypsum Trial Shows How Price-Fixing Plans Supposedly Operated," *The Wall Street Journal* (October 3, 1975), pp. 1, 19. Reprinted with permission of *The Wall Street Journal,* © Dow Jones & Company, Inc., 1975. All rights reserved.

statutes (primarily the Sherman, Clayton, and Robinson-Patman Acts) not be applied to certain marketing activities. The two major groups which have general exemptions from these statutes are agricultural cooperatives and labor unions. Agricultural groups are allowed to pool their products and bargain collectively for better prices and terms than individual farmers might get—since as individuals they would face the relatively elastic demand characteristic of a market approaching pure competition. Labor unions, too, are allowed to bargain collectively and to withhold their product from the market, i.e., to strike. (It should be noted that in return for these exemptions, both of these groups are subject to other types of laws and restrictions not directly related to marketing activities, e.g., the Taft-Hartley Act governing labor relations with management.)

The Webb-Pomerene Export Act of 1918 exempts foreign trade

activities of American firms from anticompetitive restraints. The primary purpose of this act was to permit American companies to compete with European cartels and foreign combinations on an equitable basis. However, many firms today hesitate to use this exemption for fear of possible charges of anticompetitive activities in their domestic operations.

Another type of product exempted from anticompetitive restraints is the so-called natural monopoly. Local public utilities are the clearest example of this situation, in which the scale economies of operation are so large, relative to the market to be served, that competition for these markets would not be feasible. Generally, firms providing electric power, natural gas, telephone service, water, and sometimes mass transportation are granted monopoly status by the city or county in return for agreeing to provide service to all customers and to abide by certain types of regulations imposed by the public. One sometimes hears the argument that these products are guaranteed monopoly status because they are too essential to be left to the marketplace. This argument, however, is spurious: provision of food and medical services is every bit as essential to a society as its water and power supplies, and yet these products are entrusted to the marketplace. The viable argument for the exemption of utilities from anticompetitive restraints is that the fixed costs of their operations are so large, relative to the market that they serve, that direct competition would be uneconomical.

Another exemption to anticompetitive restraints is the patent—a grant of a seventeen-year monopoly to an inventor, giving him the right to exclude others from duplicating his invention for sale or use. Public policy offers the inventor a monopoly on his invention for the purpose of encouraging innovative activity. Patents do function in this way, but the system is not without critics. Much innovative activity would continue even if patents were abolished. The simplest protective device is to keep the technical aspects of the invention secret. The classic example here is the Coca-Cola formula. Indeed, it has been said that firms keep secret what innovations they can, and patent those which they cannot. Moreover, even if the innovation can be copied, the inventor enjoys a certain amount of lead time in the marketplace. Perhaps the controversies over the patent system have been most clearly illustrated in recent years by the issue of generic versus branded drugs. Exhibit 4-20 sketches the issues here.

From the perspective of public policy, the ideal market structure and conduct is exemplified by the midpoint of the continuum, healthy competition. Firms compete vigorously, but within the constraints of law and social custom. Fortunately, this state of competition can reasonably be said to characterize many segments of industrialized economies. The role of public policy here is to administer justice in such a way as to facilitate and nurture competition. The classic example is contract enforcement in the courts.

Exhibit 4-20   The Drug Establishment

An American buying drugs is like a child who goes to the store with his mother's shopping list, which he cannot even read. He does not question the high price of the drug; he does not shop around for a cheaper variety; he does not wait for a sale; and he is usually unaware of the name of the drug he is buying, let alone the name of the manufacturer." The above statement is by Dr. James L. Goddard, former Commissioner of the Food and Drug Administration. It indicts what he calls the *drug establishment*—a closeknit, self-perpetuating power structure consisting of drug manufacturers, government agencies, and select members of the medical profession.

Dr. Goddard does not question the great contribution that drug companies have made to the nation's health over the years, but does wonder about "the enormous price tag that they place on their products." These companies, he says, earn an average 18 percent return on invested capital, as compared with 8 or 9 percent for some three dozen other major industries.

To illustrate how the drug establishment functions, Goddard describes the development of a mythical drug called *Blythophrene*. If the drug first is discovered in a company basic research project, or by an independent investigator who makes a deal with a company, the drug is simply patented. If, however, the drug is a product of government research, the company would have to show that it had discovered, at its own expense, some "new" use for the compound. This provision apparently is not a difficult one to meet. The result, says Dr. Goddard, allows the establishment to reap even larger profits by "selling back to the public results of research that was paid for primarily with public funds."

The Food and Drug Administration must evaluate this research to determine whether the drug should be marketed. Dr. Goddard says that in an attempt to impress the FDA, the companies will put together a "grab bag" containing every scrap of research done on the drug—perhaps as many as forty cartons of evidence—and then important data may be missing.

If the drug is approved for sale, Dr. Goddard claims that "the drug establishment's advertising campaigns are among the most impressive in all media. Professional journals are liberally sprinkled with drug ads that often run four to eight four-color pages (advertising revenues in the *Journal of the American Medical Association* are close to ten million dollars per year). In addition, the companies have convention exhibits, seminars, work shops, and detailing—personal selling of drugs to doctors."

The purpose of the advertising is to develop brand loyalty among physicians—the only ones who may legally prescribe drugs for patients. Dr. Goddard says that "establishment propaganda holds that only those drugs produced by research-oriented, quality-conscious companies can be said to be safe and effective." But all drugs, whether sold under brand or generic names, have to meet certain chemical standards. In addition to these standards, Dr. Goddard reports that the cheaper generics appear to be good enough to pass the rigorous tests specified by such federal agencies as the Department of Defense, which buy drugs in large quantities. For example, a drug called *prednisone*—used in the treatment of chronic arthritis, allergies, and skin and eye inflammation—was available in generic quantities for $4.53 per thousand. The Schering Corporation brand of prednisone, *Meticorten,* sold for $170.00 per thousand.

From Dr. James L. Goddard, Jr., "The Drug Establishment," *Esquire,* March, 1969, pp. 117–21, 152–53. © Dr. James L. Goddard, Jr. First published in *Esquire* Magazine. Reprinted by permission of the author.

A recent development in this area is the repeal of resale price maintenance laws, discussed earlier. Similarly, professional fee schedules and advertising bans are under attack in the courts. Although most doctors and lawyers would not agree, public policy changes of this type would further healthy competition in the markets for these services.

Unfortunately, healthy competition requires a delicate balancing of a number of factors. The balance in a given industry may be tipped one way or the other. If, for example, there are a few large firms in an industry and/or barriers to entry are high, competition may tend toward tacit cooperation. That is, companies may act in consort in their marketing efforts, particularly pricing, although executives of organizations in the industry do not actually collude. When this conduct is observed in an industry, there is pressure upon public policy makers to take steps to restructure the industry even though no laws have been broken. International Business Machines (IBM) is now in court contesting a Justice Department attempt to break it up. And there has been much discussion in Congress in the last few sessions about the desirability of breaking up the major petroleum companies. A broader measure, introduced by Senator Phillip Hart, would constitute a special commission to determine how specific companies and industries should be restructured. The seven industries designated as prime targets of the legislation are chemicals and drugs; electrical machinery and equipment; electronic computing and communications equipment; energy, iron, and steel; motor vehicles; and nonferrous metals. The legislation would affect companies such as General Electric, General Motors, IBM, Exxon, DuPont, U.S. Steel, Ford, Westinghouse, and Consolidated Edison. As of this writing, the Hart proposal is a suggestion, rather than a fact of public policy.

As we discussed in Chapter 2, it may be that public policy makers view the nature of competition in such industries too narrowly. IBM, for example, competes not only against other manufacturers of computer mainframes, but against manufacturers of mini-computers, handheld calculators, and giant government-sponsored computer manufacturers in Europe and in Japan. Moreover, as we noted in the first part of this chapter, economists have not been able to offer convincing proof that an oligopoly type of market structure inevitably lends to noncompetitive market conduct. This is a very uncertain area of public policy toward marketing at the present time. Future developments will be watched carefully.

If the balance of healthy competition tips toward more competition, it may become, in the vernacular, "cutthroat." Such competition occurred in the early days of radio broadcasting, for example, when one firm would establish a station broadcasting on a certain channel and build a profitable base of listeners. Then another firm would begin broadcasting on the same channel, in an attempt to wrest listeners and advertising revenues away from the established station. Similar patterns occurred in the airline industry and in motor freight transportation, and is presently the case in cable television.

The public policy response here, often at the behest of competitors themselves, is government regulation of competitors' conduct. For exam-

The U. S. Justice Department has filed an antitrust suit against International Business Machines Corporation (IBM), charging IBM with violating Section 2 of the Sherman Act by monopolizing the computer industry. The objective of the suit is the dissipation of the "enormous market power" of IBM by dividing its domestic and international operation into several (perhaps five) discrete, separate, independent, and competitively balanced entities capable of competing with each other and with existing companies.

If the market is defined as mainframe computer manufacturing, then there are eight firms in the industry, and IBM accounts for approximately 70 percent of sales volume. IBM, however, contends that the computer market is far larger and its share is far smaller than the government and its competitors recognize. In an industry survey IBM conducted early in 1972, 1,757 replies from 2,500 questionnaires to companies about their data processing activities showed that IBM's share of various market segments dropped to between 38 percent and 57 percent in 1970 from 69 percent or 70 percent in 1962.

There is no doubt that the case will be a landmark. The government has already obtained 27,000,000 documents pertaining to the case, and many more are expected—as well as depositions from hundreds of prospective witnesses. In an earlier case, Control Data Corporation had filed suit against IBM to prevent IBM's dominance of the computer market and growing complementary markets. Much of the data that the government planned to use in its suit had been compiled for the Control Data case. However, in a surprise move, IBM and Control Data settled their suit. One of the provisions of the settlement was the destruction by Control Data of a computerized index which it had prepared by author, subject matter, and date to some 150,000 pages of IBM internal memoranda and other documents that Control Data had obtained through court order.

From "Bigness under Attack: the U.S. Versus IBM," *Business Week* (November 11, 1972) and other news sources.

ple, the Federal Communications Commission licenses broadcasters and assigns them exclusive rights to broadcast on a certain wavelength. The Interstate Commerce Commission decides which motor freight lines may serve certain localities, and the prices they may charge. Similarly, the Civil Aeronautics Board regulates airline routes and rates.

In summary, public policy influences marketing activities in three different ways, as indicated by the three different areas of Exhibit 4-11. In the area of necessary products, public policy "intervenes" in exchange activities to influence consumption of the products in ways that society deems appropriate. In the area of prohibited products, public policy attempts to protect consumers and marketers from the high costs involved in exchanging certain types of products. And within the realm of legal marketing activities, public policy attempts to structure markets and regulate the conduct of marketers.

The crucial issue, as the diagram illustrates, is that society must determine the two boundaries. The area around the boundary separating necessary products from exchange products is characterized by transfer payments—food stamps, public education institutions, etc. The boundary between exchange products and prohibited products is characterized by black market activities. If consumers want certain prohibited products badly enough, illicit channels for delivering these products develop (e.g., narcotics, gambling). Even though prohibited by public policy, consumer demand for such products is sufficiently great to cause some organizations to produce these products despite the risks. The role public policy plays in marketing activities is significant and it is increasing.

CONTEMPORARY MARKETING/PUBLIC POLICY ISSUES

There are a great many issues here. Public policy is perhaps the dominant external factor in marketing decision making at the present time. These issues seem to be related to two major dimensions: economic and governmental. These issues are resolved in the political arena.

Government/Economic Issues

Much of the thrust of current public policy derives from the transfer-exchange and legal-illegal boundaries discussed in the previous section. Exhibit 4-22 provides a comprehensive framework for discussing these issues. Note that the economic dimension addresses the question of whether wants are satisfied by marketing or in some other way; the governmental dimension is concerned with whether such activities are satisfied in a legal or illegal manner. In the area of legal exchange, the fundamental issue for society is determining the role of regulation versus marketing incentives. The issue raised when transfer replaces exchange as the mechanism of want satisfaction is to reconcile the individual desires of consumers with the collective needs of society; this issue is often termed the micro/macro dilemma. And, as we pointed out in the previous section, there are illegal exchanges; the issue is how to control these black market operations.

No student or practitioner of marketing condones satisfying wants by force. But the problem of delineating between force and exchange is more difficult than it might appear. We look at each of these issues, in turn.

The Role of Regulation. As we noted in Exhibit 4-11, regulation can take two forms: intervention in the marketplace and consumer/marketer protection. This diagram clearly illustrates a vital point: regulation narrows the scope of marketing. The more society deems it necessary to intervene in the marketplace and the more protection it provides for consumers and marketers, the less "space" there is for marketing decision making. Beginning in 1974, for example, automobile manufacturers could not market and consumers could not buy automobiles which were not equipped with an ignition-seatbelt interlock. In 1975, all automobiles had to utilize unleaded gasoline. There is no question that society has the right—even the obligation—to regulate marketing activity. But I think it is appropriate to query the magnitude, the quality, and the timing of regulations that marketers and consumers face today.

Consider the cost of regulation. One estimate is that the federal

**Exhibit 4-22   Contemporary
Marketing/Public Policy Issues**

	Government	
	Legal Activities	Illegal Activities
Marketing Activities	*Exchange:* Innumerable products (goods, services, ideas; see Exhibit 1 - 1)	*Exchange:* Vice (prostitution, gambling, loan sharking) Smuggling (narcotics, liquor) Fencing stolen merchandise
	Issue: Role of regulation	Issue: Control of "black market" operations

Economic————————————————————————————

	Government	
Non-Marketing Activities	*Transfer:* Public Goods (highways and bridges, census data, school lunches) Public Services (police and fire protection, health care, postal delivery) Public Ideas (schools, colleges, libraries, support of religious freedom)	*Force:* Product performance (unsafe, inoperable, not as warranted) Promotion (deceptive ads, coercive selling) Distribution (non-delivery, hijacking, theft) Price (overcharging, bribery, credit refusal or executive rates, holder-in-due-course abuse)
	Issue: Micro/macro dilemma	Issue: Control of "Marketeering" without impeding marketing

government employs 63,000 workers at a cost of approximately $2 billion per year. And this direct social cost is a small proportion of the total. To comply with the regulations, marketers must fill out innumerable forms, defend themselves against lawsuits, and delay introduction of new products until federal standards have been met. All the costs will ultimately be reflected in product prices. Moreover, different regulatory agencies result in fragmented, overlapping, and sometimes contradictory regulations.

The Micro/Macro Dilemma. Public policy, by definition, is *macro*—it is designed to affect the society as a whole. It must, therefore, genuinely reflect the desires of the majority of the society. Public policy is adjusted through the political process so that generally, it does reflect the views of society reasonably well—in the long run. But consumers are satisfied, organization decisions are made, and public policy is determined on an individual basis. i.e., at the *micro* level. If, for example, prevailing public policy is to encourage competition in the provision of food products to consumers, then many consumers and most supermarket operators would argue that supermarkets are in line with public policy. Operators of independent grocery stores, however, might argue that supermarkets drive them out of business and therefore are anticompetitive. Or, the Environmental Protection Agency forcing a manufacturing plant to install expensive pollution equipment may argue that it is implementing public policy. But if the plant management decides that because such equipment is so expensive it must close the plant rather than comply—and therefore deprives employees of their means of livelihood, the employees might argue that such a requirement is contrary to public policy. In short, at the micro level, changes of any kind affect some individuals adversely (and some favorably)—long-run, macro adjustments of public policy to the desires of society may be of little comfort to individuals who feel harmed in the short run. It is necessary, therefore, that public policy be continually adjusted to meet the changing demands of consumers, organizations, and the environment in general. Consequently, the political process operates continuously to produce evolutionary (we hope) adjustments in public policy. (When the political process breaks down, the society experiences the violent change of revolution.)

Black Market Operations. The need for continual evolution in public policy toward marketing is nowhere more apparent than in societal control over illegal exchange activities. Crimes in the categories of vice, smuggling, and fencing of stolen merchandise are often referred to as "victimless crimes." That is, these are exchange transactions—presumably to expected mutual benefit—which occur outside the law. Thus, both the marketers and the consumers of illicit products share the common objective of concealing their activities from society. Such consumers forfeit society's protection against unsafe products, violent collection methods, and exorbitant prices. And these marketers cannot demand contract enforcement in the courts or protection from monopolistic or cutthroat tactics.

Illegal exchange activities arise from the fact that society has objectives in addition to effective and efficient allocations of resources to satisfy wants. All societies have religious and moral standards, for example, and chastise members of the society who violate those standards, but every society has purveyors of vice. Imports of certain products may be banned or highly taxed in order to protect the jobs of members of the society. Consumers desiring such products must get them from smugglers or fences. Control of such black market operations is necessary to protect the integrity of the society, but control raises difficult questions of definitions and enforcement.

Until a few years ago, for example, pornography was banned in most developed countries. As contemporary levels of taste changed, pornography became more and more available. To my knowlege, Denmark was the first country to legalize the sale of pornography openly, and other countries have followed suit. But what is "legal pornography" in one country or part of a country, is not necessarily legal in another country or state. A similar controversy is now raging over narcotics—should the sale of marijuana be legalized? The list of illicit products for which there is supply and demand is lengthy and does not reflect the desires of some members of the society.

Marketeering. In contrast to bona fide but illegal exchanges, there are many activities which appear to be marketing, but are in fact applications of force. Faulty or unsafe products are offered, used parts are substituted for new ones, advertisements are deceptive, lies are told by salespersons, merchandise is not delivered or is overpriced, officials are bribed, credit is refused, and so on *ad nauseam*. Such activities are not within my conception of marketing as exchange to mutual advantage; I call such activities "marketeering." Faster transportation, the long-distance telephone, and the vast impersonal nature of modern society make it possible for marketeers to operate in a more sophisticated manner than ever before. No reputable marketing scholar or practitioner would want to defend or even be associated with such illegal activities. These people satisfy their wants by force, not exchange. Legal remedies are available; more effective enforcement of existing laws in this area would be welcome to marketers as well as to consumers.

Again, however, the issues are more complex than they may seem. Distinctions between exchange and force are sometimes difficult to make. In the lumber industry, for example, the standard dimensions for 2 x 4 lumber are $1\frac{7}{8}$ by $3\frac{7}{8}$; most processed meats do not contain 100 percent meat; "diet bread" may be a regular loaf sliced thinner, and candy bars are unobtrusively reduced in size although the price is not lowered. It is possible to design an advertisement in which every word is literally true, but the context and setting imply more benefits than the product actually delivers. Are such activities illegal? When does a sales commission for legitimate services performed become an illegal bribe? Is the incorrect bill an honest mistake, or an attempt to defraud?

In short, designing, administering, and enforcing the public policy toward marketing activities is not easy. Marketing is a social activity; it must be responsive to society's objectives, as these are developed through the political process.

The Political Arena
Public policy is developed in the political arena. Marketing students must

understand the nature of the political process, and the forces which shape it. At the present time, three forces seem to dominate: rising expectations, the advocacy approach to public policy development, and perhaps some degree of misunderstanding as to how an economic system functions.

Rising Social Expectations. There is a widely held feeling that progress in one area should be paralleled by progress in others—"if they can land a man on the moon, why can't they make my dishwasher function properly?" In the last decade, there has been great progress through the political process in such areas as securing civil rights for minorities and improving minimal standards of living. So people's expectations are generally higher now than they ever have been concerning the usefulness of the political process to solve social problems.

And people are becoming more sophisticated. They generally have higher education levels, better understanding of the means of acquiring political power, and the willingness to militantly pursue their demands.

Public policy has responded. In 1962, President Kennedy articulated the rights of consumers, as excerpted in Exhibit 4-23. This statement of consumers' rights has been endorsed by every successive president. In addition, politicians in the early 1970s were increasingly prone to promise their electorates that government could solve whatever problem was brought before it. The inevitable result is more activity in public policy. There are more lawsuits: consumers sue manufacturers when products injure them, even if they have misused the product; companies sue their more successful rivals (Control Data Corporation versus IBM, Microwave Communications, Inc. versus AT&T). Congress assumes more activist postures: it threatens to break up the vertically integrated major oil companies; it creates new agencies such as the Federal Energy Administration and the Consumer Product Safety Commission; and state regulatory agencies are taking their duties more seriously. It is more difficult for private utility companies to raise their prices to offset the rising costs of energy sources and labor. Pollution control regulations are enforced more strictly, and so on.

As we have noted on several occasions, wants and desires are infinite. And that statement holds for peoples' expectations concerning public policy. "There ought to be a law" is a common refrain. There are more people today advocating that government do more specific things.

Advocacy: The "Selling" of Public Policy. Public policy toward marketing developed in an inconsistent, fragmented fashion. For example, regulations governing the manufacture and sale of automobiles are promulgated by (1) the Federal Energy Administration (which is primarily concerned with gasoline mileage), (2) the Department of Transportation, which focuses its attentions upon improving automobile safety, and

In 1962, President John F. Kennedy stated, "the Federal government—by nature the highest spokesman for all the people—has a special obligation to be alert to the consumer's needs and to the consumer's interest . . ." Kennedy maintained that the Federal government has a responsibility to consumers in the exercise of their rights. He classified these rights into four categories:

1. *The right to safety*—to be protected against the marketing of goods which are hazardous to health or life.
2. *The right to be informed*—to be protected against fraudulent, deceitful, or grossly misleading information, advertising, labeling, or other practices, and to be given the facts he needs to make an informed choice.
3. *The right to choose*—to be assured, wherever possible, access to a variety of products and services at competitive prices; and in those industries in which competition is not workable and government regulation is substituted, an assurance of satisfactory quality and service at fair prices.
4. *The right to be heard*—to be assured that consumer interests will receive full and sympathetic consideration in the formulation of government policy, and fair and expeditious treatment in its administrative tribunals.

Of course, other observers might classify consumers' rights in different ways—but this list is typical, fairly inclusive, and does have the weight of presidential authority. It has been endorsed by every president. For this reason it has become a standard by which progress in public policy toward consumers is measured.

From "Message from the President, Relative to Consumers' Protection," Document no. 364, House of Representatives, 87th Congress, 2nd session, March 15, 1962.

---

(3) the Environmental Protection Agency, which is concerned with minimizing air and noise pollution from automobiles. Each of these objectives is, by itself, commendable, but they are mutually contradictory. Automobile safety can be improved by increasing the weight of automobiles, which detracts from gasoline mileage performance. Similarly, an environmental protection device, such as the catalytic converter, adds weight, reduces gas mileage, and causes the emission of other pollutants like sulfur dioxide into the atmosphere. There is no overall objective of optimizing automobile design.

Similar examples include subsidies to tobacco growers by the U.S. government. The Department of Agriculture continues to articulate policies to improve and increase tobacco production, in the face of numerous warnings by the U.S. Surgeon General of the relationship between cigarette smoking and lung cancer. And, despite the energy crisis, there is no national energy policy.

The crux of the problem is that public policy is developed primarily through the *advocacy* process. As learned in law schools, advocacy is the vigorous and uncompromising "selling" of a particular point of view. The lawyer on the other side is expected to provide counter information, and to point out weaknesses in the argument of the advocate. There is a judge who decides, largely on the basis of legal precedents, which advocate is correct. Surely the most prominent example of advocacy in public policy today is Ralph Nader. Nader presses his contentions skillfully and vigorously, and gives no quarter. When asked once if perhaps his opponents may have had a point, Nader's response was "You do not give a burglar credit for not burglarizing, do you?" In brief, proponents of views which differ from those of the advocate are enemies to be defeated by whatever means available. The advocate has little concern for the rightness of the position in a moral sense, the economic costs and benefits of the proposal, or the importance of the issue advocated relative to others.

Of course, advocacy is not all bad. But it is at best inefficient. It was known, for example, when the 1970 automobile emission standards were promulgated that these standards would raise the cost of automobiles sold in 1975. It was expected, however, that continued economic growth would provide a cushion insulating both manufacturers and public policymakers from complaints by customers. Affluence was expected to provide customer acceptance of more expensive automobiles which polluted the atmosphere less. This expectation was wrong. Automobile sales in 1974 and 1975 were considerably below projections, as consumers strapped by the recession refused to pay higher prices for environmentally superior products.

Understanding the Economic System. Discussion of the advocacy approach to public policy development highlights a larger, and perhaps more fundamental issue. I am very much afraid that some—perhaps many—policy makers and influencers do not understand the nature of marketing and economic activities that public policy seeks to guide. The operative word is system. In any system, parts are interrelated: "everything depends upon everything else." One clear example involves the nature of the distribution system. It has been contended that if only Americans would forego using fertilizer on their lawns, then sufficient fertilizer would be available to meet grain production requirements in India. This argument is humane, but it ignores the complex problems that would be involved in redistributing fertilizer from American suburbs to Indian farms, to say nothing of the means and methods of payment to the firms supplying the fertilizer. Fertilizer in America has very little place utility in India.

Similarly, Congressmen who advocate breaking up the major oil companies do not evaluate the potential economic efficiencies generated by vertical integration in the industry. Nor do they take into account the costs of uncertainty and reorganization which divestiture would require.

In fact, the role of costs and prices in an economic system seems to be widely misunderstood. For example, consumer advocates often complain that individuals are asked to bear a disproportionate share of society's tax burden. They suggest that corporate income taxes should be raised instead. But they fail to recognize that businesses do not pay taxes; they merely collect them. A profit-seeking business must meet its costs and provide some return to its shareholders. Consequently, if taxes on a business are raised, then these taxes must be passed on to the consumer in the form of higher prices, subtracted from returns to employees in the form of lower wages, to lenders (lower interest rates), or to stockholders (lower dividends). Moreover, the costs of complying with various public policies must also be covered. If prices are to be controlled, then some employees must handle the necessary paperwork. If products are to be safer, the cost of incorporating safety features must be borne, lawsuits must be defended (and legal advice becomes more expensive each day) and so forth.

Non-monetary costs are more difficult to comprehend, but are no less real. For example, when retail gasoline prices were controlled in 1973–74, consumers were forced to wait in long lines, could not buy gasoline at night or on Sundays, and the amount of purchase was limited. Time loss and the aggravation of waiting in such lines is a very real cost, albeit a difficult one to express in terms of dollars. Similarly, it has been suggested that fluorocarbons used in aerosol dispensers may eventually weaken the ozone layer in the earth's upper atmosphere. So far, this has not been proved and it is difficult to estimate the economic impact such damage might cause if the theory proves to be true. Nevertheless, the potential risk is so great that many scientists advocate a ban on aerosol propellants, despite the enormous cost that such a ban would produce. (Already, some companies have changed products from aerosol propelled to spray pumped and use this change in their promotion messages.) This problem has a converse side: products are sometimes banned, at great cost, with insufficient documentation of the benefits claimed. A classic example here is the banning of cyclamates in the early 1970s because cyclamates were suspected of causing cancer. Subsequent research allayed such suspicions, but the ban was costly to companies, consumers, and therefore ultimately to society.

CONCLUDING NOTE

An economic system, like religion, government, and education, is a wonderfully complex social institution. And the economic system affects all members of a society. Consequently, everyone has opinions about it. Marketing activities are among the most significant and visible activities of the system, so they receive their share (some perhaps even more than their share) of criticism. It is easy to find fault, and improvements often seem slow in coming.

From a macro point of view (the perspective of a social critic or public-policy maker), the operative word is *system*. It is not difficult to advocate changes in specific aspects of the economic system to cure particular problems. The difficulty lies in determining the effects of those changes on other parts of the system. Farm price supports, for example, raise the standard of living of farmers, but cause consumers to pay higher prices for food. The small, independent businessman is a cherished part of the American tradition, but he may be performing relatively inefficiently, and so on.

Moreover, there is little question, at least in my own mind, that critics of the system would be more persuasive if they had a better understanding of the operation of the system and its limitations. This is not to say that problems do not exist or that improvements cannot be made.

In general, however, improvements in a basically market-oriented system are made not at the macro level, but at the micro level—by the decisions of individual managers, particularly marketing managers. These managers seek to obtain their own organizational objectives. Specifically, they seek some means of differentiating their product in the minds of consumers from other products that might satisfy the same wants and desires. In so doing, there is a constant search for new products, more persuasive advertisements, more efficient manufacturing processes, wider product distribution, and so on. Their purpose is not necessarily to change the system, but to operate successfully within it. It is one of the great strengths of the market mechanism that, almost as a byproduct of such operations, this system can and does improve. In public policy, as in other areas of the social environment, everyone is an expert. How many times have you heard the statement, "There ought to be a law" about whatever it is that the speaker is discussing at the moment? It is unfortunate that public policy toward marketing is sometimes shaped in this way. At any given point in time, a particular law might be passed or might be interpreted by administrators or courts in a certain way because of the actions of groups that do not reflect the majority of society. To be sure, the process of public-policy formulation tends to conform, *in the long run,* to the desires of the majority of the society. But at a given time, public policy may seem confusing and inconsistent to the marketing manager trying to operate within its constraints and yet meet his organization's objectives.

In attempting to understand public policy toward marketing, therefore, the marketing manager should remember that a particular law or court decision is seldom so bad—or so good—as it may appear to be on the surface. The realities of public policy toward marketing are very complex. Competent legal advice, therefore, is becoming an increasingly essential ingredient of successful performance of managerial tasks in marketing. I am increasingly convinced that contemporary marketing managers will need to acquire the same fundamental understanding of the law that the 1950s demanded in the behavioral sciences and the 1960s required in mathematical analysis.

KEY TERMS AND CONCEPTS

The Economic Problem
   planning (command)
   market mechanism (demand)
Economic Activity
   pure competition
   monopoly/competition continuum
   market structure and conduct
Market Structure Continuum
   pure monopoly
   oligopoly
   monopolistic competition
   pure competition
Market Concentration
   ratios
   social perception: low
      ratio = good
   empirical evidence
Functions of Government
Public-Policy Criteria
   full employment
   efficiency
   stability
   progress
   equity
   consumer sovereignty
   morality
   quality of life
Public-Policy Formulation
   inputs (environmental forces)
   economic conflict
   political activity
   policy formulation
   outputs (social, economic, marketing)
Evolution of Public Policy
   Sherman Antitrust Act
   Clayton Antitrust Act
   Federal Trade Commission Act
   Robinson-Patman Act
   Miller-Tydings Act
   Celler-Kefauver Act
Political Power vs. Economic Power
Social Perspective on Product Utility
   necessary benefits

payoffs
prohibited costs
Marketing/Public Policy Framework
intervention
protection
market guides
Contemporary Issues
role of regulation
micro/macro dilemma
black market operations
marketeering

QUESTIONS FOR DISCUSSION

1. There is little question that the concept of a command economy is easier to explain than is the market mechanism. On the other hand, economic history suggests that, on balance, the market mechanism is a bit more successful in satisfying most human wants and desires. How do you account for this apparent paradox?

2. Explain the concept of market structure in your own words. How can the marketing manager use this concept? Should he do so? Why or why not?

3. Explain, in your own words, the eight criteria for evaluating the performance of an economic system. Cite examples of specific public actions designed to improve performance according to each criterion. Have the actual results of these policies improved or impeded economic performance? Defend your assessment.

4. If, as economists aver, pure competition is ideal, why does public policy "distort" competition in farming? Should public policy strive for more or less pure competition? Why?

5. Would the performance of the U. S. Post Office (a public good) be improved if competition were allowed? Why or why not? Would your aruguments apply to other public goods, e.g., highways, schools, national defense?

6. Is concentration in the U. S. economy really increasing? What evidence do you find? Is this good or bad? Defend your views.

7. Examine such issues as the following, using the public-policy development process model: mandatory helmets for motorcyclists, legalized marijuana, registration of all firearms, no-fault automobile insurance, advertisement of prescription drug prices. Be sure to discuss inputs, economic conflict, political activity, current policy, and probable outcomes. Pay particular attention to consumer rights, the micro/macro dilemma, and possible marketing opportunities and threats. (A current

bill before Congress or your state legislature might also be worth examining in this fashion.)

8. Would you favor or oppose legislation such as the following:
   a bill requiring companies in concentrated industries to give 60-days advance notice of price changes;
   a bill to establish a cabinet-level Department of Consumer Affairs;
   a bill to abolish Sunday closing laws for retailers;
   a bill to establish a Federal Testing Bureau to examine and report on all products;
   a bill to permit class-action suits in all cases of product misrepresentation or malfunction;
   a bill requiring gasoline stations to close on Sunday.

Defend your reasoning in each case.

9. Should IBM be broken up? Why or why not? Would you extend whatever conclusion you reached about IBM to other companies or industries in similar circumstances, e.g., General Motors, United States Steel, Exxon, DuPont? Why or why not?

10. The text says that marketing activity is resented in contemporary society. Do you agree? Why or why not? What can marketers do to improve this situation?

SUGGESTED READING

1. Gilbert Burck.
"High Pressure Consumerism at the Salesman's Door." *Fortune*, July 1972, pp. 224–29; reprinted in Gabriel M. Gelb and Betsy D. Gelb, *Insights for Marketing Management*. Pacific Palisades, Calif.: Goodyear Publishing Company, 1977. Thorough, incisive examination of consumerism and its implications for public policy toward marketing.

2. Richard Caves.
American Industry: Structure, Conduct, Performance. 3rd ed., Englewood Cliffs, N.J.: Prentice-Hall, 1972. This is a widely acclaimed brief treatment of the American economic system and its relationship to public policy; contains chapters on the promotion of competition and control of monopoly, policies to restrict competition, and market performance and public policy; has extensive references for further reading.

3. Laurence P. Feldman.
Consumer Protection: Problems and Prospects. West Publishing Co., 1976. Scholarly yet readable survey of this portion of public policy toward marketing; good reference.

4. O.C. Ferrell and Raymond LaGarce, editors.
Public Policy Issues in Marketing. Lexington Books, 1975 . Thoughtfully

chosen recent essays in this area; good starting point for the serious student.

5. Hugh Furuhashi and E. Jerome McCarthy.
Social Issues of Marketing in the American Economy. Columbus, Ohio: Grid, 1971. A provocative compilation of issues faced by marketing management in contemporary society; easy reading, but does not offer pat solutions.

6. E.T. Grether.
Marketing and Public Policy. Prentice-Hall, 1966. A concise, authoritative treatment of the relationship between marketing and public policy by one of the discipline's most respected senior scholars; contains an extensive bibliography.

7. Marshall C. Howard.
Legal Aspects of Marketing. New York: McGraw-Hill Book Company, 1964. A comprehensive treatment of law as it relates to marketing activities; in need of revision in light of the increasingly rapid change in the legal environment of marketing, but valuable reading for the serious scholar in this area.

8. Earl W. Kintner.
An Anti-Trust Primer, second edition. Macmillan, 1973. The standard guide, written for the layman rather than the lawyer, but not light reading; valuable reference.

9. Thomas A. Petit.
Freedom in the American Economy. Homewood, Ill.: Richard D. Irwin, 1964. Lucid elementary treatment of the role of the economic system in an industrialized society; provides a good general foundation for the more specific study of public policy toward marketing activities.

As marketing requested it

As sales ordered it

As engineering designed it

As plant manufactured it

As field service installed it

What the customer wanted!!!

5/THE MARKETING FUNCTION IN AN ORGANIZATION

This chapter places marketing activities within the context of the overall organization. Its purpose is to demonstrate the need for careful integration of the marketing function with other functions of the organization. Major points include:

1. The organization can be viewed as a system processing inputs (human resources, physical resources, capital, information) via functions of marketing, production, and finance to produce products. Exchange of these products with customers results in attainment of organizational objectives.

2. The philosophy of the marketing concept dictates that the basic mission of the organization should be stated in terms of *generic product benefits*. Success of the product mission is then measured in terms of a basic objective criterion (profit, votes, students graduated, etc.). The organization strives for differential advantage in the way it offers products to its customers.

3. The structure of the marketing function should be derived from organizational goals and marketing objectives. The basic division of labor in marketing is between operations and services. Marketing operations may be further decentralized on the basis of geography, products and/or customers.

4. The marketing plan specifies decisions to be made in each of the functions of seeking, matching, programming, and consummating. The basic dimensions of planning for each of these functions are organizational level and timing.

5. The marketing audit is a comprehensive systematic review and appraisal of marketing activities. Ideally, the marketing audit serves as a foundation for the development of the marketing plan.

The most pervasive and active relationships that marketing management has are its relationships with the rest of the organization. Marketing management must function within the context of the larger organizational system. Therefore, marketing actions must be compatible with organizational objectives, the structure of the marketing function must fit into overall organizational design, and marketing planning must be related to corporate planning. Let us look first at the organization as a system.

THE ORGANIZATION AS A SYSTEM

It is instructive to apply the systems concept (Exhibit 2-1) to an understanding of organizational structure and functions. Exhibit 5-1 illustrates this application. The organization uses inputs of types of resources, which it processes to produce both products and information to obtain some objective.

Organizational Objectives

An organization is a group of people having a common purpose who join forces to achieve a certain objective. In profit-seeking organizations, the objective is often stated as *profit maximization.* According to the fundamental tenets of elementary economic theory, profits will be maximized if the organization produces the number of units for which marginal cost equal marginal revenue. Most profit-seeking managers declare that profit maximization is their fundamental objective, and all profit-seeking organizations pay some attention to it.

The economists' profit-maximization concept suffers from several limitations. First, it assumes perfect knowledge—of demand and cost relationships, of competitors' reactions, of customers' desires, and of the objectives of other channel members. All too often, the manager desiring to maximize profits simply does not possess such knowledge. Second, the economists' model is a static one—it assumes that changes take place instantaneously and that revenues and costs accrue at the same time. Third, the model depicts one product, demand and cost functions that can be represented by continuous curves, without constraints (e.g., absolute plant size, indivisible products), and with no influence by other marketing mix elements (promotion, product quality, distribution strategy, etc.). In short, the simple profit-maximization model is based on a number of assumptions which limit its usefulness for managerial decision making.

Because of these limitations in the profit-maximization concept, profit-seeking organizations have other objectives. Many organizations initially do not earn a profit; the major objective in the first few years is simply to survive, and perhaps to grow. Growth, often measured in terms of sales, is frequently cited as the major objective by many marketing decision makers. Many large organizations in well-established industries tend to state their objectives in terms of market share—the percentage of

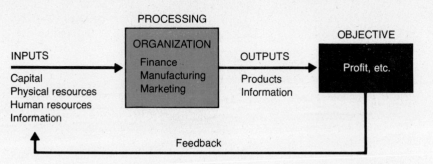

Exhibit 5-1   The Organization as a System

Exhibit 5-1 diagram content:

PROCESSING

INPUTS

Capital
Physical resources
Human resources
Information

ORGANIZATION

Finance
Manufacturing
Marketing

OUTPUTS

Products
Information

OBJECTIVE

Profit, etc.

Feedback

total industry sales obtained by the organization. Some economists argue that such objectives can be encompassed by the term profit maximization, but such a broad, long-range, all-inclusive definition would seem to rob the profit-maximization concept of much of its usefulness as a guide for actual decision making.

Marketing concepts and techniques also apply to organizations that are not profit seeking. For example, political parties, labor unions, governments, and organizations promoting social change can usefully employ various ideas from the marketing discipline. Although such organizations must generate sufficient revenues to cover their costs, it is obvious that profit maximization is not the primary consideration in such cases.

This brief review of possible objectives also illustrates the fact that any organization is almost certain to have more than one objective. In fact, most of the individuals within the organization are not cognizant of striving to achieve the organization's primary objective—whether it be profit maximization, growth, winning an election, or whatever. To reach any primary objective, certain other subordinate objectives must be met. For example, the profit-maximizing firm may have sales people whose goal is to sell a certain amount of the product, and production managers who strive to manufacture the product within certain cost constraints. In such cases, these subordinate objectives must be accomplished if the primary objective is to be reached. The attainment of subordinate objectives becomes the means for reaching goals at the next level. Exhibit 5-2 illustrates the hierarchy-of-objectives concept.

If the organization is attempting to maximize profit, it must accomplish certain subordinate objectives. For example, revenues must total a given amount. To achieve this amount of revenue, sales must reach a certain level. Consequently, most profit-seeking organizations have certain sales objectives. Similarly, at the next level, a given sales figure is obtained by generating a sufficient demand for the product. Demand is affected not only by pricing decisions, but also by the actions of the other elements of the marketing mix, for example, promotion decisions. On the

Exhibit 5-2   Hierarchy of Objectives

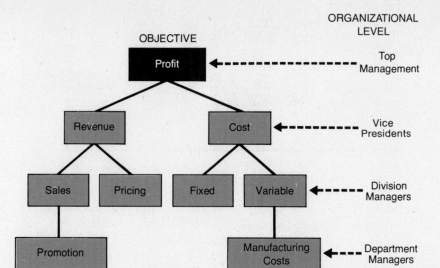

other hand, the profit objective will not be achieved—no matter how much revenue is obtained—if cost objectives are not met. For example, decisions as to the amount of plant and equipment to be used in production must be made; a certain level of *Return on Investment* (ROI) is often the specified objective here. Also, variable costs must be taken into account, e.g., the costs of manufacturing certain parts must not exceed a given percentage of the sales price if the total cost of the product is to be kept within prescribed limits.

Organizational Resources

As shown in Exhibit 5-1, there are four types of resources which become inputs into the organizational system: capital, materials, people, and information.

Capital. The term capital is used here in the accounting, as opposed to the economic, sense. Capital is those items that are entered into asset accounts (capitalized) for accounting purposes—cash; accounts receivable; land and buildings; and installations of major equipment. Capital resources generally are not managed by marketing personnel.

Physical Resources. These can be divided into four categories: accessory equipment, component parts, supplies, and energy sources. Accessory equipment includes items such as typewriters and adding machines; machine tools; desks and chairs; wheelbarrows and handtrucks; and so on. Component parts are those items that are used in producing the final product. These may include raw materials; basic items such as wire, paper, textiles or cement; assemblies such as engines, transmissions, or parts such as tires and spark plugs. Supplies are those items that are used up in the production process that do not become part of the final product. Examples are pencils, paper clips, rubber bands, sandpaper, grinding wheels, janitorial supplies. Sources of energy include coal, fuel oil, natural gas, electricity, and atomic power.

Most materials are used by production personnel. However, purchasing of materials is often the province of marketing. This area is discussed in Chapter 6, Buyer Behavior.

Human Resources. Perhaps the most important type of resource that the organization uses is the abilities, interests, and energy of the people affiliated with the organization. This includes everyone employed by the company from the president to the janitor, and the services of outside parties when needed, e.g., legal or tax advice, architectural or engineering services, temporary typing help, real estate agents, and delivery service. Personnel management is not a marketing activity, but the hiring, training, and supervising of marketing people requires close cooperation between personnel departments and marketing management.

Information. Information is not universally recognized as a resource, but it, like other organizational resources, adds value to the organization's products and is costly to procure. In this sense, information is a resource. Information can be subdivided into internal information, research, and intelligence. Internal information is primarily accounting data—balance sheets, profit and loss statements, budgets—but includes such data as sales forecasts and quotas, production estimates, personnel records, and the president's speeches. Research is information that the organization has specifically commissioned. For example, customers can be queried about their tastes and preferences, congressmen can be asked for assessments of legislative action, and products can be test marketed. The third category of information is intelligence—data that are available in the environment, but that must be captured and structured to be useful to managers.

Information management is becoming an increasingly significant aspect of marketing management. Managing marketing information and the three information types are discussed in Chapter 8.

Organizational Functions

Given the inputs into the system, the next phase of system analysis is processing. The major processing functions in an organizational system are production, finance and marketing. The production function includes designing the product, utilizing raw materials and equipment to manufacture the product, scheduling and managing work flows, and so on. The finance function involves the management of capital to enable an organization to produce and market its products; it includes working-capital procurement, analysis and budgeting of capital requirements, investment management, and so on. The marketing function, as introduced in the marketing management chapter (Chapter 2), involves identifying customer wants and coordinating production and financial activities to meet these wants: seeking, matching, programming, consummating.

ORGANIZATIONAL AND MARKETING OBJECTIVES

We noted in the previous section that there is a hierarchy of objectives within an organization. At lower levels of the objective hierarchy, the different functions may have very dissimilar objectives. The production manager may desire long production runs of a single model to minimize costs. The marketing manager, on the other hand, may like to have a number of different types of models of the product—in order to more precisely meet the various needs of different customers. At the same time, the financial manager may resist accumulating inventories, whether of a single model or of many models, because inventories tie up working capital. Exhibit 5-3 presents other examples of possible conflicts among functional managers. The possible harmful effects of suboptimization on an organization are obvious; yet such conflicts are common in organizational behavior. What is needed is some method of reconciling these conflicts.

The Marketing Concept

The method of objective reconciliation recommended by marketing scholars is *the marketing concept*. As introduced in Chapter 2, this concept states that the fundamental objective of the organization should be customer satisfaction: all activities of the organization should be devoted to identifying, and then producing products to satisfy customers' wants. This concept can be considered a basic philosophy for organizational management.

The marketing concept has two key benefits. First, the emphasis on customer satisfaction implies that all organizational activities should be focused upon this fundamental objective. With such unity of purpose and focus, organizational activities can be coordinated and conflicts minimized. Second, the emphasis on the customer should keep the organization alert to changing environmental conditions, new markets, and shifts in customers' tastes and demands. Thus, the marketing concept can be a powerful guide to managerial thinking about the basic purpose of an organization.

Exhibit 5-3 Possible Organizational Conflict Between Other Functions and the Marketing Function

Other Functions	Emphasis of Other Functions	Emphasis of Marketing
Engineering	Long design lead time Functional features Few models with standard components	Short design lead time Sales features Many models with custom components
Purchasing	Standard parts Price of material Economic lot sizes Purchasing at infrequent intervals	Nonstandard parts Quality of material Large lot sizes to avoid stockouts Immediate purchasing for customer needs
Production	Long order lead times and inflexible production schedules Long runs with few models No model changes Standard orders Ease of fabrication Average quality control	Short order lead times and flexible scheduling to meet emergency orders Short runs with many models Frequent model changes Custom orders Aesthetic appearance Tight quality control
Inventory Management	Fast-moving items, narrow product line Economic levels of stock	Broad product line Large levels of stock
Finance	Strict rationale for spending Hard and fast budgets Pricing to cover costs	Intuitive arguments for spending Flexible budgets to meet changing needs Pricing to further market development
Accounting	Standard transactions Few reports	Special terms and discounts Many reports
Credit	Full financial disclosures by customers Low credit risks Tough credit terms Tough collection procedures	Minimum credit examination of customers Medium credit risks Easy credit terms Easy collection procedures

Adapted from: Philip Kotler, ''Diagnosing the Marketing Takeover,'' *Harvard Business Review*, November–December, 1965, p. 72. Summarized with permission of *Harvard Business Review.*

Organizational Purpose

Renowned management scholar Peter Drucker is adamant on this point: "The only valid purpose of a business is to create a customer . . . what the business thinks it produces is not of first importance—especially to the business and to its success . . . what the customer thinks he is buying, what he considers of value is decisive . . ." (*Management*, p. 61).

Exhibit 5-4   Examples of Organizational Goals

Organization	Mission (generic product)	Criterion (basic objective)	Possible Marketing Objectives
1. National Household Products Manufacturer	Improve home cleanliness and/or reduce cleaning effort	Maximize shareholder wealth (profit, ROI)	Brand awareness Number of sales calls New products developed
2. Integrated Petroleum Company	Provide energy	Maximize shareholder wealth (profit, ROI)	Hold prices steady Decrease distribution costs Establish new customers
3. Political Party	Promulgate programs of interest to majority of electorate	Majority of votes cast	Campaign contributions Secure television time Register voters
4. Radio Free Europe	Change political attitudes	More positive attitudes toward the West	Secure congressional support Broadcast in appropriate languages
5. Planned Parenthood Association	Reduce population growth	Declining birthrate	Educate public Liberalize abortion laws Provide vasectomies
6. Local Chamber of Commerce	Promote economic growth	Increasing numbers of businesses, tax receipts, etc.	Provide information for businessmen Promote conventions
7. University	Produce and disseminate knowledge	More books and papers published Greater number of students graduated	Legislative liaison Promotion of programs of study

To be specific, the basic mission—the fundamental goal of the organization—must be stated in terms of the generic benefit that the organization produces and markets. Attainment of this basic objective will be measured in terms of some operational criterion. Once the basic objective has been stated in operational terms, marketing objectives (and those of other functions) can be formulated. Consider Exhibit 5-4.

A national household product manufacturer, such as Procter & Gamble or Lever Bros., has as its basic mission improving cleanliness in the home and/or reducing the effort required for cleaning tasks. The ultimate measure of how well it performs this basic mission is in terms of returns to stockholders—profit, Return On Investment, etc. The major petroleum companies such as Exxon and Texaco recognize that their basic mission is not pumping oil, but providing energy. They, too, measure accomplishment of this basic mission in monetary terms. A political party, in contrast, has as its basic mission the promulgation of programs of interest to a majority of the electorate: it measures the success of these programs in terms of votes cast. Basic missions of other organizations should be similarly stated and measured.

Then, and only then, should marketing objectives, and objectives for other functions, be stated in operational performance terms. Procter & Gamble might endeavor to increase consumer awareness of its new brand of liquid laundry detergent from 10 percent to 60 percent in a 90-day period, and the chamber of commerce might attempt to book ten new conventions next year.

Differential Advantage

In the marketing literature, the organization's mission statement is often referred to as the search for differential advantage. A differential advantage is a feature or characteristic of an organization which distinguishes it in some way from other organizations which have essentially the same fundamental mission. The differential advantage may be in terms of the organization's location (in a major metropolitan area or near a source of essential raw materials), product characteristics (Coca-Cola's secret formula), economies of scale in production (unit costs of General Motors cars are lower than those of Chrysler simply because General Motors produces more cars), and so on. The organization competes by making the most of its differential advantage.

In order to accomplish its basic mission, therefore, organization managers, especially marketing managers, must accomplish two fundamental tasks: (1) to establish a differential advantage, and (2) to nurture that advantage.

The Role of Marketing

The philosophy of the marketing concept implies that marketing should play a major role in achieving organizational objectives. This is not to say that other functions are unimportant, indeed, all functions must work together if the organization system is to achieve desired objectives. But this is a marketing book, so we focus on marketing.

The success of the marketing concept in attracting and satisfying customers has been documented. But the marketplace today requires a broader perspective. Recall from Chapter 2 the argument that the marketing concept should be interpreted generically, i.e., used to guide relationships of marketing managers with suppliers, and between marketers and society as well as with customers.

Customer-Oriented Objectives. During the early 1970s, shortages of key raw materials such as petroleum, steel, newsprint, and sugar were widespread. To solve problems created by shortages, managerial attention was shifted away from marketing and toward purchasing, inventory control, and production efficiencies. The term *demarketing* came to mean neglect of the marketing function, since the customers' demands could not be satisfied. As conditions eased in the middle 1970s, many organizations discovered to their chagrin that customers felt ill-used by demarketing, and displayed little loyalty when shortages eased. Many organizations found such customers difficult to win back. The logic of the marketing concept is not limited to stimulating and expanding markets. Its basic tenets (thorough knowledge of customers' desires and integrated organizational effort to satisfy those desires) apply in shortage situations as well as in buyer's markets. If, for example, products must be allocated (rationed), the allocation procedures should be designed with each customer's requirements in mind and should be explained as carefully as new product features are demonstrated.

Supplier-Oriented Objectives. The logic of the marketing concept applies also to supplier relations. That is, a differential advantage in the marketplace may be achieved via more efficient production processes, or cheaper raw materials. Since customers have to be satisfied, adjustments from the supply side will be most effective if marketing managers work closely with production personnel or with vendors of crucial raw materials. And marketing personnel are more likely to be effective in their dealings with production personnel and vendors if they view those groups as participants in exchange to mutual advantage. A request for a product design change, for example, may be more favorably received if it is accompanied by suggestions as to how change can be made without disrupting normal production operations.

Societally Oriented Objectives. The demands of society press upon the marketer as never before. Products must be safe, advertising must be truthful, prices must be independently set, and so on. The organization's relationships with society, especially social critics and policy makers, are becoming more numerous and more significant. Thus, explicit objectives should be set in this area. Here, too, the logic of the marketing concept can be quite helpful. In dealing with a federal agency, for example, it may be that approaching the situation from an exchange viewpoint rather than as an adversary might prove beneficial to both organization and agency. Advertising campaigns could be aimed specifically at influencing public opinion. Some companies—notably the integrated oil companies fighting possible divestiture legislation—are beginning to move in this direction. More explicit objectives need to be formulated for societal relationships.

In summary, the organization as a system operates to achieve its basic objective through the accomplishment of its primary mission. This mission should be stated in terms of generic product benefits. If the mission is so stated and is clearly understood, then the hierarchy of objectives can be operationally constructed, and the organization can be structured to achieve the basic objective.

STRUCTURE OF THE MARKETING FUNCTION

In concept, the traditional management view is that "form follows function," i.e., the way an organization is structured depends upon its hierarchy of objectives. Ideally, therefore, the organizational structure of the marketing function would be determined by the organizations' mission and hierarchy of objectives. In point of fact, most organizations are going concerns; and therefore have existing organizational structures.

Marketing Operations and Services

Design and analysis of the structure of the marketing function, therefore, depends upon understanding the existing structure and providing a rationale by which the structure can be adjusted to accommodate various marketing programs. In most contemporary organizations, the basic structure involves separation of marketing operations and marketing services. Adjustments to this basic structure are based primarily upon geography, products, or customers. Exhibit 5-5 summarizes these bases.

The basic division of marketing activities into services and operations is in essence an adaptation of the traditional line/staff division of managerial responsibilities. Operations generally is dominated by the selling function, but might also include such activities as advertising and physical distribution. The marketing services function includes such activities as marketing information, customer service, sales training, and legal liaison.

In many organizations, the marketing services manager has primary responsibility for marketing planning. It is assumed that efficiency requires that planning be separated from implementing (operations). Planners who are professionally trained and are not embroiled in day-to-day operating decisions are thought to be better equipped to plan marketing activities. While these are pertinent points, it can also be argued that this separation removes from the planning function the very expertise achieved by actual management of day-to-day problems. For this reason, some organizations place the marketing planning activity under operations, and/or make some provision for coordination of planning and operating activities.

Decentralization of Marketing Operations

As the organization grows in size and complexity, it often becomes

Exhibit 5-5 Bases for Structuring the Marketing Function

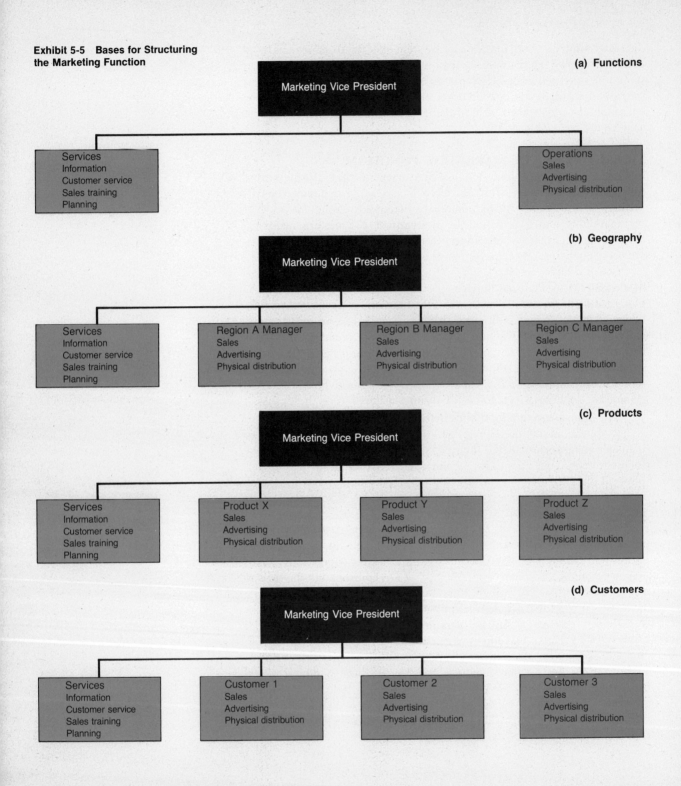

(a) Functions

Marketing Vice President

Services
Information
Customer service
Sales training
Planning

Operations
Sales
Advertising
Physical distribution

(b) Geography

Marketing Vice President

Services
Information
Customer service
Sales training
Planning

Region A Manager
Sales
Advertising
Physical distribution

Region B Manager
Sales
Advertising
Physical distribution

Region C Manager
Sales
Advertising
Physical distribution

(c) Products

Marketing Vice President

Services
Information
Customer service
Sales training
Planning

Product X
Sales
Advertising
Physical distribution

Product Y
Sales
Advertising
Physical distribution

Product Z
Sales
Advertising
Physical distribution

(d) Customers

Marketing Vice President

Services
Information
Customer service
Sales training
Planning

Customer 1
Sales
Advertising
Physical distribution

Customer 2
Sales
Advertising
Physical distribution

Customer 3
Sales
Advertising
Physical distribution

necessary to decentralize some marketing activities. This is particularly true for marketing operations; marketing services often remain centralized at an organization's headquarters. (The decentralization of marketing services is often the hallmark of a conglomerate company—such as International Telephone and Telegraph or Gulf and Western, Inc.). The most useful bases for decentralizing operations are geography, products, and customers.

1. Geographically Based Marketing Organization—Geography is perhaps the most common basis for decentralizing marketing activities. Many companies have branch sales offices; department stores and banks (in most states) have surburban branches; and magazines such as *Time* and *Reader's Digest* publish regional editions.

2. Product-Based Marketing Structure—Many companies that offer different types of products organize their marketing activities along product lines. General Motors, for example, has Chevrolet, Pontiac, Buick, Oldsmobile, and Cadillac divisions; and IBM has different sales forces for its computers, copiers, and typewriters. In the packaged goods industries—notably household products and foods—the product manager plays an important role in marketing activities. Exhibit 5-6 describes the product manager system.

3. Customer-Based Marketing Effort—When a company serves different types of customers, it may organize its marketing effort to meet the specific requirements of various customers. Electric utility companies, for example, separate marketing activities to their residential and commercial customers, aircraft manufacturers maintain different sales organizations for military and commercial activities, and steel fabricators have salespersons who specialize, e.g., in railroad, automobile, and construction industries.

These are the commonly cited textbook bases for structuring marketing activities. In fact, the structure of the marketing function of most organizations is usually some hybrid of these elementary forms. This is because every organization is unique—its historical development is not exactly like any other, its managers' skills and personalities are peculiarly their own, and its competitors and customers differ from those of other similar organizations. Particularly if the company is a large and complex one, the marketing function will not be structured in any simple way. And the structure will change with the needs of different marketing programs. However, most marketing structures are basically some combination of the elementary forms reviewed here. Now let us see how the structure of the marketing function operates: the marketing plan.

Exhibit 5-6   The Product-Manager System

The product-manager system began at Procter & Gamble in 1927, when Neil H. McElroy (later P & G president) was assigned to devote his full attention to Camay soap. He did this successfully, and the company began adding other product managers.

Responsibilities of the product manager generally break down into six tasks:

1. Developing a long-range growth and competitive strategy for the product.

2. Preparing an annual marketing plan and sales forecast.

3. Working with advertising and merchandising agencies to develop copy, programs, and campaigns.

4. Stimulating interest in and support of the product among salespersons and distributors.

5. Gathering continuous intelligence on the product's performance, customer attitudes, and new problems and opportunities.

6. Initiating product improvements to meet changing market needs.

Among the qualities needed for successful product managers are:

An obsessive fascination with marketing strategy; an *id* involvement with your brand; genuine creativity; and antigravitational ability to keep balls in the air; an unscratchable itch that makes you question both what is and what isn't; an interest in people; an innate ability to think like consumers; an inherent ability to filter out the unimportant and take action on what's left. ("Eight Traits . . .")

Advantages of the product manager system include the ability of the product manager to harmonize the various activities required for successful marketing of a product, ability to react quickly to problems in the marketplace, and intensive marketing of newer and smaller brands. Moreover, product management is an excellent training ground for promising young executives. It involves them in every area of company operations—marketing, production, and finance.

On the other hand, the product-manager system has certain disadvantages. It introduces many sources of conflict and frustration, e.g., the product manager is not given authority commensurate with his ability; he must rely upon persuasion; he is often treated like a low-level coordinator. This results in rapid turnover of product managers, with consequent damage to sound long-range

planning for the products involved. The product manager is not a real expert in any of the functions with which he must interact. And as the product-manager system becomes more prevalent in the company, costs for personnel and special studies mount. (Perhaps Parkinson's Law applies.)

Experience with market conditions in the early 1970s—rapid inflation, shortages, recession—have caused some companies to turn away from the product manager system. Notable among these are PepsiCo, Purex, Eastman Kodak, and Levi Strauss. These companies are turning more to a functional type of organization structure. And even companies retaining the product manager system, including originator Procter & Gamble, are changing the nature of the job to some extent. Today's product manager must have a broader perspective (greater awareness of supply and societal constraints), more ability in long-range planning and economic analysis, and deeper understanding of the segments to which the product is marketed. The prevailing sentiment seems to be that while the product manager is still important, he is no longer king.

Based on "Eight Traits of A Good Manager," *Marketing Insights*, 2 March 1970, pp. 15–16, copyright 1970 by Crain Communications, Inc., Chicago, Ill. and various news sources.

THE MARKETING PLAN

Planning is deciding now what actions to take in the future. We look briefly at two basic dimensions of planning, then discuss the planning process, and finally focus upon the foundation of the marketing plan: the marketing audit.

Planning Concepts

There are two basic dimensions of planning activities: time (length of planning horizon) and hierarchy (organizational level). Different types of organizational plans can be categorized along these two dimensions, as shown in Exhibit 5-7. In general, the basic classification of planning is that the longer range plans developed at higher levels of the organization are called strategy, while the shorter range, lower level plans for implementing strategy are called tactics. It should be recognized that some fairly long range plans are generated at rather low organizational levels, e.g., commitments to purchase raw materials or repayment schedules for bonded indebtedness. Conversely, at times it may be necessary for top level managers to become involved in planning on rather short notice, e.g., when disaster (a hurricane or a summons from the Federal Trade Commission) strikes. The former case is an example of routine planning; the latter is crisis.

Second, the line of demarcation between strategy and tactics should be clearly specified. In terms of timing, the traditional dividing point is one year: strategy is planning for a longer period and tactics is concerned with activities during one year. For many organizations, the long-range planning horizon is five years. But organizations vary greatly here. The forests of Weyerhauser Corporation require 40- to 75-year planning cycles, while a high-fashion merchandiser may consider the next 90 days to be long range. The organization-level dividing line between strategy (high-level planning) and tactics (lower-level implementation) is therefore difficult to generalize about, but should be defined as precisely as possible for a given organization.

Since the future is likely to bring increased scope to marketing opportunities and threats, a faster pace of environmental change, and higher costs of organizational mistakes, we can expect to see increasing attention to strategic planning in an organization. This implies more attention to formal planning processes, more operational statements of organizational objectives, more sophisticated analyses of opportunities and the organization's ability to respond to them, better integration of organizational activities, and closer control of organizational performance. Thus, the marketing planning process should be a valuable and familiar tool of marketing management.

The Marketing Planning Process

The marketing plan prescribes the specific decisions and actions to be taken as each marketing management function is performed. Exhibit 5-8 illustrates the process of marketing planning.

As we noted in opening this chapter, an organization is a system performing functions of production, finance, and marketing in order to achieve organizational objectives. Thus, the marketing plan assumes that

Exhibit 5-7   Planning Dimensions

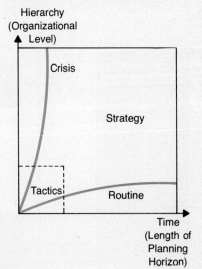

Chapter 5   The Marketing Function in an Organization   175

Exhibit 5-8   The Marketing Planning Process

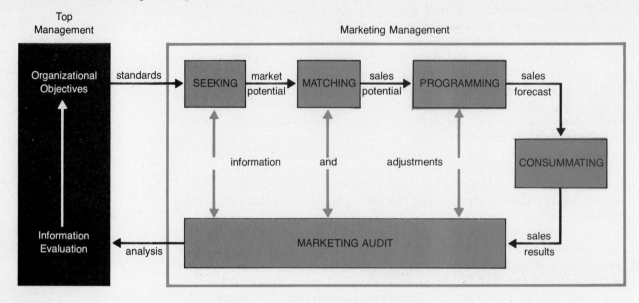

the organization's mission statement and basic objective criteria have been determined, and that a hierarchy of objectives has been formulated in operational terms for each function. Then the marketing plan can be developed in terms of the marketing management functions of seeking, matching, programming, and consummating.

The marketing plan begins with the establishment of performance standards, e.g., total sales by product line, market share in various markets, profit contributions per sales territory, and so forth. Viewing standards as objectives to be attained, marketing management seeks customers. More specifically, the first task of marketing management is to identify target market segments, to assess the responsiveness of these segments, and to determine their significance to organizational objectives. This is accomplished by estimating segment demand, i.e., determining the total demand available to all organizations offering products in this segment, given the environmental conditions and trends of a specific time period. The "output" of the seeking step is the market potential for each possible segment.

No matter how great the market potential, an organization usually cannot reasonably expect to satisfy the total market. To put it another way, no matter how much the marketing manager desires to completely satisfy the demands of target markets, relationships with the other two groups of constituents, suppliers and society, limit the manager's ability to do so.

The supply of products is determined primarily by the organizational situation. An organization may have policies prohibiting satisfaction of certain types of customers (e.g., advertising that our liquor will induce inebriation faster than Brand X), or its resources might be too limited to take advantage of opportunities offered. Even a firm with vast resources at its command would want to concentrate these resources on the most lucrative alternatives; therefore other possible markets may not be served.

On the other hand, the environmental situation may limit the ability of an organization to serve various markets. It may be that competitors are too deeply entrenched in a given market—as RCA found out when it attempted to market computer mainframes. Economic conditions deter sales of certain products, e.g., demand for automobiles and other durable goods such as dishwashers and washing machines contracts during periods of economic recession and expands during prosperity. Public policy is an increasingly stringent constraint upon the actions of many marketers. Products must be designed more carefully to meet health and safety regulations, advertising must be scrutinized for possible deception, prices must be conspicuously posted, and so on. And concern for the physical environment is rising; products must not pollute the air and water, must make less noise, and must use finite natural resources more efficiently.

The matching stage involves assessing the impact of these constraints upon target market potentials, and selecting those target markets that promise the highest level of organizational goal attainment. The output of the matching stage is projection of sales potential, i.e., the amount of sales that the organization can be expected to get, given various levels of program marketing effort.

The third stage in the marketing plan, therefore, is to determine the appropriate marketing program, i.e., mix of product features, promotion messages, distribution methods and pricing policies that will best meet organizational objectives. Developing the marketing program is not an easy task. A number of decisions must be made for each element in the mix, and then the mix must be integrated and budgeted. Chapters 9–12 are devoted to such considerations. The output of the programming step is a sales forecast. This is the amount of sales that we expect to get during the current planning period. Recall from your basic accounting classes that the sales forecast is the beginning point for production and financial planning.

All of this planning will be to no avail if the exchange transaction is not consummated. Thus the consummating step is an essential aspect of marketing management. The step consists of all those little details necessary to make the sale. More specifically, consummating is the task of making sure the four channel flows (physical product, payment, information, and use rights) have been completed. The outcome of the consummating step is sales results. Actual sales results need to be analyzed in light of performance standards so that deviations can be noted, and corrective action taken where necessary. In many organizations, such analysis is part of the consummating step. A more sophisticated approach, however, is to conduct a separate marketing audit.

The Marketing Audit

Intelligent planning must begin with an assessment of the current situation. The dictionary defines an audit as "a formal or official examination and verification of an account; a methodological examination and review." The annual accounting audit is an example familar to students of business. The marketing audit is similar in concept if less precise in execution. Specifically, a marketing audit is a systematic appraisal of current marketing activities and future prospects. Thus, the marketing audit serves as a descriptive foundation for prescribing strategy and tactics. The purpose of the audit is to define problem areas in terms of questions to which marketing managers should direct attention and specify information required to answer the questions competently.

The audit consists of two stages. The first is *diagnosis,* which involves identifying key constituents for each of the three groups (customers, citizens, and suppliers), enumerating salient environmental features for each segment (the "uncontrollable" factors with which marketing managers must deal), and reviewing the current marketing program (the "controllable" factors: product, promotion, distribution, and pricing policies currently in effect).

The second stage is *prognosis,* in which environmental forces and trends relevant to each segment are identified and then translated into specific opportunities and/or threats to the current marketing program of each segment. Finally the prognosis yields expectations—rough estimates of probable outcomes if present programs are continued and environmental trends and opportunities/threats have been correctly identified. Exhibit 5-9 provides the framework for the marketing audit.

Notice that the audit framework is a matrix identifying key members of constituent groups for diagnosis (where are we now?) and prognosis (where are we going?). This matrix provides an overall perspective on the organization's marketing activities. Such a global perspective would be appropriate for the chief marketing officer. Responsibility for various rows in the matrix would be assigned to various subordinates. In a large organization such as Procter & Gamble, for example, ultimate consumer markets might be divided into segments along the product lines: soaps and detergents, toothpaste, potato chips, etc. The brand managers could then focus on the marketing programs of different brands within each product segment. The Tide soap manager would be concerned with such decisions as the current product formula, advertising campaign, and price deals in light of external factors such as programs of competitors, views of environmentalists, and actions of public policy makers. Trends in con-

Exhibit 5-9   The Marketing Audit Matrix

CONSTITUENTS	Diagnosis				Prognosis		
	Seeking	Matching	Programming	Consummating	Trends	Expectations (Assumptions)	Threats/ Opportunities
Customers:							
Consumers							
Middlemen							
Facilitating Agents							
Suppliers							
Organizational							
External							
Society							
Competitors							
Regulators							
Influencers							

sumer demand and shifts in external factors would be translated into opportunities and threats to the Tide brand, and expectations might be phrased in terms of gains in market share, for Tide and for competitors.

On the next row of the matrix, the P & G sales force might concentrate upon middlemen. The sales force is segmented geographically, and within geographic segments along institutional lines: large retail chains, wholesalers who resell to smaller grocery stores, institutions such as schools and hospitals, and so on. The current program concern at this level would focus upon performance of salespersons in territories, in light of such external factors as competitors' salespersons, new interpretations of the Robinson-Patman Act, and strikes by railway personnel which hamper shipping. Again trends noted in the diagnosis would be translated into opportunities and threats, and summarized in terms of the general sales manager's expectations for the sales force.

Other rows in the matrix would be similarly developed. For example, the most useful facilitating agents in this case are likely to be marketing research firms, advertising agencies, common carriers (railroads, trucks), and management consultants. Performance of each of these agents would be diagnosed in terms of the programs, supplier and/or societal element that they were concentrating on.

hamper shipping. Again trends noted in the diagnosis would be translated into opportunities and threats, and summarized in terms of the general sales manager's expectations for the sales force.

Other rows in the matrix would be similarly developed. For example, the most useful facilitating agents in this case are likely to be marketing research firms, advertising agencies, common carriers (railroads, trucks), and management consultants. Performance of each of these agents would be diagnosed in terms of the programs, supplier and/or societal element that they were concentrating on.

Ideally, the marketing audit stages of diagnosis and prognosis are carried out in explicit written form for each of the constituent groups in all three categories. In fact, this is rarely the case. In the first place, the actual manager would have such familiarity with the situation that such a procedure would be unnecessarily cumbersome. Second, most managers do not yet realize the validity of examining relationships with citizens and suppliers in marketing terms.

Usual practice nothwithstanding, my strong opinion is that every marketing manager should use such a framework explicitly as a foundation for marketing decision making in the same sense that an experienced pilot always uses a checklist. Most pilots are confident that they could handle the details of take-off, flying, and landing without a checklist. But few ever do. They realize that there is always the danger that a particular item might be overlooked or performed out of sequence. The checklist serves as a comprehensive, systematic approach to the job of piloting an aircraft. In the same sense, the marketing audit framework will supplement, not supplant, managerial judgement and expertise. Even if I could not convince practicing managers to use the framework explicitly, I would strongly urge students exposed to marketing for the first time to do so.

The information in each part of the marketing audit matrix can be developed to the degree required by the manager responsible for that aspect of the marketing program, given the supplier and societal constraints that exist at a particular time. Thus, the marketing audit is potentially a powerful tool for providing a sound foundation for the development of organizational objectives and marketing strategy and tactics. We shall use this tool extensively in succeeding chapters.

CONCLUDING NOTE

It is difficult to overemphasize the importance of marketing in an organization. Whether the organization is a manufacturing giant, a multinational trading company, a corner grocery store, a political party, a labor union, a museum, or whatever—it has a marketing function. The organization has no choice about performing marketing activities; but its management does determine how well or how badly these activities are performed.

The thrust of this chapter is normative. It focuses upon how organizations should determine objectives, structure the market function, and develop the marketing plan. Most marketing managers do not approach their responsibilities in so formal a manner, but I am convinced that they should. At least the weight of the evidence seems to indicate that, by and large, the more marketing-oriented an organization's management, the more systematically it determines its objectives, and the more comprehensively it plans, then the greater is the likelihood of successful attainment of organizational objectives.

In studying marketing management, therefore, you should learn to use the concepts and techniques presented here. Learning comes from constant practice and application. Look for marketing situations which you can analyze, using the material in this chapter. As you apply this material, modify it and adapt it to increase its usefulness to you. You may find that these marketing principles become trusty companions in your quest for knowledge and understanding.

KEY TERMS AND CONCEPTS

Organizational Objectives
   profit maximization
   hierarchy of objectives
Organizational Resources
   capital
   physical resources
   human resources
   information
Organizational Functions
   production
   finance
   marketing
   organizational conflict
The Marketing Concept
   organizational purpose
   mission
   basic criteria
Differential Advantage
   customer-oriented
   supplier-oriented
   societally oriented

Structure of Marketing Function
   services
   operations
   geography
   product
   customer
Planning Concepts
   hierarchy
   timing
Planning Process
   seeking
   matching
   programming
   consummating
Marketing Audit
   constituents
   diagnosis
   prognosis

QUESTIONS FOR DISCUSSION

1. Use the systems concept to identify the components of several organizations, e.g., a local department store, a unit of a national department store chain (Sears or J. C. Penney), a retail service station, your university,

your campus fraternity or sorority, a national package goods manufacturer (Procter & Gamble), a manufacturer of rifles and hand-guns, an organization to legalize personal use of marijuana.

2. For the organizations that you listed in question 1, describe how the marketing concept might apply; also note possible supplier and societal constraints on the concept. Would some of these organizations be more likely than others to adopt the marketing concept? If so, which ones and why? If not, why not?

3. How could each of the organizations of question 1 improve its differential advantage? Consider possible customer-, supplier- and so-cially-oriented approaches. Evaluate the strengths and weaknesses of your suggestions.

4. After reviewing the marketing planning process model, close the book and describe this model verbally. With the book still closed, briefly sketch the major elements of the model. Now apply it to the marketing activities you identified in question 2, i.e., point out the marketing functions for each situation. How does this model help to structure your thinking about those situations? What modifications did you make? Why?

5. Prepare a marketing audit for one or more of the organizations examined in question 1. Be sure to identify significant constituents, and list the types of information you would need for a thorough diagnosis and prognosis.

SUGGESTED READING

1. Russell L. Ackoff.
A Concept of Corporate Planning. New York: Wiley-Interscience, 1970. Ackoff discusses corporate planning at a conceptual level; excellent, readable overview of planning concepts and a fine introduction to the work of this outstanding management scholar; extensive bibliography.

2. Peter F. Drucker.
Managing for Results. New York: Harper and Row, 1964. A masterful statement of the role and scope of the manager's job, emphasizing the importance of the marketing function. *Management.* New York: Harper and Row, 1973. Encyclopedic expansion of 1964 statement; excellent reference.

3. Fremont E. Kast and James E. Rosenzweig.
Organization and Management: A Systems Approach, 2nd ed. New York: McGraw-Hill Book Company, 1975. Standard text in organizational behavior and management, utilizing the systems perspective.

4. Warren J. Keegan.
"Multi-National Marketing Strategy and Organization: An Overview." *Changing Marketing Systems.* American Marketing Association, 1967, pp.

203–209. Overview of the management of marketing activities using international examples; reprinted in Gabriel M. Gelb and Betsy D. Gelb, 2nd ed., *Insights for Marketing Management.* Goodyear Publishing Company, 1977.

5. Betsy D. Gelb, Gabriel M. Gelb and Ricky W. Griffin.
"Managing with the Consumer's Help," *Business Horizons,* April 1976, pp. 69–74. Clear, insightful exposition of the importance of customers in attaining organizational objectives; reprinted in Gelb and Gelb, *Insights for Marketing Management.*

6. George A. Steiner.
Top Management Planning. New York: The Macmillan Company, 1969. Standard reference in the field of management planning; very comprehensive, yet not difficult reading; contains many examples and references.

CASE 4 / AT&T: COMPETITION, REGULATION AND THE JUSTICE DEPARTMENT

The American Telephone and Telegraph Company is one of the largest corporations in the United States. And it is, perhaps, the largest of a select group of the world's corporations: a privately owned, profit-seeking "natural monopoly." Few would deny its boast that it provides the world's best telephone service, and its stock is considered a safe investment for the proverbial widows and orphans. Today, however, AT&T faces troubled times.

The Company

By any measure, AT&T is the dominant company in the 40-billion dollar telecommunications industry. Although there are some 1700 telephone companies, AT&T with 140 million telephones controls 82 percent of the U.S. total. AT&T has over $100 billion in assets. It is composed of 23 operating companies (Illinois Bell, Southwestern Bell, Pacific Bell, etc.), Longlines (the long distance network), Bell Laboratories (research and development) and Western Electric (manufacturing and supply).

The company's stated objective is total telephone service—"end-to-end-responsibility." That is, AT&T wants to provide the telephone instruments, the lines, the switching equipment, and the service facilities necessary for one person to telephone another. It prefers to rent the equipment and to make monthly charges for service. AT&T's rate structure is extremely complex. It is based upon the "Uniform System of Accounts," an accounting system developed before 1900 and still in use today. Briefly, this system capitalizes virtually every type of expenditure, and slowly depreciates that capital (generally by the straight line depreciation method) over as long a period as 20 years. This system enables the company to legally report Return On Investment in the 6 to 8 percent range specified by most state regulatory commissions, while enjoying pretax profits in the 25 to 30 percent of revenue range. Although it is difficult to estimate the impact of this rate structure upon individual customers, the consensus of experts seems to be that single-line residential customers are favored by the accounting system. These customers appear to be subsidized by long-distance users, business customers, and users of such equipment as color sets, touch tone dialing, multiple extensions, and so on.

Regulation

As the world's largest profit-seeking "natural monopoly" AT&T is certainly one of the most regulated organizations in history. At the federal level, AT&T is under the jurisdiction of the Federal Communications Commission. The FCC sets overall policy for the telephone industry, including equipment standards, depreciation schedules, and rate structures for long-distance service. In addition, each of the 23 Bell operating companies is regulated by a state utilities commission in all states except Texas. In that state, there is no state regulatory body so each municipality regulates the telephone company or companies within its incorporated area. The utility commission determines rate structures for local service and intrastate calls, and they determine boundaries that divide the "natural monopolies" of the various companies.

Thus AT&T is subject to a bewildering variety of often conflicting regulatory policies. In addition, AT&T extends its natural monopoly on telephone service through its research and development subsidiary (Bell Labs) and its manufacturing and supply subsidiary (Western Electric) to telephone equipment. Thus, AT&T can set the pace of introduction of new technology and therefore control to a large extent telephone industry performance and service standards. Similarly, through its control and administration of its Longlines department which sets operating policies for the intrastate long-distance network, AT&T effectively controls other telephone companies, since the equipment of these companies must be connected to AT&T long-distance lines.

The Marketplace

There is no question that AT&T dominates the telephone industry. But competition is increasing, primarily in three areas: equipment, long-distance service, and data transmission.

Source: Adapted by the author from reports in *Business Week* July 27, 1974; November 30, 1974; March 15, 1976; and June 7, 1976; and other news sources.

In the landmark Cartefone case in 1968, the Federal Communications Commission ruled that non-Bell equipment could be attached to AT&T telephone lines. This ruling opened the market to manufacturers of telephone sets, switch boards, interoffice communications, etc. Smaller manufacturers such as Stromberg-Carlson have taken advantage of this opportunity, and large firms such as RCA are interested.

In 1969, the FCC ruled in the specialized-carrier decision that long-distance messages could be transmitted by means other than AT&T longlines and then patched into telephone equipment. The major beneficiary of this decision is Microwave Communications, Inc. MCI supplies microwave channels for carrying long-distance messages between pairs of major cities, such as Chicago and St. Louis, Houston and Dallas, New York and Washington, D.C. Needless to say, other suppliers of microwave services are extremely interested in this potentially lucrative market. Moreover, the rapid rise of citizens' band radios foreshadows additional sources of competition in the voice communications area.

The third, and potentially most significant, area of competition for AT&T is data transmission. One of the consequences of the computer revolution is the increasing need to transmit computer data over long distances. For example, a company transmits sales data from branches to the home office computer for analysis, branch banks transmit data to regional clearinghouses, the National Aeronautics and Space Administration transmits data via satellite, and so on. Provision of this service puts AT&T potentially in competition with International Business Machines, Inc. In marked contrast to firms such as Cartefone, Inc. and MCI, Inc., IBM is an industrial giant. Its revenues are in excess of $12 billion annually, and it enjoys a compound growth rate of 12 to 14 percent per year, with no sign of slowdown. And the dollar volume involved in data processing and transmission is almost $60 billion in total. Competition for so lucrative a market may become fierce in a hurry.

The telephone and data-processing industries approach their customers differently. AT&T and other telephone carriers are natural monopolies, IBM and its computer and data-processing rivals constitute one of the world's most competitive growth industries. The computer makers are determined not to be "regulated out" of the logical extensions of their market-sector of data communications equipment, computer-network systems, and a wide variety of so-called teleprocessing products that combine information processing and communications functions.

Public Policy Issues

The issues faced by public policy makers are complex and significant. Basically, the question is one of competition versus regulation. The unregulated firms, such as IBM, MCI and Cartefone, stress marketing. They are extremely sensitive to customers' desires, and gear production and financial practices to the demands of the constantly changing marketplace. For example, these firms invest heavily in research and development, and use the most-rapid depreciation policies sanctioned by the Internal Revenue Service. This results in a steady stream of technological and style of improvements in their products.

By contrast, AT&T follows the philosophy that, given its monopoly position, its markets are assured. Its top executives have almost universally risen through operating, engineering, and financial ranks. They generally are not attuned to marketing and innovations. In fact, a corporate vice president of marketing for AT&T was appointed for the first time in 1973. In the wake of the Cartefone and specialized-carrier decisions, AT&T under then-chairman H.I. Romnes took the position that competition might be advantageous for the industry. In 1973, however, new chairman John B. deButts announced that AT&T would prefer more regulation. Indeed, it never really gave up. The 1968 and 1969 FCC decisions are still under appeal.

The public policy battle is now being waged on a broader front. The U.S. Justice Department has filed an antitrust suit under the Sherman Act against AT&T. The Justice suit has two major goals: (1) divestiture of Western Electric and perhaps Bell Labs; and (2) separation of AT&T's Longlines Division from some or all of the 23 operating companies.

There are difficulties here. Western Electric alone would be ten times as large as any other current manufacturer of telephone equipment. Thus, it might be necessary to break WE into two or more independent companies. Of course, if the manufacture of telephone equipment were opened up in this way, larger companies such as RCA and General Electric might be attracted to it. Bell Labs also poses something of a problem. Much of its applied research could be incorporated into operations of Western Electric. But Bell Labs also does significant basic research, and its skills in this area are an acknowledged national resource. It has been suggested that perhaps Bell Labs should operate under government direction in much the same way as the National Aeronautics and Space Administration does. Similarly, separating the Longlines Division from the operating companies would not be easy to do. Some of the operating companies, such as New York Telephone Company and Pacific Telephone and Telegraph, are industrial giants in their own right. Each of these companies enjoys operating revenues of almost $8 billion per year.

AT&T's Position

AT&T will fight. Chairman deButts maintains that competition and/or divestiture would destroy the common carrier principle of providing phone service at roughly equal rates regardless of differences of costs. He maintains that regulation and competition do not mix. It is logical, he argues, that competitors will go after the high profit products (equipment, long distance service, etc.), while the regulated telephone companies (which by law must serve all customers) will be left with the less profitable residential and rural segments of the business.

Other telephone companies have joined forces with AT&T. Theodore F. Brophy, president of General Telephone and Electronics Corporation, which draws half its $5 billion revenues from telephone operations, notes the example of Consolidated Edison (the mammoth electric power utility in New York) which had to suspend dividends to stockholders because competition-oriented regulatory decisions "upset the delicate financial structure" of the major public utility.

In March 1976, AT&T announced that it will focus an all-out political effort on Congress to reverse recent regulatory and judicial decisions. Basically, the thrust of telephone-industry sponsored legislation would stop competition in long-distance service, permit AT&T or other traditional carriers to acquire the companies that would be put out of business, and revoke jurisdiction of the FCC over technical and operating standards that affect terminal and accessory equipment attached to local telephone facilities.

Obviously, such legislation would put companies such as MCI, Datran, and Southern Pacific Communications out of business. So the planned legislation would exempt AT&T from antitrust sanctions. Moreover,

the AT&T plan proposes to give state utility commissions, instead of the FCC, regulatory control over customer-owned equipment. This could mean that the telephone-answering machines or data terminals might be legally connected to telephone lines in some states, but not in others. Telephone companies and regulators are well aware of the difficulties any national distributor would face competing in fifty different regulatory environment dominions.

Public policy makers are quite interested, to say the least. AT&T is widely respected for its political muscle, although it seldom shows its power on a national level. This time, however, AT&T has done its homework. It is backed by most of the 1700 independent telephone companies, and such powerful unions as the Communications Workers of America. With this backing, it has already lined up 12 senators and 119 representatives to co-sponsor the bill.

In response, AT&T's competitors have banded together, and amassed a war chest of $500,000 to oppose the legislation. Known as the Ad Hoc Committee for Competitive Telecommunications (ACCT), the group is comprised of MCI, U.S. Transmissions Systems Inc. (a joint venture owned by International Telephone & Telegraph, Inc. and Transco Companies), Data Transmissions Company (Datran), Graphnec Systems Inc, and Southern Pacific Communications Companies.

ACCT plans to marshall support from users of private communication services and the companies that have entered the equipment supply field in the past five years. Such an effort could eventually result in support by such major companies as IBM, RCA, General Electric, and Honeywell. ACCT charges that "AT&T lost its battle with the FCC and the courts and now has turned to Congress as a forum of last resort." Its president calls the threat of higher home telephone rates "one of the phoniest (sic) issues I have ever heard."

At this point, no one can predict how Congress will react. The choice between monopoly and competition is a fundamental one for public policy makers. The issue is likely to be in litigation for years.

CASE 5 / CAN FREE ENTERPRISE SOLVE THE ENERGY CRISIS?

The citizens of the United States enjoy the highest standard of living in the world. Among the important foundations upon which that standard of living rests is energy usage. With six percent of the world's population, the United States consumes, in a given year, one-third of the world's total energy production. Most Americans have, until recently, taken this striking fact for granted.

Suddenly—at least it seems sudden to most Americans—energy is neither cheap nor abundant. Politicians proclaim "an energy crisis." There is much emphasis on fixing the blame for this crisis upon one group or another, and some attention is beginning to be focused on attempts to solve the myriad problems involved.

One group which has a major stake in the situation is the nation's privately owned, integrated oil companies. Their position is that their combined efforts—guided by the "invisible hand" of competition—can solve the problem. This case examines that position. It looks first at the nature of the basic problem, and the time table for solution as viewed by the oil companies. Factors influencing the solution are reviewed, and then resources and action required by various groups are analyzed. Finally, the need for a program for "marketing" their solution by the oil companies is outlined.

The Problem

The problem, as the oil companies see it, is to provide sufficient energy to maintain the life style of the United States. This objective is based on the assumption of continual growth of a basically market-oriented economy, changing and adapting in evolutionary fashion—as opposed to drastic or revolutionary shifts in styles or standards of living, multinational economic conditions, technological progress, or governmental policies. It is an ambitious goal.

Ideally, the oil companies envision a time table such as that presented in Case Exhibit 5-1. The crucial year is 1975. Because of the long lead time required for exploration and adding refinery and transportation capacity, the oil companies call for massive investments in the processes required to produce petroleum by con-

ventional methods. At the same time, they call for additional significant investments in research into alternative sources of fuel. They recognize that this will be a time of rising import costs and product prices.

Case Exhibit 5-1   Projected Timetable for Solution to Energy Crisis

---

1975 — Massive investment begins—in domestic, offshore, and international oil exploration; in conventional refinery and transportation capacity; in research. Rising petroleum import costs and product prices.

1980 — Imports provide 40 percent of U.S. domestic needs. Situation improves as crude from Alaska and expanded use of coal add to supplies.

1985 — Oil imports reduced to 15 percent of total domestic needs as earlier exploration, increased capacity and improved recovery techniques boost domestic supplies. Beginning contributions by nuclear power, coal liquification and gasifition, and oil shale.

1990 — Research in alternative energy sources—geothermal, synthetic fuels (urethane from garbage, ethanol from trees), nuclear power, begins to contribute to supplies.

1995 — Oil production peaks. Alternative forms of energy perfected to replace dependence on petroleum.

2000 — Long range research in alternative fuel sources pays off—declining oil production supplanted, chiefly by nuclear fusion and solar power (which are virtually inexhaustible).

Provided that these commitments are made in the 1970s, the companies see the situation worsening through the early 1980s, then beginning to improve as conventional petroleum production methods increase supplies. By 1985, alternative sources of supply will begin to appear, so that when petroleum production peaks in the 1990s, alternative fuel supplies will have taken up the slack. This is an optimistic scenario. Its achievement will depend on many factors.

Factors Influencing the Situation

The number of factors which influence this situation is large. To facilitate discussion, these factors have been grouped into four categories: economic, sociocultural, physical, and governmental.

Economic Factors.   The economic situation in the

Source: Prepared by the author from various news sources.

U.S. is difficult at the moment. In early 1975, the inflation rate was down (!) to seven or eight percent from the 1974 high of 12 to 14 percent. But this reduction has been achieved mainly at the expense of lower productivity; many industries are operating far below capacity and the general unemployment rate is in the neighborhood of eight percent. In addition, the international economic situation is at least as bad as that in the United States. Worldwide demand for oil has expanded greatly, and much of the petroleum available for export is controlled by a classic monopoly cartel—the Organization of Petroleum Exporting Countries (OPEC). Hard times generally focus attention upon short-range actions. The kind of long-range, far-seeing economic decision making envisioned by the oil companies is difficult in this kind of economic climate.

Sociocultural Factors. There is no question that public opinion toward the oil companies is generally unfavorable, perhaps even hostile. John E. Swearingen, Chairman of Standard Oil Company (Indiana), contends that allegations against the oil industry portray it as using objectives and methods that differ little from those of organized crime. To some extent, this attitude is the result of rather low levels of economic literacy on the part of the public, he believes.

Swearingen points out, for example, that dramatic gains in the oil company earnings in the past two years have to be put into perspective. "A motorist who spent an hour in a line at a service station in order to reach a pump at which he was allowed to buy ten gallons of gasoline at a higher price than he ever paid before could be expected to react strongly to dramatic reports of record oil company earnings." Swearingen maintains that it is no trick for "demagogues" to attack the oil companies as profiteers, and perhaps as having engineered the entire shortage situation.

Of course, some of these charges are exaggerated. The energy crisis is real, and the dramatic earnings gains by oil companies in the last two years have only raised them to average profitability among U.S. corporations. But the oil companies have contributed to their own image problems. They have tended to emphasize their responsibilities to shareholders, perhaps at the expense of responsibilities to customers, employees, and the public at large. Such factors as illicit campaign contributions, pressure upon independent distributors, and bribery-tainted agreements with for-

eign governments have not cast the oil companies in a very favorable light.

Physical Factors. The fact is that most of the oil that is easy to find and extract from the earth has been found, and much of it is under the control of foreign governments. The development of new petroleum resources, therefore, becomes increasingly more difficult and more expensive. At the same time, there is emphasis upon environmental protection, e.g., pollution control, maintenance of wilderness areas, safeguards against catastrophe, and so on.

Public Policy. Perhaps the most pervasive set of factors influencing the energy situation is in the area of public policy. The oil industry is regulated by a bewildering variety of agencies, statutes, and jurisdictions—both domestic and international. The petroleum industry was one of the first to be placed under federal price controls, and is one of the few remaining industries so controlled. Agencies ranging from the Environmental Protection Agency to the Federal Trade Commission to state utilities commissions regulate every phase of oil industry activities. Economist Paul Crawford of Texas A&M University estimates that this "red tape" increases by 10 to 25 percent the cost of providing oil and gas. And the oil companies with multinational operations must also cope with the laws and regulations of other nations.

In spite of the heavy emphasis upon regulation, there is no unified, coordinated national policy with respect to energy development and usage. Energy affects national security and the balance of payments, as well as domestic standards of living and rates of productivity and growth. Thus, solving the energy crisis is no easy task. The requirements for a viable solution are not simple.

Requirements for a Solution

The first and most obvious requirement to solve the energy crisis is capital, lots of capital. Estimates range from $1.0 to $1.5 trillion dollars in free-world investments over the next ten years in energy productions. For example, Roscoe Murray of Mobil Oil has calculated that to increase present U.S. refining capacity of 14.3 million barrels of oil per day to 21.4 million barrels of oil per day by 1984, refining capacity must be increased at the rate of 700,000 barrels of oil per day each year. This is equivalent to completing two refineries of 350,000 barrel capacity each year between now and 1985. Each such refinery would cost upwards of half a billion dollars. Ten million tons of steel would be required to build these 20 refineries. And they would take 41,000 man-years of effort on the part of technical personnel, and 306,000 man-years of skilled labor, if construction were to proceed on a uniform scale. In addition, capital must be raised for exploration, for increasing transportation capacity, and for basic and applied research. At a time when the federal budget deficit is estimated to be in the range of 60 to 70 billion dollars (raising fears that private capital requirements will be "crowded out" of capital markets), the capital requirements of the energy industry seem enormous.

A second major requirement, therefore, is that public policy toward the oil business be structured so as to facilitate the free-enterprise approach to the energy crisis. Oil men, for example, would like price controls on "old oil" and on natural gas at the wellhead removed. They would like an easing, or a least a moratorium, on air pollution standards, so that high sulphur fuel oil and coal could be burned for fuel. Oil men would welcome fewer directives from the Federal Energy Administration, and would be very happy if such proposals by the Federal Trade Commission as the "line of business" reporting regulations, and the antitrust suit against the eight major oil companies were dropped. They argue for streamlining procedures to get refinery construction and operating permits, and to settle complaints by environmentalists. The "wish-list" of specific de-regulations goes on and on.

At the same time that oil men argue for less interference with the market mechanism, they lobby strongly for a floor on oil prices—to protect domestic investments in high-cost recovery of oil, and in alternative power sources such as coal liquification and gasification. Most oil officials feel that a price in the range of seven to eight dollars per barrel would be required to assure decreasing dependence upon foreign supplies of oil. They point out that farmers seek such price supports for their crops, and that energy is as essential to modern civilization as food. And they stress the significant national security implications of being dependent upon foreign oil.

The Marketing Challenge

As these reviews of capital and public policy requirements illustrate, the key requirement for a private-enterprise solution to the energy crisis is public confidence in the oil industry. Perhaps the most fundamental requirement of this approach is that the public understand the role of free enterprise. This involves educating consumers, public policy makers, and society in general as to the role of competition in promoting progress, and the role of profits in generating capital for investment and stimulating investor confidence.

Oil company officials for too long have talked to each other and rarely to anyone else. The current energy shortage was forecast as early as the 1950s, but company figures were proprietary. The public was not informed. This is changing. The industry is now attempting to market the idea that the free enterprise system can solve the energy crisis.

CASE 6 / ARMCO STEEL CO.: FROM POLLUTION TO PATRON

Armco Steel Corporation is the fourth largest steel company in the U.S. Its home offices are in Middletown, Ohio. The Houston works, Armco in Houston, is the largest integrated steel manufacturing plant on tidewater west of the Mississippi River. The Houston works employs 4,500 people, has an annual payroll of over $60 million, and pays more than $4 million in state and local taxes.

Generally, a company of such substantial stature in the community is regarded favorably by citizens. Unfortunately, this generalization could not accurately be applied to Armco Steel in Houston. In the late 1960s and early 1970s, Armco was Houston's horrible example of community relations. Armco had an image problem.

The Problem

Almost from the day that pollution became an issue in Houston, Armco has been identified with it. Between 1968 and 1972, the company faced both air and water pollution suits.

A survey of newspaper clippings from the local press during the 1968–72 period, as they reported on the charges and countercharges and the ensuing litigation, showed but one favorable mention of Armco. More than one hundred articles reported Armco unfavorably. This trend is best exemplified by the comments of Harold Scarlett, the respected environmental editor of the *Houston Post*:

> Armco is the number one polluter. They are on the ship channel [the manmade canal connecting the Port of Houston with the Gulf of Mexico]. Armco and other companies on the channel do as little as they can to comply, and then they scream bloody murder when the rules are changed. This is not short-sighted on their part so far as dividends to stockholders are concerned. We need an enforcement agency. The polluters are caught and tagged, and then escape in the court battles . . .

In 1972, Armco settled the water-pollution suit, paying a penalty of $125,000, the largest fine assessed, as of then. A second suit, concerning the alleged violation of Texas Air Control standards, was settled with payment of a $250,000 penalty. These facts made news, and Armco's image sank.

The Players

The players in this drama included the public, reporters for the broadcast and print media, various courts and county pollution control officers, and responsible Armco officials. Armco management knew that public opinion was unfavorable, but they did not realize how bad an image Armco had until it conducted a telephone survey. Results of the survey are shown in the accompanying table. The survey showed clearly that Armco's image was much worse than that of four other companies of comparable size and community stature.

Because environmental pollution was (and is) an issue of public concern, reporters took an active interest in it. Armco, largest company on the most polluted body of water in Houston, became a favorite "whipping boy." Public officials took up the challenge. Harris County Attorney Joe Resweber and County Pollution Control Director Dr. Walter Quebedeaux filed several suits; even Texas Attorney General John Hill used Armco as an example of socially irresponsible management.

In early 1973, Armco dispatched to the scene George Hansen, a tall, blunt-spoken steel man with the title of Vice-President, Western Division, and the responsibility for operations of four of its eight major plants, including the Houston Works, the third largest Armco facility. Hansen immediately began to improve the Armco-in-Houston image.

The Plan

Hansen and his public relations counsel, Dale Henderson, Inc., with Ogilvy and Mather, Inc., advertising agency, unveiled Armco's policy for dealing with the problem: *the new broom*. Hansen would sweep away the old problem, and would pull the Houston company into the mainstream of public affairs.

The first sweep of the new broom was a press conference announcing settlement of the air pollution case. This conference was used to squelch rumors and give additional facts to demonstrate the company's

Source: Prepared by the author from interviews with Dale Henderson, Inc. Public Relations and Marketing Counsel.

Case Exhibit 6-1 Company Image Profiles

Houston Company	Doing its best to avoid pollution	Believe official statements made in newspapers	Treats its employees fairly	Would buy stock in this company	Company is asset to Houston
Armco Steel Co.	11%*	20	30	31	46
Giant Steel Co.	25	28	43	51	57
Major Oil Co.	29	30	37	48	69
General Oil Co.	39	43	58	59	76
Power Elec. Co.	50	35	52	49	77

*Table reads "11 percent of a random sample of 208 Houston telephone subscribers agree that Armco is doing its best to avoid pollution."

desire to cooperate with pollution authorities to the fullest extent. Hansen said in part:

> from about the same point in time that pollution became an issue in Houston, our name has been linked with it. The reason we have been identified with pollution right from the start is quite simple— we have been polluting . . . Historically, steel-making has been associated with flame, smoke, and the emissions produced by integrated steel mills. Our plant at the ship channel, with its coke ovens, blast furnace, and related facilities has been highly visible. As steel mills go, the Houston works is one of the cleanest in the world, but that does not necessarily make it clean enough.
>
> We now have a clear directive agreed upon with the state . . . the agreement is tough . . . but realistic . . . it will require an expenditure of $3.5 million for air pollution control equipment, but this figure may be considerably higher, with another $35 to $50 million to follow on our coke-making facilities.

This straight-from-the-shoulder talk caused environmental writer Harold Scarlett to remark, "It looks like Armco has gotten a new lawyer and a new public relations counsel." There were additional press conferences, featuring Hansen and other Armco officials with the same brand of straight talk on the "rocky road to Zero Pollution by 1985." In addition, Armco officials

accepted invitations to speak to community and professional groups, and began mailing a newsletter, the Armco *Communique,* to Houston business and community leaders, and members of the press.

Communication with Armco employees also was vitally important. Armco employees were embarrassed over Armco's reputation, and concerned that the company might solve its problems by closing the Houston works. A series of communiques assured them that the latter was not true, and that steps were being taken to correct the former. These communiques were titled "Speak Up for Armco" (see Case Exhibit 6-2).

As further evidence of Armco's determination to be a good citizen, the company co-sponsored the production of a four-part documentary entitled "TEXAS." Each part was an hour-long outdoor film, written and narrated by popular Houston newscaster Ron Stone, designed to capture the "awesomeness of a state whose boundaries stretch from the Gulf of Mexico to the arid western plains to the far reaches of the Panhandle to the Rio Grande Valley." On the day after the series ran on local television, Armco's community relations advisor, David Haines, personally took 55 phone calls in the first two hours of the business day from schools asking for a print of the documentary to use as a teaching aid.

Case Exhibit 6-2 Speak Up for Armco

"SPEAK UP FOR ARMCO."

This is first in a series of short memos which will keep you from being caught with your facts down the next time someone buttonholes you at a party and starts razzing you about Armco.

Friend says: *Oh, you work for Armco, huh? You're the guys who dump cyanide into the ship channel – right?*

You say: *Wrong! We did at one time but we don't any more. Haven't dumped any since July 1972. The cyanide is being incinerated these days – just like the government asked us to do. We're clean.*

George W. Hansen

GEORGE W. HANSEN

ARMCO IN HOUSTON.

Progress: From Polluter to Patron

The film orders were the first indication that the new broom was beginning to clean up. Armco commissioned a second survey of public attitudes toward its operations. In August, 1973, the follow-up survey showed a significant increase in evaluations of Armco's "efforts at controlling pollution," one of the key criteria. Favorable ratings increased from 34 percent before the new broom to 41 percent. Armco was the only one of the companies surveyed to register a gain on this criterion. Armco's image also increased on the dimension of "believability of public statements made by officials." Results were not totally favorable, however. The company's rating of "fairness to its employees" decreased, and "chances of buying its stock" also fell slightly. Perhaps these results indicate that the new broom was paying too much attention to pollution and not enough to other aspects of corporate image.

Armco's many contributions to socioeconomic gains in the Houston community had been obscured by its dominant identity as a polluter. It was not known as the world's largest buyer of scrap metal, and thus a recycler of millions of tons of junk from urban areas. Nor were its employees properly recognized for their above average contributions to the United Fund. And the thousands of man-hours of labor devoted annually to special community projects were done with nearly complete anonymity.

Moving from strict response to the pollution theme, Armco became Houston's most generous supporter of the opera, became the major contributor to a struggling, youth-oriented drug abuse program, and assured restoration of the area's first black school with a responsible contribution of labor and money. These and other works helped broaden Armco's image as a responsible corporate citizen.

And there were other problems. In building a bag house to catch pollution from one of its plants, Armco ran into successive delays in deliveries of key components, including steel framing and plating for the structure. Trying to end the delays, Armco traced the tardy steel through its contractor down to the subcontractor who placed the order, and found that it had gone to— Armco Steel Corporation! This snafu was typical of the delays and frustrations, the problems and the pitfalls, involved in implementing any program of such scope.

But on the whole, Armco officials were satisfied that progress was being made in changing Armco's image from polluter to community patron. Perhaps the clearest example of the changing image occurred about eight months after the announcement of settlement of the pollution suit. On Thanksgiving Day, 1973, a waterside worker telephoned Works Manager W.N. Rankin to report that thousands of seagulls had appeared on the channel. A closer check showed that the seagulls were feeding on shrimp. Never one to waste an opportunity, Rankin invited Harold Scarlett and other representatives of the Houston media to catch some Ship Channel shrimp at the Armco dock, and join him in a shrimp boil. Scarlett reported that the shirmp, cooked in the plant cafeteria, were "small but succulent, with perhaps a faint taste of oil."

Commented Works Manager Rankin as he nibbled on a shrimp, "We may have to start a seafood division."

QUESTIONS FOR ANALYSIS OF CASES

1. Briefly describe the organization in terms of the marketing relationship framework presented in Chapter 2. Discuss the major constituents in each of the three groups (customers, citizens, and suppliers).

2. What are the major market segments in each group? What is the structure of each market? What are the major environmental trends that influence this market? What opportunities and threats result from these trends?

3. Comment upon the role that public policy plays in this case. Forecast the most likely direction of future public policy as it affects the case. Defend your forecast. In your opinion, which groups in society would be helped, and which would be hurt, if your forecast of public policy impact upon the company in question proves accurate?

4. Consider the organization in the case as a system, as discussed in Chapter 5. Discuss organizational objectives, resources, and functions as they relate to the situation of the case. How would you apply the marketing concept to each situation?

5. Select one market segment and trace the marketing planning process: organizational objectives, seeking, matching, programming, consummating, and the market audit for that segment.

PART 3 MARKETING ANALYSIS AND STRATEGY

After studying this part, you should be able to:

1. Describe the basic buying procedures that individuals or organizations engage in.

2. Explain and analyze the general marketing strategies followed by organizations with which you come in contact.

3. Structure marketing problems in basic, comprehensible decision format.

4. Discuss knowledgeably types, sources, and uses of marketing information.

Wagner International Photos

Editorial cartoon by Pat Oliphant; Copyright ©1973 *Washington Star;* Reprinted with permission of the Los Angeles Times Syndicate.

'FILL 'ER UP, CHECK THE OIL, AND REMOVE THE BUMPER-STICKER!'

6/BUYER BEHAVIOR

We discussed the marketing manager's relationships in Part Two. Now we examine the "target"—the other direct participant in the exchange process: the buyer. Fundamental points covered are:

1. Buying behavior is a process. The stages in the process are perception of want, search, purchase decision, and product use and evaluation.

2. The *economic man* concept sees the buyer as a rational, calculating machine seeking maximum satisfaction. This theory is oversimplified, but it provides a foundation for studying buyer behavior.

3. Personal influences can be categorized as cognitive, affective, and conative. The processes of perception, motivation, and learning shape these components.

4. Interpersonal influences upon buyer behavior operate through norms, reference groups, and opinion leadership. Significant groups in modern society include the family, social class, and culture (including subcultures).

5. The systems approach provides a simple overview of the buying decision. A more sophisticated model is offered by Howard and Sheth.

6. Outputs of the buying decision are attitudinal and/or behavioral changes. Attitudes can be confirmed, created, or changed and behavior may or may not develop regular patterns as the buyer searches for satisfaction.

A housewife selects Cap'n Crunch cereal.

A hospital purchasing agent orders bandages from Americal Hospital Supply.

A family moves into their new home.

An engineer rejects a carload of steel when a sample fails a tensile strength test.

These are examples of the many types of buyer behavior. This topic is of paramount importance to marketing managers because *nothing moves until the sale is made.* Although products are bought for a bewildering variety of reasons and it is difficult to understand completely any given purchasing decision, there are underlying principles of buyer behavior. This chapter focuses on these principles, drawing examples from different types of buying situations. We begin with a look at the nature of buyer behavior.

THE NATURE OF BUYER BEHAVIOR

In this chapter, we are looking at the exchange transaction from the buyer's viewpoint. We look first in this section at the types of buying units, then at the economists' explanation of buyer behavior. A more realistic representation of this type of behavior is the buying process.

The Buying Unit

The chapter opens with four examples of buyer behavior. We chose these examples purposely to illustrate the diverse nature of this type of behavior. The common element in each example, however, is the basic unit of buyer behavior, the buying unit. Exhibit 6-1 categorizes the four types of buying units.

The two characteristics of buying behavior which distinguish types of buying units are the purpose of the purchase and purchase authority. As we noted in Chapter 3, a product may be purchased for consumption, or may be purchased by an organization for use in manufacturing and marketing other products in order to reach its objectives. Purchase authority may be delegated to one individual, or may be shared by two or more people.

The classic example of an individual exercising delegated authority for consumption is the housewife. She may be purchasing a product for her own use, or for consumption by her family, e.g., breakfast cereal. In contrast, when two or more family members share purchase authority, the actions of the buying unit become more complex—as in the case of the family purchasing a new home. Purchasing by organizations can also be accomplished by one individual. This is the case when a hospital purchasing agent orders bandages and other supplies. When the organization purchases more expensive or unusual products, authority to purchase

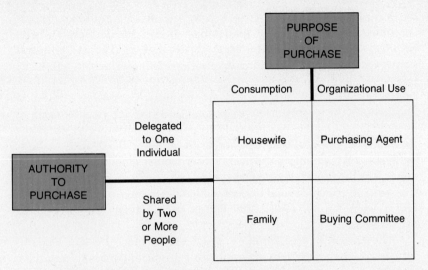

Exhibit 6-1 The Four Types of Buying Behavior

may be shared among members of a buying committee.

In Chapter 3, we defined effective demand to result from the buying unit's having Money, Authority, and Desire. The major question at issue in this chapter is how does the MAD buyer (the buyer having effective demand) behave, and why? The traditional explanation of buyer behavior is that offered by economists, who postulate the existence of "economic man."

Economic Man

Economic theory holds that a buyer will act so as to maximize the total utility that he/she obtains from all products consumed. Although this conception of buyer behavior is incomplete, it provides a starting point for an examination of the buying process.

Utility—the ability to satisfy wants—is a concept postulated by such writers as Jeremy Bentham to explain the demand for products. Bentham's "felicific calculus" viewed people as carefully weighing and calculating the expected pleasures and pains of every contemplated action. Bentham assumed that people's wants are infinite, while their sources for satisfying these wants are finite: consequently, each person must make choices among alternative means of obtaining satisfaction.

In the late nineteenth century, Bentham's work was specifically applied to consumer behavior. This application was formulated independently by several economists, notably Alfred Marshall. Exhibit 6-2 presents the Marshallian conception of utility, as it is usually presented in elementary economics textbooks.

Note that as the quantity of the product consumed increases, utility increases, but at a decreasing rate. This means that the marginal utility—

Exhibit 6-2   The Utility Function

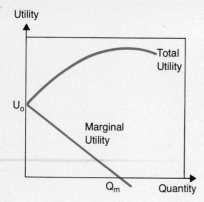

the increment of utility contributed by the last unit of the product consumed (the derivative of total utility, if you are comfortable with calculus)—diminishes as quantity consumed increases. The usual illustration—perhaps because it conjures up pleasant feelings which hopefully are transferred to the subject matter—is beer consumption. The total utility curve indicates that the first tall cool one affords U_o units or "utiles" of satisfaction. The next beer increases total satisfaction to some extent, as does the third, and the fourth, etc. There comes a time, however, when the individual would really rather not drink another beer—after perhaps fourteen or so, adding that fifteenth beer would actually decrease total utility. The function begins to turn down. This point occurs at quantity Q_m. Consequently, the marginal utility function decreases from U_o for the first unit consumed to Q_m units. After that point, marginal utility is actually negative.

The economist's assumptions about utility, then, are that an individual can express his/her total utility for a product in quantifiable terms, and that total utility increases at a decreasing rate. Given this set of assumptions about utility functions, and the consumer's postulated desire to maximize total utility, then the behavior that the consumer should follow is fairly clear: he/she should consume Q_m units of beer, and should adjust that quantity as his/her buying power and/or the price of beer changes—ceteris paribus (we return to the "all other things being equal" assumption presently).

This theory can be extended to encompass consumption of more than one product. The problem is to weight the marginal utility of each product by its price, and then to equate the ratios for all products that the consumer desires. For two products, this ratio can be expressed in symbols:

$$\frac{MU_X}{P_X} = \frac{MU_Y}{P_Y}$$

This equation says that the marginal utility for product X divided by the price of product X should be equal to the marginal utility of product Y divided by the price of product Y. It is easy to see why this decision rule must hold, given the economist's assumptions. If the ratio is larger for X than for Y, then the consumer should increase his consumption of product X. As he does so, the marginal utility of X will fall, which tends to equalize the terms of the equation. Only when the ratios are equal has the consumer maximized his total satisfaction. This decision rule could be extended to as many products as the consumer desires to purchase. Alternatively, generality can also be achieved by letting product Y be money, and comparing money against any other single product.

The economic man concept has been refined by economists in many ways, e.g., indifference curves, budget constraints, product substitutability differentials, and revealed preference. (If you are interested in this area, you might start with the Leftwich text annotated at the end of the chapter.) From the viewpoint of marketing management this theory of buyer behavior has severe limitations.

The economic man concept is based upon a number of assumptions—basically the same assumptions that underlie the theory of pure competition discussed in Chapter 4. For example, individuals are presumed to be so numerous that one individual cannot influence general market conditions. When an individual automobile buyer deals with Ford or General Motors, he/she has relatively little bargaining strength. Similarly, when a small manufacturer negotiates with Sears or A & P, his/her bargaining position is relatively weak. Moreover, other assumptions similar to those of the purely competitive market do not often hold: instantaneous, costless transactions; infinitely divisible products (e.g., one is able to purchase half a Cadillac); products that never change, i.e., no product development; and so forth.

Second, the theory assumes that individuals are all-knowing—which contradicts what we know about selective perception and about how different individuals respond to decision-making risks. Third, the consumer is assumed to be rational: if he prefers product X to product Y, and prefers Y to Z, then he will prefer X to Z. He will not make a mistake, and this preference will not change. This assumption ignores what we know about human analytical ability and about learning. Fourth, the theory assumes that the consumer is not influenced by other consumers—a direct contradiction of all that we know about interpersonal influence. And, as we discussed in Chapter 4, the theory assumes that there is no marketing effort: no product development, no advertising, no personal selling, no distribution strategies. Thus, marketing students may well be tempted to dismiss the theory of economic man as a figment of the ivory tower imaginations of armchair economists.

But this judgment may be a bit harsh. The theory does stress the fundamental importance of buying power (economists talk about "income," but income is only one component of buying power—the others being assets held and credit worthiness). Without buying power there can be no sale. Consequently, concepts from economics provide some useful insights. The classic example is the relationship between income (buying power) and buying behavior generalized by the German statistician Ernst Engel. Engel's laws are as follows:

As income rises, family expenditures tend to increase in all categories, but the percentage spent on food tends to decline, the percentage spent on housing and household operations tends to remain constant, and the percentage spent on other categories and savings tends to increase.

Exhibit 6-3   Protocol of a Car Buyer's Experience

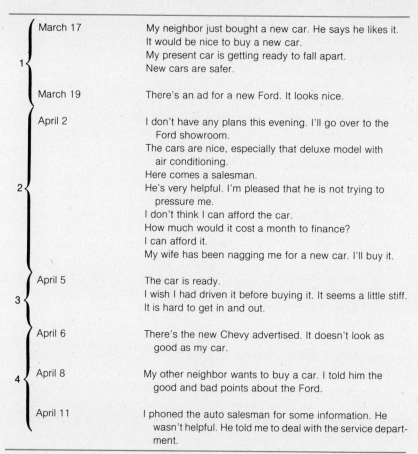

1	March 17	My neighbor just bought a new car. He says he likes it. It would be nice to buy a new car. My present car is getting ready to fall apart. New cars are safer.
	March 19	There's an ad for a new Ford. It looks nice.
2	April 2	I don't have any plans this evening. I'll go over to the Ford showroom. The cars are nice, especially that deluxe model with air conditioning. Here comes a salesman. He's very helpful. I'm pleased that he is not trying to pressure me. I don't think I can afford the car. How much would it cost a month to finance? I can afford it. My wife has been nagging me for a new car. I'll buy it.
3	April 5	The car is ready. I wish I had driven it before buying it. It seems a little stiff. It is hard to get in and out.
	April 6	There's the new Chevy advertised. It doesn't look as good as my car.
4	April 8	My other neighbor wants to buy a car. I told him the good and bad points about the Ford.
	April 11	I phoned the auto salesman for some information. He wasn't helpful. He told me to deal with the service department.

Adapted from Philip Kotler, *Marketing Management: Analysis, Planning, and Control*, 3rd ed. (Englewood Cliffs, N.J., Prentice-Hall, 1976), p. 86. Reprinted by permission of Prentice-Hall.

These laws have generally been validated in subsequent studies. Moreover, there is some validity in the concept of maximization of satisfaction as the goal of consumer behavior. And the concept of diminishing marginal utility, especially when buying power is limited (as it is for most of us) is very pertinent to our discussion.

The concept of economic man, in summary, is relatively simple. It omits several relevant variables, but it does provide both foundation and guidelines for further examination of buying behavior. Examining the buying process provides a more realistic viewpoint.

The Buying Process

Consider Exhibit 6-3, a protocol or internal monologue of a hypothetical car buyer's experience. Note that, as time passes, the buyer progresses from recognizing the desire for a new automobile to purchasing an

BUYING PROCESS

Exhibit 6-4   Stages in the Buying Process

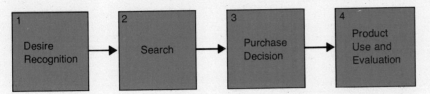

automobile and then evaluating that decision. The stages in this progression are numbered; Exhibit 6-4 formalizes these stages of the buying process. There are alternative formulations of this process; Exhibit 6-5 presents several examples. Our formulation includes four stages: desire recognition, search, purchase decision, and product use and evaluation. Let us examine each of these stages.

Desire Recognition. The process begins when an individual begins to feel that a certain want or desire must be satisfied. This feeling is triggered, in psychological terms, by differences between the individual's desired level of satisfaction and his/her actual level of satisfaction with respect to a certain product or situation. In the car protocol, for example, the discrepancy between the individual's actual and desired satisfaction with his/her automobile becomes apparent in his/her first (3/17) statements.

Search. Once the individual has recognized a want or desire, he/she will search for ways of satisfying that want or desire. The search may be conducted rapidly and intuitively, or it may involve extended effort and analysis of information.

One major source of formal information is the marketing efforts of firms serving a particular market—advertising, personal selling, and distribution outlets. In organizational buying situations, many organiza-

Exhibit 6-5   Hierarchy of Effects Models

Dagmar(1)	Lavidge-Steiner(2)	AIDA(3)	Adoption Process(4)
Awareness	Awareness	Attention	Awareness
Comprehension	Knowledge	Interest	Interest
Conviction	Liking	Desire	Evaluation
Action	Preference	Action	Trial
	Conviction		Adoption
	Purchase		

Sources: 1. Russell H. Colley, *Defining Advertising Goals for Measured Advertising Results* (New York: Association of National Advertisers, 1961).
2. Robert J. Lavidge and Gary A. Steiner, "A Model for Predictive Measurements of Advertising Effectiveness," *Journal of Marketing*, October 1961, pp. 59–62.
3. E.K. Strong, *The Psychology of Selling* (New York: McGraw-Hill Company, 1925), p. 9.
4. *The Adoption of New Products* (Ann Arbor: Foundation for Research on Human Behavior, 1959); and Everett Rogers, *Diffusion of Innovations* (New York: Free Press, 1962).

Exhibit 6-6   Sources of Buying Information

Formal Sources	Informal Sources
Marketing Effort Advertising, personal selling, distribution, etc.	**Personal Experience** previous use of product, patronage of firm, etc.
Organizational Sources Engineering specifications, sampling and testing, performance reports	**Word of Mouth** experience and opinions of friends, relatives, acquaintances
Published Material *Consumers' Report*, industry trade associations	**Opinion Leadership** reference groups, journals or magazines
Governmental Effort Standards and grades, truth-in . . . legislation, FTC scrutiny of advertising	

tions have extensive information-generating and analyzing capabilities. For example, when General Motors buys material from U.S. Steel, it does not rely on assurances from the steel company that shipments will be "new and improved with twice the active ingredients" of competitors' products.

In addition, as we noted in Chapter 4, public policy is increasingly moving to organize and formalize the kinds of information available to consumers. Truth in lending and packaging laws, standards of advertising truthfulness, and so forth, are providing increasingly better organized information for the buying process. And there is increasing interest in such private sources of product information as *Consumers Report*.

Despite these advances in formal information for the search stage of the buying process, it is likely that the majority of information for many buying situations (particularly those faced by final household consumers) comes from informal information sources. The major categories are the personal experience of the buyer—previous use of the product, former patronage of the firm and so forth; word-of-mouth—the experiences and opinions of friends, relatives, acquaintances; and opinion leadership—buying decisions by reference groups, advice from trade journals or fashion magazines, and so forth. Exhibit 6-6 illustrates these sources.

Purchase Decision. Information search culminates in the third stage of the buying process: the actual purchase decision. A decision is a commitment to a course of action—in this case, agreement to purchase a certain product. The purchase decision involves evaluation of information obtained in the search stage in light of the individual's recognized need. Obviously, this decision is the focal point of considerable marketing effort. We consider the purchase decision in some detail later in this chapter.

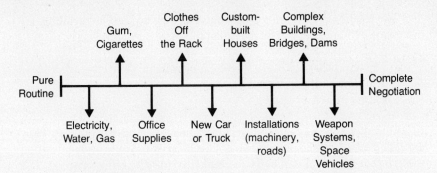

Exhibit 6-7   Continuum of Buying Process Effort

Product Use and Evaluation. Once the purchase decision has been made, the next stage in the buying process is to use the product, i.e., to extract utility from it. Given a wide variety of products and a variety of uses for each product to satisfy individual wants and desires, it is difficult to generalize about the product usage stage of the model. It is often worthwhile, however, for the marketing manager to study the specific uses to which buyers put his product. All baby food is not consumed by babies, and women use hairpins for many different purposes. Perhaps the classic here is the use of foam rubber "falsies" as extra padding in baseball catchers' mitts.

Product usage generates experience with the product, which is one basis for evaluation. Product evaluation may be very formal, lengthy and complex—or relatively informal, quick and simple. The scope of the evaluation includes not only the product itself, but also a reexamination of sources of information about the product, with respect to satisfaction of the desire(s) which triggered the buying process.

The buying process may be completed rapidly and with very little conscious thought or effort, or it may be quite lengthy and involved. The amount of effort devoted to the buying process for a particular product can be conceived as a continuum stretching from complete routine (purchases of electricity, gas, water, and other utilities which are automatically consumed as needed) to complete negotiation (unique exchange activities such as those involved in the design and purchase of a new weapon system or a vehicle for space exploration). Between these extremes are products that require varying degrees of effort in the buying process. Exhibit 6-7 provides examples of types of products located at different points on the buying process continuum.

Roles in the Buying Process. The discussion to this point has focussed upon the role of *purchaser* of the product. Two other roles may be directly involved. These are the *user* (the person or persons who consume the product) and the *decider* (the individual or group that actually makes the decision to purchase the product).

The relationships among these roles can best be seen by recalling our discussion (Chapter 3) of effective demand. The acronym was

Money (buying power)—the decider role,
Authority—the purchaser's role, and
Desire—the user's role.

In addition, others may play indirect roles in a given buying process. They are called *advisors* (persons who do not necessarily buy, use or decide upon the product, but who explicitly or implicitly influence the process). For some products, all of these roles may be performed by one individual. The more usual case, in families or organizations, is that different individuals assume the various roles in the purchase decision.

In the purchase of a child's toy, for example, the child is the product user. Advisors might include other children, teachers, and authorities on child rearing. The purchaser's role will probably be played by the child's mother, who might have primary responsibility for information search and in actually making the purchase. The decider, however, may be the child's father, who must weigh the toy's cost against other budget considerations in making the decision. Although specifics would differ, the same roles would occur in choosing subcontractors for electronic assemblies, naming a candidate to represent the party in the next election, selecting a meal in a restaurant, or ordering office supplies.

The Organizational Buyer
It may be prudent at this point to state my position on a somewhat controversial issue. In this chapter, I say that buyer behavior may be for either consumption or organizational purposes. Similarity of behavior is implied, but marketing students argue that organizational buying is quite different.

There is no question that the tasks and responsibilities of the organizational buyer are varied and exacting, as Exhibit 6-8 demonstrates. Thus the picture emerges of a person who emotionlessly sifts vast quantities of technical data in preparation for protracted negotiations involving millions of dollars.

This picture is, of course, a stereotype. As we shall see, organizational buying behavior is not motivated solely by economic considerations, nor is consumption buying irrational. The buying process proceeds in the same manner for both. There are differences to be sure, but the differences are of degree rather than kind.

In summary, buying behavior can best be studied if viewed as a process leading to and resulting from the purchase decision. To understand the decision, we must study the factors that influence the process. In broad terms, there are personal influences and group influences. We look at each in turn.

Webster and Wind list six responsibilities of the organizational buyer:

1. Negotiating prices and other terms of sale with vendors.
2. Generating alternative solutions to the buying problem and keeping organization members informed of market conditions.
3. Protecting the organization's cost structure, especially if it is influenced by the prices paid for purchased goods and services and more generally as it is influenced by the effect of purchased goods and services on the cost of performing the work of the organization.

4. Assuring long-term sources of supply for those goods and services necessary for organizational functioning.
5. Maintaining good relationships with suppliers.
6. Managing the mechanics of the procurement process, including establishing reorder points on routinely purchased items, placing orders with suppliers, expediting orders, checking orders when received, maintaining records of transactions with suppliers, and so forth.

"In order to perform his functions most effectively, the organizational buying agent typically feels that he must be involved in the buying process at its earliest stages—that is, at the stage of defining the need for purchased products or services. He wants to participate actively in the determination of specifications

and then the identification of alternative buying actions. He wants to avoid specifications or delivery requirements that unduly limit the number of alternative objectives that can be considered.

"Especially if the buyer is ambitious, he will want to achieve management recognition and enhanced status within the organization and, identifying with the profession of purchasing, he will actively seek to enlarge the scope of his authority and responsibility. He will actively fight any tendency to keep the purchasing function from being involved before final stages of placing orders and he will resist specifications that limit the alternatives that he can consider."

Adapted from Frederick E. Webster, Jr., and Yoram Wind, *Organizational Buying Behavior*, pp. 81–82, © 1972. Reprinted by permission of Prentice-Hall, Inc., Englewood Cliffs, New Jersey.

PERSONAL INFLUENCES

There is no doubt that the internal mechanisms employed by the consumer to satisfy his/her wants are much more complex than the simple rational calculations envisioned by economists. Nor is there any question that an understanding of these mechanisms would improve managerial decision making in marketing. There is controversy, however, over how much we know about these mechanisms and how best to apply them to marketing decision making.

Behavior is complex. The separation of behavior into elements is necessary for studying behavior, but it makes that study somewhat artificial. Moreover, it is difficult to obtain agreement among experts regarding the essential elements of behavior. Our overview of buyer behavior, therefore, is somewhat arbitrary and certainly oversimplified, yet it provides useful insights for managerial decision making.

We view personal influences upon buyer behavior as a set of attitudes which change as a result of certain processes. Specifically, the attitude set has cognitive (thinking), affective (feeling), and conative (doing) components which are interrelated to form an individual's personality, and which are acted upon by processes of motivation, perception, and learning. We discuss these components and processes separately, but they are interrelated.

Components of Individual Behavior

In simplest terms, behavior is response to stimuli. For buyer behavior, the usual stimulus is a product. In Chapter 1, we defined a product as anything possessing potential want-satisfying capability. Thus, the individual responds by recognizing the want, searching for information, making the purchase decision, and using and evaluating the product.

The crucial questions then become: how does a given individual respond to a certain product, and why? Of course, different individuals respond in various ways to product stimuli. Explaining and/or predicting individual behavior in buying situations is the objective of the study of buyer behavior.

Roughly speaking, psychologists postulate the construct of attitudes to account for differences in responses among individuals. An attitude is a predisposition to respond to a stimulus in a certain way. An individual has sets or clusters of attitudes which have cognitive, effective, and conative dimensions integrated to form his/her personality.

Cognitive. The cognitive or mental portion of an individual's makeup includes the ability to think and reason, memory, and judgment. This component obviously plays a part in buying behavior—the individual must know about the product. Thus advertising copy, product labels, and operating instructions must be presented in such a way that they can be comprehended by the individual.

One result of attempts by marketing managers to take the cognitive component into account is reflected in the literacy level of most broadcast and printed advertising copy. As shown in Exhibit 6-9, human intelligence as defined by the Stanford-Binet Intelligence Scale is distributed in *normal* fashion, with a mean of 100—50 percent of the distribution having an intelligence quotient between 90 and 110. Consequently, most advertising copy is designed to be comprehended by people with intelligence in this range. The problem is that many students of marketing, marketing managers, and public policy makers have IQs higher than 110. They tend to find the bulk of advertising copy boring, tasteless, and simplistic. When advertisements are designed to appeal to the upper end of the intelligence scale, however, the ads cannot be easily comprehended by the majority. One classic example here is provided by Alka Seltzer: "Try it, you'll like it"; "I can't believe I ate the whole thing."

Affective. Influencing buyer behavior is more than a matter of matching marketing strategy to the buyer's cognitive capabilities. The affective dimension—the individual's feelings and emotions and values—also influ-

Exhibit 6-9   Normal Distribution of Human Intelligence

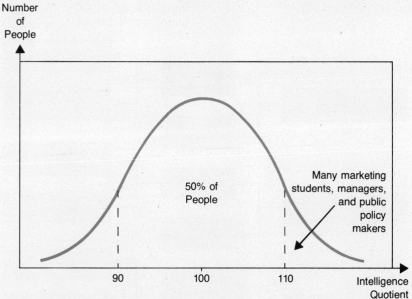

ences his/her buying behavior. One example here is that many people have favorable attitudes toward products of their own country relative to products of other countries, e.g., Chevrolet's "Buy American" campaign and the Common Agricultural Policy of the European Economic Community.

It is at this point that many critics of marketing attempt to make a distinction between cognitive and affective attitude components—between thinking and feeling. An individual is said to be "rational" if thinking predominates, and "irrational" if guided by feelings. It may be said, for example, that while an individual would cite such factors as durability, safety, and trade-in value as reasons for buying a big luxury automobile, the individual's "real" reasons may involve desire for status and prestige.

Such explanations have intuitive appeal, but are gross oversimplifications. Attitudinal components are not so easily separated and categorized. An individual's thoughts and emotions are linked in complex fashion and must be considered in light of his/her action tendencies.

Conative. The conative dimension of attitudes is the action-tendency or behavioral component. The conative dimension reflects an individual's expectations about possible consequences of his/her behavior, i.e., his/her attitude toward risk. In broad terms, risk-taking is a function of the magnitude of the consequences of an act, and the likelihood that such consequences will be experienced. Risk-taking involves evaluating both the payoffs resulting from a given action and the degree of probability that payoff will occur. Thus, sampling a new type of candy bar or cigarette

Exhibit 6-10 Comparison of Buying Intentions and Purchase Behavior

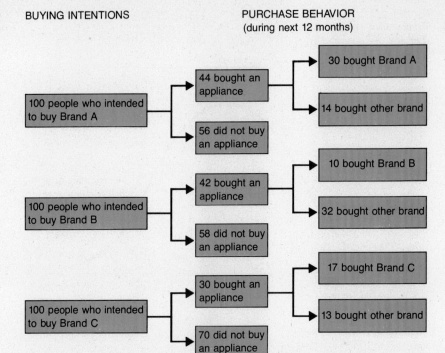

BUYING INTENTIONS

PURCHASE BEHAVIOR
(during next 12 months)

100 people who intended to buy Brand A

44 bought an appliance

30 bought Brand A

14 bought other brand

56 did not buy an appliance

100 people who intended to buy Brand B

42 bought an appliance

10 bought Brand B

32 bought other brand

58 did not buy an appliance

100 people who intended to buy Brand C

30 bought an appliance

17 bought Brand C

13 bought other brand

70 did not buy an appliance

Adapted from Robert W. Pratt, "Understanding the Decision Process for Consumer Durable Goods," reprinted in *Marketing and Economic Development,* Proceedings, ed. Peter Bennett (Chicago: American Marketing Association, 1965), pp. 244–260, with permission of the publisher, the American Marketing Association.

involves relatively little risk if it is unsatisfactory. On the other hand, if a new automobile is a lemon, the loss is great. So one might "invest" considerably more time and effort in information search to reduce the uncertainty associated with the choice of automobile to be purchased.

As a measure of the conative components, the marketing manager might turn to data on intentions. Intentions may be defined as planned actions to be taken at a specified future time. These self-predictions of behavior may be very pertinent marketing data, but the marketing manager must realize that they are conditional predictions. That is, planned actions of necessity include assumptions, e.g., expectations about general economic conditions, level of other wants and desires, and fashion trends. If such assumptions prove incorrect at the time when the planned action is to take place, then the action may be modified.

Exhibit 6-10 illustrates this situation and shows a divergence between buying intentions and actual buying behavior. Since marketing decision making is concerned with future behavior, buying intention information should not be ignored. Political polling measures intentions, in a number of ways. Political pollsters like Gallup, Harris, and Roper have developed interviewing techniques in which voting intentions of respondents have been used with considerable success as predictors of actual voting behavior. The Survey Research Center at the University of Michigan has for a number of years conducted a quarterly survey of the buying intentions of consumer durables. And business-oriented journals such as *Business Week* and *Wall Street Journal* periodically publish surveys of executive opinion about the intentions of organizational buyers in various fields.

Personality. There are numerous and complex cognitive, affective, and conative influences upon buying behavior. For this reason, the individual must have some means of organizing and integrating these various influences upon his/her behavior. Generally speaking, the manner in which he/she does this is called *personality*—character traits, soul, his/her self-concept. Personality is a complex psychological construct. Its primary features are self-concept, roles, and levels of consciousness.

Every individual has an idea of what he/she is like. In fact, some authorities think that the self-concept may have three parts: the idealized self—what he/she would like to be like, the looking-glass self—how he/she thinks others see him/her, and the self-self, his/her own conception of what he/she is like. It is easy to see potential marketing implications in the self-concept. For example, an individual who sees himself/herself as friendly, extroverted, and outgoing is more likely to be a potential buyer of products that involve him/her with other people, e.g., night clubs and outdoor cooking equipment. A more shy and introverted person, on the other hand, might be a better prospect for books or theater tickets.

Each individual plays many roles—loving parent, efficient administrator, friendly co-worker, prudent household manager, rabid sports fan, etc. Buying behavior is likely to be influenced by the particular roles upon which he/she is concentrating at a given time. These roles may conflict. For example, the loving parent may want the most exclusive and expensive summer camp for the children, but the prudent household manager may feel that he/she cannot afford such activities.

Moreover, many authorities believe that an individual does not have full knowledge and understanding of his/her psyche. Some part of the personality is hidden in the unconscious or subconscious—where its influence is difficult to determine. In his classic id-ego-superego model of the psyche, Freud postulated that each individual comes into the world with a personality consisting only of mindless desires that it seeks to satisfy. This mindless primitive part of the psyche he called the *id*. As the individual develops, his/her psyche soon learns that behaviors leading to immediate and total gratification of desires are unacceptable to other human beings. Consequently, two additional portions of his/her psyche develop. The first is the *superego,* composed of idealized behavior patterns, and a conscience that measures actual behavior against this ideal. Thus the superego acts in opposition to the id. To mediate or balance the id and superego, the individual develops an *ego*—a conscious, rational psychic component to direct behavior so as to satisfy both id and superego.

An individual's use of credit is often utilized to illustrate the effect of the three parts of the psyche upon buying behavior. The id would influence the individual to use as much credit as possible in order to satisfy desires immediately. A superego, particularly one developed in a religious atmosphere, might regard credit as sinful and as a circumvention of the Protestant ethic—and therefore would militate against the use of credit. Ego-based considerations of credit, however, might focus upon the individual's financial condition and his/her ability to meet credit terms without straining the budget.

Let me reemphasize that while the cognitive, affective, and conative components of the individual's personality have been separated in this discussion, their influence upon buying behavior cannot be so neatly categorized. And single attitudes are not simple determinants of buying behavior. Prospective automobile purchasers, for example, are likely to exhibit rather strong attitudes toward safety, but manufacturers have seldom been successful at using safety features as sales appeals. Perhaps this illustrates two basic points about attitudes. First, a buyer is likely to have a great many feelings toward a product; no one attitude, therefore, is likely to be the determining one. Second, a given attitude may be widely held in the population, and therefore reflected in the features of most products in the market. In such a case, that attitude would provide relatively little information regarding choices between different brands and types of products by members of that population. Moreover, attitudes and behavior change as they are affected by the processes of motivation, perception, and learning.

Processes of Motivation, Perception, and Learning

Although it is possible to discuss the components of intrapersonal influences upon buying behavior as they exist at a given moment, the question inevitably arises as to how and why these factors operate. That is, where do knowledge, emotions, and intentions come from? What causes the individual to respond in certain ways? And how do these response patterns change over time?

Motivation. Motivation is the drive to act, to move, to obtain a goal or goals. Motivation arises within the individual; it is affected by attitudes, and by outside influences such as culture and marketing effort.

Students of marketing have for a number of years been fascinated by lists of different motives and their impact upon buying behavior. Many such lists have been proposed, with the number of motives ranging from three to well over a hundred. Probably the best known and perhaps the most useful list for marketing purposes is that proposed by Maslow. Exhibit 6-11 illustrates Maslow's approach to motivation; part (a) presents his basic hierarchy of human needs.

The physiological needs—food, water, sleep, etc.—are essentially tension-reducing mechanisms. They are most fundamental or prepotent— if they are not satisfied, the individual thinks of little else. When a man is hungry, notes Maslow, his consciousness is almost preempted by hunger— "the urge to write poetry, the desire to acquire an automobile or a new pair of shoes, are forgotten or are of secondary importance." In industrial societies, physiological needs rarely are sufficiently strong to be of concern for marketing strategy. To be sure, there are individuals whose physiological needs are sometimes not completely fulfilled, but the number of these individuals in an industrial society is rather small.

If physiological needs are relatively well gratified, the individual begins to seek physical safety and security, stability in his world, and so on. As these needs become relatively well satisfied, the individual begins to realize needs for love, affection, and belonging—he will want to attain such relations more than anything else in the world and may even forget that once, when he was hungry, he sneered at love. As the love needs become satiated, the individual's need for a stable, firmly based, high evaluation of himself becomes apparent. He has a desire for self-respect, for reputation and prestige, for recognition, attention, and appreciation. Finally, even if all of these needs are relatively well satisfied, the individual may become discontented and restless unless he is doing what he is fitted for—"What a man can be, he must be." (And woman, too, of course—We assume that Maslow used the term *man* generically.)

Maslow recognized that lower-level needs do not have to be completely satisfied before the individual begins to feel desires at the next level. A more realistic portrayal of Maslow's hierarchy is shown in part (b). In terms of psychological development, physiological needs are most important, but as they are fulfilled they begin to taper off, and attention turns to safety needs. As these are fulfilled, belongingness and love needs become prepotent (as indicated by the height of that curve), and so on. In industrial societies, most of the physiological and many of the safety needs of the majority of members of societies are largely fulfilled. On the other hand, few people have reached self-actualization. According to Maslow, most people are striving for belongingness and love and esteem. There are obvious implications here for marketing strategy. Food ads on television, for example, generally do not stress basic nutrition; they stress family approbation or the contribution that the product will make to the consumer's next party.

Exhibit 6-11 Maslow's Hierarchy of Needs Concept

(a) Basic Hierarchy

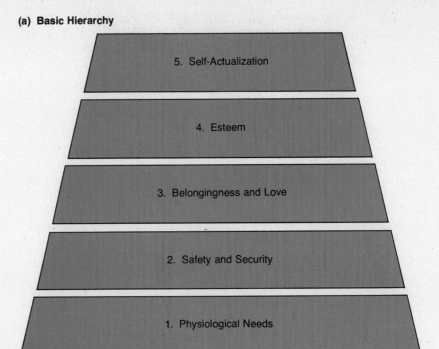

Data from pp. 35–46, *Motivation and Personality*, 2nd ed., by Abraham H. Maslow (Harper & Row, 1970), reprinted with permission of the publisher.

(b) Prepotency of Needs

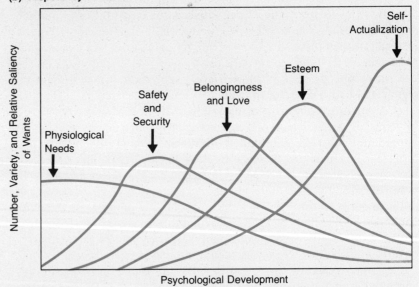

Adapted from David Krech and others, *Individual in Society* (New York: McGraw-Hill, 1962). p. 77, with permission of the publisher.

Exhibit 6-12
The Dependence Effect

The notion that wants do not become less urgent the more amply the individual is supplied is broadly repugnant to common sense . . . if the individual's wants are to be urgent they must be original with himself. They cannot be urgent if they must be contrived for him. And above all they must not be contrived by the process of production, by which they are satisfied . . . A man who is hungry need never be told of his need for food. If he is inspired by his appetite, he is immune to the influence of Messrs. Batten, Barton, Durstine and Osborn. The latter are effective only with those who are so far removed from physical want that they do not already know they want. In this state alone men are open to persuasion," says economist and social critic John Kenneth Galbraith.

. . . "One must imagine a humanitarian who was long ago persuaded of the grievous short-age of hospital facilities in the town. He continues to importune the passers-by for money for more beds and refuses to notice that the town doctor is deftly knocking over pedestrians with his car to keep up the occupancy." Galbraith's general conclusion is that, "As a society becomes increasingly affluent, wants in-creasingly come to depend on output."

Nobel prize-winning economist Hayek agrees that we as individuals would not "desire any of the amenities of civilization—or even of the most primitive culture—if we did not live in a society in which others provide them. Innate wants are probably confined to food, shelter, and sex. All the rest we learn to desire because we see others enjoying various things. To say that a desire is not important because it is not innate is to say that the whole cultural achievement of man is not important . . . most needs which make us act are needs for things which only civilization teaches us exist at all, and these things are wanted by us because they produce feelings or emotions which we would not know if it were not for our cultural inheritance.

"How complete a non sequitur Professor Galbraith's conclusion represents is seen most clearly if we apply the argument to any product of the arts, be it music, painting, or literature . . . the argument could easily be employed without any change of the essential terms, to demonstrate the worthlessness of literature or any other form of art. Surely an individual's want for literature is not original with himself in the sense that he would experience it if literature were not produced. Does this then mean that the production of literature cannot be defended as satisfying a want because it is only the production which provokes the demand?"

Adapted from John Kenneth Galbraith, *The Affluent Society* (Boston: Houghton-Mifflin Company, 1958, 1969), pp. 152–160; and adapted from Frederick A. von Hayek, "The Non Sequitur of the Dependence Effect," *Southern Economic Journal,* April 1961, pp. 346–48, with the permission of the publishers.

You have no doubt noted that the discussion has shifted from "want satisfaction" to "need satisfaction." We have avoided this distinction so far, but now this issue should be faced. Although it is difficult, as Maslow points out, to isolate particular types of motives in a given situation, there is an extremely appealing distinction between needs which have a physical basis—physiological and safety needs, and those that are more psychologi-cal in character—the love, esteem, and self-actualization needs. Marketing activities in industrial societies generally focus on satisfying the latter type of needs or wants, a condition which Galbraith calls *the dependence effect.* Exhibit 6-12 presents Galbraith's thesis, and a rebuttal by Hayek.

In my opinion, Hayek is persuasive—it appears to be exceedingly difficult for different people to agree upon a workable distinction between motives that an individual *needs* to satisfy, and motives less necessary that the individual only *wants* to satisfy. (As a nonsmoker, I really cannot believe that anyone truly needs a cigarette. But many of my friends rank cigarettes rather high on their list of purchase priorities.) In this book, I interpret wants or desires to include innate needs. Motivation for want-satisfaction is triggered by perception.

Perception. Perception is the sensing of stimuli external to the individual organism—the act or process of comprehending the world in which the individual exists. The individual must organize and integrate innumerable sights, sounds, odors, tastes, and tactile impressions. For example, an individual looking at a new automobile does not perceive a random collection of paint, tires, glass, and steel. He/she perceives an integrated entity designed to perform certain functions—transportation, conferring of status on the driver, comfort, convenience.

Perception is more than ordered sensations. The sensory inputs are altered by the individual's knowledge and past experiences, feelings and attitudes, and personality. If, for example, an individual observes someone driving a new Continental or Cadillac, the individual might perceive the driver to be someone of wealth, power, and influence. Perceptions can also lead to stereotyping; if the driver of the Continental or Cadillac is wearing some type of uniform, he/she will probably be perceived as a chauffeur. Moreover, perception may have no objective basis in reality. For example, research has shown that some drivers perceive improved acceleration from their automobiles when the accelerator is made easier to depress; that salad oil is perceived to be thicker if it is darker in color than usual; and that vacuum cleaners are perceived to be less efficient if they are less noisy than usual. The marketing manager must understand how his/her marketing effort is perceived by the consumer. One frequently mentioned technique—that does not work—is *subliminal perception*. This topic is reviewed in Exhibit 6-13.

Learning. Learning is defined as changes or alterations in cognitive, affective, or conative components of the individual—as these are manifest in behavioral changes. Many psychologists believe that learning is the most fundamental process in human behavior. The higher order "needs," for example, are learned, and selective perception—a function of past experiences—is learned. Learning theory is a large and diverse discipline, and not without internal contradictions. The stimulus-response school of learning theory seems most useful to marketing managers at the present time.

You probably recall Pavlov's classic stimulus-response experiments. By ringing a bell before he gave food to a dog, Pavlov established a relationship between the sound of the bell and the forthcoming food. The dog learned to expect food when it heard the bell. In the terminology of

Exhibit 6-13   Subliminal Perception

The possible use of subliminal perception in advertising received widespread attention in 1958. Reports indicated that, during a six-week period, 45,699 people attending a motion picture theater in New Jersey were exposed to one of two subliminal messages, "Hungry? Eat Popcorn" or "Drink Coca-Cola." Sales figures during the test period were compared with previous sales records. Most reports stated that popcorn sales increased 58 percent and Coca-Cola sales increased 18 percent.

Subliminal perception—perception of stimuli without conscious awareness—does exist. Studies done in 1939 by J.G. Miller showed that people could accurately identify geometric forms shown on a screen for periods too brief to be consciously comprehended. Moreover, this subliminal perception was improved under strong motivational conditions (money and fear of shock). But what is subliminal for one person may be above the threshold of consciousness for another.

Clearly, then, there would be technical problems associated with keeping stimuli subliminal for any large group. Moreover, subliminal messages are likely to be ambiguous. The further below the threshold a given message is presented, the greater the capacity for a distortion. "Drink Coca-Cola," for example, might be read subliminally as "Drink Pepsi-Cola," "Drink Cocoa," or even "Drive Slowly." In addition to these technical problems, the report from the New Jersey movie theater raises many questions on methodological grounds. First, the movie was "Picnic"—Coca-Cola and popcorn sales would be likely to increase during the showing of this film. Moreover, there was no control over extraneous variables. Barthol and Goldstein conclude that there is small danger to the consumer from subliminal stimulation . . . "(people) are staunchly protected by our inefficient nervous systems, our prejudices, our lack of attention, and the inalienable right to completely misunderstand, misinterpret, and ignore what we do not see clearly."

Adapted from Richard P. Barthol and Michael J. Goldstein, "Psychology and the Invisible Sale," *California Management Review*, Vol. 1 No. 2, Winter 1959, pp. 29–35, with permission of the publisher.

learning theory, the dog was motivated by the drive to reduce hunger; the environmental stimulus (the bell) is called a *cue;* the organism's response (salivation in the case of the dog) indicates that learning has taken place; finally, learning is reinforced if it is rewarded (the dog was given food).

Implications for marketing management here are obvious. Advertising can provide the cue for the motivation to satisfy various wants. If the product is purchased, reinforcement occurs to the extent that the product does indeed provide the expected satisfaction. The conceptual usefulness of learning theory has been translated into formalized terms. The Howard-Sheth model of buyer behavior, discussed later in this chapter, is basically a learning model.

From the point of view of the marketing manager, three concepts in learning theory should be stressed. First is *reinforcement*, which we have already described—the buyer's purchase response must be reinforced—with adequate product performance, satisfactory service, reminder advertising, and so forth. Second is *repetition*. Although there are studies supporting the theory that excessive repetition may reduce learning, the majority of marketing managers seem to rely on its effectiveness. The strength of learning is usually directly correlated with the amount of *repetition* of the cues—thus we have advertising jingles continually repeated—sometimes to the point of nausea. And third, learning is increased if the individual *participates* in the process. Free samples, for example, are more likely to be effective in evoking the response of product trial than are other types of promotion. This is one reason why the automobile salesperson is continually coaxing you to test drive his/her car: "Keep it overnight."

In this necessarily brief overview of personal influences upon buyer behavior, the components and processes are separated for clarity and easy explanation. However, in marketing situations these factors influence buyer behavior simultaneously and in rather complex ways. They may also be intertwined with—and difficult for the marketing manager to distinguish from—group influences upon buyer behavior.

GROUP INFLUENCES

Buying behavior is influenced by the activities, interests, and opinions of other people. Almost everyone comes into contact with other people; *Robinson Crusoe* was fiction and there are few true hermits. In general, interpersonal influences are manifest by the groups to which an individual belongs. Let us look at the nature of groups (the sociological basis for behavior), and then at significant social groups, or reference groups.

Nature of Groups

By definition, a group is two or more individuals who interact for some purpose. Thus, a collection of individuals, e.g., passengers in an elevator, is not a group. If the elevator becomes stuck between floors, and the passengers work together to escape from it, they become a group. In the most general terms, the purpose of any group is to create a surplus. That is, an individual joins a group because he/she expects the benefits of group membership to outweigh the costs. To achieve its goal or goals, a given group has functions, a structure, and patterns of influence.

There are basically two group functions: the utilitarian, or goal-seeking, function, and the contact, or interaction, function. For goal-seeking, division of labor is required; consequently each individual performs a role or roles which contribute to goal attainment. Of course, a given individual may perform different roles in the same group at different times. In connection with the interaction function, the group develops a status hierarchy in which some group members are accorded more prestige than others. Status refers to an individual's position in the structure of the group and the corresponding prestige attendant to that position.

The structure of the group may be formal (functions are clearly specified) or informal (functions are not clearly specified). Friends conversing at a party or co-workers in an office or shop are examples of informal groups. If the friends belong to a professional organization, then they are also members of that formal group. Also, the co-workers belong to the formal group composed of the organization's employees. The group develops patterns of influence on individual behavior. These patterns take the form of norms, reference groups, and opinion leadership.

Norms. A norm is an expected pattern of behavior to which all group members should adhere. The transmission of norms to a group member is called socialization.

There are a number of experiments in psychological literature that illustrate the development of group norms. The usual experiment procedure is to have one of a group of subjects serve as the object of the experiment; the other subjects of the group are confederates of the researcher. The confederates insist that certain correct information is not so. In most cases, the naive subject can be persuaded to change his/her opinion to match the incorrect group consensus.

This little experiment has been conducted with matching lengths of line segments, persuading homemakers to use cheaper cuts of meats, and designating one of three identical suits as being of superior quality and workmanship. Group pressure to conform can be very strong. When faced with ambiguous stimuli, the naive subject often comes to rely upon group judgment. This is similar to the situation that consumers of different products frequently face, so the concept of group norms is an important one for marketing management. The idea of conformity to group norms can be extended to reference groups, and then to opinion leadership.

Reference Groups. From the perspective of one individual, a reference group is a set of people to whom he/she looks for advice and guidance concerning his/her thoughts and actions. Any type of group can be a reference group. For example, housewives may belong to a bridge club or a sewing circle; professional people may belong to organizations such as the American Medical Association or the American Marketing Association. But the individual need not be a member of a group to look to it as a reference point for his/her own guidance. Young people may revere athletes, movie stars, musicians, and—closer to home—coaches, teachers, and other adult acquaintances.

The relevance of reference groups to marketing activities, therefore, is quite strong. Whether a family drives a Ford or a Datsun, reads *Time* or *Newsweek,* serves instant or ground coffee, or takes vacations in a camper or in a luxurious hotel, depends at least in part upon what the people whom they would "like to be like" do in these matters. Consequently, one sees a great many advertisements portraying products used in socially pleasant situations, prominent people endorsing products, and so forth.

In addition, family members can be seen as a reference group for buying behavior. Another reference group is the work group in an organizational buying situation. The organizational buyer, or purchasing agent, would like to have the rewards, both financial and otherwise, that result from effective performance of the buying function. Although a part of the buyer's job can be evaluated in dollars-and-cents terms, much of the work involves relationships with others—engineers, foremen, workers, maintenance men—who evaluate him/her in interpersonal terms.

Opinion Leadership. It is clear that interpersonal relations in general and reference groups in particular are significant influences upon the buying process. The marketing manager, therefore, would like to know who the most influential people are, and what marketing efforts would be most successful with these people.

Unfortunately, the considerable amount of research done in these areas has not yet provided clear-cut, general answers to such questions. Given the present state of this type of research, as reviewed in Exhibit 6-14, the marketing manager probably would not be able to identify individuals who would be reference group role models or opinion leaders in all situations.

If we cannot identify people who are likely to be opinion leaders in all situations, perhaps we can find certain types of products for which reference group influence and opinion leadership are most important. The classic study here is outlined in Exhibit 6-15. In this table, products are classified as either weak or strong along two dimensions: the nature of the product measured horizontally, and the brand or type of the product measured vertically. Each dimension is categorized as weak or strong on

Exhibit 6-15 Reference Group
Influence on Product and Brand

		Reference Group Influence Relatively:	
		Weak-	Strong +
	Strong +	clothing furniture magazines refrigerator (type) toilet soap	cars* cigarettes* beer (prem. vs. reg.)* drugs*
Reference Group Influence Relatively:	Weak -	soap canned peaches laundry soap refrigerator (brand) radios	air conditioners* instant coffee* TV (black & white)

*The classification of all starred products is based on actual experimental evidence. Other products in this table are classified speculatively on the basis of generalizations derived from the sum of research in this area and confirmed by the judgment of seminar participants.

Adapted from *Group Influence in Marketing and Public Relations* (Foundation for Research on Human Behavior, 1956), p.8.

the basis of significance of reference group influence. The *plus-plus* category, for example, means that reference group influence is strong for, say, cars both in terms of a product class, and in terms of the brand of car a person might select. That is, how much one drives, and what brand of car one drives, are decisions that are subject to considerable reference group influence.

On the other hand, for certain products neither the product class nor the brand or type is socially conspicuous. For example, items such as salt, peaches, and laundry soap generally fall into this category. In addition, there are some products, e.g., clothing and furniture, which everyone owns, so the product class is not susceptible to reference group influence, but the type and brand of clothing or furniture bought very definitely is influenced by reference group preferences and opinions. Conversely, while consumption or nonconsumption of such products as room air conditioners and instant coffee was influenced by group opinion leaders, the product brand was not a significant factor. If, for example, instant coffee was accepted by a group, the brand of coffee was immaterial.

To the marketing manager, this study indicates that certain product classes and/or brands of products are more susceptible to reference group influence than are other products. The manager with a strong product class or a strong brand (in the reference group sense) might, therefore, pay considerable attention to the reference group concept.

Note, however, that this study was done years ago. It is likely, for example, that black and white television sets are no longer a *plus* type of product. It is interesting and enlightening to insert contemporary product examples into each of the four categories in the table—for example, video cassettes are probably a strong *plus, plus* product today; the introduction of precision radios from West Germany and Japan into the U.S. market may have moved radios into the brand *plus* category. The point is that groups do influence buying behavior. There are several significant groups in modern society.

Groups in Society

The way that people live together in society, their shared values, their roles, their perceptions of space and time, and how they relate to each other are manifestations of the society's culture. *Culture* is the intellectual and social heritage of a specific society.

Culture. Most Americans speak English, wear trousers or dresses and shoes, and know how to operate an automobile, a television set, a telephone, and an elevator. They more or less understand income taxes, the democratic political process, and various spectator sports and card games. With the exception of language, members of other industrial societies also share these traits—and even language is becoming less significant as English becomes more universally accepted. By contrast, most members of these societies would not be comfortable nude or in a grass skirt or toga, could not find potable water in a jungle, and would not enjoy a meal of whale blubber or human flesh. An individual's culture conditions not only his/her values and attitudes as discussed above, but also the kinds of actions he/she considers socially acceptable in given situations, how he/she interprets time and distance, what he/she considers edible, and so on. Specifically, culture influences product preferences and consumption patterns. The marketing manager needs to study the culture of any society in which he/she expects to market products.

Culture is generally studied in terms of three dimensions: the distributive dimension, the normative dimension, and the structural dimension. The distributive dimension reviews culture in terms of the way certain characteristics are distributed in the society. The usual distributive variables are the ones we discussed in Chapter 3: demography, income patterns, and stages of economic growth.

The normative dimension explores the values and customs of the society. As each individual develops and matures, the personality characteristics that he/she inherited from his/her parents interact with his/her experiences to form values and attitudes—the structure of concepts, beliefs, habits, and motives associated with particular objects. Thus, the individual's values and attitudes determine the way in which he/she thinks about particular objects and events, including products of various types.

Exhibit 6-16 The American Core Culture: General Attitudes Shared by the Majority of Americans

Nativity: Native-born of native-born parents.

2. Culture of Origin: Born and educated in the American culture.

3. Attitude toward American Culture: Unaware of cultural differences. American culture only one known to individual.

4. Attitudes toward Parents and Family Structure: Parents are primarily friends and guides rather than punitive authority. Matriarchal family structure or authority evenly divided between parents.

5. Religion: Member of any of large Protestant denominations.

6. Name: First, middle and last name according to Anglo-Saxon use.

7. Mother Tongue: American, English, Scottish, Irish, Canadian-English, New Zealandish-English.

8. Accent: No discernible accent.

9. Reading: Reads American papers and books only, exclusive of foreign professional publications.

10. External Appearance: Style of dress reflects American local standards and fashions; posture, relaxed, casual and informal; gestures, minimal; physical culture conforms to American ideals of slender, youthful appearance.

11. Choice of Menu: Protein eater.

12. Preparation of Food and Use of Condiments; Quickly prepared dishes; no sauces; no spices; catsup and other condiments added at time of meal. Food served in large pieces. Leftovers thrown away.

13. Attitude towards Food: Food is nourishment, but provides no particular sensual gratification. Convenience and expediency greatest concern. Emphasis on food hygiene, vitamins and calories.

14. Non-Alcoholic Drinks: Coffee, milk, fruit juices, cola drinks, milk shakes.

15. Drinking Habits and Alcoholic Beverages: No separation of sexes for alcohol consumption. Cocktails before dinner, highballs after dinner. Preference for cocktails made of whiskey, gin, rum. Beer with food.

16. Recreation: Passive, non-organized types of relaxation; spectator sports and gambling enjoyed. No separation of sexes except for occasional hunting or fishing trips of men and sewing and knitting of women.

17. Characteristic Personal Traits: Sense of humor, casual, warm, conformist, playful, fair, vivacious, healthy, good sport, happy-go-lucky, self-sufficient, tough.

18. Ideal Traits Wished for: Relaxed, democratic, casual, successful, easy-going, energetic, fair-minded, tough, flexible, cheerful, enterprising, non-argumentative, resourceful.

19. Attitudes toward Women: Women emancipated; they vote and work. Status not related to marriage. Women considered equal to men.

20. Attitudes toward Public and Success: Winning the public is of prime importance. Success measured in terms of money and popularity.

21. Residence: Resides in areas determined by class membership. If member of lower class, less separation from minority ethnic groups than if member of middle or upper class. Mixes with neighborhood group.

22. Associations: If a joiner, belongs to American type of lodge, club, or association with ethnic slant. Same friends as in childhood. No members of minority groups among close friends.

23. Festivities and Special Occasions: Celebrates official or local holidays of American character, e.g., Thanksgiving, Fourth of July, July 24 (Mormon holiday), etc.

24. Music: Prefers popular American music: jazz, jitterbug, musical comedy, swing, boogie-woogie, Bing Crosby, Negro spirituals, etc.

Excerpted from J. Ruesch, A. Jacobsen, and M.B. Loeb, ''Acculturation and Illness,'' *Psychological Monographs,* Vol. 62 (1948), pp. 1–40. Copyright 1948 by the American Psychological Association, and reprinted by permission.

One view of the generally accepted value-and-attitude pattern of Americans (the American culture) is presented in Exhibit 6-16. This summary was originally prepared in 1948 as a measurement device to determine the degree to which an individual fits the American cultural pattern. It provides a basic description of the cultural traits that are considered characteristic of the contemporary American society. For example, most Americans are native-born of native-born parents, generally speak English only, eat relatively large amounts of protein, and usually are "joiners." Careful study of Exhibit 6-16 can be quite valuable in reviewing usual American beliefs and attitudes. It is not difficult to see how many American marketing practices derived from these values and attitudes. For example, the very rapid rise in fast food outlets is a reflection of the American attitude that food is for nourishment but provides no particular sensual gratification—"hurry up and eat, Fred, so we can get to Mother's."

Of course, these values and attitudes are generalizations—they do not hold for every member of a society at a given time. Moreover, values and attitudes do change. Two examples of significant trends in American values and customs are growing hedonism and mounting security-consciousness.

It has been said, not entirely in jest, that Americans have been brought up to conform to the ideals of the Boy Scout law: loyal, trustworthy, helpful, friendly, courteous, kind, obedient, cheerful, thrifty, brave, clean, and reverent. A more serious label for this set of values and attitudes is "the Protestant ethic"—hard work, sober dedication to duty, thrift, respect for age and authority, lack of ostentation, etc. Today, however, there is a definite trend in American society away from these ideals and toward pleasure. Evidence of this shift in values includes more open acknowledgement of sexual freedom, declining interest in organized religion, desire to remain young, immediate gratification of sensual appetites, and so on. People in general want to spend fewer hours working, save a smaller proportion of their incomes, and worry less about the future—particularly about what will happen to their souls after death.

A related shift in contemporary Western values and attitudes is the drive to reduce risks. From the dating custom of going steady to social security taxes to preventive dentistry to service contracts on new appliances, people generally want less uncertainty and instability in their lives. This trend is in line with the hedonistic desire to enjoy life without fear of catastrophe, and reflects the growing trend of relying on others—particularly large, impersonal organizations like banks, insurance companies, and department stores—rather than one's own resources to provide that security.

For marketing management, this means, for example, that the emphasis is shifting from the repair and replacement of products when they break down or wear out to preventive maintenance and periodic replacement. Fire and burglar alarm protection systems are selling well, and there is a whole spate of *truth-in* laws, e.g., truth in packaging, truth in lending, that reflect the consumer's desire for a more secure and stable environment.

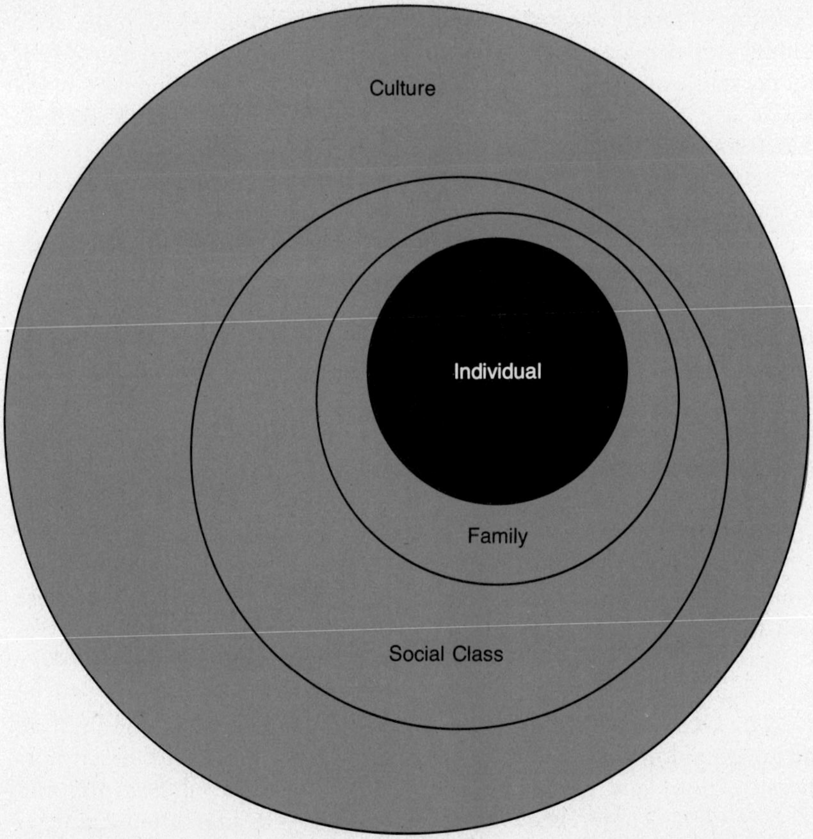

Exhibit 6-17   Relationships among Major Groups in the Social Structure

Social Structure. Social structure can best be examined by looking first at the individual, and then seeing how groups of individuals are aggregated to form parts of the society. Exhibit 6-17 serves as a focal point for our discussion.

At the center of Exhibit 6-17 is the individual—with his/her personality traits, experiences, and attitudes—surrounded by aspects of the social structure. The societal unit most closely related to the individual is his/her family; then in approximate order of importance to the individual come other reference groups (which may cut across other elements of the social structure), social class, and his/her culture.

The family is probably the most significant single determinant of an individual's values and attitudes; therefore, the collective values and attitudes of the society derive in no small measure from the way in which the family is viewed by its members. In Western society, families tend to be nuclear (mother, father, children, if any) as opposed to extended (grandparents, aunts and uncles, etc.).

In contemporary societies, however, the trend seems to be toward the loosening of family ties, reflecting a shift to reference group (as opposed to family) guides to behavior and attitude formation. Moreover, marriage is not the stable institution that it once was. Divorce is more frequent, many people live together without marriage (including homosexual relationships), and group familylike arrangements are more common today. Whatever its makeup, the family is often the basic buying unit for many products.

Social class is the concept that there are layers or strata of society, i.e., groups of people who share attitudes and values which differ from those of people in other layers. In more traditional societies, class structure is a function of birth, e.g., the Indian caste system and the medieval king-nobles-yeomen-serfs structure. In contemporary society, social classes are less rigid; it is possible to move from one class to another, but the phenomenon of classes in society is no less pervasive.

Perhaps the six-level classification system developed by sociologist Lloyd Warner is the most widely used indicator of social class in the United States. It divides the social structure into classes on the basis of four variables: occupation, source of income, house type, and dwelling area. Exhibit 6-18 summarizes American social classes according to these indicators. Note that the table indicates that the three upper classes comprise about one-sixth of American population, but include most of the business and social leaders.

The most important classes for marketing managers to consider are the lower-middle and the upper-lower classes. Perhaps better descriptors (because they lack the connotation of ranking) are *middle class* and *working class*. These classes are important to the marketing manager because they contain the bulk of the population in an industrial society. The marketing manager needs to understand how social class influences the buying behavior of these two major groupings.

Differences in these two classes can be briefly illustrated by considering two popular contemporary television comedies: "The Mary Tyler Moore Show" and "All in the Family." Mary is a producer for a television station, clearly a middle-class job; she is relatively well educated, "liberated," and lives in a tastefully decorated, modernized apartment. Archie Bunker, on the other hand, is a first-level foreman—a rather successful working-class occupation. He is not well educated, is a bit of a tyrant to his family, and lives in an older house which contains rather drab furnishings.

Here, gleaned from several different sources, are some of the differences between the middle class and the working class. Occupation is perhaps the primary differentiating factor. Although two family heads may live in similarly priced houses and earn approximately the same income, the way that they make this money differs. The middle-class breadwinner may be a bank teller, an accountant, a school teacher, a

Exhibit 6-18   Indicators of Social Class in America

Social Class	Proportion of American Population (percent)	Indicators			
		Primary Occupations	Income Source	House Type	Dwelling Area
Upper-upper	0.5–1.0	Investments Civic work	Inherited wealth	Family mansions	Older affluent areas
Lower-upper	1.5–2.0	Professionals Corporation heads	Salary Dividends	New mansions	Newer affluent areas
Upper-middle	10–12	Professionals Businesspeople	Salary	New "split levels"	Better suburbs
Lower-middle	25–35	White collar workers	Salary	Tract houses	Suburbs
Upper-lower	35–45	Blue collar workers	Wages	Older frame houses	Areas of central city
Lower-lower	20–25	Laborers Janitors, etc.	Wages	Tenements	Slums

Note: Table entries are illustrative of generalizations about social classes, but are not complete descriptions.

Prepared by the author from various discussions of the concept of social class; based on W. Lloyd Warner and others, *Social Class in America* (Science Research Associates, Inc., 1949).

middle-manager paid by the week. The working-class household head is an electrician, baker, appliance service man, or skilled factory worker; he/ she is probably paid by the hour. The working-class husband is likely to turn his entire paycheck over to his wife, who manages the family budget. In the middle-class household, budgeting and financial affairs are more likely to be joint decisions. The working-class house is probably older, and located in a lower-status neighborhood than the middle-class house—but it probably has newer and more expensive appliances in it. The working-class wife is likely to be pretty good with the sewing machine, and her husband spends a considerable amount of time in do-it-yourself chores around the house. Both are generally more proficient at this type of task than are their middle-class counterparts. Style and fashion in clothes and furniture is probably of greater significance to the middle class than to the working class. The middle-class family is likely to take a vacation at the beach or in the mountains. Working-class vacations are likely to be spent at home or with relatives.

Of course, these are generalizations, and there are exceptions, but the point is: the marketing manager should know the social class from which his customers hail. Exhibit 6-19 describes a classic example here.

Exhibit 6-19 Social Class and Store Patronage

Patrons of Chicago retail organizations were asked, "If you were going to buy new living room furniture for your home, at which store would you be most likely to find what you want?" The figure below summarizes the answers for two leading stores. If the customer body of each store had been truly representative of the social classes in the metropolitan area, the result would have shown up as the horizontal broken line opposite the figure 100. But Store A appealed strongly to people in the upper and middle classes, and Store B appealed strongly to

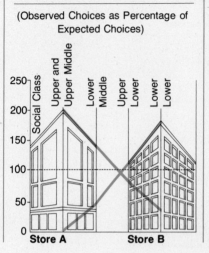

(Observed Choices as Percentage of Expected Choices)

shoppers from the lower (working) social classes.

Yet the advertising director of Store A, a leading department store with a broad range of price lines and a basement store, was astonished to learn that not every person read his store's advertising. And the executive Vice President of Store B, one of the chain of retail furniture stores, was on record as saying, "We sell everybody. We have stores throughout the area, we advertise in the mass-media, we have furniture in all price ranges."

Adapted from Pierre Martineau. "The Personality of the Retail Store," *Harvard Business Review*, January–February 1958, pp. 47–55, with permission of the publisher.

In this section on group influences, and in the previous section on personal influences, we have discussed the major factors that influence the purchase decision. Now we turn to that decision.

THE BUYING DECISION

In terms of the exchange notion, the focal point of marketing is the buying decision. We have outlined the psychological and sociological basis for understanding some of the factors that influence the buying decision. In this section, we use the systems concept to integrate that discussion with other types of factors that influence the buying decision. This discussion sets the stage for a brief look at a more sophisticated model of the buying process. We close with some comments on the diffusion of innovations.

Systems View of the Buying Process

That most useful of analytical tools, the systems approach, can be applied to the buying decision. Exhibit 6-20 depicts the major elements and their interrelationships. The objective of the buying decision is buyer satisfaction. Thus, the purpose of the process leading to and resulting from the buying decision is to procure products that satisfy the wants and desires of the buyer.

In order to achieve this objective, five basic types of inputs enter the decision process: (1) effective demand, (2) personal influence, (3) group influence, (4) marketing and other types of organizational effort, and (5) other environmental factors. Earlier in the chapter, we used the acronym

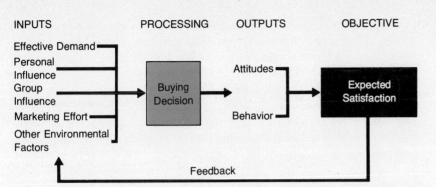

INPUTS   PROCESSING   OUTPUTS   OBJECTIVE

Effective Demand
Personal Influence
Group Influence
Marketing Effort
Other Environmental Factors

Buying Decision

Attitudes
Behavior

Expected Satisfaction

Feedback

Exhibit 6-20   Systems View of the Buying Decision

MAD to represent effective demand, and we discussed personal and group influences upon the buying decision.

The fourth type of input into the buying process is generated by the effort of organizations offering products to satisfy the buyer's wants and desires. We discussed marketing functions in Chapter 2 and placed these functions within the context of the organizational system in Chapter 5; the material in the chapters following this one are devoted to examining marketing effort in more detail.

The fifth set of inputs into the decision process stems from environmental factors not directly related to effective demand, personal or marketing effort—such factors as general economic conditions, pending legislation, fashion trends, and technological advances. Even when these factors do not directly influence the buying power or behavior of individuals or the marketing efforts of firms, they affect the buying process—therefore, they must be considered by anyone wishing to understand that process.

Earlier, we commented that the process leading to the buying decision is a response triggered by product stimuli. The five types of inputs represent an elaboration of the types of product stimuli that trigger the buying process. The outputs of this process are of two types: attitudes and behavior.

Attitude Change. The marketing manager is interested in the buyer's attitudes. The attitudinal output of the purchase decision can take one of three forms. The buying process might confirm existing attitudes, change those attitudes, or create new attitudes. Attitude confirmation is the easiest output, from the marketing manager's perspective. A great deal of marketing effort has the basic objective of confirming favorable attitudes toward well-established products.

Attitude change means alteration of the disposition to act in a certain way. One obvious example is the change from negative to positive attitudes about a product. Attitude change is not easy. There are a number of different approaches to the problem of changing attitudes. It might be easier to create a new attitude by introducing a new product. We discuss approaches to attitude confirmation, change, and creation in Chapter 10 on promotion.

There is considerable discussion in marketing literature as to whether attitude confirmation, change, or creation precedes or follows purchase behavior. Evidence shows that in many cases attitudes toward a product must be favorable before it is purchased. On the other hand, purchase of some products leads to positive or negative attitude formation.

Purchase Behavior. From the point of view of marketing management, the most significant consequence of the buying decision is the action that the buyer takes: What product will he/she buy? What store will he/she patronize? What brand will he/she choose? What price will he/she pay?

Answers to these questions take the form of analyses of behavior patterns over time. Information about past behavior is useful for marketing decision making—provided that future conditions resemble those of the past. The frequent use of past behavior information by marketing management is based on the assumption that there is some relatively stable relationship between past and future behavior. Given this assumption, it makes sense to look systematically at past behavior, particularly loyalty patterns.

Much work has been devoted to the investigation of the strength of the buyer's preference for a particular brand of product or store in which to shop. It is to the marketer's advantage to increase his/her customer's loyalty if possible. Unfortunately, however, an empirical grasp of the loyalty concept has proved difficult because loyalty can be defined in a number of ways. Three of the most common definitions are:

1. *Percent of budget devoted to given brand or store*—the higher the percentage of total budget for that product category devoted to a particular brand or store, the more loyal the consumer is said to be.

2. *Number of brands used or stores patronized*—the fewer brands used or stores shopped, the higher the consumer's loyalty to one brand or store is said to be.

3. *Pattern of repeat purchases*—the more consecutive times the consumer buys a given brand or shops in a given store, the higher his loyalty to that brand or store is said to be.

Each of these definitions of loyalty has some intuitive plausibility, but note that they are not necessarily the same. For example, a consumer may spend 80 percent of his/her budget on one brand, but split the remaining 20 percent among five other brands. He/she would, therefore, be rated highly loyal on the percentage-of-budget comparison, but relatively disloyal on the number-of-brands-used criterion.

Despite this disparity of definitions, a great deal of work has been done on brand and store loyalty. These attempts (usually based on frequently purchased products of small unit value, such as dry groceries) have tended to focus on determining a relationship between loyalty and consumers' socioeconomic or psychological characteristics. Such research has attempted to identify people who might be highly loyal to a particular product or store. Hypothetically, this research might indicate that consumers in a certain age group, or those without an automobile, or those with a high need for order or deference, would tend to purchase regularly a given brand or to patronize frequently a particular store. Unfortunately, this research to date has not shown that generalized loyalty proneness exists. Given our present knowledge of consumer loyalty, it would seem that the best way for the marketing manager to determine loyalty to his/her brand or store is to study the customers and to adjust his/her marketing efforts to please the most regular patrons.

Outputs of the buying decision are assessed in terms of the buyer's level of satisfaction. If the actual consequences of the buying process are judged by the buyer to be better than or equal to the expected consequences, the buyer will feel satisfied with the process. Conversely, if actual outcomes are less rewarding than expected, the buyer will feel dissatisfied. Satisfaction must, of course, be evaluated relative to the buyer's expenditure of effort and money during the buying process.

It is easy to grasp the concept of satisfaction but difficult to document it empirically. This is because satisfaction is the net result of many factors—the product itself, the environment surrounding the buying experience, the marketing effort expended on the product, and so on. Satisfaction is a complex phenomenon; a buyer might experience inconsistent thoughts or cognitions about the buying process he/she has just completed. This is particularly true if the decision is an important one—an automobile, a home, a major appliance—and if the rejected alternatives are numerous or attractive. Conceptually, it would be possible to construct an index for measuring the degree of satisfaction experienced in a particular buying situation, but little empirical progress has been made on this monumental task.

Some work has been done, however, in the area of consumer dissatisfaction or dissonance. In psychological terms, dissonance—post purchase anxiety—results in a state of tension in the individual, with a consequent drive to alleviate the tension by reducing the dissonance. He/she may do this by revoking the purchase decision, i.e., returning the product and demanding payment back. More commonly, however, the consumer will seek to reduce dissonance by reading advertisements for the product, by speaking favorably of it to others, and so forth.

Although subsequent research has not been entirely consistent in determining the extent and magnitude of dissonance resulting from purchase decisions, the concept is useful because it suggests that automobile and appliance salespersons should make follow-up telephone calls or send letters to purchasers, and that some part of the advertising budget should be devoted to reminder advertising.

In the final stage of the systems view of the buying decision, the buyer's level of satisfaction becomes information that is fed back into his/her buying process. In addition, as we discussed in the section of the chapter on search in the buying process, this information may be communicated either formally or informally to other current and potential buyers.

I believe that this systems view of the buying decision is a useful one for marketing management. It presents a relatively simple framework for thinking about buyer behavior. Because it is simple, however, it is also crude. Howard and Sheth have developed a more elaborate model of the buying decision.

Howard/Sheth Model of Buying Behavior
Exhibit 6-21 presents the Howard/Sheth model of buyer behavior. A complete explanation of the model is beyond the scope of this book, but note that it conforms in major features to the systems view. There are four sections of the model. The most important is the buyer's information and decision process, represented by the area within the heavy black border in the center of the diagram. The variables within this (black) box are called "endogenous variables." Inputs into the decision process are shown at the left. Howard and Sheth classify these input stimuli as brand information (significative) stimuli, marketing effort (symbolic) stimuli, and informal communications (social environment) stimuli. The decision process is affected by seven external (exogenous) factors—importance of purchase, personality variables, social class, culture, organization (group influences), time pressure, and financial status. The output of the decision process is the buyer's response to the input stimuli. Note that these outputs are phrased in terms of the hierarchy of effects (Exhibit 6-5) that we discussed earlier in the chapter.

These outputs can also be viewed as stages in the adoption of the product. This perspective is called diffusion of innovations.

The Diffusion Process
Diffusion is the process by which something spreads, e.g., language, religion, and technological advances, both among and within societies. The pioneer in diffusion theory is Rogers; Exhibit 6-22 shows the fundamentals of his work on the diffusion process. In marketing, diffusion is the acceptance of new products. The group of most interest to marketing managers is the *early adopters* (the innovators are likely to try a product

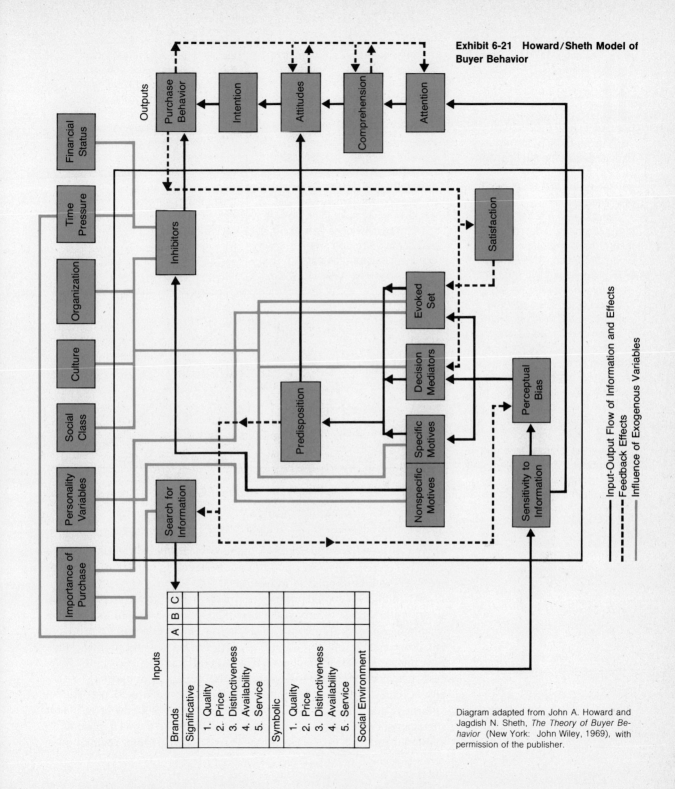

Exhibit 6-21   Howard/Sheth Model of Buyer Behavior

Outputs

Inputs

Legend:
—— Input-Output Flow of Information and Effects
- - - Feedback Effects
—— Influence of Exogenous Variables

Diagram adapted from John A. Howard and Jagdish N. Sheth, *The Theory of Buyer Behavior* (New York: John Wiley, 1969), with permission of the publisher.

Exhibit 6-22   The Diffusion Pattern

On the basis of his research, Rogers represents the adoption process as a normal or near normal distribution when plotted over time.

The adopters are categorized in terms of standard deviations of the normal distribution. The *innovators* are those whose adoption time is more than two standard deviations before the average adoption time. The next class is *early adopters,* those who adopt between one and two standard deviations before the average adoption time. The third category is the *early majority,* those between the average adoption time and one standard deviation; the *late majority* consists of those whose adoption time is between the average time and one standard deviation after, and those whose adoption time is greater than one standard devia-tion after the mean are termed laggards.

In trying to identify the characteristics of each adopter category, Rogers assigned "ideation values" to each group. The innovators are characterized by *venturesomeness*—they like new ideas, even at some risk. The early adopters are characterized by *respect*—they enjoy position in the community as opinion leaders: they adopt new ideas early, but with some discretion. The dominant value of the early majority is *deliberateness;* they are, as Shakespeare said, "not the first by whom the new is tried, nor the last to put the old aside." For the late majority, the dominant value is *skepticism*—they do not adopt an innovation until the weight of majority opinion seems to endorse it. Finally, the dominant value of the laggards is *tradition*—they are suspicious of change and adopt an innovation only when it has been accepted by the community.

Adapted from Everett M. Rogers, *Diffusion of Innovations* (New York: Free Press, 1962), p. 162 ff, with permission of the publisher.

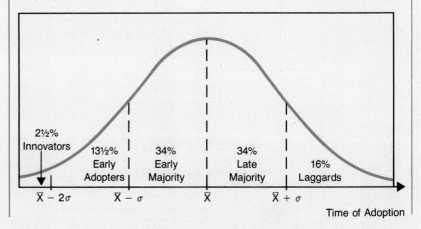

without the efforts of marketing managers). Early adopters have the respect of society—they are opinion leaders, hence an important group for marketers to identify and to influence.

A number of studies have attempted to rate buyer characteristics according to degree of innovativeness. The innovators seem to be some-what higher in education and income, to have more exposure to print and broadcast media, and to be more gregarious and socially mobile. How-ever, this evidence is inconclusive. The general characteristic—innovative-ness—has been difficult to isolate in the general population. Within product categories, however, innovators have been identified, e.g., studies of farmers adopting new fertilizers, or doctors adopting new drugs. Once characteristics of early adopters are identified for a given product, a marketing program can be developed to reach these people. Segmentation decisions and information needed to develop such a program are the subjects of the following chapters.

CONCLUDING NOTE

Throughout this chapter, we have referred to buyer behavior in terms of customers of an organization's products. In line with the generic interpretation of the marketing concept, the term *buyer* could also connote organizational relationships with other constituents, e.g., public policy makers, employees, stockholders, vendors, etc. Conceptually, the term *buying process* would be correctly applied to all constituents. In application, however, differences would inevitably arise.

Buyer behavior, however defined, is interesting and complex. We could say much more about it—indeed, an economist, a psychologist, a sociologist, or an anthropologist would no doubt accuse us of slighting his/her area in this overview of consumer behavior. I certainly encourage you to read further in this field. The suggested readings at the end of this chapter provide a good starting point, and these sources contain further references.

Extensive study in buyer behavior can be frustrating, however. You may find that more knowledge does not necessarily mean better managerial performance, or even increased understanding of buyer behavior. Much specific information and many generalizations exist regarding buyer behavior, but relatively little of this knowledge translates to an operational level—little is known about why a given consumer behaves as he/she does. Drawing useful policy guidelines for future marketing actions from behavioral analyses is not easy. The risks (and rewards) from translating generalized trends into products that satisfy individual wants are great—because the job is complex and difficult. Fortunately for the marketing manager, knowledge of specific individual behavior is usually not necessary. The marketing manager works with groups of individuals and markets. Here the law of large numbers tends to work: individual differences and the influence of random factors in the environment tend to cancel out. Thus, it is usually not necessary to say *who* will buy, simply how many. For such a task, the material in this chapter, from the marketing manager's point of view, is good general background. This material also provides the basis for our discussion in following chapters of market segmentation, decision making and forecasting.

KEY TERMS AND CONCEPTS

Buying Process
    desire recognition
    search
    purchase decision
    product use and evaluation

Economic Man Concept
    rationality
    assumptions

Utility
  measure of satisfaction
  diminishing marginal
Intrapersonal Behavior Components
  cognitive
  affective
  conative
  personality
Processes of Behavioral Change
  motivation
  perception
  learning
Groups
  function
  structure
Group Influence
  norms
  reference groups
  opinion
  leadership

Culture Dimensions
  distributive
  normative
  structural
Social Structure
  family
  social class
  culture
Systems View of Buying Behavior
  objective
  inputs
  processing
  outputs
Model of Buyer Behavior
  Howard-Sheth
Outputs of Buying Decision
  satisfaction
  dissonance
  loyalty
  intentions
Diffusion Process

QUESTIONS FOR DISCUSSION

1. A woman enters a grocery store with her child. The child hands her a box of cereal. She reads the label, then returns the box to the shelf. The child hands her another brand, which she accepts. Use the buying process model (Exhibit 6-4) to examine this situation.

2. Using Exhibit 6-6 as a guide, evaluate various formal and informal sources of information for such products as life insurance, a new automobile, structural steel shapes, a restaurant, and a candidate for the state legislature.

3. The position taken in this book is that the processes of organizational buying and the buying for household consumption are basically similar. Argue that this position is valid; now argue that it is not valid. What is your opinion?

4. We also take the position that distinguishing *needs* from *wants* is not useful to marketing managers. Look at both sides of this issue, too. What is your opinion?

5. The text states that contemporary society is placing less value on organized religion. On the basis of your personal knowledge and experience, would you agree or disagree? Why? If such a trend is occurring, and you were the "marketing manager" (pastor, priest, rabbi, or lay leader) of

a religious organization, what marketing-oriented actions would you recommend? Why?

6. Contrast consumption patterns of the middle-class and working-class housewife, as portrayed in the text. Why is such a study of interest to marketing decision makers?

7. Some of the examples given in the text are classic, but a bit dated. Give contemporary examples of:

(a) reference group influence (Exhibit 6-15)

(b) diffusion of innovations (Exhibit 6-22)

8. Using the situation in question 1, identify inputs, processing, and outputs according to the Howard/Sheth model.

SUGGESTED READING

1. James F. Engel, David T. Kollat, and Roger D. Blackwell. *Consumer Behavior.* 2nd ed. New York: Holt, Rinehart and Winston, 1973. This is perhaps the standard general reference in the area of buying behavior at the present time; it is encyclopedic, and contains numerous references.

2. Peter D. Bennett and Harold H. Kassarjian. *Consumer Behavior.* Englewood Cliffs, N.J.: Prentice-Hall, 1972. This book is a 132-page overview of the area of consumer behavior; it devotes a chapter to the economic theory of demand, and is heavily psychologically oriented; easy, entertaining reading; good quick introduction to the field.

3. Harold H. Kassarjian and Thomas S. Robertson, eds. *Perspectives in Consumer Behavior,* 2nd ed. Chicago: Scott, Foresman and Company, 1973. Perhaps best general anthology of articles on consumer behavior; many of the examples in the text can be found in the various articles in this volume.

4. David Krech, Richard F. Crutchfield, and Egerton L. Ballachey. *The Individual in Society: A Textbook of Social Psychology.* New York: McGraw Hill Book Company, 1962. Classic textbook in social psychology; good general background for the more specific study of buyer behavior.

5. Richard H. Leftwich. *The Price System and Resource Allocation,* 3rd ed. New York: Holt, Rinehart and Winston, 1971. This is a very readable standard reference in microeconomic theory; contains a relatively lucid treatment of the economic theory of demand, good background reading for the serious student of buyer behavior.

6. Thomas S. Robertson. *Consumer Behavior.* Chicago: Scott, Foresman and Company, 1970.

Another short overview of the field; this one is written at a somewhat higher level, with greater attention to research concepts and findings than the Bennett and Kassarjian book; probably a better introduction to the area for the aspiring researcher.

7. Frederick E. Webster, Jr. and Yoram Wind.
Organizational Buying Behavior. Englewood Cliffs, N.J.: Prentice-Hall, 1972. This short overview is oriented toward organizational, as distinguished from household, buying behavior; well-written and extensively referenced; no really different concepts, but the difference in perspective is instructive.

"This is Barbara Walters. Fighting continues in the streets of Beirut..."

7/ MARKET SEGMENTATION

This chapter in the Market Analysis and Strategy part of the book integrates the material on marketing functions and buyer behavior that we have covered to this point. Its purpose is to structure this material in a manner useful for marketing strategy formulation. Major points include:

1. Market segmentation strives for successful attainment of organizational objectives by identifying and serving groups of people with similar wants. It is a compromise between the ineffectiveness of treating all consumers alike and the inefficiency of treating each one differently.

2. The criteria for successful segmentation include identification, responsiveness, and significance. Bases for segmentation include customer state-of-being characteristics, customer state-of-mind characteristics, product usage, and product benefits.

3. Segmentation strategy formulation involves four steps. First, market segments must be delineated. Second, a target market is selected by matching organizational products to the wants of certain segments. Third, a marketing program is developed to serve the target market. Fourth, the program is implemented and controlled.

4. The marketing planning process provides the structure for strategy development. Concepts for measuring consumer demand in a segment are buying power, market potential, and sales potential.

The economic theory of pure competition assumes that all buyers are alike. In the preceding chapter, on the other hand, we indicate that all buyers are different. From the point of view of marketing management, neither perspective is particularly useful. While it would not effectively serve the wants and desires of customers to treat them all alike, it would not be efficient to produce a different product to satisfy each consumer in the market.

Market segmentation is concerned, therefore, with identifying and serving meaningful customer groups in the market. We look first at the concept of market segmentation, review the bases of market segment delineation, and then discuss target market selection and demand estimation.

CONCEPT OF MARKET SEGMENTATION

The need for market segmentation strategy derives from the heterogeneity of supply and of demand. A market segment is a group of people with homogeneous wants—for which an organization might provide a product. Segmentation strategy generally improves the effectiveness of marketing performance, but at some cost in production and marketing efficiencies.

The Need for Segmentation Strategy

Recall from Chapter 4 that the economic theory of pure competition assumes the homogeneous products of suppliers will be matched with the homogeneous wants and desires of consumers through price adjustments. The real world is a bit more complex. On the supply side, products may differ for a number of reasons, e.g., composition of raw materials, manufacturing techniques, advertising campaigns, geographic location of the organization. On the demand side, the wants and desires of consumers are diverse. Consequently, the real world is characterized by heterogeneous markets, in which the demands of each consumer are somewhat different. Exhibit 7-1 illustrates the two extremes.

The economist sees a perfectly homogeneous market in which demands of all consumers are identical; the student of buyer behavior sees each individual's demand as unique. The marketing manager's view is between these extremes. The manager is interested in disaggregating perfectly homogeneous markets in order to serve consumers more effectively. At the same time, heterogeneous demands must be aggregated into meaningful groups so that products can be efficiently produced. Thus, beer is seldom brewed to an individual's taste, but neither is there one beer for all consumers. The beer market now offers regular, light, premium, malt liquor, and near-beer products.

From the perspective of the marketing manager, market segmentation involves two closely related ideas. First, the total market for any product can be subdivided or segmented into groups of potential custom-

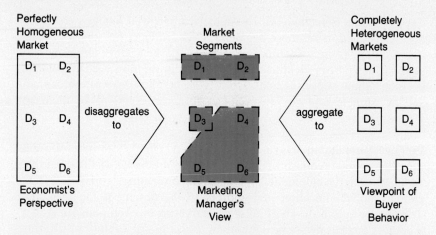

Exhibit 7-1   How Markets Are Viewed

Perfectly Homogeneous Market

Market Segments

Completely Heterogeneous Markets

D_1 D_2

D_3 D_4

D_5 D_6

disaggregates to

D_1 D_2

D_3 D_4

D_5 D_6

aggregate to

D_1 D_2

D_3 D_4

D_5 D_6

Economist's Perspective

Marketing Manager's View

Viewpoint of Buyer Behavior

ers who are homogeneous with respect to certain wants or desires. Second, it might be advantageous to the organization (in terms of meeting its objectives) to serve one or more of these market segments. Market segmentation can be defined as:

> the delineation of a customer group or groups with homogeneous wants which the organization might successfully satisfy.

Note the emphasis on two terms in this definition. First, homogeneous means that the wants of the segment are similar relative to the wants of the total market. Second, successful indicates that there must be some expectation on the part of the organization that, by satisfying the wants of the segment, it can obtain its objectives. Thus, the marketing manager must weigh the benefits and costs of segmentation.

Segmentation Benefits . . .
Segmentation generally improves the effectiveness of the marketing program. The benefits of segmentation strategy relate basically to the marketing management functions of seeking, matching, and programming.

Customer Focus. The process of identifying segments and determining their accessibility necessitates focusing upon consumer wants and desires. This, of course, is the essence of the marketing concept. It encourages the organization to keep up with who buys its products where, when, how, etc. Segmentation, therefore, keeps the organization alert to changes in market conditions, competitors' actions, and other environmental opportunities and threats. For example, competitive analysis may indicate which segments of the market are controlled by strong, entrenched competitors and which segments' needs are not fulfilled by present product offerings.

Target-Market Selection. This customer contact and analysis results in the determination of those segments that can best be served by the organization. These segments are the target markets. Once target-market segments have been identified, the types of information needed to make decisions about those segments is fairly clear. The organization can get specific estimates and can set specific performance standards on the basis of its objectives.

Program Formulation. Having selected its target market, the organization can develop marketing programs tailored to the needs of those market segments. This development involves careful budgeting of total marketing effort, rational allocation of resources to the design of the program, decisions on specific levels of different marketing mix components. And it pinpoints tactical decision alternatives, e.g., the advisability of offering another brand, or whether or not to increase the intensity of distribution.

. . . and Costs

Increases in effectiveness, however, are generally achieved at the expense of efficiency. Segmentation is expensive, and the resulting pattern of market coverage may be less than ideal.

Segmentation Expenses. Clearly, it is less efficient to produce different models and variations of a product than to produce one standard model—it is certainly cheaper to produce only black automobiles. Moreover, the development costs of different models generally involve research and design expenses, and engineering and tooling costs. Marketing costs also are likely to be higher. For example, inventories of each of the different products will have to be maintained, it may be necessary to design different promotional campaigns to reach the different segments, and salespersons will have to become proficient in explaining and demonstrating different models of the product. The administrative costs of these activities will also rise. The company will need to develop separate marketing plans, production schedules, personnel hiring practices, and so on. In short, market segmentation is likely to lead to higher sales of the organization's product, and to higher costs of making these sales.

Market Coverage. The concept of segmentation underscores the point that no one product can please everyone. Consequently, if a company desires to serve an entire market, it must have more than one product. Procter & Gamble, for example, markets *Tide*, *Cheer*, and *Ivory Snow* detergents. General Motors offers Buick, Pontiac, Chevrolet, and Oldsmobile automobiles to middle-income market segments. On the other hand, the strategy of maximum market coverage might result in *cannibalization* of an organization's market—the situation in which one of an organization's products takes sales away from another product of that same organization. The classic example here is the Ford Falcon. The Falcon was introduced in 1960 as an economy car for lower-income consumers. It turned out to have a much broader appeal, however; many middle-income consumers purchased it as a second car. This wider appeal cut into the market for Ford's traditional, standard-size automobiles. General Motors seems not to have learned from Ford's mistake. The Cadillac Seville probably takes away as many Coupe De Ville sales as it does sales from Mercedes 450 SLs.

Thus, segmentation strategies must be carefully examined in light of the organization's objectives. The basic question is: Will a strategy based on this target-market segment contribute to organizational objectives? To answer this question, we look next at the criteria for segmentation.

Segmentation Criteria

Segmentation strategy rests upon the delineation of meaningful market segments and uses these three criteria: identity, responsiveness and significance.

Identity. The marketing manager interested in segmentation must first have some means of identifying members of the segment—some basis for classifying an individual as being or not being a member of the segment. That is, there must be some evident want or desire, or at least some common characteristic or behavior pattern. For example, certain people may want pollution-control equipment, or sugarless gum, or they may have a psychological obsession with cleanliness, or they may all belong to the same religion. The relevant question here is: How can the members of the segment be identified?

Responsiveness. If the segment can be identified, the next criterion to consider is whether or not the segment can be communicated with and how it will react to marketing effort. For example, certain product features, a lower price or more service, may more precisely satisfy the needs of a given segment than would a general marketing effort. The relevant question is: What are the purchase motivations of the members of the segment under scrutiny?

Significance. Suppose that a segment meets the first two criteria, i.e., it can be identified and reached with marketing effort, and would respond to that effort. The last and most crucial question, from marketing management's point of view, is: Is it worth it? The segment must possess sufficient buying power (willingness to buy plus ability to buy) to make a worthwhile contribution to the organization's objectives. Whether it is worth the effort or not generally depends on the number of people in the segment. But it may be that, in a segment small in number, a few

Exhibit 7-2   Hierarchy of Segmentation Bases

CUSTOMER SATISFACTION

4. Product Benefits

3. Product Usage

2. Customer State-of-Mind

1. Customer State-of-Being

customers each have sufficient buying power to make the segment worth significant marketing effort.

In summary, the concept of market segmentation is rapidly becoming the basic point of origin for all marketing strategy. The remainder of this chapter is devoted to explaining segment identification, responsiveness and significance in terms useful for guiding marketing strategy formulation. Identification is based upon four types of variables.

BASES FOR SEGMENTATION

The foundation for market segmentation strategy is the base upon which the segments are built, i.e., the variables used to identify the segments of interest. The ultimate purpose of market segmentation is increased consumer satisfaction. Satisfaction is the result of product benefits, which in turn result from product use. Product usage is related to certain customer characteristics—state-of-mind (attitudes, values, perception) and/or state-of-being (geographic location, demographic characteristics). These four factors, therefore, form a hierarchy of possible segmentation bases leading to customer satisfaction. This hierarchy is presented in Exhibit 7-2.

Customer state-of-being characteristics are relatively easy to identify, but they are rather far removed from customer satisfaction. State-of-mind characteristics, such as attitudes toward products or brands, store preferences, and so forth, are somewhat closer to customer satisfaction, but are a bit more difficult to measure. Even closer to customer satisfaction is product usage, but this requires an after-the-fact measurement of consumer behavior. Most closely related to consumer satisfaction are the product benefits which the consumer derives from the product. Segmentation on the basis of these benefits requires very specific measures of expectations and evaluations of product performance. Of course, this is not the only way segmentation bases can be categorized, but it is useful in separating the various bases for market segmentation strategy so that we can study them. Exhibit 7-3 provides structure for our discussion.

State-of-Being Segmentation Bases

State-of-being information refers to physical or demographic characteristics of individuals or organizations. Early segmentation strategy efforts focused on this type of variable—because it is relatively easy to identify. Commonly employed state-of-being segmentation variables include geography, demography, and customer type.

Geographic Segmentation. Geography is a very common and useful basis for market segmentation. Individuals who are located in close proximity to an organization are more likely to be its customers than are more distantly located individuals—other things being equal. Also, a particular geo-

Exhibit 7-3 Structure of Segmentation Strategies

Segmentation Base	Common Variables	Examples
1. State-of-being	Geography	Region, city, neighborhood
	Demography	Age, sex, race, income
	Customer type	Government body, institution, specific industry
2. State-of-mind	Psychographics	Personality traits, life style
	Perceptions and preferences	Multidimensional scaling, cluster analysis
3. Product usage	Volume	"The heavy half"
	Market factors	Sensitivity to advertising
	Loyalty	Budget allocation, switching
4. Benefits	Situation-specific measures	Economy, function, style, sociability

graphic region may represent a potentially successful market segment for a firm because few competitors are located in the region. Conversely, a particular institutional pattern may be so entrenched that penetration of the region by a new firm is unlikely to prove successful.

National organizations also practice geographic segmentation. Many magazines, from *Time* to *Playboy* to *Reader's Digest,* publish regional editions. Advertisers can purchase space in all editions or can tailor advertisements to specific sections of the country. And the sales force of many a company is structured on a territorial basis. Exhibit 7-4 describes *Sales Management* magazine's "Buying Power Index," a geographically oriented method of estimating purchasing power.

Demographic Segmentation. Demographic information is often used to develop customer segments; race ("soul" radio stations), religion (Kosher foods), and sex (feminine hygiene products) are typical examples. As we discussed in the previous chapter, such elements as social class and family life cycle influence buyer behavior.

Customer-Type Segmentation. In some markets, a single customer or type of customer is so large that it is worthwhile to consider that customer or customer type as a segment. Steel companies, for example, mount separate marketing efforts for the automobile, railroad, and bridge building industries. The Standard Industrial Classification (S.I.C.) code system described in Exhibit 7-5 provides a means of identifying customer types for possible segmentation strategies.

Institutions—hospitals, colleges, libraries, prisons, government agencies—are often treated as separate market segments by organizations marketing to them. This is because the buying procedures of these institutions are relatively complex. Consider a university, for example. Each academic department is a separate administrative unit with its own budget. Some items, e.g., mimeograph paper, pencils, and paper clips, can be purchased by the carload for the entire university. But items such as visual aid materials and books for the library must be requisitioned separately by each department. Textbooks are often chosen by individual professors. Any large organization is likely to have relatively complex procedures for getting anything done, but the difficulties seem to be multiplied in not-for-profit institutions. Designing a separate marketing program specifically for an institutional segment, therefore, is found by many marketing managers to be a sound practice.

The largest institution of all is government, at federal, state, and local levels. Although governmental agencies buy almost every product imaginable, their procurement procedures are usually so complex and specialized that many organizations marketing to governmental units have separate staffs and programs to cover this segment. At the federal level, there are three broad categories of government markets: the General Services Administration which buys, stores, and disburses items in general use by all government agencies, civilian agencies, such as the departments of Commerce and the Interior, agencies such as the Federal Aviation Agency and the Federal Trade Commission, administrations such as the National Aeronautics and Space Administration, and military buying.

The assumption underlying segmentation on the basis of state-of-being information is that these characteristics are related to customer satisfaction. There is some validity to this assumption. However, custom-

Exhibit 7-5 Example of the Standard Industrial Classification System

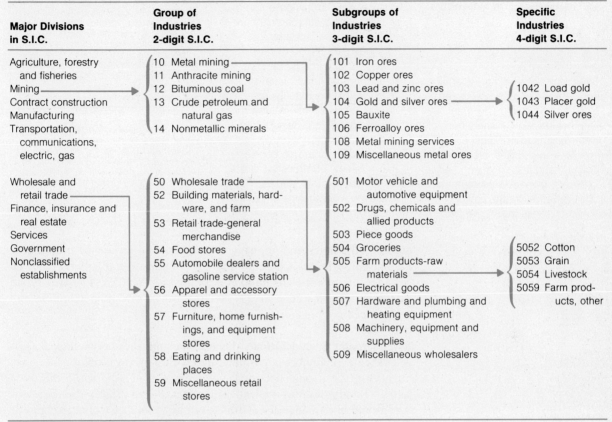

Major Divisions in S.I.C.	Group of Industries 2-digit S.I.C.	Subgroups of Industries 3-digit S.I.C.	Specific Industries 4-digit S.I.C.
Agriculture, forestry and fisheries	10 Metal mining	101 Iron ores	
Mining	11 Anthracite mining	102 Copper ores	
Contract construction	12 Bituminous coal	103 Lead and zinc ores	1042 Load gold
Manufacturing	13 Crude petroleum and natural gas	104 Gold and silver ores	1043 Placer gold
Transportation, communications, electric, gas	14 Nonmetallic minerals	105 Bauxite	1044 Silver ores
		106 Ferroalloy ores	
		108 Metal mining services	
		109 Miscellaneous metal ores	
Wholesale and retail trade	50 Wholesale trade	501 Motor vehicle and automotive equipment	
Finance, insurance and real estate	52 Building materials, hardware, and farm	502 Drugs, chemicals and allied products	
Services	53 Retail trade-general merchandise	503 Piece goods	
Government	54 Food stores	504 Groceries	5052 Cotton
Nonclassified establishments	55 Automobile dealers and gasoline service station	505 Farm products-raw materials	5053 Grain
	56 Apparel and accessory stores	506 Electrical goods	5054 Livestock
	57 Furniture, home furnishings, and equipment stores	507 Hardware and plumbing and heating equipment	5059 Farm products, other
	58 Eating and drinking places	508 Machinery, equipment and supplies	
	59 Miscellaneous retail stores	509 Miscellaneous wholesalers	

Adapted from *Standard Industrial Classification Manual* (Bureau of the Budget, 1967).

ers with different state-of-being characteristics can be satisfied with the same type of product (invalids, as well as infants, may consume baby food); conversely, customers with similar state-of-being characteristics may have different wants and desires (not every suburban housewife wants a station wagon). Segmentation in this fashion is rather crude. These characteristics are simple and easy-to-use segmentation bases, but they provide only general guidance for marketing decision making.

State-of-Mind Segmentation Bases

State-of-mind characteristics are mental attributes of individuals—personality traits, attitudes, decision processes, images, and product preferences. As we discussed in the previous chapter, it is clear that state-of-mind characteristics do influence buying behavior, but we really know relatively little about how these influences operate in specific cases. We also pointed out that it is usually unnecessary to understand individual mental

Exhibit 7-6 Psychographic Segmentation in Automobiles

Evans attempted to determine personality differences between owners of Ford and Chevrolet automobiles. Ford owners had been described as "independent, impulsive, masculine, alert to change, and self-confident," while Chevrolet owners were seen as "conservative, thrifty, prestige-conscious, less masculine, and seeking to avoid extremes." Evans examined this assertion by administering a standardized personality test, the Edwards Personality Profile, to owners of Fords and Chevrolets. He concluded, on the basis of statistical analysis, that personality variables were of relatively little value in differentiating Ford owners from Chevrolet owners.

This study generated considerable scholarly controversy, and several subsequent studies. The result: no relationships of practical value for marketing management.

Based on articles in the *Journal of Business:* Franklin B. Evans, "Psychological and Objective Factors in the Prediction of Brand Choice: Ford vs. Chevrolet," October 1959, pp. 340–69; Gary A. Steiner, "Notes on Franklin B. Evans—'Psychological and Objective Factors in the Prediction of Brand Choice,'" January 1961, pp. 57–60; Charles Winick, "The Relationship Among Personality Needs, Objective Factors, and Brand Choice: A Re-examination," January 1961, pp. 61–66; Evans, "You Still Can't Tell a Ford Owner from a Chevrolet Owner," January 1961, pp. 67–73; Alfred A. Kuehn, "Demonstration of a Relationship between Psychological Factors and Brand Choice," April 1963, pp. 237–41; Evans and H.B. Roberts, "Fords, Chevrolets, and the Problem of Discrimination," April 1963, pp. 242–49. And in *Journal of Marketing:* Ralph Westfall, "Psychological Factors in Predicting Product Choice," April 1962, pp. 34–40.

makeup—the marketing manager is interested in groups of individuals, i.e., market segments. Consequently, state of mind variables have received considerable attention in market segmentation studies. The two broad categories of such studies are (1) psychographics, and (2) perceptions and preferences.

Psychographic Segmentation. The intuitive appeal of psychological characteristics as predictors of customer behavior patterns is obvious. Is it not likely that the young, liberated woman will read *Ms.,* while the more settled, family oriented matron will prefer *Better Homes and Gardens?* And would not an advertisement for Virginia Slims—a woman's cigarette that stresses "You've come a long way, baby"—be more likely to influence readers of *Ms.* than *Better Homes and Gardens?*

The answer to these questions is probably affirmative—but this is an extreme example. Marketing managers need more general knowledge about the nature and strength of the relationship between psychographic variables and potential consumer behavior. Many studies have been conducted along these lines. Exhibit 7-6 presents one of the classics in this area. Although such work is extremely interesting to marketing scholars, the general conclusion has been that relationships between psychographic variables and consumer behavior are too weak to be of value in guiding marketing strategy formulation.

Preferences and Perceptions. Consumer perceptions of various products, and their preferences for various brands within a product category, would also seem intuitively to be related to consumer behavior. With the aid of the new fourth-generation computers, researchers have been able to measure customer perceptions and preferences mathematically. Since

Exhibit 7-7   Segmentation via Perceptual and Preference Mapping

In market segmentation analysis, a manager might want to:
1. determine how brands or products in a class are perceived with respect to strengths, weaknesses, similarities, etc.
2. learn about consumers' desires, and how these are satisfied or unsatisfied by the current market.
3. integrate these findings strategically to determine opportunities for new brands of products and how a product or its image should be modified.

Multidimensional scaling techniques can be used to provide information for such purposes. For example, consider the two-dimensional product space for beer shown below. The dimensions are mildness and price. The space was obtained by asking beer drinkers to rate each beer on scales of mildness and lightness. Computer routines then average these ratings to produce a rectangular geometric space with the products positioned as shown.

Note that the beer drinkers surveyed perceived Schlitz and Budweiser to be very similar

products—both prestige beers somewhat on the heavy side. Relative to Budweiser, Miller is seen as a much lighter beer, and Brand A is perceived as considerably more of a price beer.

The second purpose of the study is to determine consumer preferences for beer. This is done by asking the responders to rate their ideal brand of beer on the mildness and lightness scales. These ratings are then averaged. In this study, the ideal points tended to cluster at several different points in the space. Clusters 1 and 2 are the largest. Note that these clusters are near the two largest selling brands of beer, Budweiser and Schlitz. Consumers in Cluster 1

apparently would like both Schlitz and Budweiser to be a little heavier, while those in Cluster 2 would prefer a lighter brew.

Third, note that several clusters of ideal points are not close to any brands in the market. This indicates a possible opportunity to introduce a new brand close to one of these points—or to reposition an existing brand here. For example, Brands A and B are not particularly close to anyone's ideal point—perhaps these beers exist in the market because they are low-priced products.

Adapted from Richard M. Johnson, "Market Segmentation: A Strategic Management Tool," *Journal of Marketing Research*, February 1971, pp. 13–18, with permission of the publishers, the American Marketing Association.

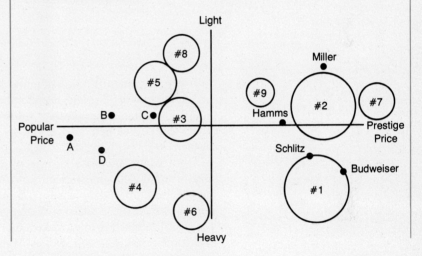

perceptions and preferences are likely to be rather complex, presenting them in several dimensions should improve understanding of their relationships to consumer behavior. The analytical procedures involved here are quite complex, but managerial interpretations of the results may prove useful. Exhibit 7-7 presents one example of this type of segmentation research.

As with state-of-being bases, state-of-mind segmentation studies are undertaken in the belief that a knowledge of such characteristics will lead

Exhibit 7-8 Examples of Product Usage Segmentation

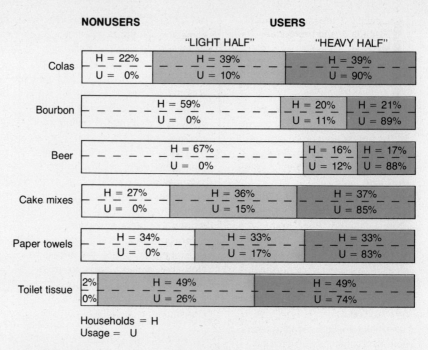

NONUSERS   USERS

"LIGHT HALF"   "HEAVY HALF"

Colas
H = 22% | H = 39% | H = 39%
U = 0% | U = 10% | U = 90%

Bourbon
H = 59% | H = 20% | H = 21%
U = 0% | U = 11% | U = 89%

Beer
H = 67% | H = 16% | H = 17%
U = 0% | U = 12% | U = 88%

Cake mixes
H = 27% | H = 36% | H = 37%
U = 0% | U = 15% | U = 85%

Paper towels
H = 34% | H = 33% | H = 33%
U = 0% | U = 17% | U = 83%

Toilet tissue
2% | H = 49% | H = 49%
0% | U = 26% | U = 74%

Households = H
Usage = U

Adapted from Dik Warren Twedt, "How Important to Marketing Strategy Is the 'Heavy User'?" *Journal of Marketing,* January 1964, p. 72, with permission of the publisher, the American Marketing Association.

to more precise identification of market segments. This is a very appealing notion, but empirical results useful in managerial decision making have to date been rather disappointing. Improvements are likely as these techniques are developed and tested in various situations. A significant problem remains, however. It is not altogether clear how the marketing manager would translate knowledge of a relationship between certain state-of-mind characteristics and consumer behavior into a useful marketing program. For example, suppose that consumers of a certain product were shown to have a relatively high need for dominance. How a manager would utilize this fact to produce a marketing program to take advantage of this relationship is not obvious from this information.

Product Usage Segmentation

As noted above, attempts to relate customer satisfaction to state-of-mind or state-of-being characteristics have provided some general information, but have not been particularly valuable for specific strategy formulation. Consequently, some marketing researchers have looked directly at product usage rates. As shown in Exhibit 7-8, it is possible to take panel data on product purchases and array them according to amount of product usage. For the first product category (colas) note that 78 percent of the panel members use the product. Of those, half—the "heavy half"—purchased 90 percent of all cola drinks. The "heavy half" phenomenon is relatively consistent across all product categories: heavy users purchased from 4 to 10 times as much of the product as light users. Clearly, these would be good prospects to focus marketing effort upon—if they are a responsive segment.

One approach to responsiveness has been to search for relationships between product usage and marketing mix influences. For example, Brand Rating Research Corporation began in the early 60s to identify relationships between heavy users and their media preferences—the television programs they watch, the radio programs they listen to, the magazines and newspapers they read. By combining this information with the demographic characteristics of the heavy user (age, family life cycle stage, income level, education level), the marketing manager can obtain useful information upon which to base advertising campaign strategy, as we discuss in Chapter 10.

A related approach to product usage segmentation is to examine the sensitivities of different user segments to various marketing mix factors. For example, is there a price-conscious segment for a particular product? Or a segment that responds to personalized service? Recall from the last chapter that these types of buyer preferences were postulated—but the task is to relate them to meaningful market segments.

As we noted in the last chapter, customer loyalty to store and brand is a real phenomenon in the marketplace. Many studies have attempted to use customer loyalty as a basis for market segmentation. However, research efforts aimed at identifying the brand-loyal customer have not been notably successful. Loyal customers do not seem to form a responsive market segment. This may be because the general concept of loyalty is ambiguous. Recall first that there are three different generally accepted ways of defining loyalty. Moreover, what may appear to be genuine loyalty toward a brand or store may reflect indifference, habit, a lower price, or a lack of available substitutes. Product usage segmentation has generally been successful when it has been limited to specific products and particular marketing situations. Attempts to generalize the findings of these specific studies usually have not worked particularly well.

Benefit Segmentation

Benefit segmentation strategies focus upon the benefits that consumers derive from products. Marketing programs can then be designed to create and emphasize these benefits. This approach is conceptually superior to the other segmentation strategies discussed above, in that it emphasizes directly the wants and desires of consumers, rather than any characteristic or behavior pattern related to the satisfaction of these wants and desires. One difficulty with volume segmentation, for example, may be that all

Exhibit 7-9   Example of Benefit Segmentation

Toothpaste Market Segment Description

Segment Name:	The Sensory Segment	The Sociables	The Worriers	The Independent Segment
Principal benefit sought:	Flavor, product appearance	Brightness of teeth	Decay prevention	Price
Demographic strengths:	Children	Teens, young people	Large families	Men
Special behavioral characteristics:	Users of spearmint flavored toothpaste	Smokers	Heavy users	Heavy users
Brands disproportionately favored:	Colgate, Stripe	Macleans, Plus White, Ultra Brite	Crest	Brands on sale
Personality characteristics:	High, self-involvement	High sociability	High hypochondriasis	High autonomy
Life-style characteristics:	Hedonistic	Active	Conservative	Value-oriented

Reprinted from Russell I. Haley, "Benefit Segmentation: A Decision-Oriented Research Tool," *Journal of Marketing,* July 1968, p. 33, published by the American Marketing Association. Reprinted by permission of the publisher.

heavy users are not seeking the same benefits. The heavy beer drinkers, for example, may be divided generally into two groups: those who believe all beers taste alike (these people are likely to purchase lower-priced beers) and those who may be loyal to a particular brand of beer because they like its taste. Thus, benefit segmentation is based upon the premise that the benefits which people are seeking in consuming a given product are the basic reason for the existence of true market segments. In contrast, such factors as state-of-being or state-of-mind characteristics, or product usage, are at best descriptors of people seeking certain types of benefits.

Exhibit 7-9 presents a well-known example of a benefit segmentation study. This example is hypothetical, but is based on actual segmentation studies. The procedure is to identify users of the product, and then to research, in depth, their socioeconomic characteristics, psychological characteristics, behavior patterns, and product preferences. When all of this information is analyzed and evaluated, it is possible to group the users into various segments. As shown in the table, one segment (predominantly children) is primarily seeking flavor and appearance benefits from its toothpaste. Another group is primarily seeking decay prevention, and a third group is interested in having its teeth cleaned at the lowest possible price. Each of these segments has various behavioral, personality, and lifestyle characteristics. Consequently, it is possible to design marketing programs to appeal to these groups. Advertisements to the sensory segment, for example, will be pitched to a child's level of understanding; price-dealing will be used to reach the independent segment, and so on. Exhibit 7-10 presents a recent example of benefit segmentation.

While this approach seems particularly useful for strategy formulation, it does have certain disadvantages. First, choosing the benefit to emphasize is not always a straightforward task. Because of the complexity of human motivation, emphasis upon a single benefit may not reach a sufficiently large market segment. Moreover, obtaining enough information to be sure that real benefits have been identified can be quite expensive. In fact, this approach requires considerable research into the "life styles and psychographics," to use the current jargon, of potential customers. The marketing manager must determine in each case whether the information obtained is worth the cost.

In summary, there are four general bases for market segmentation strategy. The concept of market segmentation has proved its value, but there are few generalized guidelines for the formulation of market segmentation strategy. The marketing manager must examine each situation to determine the type or types of segmentation strategies that would be best for that situation. Crude measures such as geography or demographic characteristics may be useful for a particular product or organization. Large-scale research to determine benefit-based segments may be worthwhile in some cases. While segment identification is necessary, it is only the first step in strategy formulation. The next section places segment identification within the context of segmentation decisions.

SEGMENTATION DECISIONS

Market segmentation involves managerial decisions at several levels. First, the marketer must decide upon a general segmentation policy for all markets. Then, within each market, market segmentation strategy must be formulated. Finally, tactics for implementing the segmentation strategy in a particular market can be devised.

Segmentation Policy

Broadly speaking, an organization has two basic levels of segmentation policy decisions. First, it must decide whether or not to segment. A policy of not developing different marketing programs for various market segments is not as prevalent as it used to be (home appliances used to be uniformly white enamel; Coca-Cola used to come only in six-ounce glass bottles). This approach, called *undifferentiated marketing* or *market aggregation,* is still practiced consciously by some organizations primarily for tangible commodities such as industrial chemicals and raw agricultural products. Some firms do not consciously design segmentation strategies because they do not realize they appeal primarily to certain market segments—recall Martineau's description of the social-class appeal of two furniture stores in Exhibit 6-19.

More and more organizations, however, are recognizing the necessity of market segmentation. To compete effectively in most markets, the question is not whether, but how, to segment. There are two policies: *differentiated marketing* and *concentrated marketing.* Differentiated marketing attempts to appeal to the entire market by designing different products and marketing programs for different segments of the market. Concentrated marketing attempts to appeal only to a few of the most promising segments in the market. Exhibit 7-11 presents examples of these segmentation philosophies. In computers, for example, IBM offers the System II to its largest users and the 5100 to those who need a small computer. In contrast, Sperry Univac concentrates on the large computers, while Digital Equipment Corp. produces only desk-top computers that compete with IBM's 5100. In the automobile market, General Motors, Ford, and Chrysler have entries in all market segments from luxury sedans to minicompacts. On the other hand, Mercedes Benz produces luxury cars, the Checker Motor Corporation produces vehicles primarily for taxicab fleets, and Mack Motors is a truck manufacturer.

Differentiated marketing, of course, provides more opportunity for an organization to sell its products. But this approach requires that the organization design and implement different marketing programs for the various segments, a process which can be very expensive and time consuming. Concentrated marketing, by contrast, permits the firm to focus its energies upon one or two marketing programs and develop them to a higher degree, but there is the danger of "putting all one's eggs in one

Exhibit 7-11   Examples of
Segmentation Philosophies

Segmentation Policies

Industry	Differentiation	Concentration
Computers	IBM, Honeywell	Sperry Univac, Digital Equipment Corp.
Automobiles	GM, Ford, Chrysler	Mercedes Benz, Checker, Mack Trucks
Soft Drinks	Coca-Cola	Dr. Pepper, 7-Up
Retailing	Sears, Montgomery Ward	Hallmark Card Shops Wicks-N-Sticks Candle Shops

basket." Consequently, organization management must examine specific market segmentation strategies within the context of these general policy guidelines.

Segmentation Strategy

If an organization does decide to segment its market, it must first identify possible market segments—using the segmentation bases discussed in the previous section. The segments identified are possible target markets, i.e., segments upon which marketing efforts could be focused. As we noted earlier in the chapter, target market segments require not only identifiability, but also responsiveness and significance.

Recall from Chapter 3 our discussion of effective demand in terms of the acronym MAD. A segment is said to be responsive if it demonstrates effective demand, i.e., Money (income, assets and/or credit worthiness), Authority to buy, and Desire to buy. A segment of consumers with effective demand will respond to marketing effort by the organization.

The final segmentation criterion is significance—will demand be great enough to be worthwhile? This is a question about the market potential of the segment. Market potential is defined as all customers who could benefit from an organization's products. Potential, therefore, is a measure of the total possible demand in a given segment. Potential must be specified in terms of three dimensions: boundaries, size, and time.

Segment boundaries may be drawn geographically, by enumeration, or listed according to a specified criteria. For example, a distributor of oil-drilling tools and supplies may consider the potential market to be all drilling operators in the states of Texas, Oklahoma, and Louisiana. A political party might consider as "customers" all qualified individuals living in a given precinct (eighteen years or older, having citizenship, etc.). For many types of marketing, a complete list of customers is available: owners of automobiles, students at a given college, users of telephone service. Finally, market potential may be bounded by some criterion, a

Exhibit 7-12 Approaches to Product/Market Matching

Markets	Products		
	Present	Differentiated	New
Current	*penetration* (Coke—the real thing)	*extension* (Coke in resealable bottles)	*replacement* (Tab—without cyclamates)
New	*expansion* (Coke in Eastern Europe	*growth* (Tab—diet cola)	*diversification* (Mr. Pibb)

Source: Suggested by Professor Keith K. Cox.

given S.I.C code, all holders of an American Express credit card, or all individuals with intelligence quotients greater than 140.

Within these boundaries, the size of the market segment can be given in terms of physical units, dollars, or proportions. For example, automobile sales for the coming year in the United States might be estimated at 12 million units. The total market for liability insurance of those automobiles might be estimated at $36 million. Those totals could also be expressed as a proportion—a 25 percent increase in last year's sales.

This suggests the third dimension of market potentials: the time frame. To be meaningful, market potentials must be stated in terms of a given time period: next year, the fall quota, the third week in December. Once the three segmentation criteria—identity, responsiveness, and significance—have been met, the potential target market has been specified. As you may have noted by now, target market specification is the culmination of the seeking step in market planning. This step can now be related to the other marketing management functions of matching, programming, and consummating.

The second part of segmentation strategy is matching of segment characteristics and product benefits. The target market may be one currently being served by the organization, or it may be a new one. The product may take one of three different forms: the present product, a differentiation of that product, or a new product. Thus, there are basically six ways in which markets can be matched with products. Exhibit 7-12 illustrates approaches to product/market matching.

For current products in present markets, the market potential is fixed. However, sales of the products of a given organization can be increased if more of the potential customers in the market are served, and/or if the usage rate of the product by current customers can be increased. Marketers generally call this approach *market penetration*. The Coca-Cola Company continuously seeks to penetrate its existing markets; new advertising slogans are frequently employed for this purpose.

A second approach to customers in current markets is to differentiate the product in some way. This approach is generally called *market extension.* Coca-Cola, for example, recently brought out resealable 32-ounce returnable bottles—extending product benefits to that segment of the market that desires such product features. A third approach to current markets is to replace one product with another. Coca-Cola did this with its diet drink Tab in the early 1970s, when the sweetening agent cyclamates were declared unfit for human consumption by the Food and Drug Administration. The drinks containing cyclamates were taken off the market, and replaced with a diet cola drink that did not contain cyclamates.

An organization might also select as a target market a segment that it is not presently serving—a new market. One approach is to offer the present product to the new market; this is called *market expansion.* Coca-Cola has recently opened bottling plants in such Eastern European countries as Hungary and Czechoslovakia. Offering a differentiated product to a new market is a growth strategy. Coca-Cola did this when it first brought out its diet cola, Tab. Tab is a cola drink, but differentiating it by lowering the calorie content enabled the Coca-Cola company to go into the diet segment of the market. A final approach is to offer a new product to a new marketing segment. This approach is called *diversification.* Coca-Cola did this two years ago when it introduced its Dr. Pepper-like soft drink, Mr. Pibb. Mr. Pibb is a new product in that it consists of a new formula, and it allowed Coca-Cola to diversify into the segment of the market which prefers soft drinks not based upon colas. We will have considerably more to say about new product development and product policies in Chapter 9.

The determination as to which of these approaches to the product/market match will be taken by an organization depends upon the organization's objectives, constraints, and alternatives. First, the organization seeks to achieve its objectives. The significance criterion for segment delineation links the target-market segment to the organization's objectives. Before choosing a segment as a target market, therefore, the market manager will very carefully assess that segment in terms of its possible contribution to profit, return on investment (ROI), market share, sales volume, voting percentage, or other basic organizational objective criterion.

Even though a segment would appear to be a significant contributor to an organization's objectives it may not necessarily be selected as a target market. Serving this segment, for example, might require types or amounts of resources which are unavailable to the organization. For example, product design and manufacture might require capabilities of skilled personnel which the organization does not presently employ, or the capital needed to exploit the market segment may be beyond the present credit capability of the organization. In theory, resources will be attracted to organizations that demonstrate significant potential—but in the real world this takes considerable time and effort; an organization's management may simply feel that it is not worthwhile to attempt to secure the resources necessary to exploit the opportunity that the segment presents.

Another constraint upon target-market selection is the organization's current commitments. A potentially significant segment in another region of the country, for example, might entail relocation expenses, or possible loss of contact with existing customers. The new segment may not fit the company's image—Brooks Brothers, for example, remains strongly committed to the traditional style of clothing—refusing to alter its line of men's suits and sport coats to remain abreast of every new fad and fashion. Environmental constraints such as actions of competitors, general economic conditions, government regulation, the number of consumers in the potential market, their loyalty, taste, and fashion trends must all be considered in the selection of a given market segment as a target market.

Finally, even if analysis shows that the segment's contribution to organizational objectives is significant, and organizational constraints do not rule out the segment, segmentation strategy should not be developed in isolation for one segment. An organization nearly always has alternative segments to which it could direct its efforts. Consequently, the consideration of organizational objectives, constraints, and decision alternatives for market segmentation-strategy formulation requires a systematic approach. Exhibit 7-13 depicts our approach. Note that the exhibit summarizes the discussion of market segmentation strategy in terms of both seeking and matching. The culmination of strategy is the estimate of sales that the organization could obtain from the target market selected. This estimate is called *sales potential*.

Realization of sales potential depends upon the tactics employed to carry out the segmentation strategy. Tactics involve the marketing functions of programming and consummating. Programming is the selection and integration of various elements of the marketing mix.

The Marketing Mix. Once an organization has formulated its strategy to the point of target-market selection, a marketing program must be formulated to serve the wants and desires of the market segment. The heart of any marketing program is the development of the marketing mix, which involves decisions in basically four areas:

1. Product—decisions about the design of the product, its manufacture, packaging, and branding. Product decisions are the subject of Chapter 9.
2. Promotion—the content, media used to convey the content, and timing of advertising, personal selling, sales promotion, and publicity efforts. Chapter 10 is devoted to these types of decisions.
3. Distribution—the design, management and maintenance of channels of distribution. Channel management is discussed in Chapter 11.

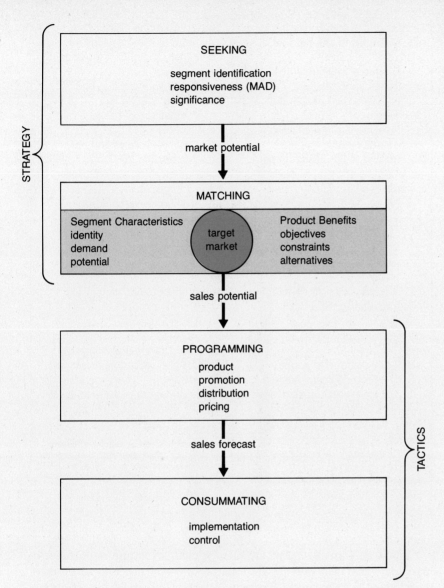

Exhibit 7-13 Segmentation-based Marketing Planning

STRATEGY

SEEKING

segment identification
responsiveness (MAD)
significance

market potential

MATCHING

Segment Characteristics
identity
demand
potential

target
market

Product Benefits
objectives
constraints
alternatives

sales potential

PROGRAMMING

product
promotion
distribution
pricing

sales forecast

CONSUMMATING

implementation
control

TACTICS

4. Price—determination of the level of price with respect to consumer price perceptions, competition, and costs of the product; suggested profit margins for channel members; and the finalization of specific price lines. This material is covered in Chapter 12.

Of course, the various elements of the marketing program could be expressed in different ways. Exhibit 7-14 presents Borden's classic statement of the concept of the marketing mix.

Marketing-mix decisions are of such complexity and importance to marketing management that we separate them in order to study them thoroughly—but the marketing manager must integrate marketing-mix elements to develop an effective and efficient program for reaching target markets. Examples of the lack of program integration are easy to find: the comprehensive, effective national campaign advertising a new product that is not yet on the store shelves; the salesperson who cannot demonstrate the product to customers; and the manufacturer's warranty that is not backed up by the dealer. These experiences are familiar to all consumers. We return to program integration and implementation and control of the marketing program in Chapter 13.

Sales Forecasting. One of the most important aspects of programming is forecasting—predicting—how the program will actually turn out when it is implemented in the marketplace. Measurement of objective attainment requires performance standards, forecasts of sales, of resulting revenues, and of costs—and the impact of these revenues and costs upon profits, return on investment, or other statements of organizational objectives. The sales forecast is derived in three stages:

1. *Estimates of market potential*—predictions of total market demand in terms of boundaries, size, and timing. Market potential serves as an upper limit on—
2. *Estimates of sales potential*—prediction of sales of a product of a given organization as a function (curve) of the marketing effort of the individual firm; from this curve comes—
3. *Sales Forecasts*—estimate of the particular amount (point on a curve) of sales of an organization that will be generated by the programmed level of marketing effort. These relationships are shown in Exhibit 7-15.

Note that market potential is graphed as a straight line; sales potential cannot be greater than market potential. The market potential line in this diagram slopes slightly upward. The degree of slope has meaning. If an organization were relatively small, then its marketing effort would have no appreciable effect upon the size of the total market. In such a case, the market potential line would be horizontal. On the other hand, marketing effort by a large firm expands the total market; this is represented by an upsloping market potential line. When there was a strike of the United Auto Workers at General Motors in the early 1970s, sales of GM cars fell. But sales of other brands of autos also fell. When General Motors ceased marketing for the duration of the strike, many buyers simply withdrew from the market to await GM's return. Consequently, the entire market contracted; market potential was lessened while General Motors was not exerting marketing effort.

Sales potential, the share of total market potential that a given organization could attain, depends primarily upon the level of the amount of marketing effort expended. In general, the relationship is a positive one: the greater the effort, the more the sales. This relationship is probably not a linear one. For most organizations, sales are likely to be quite small at low levels of marketing effort, and they probably grow rapidly as marketing effort is increased. There comes a time, however, when increasing marketing effort does not increase sales. In fact, extremely high levels of marketing effort might acutally turn away some customers.

Finally, note that the sales forecast is a dependent variable. This third interpretation of the term *forecast* is of special interest for completing the marketing program. In this view, the sales forecast is a dependent

Exhibit 7-15   The Sales Forecast—Result of Programmed Marketing Effort

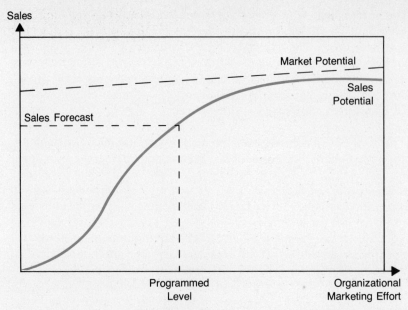

Adapted from Philip Kotler, *Marketing Management: Analysis, Planning and Control,* 2nd ed., © 1972, Prentice-Hall, Inc., pp. 215, by permission of Prentice-Hall, Inc.

variable—the result of the organization's marketing plan—given the sales potential function for that organization.

To repeat, for emphasis, the amount of sales actually obtained by an organization depends upon organizational sales potential (demand for the organization's product) as well as upon the amount of effort expended by the organization in that market. The classic example here is the inventory stocking problem: a baker must decide how many cakes to bake each day. If there is demand for more cakes than he bakes, he will lose sales—he has not expended sufficient effort to realize his sales potential. But if he bakes more cakes than the market demands on a given day, he will have cakes left over—too much effort expended. Amount of effort to be expended is a managerial decision; once this decision has been made, i.e., a marketing mix has been determined, the sales forecast can be developed to meet the target market demand.

CONCLUDING NOTE

The strategy of market segmentation is fundamental to marketing management. Most organizations, at the present time, segment intuitively, e.g., by trial and error. They do not precisely identify their prime segments. However, this is an area of marketing in which considerable scholarly work is in progress and is beginning to show important successes. We can expect rapid increases in the use of scientific segmentation procedures as computer capacities expand, as better data become available, and particularly as marketing managers become more proficient in utilizing scientific research procedures and results in making their decisions.

In view of the importance of the market segmentation concept to marketing management, you might become more familiar with it by looking for examples of segmentation strategies in the marketing efforts of organizations with which you come into contact. Examine these strategies critically—but do not be too quick to pronounce a given strategy a success or a failure. Segment delineation, target market selection, market program formulation, and implementation and control of that program involve many complex and difficult decisions. We examine some of these difficulties and procedures for dealing with them throughout the remainder of the book.

KEY TERMS AND CONCEPTS

Matching Supply and Demand
  homogeneous markets
  heterogeneous markets
  market segmentation
Segmentation Concept
  definition
  homogeneous wants
  target market
Segmentation Criteria
  identity
  responsiveness
  significance
Segmentation Bases
  customer state-of-being
  customer state-of-mind
  product usage
  product benefits

Segmentation Policies
  undifferentiated
  differentiated
  concentrated
Segmentation Strategy
  segment delineation
  target-market selection
  marketing program
  implementation or control
Marketing Mix
  product
  promotion
  distribution
  price
Types of Forecasts
  market potential
  sales potential
  sales forecast

QUESTIONS FOR DISCUSSION

1. Describe the concept of market segmentation in your own words. Ignore phraseology and conciseness—explain the concept to your own satisfaction. Use examples with which you are familiar.

2. Consider the following organizations: a local department store, your university or college, a franchised hamburger chain, the professional football team located nearest to you, a men's hairstyling salon, the minority party in your city's next election, and the U.S. Army. What possible market segments could each of these organizations serve? Note: apply the segmentation criteria in answering this question.

3. How would you use the four segmentation bases to identify market segments for one or more of the organizations mentioned in question 2? For example, at the state-of-being level, how could the Buying Power Index or Standard Industrial Classification codes be used to identify segments?

4. For the segments you identified in question 3, list the factors that might influence market potential and sales potential.

5. Using Exhibit 7-13 as a guide, outline a marketing strategy for the segments examined in question 4.

6. Examine a marketing situation that you are familiar with (personal experience, current news, or *Marketing Is Everybody's Business*) and, using Exhibit 7-13 to guide you, formulate strategy for the marketing situation.

SUGGESTED READING

1. James F. Engel, Henry F. Fiorillo, and Murray A. Cayley, eds. *Market Segmentation: Concepts and Applications*. New York: Holt, Rinehart and Winston, 1972. Well-chosen anthology of articles related to market segmentation; good general source of material in this area, including the following classics:

    (1) Ronald E. Frank. "Market Segmentation Research: Findings and Implications," in Bass, et al., eds. *The Application of the Sciences to Marketing Management*. New York: John Wiley and Sons, 1968, pp. 39-68.

    (2) Russell I. Haley. "Benefit Segmentation: A Decision-oriented Research Tool." *Journal of Marketing,* July 1968, pp. 30-35; reprinted in Gabriel M. Gelb and Betsy D. Gelb. *Insights for Marketing Management,* 2nd ed. Goodyear, 1977.

    (3) Wendell R. Smith. "Product Differentiation and Market Segmentation as Alternative Marketing Strategies." *Journal of Marketing,* July 1956, pp. 3-8.

    (4) Daniel Yankelovich. "New Criteria for Market Segmentation." *Harvard Business Review,* March-April 1964, pp. 83-90.

2. Ronald E. Frank, William F. Massy, and Yoram Wind. *Market Segmentation*. Englewood Cliffs, N.J.: Prentice-Hall, 1972. A review and synthesis, at a rather rigorous level, of market segmentation research; not easy reading, but a valuable source for the student and researcher in this area.

3. Cecil V. Hynes and Noel B. Zabriskie. *Marketing to Governments*. Grid, 1974. Concise primer on government market segments.

4. Philip Kotler. *Marketing Management: Analysis Planning and Control*. 3rd ed. Engle-

wood Cliffs, N.J.: Prentice-Hall, 1976. Kotler's chapters 6, 7, and 8 treat, in greater depth, material covered in this chapter.

5. William D. Wells, editor.

Life Style and Psychographics. American Marketing Association, 1974. Collection of papers on the frontiers of segmentation research; requires some knowledge of statistical techniques; voluminous references.

"And so, extrapolating from the best figures available, we see that current trends, unless dramatically reversed, will inevitably lead to a situation in which the sky will fall."

8/INFORMATION FOR MARKETING DECISIONS

This chapter provides a conceptual framework for marketing decision making. With this background, we can discuss information procurement and analysis procedures for making decisions. Fundamental points include:

1. Decision making is a process which can be formalized. But formal decision-making procedures are difficult to employ in marketing. Marketing decisions, by their very nature, are complex, uncertain, and dynamic.

2. Despite these difficulties, we focus upon formal decision making in marketing for three reasons: formalized procedures provide a framework for structuring intuitive judgments; they constitute a basis for communication of such judgments; and recent developments indicate that more formalized procedures will be used by marketing managers in the future.

3. One useful formalized decision-making model is the seven-step information/decision model presented in this chapter. This model forms the basis for our discussion of information needs and decision making.

4. Information assembly should be approached in a systematic fashion. Information needs should be derived from the definition of the decision problem, and should take cognizance of analytical techniques to be used and managerial implications of possible results.

5. Information assembly involves balancing questions of appropriate techniques to use in gathering the data, the sources from which data are to be obtained, and whether or not the data are to be manipulated—experimentation.

6. Analysis for marketing decisions should also follow logically from the definition of the problem to be analyzed. Analytical techniques include summarization procedures and statistical inference.

7. The marketing information system (MIS) is a conceptual framework for formally managing marketing information. Its components are the data bank, analytical bank, and model bank; it performs functions of assembly, processing, analysis, evaluation, storage and retrieval, and dissemination of information.

Decision making is the essence of management. Managers of all types probably spend more time defining, making and implementing decisions than in any other activity. Marketing decisions are perhaps the most complex managerial decisions of all. In spite of this fact, perhaps because of it, marketing managers are just beginning to use systematic information and analytical procedures. Such procedures are becoming increasingly important in marketing decision-making.

THE NATURE OF MARKETING DECISIONS

All managers make decisions. In many fields, formalized procedures have greatly improved decisions in those fields: statistical quality control in manufacturing, linear programming in refinery operations, PERT in construction scheduling, preflight checklists for aircraft pilots, game theory in military strategy. The list of successful applications of formal decision procedures is impressive. But many marketing managers feel that their field is different. And it is—to some extent. We examine the nature of marketing decisions, and the barriers encountered by formalized decision procedures in this field. We also see, however, that such procedures can be very useful to marketing management.

The Context of Marketing Decisions

Marketing decisions involve many variables, which are difficult to measure, which interact in complex fashion, and which change rapidly. Most marketing decisions require at least some understanding of how and why people act in a certain way at a given time; a knowledge of buyer behavior is particularly important. But sometimes buyers do not know or cannot articulate their wants. Consider, for example, how one might make known a desire for electric light to an eighteenth-century candlemaker. And the wants of some customers may not be worth satisfying—"Lady, they don't make shocking-pink golf balls." Or a competitor may be too solidly entrenched—"We leave the custom dyeing to Al's Pro Shop." Or the required technology may not be available—"No we do not have one that comes back when you press a button." In addition, our measures of human behavior, relative to the measures of other types of variables, are rather poor. By contrast, decision making in the area of inventory control is fairly precise; this precision would be greatly decreased if the inventory manager had to rely on the verbal reports of his clerks to know what items were in stock last week.

Marketing managers must consider the influence of a great many variables upon a given decision. Within the marketing function, there are the marketing-mix variables: product, promotion, distribution, and price. Actions by managers in other units of the organization—finance, engineering, production, legal—affect marketing decisions. Outside the organization, there are the actions of suppliers, distributors, stockholders, trade associations, and customers. And other influences on marketing decisions include such factors as competitors' actions, general economic conditions, governmental regulations, and fashion trends.

The marketing manager must also be aware of interrelationships among these variables. For example, a brilliant, well-executed advertising campaign will not result in increased sales unless the product has been distributed so as to be conveniently available for purchase. In addition to these difficulties, conditions affecting marketing activities are constantly changing—technology develops new products, competitors increase their marketing efforts, new governmental regulations are promulgated, and consumers' wants and tastes are constantly shifting.

Barriers to Formal Decision Procedures

Marketing managers learn to live with such conditions. Indeed, the stereotype is that marketing managers truly enjoy such situations. Lee Adler ("Systems Approach . . ." p. 116) has commented that:

> a good many marketing executives, in the deepest recesses of their psyches, are artists, not analysts. For them, marketing is an art form and, in my opinion, they really do not want it any other way. Their temperament is antipathetic to system, order, knowledge. They enjoy flying by the seat of their pants—though you will never get them to admit it. They revel in chaos, abhor facts, and fear research. They hate to be trammeled by written plans. And they love to spend, but are loath to assess the results of their spending . . .

The decision-maker who fits this description is not likely to willingly embrace formalized decision procedures. In fact, there are several barriers to the adoption of formalized decision procedures by marketing managers. First, most marketing managers have had relatively little education or experience with such procedures. In terms of the total careers of most marketing managers, the movement toward the teaching of formalized decision procedures in college curricula and in management short courses is a relatively recent development. Many marketing managers simply do not completely understand this approach.

In addition, marketing managers face a great number of diverse problems every day. If they lack formalized training, therefore, they probably also lack the time to obtain this training. Most marketing managers are so immersed in their day-to-day problems that they cannot see their way clear to spend the time learning to apply formalized procedures, even if they recognized the value of such techniques.

Third, there is no doubt that the real, practical benefits of formalized decision procedures for marketing problems have been exaggerated by some experts. Marketing problems are more diverse and more complex

Exhibit 8-1   Systems Perspective of Decision Making

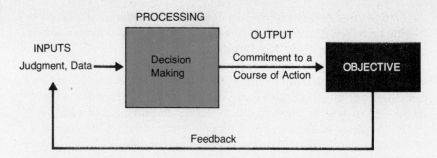

than most decision problems. Many of the standard formalized decision procedures simply are not applicable to marketing situations.

Finally, no matter how sophisticated the formalized procedure, the results are no better than the input into the process. "Garbage-in, garbage-out" (GIGO) is a familiar term; no procedure will generate good answers from bad data. Less obviously, and perhaps more importantly, the objectives of the decision maker using a formalized procedure must be very carefully specified. It is very difficult, for example, for the decision maker to express his attitude toward risk in formalized terms. Moreover, most decision makers have personal objectives which may or may not parallel organizational objectives. Many a marketing executive has fought fiercely for his pet project or product, even when rational analysis indicated that his idea would have very little chance of success.

And now the good news: the foregoing comments notwithstanding, there is little doubt that formalized decision procedures can be very helpful to marketing decision makers. Such procedures cannot replace managerial judgment, but they can extend and supplement it. A useful analogy here is the aircraft pilot. In times past, a pilot simply went into an open field and learned to fly a biplane "by the seat of his pants"—by trial and error. We now have faster, more powerful, and more complex aircraft. No one would ride in such a plane with a pilot who had learned to navigate with his backside. The flying skills of modern pilots have been extended and supplemented by flight simulators, extensive checklists, and precise instruments. But the pilot remains. His judgment has not been replaced; it has been supplemented.

Consequently, the remainder of this chapter focuses on the use of formalized techniques for marketing decision making. There are three reasons for using formalized techniques. First, formalized procedures do provide a general framework to guide individual intuition. Second, informal techniques, by their very nature, cannot be generalized. It is very difficult to explain how one's own intuition and judgment operate. Formalized procedures can be communicated to others. (Again, we are not saying that intuition and judgment can be replaced by formalized procedures, but that they can be organized and structured for clearer communication, increased comprehensiveness, and logical consistency.) Third, as the educational level of managers rises and the cost of making incorrect decisions increases, we can expect greater usage of formalized procedures.

Consequently, the marketing manager of the future will no doubt need a better grasp of formalized decision procedures than do current marketing managers. The foundation for any formalized approach to decision making is the systems concept (recall Exhibit 2-1).

Systems View of Decision Making

Decision making can be viewed from a systems perspective. As shown in Exhibit 8-1, the inputs are judgment and data. Judgment is that intangible blend of intellectual ability, past experience, and intuition that separates man from machine. Data, as we discuss in detail in the next section, can take four forms: facts—known events or conditions; opinions—unverified facts; estimates—inferred facts; and predictions—estimates of future facts. These inputs are processed by thinking—summarizing, evaluating, weighing—to produce the output: a commitment to a course of action. Measuring the results of this decision, in light of the decision maker's objectives, provides data to be fed back into the process of future decision making. This view of managerial decision making is somewhat simplified, but it does serve to highlight the elements and emphasize the process nature of decision making.

The Decision-Process Model

Many authors have written about the decision-making process. While specifics differ, there is general agreement on the essentials. The model presented in Exhibit 8-2 is representative of such work.

As the figure shows, the first step in decision making is to carefully define the problem. The manager must determine what it is that he/she is trying to accomplish, and what alternative methods are available for attaining this objective. Until the problem is well-defined, no formal decision making procedure can be of any value to a manager.

The next step is to assess available information. The manager must determine what he/she already knows about the problem, preferably expressed in quantitative (e.g., dollars-and-cents) terms. After available information is assessed the manager faces a two-faceted question. First, if he/she decides to act on the basis of available information, which action should be taken? Second, should he/she take that action, or should additional information be assembled? Information is a resource—it is costly and time consuming to obtain. In terms of decision making, additional information should be assembled only if it is expected that its value will exceed its cost.

If the decision maker determines that additional information is

Exhibit 8-2 Decision Process Model

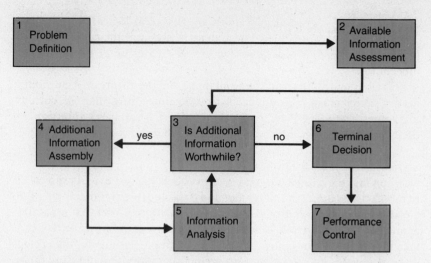

Adapted from Keith K. Cox and Ben M. Enis, *The Marketing Research Process* (Goodyear Publishing Company, 1972), p. 55.

worthwhile, he/she will assemble—or cause to be assembled—the information wanted. Then that information must be analyzed, after which the decision maker again faces the twofold question. Should he/she make the decision on the basis of the information now available, or should an additional round of information be secured? Conceivably, the decision maker might assemble several rounds of additional information. The time must inevitably come, however, when he/she feels that the cost of assembling another round is greater than the expected benefit. At that point he/she makes the decision, and then must control the performance of that decision.

Thus, information is absolutely essential to formalized decision-making procedures. Let us look at the major types of marketing information, and the roles that such information can play in the decision process.

MARKETING INFORMATION

The marketing manager has access to a bewildering amount and variety of data. But not all data contribute to effective decision making. Our first step, therefore, is to distinguish between data and information.

Information, as we will use the term, is data that a manager expects will reduce the uncertainty involved in making a correct decision. Data, as we noted above, can take four forms (facts, opinions, estimates, and predictions). Information defined in this way is a very broad area to study. To facilitate our work, we will look at information in terms of the three major roles that it can play in the decision-making process. First, information can be useful in defining problems for analysis. Second, information can be used to solve the problems defined. Third, information

Marketing Department

How many salesmen should we hire?

Should we use a red package or a
blue one?

How effective is the new advertising
campaign?

Which marketing research firm should
we engage?

Internal Suppliers

Can we standardize this model to
achieve production economies?

The comptroller has cut 10 percent from the
advertising budget.

Please be more careful in granting
credit; bad debt losses are up 20 percent
over last year.

External Suppliers

The price of that material
is up 15 percent.

The prime interest rate went up .5 percent
today.

Some of the stockholders are demanding a biodegradable package.

Customers

This shipment is not up to contract
specifications.

Does the warranty cover dropping it
in the swimming pool?

Could we pay you in 90 days?

Does this model come in blue?

Middlemen

We are doubling our minimum
order size.

The parts for the special assembly our
biggest customer ordered will be
two weeks late.

Society

The railroad strike will affect deliveries
of the new model.

That material is out of style.

Your competitor's price is $2 / unit less.

The Justice Department will not like this.

Source: Adapted from Keith K. Cox and Ben M. Enis, *The Marketing Research Process* (Pacific
Palisades, Calif: Goodyear Publishing Company, 1972), p. 66.

is essential in monitoring the implementation of decisions. We shall have
more to say about the latter two roles that information plays in the
decision process. Let us look first at problem-defining, or exploratory,
information.

Problem-Defining Information

The first step in decision making is to define the problem. Since this is the
initial step, useful information here is likely to be unstructured, qualitative, tentative—exploratory. Indications of possible problems arise from
many sources. Exhibit 8-3 provides examples.

In its broadest sense, the term *problem* connotes a situation that
appears to warrant further investigation. Marketing managers face numerous problems each day. Three comments on the relationship between
problems and decisions are pertinent at this point.

1. Not all problems require decisions by management. Some of the
questions that a manager faces are trivial; others represent essentially
random fluctuations in an otherwise stable situation. A question may be
one about which the manager can do nothing at the present time. In these
situations, no decision is required.

2. Many, perhaps most, of the problems marketing managers face are

handled then and there. Judgment, that unique blend of intuition, experience, and guesswork, is substituted for information about these situations simply because the manager does not have the resources (time, energy, money, manpower) to fully investigate every problem that comes up. Consequently, the decision maker must determine which of the problems visible at a given time are worthy of further investigation.

Although this step is important, a textbook can offer relatively little guidance to the manager in this area. We are talking about the essence of managerial judgment. There are no formal procedures to follow. Basically, however, the decision maker views the problem in light of organizational objectives—what are the possible consequences of this problem? How does it relate to other organizational activities? and so on.

3. Our third comment about the importance of exploratory research is that if the manager does deem a problem to be of sufficient importance to begin the process of converting data into information, problem definition should begin broadly. The initial manifestation of the problem may be only a symptom rather than a cause for managerial concern. For example, declining sales are usually a result of some cause. The search for this cause should be undertaken creatively. That is, the decision maker should attempt new approaches, seek fresh ideas, and find previously unrecognized relationships, to identify actual causes of problems. This requires innovative, as distinguished from critical, thinking. It is not easy to think creatively, but various techniques are available to aid the manager who attempts it. Exhibit 8-4 provides examples.

If the creative search for problem causes indicates information might improve the likelihood of making a good decision, then the project to generate that information must be undertaken.

Decision-Making Information

If a manager is contemplating performing (or more likely having performed) a project to generate information about a problem, the first step is to carefully define the project. This step generally involves specification of two key elements: the objective that the decision maker is trying to reach, and alternatives available for reaching the objective. A profit-seeking objective, for example, might be furthered either by raising revenues or by lowering costs. A political party seeking votes might design a platform to appeal to either liberals or conservatives. These examples suggest that decision alternatives are not necessarily mutually exclusive, but do involve different directions or emphases. The purpose of gathering information, therefore, is to enable the decision maker to better determine which alternative will best attain the objective.

After problem definition, preparation for conducting the information-generating project proceeds in two stages. The first is *hypothesis hunting,* i.e., the examination of available data to determine directions for

Exhibit 8-4   Methods of Stimulating Creative Thinking

1. *Brainstorming:* An intentionally uninhibited, either individual or group approach. The objective is to produce the greatest possible number of alternative ideas for later evaluation and development.

2. *Reverse Brainstorming:* Sometimes useful prior to a brainstorm session. It consists of being critical instead of suspending judgment:

(a) List all the things wrong with the operation, process, system, or product.

(b) Systematically take each flaw uncovered and suggest ways of overcoming it.

3. *Catalog Technique:* Stated simply, the reference to various and sundry catalogs or other sources of printed information as a means of getting ideas that will, in turn, suggest other ideas. May be used in combination with the forced-relationship technique.

4. *Checklist Technique:* A system of getting idea-clues or leads by checking the items on a prepared list against the problem or subject under consideration. The objective is to obtain a number of general ideas for further follow-up and development into specific form.

5. *Free Association:* A method of stimulating the imagination to some constructive purpose:

(a) Jot down a symbol—word, sketch, number, picture, which is related in some key way to some important aspect of the problem or subject under consideration.

(b) Jot down another symbol suggested by the first one.

(c) Continue as in Step 2—ad lib—until ideas emerge. The objective is to produce intangible ideas, advertising slogans, designs, names, etc.

6. *Attribute Listing:* A technique used principally for improving tangible things:

(a) Choose some object to improve.

(b) List the parts of the object.

(c) List the essential, basic qualities, features, or attributes of the object and its parts.

(d) Systematically change or modify the attributes. The objective is to satisfy better the original purpose of the object, or to fulfill a new need with it.

7. *Forced Relationship:* A method which has essentially the same basic purpose as free association:

(a) Isolate the elements of the problem at hand.

(b) Find the relationships between/among these elements (similarities; differences; analogies; cause and effect).

(c) Record the relationships in organized fashion.

(d) Analyze the record of relationships to find the patterns (or basic ideas) present. Develop new ideas from these patterns.

8. *Synectics:* A structured approach to creative thinking. Operational mechanisms:

(a) Making the strange familiar (through analysis, generalization, and model seeking).

(b) Making the familiar strange (through personal analogy, direct analogy, and symbolic analogy). The objective usually is to produce one best idea and to carry it through to testing, verification, development, and production in final form.

9. *Bionics:* Ask yourself, "How is this done in nature?" Nature's scheme of things is revealed to those who search. (Note: This technique may come into play in synectics when utilizing analogies.)

10. *Value Analysis (or Engineering):* A specialized application of creative problem solving to increase value. It may be defined as an objective, systematic, and formalized method of performing a job to achieve only necessary functions at minimum cost. Six questions are evoked concerning each part:

(a) What is it?

(b) What must it do?

(c) What does it do?

(d) What did it cost?

(e) What else will do the job?

(f) What will that cost?

Adapted from M.O. Edwards, "Solving Problems Creatively," *Systems and Procedures Journal,* January–February 1966, pp. 61–76, with permission of the publisher.

the project. The traditional literature review is the standard approach at this stage. Examination of published research and past projects conducted on topics similar to the current problem is essential. An examination can save time and energy that might otherwise be invested in "reinventing the

In many decision situations, the manager feels that information would be useful, but is not sure exactly what kind of information would be best. The focused group interview technique can be very effective in such cases.

The technique involves a group moderator who leads eight to twelve people through an unstructured discussion. The focused group gets its name from the moderator's objective: to focus the discussion on relevant subjects in a nondirective manner. Such interviews can be used to identify content areas for more specific research projects, and they may develop fresh ideas for new products, advertising themes, packaging alternatives, and other possible marketing decisions.

In one application, the Alpha Power and Light Company requested an increase in its electricity rates from the State Utilities Commission. In preparing arguments for the utilities commission, Alpha managers wanted to know the following:

1. Why were those consumers who opposed the rate hike really opposed?
2. What information should be communicated to those consumers opposed in order to justify a rate increase to them?
3. What reasons were given by consumers not opposed to rate increase?
4. How important were general service problems in influencing customer opinions about the rate increase?

The focused group interviews uncovered a "rate bargaining" phenomenon among the groups, which could be traced back to fear of an energy shortage, and the possibility of fast-rising prices for consumer goods and services. In general, consumers wanted assurances of available utilities and were willing to pay for services, but they felt price changes should be negotiated. As a result of these interviews, a questionnaire for telephone interviews was developed. In addition, advertising communication themes regarding consumer resistance to the rate increase were suggested by the interviews.

Source: Keith K. Cox, James D. Higginbotham and John Burton, "Applications of Focused Group Interviews in Marketing," *Journal of Marketing* (January 1976), pp. 77–80.

wheel," and may also provide new insights into the current problem. Increasingly, literature review is supplemented by other methods of data generation for guiding research projects. Perhaps the current favorite is the focused group interview, which is illustrated in Exhibit 8-5.

The final stage is project design. At this point, the specific nature and directions of the project are stated. In general, the project design should answer the tried and true questions: what, where, when, how, why, and who? Specifically, project design contains a statement of content—the information sought. Content answers the questions: what is to be done, and why? Second, the research design states the methodology—the procedure to be employed. This answers the "how" question. Third is the project schedule: who is going where, and when? Finally, the project budget must be specified—how much is this going to cost?

RESEARCH FOR MARKETING DECISIONS

Once the project has been designed, the assembly of information to aid the decision maker begins. This is marketing research. It is so broad an area that we can do no more than overview it. We look first at the issue of secondary versus primary data, examine each of the three dimensions of

There are essentially seven categories of secondary information:

1. *Internal information*—as discussed in the chapter, the most common type of secondary information is the sales invoice, and other types of accounting records. Data may also be procured from previous marketing research studies, the personnel department, legal office, and so on. Often internal information must be re-analyzed to be useful for a given marketing decision.

2. *Consultants*—a consultant is quite likely to have data on projects of a similar nature, broad experience in the area, and/or contacts that can provide useful information.

3. *Affiliates of the organization*—trade associations in many industries publish data on industry growth patterns, performance norms, and relationships with government agencies. Suppliers, stockholders, and distributors may also be able to provide useful information.

4. *Government agencies*—the largest single source of external secondary information is federal, state and local government agencies. Census bureau compilations include publications on population, housing, business, manufacturing, and government. The standard industrial classification (S.I.C.) codes can also be very useful.

5. *Published sources*—(1) journals: scholarly, e.g., the *Journal of Marketing* and *Harvard Business Review;* general commercial publications such as *Fortune, Business Week, Wall Street Journal,* and the *National Observer;* specific trade journals in various fields, e.g., *Aviation Weekly, Progressive Grocer,* (2) books, and (3) reports and monographs.

6. *Syndicated services*—a number of firms collect data about various phases of marketing activity, and sell this information on a subscription basis. The Market Research Corporation of America, A. C. Nielsen Company, and Audit and Surveys, Inc., are prominent in this field.

7. *Nonprofit agencies*—educational institutions; foundations, e.g., Ford, Carnegie, National Industrial Conference Board, and the Marketing Science Institute; local Chambers of Commerce, Nader's Raiders.

primary information, and then briefly review the basic techniques for analyzing data.

Secondary versus Primary Data

Information costs money. Prudent information management therefore dictates that, for a given amount and quality of information, information costs should be minimized. One obvious cost minimization technique is to use information assembled for some purpose other than the problem at hand—provided that the information is useful, i.e., reduces the uncertainty associated with the given problem. Information assembled expressly for the problem at hand is called primary; information assembled for any other purpose is secondary.

Thus, secondary data may be available internally (e.g., accounting records), or it may have been collected outside the organization. Census data is the classic example; these data are collected originally for legislative reapportionment, but can be very useful for many other purposes, when properly analyzed. Exhibit 8-6 presents examples of secondary information. In examining a given problem, secondary information should always be considered. In the first place, the problem may be satisfactorily resolved using secondary information alone, with resulting savings in time and resources. Even if secondary information by itself is not sufficient to solve the problem, it may contribute to that solution—by clarifying primary information needs and suggesting methods of data collection and analysis.

The major benefit of secondary information is that it can almost always be procured faster and with less expense than can primary information. However, because secondary information was originally assembled for some other purpose, it may not meet the needs of the present problem. Consequently, secondary data must be evaluated by the decision maker. In making this evaluation, three criteria should be considered:

> *Relevance*—Do the data relate to the problem at hand?
> *Credibility*—Is the source of these data trustworthy?
> *Accuracy*—Are the data free from significant error? Up to date? etc.

Secondary data must meet the needs of the problem at hand. The point cannot be too heavily stressed that a manager's judgment as to the potential value of any additional information is a function of the way that particular problem is defined. If, for example, different price levels were not considered as alternative courses of action when the problem was defined, then information about the effect of price on demand will not be assembled. Although this point may seem a bit elementary, in actual situations information all too frequently does not contribute to the solution of the problem at hand. If secondary data do not meet these criteria, then primary data must be sought.

The heart of traditional marketing research is the assembly and analysis of primary information. Many references in this area indicate that the three methods of assembling additional primary information are questioning, observation, and experimentation. In point of fact, however, these methods are merely aspects of the three dimensions of primary information assembly: how the data are to be collected, the sources from which the data are to be procured, and whether or not the data are to be manipulated during collection—in short, questioning and observation, sampling, and experimentation. Exhibit 8-7 presents examples. We examine each dimension separately in the following paragraphs. In an actual situation, however, decisions about each dimension must be integrated in a single information assembly procedure.

Data Collection

There are basically two ways of collecting marketing information: questioning and observation. The questioning method seeks to obtain verbal or written responses from people. A format of organized, written questions is

Exhibit 8-7 Examples of Primary Information Assembly in Marketing

Data Collection Method	Audience to be Studied			
	Population		**Sample**	
	Experiment	Survey	Experiment	Survey
Questioning	An industrial company wanted to evaluate three sales incentive programs. All 60 salesmen were randomly divided into three groups. Each group filled out a questionnaire about one of the three incentive programs.	An industrial equipment manufacturer needed information about customer usage of the equipment. Personal interviews were conducted with the purchasing agents of all 50 companies in the population.	An advertising agency wanted to evaluate three different advertising campaigns. A group of housewives were randomly divided into three test groups, each of which was asked to evaluate one of the ads.	An oil company wanted to estimate the trading area of its retail service stations. A sample of customers buying gasoline in the company service stations were interviewed.
Observation	A retail chain wanted to measure the effect of a new package for an existing product. Half of the 100 stores in the chain stocked the product with the new package, while the other stores continued to stock the old package. All stores were audited for sales of the product.	A franchiser wanted to know how all 20 franchises were using sales promotional materials in the retail locations. In all 20 stores, the use of sales promotional materials was physically observed.	In testing two new products, each product was introduced in several test markets. Sales results were obtained by auditing the retail stores in each test market.	An oil company wanted to estimate the trading area of competing stations. The license plates of a sample of cars in competing stations were recorded. Using state license records, the home addresses were plotted on a city map.

Reprinted from Keith K. Cox and Ben M. Enis, *The Marketing Research Process* (Pacific Palisades, Calif.: Goodyear Publishing Company, 1972), p. 329. Reprinted by permission of the publisher.

called a questionnaire. It can be read to the respondent by an investigator who records the respondent's answers, or it can be self-administered by the respondent. Observation is recording and measuring the actions of people or the states of physical phenomena. We look briefly at each of these aspects of data collection.

Questionnaire Design. Questioning methods have great versatility. They can be used to procure data for almost any type of marketing problem. The first step in employing the questionnaire is to design its structure, wording, and sequencing.

In studying question structure, it is useful to classify questions and answers according to degree of structure: unstructured, semistructured and structured. Exhibit 8-8 provides examples. Unstructured questions and answers give both the investigator and the respondent freedom to communicate information, i.e., both questions and answers are open-ended as opposed to being cast in any certain format. Unstructured questions are by scope and nature exploratory—designed to identify problems rather than to provide definite solutions. The major difficulty

Unstructured

Word Association (In a home sewing study, respondents were asked to give their immediate reactions to the following words and phrases):

Zippers   Making a dress

Buttons   Snaps

Incomplete Sentences (Respondents asked to complete):

People who drive convertibles . . .

Insurance of all kinds is . . .

Narrative Projection: "A friend of yours has just bought his first car. He asks you what he should do about getting insurance on it. What would you tell him?"

Thematic Apperception: A woman is pictured working at a sewing machine. Respondents were asked what the woman was thinking as she worked.

2. Semistructured

Essay-type Questions (Respondents not limited in length of answers to such questions as):

What is your opinion of this company?

What should this store do to keep you a loyal customer?

What is candidate X's biggest weakness?

3. Structured

Multiple-choice Questions (Respondents asked to check one):

What is your general impression of the advertisement now appearing on the screen?

Fantastic
Delightful
Pleasant
Neutral
Moderately Poor
Bad
Horrible

Adapted from Keith K. Cox and Ben M. Enis, *The Marketing Research Process* (Pacific Palisades, Calif.: Goodyear Publishing Company, 1972), pp. 209–12, with permission of the publisher.

with unstructured questions and answers lies in interpreting the results. It is not uncommon for different interviews on the same topic to develop along very dissimilar lines. This makes comparisons of answers difficult, particularly if statistical summaries are needed.

Semistructured questions are precisely stated, but the respondent is allowed to answer in his/her own words. This approach gives the respondent maximum latitude in framing an answer. Consequently, a breadth of information is usually obtained, and fresh insights sometimes emerge. One limitation of this approach is that its effectiveness is related to the respondent's educational level—the better-educated respondent tends to give articulate and complete replies. Also, effectiveness is directly related to the amount of interest in the question asked. Another difficulty lies in interpreting the answers obtained: one hundred respondents may furnish one hundred different answers which must be summarized and evaluated.

The structured approach is one in which both questions and answers are specifically stated. The most common types of structured questions are multiple-choice and dichotomous questions. Multiple-choice questions offer the respondent a number of alternative responses to a question. Dichotomous questions are limited to a two-choice answer, such as yes-no, agree-disagree, true-false, male-female, or cash-credit.

As compared to semistructured and unstructured approaches, structured questions and answers allow more control over the respondent's answers and minimize the potential bias interjected by the investigator's words, demeanor, or gestures. Other advantages of the structured approach include lower cost in tabulating responses and less ambiguity in the answers. The major disadvantage is the narrow range of response permitted by structured questions and answers. A yes-no answer does not allow the respondent much latitude in expressing his opinion or belief. Unstructured and semistructured questions and answers permit breadth, but are relatively costly, and are difficult to interpret and classify.

Question scaling is an attempt to achieve the advantages of both unstructured and structured techniques. A scale permits a range of responses, while providing a common-response format. There are a number of scaling techniques, but perhaps the most widely used in marketing research is the semantic differential. The procedure is to have the respondent convey his/her opinion on a given topic by indicating one of seven positions on a scale of bipolar adjectives. A typical scale is

| +3 | +2 | +1 | 0 | –1 | –2 | –3 |

The intervals are usually interpreted (from left to right) as extremely good, very good, slightly good, both good and bad, and slightly bad, very bad, and extremely bad. The semantic differential has been adapted for use in marketing to measure consumer opinions about stores, policies, brands, and companies. Exhibit 8-9 presents the classic example of the use of the semantic differential in marketing research.

The major advantage of the semantic differential is its simplicity; this technique can be adapted to many marketing problems. Since the questions and answers are completely structured, the cost of tabulating the answers is low. Interpretation of the tabulations, however, raises interesting technical questions. [Pedantic aside: the issue (explored in some depth in such sources as Cox and Enis, Green and Tull) is whether the scales can be measured numerically or only in ordinal fashion.]

Question wording can significantly affect meaning. There are basically four ways in which questions can be worded improperly. These are:

1. *Ambiguous questions:*
   What do you usually have for lunch?
   Tell me all you know about this company.

2. *Exceeding the respondent's ability to answer:*
   What is your husband's favorite brand of golf balls?
   How much laundry detergent did you use last year?

3. *Exceeding the respondent's willingness to answer:*
   What is your family income?
   How often do you have sexual intercourse?

Exhibit 8-9   The Semantic Differential in a Brand-Image Study

Mindak used the semantic differential to determine beer drinkers' reactions to the personalities of three brands of beer. An example of the approach is the profile shown at right.

The profiles represent mean ratings of all respondents for each brand of beer. Company X's product is most favorably regarded on all scales except aging. Brand Z's product has the least favorable image. Note that none of the profiles are on the negative side of the set of scales.

Adapted from William A. Mindak, "Fitting the Semantic Differential to the Marketing Problem," *Journal of Marketing*, April 1961, pp. 28–33, with permission of the publisher, the American Marketing Association.

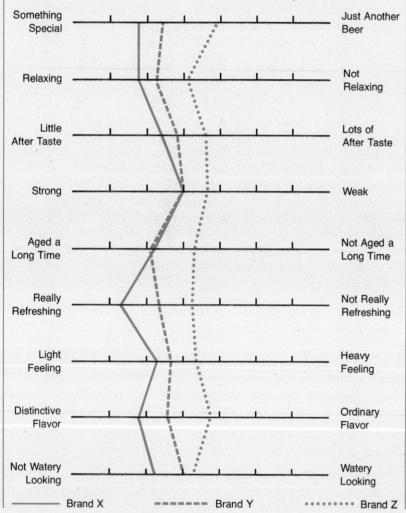

4. Influencing the respondent:

Do you think it is right as a loyal citizen to buy foreign products that put Amerians out of work?

Do you favor the installation of seat belts in cars to save lives?

Another important factor in questioning is the sequence of items in the questionnaire. Several points are of interest here. First, the opening question should catch the respondent's attention and encourage him/her to answer the remaining questions. Consequently, it should be short and interesting. In one rather successful survey of dairy patronage conducted by the author, the first question was, "Do you own a milk cow?"

Once attention is gained, questions generally proceed from the general to the specific, for two reasons. First, that order appears logical to most people. Second, answers to later questions are influenced by earlier questions. For example, an automobile preference survey which disclosed sponsorship by Ford at the beginning would probably bias subsequent questions either in favor of or against Ford products. Considerable psychological research has shown some personality types tend to respond positively to such influences (yeasayers), while others react negatively (naysayers). Consequently, the name of the company or product sponsoring the survey is usually withheld until the end of the questionnaire, or is not mentioned at all.

Bias can also result from the position of the question relative to other questions. Politicians generally prefer to be first on a ballot, and respondents tend not to select the first or last choice in a multiple-choice answer. This bias can be controlled to some extent by a careful question sequencing and by rotating the sequence of questions as the questionnaire is printed.

A final point on question sequencing is that most questionnaires ask for data about the respondent for the purpose of cross-classification. For example, age, sex, income level, occupation, education, place of employment, and so on may be potentially useful in a given survey in terms of providing categories for classifying the information obtained. People, however, sometimes resent or become suspicious of personal questions. Consequently, classificatory questions are generally placed at the end of the questionnaire.

In summary, designing questions which generate useful information can be a very complex task. For this reason, the manager is usually well-advised to consult an expert in this area. Moreover, even the most expert researcher will pretest the questionnaire, perhaps more than once, in order to minimize potential biases.

Collection Alternatives

Two approaches to collecting answers to questions are interviewing (verbal responses) and self-administered questions (written responses). Verbal responses may be obtained by interviewing respondents in person or by telephone.

The interview is a social process in which the investigator and the respondent interact, i.e., influence each other's attitudes and behavior. The respondent's role in this process is to supply useful information. The investigator's task is twofold: (1) to get the respondent to accept his/her role and participate in the interview, and (2) to obtain the information at minimum cost. More information can usually be obtained from personal interviews than from telephone interviews. Personal interviews tend to be granted for longer time periods and are more difficult for the respondent to terminate before the investigator is ready. The personal approach also permits the use of visual aids and allows the investigator to evaluate the background (dress, size and appearance of dwelling or office, type of reading material visible, etc.) of the respondent. The personal interview enables the researcher to obtain information from respondents who do not have access to a telephone. Telephone interviews, on the other hand, are usually faster and less expensive. Respondents can be contacted quickly, with no travel cost, and the individual who does not answer can easily be recontacted at a later time.

In the case of self-administered questions, the respondents receive a questionnnaire and answer it, having no verbal interaction with the questioner. Self-administered questionnaires may be mailed to individual respondents or handed out to groups of people. So-called mail questionnaires include those inserted in newspapers or magazines, tucked under automobile windshield wipers, etc. Mail questionnaires are characterized by constant cost per return, regardless of the geographic location of the respondent. Also, since respondents can remain anonymous, their motivation to reveal confidential information may be enhanced. Response rates for mail questionnaires, however, are generally much lower than for personal or telephone interviews. The length of time required to receive return mail questionnaires requires that lead time be budgeted in the project schedule.

Questionnaires are frequently given to a group of people assembled at a given place at a certain time. Perhaps the best example of this is college students who are continually answering self-administered questionnaires in their classrooms. Since groups of consumers, salespersons, or business people are often assembled at one time and place, this method can be an efficient way of collecting information. Having people assemble expressly for the purpose of completing a questionnaire, however, is costly. If the information is worth the expense, a personal interview may yield more information.

The major disadvantage of both types of self-administered questionnaires relative to interview methods is the limited information which can

Exhibit 8-10 Classification of Observation Methods

Methods of Observation

Object Being Observed	Personal Observer	Mechanical Device
People	A sales supervisor accompanies a new salesperson and observes the salesperson's behavior with customers.	An eye camera records changes in pupil size of a subject looking at different advertisements.
Physical Phenomena	An investigator counts inventory for a store audit.	An audimeter notes times when a television set is on, and the television channels to which it is tuned.

be obtained from self-administered questions. Long questionnaires may simply be thrown away. Moreover, various authorities have estimated that 10 to 20 percent of the adult population in the United States lacks the degree of literacy required to complete the typical questionnaire unassisted.

Data Collection Using Observation

As opposed to verbal questioning, data collection by observation includes counting, measuring, and recording. Observation methods may be classified by the object being observed, and by the method of observation. Objects being observed may be people or physical phenomena; the method of observation can be by personal observer or by mechanical device. Exhibit 8-10 provides an illustration of each type of observation.

One of the major advantages of direct observation is that it measures actual behavior rather than what people say they prefer or intend to do. An offsetting disadvantage of observing people is that only overt behavior can be studied. Motivation for the behavior patterns observed can only be inferred. Another disadvantage of observation of people is that two observers may interpret similar behavior differently, or may see similarities in behavior patterns that are in fact different. Also the observer, through boredom or fatigue, may make errors. These limitations can be minimized by careful observer training and supervision.

A second way of observing the behavior of people is by means of mechanical devices. A number of physiological research measures, notably the pupilometer and the galvanic skin response, are employed in advertising research. The assumption underlying the pupilometer or eye camera is that changes in pupil diameter measure interest. The galvanic skin response or lie detector measures involuntary changes in electrical resistance on the skin. Changes in this resistance are thought to correlate with arousal or interest. Other mechanical devices used to observe people include photographs, tape recordings, cameras, and the tachistoscope—a projection device which presents visual stimuli to subjects for very short (thousandths of seconds) and carefully timed intervals. The tachistoscope is commercially applicable to recognition of brand symbols and packaging research. Mechanical devices provide complete and accurate observation of the overt behavior for which they were designed. They are relatively expensive, however, and the results must be interpreted for marketing decision making. Despite these limitations, use of mechanical observation devices for marketing information seems to be on the increase.

Useful information can often be obtained by observing (studying) physical phenomena. Three broad categories of physical phenomena are documents, physical characteristics, and inventory. Documents of potential usefulness in marketing include shipping invoices, tax returns, automobile registrations, building permits, subscriber lists, and on and on. We are a well-documented society.

A related type of marketing observation that, unfortunately, does exist is industrial espionage. This type of observation includes such techniques as photographing documents, bugging telephones, tape recording competitors' meetings, screening rivals' trash, and eliciting information from their employees. To my personal distress, covert information is becoming increasingly important for marketing decision making, and observation techniques are well-suited to this task.

The second category of phenomena which can be observed by people is physical characteristics. A fine contribution to this area of research is the book by Webb and his colleagues. Here are two examples of physical-characteristic observation from this book:

> An observer wanted to measure the amount of liquor consumption in a city which was officially dry. He counted the number of empty liquor bottles in the trash cans.

> Researchers wanted to measure the effect of a newspaper strike upon retail shopping. Revenue collected from parking meters in the downtown shopping area was used as an index of the effect of the strike.

The third category of physical-phenomena observation is the counting of inventory and other indicators of consumer behavior. Store audits in retail stores and pantry audits in consumers' homes are examples of counting purchase behavior. Packaged-goods manufacturers frequently buy syndicated store audits from such research firms as Nielsen Company and Audits and Surveys, Inc. The continuous audit of sales in the marketplace is one of the major responsibilities of salespersons for food manufacturers.

Observation of physical characteristics can provide interesting marketing information at low cost. However, this type of information generally is most useful for the exploratory phase of the project; that is, observation of physical characteristics can suggest trends, but it provides only tentative answers.

A typical mechanical device for recording physical phenomena is the traffic counter, which records the number of cars passing a certain location within some time period, or the number of theater or store patrons passing through a turnstile during a given time period. This type of information is frequently obtained for retail location decisions and store expansion plans. Another mechanical device is the Nielsen Company audimeter which records the times that a television set is on and the channel to which the set is tuned. There is no differentiation between having the set on while reading or cleaning house and a room full of people whose attention is riveted to the program. However, a technique which rates the Howard Cosell Show dead last cannot be all bad. Based upon the information obtained through this mechanical device, projections are estimated for total national audiences of television programs. These devices are accurate, but relatively expensive. Moreover, they report only overt behavior. It is up to the marketing manager to determine possible decision implications of such information.

Observation methods have been used relatively infrequently in marketing. In general, questioning methods have been heavily relied upon, with observation techniques used to obtain supporting data. This trend is likely to continue, but perhaps observation will play a more significant role. For one thing, questioning can produce false or misleading information. Also, it may be feasible in some situations to obtain the advantages of both questioning and observation techniques. No one data collection technique is applicable to all situations; various techniques should be considered in each case. In some cases a combination of methods might be useful. The decision maker needs a basic understanding of data collection techniques because he/she is responsible for specifying the information needed, and for ascertaining that the information is worth more than it costs to assemble.

Sources of Information: Sampling

The source (called the population) from which the data are to be obtained is determined by the relevant information desired by the decision maker. Exhibit 8-11 illustrates the diversity of populations that could be studied. When the number of units in the population is small, such as salespersons for ABC Wholesale Distributors, the researcher may want to assemble information about all units in the population. However, the entire population is addressed infrequently, for several reasons.

One problem marketing researchers face is that the number of units in the defined population may not be known. This problem arises all too often, leaving the researcher little choice but to use a portion of the units

Exhibit 8-11   Examples of Different Populations in Marketing Decision Making

Defined Population Source of Subjects	Number in Population	List or Frame Possible Information Source
Students in Utopia University	25,000	Student directory
Total work force in the United States	80,000,000	Census Bureau
Beer drinkers in your trade area	?	City telephone directory
Retail stores of XYZ Drug Chain	52	List of stores
Salespersons for ABC Wholesale Distributors	28	List of salespersons
Customers of antimissile weapon system	6	List of governments

from a defined population. Another difficulty lies in matching the source of information (the list or frame) with the population as defined. For example, at any large university, the student directory (frame) probably differs from the actual student population at any time. Consequently, the population is often sampled.

The Concept of Sampling. Sampling is a familiar idea; the swimmer tests the water with a toe before diving in, the diner sips the wine before accepting the bottle, the prospective purchaser takes the new automobile for a drive before signing the contract. The purpose in each case is to learn something about the entity in question quickly and with relatively little expenditure of effort. Sampling is, therefore, a compromise between the high cost of being certain and the high risk of guessing.

The objective of sampling procedures is to maximize the accuracy of the information obtained, subject to cost constraints. Sampling accuracy is affected by two types of factors. First is bias, the difference between the true value and the measured value of a certain piece of information. The second is sampling error, which is the difference between the measure obtained from the sample and the measure that would have been obtained from all units in the population. There are basically two approaches to sampling accuracy: researcher control and probability.

Researcher-Controlled Sampling. When the researcher selects the units to be included in the sample, the sampling procedure is called researcher-controlled, or nonprobability sampling. In fact, the latter term is more common, but defining concepts in terms of what they are not can be confusing. By whatever name, the essence of researcher-controlled sampling is that the researcher determines the units to be included in the sample.

Three of the most commonly used types of researcher-controlled sample designs in marketing research are:

1. Convenience Sampling: A convenience sample is exactly what the name implies—a sample selected on the basis of speed and ease of contact with the respondent. Therefore, it is convenient for the researcher. This type of sampling is practiced every day by everyone. When purchasing a new fall suit, for example, one does not ordinarily shop in more than two or three stores. Many man-on-the-street interviews are basically convenience samples.

2. Judgment Sampling: One method of increasing the representativeness of the sample is to match the qualifications of the respondent with respect to the characteristic in question. Thus, *Business Week* or *Fortune* might choose a sample of 25 leading economists to estimate Gross National Product for next year. Many fashion magazines have a panel of experts who comment on next year's fashions, and the Associated Press and United Press International football ratings are examples of judgment sampling in sports.

3. Quota Sampling: The quota sampling technique consists of identifying features of the population which are related to the characteristic of interest, and structuring the sample so that it reflects the proportions of each of these characteristics that exist in the population. For example, if women constitute half the population, then the sample should be half women; if senior citizens constitute 20 percent of the population, then one-fifth of the sample should be senior citizens, and so forth. Quota samples are more representative of the population than are judgment or convenience samples, but are also more difficult to select—particularly as the number of quotas increases.

The main advantage of a convenience sample is that it is indeed quick and easy to select. However, the researcher usually sacrifices sample accuracy to reduce the time and cost of obtaining the data. Judgment samples provide expert opinion at relatively low cost, but can be biased by the experts selected. (Would you trust a football rating compiled entirely by Ivy League coaches?) Quota samples cost more, but are assumed to be generally more representative of the population. Since "generally more representative" is imprecise, researchers have sought ways of quantifying the representativeness of a sample. To put it another way, researchers want to measure the amount of error in a given set of sample data. This desire for quantification provides the rationale for probability sampling methods; i.e., sampling based on random choice of units to be included in the sample as opposed to researcher-controlled selection.

Probability Sampling. The distinguishing feature of probability sampling methods is that, when a chance mechanism is employed in the selection of population units to be included in the sample, the mathematical theory of probability can be used to determine the sampling error in the data. Researcher control, however objectively administered, may result in introduction of the researcher's biases into the sample. When chance governs selection, provided that there are no biases in the data, errors should occur only on a random basis—and random error can be measured precisely using probability theory.

The three types of probability samples most used in marketing are:

1. Simple Random Sampling: The distinction between probability samples and researcher-controlled samples is in the method of sample selection. In probability sampling, some random or chance mechanism is employed in selecting the sample from the sampling frame. In simple random sampling, each element in the population has a probability given by 1/n (where n = sample size) of being included in the sample. The classic example is selecting one of two items by flipping a coin.

2. Stratified Sampling: A stratified sample is obtained by dividing the total population into subgroups or strata and treating each stratum as a separate random sample. This is done to decrease the size of the sampling error caused by skewed distributions—a few large values and many small values. Populations of individual incomes, grocery store sales, and shopping distances traveled tend to be skewed.

3. Area (Cluster) Samples: In many cases it is difficult to secure a precise list of the population, but geographic areas (or clusters by alphabet or rank) are easy to obtain. The rationale for sampling without a list is that everyone lives somewhere. As long as the researcher has blocks or tracks of geographical territories which delineate them in a definite way he can use census track information to select a random sample. Other examples include a sample of sales invoices taken from a numerical list, or a sample of customers taken from an alphabetic list. Random samples within areas are true probability samples, although the sampling error of such procedures is relatively large. Despite this inefficiency, area or cluster samples are often used because they are relatively inexpensive.

Experimentation

In many cases, the most useful information that a decision maker can have is knowledge of the factors which caused a certain event to occur. The process of relating cause and effect is called experimentation. Scientific advances have been rapid in fields where causal factors have been correctly identified, notably in the physical sciences and in medicine.

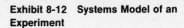

Exhibit 8-12 Systems Model of an Experiment

INPUTS   PROCESSING   OUTPUT

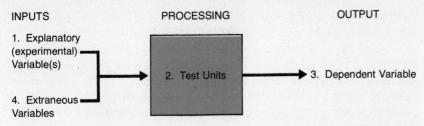

1. Explanatory (experimental) Variable(s)

2. Test Units

3. Dependent Variable

4. Extraneous Variables

Where cause and effect are difficult to relate—as, for example, in economic policy and in treating mental illness—progress is slow. Experimentation can be a very useful information generating procedure for marketing decision making.

Experimentation seeks to establish causal relationships among variables. By definition, then, an experiment is performed when explanatory variables are manipulated, and the effects of this manipulation upon a dependent variable are measured. Note that the distinguishing characteristic of an experiment is the manipulation of the explanatory variable before measuring the effect upon the dependent variable. Unfortunately, identifying and understanding the consequences of this manipulation are often complicated by the effects of other (extraneous) variables. One way of simplifying this task is to view the experiment from a systems perspective: inputs processed to produce outputs, as shown in Exhibit 8-12.

The four elements of the experimental model are interpreted as follows:

1. Explanatory Variable: The independent variable or variables which the experimenter will manipulate. In marketing, explanatory variables are generally some aspect of the marketing mix (product quality, price level, promotion strategies, or distribution decisions).

2. Test Units: These are the entities affected by the manipulation of the explanatory variables and the influences of extraneous variables. In marketing, the two broad classes of test units are people (customers or potential customers) and physical entities (stores, sales territories, product lines, etc.).

3. Dependent Variable: This is the criterion or standard for measuring attainment of the experimental objective. In marketing, the ideal dependent variable is sales or profit, but the effect of various extraneous variables upon sales is often difficult to determine. Consequently, other variables such as advertising recall scores, brand preference ratings, and customers' attitudes are also used.

4. Extraneous Variables: These are factors other than the explanatory variable that affect the dependent variable. In marketing, there are so many such influences that it is useful to categorize them. Following our basic marketing management model, the categories are internal (organizational) and external (environmental). The internal extraneous variables are product, price, promotion, and distribution that are not manipulated in a given experiment. The external category can be subdivided into customer variables (individual attitudes and actions, and group influences), competitors (marketers of similar products, and other products that satisfy the same generic need), and other environmental influences, e.g., economic trends and conditions, actions of governmental bodies, technological advances, seasonal variations, etc. Using these definitions, the experimental model shown in Exhibit 8-12 can aid in comprehending any marketing experiment. The best way to understand marketing experiments is to examine a few of them using the system model to guide your thinking. Sevin's work (Exhibit 8-13) provides a good example.

Analysis of Marketing Information

After the information has been assembled, it must be analyzed. Informa-

---

Exhibit 8-13   Product Line Modification: Example of a Marketing Experiment

The purpose of this experiment was to measure the effect upon profits of dropping unprofitable products from the total product line. The systems view is:

| Explanatory Variables (elimination of unprofitable products) | → | Test Units (Sales Territories) | → | Dependent Variable (profit contribution) |

Two sales territories were randomly selected as experimental and control territories. In the experimental territory 592 unprofitable items were eliminated from the original product line of 875 items. No product changes were made in the control territory. The profit contribution was measured for 18 months before and after eliminating the unprofitable items.

The experimental results indicated an increase of almost 24 percent in profit contributions when the unprofitable products were eliminated. Consequently, the unprofitable products were eliminated in all sales territories.

Adapted from Charles H. Sevin, *Marketing Productivity Analysis* (New York: McGraw-Hill Company, 1965), pp. 90–91, with permission of the publisher.

Test Units	Profit Contribution Before Change	Profit Contribution After Change	Change	Effect of Eliminating Unprofitable Products
Experimental Territories	100.0	123.4	+ 23.4	+ 23.9
Control Territories	100.0	99.5	–.5	

tion analysis is a broad and complex field. The marketing manager cannot be expected to be proficient in information analysis, but should be sufficiently well-versed in the fundamentals of information analysis to communicate with expert analysts. In general, there are two basic approaches to marketing information analysis: description and inference.

Descriptive Procedures. These are methods of summarizing and simplifying information for the purpose of improving user comprehension. The most common types are percentages, measures of central tendency (mean, median, mode), and trend analysis. Descriptive statistics are perhaps the most widely used of all analytical procedures in marketing. Much marketing information is analyzed by these methods alone. One cannot pick up a copy of *The Wall Street Journal* or *Business Week* without encountering presentations of percentages, discussions of averages, and evaluations of trends.

Descriptive statistics can be misleading. "Seventy-five percent of the voters support Blimp for Senator" is an impressive claim until you learn that the sample size for this statement is four. Also, the tabulation may mask the influence of variables not explicitly analyzed. For example, relationships between a larger advertising budget and an increase in sales may really be no more than reflections of growth in Gross National Product. And there is danger in extrapolating present trends into the future. Improper extrapolation of market trends is considered a primary reason, as discussed in Exhibit 8-14, for the failure of the Edsel.

Statistical Inference. These procedures involve the use of sample data to make inferences about populations of interest. There are three basic approaches: estimates of population values, hypotheses about population values, and tests of association between values in the population. Estimation involves the use of point estimates and confidence intervals; tests of hypotheses generally use t, Z or F probability distributions; and analysis of associative data involves such techniques as Chi-square, regression, correlation, and sophisticated variations of these techniques. These terms may have very little meaning to you unless you have had a basic statistics course. Marketing managers are increasingly taking such courses because statistical inference is becoming more and more accepted as an analytical technique for marketing decision making. Exhibit 8-15 presents one classic example.

Perhaps the fundamental issue in marketing research today is getting marketing decision makers to fully utilize systematically collected and scientifically analyzed marketing information. There is no doubt that much progress toward this end has been made in the 1970s, but it is also true that many managers still make crucial decisions primarily by guesswork and intuition. To accelerate the former trend and diminish the

Exhibit 8-14   The Edsel: An Example of Extrapolation Error

In the mid 1950s, Ford had about 25 percent of the automobile market, Chevrolet another 25 percent, the Buick-Oldsmobile-Pontiac ("B-O-P") cars a third 25 percent, and the final 25 percent was shared by all other car makes. The Ford Motor Company had only the Mercury, a weak competitor in the B-O-P market. Moreover, Ford researchers estimated that in 1955 the number of cars in operation would be 70 million—up 20 million. More than half the families in the nation would have incomes of over $5,000 per year, and 40 percent of all cars sold would be in the medium price range or better.

Ford executives decided to bring out a car to capture a portion of this market—differentiated from the "stodgy" B-O-P's with a youthful and elegant personality—"The Smart Car for the Younger Executive or Professional Family on Its Way Up." Ford did an incredible amount of marketing and product research on this automobile. Automobile images were researched, demographic trends were carefully analyzed, and a massive effort was made to name the new car. This latter effort included computer-generated names and correspondence with poet Marianne Moore, who suggested such names as Intelligent Bullet, Utopian Turtletop, Bullet Cloisonne, Pastelogram, Mongoose Civique, and Andante Con Motor. Nevertheless, the car was named Edsel—"for the only son of the founder Henry." Moreover, for security reasons, styling was handled internally. This caused problems—the grill, particularly, was peculiar-looking; it became the subject of countless Freudian jokes.

Reynolds, a former Ford executive, believes, however, that the concept of the Edsel was not bad. He acknowledges mistakes in execution of the Edsel's marketing plan—such as a thin, under-financed dealer organization, and Ford's agreement to stop competing in stock car races and advertising power and performance—but argues that the major factors contributing to the Edsel's failure were beyond Ford's control.

First, the B-O-P market simply did not grow as rapidly as Ford researchers expected. With the onslaught of the recession in the 1950s people began to look for cheaper means of transportation. Sales of American Motors' Rambler and of the German Beetle—the Volkswagen—made impressive gains during this period. Second, the love affair between Americans and their automobiles began to come to an end. A rash of "hate Detroit" articles and books began to appear. John Keats published his *Insolent Chariots,* and people began deriding our "tailfin" culture. Young men customizing their cars began to remove chrome, take out grills, take off wheel covers, and perform surgery on tailfins. The flashy Edsel was utterly out of tune with this trend in taste. Reynolds comments, "it is hard to see how anyone could, given the kind of car market that existed in 1955 and 1956 . . . have anticipated such trends."

Perhaps so, but the dangers of simply extrapolating past trends have never been so clearly demonstrated. The Edsel was a marketing disaster. It may have been the costliest flop in marketing history. Henry J. Kaiser, in his farewell to the car business, stated, "we expected to toss 50 million dollars into the automobile pond, but we didn't expect it to disappear without a ripple." Ford admits to spending five times that amount, and some authorities estimate the loss at closer to 350 million.

Adapted from William H. Reynolds, "The Edsel Ten Years Later," *Business Horizons,* Fall 1967, pp. 39–46, with permission of the publisher.

latter, organizations are beginning to consider information as a resource to be managed.

MANAGING MARKETING INFORMATION

Information is an organizational resource that must be carefully managed for maximum effectiveness and minimum cost. Many organizations are

Exhibit 8-15 Forecasting with Regression Analysis

alda used regression analysis to develop an estimating equation for Lydia Pinkham's Vegetable Compound. Between 1908 and 1960, this company spent 40–60 percent of its sales on advertising, but did not employ many of the other usual types of marketing effort (e.g., sales force, credit, package changes, and special deals). Also, the product had no close substitutes. Consequently, it was reasonable to assume that advertising did have a substantial effect on sales.

Regression analysis yielded the following predicting equation for sales of the compound:

This equation accounted for most of the variation in sales of the compound between 1908 and 1960. It can be used to predict sales of the compound in future years.

$$Y_c = -3649 + .665X_1 + 1180(\log X_2) + 774X_3 + 32X_4 - 2.83X_5$$

where: Y_c = predicted yearly sales (in thousands of dollars)—the dependent variable

X_1 = last year's sales (thousands of dollars)

X_2 = current year's budgeted advertising expenditures (thousands of dollars)

X_3 = a dummy variable $\begin{cases} 1 \text{ from 1908 to 1925} \\ 0 \text{ from 1926 on} \end{cases}$

X_4 = year (1908 = 0, 1909 = 1, . . .)

X_5 = current year's disposable personal income (billions of dollars).

Adapted from Kristian S. Palda, *The Measurement of Cumulative Advertising Effects* (Englewood Cliffs, N.J.: Prentice-Hall, 1964), pp. 67–68, with permission of the author.

beginning to move toward the Marketing Information System (MIS) concept as a means of managing marketing information.

Information Costs and Values

As noted above, there are many types of data that could be useful for marketing decision making. To better determine cost and value, information can be grouped into three categories: internal information, intelligence, and marketing research.

Internal Infomation. Internal information is data that are generated within the organization. The major source of such information is the accounting department, which captures and reports orders, sales, inventory levels, accounts receivable, accounts payable, and so on. Analysis of this type of information can identify opportunities and problems, and compare actual to expected levels of performance. Other sources of internal information include personnel records, the public relations department, the financial vice-president's office, and various operating units such as production, traffic, and engineering.

Marketing Intelligence. Intelligence is data from external sources. There are three types of marketing intelligence. First, overt information is intelligence that can be obtained from public sources, for example, census reports; trade papers; trade shows; newspapers and magazines; books; and company annual reports. Covert information is procured from unknowing or uncooperative sources. It is also called industrial espionage, everal items of fictitious information were "planted" by customers of six salesmen of an electrical-components manufacturing company. For example:

changing customer requirements; competitor's construction of a new plant; competitor's price quote; availability of a new raw material; development of a new product by a competitor.

After planting the information with a salesman, each customer notified the researcher. Each of these items of information would be extremely useful to decision makers in one of the company's operating units. Albaum wanted to determine whether this unsolicited information would flow to those decision makers.

Of the six items of information, only one arrived as planted—a full ten days after the salesman heard the information. Moreover, that salesman had previously sold the product which was the subject of the plant, and was a personal friend of the manager of the operating unit. He had, therefore, extraordinary incentive to make the report. One other item of information did arrive, but in so distorted a fashion as to be dangerously misleading to the decision maker receiving it.

The other four items never reached the target managers, even after the company sent a questionnaire asking specifically about such items to all salesmen (including the test subjects). The need for effective management of such information (from assembly to dissemination) is apparent.

Adapted from Gerald Albaum, "Horizontal Information Flow: An Exploratory Study," *Journal of the Academy of Management,* March 1964, pp. 21–33, with permission of the publisher.

e.g., bugging (placing a microphone or camera in the headquarters of a customer or competitor), romancing a competitor's secretary or hiring one of his employees, or sifting through his trash. Distasteful as it may seem, covert information is extremely useful in some marketing situations. This source of information has obvious ethical implications.

The third category of marketing intelligence is unsolicited information. This is information that would be of value to the organization if the information were known before it became public knowledge (overt intelligence). For example, a salesperson may hear that a new plant is moving to town, or that a competitor has developed a technologically superior product. Exhibit 8-16 presents a classic study of unsolicited information.

Marketing Research. Research is specifically commissioned, information-seeking activity. Internal marketing research might involve special studies on the profitability of certain products or the feasibility of changing packages. Most research in marketing, however, involves buyer behavior studies—concept testing, product preference studies, usage patterns, advertising awareness studies, and so on.

Obtaining information is not without cost. Four types of costs should be considered:

1. Cost of Assembly: The actual costs associated with assembling the information: consultant's fee, staff time, printing and mailing, samples, computer programming, etc.

2. *Time Delays:* Implementation of a course of action is held pending the result of the assembled information; consequently, all revenues accruing from that course of action are postponed, lowering their present value.

3. *Risk of Adverse Environmental Change:* While the decision is pending, the situation may deteriorate; e.g., a competitor may increase marketing effort, or inflation may increase costs. (Of course, a change for the better may also occur.)

4. *Cost of Error:* It is possible that by chance or because of some bias, the assembled information could be incorrect. Erroneous information could lead to wrong decisions, with costly consequences.

Determining costs is often a rather pragmatic undertaking. In my experience, both personal and from marketing literature, most decision makers in actual situations ask: How much will the information cost and how long will acquiring it take? The answer is then compared to the total budget for marketing research. Thus, explicit account is taken of out-of-pocket costs of information assembly, and revenue delays are recognized. If considered at all in a given case, costs associated with erroneous information and with adverse environmental change are handled intuitively.

There are, of course, both advantages and disadvantages to intuitive determination of the value of additional information. Managerial intuition is relatively fast and inexpensive; and it is a decision-making aid with which the manager feels comfortable. Moreover, formal calculations require some knowledge of probability theory and an amount of hard data; many marketing managers have neither. On the other hand, as we have noted earlier, intuitive assessments may lack consistency, comprehensiveness, and communicability. Thus, many organizations are beginning to consider a systemic approach to marketing information management.

The Marketing Information System (MIS) Concept

The 1960s witnessed the conception of the Marketing Information System. An MIS is an organizational entity whose purpose is to aid marketing managers in processing data for decision making. Precise definitions of the concept tend to be a bit lengthy (see Exhibit 8-17), because the concept is complex. A picture is useful here; Exhibit 8-18 illustrates the concept. As the figure shows, the concept expands the processing stage of decision making (review Exhibit 8-1) by interposing an MIS between the inputs of data and judgment, and the manager's own thinking.

Consider, for example, a contemplated decision to increase the price of a particular product. Relevant data might include past sales and costs figures for this time, competitors' prices, general economic conditions, and possible reactions by the Federal Price Board. The amount, diversity, and

Exhibit 8-17   Definitions of the Marketing Information System

Brien and Stafford have defined the Marketing Information System in these terms:

a structural, interacting complex of persons, machines and procedures designed to generate an orderly flow of pertinent information, collected from both intra- and extra-firm sources, for use as the bases for decision-making in specific responsibility areas of marketing management.

And Kotler has proposed a *marketing nerve center* which he describes as follows:

this unit is a generalization of the marketing research department into something infinitely more effective known as the Marketing Information and Analysis Center (MIAC). MIAC will function as the marketing nerve center for the company and will not only provide instantaneous information to meet a variety of executive needs but will also develop all kinds of analytical and decision aids for executives—from computer forecasting programs to complex simulations of the company's markets.

These are perhaps the most often cited definitions of the MIS.

From Richard H. Brien and James E. Stafford, "Marketing Information Systems: A New Direction for Marketing Research," *Journal of Marketing* (July 1970), pp. 19–23; and Philip Kotler, "A Design for the Firm's Marketing Nerve Center," *Business Horizons* (Fall 1966), pp. 63–74.

complexity of such data might literally defy managerial understanding.

To be useful to the manager making this decision, the data must be analyzed—simplified, organized, summarized, correlated, etc. He/she might ask, for example, for a graph of sales by years, a list of competitors' average prices, or a one-page summary of previous Price Board decisions in this area. There are numerous analytical techniques available.

The crucial question is that of determining which analytical techniques to apply to the data in a given situation. This determination is guided by the decision maker's *models*—perceptions, ideas, stereotypes, generalizations—of phenomena relevant to the situation. With respect to the pricing decision, for example, one model provided by economic theory says that, ceteris paribus, less of the product will be demanded if price is raised. Another model may be that the manager sees his firm as an industry leader, and reasons that competitors would follow his lead in raising prices.

In concept, then, the MIS should have three components: an analytical bank (collection of routines, preferably computerized, for analyzing data), a data bank (accumulation of raw data for analysis), and a model bank (set of guidelines for appropriate analyses of various marketing situations). When these components are functioning properly, marketing information can be managed to aid decision making. The MIS should perform six functions:

> *assembly*—the search for, and gathering of, marketing data
> *processing*—the editing, tabulating, and summarizing of data
> *analysis*—the computation of percentages, ratios, tests of statistical significance, solution for optimal values, etc.
> *storage and retrieval*—the indexing, filing, and relocating of data

Exhibit 8-18 The Marketing Information System Concept

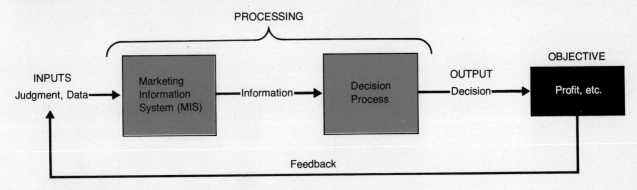

evaluation—the statement of the quality of the information, i.e., the amount of faith that the decision maker can have in the accuracy of the information

dissemination—the routing of useful information to the appropriate decision maker

These functions relate to the three MIS components, and support the marketing decision process, as shown in Exhibit 8-19. The model bank determines what information will be assembled and processed, the techniques stored in the analytical bank are used in analysis and evaluation, and the information itself is stored in, retrieved from, and disseminated by the data bank.

The MIS is an excellent concept. Once the marketing managers in an organization begin to think about formalizing their decision processes and specifying their information needs in explicit detail, the potential benefits of an MIS become obvious. If a significant portion of the marketing managers in a given organization begin requesting more information, analyzed with more sophistication and less delay, then an effective and efficient way of meeting these needs should be developed. But a decade or so of experience has shown that designing and operating such a system entails greater costs and returns fewer benefits, at least in the short run, than many marketing managers initially expected.

CONCLUDING NOTE

This chapter was not an easy one to write, and perhaps it is not easy to read. A great deal of work is going on in the area of formalized decision procedures; it is absolutely essential that marketing students be exposed to such work. One chapter can do little more than overview so broad and complex an area, but perhaps it does serve to introduce you to work in a field of vast *potential* significance to marketing management.

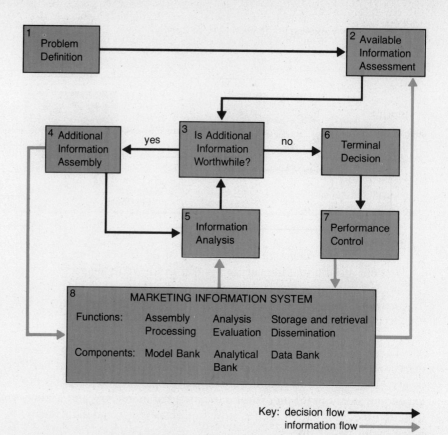

Exhibit 8-19 The Management of Marketing Information

1 Problem Definition

2 Available Information Assessment

4 Additional Information Assembly

yes

3 Is Additional Information Worthwhile?

no

6 Terminal Decision

5 Information Analysis

7 Performance Control

8 MARKETING INFORMATION SYSTEM

Functions: Assembly Processing | Analysis Evaluation | Storage and retrieval Dissemination

Components: Model Bank | Analytical Bank | Data Bank

Key: decision flow ⟶
information flow ⟶

Note that we have emphasized the word *potential*. Formalized decision making procedures beyond simple break-even analysis and other accounting-oriented techniques have really not contributed greatly to marketing management to this point. Only in the larger and better managed firms have formalized decision procedures been utilized to any significant extent. The gap between information users and information suppliers is both wide and deep in most organizations. Most marketing managers do not use formal information assembly and analysis procedures to nearly the extent they should. Decisions of great significance are sometimes made on the basis of intuition aided by only the skimpiest of informal data.

This situation must change. Increasingly, marketing decisions become the core of the organization's activities, and costs associated with making incorrect marketing decisions are rising rapidly. To make the marketing research process viable for marketing decision making will require the concentrated effort of both users and suppliers of marketing information.

Users must understand the marketing research process, and the functions of the marketing information system in implementing this process. They must learn the fundamentals of the process by careful study of textbook principles, and by giving serious thought to how those principles relate to the specific organization with which they are concerned. Second, decision makers must cooperate fully in the explication of their decision processes and information needs. Third, they must use the system and feed back suggestions for modification and improvements.

The information supplier's responsibility for bridging the gap is also basically threefold. First, of course, he/she must have a high degree of competence in assembling, analyzing, and evaluating marketing information.

Second, the information supplier must understand the organization's goals, functions, and environmental characteristics. Marketing packaged goods to final household consumers is different from supplying the needs of oil field drilling operations—and both differ from a campaign to elect a person to public office. To be sure, similar marketing principles underlie each of these situations, but jargon, trade practices, and the backgrounds of individuals in these fields differ. The information supplier must learn the specifics of his/her organization's situation.

Third, and perhaps most important, the supplier must strive to develop in the user a sense of confidence in the formal processes employed to obtain the desired information. This involves holding training sessions, giving demonstrations, and being genuinely receptive to questions that are often elementary and sometimes plain foolish. Moreover, the supplier must develop and maintain relationships with the user based on mutual respect for the other's skills. This statement may be trite, but its importance cannot be overemphasized. Final decision-making responsibility rests with the manager; if he/she does not trust formalized information and decision procedures, he/she will not use them.

Systematic processes for decision making should be evaluated at two levels: conceptual and operational. At the conceptual level, i.e., as a guide to thinking, systematic procedures for marketing decisions can be very useful. They encourage logical and consistent patterns of thought, tend to improve the comprehensiveness of factors considered, and facilitate communication among managers. At the operational level (actually implementing formal procedures), the record of systematic decision procedures to date has been less impressive in marketing than in other fields, but progress is being made.

In subsequent chapters, many types of decisions in market analysis, programming, implementation, and control are discussed. Keep in mind the concepts presented in this chapter, and apply them to these decisions. This exercise will help in analyzing the strengths and the weaknesses of systematic decision procedures in marketing situations.

KEY TERMS AND CONCEPTS

Context of Marketing Decisions
  lack of consumer knowledge of wants
  crude measures of behavior
  large number of variables
  interrelationships
  rapid change
Barriers to Formal Decision Procedures
  lack of knowledge
  press of day-to-day affairs
  exaggerated claims
Uses of Formal Decision Procedures
  supplement to judgment
  communication
  reduce costs
Systems View of Decision Making
Decision-Process Model
  problem definition
  available information
  is additional information worthwhile?
  additional information assembly
  information analysis
  performance control
Information Uses
  exploratory (decision defining)
  problem solving (decision making)
  decision monitoring
Project Design
  hypothesis hunting
  literature review
  content
  methodology
  schedule
  budget
Data
  facts
  opinions
  estimates
  predictions
Secondary Information
  relevance
  credibility
  accuracy

Questionnaire Design
  structure
  wording
  sequencing
Collection Alternatives
  interview
  self-administered
Observation
  people
  physical phenomena
Information Source
  population
  samples
Sampling
  concept
  researcher-controlled
  probability
Experimentation
  definition
  internal validity
  external validity
Analytical Techniques
  summarization
  statistical inference
Types of Information
  internal
  intelligence
  research
Information Costs
  assembly
  time
  adverse changes
  error
MIS Concept
  definition
  components
  functions

QUESTIONS FOR DISCUSSION

1. Are the decisions that a marketing manager faces more difficult than those of production, finance, or personnel? Why or why not?

2. Using Exhibit 8-2, examine some decisions that you have made, e.g., ordering a meal, buying a car, choosing a major in college. Identify all seven steps of the decision process for each type of decision. Would such an approach be helpful in marketing decision making, e.g., what styles to order, what prices to charge, what salespersons to hire?

3. Define the problem, in terms of objectives and alternatives, for the decisions you considered in question 2. What types of exploratory information would be useful in defining each problem?

4. You are a marketing decision maker who has requested certain information. The marketing research department has prepared a questionnaire and sent it to you to examine. What do you look for? Why?

5. Consider the following types of marketing situations: evaluating a new toy designed for preschoolers; determining voter preferences for a coming election; evaluating consumer acceptance of an automatic nailing machine designed for faster home building; estimating extent of interest in a proposed resort community.

a. Select one or two of these situations and evaluate alternative structures of questions and answers to generate the information you want.

b. Evaluate the various methods of assembling questionnaire data for the marketing situations you selected in part (a). Compare your answers.

c. Evaluate observation as a means of obtaining the necessary information. Compare your answer to the answers for (a) and (b).

6. For each of the populations in Exhibit 8-11, identify a sample frame. Evaluate the various sample designs discussed in this chapter as ways of securing information for those two populations. Compare your answers.

7. Explain the difference between information assembly by survey (questioning and observation) and by experimentation. Give examples of marketing situations in which each type might be useful. Review advantages and limitations of both types of information.

8. Examine the Sevin experiment presented in Exhibit 8-13, using the model of an experiment given in Exhibit 8-12. Identify independent (explanatory and extraneous) and dependent variables and test units. What was the purpose of this experiment? What were the results? Comment on the validity of this experiment.

9. Discuss the material in this chapter with someone who has marketing decision-making responsibilities. First, describe the approach to him/her. Then get his/her reactions. Compare his/her comments with the material in the chapter.

10. How would the Marketing Information Systems of A & P, the corner grocery store, and a political candidate be alike? How would they differ?

SUGGESTED READING

1. Lee Adler.
"Systems Approach to Marketing." *Harvard Business Review,* May–June 1967, pp. 105–18. Masterful integration of marketing decisionmaking, information systems, and research needs; reprinted in Gabriel M. Gelb and Betsy D. Gelb, *Insights for Marketing Management,* 2nd. ed. Goodyear Publishing Company, 1977.

2. Harper Boyd, Jr. and Ralph Westfall.
Marketing Research: Text and Cases. 3rd ed. Irwin, 1972. Standard textbook in marketing research techniques.

3. Keith K. Cox and Ben M. Enis.
The Marketing Research Process: A Managerial Approach to Purchasing Relevant Information for Decision Making. Pacific Palisades, Calif.: Goodyear Publishing Company, 1972. I am, of course, inclined to think that this is a good book. It is the major source for material in this chapter; somewhat more advanced and detailed in scope and presentation than the present text.

4. Paul E. Green and Donald S. Tull.
Research for Marketing Decisions. 3rd ed. Englewood Cliffs, N.J.: Prentice-Hall, 1975. Standard textbook of marketing research procedures and techniques; written at a more advanced level than the Cox and Enis reference—requires some familiarity with matrix algebra and statistical inference.

5. James H. Myers and A. C. Samli.
"Management Control of Marketing Research." *Journal of Marketing Research,* August 1969, pp. 267–77. Clear exposition of techniques for managing marketing information; good bibliography; reprinted in Gelb and Gelb, *Insights for Marketing Management.*

6. Stanley Payne.
The Art of Asking Questions. Princeton, New Jersey: Princeton University Press, 1951. This small book is still the best available source on the practical aspects of designing and asking questions; delightfully easy reading.

7. Eugene Webb, Donald Campbell, Richard Schwartz, and Lee Secrest.
Unobtrusive Measures: Nonreactive Research in the Social Sciences. Chicago: Rand McNally, 1966. This book makes a delightful and eloquent plea for considering observation data collection methods in addition to questioning; numerous interesting examples are described.

CASE 7/ THE SATURDAY SUNRISE CHRONICLE

Houston is one of the relatively few remaining cities to have two independent newspapers: the morning *Post* and the evening *Chronicle*. Both are relatively successful newspapers. The *Chronicle* leads the state of Texas in total circulation and advertising linage in both its weekday and Sunday editions. Up to 1974, however, the Saturday afternoon edition was not doing nearly as well.

The Situation

The *Chronicle* managers unanimously recognized that the Saturday afternoon paper was a problem child. It was not doing as well as desired, and the various editors regarded it, bluntly, as an inferior product. They ignored it as much as possible. In fact, the Saturday afternoon edition would have been a very small paper indeed had it not been for the fact that the *Chronicle* sold classified advertising by the seven-day week. The classified section was often more than half the total paper on Saturday afternoon.

There was less unanimity, however, about what to do with the problem child. *Chronicle* top management did not want to cease publishing a Saturday paper for fear that the image of the *Chronicle* as a progressive metropolitan daily paper would be damaged. On the other hand, there was little enthusiasm for continuing the product in its existing form.

A third possibility was to publish the Saturday paper in the morning. Several other newspapers, notably the Oakland *Tribune* and the Fort Lauderdale *News,* had made such a change in their Saturday publication schedules. But results were mixed. Some such papers did well, but others not so good. The *Chronicle* managers believed that such a product modification might have possibilities, in that some social observers had been claiming in recent years that weekend life styles were changing. Saturday was no longer considered a workday, and Sunday was no longer the exclusive leisure day. To test this premise and to develop information for guiding the possible "facelift" of the Saturday paper, management turned to research.

Research

The key questions to be answered were: how does the public feel about the Saturday afternoon paper,? what did people think about the idea of changing to Saturday morning,? and what specific changes would they desire?

The information was obtained from eight groups of respondents who met as a group to discuss the key questions and related issues. In addition to the three key questions, respondents were given samples of parts of newspapers from different parts of the country as examples of different types of editorial features that the new Saturday edition might contain. This technique is termed a focused group interview. But the *Chronicle* research staff added two new elements. First, they included *Chronicle* observers in each group which observed while the inner group discussed the questions. The inner group was told to disregard the observers, and that they would be introduced to the observers in due time. Second, each focused group session ended with members of the inner group filling out self-administered questionnaires so that the results of the sessions could be quantified. Each session lasted one and one-half to two hours.

A total of more than 100 respondents were included in the eight groups. These respondents were chosen from participants in previous studies of newspaper readership. Thus, they were not statistically representative of the population, but could be stratified on the basis of newspaper preference, income, and location of residence. Consequently, the respondents chosen were thought to be fairly representative of the market for a new newspaper product. The respondents were readers of either the morning *Post* or the evening *Chronicle,* or in some cases (18 percent of the total) subscribers to both Houston dailies.

The type of information elicited in the sessions is illustrated by the following verbatim comments from panelists:

> Moderator: Let's talk about the kind of news you read on Saturday compared with news in the paper during the week. How much of the latest news should you get in your paper on Saturday? How important to you is news on Saturday?

Written by Ben Enis, based on an interview with August Galiano, the *Houston Chronicle*. Courtesy of the *Houston Chronicle*, research division.

Replies: On Saturday we want different news instead of the mass hysteria the media is bombarding us with all the time . . . I mean the Doomsday Machine . . . There's got to be something besides murder, rape, and Watergate that could be in the paper . . . Why not make Saturday be the good guys' paper?

In other words, the appetite of the reading public shifts away from hard news to more tranquil leisure-oriented contents when the week-end arrives.

From analysis of these and other comments and the self-administered questionnaires, *Chronicle* researchers concluded that they had a special opportunity to capitalize on the potential for a Saturday paper, tailored to a change of pace in readers' lifestyles. This would involve (1) substantial modification of the content and tone of the Saturday paper, and (2) a change in delivery time from afternoon to early morning—before 7 a.m.

The New Product

The necessary changes in the content of the Saturday paper were obvious from analysis of the research. First, because the public pursued a wide spectrum of activities based on individual needs rather than events on the weekend, *Chronicle* researchers were convinced the new Saturday *Chronicle* should focus largely on reader service features. For example, the inside front page of the new paper could be devoted to a schedule of events taking place in Houston on that weekend: one paragraph summaries of plots of first run movies, plays and musical events; lectures and seminars; professional sports schedules, and so forth. A second suggestion was the inclusion of more material for younger people, especially pre-schoolers. The Mini-Page was adopted. This was a double tabloid page feature of material aimed at the early school and pre-school child. It included synopses of news written in a style comprehensible to this age group, crossword puzzles and jokes, and profiles of important newsmakers.

The research also determined that subscribers were still interested in the news, but that they preferred capsule summaries to indepth treatments. Thus one page in the new Saturday paper could be devoted to summaries of world and national news events, and another page to state and local happenings.

It is not unusual in marketing to find a significant gap between research conclusions, and the actions taken by responsible managers. The *Chronicle* bridged this gap by using the "observer" concept to supplement the focus group interviews. The outer group was made up of *Chronicle* editors. Thus, the individuals who would actually implement product changes essential to the success of a new Saturday format were present as the existing product was criticised and suggestions for improvements were made.

Of course, some inner group respondents were embarrassed when introduced to employees of the paper they had faulted. But the procedure proved quite useful in sharing ideas to be implemented by the *Chronicle*. The editors heard first-hand what respondents liked and did not like about the product. This is not to say that the *Chronicle* always followed respondents' suggestions, but the paper was exposed to the viewpoints of the ultimate consumers. The *Chronicle* can trace many new editorial ideas to these focused group sessions.

The research was conducted in early 1974. During the ensuing six months, the decision was made to change the Saturday paper to a "Sunrise Edition." Considerable planning went into the changeover: production schedules had to be revamped, and new delivery schedules arranged. Moreover, editorial policies had to be altered for the Saturday paper. Additional use was to be made of color in the sunrise edition, and this necessitated changes in production procedures. The new product was launched in October of 1974.

Results

The Saturday Sunrise Edition was an immediate success. After three months of publication, circulation of the Saturday paper outstripped daily circulation, and readership, as measured by an independent survey, had increased substantially. Most importantly, the advertising content of the Saturday paper—the profit producing portion—had almost doubled over the same period during the previous year. The following table shows comparisons of the *Chronicle* with the morning *Post*.

Not all of the 20 percent increase in circulation could be attributed to product changes, since a combination Saturday-Sunday subscription rate was instituted in October, 1974. However, all of the readership increase was attributable to the change in product and delivery time.

Saturday October 5 thru Saturday December 28, 1974
versus
Saturday October 6 thru Saturday December 29, 1973

Total Advertising Linage

	1974	1973	+ or −
CHRONICLE	1,689,644	876,272	+ 813,372
POST	1,965,766	2,202,210	− 236,444

Classified Linage

	1974	1973	+ or −
CHRONICLE	969,526	735,071	+ 234,455
POST	895,634	1,042,378	− 146,744

Retail Linage

	1974	1973	+ or −
CHRONICLE	654,995	100,656	+ 544,339
POST	1,040,872	1,116,682	− 75,810

Success, however, must be continually nurtured. Since the Saturday paper was no longer an editorial stepchild, the distinguishing features of the Saturday Sunrise Edition—the bold and breezy editorial style, the minimization of ''hard news''—were beginning to give way to the more traditional front page.

CASE 8 / WORTHINGTON FOODS

Worthington Foods, Inc., a subsidiary of Miles Laboratories, stands in 1973 as a pioneer and leader in the field of researching and test marketing vegetable protein meatless meats known as meat analogs. These various analogs closely simulate the taste, texture, and appearance of nearly every meat product now available.

One of the prime markets for these meat analogs is the institutional field. With the costs of meat soaring and the labor problem becoming more acute, the popularity and acceptance of this alternative source of economical protein are growing in nursing homes, hospitals, schools, and other institutions across the nation.

BACKGROUND INFORMATION
The Company
The company was first organized in 1939 under the name "Special Foods, Inc." by a group of Seventh-Day Adventist business and professional men. Originally, the firm was founded to meet the vegetarian needs of this religious group. In 1945, the company was incorporated under the name Worthington Foods, Inc. Worthington merged with and became a subsidiary of Miles Laboratories in March of 1970.

Product Development
Worthington products are developed primarily from soy and wheat protein. The basic raw ingredients are combined with flavorings, binders (high protein egg white), and emulsifiers to produce the meat analogs. They are strikingly similar in taste, texture, and appearance to beef, pork, and poultry products. No meat, meat derivatives, or preservatives are used in any of these foods.

Although Worthington began manufacturing vegetable protein foods in 1939, the revolution in textured protein products did not come about until 1957. At that time, Dr. Robert Boyer developed the process that allowed protein from soy beans to be spun into a fiber. Worthington's food technologists could now develop foods that approximated much more closely the fibrous texture of animal protein. In this process, a solution of soy protein isolate is pumped through metal spinnerettes containing thousands of tiny holes, each about four-thousandths of an inch in diameter, and into a bath that causes the extruded solution to coagulate into thread-like fibers. At this point, these filaments are essentially colorless, tasteless, and odorless. This bland high-protein substance is then turned into a variety of different foods by adding flavors, colors, nutrients, and other ingredients, then by cutting, cooking, and shaping to produce the final product.

Product Offering
Today, the company has over 40 alternative product offerings of meatless versions of ham, beef, corned beef, chicken, turkey, bacon, and even seafood.

Worthington's products are formulated scientifically to provide good nutritional levels of protein, fat, and carbohydrate. They are lower in total fat (with polyunsaturates predominating) and calories than most of their animal meat counterparts. For example, Stripples, the firm's hickory smoke-flavored bacon-like product, has only 16 calories per strip compared with about 49 for bacon. Stripples contains 23.3 percent protein by weight, 10.9 percent fat, 11.6 percent carbohydrate, and virtually no cholesterol, since vegetable fats are used instead of animal fats.

Many of the products are fortified with vitamins and minerals in accordance with government recommendations. Product quality is precisely controlled to assure consistent nutrition, flavor, and tenderness. Flavorings are derived primarily from natural plant extractives and, in some instances, from imitation flavor enhancers.

The vegetable protein foods are precooked, experience little or no shrinkage when prepared, have no bones, gristle, or excess fat. The price per edible pound of vegetable protein is usually significantly lower in cost than most animal protein. Products are also preportioned to reduce preparation time and waste, and have a long shelf life.

In summary, the main characteristics of meatless meats are:

They contain no meat or meat derivatives.
They are a rich protein source (soy and wheat) comparable to meat.
They are lower in total fat (with polyunsaturates predominating).
They are lower in calories.
They have virtually no cholesterol.

From *Contemporary Cases in Marketing* by W. Wayne Talarzyk. Copyright © 1974 by The Dryden Press, A Division of Holt, Rinehart and Winston, Inc. Reprinted by permission of Holt, Rinehart and Winston.

They contain no preservatives.

They have a longer shelf life.

They are economical (precooked, little or no shrinkage, no excess fat, no gristle, no waste).

Worthington also has diversified somewhat to become a supplier of texturized vegetable proteins to other food processors and manufacturers. One of the items marketed is extenders for meat, chicken, and seafood. With meats, these extenders reduce shrinkage and increase fat and moisture-holding capacities. The red meat extenders comprise a mixture of spun protein fibers, binders, emulsifiers, red coloring, and, in some instances, an added beef-like flavor. It is economical to use such extenders and formulas for the less expensive and higher fat meat cuts. The extenders can also nutritionally upgrade hamburger, sausage, and patty formulas.

Chicken-type extenders comprise a mixture tailored for addition to chicken meat. Extenders also provide an opportunity to retexturize and nutritionally upgrade chicken and turkey byproducts.

Product Significance

Every day brings an estimated 180,000 new mouths to feed throughout the world. By the year 2000, nearly 7 billion persons are likely to inhabit the earth. Few experts believe it will be possible to feed all of them without massive assistance from vegetable protein. Fortunately, soy protein production offers some key economies. One acre of grazing land, for example, can produce an estimated 50 pounds of food protein when fed to beef cattle. If, however, this same acre is planted in soy beans, the yield of vegetable protein is over 500 pounds.

Additionally, since texturized vegetable protein foods are manufactured, their nutritional content as well as other factors are totally controllable. Protein, fat, carbohydrate, calories, and other nutrients can be easily adjusted to meet specific dietary needs. Also, unlike meat, quality control standards assure that preestablished nutritional levels can be maintained at all times.

Vegetable protein foods have achieved rapid acceptance and use and will become an increasingly important food source because of several main reasons: (1) The world's population is expected to double by the year 2000, as already stated, and, unless additional sources of protein are utilized, the protein shortage will become more acute; (2) The number of people preferring to reduce or eliminate meat from their diet for philosophical, medical, or religious reasons is increasing rapidly; (3) The cost of meat is continuing to spiral upward as demand outstrips supply; and (4) There is an expanding awareness and concern with regard to the nutritional adequacy of all prepared foods.

The Industry

The vegetable protein industry produced sales in 1968 of approximately $10 million. By 1972, the total sales were estimated at over $50 million. According to a study by the Stanford Research Institute, this sales volume will possibly climb to as high as $2.0 billion by 1980. A study by Cornell University predicted that by 1985 soy protein products will be at 145 million pounds and will account for 10 percent of all domestic meat and poultry consumption. Even further in the future, volume was estimated to reach an annual rate of 2.45 billion pounds by the year 2000. Although Worthington Foods is the pioneer in this field, General Mills, Archer-Daniels-Midland, Swift and Company, Griffith Laboratories, and A.E. Staley are also becoming deeply involved in vegetable proteins.

THE INSTITUTIONAL MARKET

Institutional markets utilize the vegetable proteins in two basic fashions. In some instances, they are used to extend meat and seafood proteins, and in others they are direct replacements for meats and seafoods. For both of these applications, the primary institutional markets are state, federal and municipal hospitals, colleges and universities, schools, in-plant feeding operations, prisons, and nursing homes. Meat packers and processors are also important markets for the protein extenders. Advertisements used to reach institutional markets explain how these vegetable proteins can be incorporated into meal planning.

A key element in the marketing of vegetable proteins is to utilize the right approach with the right account. For example, cost savings and palatability are important to all potential users. But institutions, especially schools, are concerned with nutritional benefits and convenient preparation, while meat processors are usually more concerned about USDA labeling requirements and how the average consumer will react when he discovers that there is soy in his hamburger.

MARKETING STRATEGY

In early 1973, Miles Laboratories switched from a part-time to a full-time protein sales effort and consolidated its industrial and institutional account development by creating a protein products group within its Marschall Division. This new group involved a six-man sales force and a national sales manager, Doyle Ramey, formerly Worthington's marketing manager.

One of Miles' major marketing thrusts is designed to secure a trial order for the purpose of evaluation. Experience has demonstrated that when the company persuades a potential account to at least try this ''new foods concept,'' and usage instructions are then followed, the results of the evaluation are usually favorable. The key is to achieve the trial usage.

The company has been most successful in selling this ''new foods concept'' by making large-scale presentations to state dietary groups, regional food service directors, and state and regional meetings involved in food service. The format of these presentations has been to make a short talk, followed by a film on the food industry and what is projected for the 1970s and beyond, and to conclude with a buffet. This buffet may include a 100-percent substitute foods-type smorgasbord or it may involve certain combinations of meat substitutes, extended meats, and other dishes.

Company representatives also attend many national food shows such as the National Restaurant Show, American Dietetics Association, Mid-Atlantic Health Congress, Great Lakes Health Congress, New England Hotel & Motel Show, National Independent Meat Packers Association, and American Meat Institute, as well as many state and regional shows. At these shows, the company generally offers literature or accepts requests for literature and samples for certain products currently being promoted.

A major promotional activity was undertaken prior to the 1972 annual meeting of the American Meat Institute. This campaign was designed to build awareness and interest in Pro-Lean 45, a meat extender that the company claimed would save meat processors a minimum of 2 cents per pound—a significant figure in a thin margin industry—yet maintain the texture and quality of the end product. The company began by sending four direct mailings to a list of key accounts submitted by the sales force.

The last mailing, sent shortly before the show opened in October 1972, was a handsome briefcase and clipboard. Attached were copies of Miles' guarantee for the product, technical data sheets and instructions, a reprint of a four-page product advertisement, the USDA formula and label approval statement, a sample label for beef patties containing Pro-Lean 45, and a response card and order form.

The results were very impressive. With an objective of 150 trial orders, the campaign actually generated over 400. Meat processors came to Miles' display at the show highly skeptical but left willing to give the product a try after tasting the patties cooked by the company representatives.

In terms of advertising, the Marschall Division primarily uses *School Lunch Journal, Meat Processing,* and *National Provisioner.* The company plans to expand its advertising into other institutional publications in the near future.

PRELIMINARY INFORMATION

From September 1968 through February 1969, Worthington Foods test marketed its new bacon analog, Stripples, in Fort Wayne and South Bend, Indiana as well as in Columbus, Ohio. The product was introduced with a substantial promotional campaign that emphasized the analog's uniqueness in relation to health and economy. Resulting sales data from store audits indicated a fairly favorable response by consumers. With national bacon consumption estimated to 1.45 billion pounds for 1968, the market potential of this type of product becomes very significant.

Characteristics of the Analog

Stripples simulates the form, texture, color, and taste of bacon and can be used as bacon by consumers. The product contains the following ingredients:

Wheat proteins
Soy proteins
Yeast proteins
Water
Corn oil
Egg albumen
Brown sugar
Salt
U.S. certified color
Seasonings
Monosodium glutamate
Vegetable gum

Flavorings
Nucleotides

The major differences between Stripples and bacon were stressed in the advertising directed to consumers. The analog is precooked and does not shrink during cooking. It contains little or no cholesterol, and has only one-third the calories of bacon (65 calories per four strips of the analog). In addition, throughout the test period, the price of the analog was held constant at 69 cents for an 8-ounce package. Newspaper advertisements stressed that the 8-ounce package contained 32 slices in contrast to the 20 slices usually found in a 1-pound package of bacon and that bacon experienced shrinkage of about 75 percent. On an as-served basis, therefore, the analog costs approximately half as much as bacon. Another unusual feature was that the bacon analog was sold as a frozen food, whereas bacon stocks were usually displayed in refrigerated cases in a separate section of each store.

Test Market Objectives

The basic objectives of the test market were (a) to determine the sales potential of Stripples, (b) to compare the product's sales with those of bacon, (c) to evaluate the relationships between store characteristics and sales of the new product, and (d) to assess the market prospects for this type of product.

RESEARCH METHODOLOGY

Market Environment

Fort Wayne, the test market utilized by Worthington Foods for this study, is located in the northeastern part of Indiana and has a diversified industrial economy. The city's 1968 population was estimated to be 176,000 compared with a 1960 population of 161,800.

Forty supermarkets in national, regional, and local chains were selected for the test. For analytical purposes, test stores were classified on the basis of seven major characteristics. Three of these—average weekly dollar sales, neighborhood median income, and type of store—remained the same throughout the 6-month test. These store characteristics are generally stable over short time periods. The remaining characteristics— meat case dollar sales, pounds of bacon sold, average price of bacon, and number of bacon brands available— were not the same throughout the test period. These store characteristics usually change fairly rapidly. Since the number of stores in each class was not constant during the entire test period, the analysis was based on average sales of the analog and of bacon per store as indicators of possible market relationships.

Two Phases

During Phase I (the first 3 months), in-store displays and stocks of Stripples were checked and maintained each week by contract personnel. Intensive promotion and advertisement of the analog consisted of in-store shelf talkers, weekly quarter-page newspaper advertisements, and frequent TV spot advertisements. During Phase II (the second 3 months), food brokerage and store personnel maintained in-store displays and stock. There were few newspaper, TV, and radio advertisements. Marketing of the bacon analog was similar to that for a long-established product; that is, considerably fewer inputs of promotion and merchandising.

Consumer Research

In addition to the store audits, buyers and nonbuyers of Stripples were interviewed by telephone. During the initial weeks of the study, about 500 cards were placed in the new product packages offering purchasers a small gift for filling out their name and address and mailing the card. About 300 cards were returned, and these people were interviewed to determine their reaction to the analog. A sample of 100 people who were aware of the analog but had not tried it were selected from the Fort Wayne telephone directory, and these people were interviewed. Information obtained included initial purchase rate, repeat purchase rate, intentions to buy, problems in use, reaction to price level, household use patterns, and overall satisfaction with the product.

TEST MARKET RESULTS

Consumer Acceptance

A consistent pattern of sales for Stripples emerged from the test market with the product being purchased each of the 6 months in 38 of the stores. In the other 2 stores, it was purchased in each of 5 months.

Results from the consumer surveys indicated, in general, a high level of acceptance for the product. The product's strongest attributes were ease and speed of preparation and good cooking qualities. A large proportion of the users found nothing that they disliked about the product. A substantial majority of the Stripples users indicated that they would purchase the product again. Buyers' initial and repeat purchase rates as determined by the consumer surveys reinforced the pattern noted in the audited sales data.

Most consumers indicated that they used the product at breakfast, generally as the main meat course. Survey results also showed that many users were attracted to Stripples because of its advertised low-calorie and low-cholesterol values. The consumer survey also indicated that price was an important consideration for buyers. An overwhelming majority of buyers of Stripples regarded the price as reasonable.

Sales and Store Characteristics

Sales of Stripples and bacon were not the same for all of the stores in the test market. In fact, some interesting and significant relationships emerged when sales were related to store characteristics. The following statements briefly indicate some of these relationships:

Neighborhood income—Bacon and Stripples sales were greater when the median income for the neighborhood was above $6000.

Type of store—The average sale of Stripples per store was greater in local and regional chains than it was in national chains.

Weekly dollar sales—The ratio of bacon sales to Stripples sales was greater in stores having high average weekly sales than in other stores.

Monthly meat sales—Stripples and bacon sales increased as other meat sales increased.

Bacon sales—Sales of Stripples per store increased as sales of bacon increased.

Price of bacon—Both products showed little variation in sales among stores grouped by average price of bacon per pound.

Brands of bacon available—Average sales per store for both products were larger where more than five brands of bacon were available.

INFORMATION ON THE CONSUMER

Several years ago, a number of consumers familiar with vegetable protein products were questioned concerning their opinion of these types of foods. Many details of the study were interesting although not particularly significant, but the market prejudice of most women against meat substitutes was very convincing.

Of the consumers responding, 41 percent said they would not give their family any new meat substitute regardless of how good the product tasted; 5 percent said they knew it would not taste as good as the natural product; and 25 percent said they might try it once, but they were certain they would not like it. This 71 percent bias against a product even before trying it was reduced to 58 percent after several exposures to a good meat analog. Such attitudes, however, are still very limiting to the consumer market.

These persons who did or would buy the meat analog if it were available gave the following reasons for their potential purchase: low calories 47 percent, economy 28 percent, high protein 13 percent, convenience 12 percent, and taste 5 percent. It is also important to point out that another recent survey indicated that very few consumers currently have any basic technical knowledge of good nutrition and food quality.

While these results may be viewed as preliminary, they do seem to point out that a good consumer education program in nutrition would be necessary before any successful penetration of the vegetable protein meat analogs could be expected in the consumer area.

CASE 9 / COTTONWOOD VILLAGE

A half century ago there was a stop on the interurban railway running south from Edwardsville, Illinois, that was named Cottonwood Station. This name recently was revived by Dr. Merrill Ottwein for his real estate developments in the vicinity of the old interurban stop, and the name of the corporation he founded was Cottonwood Station, Incorporated.

In the late 1960s Dr. Ottwein had sold his flourishing veterinary practice and turned to other activities, of which the outstanding was land development. He had developed, on a tract of land about two miles south of Edwardsville, Lakewood subdivision. This was a charming subdivision designed for high-class homes, and all of its lots had been sold in 1971 despite their premium prices. At that time Dr. Ottwein and his colleagues were proceeding with an addition to Lakewood, including another small lake, and with different sorts of utilization of the large area of over 800 acres that had been brought together under Cottonwood Station, Inc. One venture was intended for economy-priced housing, for there was an obvious scarcity of new housing in that price bracket in the area. It would be located in rolling terrain at the far eastern end of the property, the opposite from Lakewood, and it was given the name of Cottonwood Village.

INITIAL DEVELOPMENT

Land planning for Cottonwood Village had begun some time earlier, and a small lake was being filled a short distance north of the site. This was an area on the west side of a circling road around the eastern acreage, at the entrance to which would be a reception center that also could serve to control privacy. As landscape planning was very important in the developer's personal value system, shrubs and trees were being grown in a nursery area for later transplanting to the Village. Underground utilities and other site requirements were planned or under way, but the major step would be selecting and procuring the housing units.

An exhaustive effort was made to determine the ideal available type of housing. The Cottonwood people estimated that truly economy housing should cost somewhat under $10,000 for a two-bedroom unit. On-site construction, even of precut houses, soon was

found to be infeasible for such a figure. Modular units seemed desirable, but no manufacturer could be found in the Midwest who would be able to make and deliver units within the necessary time—and the costs were too high. All possibilities except mobile homes were eliminated, and the products of all leading and reputable manufacturers were given thorough comparison before one manufacturer in southern Michigan was determined to offer the quality, price level, and attractiveness needed.

Sites for the units and for other installations were mapped out and their preparation started. The circling road through the property was blacktopped, signs and lighting erected, and development was proceeding well when the first mobile homes were delivered in August, 1971. Soon four units, which had various options of size and luxury features, had been placed at the reception center and were ready for exhibit. Advertising was published in two area newspapers, radio commercials broadcast, literature ready and mailed, and Cottonwood Village was open for prospective customers.

SITUATION OF THE PROBLEM

The first visitors during the opening on a Sunday near the end of September comprised a variety of age levels, economic levels, place of residence, and other aspects. It had been expected that young married people would be the most interested, but in the early showings the salespersons could discern no predominant type. Sales were quite slow and when the first one was closed, it was with an elderly retired couple. There was no indication of whether the advertising had been effective, and the fact that people were coming from towns where there had not been advertising added mystery.

Dr. Ottwein knew well from his own experience that a proper and strong marketing campaign was essential in attaining sales in real estate. At this point he recognized that he had insufficient marketing information for making vital decisions on the campaign to sell Cottonwood Village. Therefore, he turned to marketing professionals for counsel. They naturally had to become well apprised of the nature of Cottonwood Village and its situation, a background that we now will summarize. The Village was connected by a short paved road with a State highway running into Edwardsville, a county seat

Source: Adapted from David J. Luck, *et al.*, *Marketing Research*, 4th ed., Prentice-Hall, 1974, pp. 89–93.

city of around 12,000 population—and southward into Collinsville, which had a population of 18,000. At the southwestern limits of Edwardsville was the new campus of Southern Illinois University, whose enrollment ran around 12–13,000. Only a handful of less than 2 percent of the students were housed on the campus, which had been intended mainly to be a commuting university, but a larger number lived in mobile home parks and other dwellings in the immediate area. Edwardsville was in the metropolitan area of St. Louis but not a suburban or bedroom community, as one would expect from its nearness, because most of the suburban sprawl had moved into Missouri rather than Illinois.

Within that county (Madison) was a large industrial population of over 200,000, and there were many executive and professional employees of those industries who moved into the hilly land around Edwardsville and Collinsville—which were from seven to twenty miles from their work. The Village was less than two miles from Interstate-270 on which the northern metropolitan area of St. Louis and many industries could be reached in fifteen to thirty-five minutes. Also by Interstate highway downtown St. Louis could be driven to in twenty to twenty-five minutes. And so there seemed to be a wide area from which Cottonwood might draw residents.

CHARACTERISTICS OF HOMES

The units in Cottonwood Village were indeed mobile homes, but Dr. Ottwein had improved them after arrival in several ways. A conspicuous change was the application of Masonite type paneling on their exteriors, giving them a wooden appearance and avoiding the garish whites and bright colors of normal mobile homes. When placed on their sites, the wheels were removed and the grading of dirt and the shrubbery concealed the usual open space at the bottom—which also avoided the mobile home look. An important departure from the usual dreary mobile homes court was placing the units at various angles in clusters. Thus, while the oblong boxiness of the unit could not be avoided, in other respects the Village appeared more like a community of houses than a congested mobile homes park. This was enhanced by providing parking areas for the automobiles, so there were no driveways running alongside the units.

The units were available in 2-bedroom or 3-bedroom models, with or without furniture, and with options of air conditioning, porches, and patios. Prices with furniture for 2-bedroom homes ranged from $9,000 to $11,500 and those for 3-bedroom homes from $9,700 to $12,200. The land, however, was leased from Cottonwood Station, Inc., which charged a space rental including water, sewers, trash pickup, and care of lawn and landscaping. An example of average costs was the following:

Purchase price	$10,000
Percent downpayment	20%
Amount of loan	$8,000
Years to repay	12
Monthly payment on loan	$86.90
Space rental	$65.00
Estimated insurance and taxes	$20.00
Total living costs	$171.90

For this price Dr. Ottwein believed that he was offering a very unusual combination of features perhaps unique for such low-cost home ownership and unmatched by any mobile home park in the Midwest. These features were cited:

The Environment

1. Mobile homes arranged in clusters of 3 to 5, not in rows.
2. Natural wood exteriors (20-year guarantee) in subdued woodland colors (dark green, brown, tan).
3. Natural landscaping, trees left undisturbed, utilities underground, 25-acre private natural park. Patios and decks at each site.
4. Small lake for fishing and ice-skating.
5. Mobile homes tied down with cables to concrete piers, not set on wheels on concrete pads. Wheels are stored for owners.
6. Paved roads and sidewalks.
7. Twenty to thirty minutes to downtown area of major city.

Mobile Modular Homes

8. Everything electric— no combustible fuels.
9. House-type furniture (rather than mobile home furniture). Basset and other name brands.
10. Forty-two gallon water heater (many mobile homes have 30 gallon).
11. Attached storm windows and extra insulation.

(Ceilings and floors 6″, walls 3″; Mobile Home Manufacturer's Assn. standard is 3″ and 1½″.)

12. One-quarter inch natural wood paneling throughout interior.

13. Carpeting throughout interior (except bathroom).

14. House-type exterior doors with wood interior doors on all cabinets and closets.

15. Two door refrigerator and freezer, 30 inch electric range and oven.

Services

16. Security provided (guard, entrance control, and lighting at control points).

17. Storage area and building away from living area.

18. Gardening area for residents' use.

19. Car wash facility on premises.

20. Lawn and yard care provided by management.

21. Adjacent shopping and laundry.

22. Restrictions on noxious or offensive use of facilities.

23. Buy-back provision. Owner has right to sell, but management agrees to buy back at agreed-upon depreciated value.

The unusual character of Cottonwood Village added to his own limited experience in marketing real estate contributed to the complexity of Dr. Ottwein's decision outlook. A problem that we have not yet mentioned was that many of the features listed above were still quite optional and could be omitted, if not justified. For instance, an ordinary sized water heater could be offered or the car wash, laundry, or storage facilities could be excluded. A number of variables in the Cottonwood Village market mix needed decisions—in product, price and promotion, and in the basic question of markets.

QUESTIONS FOR ANALYSIS OF CASES

1. Use the buying process model to describe the buying behavior of a "typical" consumer of the product mentioned in the case. Identify internal and external influences upon the process, and specify the nature of the influence for each variable. Identify outputs of the process.

2. Evaluate the possible market segments upon which this organization might focus its marketing effort in terms of identifiability, responsiveness, and significance. Discuss bases upon which market segmentation strategies might be built, and comment upon effective demand in the segment, and point out ways of measuring market potential.

3. Examine the market information needs of this organization. Identify internal, research and intelligence data that might prove useful for marketing decisions, and note possible sources of such data. What cost would be associated with the data? How would management determine the value of the data? What role could a marketing information system play here?

4. Given your analysis, outline the market strategy that you would recommend this organization follow. Defend your recommendations.

PART 4 THE MARKETING PROGRAM

After reading this part, you should be able to:

1. Explain the major elements of the marketing program for a product (you might select a particular product to think about as you are reading these chapters).

2. Discuss the basic decisions to be made within these major areas and the integration of these decisions into a marketing program.

3. Point out possible problems in implementing and controlling the program.

4. Identify environmental factors that could affect the program.

Magnum Photos, Inc.

The taste people hate. Twice a day.

The taste

LISTERINE

First published in *Esquire* Magazine.

"I had a feeling they wouldn't stop at artificial turf."

9/PRODUCT DECISIONS

This chapter is the first of four devoted to development of the marketing program. The material is separated into chapters for ease of exposition. In an actual situation, the marketing manager must consider product, promotion, distribution and pricing decisions more or less simultaneously. Product decisions form the basis of the marketing program, so we begin with them. Major points in the chapter include:

1. The consumer views a product as a bundle of utilities for providing satisfaction. The producer sees a product as the culmination of the processing of resources.

2. The product life cycle postulates that product brands pass through stages of introduction, growth, maturity, and decline. This concept provides guidance for decisions over time.

3. The product portfolio must be formulated with respect to the width, depth, and dynamics of the product mix. Products must also be identified by branding, and product extensions (design, packaging, services) must be determined.

4. Product decisions must be integrated with promotion, distribution, and pricing to formulate the marketing program. Classifications-of-goods concepts offer some general guidelines for this integration.

An organization's *product* (good, service, or idea) is the fundamental basis of its existence. The product is the medium through which the organization attains its objectives by satisfying the wants and desires of its customers. Product decisions, therefore, are of paramount importance to the organization. So we begin by examining the basic nature of the product, as seen by the customer and by the organization.

NATURE OF THE PRODUCT

"In the factory, we make cosmetics; in the store we sell hope," said Charles Revson, of Revlon, Inc. Marketing observer Theodore Levitt states, "Purchasing agents do not buy quarter-inch drills; they buy quarter-inch holes." And Elmer Wheeler, early pioneer of successful sales techniques, used to say, "Don't sell the steak—sell the sizzle." The message is clear: the consumer and the producer may view the product in very different ways.

Consumer's View of the Product

The consumer buys expectations of benefits. A product is seen as a *bundle of utilities* capable of supplying expected benefits. Any entity (good, service, or idea) that the consumer believes will satisfy a want or desire is a product.

Products that a producer might think are very different may be perceived as similar in the eyes of the consumer (recall Exhibit 2-4). For example, Yoga lessons and sleeping pills may be alternative ways of satisfying the desire for a sound night's sleep. To fulfill his/her desire for recreation, a consumer might weigh the merits of a backyard swimming pool versus a membership in a country club. And season tickets to the local team's home games might be weighed against a new set of golf clubs as alternative ways of satisfying a desire for recreation.

Conversely, products that the producer believes to be similar may be perceived as completely different by the consumer. Perhaps the classic example here is mass transit. Many social critics and public policymakers see mass transit (buses, subways, commuter trains) as alternative means of transportation to the private automobile. But to many potential mass-transit consumers, the automobile provides many benefits other than transportation, e.g., ease of mobility, privacy, freedom from schedules, and door-to-door transportation. Though the costs of these extra benefits are very expensive on a per-mile basis, a product that does not offer these benefits is simply not, to many consumers, a substitute for a car.

Producer's Perspective on the Product

The producer is quite likely to think of his product in terms of the inputs and processes required to produce it. For example, steel, a motor, bearings and valves, human labor, capital, information, and administrative effort are required to manufacture a washing machine. To the manufacturer, the sum total of the processing efforts lavished upon these resources is the product—a device that washes clothes. The housewife, however, is not the least bit interested in these resources or this effort; nor is she particularly concerned about the fine quality of the materials, the quality of the craftsmanship, or the manufacturer's long experience in producing such machines—except as these factors contribute to her desire for satisfaction: clean, sweet-smelling clothes, convenience, approval of her family, etc.

And so it is with services. The customer in the barber chair, for example, really does not care how long the barber has worked to learn his trade, nor how badly the barber's feet hurt; he is concerned that the results of the barber's services will be a handsome head of hair. This sort of concern is fundamental with respect to ideas—anyone attempting to solicit votes or charitable contributions must focus upon the benefits the voter or donor (consumer) is expected to receive in return. Of course, we are simply reaffirming here a basic theme emphasized throughout the book: *Customer satisfaction—the customer's belief that the benefits of a given exchange exceed the cost of making that exchange—is paramount.* Customer satisfaction is paramount because customer satisfaction is the key to successful attainment of the organization's objective, e.g., profit, return on investment, increased market share, winning the election, or whatever.

Product decisions play a fundamental role in effecting customer satisfaction and organizational objective attainment. As we discussed in Part III, the organization selects a target market by matching its objectives and capabilities with characteristics of various market segments, and then designs a marketing program to satisfy the wants and desires of that segment. Now we are in a position to see clearly the fundamental role that product decisions play in such a process.

In the study of product decisions, confusion sometimes arises from the fact that such decisions must be made at three different levels. Each individual product must be managed through its life cycle. The product portfolio (total assortment of products offered by a given organization) must be determined. These product decisions must then be integrated with promotion, distribution, and pricing decisions into a marketing program that energizes the marketing plan.

THE PRODUCT LIFE-CYCLE CONCEPT

The marketing manager must be concerned with the dynamics of his product—its product life cycle. We examine this concept and discuss its usefulness for guiding marketing decisions, particularly at the beginning of the cycle (new product development), and as the cycle matures. Exhibit 9-1 illustrates the product life cycle concept. Note the four stages:

1. Introduction—the product is brought to market; sales are slow as demand is developed and the product is improved technically.

Exhibit 9-1 The Product Life Cycle Concept

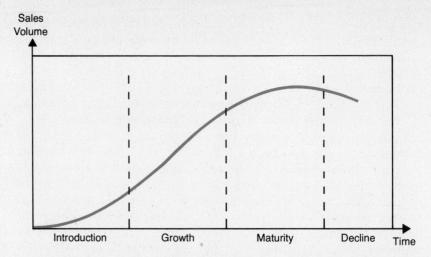

2. *Growth*—the product catches on; sales rise rapidly and the total market expands.

3. *Maturity*—growth in sales volume levels off; competitors enter the market; many sales are of the replacement type.

4. *Decline*—sales fall off as new products enter the market, consumers' tastes change, etc.

Clearly, the emphasis upon each of the four marketing mix elements might vary in different stages of the cycle. For example, in the introductory stage, promotion (advertising, free samples, direct mail, intensive personal selling) may be necessary to gain the attention of consumers. As the growth stage begins, the focus of marketing effort might shift to widespread and rapid distribution patterns. In the maturity stage, differentiating the product from other products through packaging, service, or functional adaptations might be useful. Price cuts may be the most effective way of halting or at least slowing down a sales decline.

Is the product-life-cycle concept really useful to marketing managers? A number of empirical studies have traced the sales histories of various types of products. The patterns vary. Only a few resemble the generalized product life cycle of Exhibit 9-1. Attempts to explain the discrepancies have focused upon differences among product forms (whiskey, automobiles, cigarettes), classes (Scotch whiskey, sedan automobiles, filter-tipped cigarettes), or brands (J&B, Chevrolet, Marlboro).

My own opinion is that the product-life-cycle concept is of limited usefulness for product forms or product classes. It can be very helpful in planning marketing strategies for marketing brands, provided that one key point is clearly understood. Products are not organisms. They do not have innate life cycles, as plants and animals do. On the contrary, products

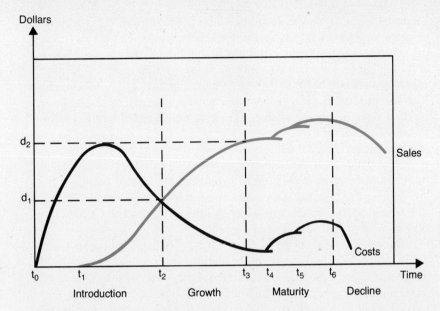

Exhibit 9-2   Using the PLC for Marketing Planning

Dollars

d_2

d_1

Sales

Costs

t_0 t_1 t_2 t_3 t_4 t_5 t_6 Time

Introduction   Growth   Maturity   Decline

are introduced, grow, mature, and decline as the result of decisions by marketing managers as these decisions are affected by competition and other environmental forces.

In analytical terms, the product life cycle as shown in the graph of Exhibit 9-1 is the *dependent variable:* sales as a function of time. The independent variable, time, is a proxy variable for the amount of marketing effort programmed and budgeted for the product. Viewed in this way, the product-life-cycle concept becomes a useful planning and forecasting tool for marketing decisions regarding individual products. Exhibit 9-2 shows how this refinement of the PLC concept could be used.

Note first that the product life cycle actually begins before the product is introduced into the market. There must be a period of product development before any sales can occur. This time period is shown on the graph by the distance from t_0 to t_1. Costs of product development, however, do accrue during this time period. Indeed, costs may be highest during this time period. The product is introduced according to a marketing plan which specifies some level of sales (d_1) by a certain time, designated t_2. The planned sales figure may be in dollars or in terms of market share.

If sales do rise according to the plan, the product is advanced to the growth stage in managerial thinking. Note that the product does not automatically change from introduction to growth like a child reaching puberty. It is advanced to the growth stage if, and only if, the marketing manager is satisfied with its progress during the introductory stage. Managerial satisfaction is usually the result of profitable performance. It is generally useful to view the product's advancement from the introductory stage to the growth stage as occuring when its breakeven point is reached.

During the growth stage, it is hoped that sales will continue to rise and costs will continue to fall. At some point, designated t_3 on the graph, the rate of growth will begin to decline. When sales have obtained some level (d_2), the product is said to have reached its maturity stage. Again, the product does not reach maturity as a result of some internal organic process. Maturity is a management decision, influenced by such factors as product profitability, marketing strategies for other products, organizational priorities, and the effect of external factors such as competitive marketing strategies, legislation, consumer tastes, and so on.

During the maturity stage, marketing strategy might be focused upon differentiating the product to increase sales. For example, a new flavor may be added or a package redesigned.

Such adjustments cause costs to increase, as shown at points t_4 and t_5 on the graph. Finally, at some point (designated t_6) sales begin to decline. The decline may be the result of external factors, or it may be a specific managerial decision. The product may be allowed to "die" by continuing to offer it but with vastly reduced levels of marketing effort. Or the death of the product may be followed immediately by the "birth" of a new and improved version. We examine managerial decisions appropriate to each of these planning stages in the remainder of this section of the chapter.

Introduction—New Product Development
Product innovation is essential. The product life cycle says so; an organization's competitors require it; and consumers' changing wants and desires compel it—but what is a new product? For purposes of this discussion, a *new product* means a product new to the organization under consideration. Four types can be distinguished. First, the product may involve a new concept, a completely different approach to satisfying customer desires. Examples include the typewriter, television, the polaroid camera, and the xerox process. Second, the product may involve a new process which replaces an existing way of satisfying a particular desire. For example, the calculator has replaced the slide rule, electric toothbrushes have replaced manual ones, and transistors have replaced vacuum tubes. Third, the product may be new to the company, i.e., a new brand, even though other companies may already be producing a similar product. For example, both Schick and Persona now offer double-bladed razors to compete with the Gillette Trac-II. And General Motors offers the Chevette to compete with imported small cars. Finally, a company may bring out a new model or improved version of an existing product: the 1976 Maverick or "new improved" Cheer.

New product development is big business. After some slowdown during the 1974–75 recession, firms in the U.S. alone are spending in the

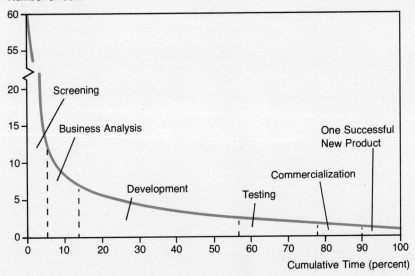

Number of Ideas

Adapted from *Management of New Products*, 4th ed., (New York: Booz, Allen & Hamilton, 1965), p.9, with permission of the publisher.

Exhibit 9-3   Mortality Curve of New Product Ideas

neighborhood of $18 billion annually for new product development. These expenditures contribute to sales and profits. Despite these impressive figures, the new product development process is not particularly efficient. There appear to be three reasons for this inefficiency. First, most new product ideas do not reach the market. The classic study, by the management consulting firm of Booz, Allen & Hamilton, is shown in Exhibit 9-3. It indicates that only about one idea in sixty survives from original conception to successful commercialization. Exhibit 9-4 presents one company's experience. Second, many products that do reach the market fail. Exhibit 9-5 presents a list of notable product failures that did not attain organizational objectives. And third, even products that do perform satisfactorily encounter stiff competition. General Electric introduced the electric toothbrush in 1962—by 1964 it had 52 competitors. The Gillette Trac-II razor was introduced during the 1971 World Series; six months before that the company had only an unnamed, handmade prototype. Six months after the Series, the Schick Double-Blade razor was on the market.

Consequently, the general process of new product development is worthy of serious consideration. As defined by Booz, Allen & Hamilton, this process involves six stages: idea generation, screening, economic analysis, development, testing, and commercialization.

1. Idea generation. New products begin with ideas. Since it takes many

Exhibit 9-4   New Product Mortality in One Major Company

New Product Development Stage	Cost	
Screening and Analysis:		
more than 600 new product ideas	Technical research	$ 30 million
(during a recent, typical 10-year period)	Marketing research	46 million
	Total	$ 76 million
resulting in		
Development:		
118 concepts, of which 31 were eliminated,	Technical research	$ 5 million
at a cost of	Marketing research	5 million
	Capital investment	1 million
allowing	Total	$ 11 million
Test Marketing:		
of the 87 products tested, 47 failed	Total	$156 million*
leaving		
Commercialization:		
40 products introduced into the market		
Result:		
10 commercial failures and 30 successful		
products, representing a total investment of		$243 million

*This figure was not decomposed.

Based on data from A.S. Clausi, Vice-president for Corporate Research, General Foods Corporation, reported in "The Rebuilding Job at General Foods," *Business Week,* August 25, 1973, p. 50.

ideas to generate one successful product, it is to the organization's advantage to have as many ideas as possible. Possible sources include research and development by the organization or by other agencies (see Exhibit 9-6); customers (particularly through contact with salespersons); secondary sources, e.g., the U.S. Patent Office, and the *New Products Digest* published by Batten, Barton, Durstine and Osborn, a New York advertising agency; and competitors (by methods ranging from analysis of competitors' commercial products to industrial espionage). New product ideas constitute information, and, therefore, should be managed via the Marketing Information System. At the very least, someone within the organization should be designated to receive new product ideas and route them to appropriate decision makers.

2. Screening. As opposed to the creative thinking needed in the idea

Exhibit 9-5 Some Examples of Product "Failures"

Packaged Goods:	Automobiles (Since WW II):	Other Products:
Campbell Red Kettle Soups	Allstate	Du Pont Corfam
Lever Bros. Vim tablet detergent	Avanti	Sylvania Colorslide TV viewer
Colgate Cue toothpaste	Corvair	Convair 880 and 990 jet planes
Best Foods Knorr Soups	Crosley	Electra prop-jet planes
GF Post Cereals with freeze-dried fruit	Edsel	Supersonic transport plane
Bristol-Myers aerosol Ipana toothpaste	Frazer	Dowgard antifreeze
Rheingold Gablinger's Beer	Henry J	Bell Labs Picture Phone
Hunt flavored ketchups	Hudson	Golden ESSO EXTRA gasoline
Bristol-Myers Resolve analgesic	Kaiser	Shell of the Future gasoline
Scott Papers Babyscott diapers	Marlin	Three dimensional movies
Gillette Nine Flags men's cologne	Nash	*Life, Saturday Evening Post, Collier's*
Hunt-Wesson Suprema spaghetti sauce	Willys	magazines
Warner-Lambert Reef mouthwash		Keedozzle (automated super-
Listerine toothpaste		market)
B&W Lyme (lime flavored cigarette)		Philco Instant Dividend Plan
Frost 8-80 "white" whiskey		
L&M Devon menthol cigarette		

Note: The purpose of this list is to illustrate with familiar examples the text point that not all products live up to expectations. *Failure* is used in this sense only— no criticism of individuals or companies is implied. Many of these organizations can also point to outstanding product successes.

Adapted by the author from various sources, including "New Products: The Push Is on Marketing," *Business Week,* March 4, 1972, pp. 72–7; and Thomas L. Berg, *Mismarketing: Case Histories of Marketing Misfires,* Doubleday and Co., 1970.

generation stage, the screening stage must be characterized by critical thinking. Successful screening involves avoiding two types of errors: eliminating good ideas, and passing bad ones along. The first error is probably more significant (bad ideas can be eliminated at a later stage). For example, RCA Corporation saw the potential of radio; the Victor Talking Machine Company did not. Volkswagen showed American automobile manufacturers that a market existed for an economy car, and both IBM and Eastman Kodak Corporation turned down Carlson's Xerox copying process. A formalized screening procedure is generally recommended; the classic procedure is a checklist, such as shown in Exhibit 9-7.

3. Economic Analysis. If a product survives the screening stage, the next task is to determine how it will contribute to the organization's objectives. For the most part, the concepts and techniques discussed in the chapters on market segmentation, planning, and decision making are applicable here. Sales potentials are forecast, cost estimates are made, breakeven points are calculated, and in some cases more comprehensive decision procedures, such as Bayesian analysis, are used.

4. Development. If the result of the analysis stage is positive, the product idea will be developed into a prototype. Both the technical and the any new product ideas have been generated by research for the space program. Several examples are given below.

Medicine. In some hospitals, a single nurse can watch dozens of intensive-care patients simultaneously by glancing at a vital-signs board. Each patient is fitted with electronic sensors which track heartbeat, respiration, and blood pressure. The eye-control switch—developed so astronauts could operate a spacecraft while unable to move their arms because of gravitational forces—is being used to allow totally paralyzed individuals to tune a TV, open a window, turn off a light,

etc. Doctors soon will be able to watch an animated movie of a patient's heart in action. This will be done by feeding pulse information into a computer which translates the heartbeat into a picture. Many heart troubles can be spotted by watching the movie.

Clothes. Scientists developed a teflon-coated fabric called "Beta fiber" which will not burn or emit toxic gases. This fabric can provide nonflammable protection for fire fighters, babies, and office draperies. Also, a space-blanket, made of laminated plastic and a layer of aluminum half-a-thousandth of an inch thick, gives excellent protection from both heat and cold.

Food. Food that is high in nutrition, crumble-free, nonperishable, lightweight, low in volume, and easy to prepare and digest was required for space

flight. Already on the shelves of many local grocery stores are high-nutrition, meal-in-one food sticks, and artificial fruit juices used by the astronauts in space. Yet to come are such space-agency creations as instant applesauce, bacon bars, cheesecake cubes, sweet-pea bars, and strawberry-cereal cubes. Scientists also learned how to keep slices of bread fresh at room temperature for fourteen weeks.

Building Construction. Fire-resistant paints and building materials are now widely used in construction. In electrical wiring, a "flat conductor cable" which can be stuck to a wall like adhesive tape is likely to replace the bulky cables running through walls, and the switch boxes of present electrical installations.

Adapted by the author from various sources.

marketing aspects of the product must be developed and coordinated. Technical development involves such considerations as manufacturing efficiency, performance reliability, product durability, ease of maintenance, and so on. Marketing considerations involve branding, packaging, design modifications as a result of consumer tests. The end result of this stage is a basic Go/No-Go decision. If the product is not eliminated at this stage, it will be produced at least in sufficient quantities for test marketing, if not for complete distribution.

5. Test-Marketing. Not too many years ago, nearly every product was subjected to some sort of test-market experiment. Using the techniques of experimentation described in Chapter 8, products were placed on the market in certain cities and sold under carefully controlled conditions. Test-marketing is useful because it provides data for estimates of potential product sales and allows pretesting of alternative formulations of the marketing program. On the other hand, many organizations today are finding that testing does not always pay off. The classic case here is General Foods Corporation's cereal incorporating freeze-dried strawberries. The product passed all test markets with flying colors, but failed

Exhibit 9-7 An Appraisal Form for New Product Development

A simple checklist can be used to compare different product ideas. The figure below shows the rating patterns for two products rated in terms of nine characteristics on a five point scale.

Of course, a checklist is a rather crude device. The procedure could be improved by assigning weights to the various criteria, and coming up with a numerical ranking for the various products. However, even in its crude form, a checklist can be very helpful in evaluating new product ideas.

Adapted from Charles H. Kline, "The Strategy of Product Policy," *Harvard Business Review,* July-August 1955, pp. 91–100, with permission of the publisher.

Case A: A Generally Favorable Pattern

	Very Good	Good	Fair	Poor	Very Poor
Sales volume	✓				
Type and number of competitors	✓				
Technical opportunity	✓				
Patent protection		✓			
Raw materials		✓			
Production load		✓			
Value added		✓			
Similarity to major business				✓	
Effect on present products			✓		

Case B: A Generally Unfavorable Pattern

	Very Good	Good	Fair	Poor	Very Poor
Sales volume	✓				
Type and number of competitors					✓
Technical opportunity				✓	
Patent protection					✓
Raw materials		✓			
Production load			✓		
Value added		✓			
Similarity to major business	✓				
Effect on present products	✓				

miserably in the marketplace (an estimated $15 million loss). Moreover, competitors increasingly attempt to disrupt test-market results, and there is a time lag while test-market results are being evaluated. Consequently, test-marketing should be systematically approached; Exhibit 9-8 presents one suggestion.

6. Commercialization. If the product passes all of the above stages, as summarized in Exhibit 9-8, it is introduced into the marketplace—a marketing plan is formulated, implemented and controlled. Hopefully, the product is a successful one, and is moved into the growth stage of the product life cycle.

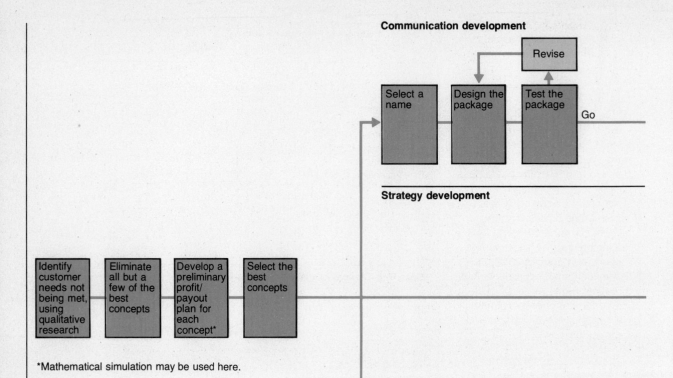

Communication development

Revise

Select a name → Design the package → Test the package → **Go**

Strategy development

Identify customer needs not being met, using qualitative research → Eliminate all but a few of the best concepts → Develop a preliminary profit/payout plan for each concept* → Select the best concepts

*Mathematical simulation may be used here.

▌**Exhibit 9-8   Test Marketing in New Product Development**

Ideally, test marketing is the culmination of the new product development process. It is a "dress rehearsal" of the entire marketing plan (in the terms of this text, seeking, matching, and programming of all four elements of the marketing mix) just prior to actual introduction of the product.

Test marketing is not indicated in all cases. Test marketing is, in fact, a compromise between collecting more information—at considerable direct and indirect cost—and the expense of product failure. The direct cost can be calculated in dollars and cents. But there are also indirect costs: the new product idea will be revealed to competitors, employee time and activities must be spent on the product, and management must also devote attention to it. So the entire product development process should be carefully and comprehensively considered. The figure outlines one approach.

Product development

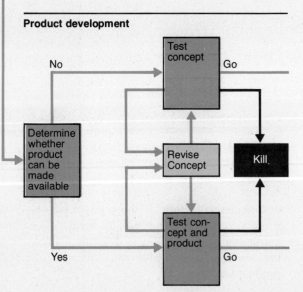

No → Test concept → **Go**

Determine whether product can be made available → Revise Concept → Kill

Yes → Test concept and product → **Go**

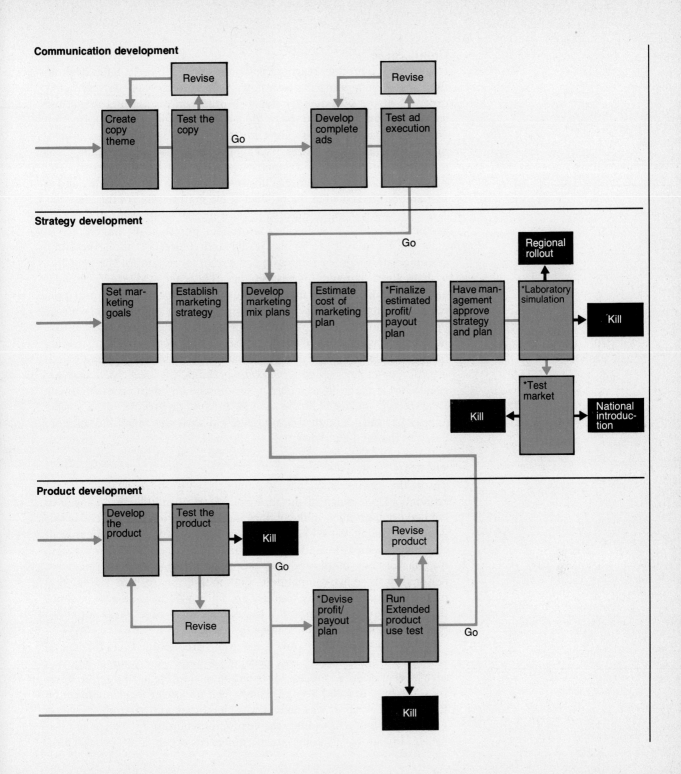

Communication development

Revise

Create copy theme → Test the copy — Go → Develop complete ads → Test ad execution — Revise

Strategy development

Go

Set marketing goals → Establish marketing strategy → Develop marketing mix plans → Estimate cost of marketing plan → *Finalize estimated profit/ payout plan → Have management approve strategy and plan → *Laboratory simulation

Regional rollout

Kill

*Test market → National introduction

Kill

Product development

Develop the product → Test the product → Kill

Go

Revise

*Devise profit/ payout plan → Run Extended product use test — Go

Revise product

Kill

Growth Stage

Happiness is a product reaching this stage in the life cycle. Sales begin to rise rapidly, generating the cash flows needed to recover the very heavy expenses of the introductory stage. Information on product usage and consumer attitudes toward the product can be obtained. This information and experience with the product can be used to make program adjustments—new models and sizes, packaging changes, advertising campaigns tailored more expressly to customer wants and desires, and so forth. The marketing manager's purpose in this stage is to keep the ball rolling and to prepare for the arrival of the product at the mature stage of the life cycle.

On the other hand, an organization may actually want to limit the product's growth. For example, a resort hotel or restaurant that catches on may not be able to serve the wants and desires of all its potential customers. If expansion is infeasible, the resort or restaurant manager may wish to limit demand for his product. The energy shortage provides another possible example here. Electric utility companies—who until quite recently promoted the use of electric power with discounts on volume purchases and extended payment plans for new electric appliances—are now encouraging consumers to conserve electricity, and are making positive suggestions for this conservation. A marketing plan to limit growth—sometimes called *demarketing*—should be developed and executed just as carefully as a plan to sustain and augment product growth. Demarketing seems likely to assume greater importance as a society approaches the postindustrial phase. We discuss this possibility in more detail in the final chapter.

The Maturity Stage

This is the inevitable stage for the majority of products in an industrial economy. Thus, much of the time and effort of marketing managers is focused upon products in the mature stage of the product life cycle. In this stage, the product is well known, has some loyal customers, and has well-entrenched competitors—the product has achieved a position, or niche, in the market. For most products, this stage also means that prices are reasonably close to competition, that market shares are stable, that production and marketing routines are fairly well worked out—in short, that the product is contributing to organizational objectives, but is not particularly exciting or challenging to manage.

Products reach the mature stage in the product life cycle for several reasons. First, the market may become saturated—the product enjoys a high level of brand awareness, distribution is widespread, and repurchases form the bulk of sales. Second, middlemen no longer focus attention on the product. When it was new, it was glamorous and exciting; now it is commonplace. It will seldom receive promotional support except as a loss leader. Inventory stockouts are permitted to occur, and so on. Third, competitive versions of the same product are available—from other competitors who introduced and developed their own versions of the product, from middlemen who offer private brand versions of the product, and from imitators. The life cycle of a mature product can be extended—perhaps even improved. Three basic approaches should be considered: new market segments, product differentiation, and recycling.

Penetrating New Market Segments. An organization may find that its products appeal to market segments other than its existing target markets. For example, such leisure time activities as watching wrestling matches and playing billiards experienced new growth in the early sixties when these products were marketed to women as well as men. Conversely, the rapid growth of men's beauty aids (deodorants, hair spray, cologne, etc.) illustrates the potential for rapid growth in a new market segment. And the success of Arm & Hammer baking soda promoted for such uses as absorbing food odors is fast becoming a marketing legend.

Product Differentiation. Sometimes a change in the marketing program of a product can improve its sales or profits. For example, appliance manufacturers, particularly in Europe, are finding a ready market for smaller-sized refrigerators, stoves, and washers and dryers. A packaging change might be beneficial—soft drinks now come in large-sized resealable containers for home use. Or the organization might desire to change the image of a product. This may involve nothing more than a different promotional theme. One of the classic applications of motivation research in marketing was the finding that most people considered tea to be the drink of weaklings and invalids. A hard-hitting advertising campaign was designed, featuring the theme that tea is "hefty, hot, and hearty"—and, therefore, should be drunk by everyone. On the other hand, changing the product's image may involve substantial modification of the product itself. In the middle 1950s, Ford introduced the two-seater Thunderbird—a classic sportscar. By the late 1950s, sales had leveled off. Ford then switched to a four-door Thunderbird—altering the car's image to that of a personalized luxury car and substantially increasing its market potential.

Recycling. This term is used to designate the marketing strategy of finding new uses for products. Nylon is perhaps the classic example here; see Exhibit 9-9. Similarly, steel makers have found a number of new uses for different kinds and tensile strengths of steel. Petroleum jelly, introduced for surgical dressing, is now used to lubricate machinery. New product uses are not always intentional, e.g., some people use model airplane glue as a narcotic.

Decline Stage
The basic indicator of entry into this stage is falling sales. But management

The figure below illustrates possible extensions of the life cycle for nylon.

Recycles A, B, C, and D result from marketing actions 1, 2, 3, and 4:

1. Promoting more frequent usage of the product among current users—reiterating the social necessity of wearing stockings at all times. Although obviously difficult and costly, such an approach could have built sales.
2. Developing more varied usage of the product among current users—this strategy was to promote the fashion smartness of tinted hose and later of patterned and highly textured hosiery. This would not only expand a woman's hosiery wardrobe, but would open the door for annual tint and pattern obsolescence.

3. Creating new users for the product by expanding the market—expanding the market for nylon hosiery might have taken the form of attempting to legitimize the necessity of wearing hosiery among early teenagers and preteenagers.
4. Finding new uses for the basic material—for nylon, this tactic has had many trials: stretch stockings

and socks, rugs, tires, bearings, etc.

Levitt emphasizes that the use of nylon as an illustration is purely hypothetical, but it does serve to emphasize the possibility of recycling the mature product.

Adapted from Theodore Levitt, "Exploit the Product Life Cycle," *Harvard Business Review,* November-December 1965, pp. 81–94. Copyright © 1976 by the President and Fellows of Harvard College; all rights reserved.

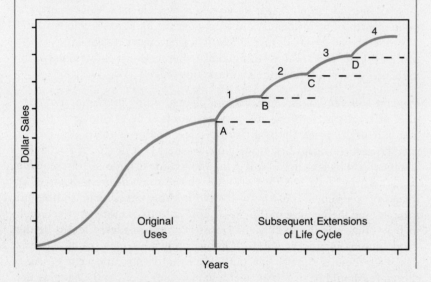

should investigate carefully to be sure that the sales decline is permanent, and not just a fluctuation in the maturity stage. Other useful indicators of this stage include severe competition, perhaps with superior products; considerable price-cutting; large investments in resources, particularly executive time; and, consequently, a price-cost-profit squeeze.

Products in the decline stage of the product life cycle require managerial action, essentially one of four possible strategies: re-enter with an improved version, phase the product out, modify it, or eliminate it.

Re-entry. Decline can be abrupt. The product can be removed from the market. Removal is frequently followed immediately by the re-entry of a "new and improved" version of the dying product. For example, annual automobile model changes, while less prevalent than in years past, still call for the formulation and implementation of new marketing strategies each year. Similarly, Maxwell House coffee is replaced by New Maxwell House coffee, the 1976 television receivers feature significant improvements over their 1975 counterparts, and so on.

Phase Out. A product may be declining, yet may still serve the wants and desires of a target market, therefore contributing something to organizational objectives. There is a company, for example, that still manufactures detachable paper shirt collars and cuffs. Certain health and beauty aids, e.g., proprietary soaps and tooth powder, are no longer promoted heavily or distributed widely, but remain on the market to serve the needs of the few remaining loyal customers. One interesting example here is Ipana brand toothpaste. Bristol-Myers produced Ipana until 1968, when it abandoned it in favor of other brands. The brand name was bought by another company, which produced a different formula toothpaste, but with the same packaging and branding; the new company earned $250,000 from Ipana in the first seven months. Some writers refer to this as a period of "product petrification" within the decline stage, in which the demand of some very loyal customers is simply frozen or petrified. An organization may wish to take advantage of this continuing demand for a product in the decline stage by phasing out the product gradually.

Product Modification. It may be possible to arrest the decline of a particular product. Drucker (*Managing for Results*) refers to this decision as a *repair job*. In order to qualify as a candidate for a repair job, a declining product should have the expectation of considerable growth opportunity and substantial volume, if the repair is successful, and the probability of success should be rather high. Furthermore, the product should suffer from one and only one major defect which is clearly definable and relatively easy to correct. Analysis of one industrial product, for example, indicated that it was being supplanted by more sophisticated models; however, careful examination showed that its simple design and manual operating characteristics made it ideal for export to Latin America. In another case, a company found that its door-to-door sales people were selling a substantial proportion of their calls, but the product was losing money. Analysis disclosed that sales calls took over an hour to complete, because the salesperson had to demonstrate the product and answer many questions about it. When the salesmen were given other products to sell along with the basic product, and a small truck to carry them on, the door-to-door operation became profitable.

Product Elimination. While petrification or modification are more pleasant alternatives than elimination, the sad fact is that many products in the decline stage should be withdrawn from the market. This is never an easy decision. There is always someone in the organization who will defend the declining product—even after a repair job has been attempted, and no petrified demand exists. "The portable, six-sided pretzel polisher is the first product the company ever made," or "That product is our company—without it, our company image will not be the same," or "That product may not be profitable in itself, but it gives us a full product line to offer to customers."

These arguments may or may not be valid; they should be carefully investigated. After all, organizational change of any type is potentially disruptive. If a product is abandoned, personnel may have to be shifted to other duties or released. Sales contracts may have to be renegotiated with customers or middlemen. Inventories may have to be disposed of at a loss, and so on. Consequently, a comprehensive, systematic product elimination procedure should be followed. Product elimination is one type of control decision discussed in Chapter 13.

In summary, the product life-cycle concept can be a useful device for structuring managerial thinking about a single product. Products, unlike people, do not have inherent life cycles. They progress from stage to stage as the result of marketing decisions. Decisions about individual products are not made in a vacuum—almost all organizations have assortments or portfolios of products to be managed.

MANAGING THE PRODUCT PORTFOLIO

Most organizations offer a variety of products to the marketplace. The average supermarket carries 10,000 or more products, a political party fields candidates at local and national levels; a university offers courses in fields ranging from anthropology to zoology, and a major manufacturer such as General Electric has over a quarter of a million different products. Attention must be given to the composition of the product mix. In addition, decisions must be made about branding, and about various product extensions.

The Product Mix

The total composite of products offered by a particular organization is termed the product mix. The mix consists of product lines and product items. A line is a group of products considered to be similar for customer, marketing, and/or technical reasons. A product item is an individual member of a product line. For example, all the courses that a university offers constitute its product mix; courses in the marketing department constitute a product line; and the basic marketing course is a product item. Product decisions at these three levels are generally of two types: width and depth of the product line, and changes in the mix over time.

Width and Depth of Line.
The width of the product mix refers to the number of different product lines found within the organization. Depth of the product mix refers to the number of product items offered within each

Exhibit 9-10 The Product-Mix
Concept

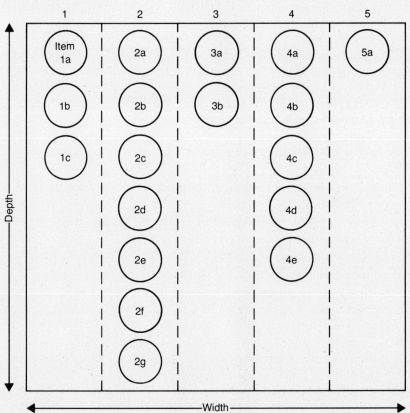

PRODUCT LINES

Adapted from Philip Kotler, *Marketing Management: Analysis, Planning and Control*, 2nd ed., © 1972, Prentice-Hall, Inc., p. 440, by permission of Prentice-Hall, Inc.

line. For example, a large state university with many departments would be said to have a wide product line. On the other hand, a small, private, liberal arts college would probably offer courses in only a few disciplines. Its product line would be considered narrow.

That liberal arts college, however, might have a very well-known, productive department of philosophy. The philosophy product line, therefore, would be considered deep. By the same token, the large state university may have several departments, each having only a few faculty members and a relatively small budget. The depth of these product lines would not be too great. Exhibit 9-10 summarizes these points.

Product Mix Dynamics. Our earlier discussion of the product life-cycle concept indicated that the individual products or items are changed over time. These changes should not be made in isolation for individual product items. Ideally, changes in the life cycle of individual products should be made with regard to the total product mix. That is, new products should be developed, weak products strengthened or abandoned, and/or existing products changed in such a way as to optimize customer and organizational satisfaction, but this is easier said than done.

At the very least, product items and lines should be analyzed in terms of present or potential contributions to the product mix. Drucker *(Managing for Results)* suggests such categories as:

1. Tomorrow's Breadwinners—new products or improvements on present products.

2. Today's Breadwinners—the current contributor, but these are the innovations of yesterday.

3. Repairables—products capable of becoming breadwinners if a repair job (recall our earlier discussion) is done.

4. Yesterday's Breadwinners—formerly high volume products badly fragmented today into special deals and small orders.

5. The "Also-rans"—yesterday's high hopes which have not been outright failures, but which have not contributed as expected, and realistically speaking, have little chance of ever doing so.

If the product mix currently consists largely of the breadwinners of today and yesterday, the current sales picture may look rosy, but trouble looms in the future. Conversely, the company investing considerable sums in research and development on tomorrow's breadwinners and repair jobs in hopes of a brighter tomorrow will face hard times today. A productive balance is not easy to maintain.

Much of the success of many American companies can be traced to emphasis upon innovation. Fortunes were made and lost as the diesel locomotive of General Motors replaced the steam locomotives of Baldwin; Japanese radios using Bell Laboratories' transistors replaced the vacuum tube radios of General Electric, Westinghouse and Sylvania; calculators with integrated circuits by Texas Instruments replaced the mechanical machines of Friden, Monroe, and NCR; and the huge Swiss watch industry is losing out to digital watches marketed by names no watchmaker would recognize: Pulsar, Intel, and Litronix.

Innovation can be profitable. On the other hand, innovation requires extensive effort. One package goods manufacturer, for example, decided to put considerable funds into developing a lemon-lime cake mix rather than into a synthetic meat product. Its management knew what the profit return from the cake mix would be, but the synthetic steak would have taken longer, required a bigger investment, and faced a higher risk of failure.

In summary, the product mix is determined with reference to three dimensions: the depth of individual lines, the number or width of those lines, and changes in width and depth over time. Determining the proper mix in light of these three dimensions requires considerable management attention. And the organization's products, from total mix to individual time, must be identified.

Branding

The general area of establishing a product identity is termed branding; Exhibit 9-11 presents precise definitions of several branding terms. The basic purpose of branding is to fix the identity of the producer of a given product. This practice began during the Middle Ages, when craft guilds were formed to control the quality and quantity of various products. The guilds required each producer to affix to his product the mark of his hall— his hallmark—so that his products could be identified. This practice prevented inferior products from reflecting upon the entire guild. Similarly, in more recent times, Russian citizens began to use the factory numbers attached to products to identify those factories which produced poor quality products. The Soviet government subsequently established state-sponsored advertising agencies to streamline the process of identifying products and communicating about them to consumers. In a mature industrial economy, hardly any product remains unbranded. Even products that economists label commodities, e.g., raw foodstuffs, such as oranges and bananas, extracted materials such as coal, steel, and fuel oil, are branded.

The organization brands its product for three reasons: physical identification, legal protection, and as a basis for marketing effort. The physical identification of individual products and product lines can be quite important in shipping, storing, grading, labeling, and managing the inventory of various products. Legal protection is vested in the trade-

Exhibit 9-12 The Development of Brand Loyalty

Tucker contacted a group of housewives who had just moved to town, and arranged to deliver bread to them each week. Through the cooperation of a local bakery, Tucker was supplied each week with freshly baked loaves of bread in clear polyethylene wrappers. Just before calling on each housewife, Tucker placed a "brand"—letter of the alphabet—on each of the four loaves. Otherwise, the loaves were identical. He then asked each housewife to select one of the brands of bread. Each housewife was called upon 12 times. Brand loyalty was measured by the number of times in succession that the same "brand" was chosen.

Tucker found that the housewives tended to purchase one preferred brand much more often than would have occurred by chance, even when pennies were attached to other brands—thereby raising the price of the chosen brand. Tucker concluded that consumers will develop brand loyalties for bread even when no physical differences exist among products.

Adapted from W.T. Tucker, "The Development of Brand Loyalty," *Journal of Marketing Research,* August 1964, pp. 32–5, with permission of the publisher, the American Marketing Association.

mark—that part of the brand that is by law the organization's exclusive right to a particular brand and all that the brand connotes.

The most important reason for branding is a marketing one—the brand provides a means of identifying a product so that a meaningful marketing program can be designed and implemented for the product. The purpose of the marketing program is to convince the consumer that the organization's product will best satisfy his wants and desires. If this purpose is to be accomplished, the consumer must first be able to recognize the products of a particular organization and to associate particular benefits with that recognition. The vehicle for this association is the brand of the product.

Thus, the consumer also has reason to make use of the brands of products. First, brands make shopping feasible. For example, brands guide consumer selection among the ten thousand or so items in a modern supermarket—facilitating repeat purchases. A consumer who has tried a new product and is satisfied with it is likely to purchase that same brand of product next time. Conversely, if the first experience was not satisfactory, the brand serves as a beacon by which the consumer steers away from the product. Consequently, the consumer tends to develop brand loyalty, even when the brand means nothing more than psychological differentiation of homogeneous products; Tucker's bread study, Exhibit 9-12, is a classic example of this point.

Thus, branding is an important product policy decision for the organization. One of the major controversies in branding is the so-called *battle of the brands*—whether the manufacturer or the middleman will affix the brand to the product. Our discussion so far has tended to emphasize branding as a manufacturer's prerogative, but many large organizations that act as middlemen affix their own brands to products—e.g., grocery

Exhibit 9-13   Developing a Brand Name

Selecting a brand name can be a tricky and frustrating undertaking. Among the guidelines usually suggested are the following:

1. *The brand should suggest product benefits or qualities.* Examples here would include Coldspot and Frigidaire refrigerators, Craftsman tools, Accutron watches, and Spic and Span detergent.

2. *The brand should be easy to spell, remember, and pronounce.* Simple, crisp, one-syllable names are best here: Tide, Crest, Gleem, etc.

3. *The brand should be distinctive.* Examples here might include Mustang, Kodak, Exxon.

4. *The name should have no negative connotations.* Before the name Exxon was chosen, the company considered Enco—a name it had been using in some states. However, it turned out that *Enco* is part of a phrase which means *stalled car* in the Japanese language. When the Pet Milk Company introduced its liquid low-calorie diet food, its research disclosed that the name *Pet* should not be part of the brand, since that name connoted calorie-rich Pet Evaporated milk. The company chose Sego Liquid Diet Food.

5. *The name should have no legal restrictions.* This is perhaps the most significant and stringent test of a brand name. On the one hand, the brand must not be too closely associated with an existing brand. For example, in a case in Houston, the courts enjoined a woman named Avis Thornton from advertising her stables as "Avis Rent-a-Horse." Although Avis was her legal name, the court found the slogan too close to the Avis Rent-a-Car slogan and brand.

On the other hand, there is a danger that a brand may become so identified with a product that it becomes the generic label for that product class. When this happens, the brand passes into common usage, and no longer affords legal protection to the organization. Examples of brand names to which this has happened include linoleum, aspirin, celluloid, cellophane, kerosene, shredded wheat, and nylon. Brand names that are in danger of becoming generic include Frigidaire, Scotch Tape, Kleenex, and Xerox. Xerox ran ads in business periodicals emphasizing the point that its name is a brand, not a generic description of the photocopying process.

Compiled by the author from several sources, including Philip Kotler, *Marketing Management: Analysis, Planning and Control,* 2nd ed., © 1972, Prentice-Hall, p. 493, by permission of Prentice-Hall, Inc.; and Stanton. *Fundamentals of Marketing* (New York: McGraw-Hill, 1971), 3rd ed. p. 243, with permission of the publisher; and William Mathewson. "Trademarks are a Global Business These Days . . ." *The Wall Street Journal* (Sept. 4, 1975), p. 24.

merchants such as A & P, IGA, and Safeway; and retailers such as Sears and J.C. Penney's. (The brands of middlemen are sometimes called private brands or dealer brands, as distinguished from manufacturer's brands, sometimes called national brands.) This issue is really one aspect of the continual struggle for control of the channel of distribution, which we discuss in Chapter 11.

Developing a brand name and branding strategy are important aspects of product policy. Brand naming is discussed in Exhibit 9-13. In terms of strategy, there are three general possibilities: branding each individual item, creating brand families, and using a single brand for all of the organization's products. These possibilities are analogous to the three levels of product aggregation—individual item, product line, and marketing mix. Exhibit 9-14 presents examples of organizations following each type of strategy—at the manufacturer, and at the middleman's level. Procter & Gamble, for example, uses different brands within its line of detergents: Tide, Bold, Cheer, Duz. Similarly, A & P might offer both Iona and

Exhibit 9-14 Examples of Branding Strategies

Branding Strategy	Manufacturer's Brands	Middlemen's Brands
Individual Item	Tide, Bold, Cheer, Duz (Procter & Gamble)	Ann Page, Iona, Sultana (A & P)
Brand Family (product line)	Chevrolet, Pontiac, Cadillac (General Motors)	Kenmore, Craftsman, Kerrybrook (Sears)
Single Name (marketing mix)	GE appliances (General Electric)	IGA groceries (Independent Grocers Alliance)

Sultana brands of green beans. This strategy allows the organization to develop a separate identity and image for each product. Products are not readily associated with other products that the organization offers, nor with the general reputation of the organization itself.

When there are similarities among products in a given product line, many organizations use what is called a "family branding" strategy, i.e., products within a given product line carry the same brand name. One example on the manufacturer's side is General Motors, which produces Chevrolet, Pontiac, Cadillac—lines of automobiles. At the middleman's level, Sears uses the Kenmore name for its major appliances, the Craftsman brand for its power tools, and Kerrybrook for its line of women's clothing. This strategy permits brand indentification of similar types of products, but does not necessarily associate that line with other lines that the organization offers. Finally, at the other end of the scale, many organizations simply use one brand name for all of their products: General Electric appliances at the manufacturer's level, and IGA—the brand of the independent grocers alliance.

In practice, the strategies sometimes become blurred. For example, an increasing number of organizations are associating their names with their products: Kellogg's Rice Krispies, IBM 5100 computers. In perhaps the most significant brand strategy decision in marketing history, Exxon has become the corporate name, and brand, for all products of Standard Oil of New Jersey marketed in the United States. Moreover, companies that have successful brands often try to extend this success to other products by assigning the same brand name to them. For example, the success of Quaker Oats' Cap'n Crunch breakfast cereal spawned a whole host of related products—including T-shirts. Also, Armour, basically a meat-packing company, produces Dial soap—a very successful product. The Dial brand has been extended by Armour to other health and beauty aid products.

On the other hand, an organization might follow a multibrand strategy. That is, it might deliberately develop two or more products which in effect compete with each other. This strategy is often used by Procter & Gamble. Other companies, particularly in the packaged grocery field, have tended to follow suit. This strategy may enable the organization to increase the total retail shelf space allocated to its products. It also permits somewhat different promotional appeals to be designed for the various products of a single manufacturer, and in the intensely competitive environment of retailing, a new brand can generate a sense of excitement among dealers and consumers. The cliché in the packaged-goods industry is: If it doesn't say new, it had better say 10 cents off.

Product Extensions

There are several ways in which the manufacturer can extend his/her product to more completely meet the wants and desires of the target-market segment. The three major approaches involve changes in product design, packaging, and service.

Product Design. The utility of many products can be improved through product design. For example, products can be custom-tailored to the needs of specific markets. There are left-handed golf clubs, dentist's equipment, and scissors. Most clothing stores will make alterations in suits and dresses, and many products come in different sizes, colors, and fabrics. Buyers of homes and automobiles often specify type and number of accessories, e.g., dishwasher, air conditioning, automatic transmission.

A second aspect of product design, product obsolescence, generates a certain amount of controversy. New products are constantly being developed. Sometimes, it is charged that the new products are only superficially different from the old ones, that there is a deliberate policy of *planned obsolescence.* The annual automobile model change is perhaps the most frequently cited example here. Others include changes in the fashions of clothes—particularly women's hemlines—new models in major appliances, and the updated edition that makes a textbook obsolete.

Planned product obsolescence can be a boon to a particular organization or industry. But it may not be a managerial decision. The conditions which result in product obsolescence are more often than not external to the organization. For example, technological advances compel product design changes, if only to meet competition. Two classic examples here are the transistor and the radial tire. American manufacturers were quite satisfied with vacuum tubes and cloth-ply tires. But competition from abroad, primarily from Japan in the case of transistorized portable radios and from Europe in the case of radial tires, caused American manufacturers to redesign their own radios and tires. Second, governmental regulations are increasingly requiring product design changes. Automobile safety and pollution laws, for example, have literally forced major improvements in bumper design, safety belts, and gasoline emission control devices. Third, as we discussed in Chapter 6, consumer tastes do change. Last year's fashion is just that—out of date. And there is no question that ownership of the latest style or fashion is often perceived as a status-augmenting characteristic in mature industrial societies.

To be sure, marketing effort can accelerate and increase the influence of these basic factors. Polaroid cameras, for example, always seem to be improved just before the Christmas season starts. The instant-on television set is a real technological breakthrough—but how much utility does it really provide for the average household? On the whole, however, planned product changes seem to be a permanent characteristic of marketing activity in any mature industrial economy.

Packaging. Very few products are delivered to buyers without some form of packaging. In fact, the amount spent on packaging materials approached 26 billion dollars in 1976. Consequently, packaging considerations are an integral component of product policy decisions.

The traditional packaging decision is a cost/protection tradeoff: the package must be sufficiently strong, durable, and climate-proof to protect the product. At the same time, the cost of this protection should be minimized. In addition to these considerations, however, modern packaging policies recognize two additional possible purposes. First, the package can add significant consumer utility to the product. Sugar packaged in hundred-pound sacks, for example, is inexpensive, but relatively awkward for the average household. A five- or ten-pound sack may be considerably more useful, although packaging costs as a percentage of the total cost of the product would increase. Similarly, many restaurants use individually packaged teaspoonfuls of sugar. In this case, the package is a significant portion of total product cost, but customers find it more convenient and sanitary, and the restaurant saves on other costs, e.g., sugar bowl cleaning and maintenance. Frozen boil-in-the-pack vegetables, aerosol shaving cream, and cargo containers for ocean shipping are other examples of packaging policies that increase the utility of the product for the consumer.

Another dimension of packaging-policy decisions is that the package can be used as a promotional tool. This is particularly true for products sold at retail, since the bulk of retailing is self-service. The package must attract and hold the consumer's attention at the point of purchase. Color and distinctive shape (e.g., L'eggs hosiery), and useful labeling (e.g., unit costs and recipes) can be used to promote the product.

Services. The third major type of product extension is various kinds of services that the organization provides with the product. Many products are installed by the seller. Technicians for a computer manufacturer, for example, may spend many months on a customer's premises installing, checking, and debugging the computer system. In the home, the new television set, dishwasher, or washing machine is usually delivered, set up, and checked out by the retailer who sold the appliance.

Many organizations maintain extensive repair facilities to keep products in working order. As many products become technologically more complex and sophisticated, the necessity for repair work inevitably increases. This need has prompted many organizations to offer regular maintenance on their products. For example, many automobile and truck fleets, computers, and telephone equipment are leased rather than sold. In many cases the owner maintains these products as part of the lease contract. Moreover, many appliance dealers are offering maintenance contracts—a form of insurance—in lieu of payments for specific repairs when needed.

One of the most interesting developments in service in the 1970s is the spread of self-service, particularly in gasoline retailing. Before the OPEC embargo in 1973 led to a doubling of gasoline prices in the United States and even more severe increases in most other developed countries, most customers patronized "service" stations. While the tank was being filled, a cheerful attendant cleaned the windshield, checked the oil and battery, gauged tire pressure, and even swept out the car's interior. No longer. Today that service generally comes at a higher price, often 5 or 6 cents per gallon. So, many drivers are pumping their own gas. One survey showed that 18 percent of all stations in the United States have self-service pumps, and that self-service accounts for nearly 30 percent of all gasoline sold. The do-it-yourself trend is manifest in other areas such as home and automobile repair, furniture refinishing, and household moving. Just as gasoline retailers are evolving from service stations to either gasoline dispensers or total car clinics, home and automobile repair centers furnish raw materials, parts, tools, and even expert advice to the do-it-yourselfer. And the orange U-Haul truck or trailer is a familiar sight on American highways.

Another service feature is the product warranty. Firms are now required to state clearly what the warranty does and does not cover. In addition, the marketing research practice of obtaining information about the consumer under the guise of warranty validation has been outlawed. Nor is the manufacturer's implied liability to the final consumer vitiated by resale of the product. There was one case in which a manufacturer of printing presses was held liable for injuries suffered by an operator seventy years and four changes of ownership after the manufacturer had sold the press. Exhibit 9-15 summarizes product liability and other legal aspects of product mix decisions.

In summary, product mix decisions are the heart of the marketing program. In fact it has been cogently argued that decisions about the product mix determine the upper limit of possible objective obtainment

Product Design—Product design and branding are protected by patent, trademark, and copyright legislation. As discussed in Chapter 4 and in this chapter, such legislation provides the product manufacturer with a legal monopoly over that product design or brand. Competitors desiring to introduce similar products or brands must pay royalty fees, or differentiate their products in some way from the patent, trademark, or copyright.

2. *Product Liability*—One of the strongest areas of consumerism is product liability. In recent years, the liability of the producer of the product, as well as middlemen involved in its distribution, has increased markedly. There seem to be three general guidelines: (1) A warranty, whether express or implied, accompanies every product; (2) Any product that could be dangerous if made defectively will subject the manufacturer to liability, even if he used the utmost care in producing it, and disclaimed liability in advance; and (3) The manufacturer may be liable for "economic loss" to the purchaser if the product does not perform as it should, even if there is neither injury nor warranty. In addition to these developments, there are an increasing number of laws that deal directly with product safety and liability, e.g., the Flammable Fabrics Act, the Federal Traffic Safety Act, the Natural Gas Pipeline Safety Act, and so on. Moreover, the Federal Trade Commission has inspired recalls of many products suspected of being defective, e.g., automobiles, tires, and canned food products.

3. *Product Packaging and Labeling*—Many products are federally inspected and graded, e.g., meats and other foodstuffs. Moreover, the Fair Packaging and Labeling Act prohibits exaggerations, e.g., "the giant quart," packaging to price (reducing the contents of a package without reducing the price or package size) and "cents off" sales that do not represent real savings. Moreover, products that may be injurious to health must be clearly labeled, and there is legislation before Congress now to require childproof packaging of such products as proprietary medicines.

There is no question that consumers increasingly demand products that are safe, that perform as advertised, and that can be replaced or serviced when shown to be defective. Given the increasing number of new products offered to the market each year, we can expect increased attention to public policy regulation upon product decisions. The marketing decision maker, therefore, should seek competent legal counsel for his/her decisions, particularly in the three areas outlined above.

Compiled by the author from various sources including David L. Rados, "Product Liability: Tougher Ground Rules," *Harvard Business Review*, July-August 1969, pp. 144–52; "The Lengthening Reach of Liability," *Business Week*, 16 September, 1967, pp. 100ff; Louis W. Stern and John R. Grabner, *Competition in the Marketplace*, Scott, Foresman and Co., 1970; and Paul H. Weaver, "The Hazards of Trying to Make Products Safer," *Fortune* (July 1975), pp. 135ff.

by the organization, and decisions with respect to other aspects of the marketing program determine how closely the organization comes to that upper limit. The final section of the chapter explores the integrations of the product decisions into the marketing program.

PRODUCT DECISIONS AND THE MARKETING PROGRAM

The marketing program is formulated as a result of the seeking and matching stages in marketing planning. In formulating the program, product decisions generally precede decisions about other marketing mix elements. Thus, classifications of product types can provide guidelines for development of the other aspects of marketing mix.

Product/Marketing Mix

Exhibit 9-16 depicts the steps in the marketing plan, highlighting the

Exhibit 9-16 Importance of Product Decisions in the Marketing Program

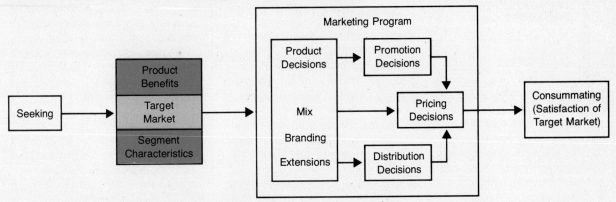

relationships between the target market and marketing programming decisions. The matching of product benefits and market segment characteristics results in selection of the target market. The marketing program to satisfy the wants and desires of the target market begins with the product decision, aligning the product mix, brand and specific product extensions with the consumer's perception of the product as a bundle of utilities.

These product extensions are then related to promotion, distribution and pricing decisions. The ordering of elements in the marketing program has meaning. Product decisions are generally made first, then promotion and distribution are made and the process of setting the price is begun. The final product price, however, is usually the last programming decision made. Price adjustments are generally used to achieve consummation of the exchange process. Exhibit 9-16 again emphasizes the fundamental point that marketing planning first identifies customer wants and desires, and then systematically satisfies them.

The American Airlines example of Exhibit 9-17 illustrates one systematic approach to marketing programming formulation. It is to design a marketing program specifically for an individual customer. In most cases, however, a tailor-made system is not feasible. There is need for a generalized approach to integrating product decisions with other types of decisions in the marketing program. In the literature, work in this area is called classification-of-goods theories.

Classifications-of-Goods Theories

There are many different types of products (recall Exhibit 1-1). Ideally, the marketing program for each one is a coordinated, integrated set of decisions. In order to think in general terms about marketing programs, therefore, we need some sort of theory about how consumers will react to different program formulations. The usual basis for such theorizing is a product category system or taxonomy.

The necessity for correctly identifying the wants and desires of a target market segment, and then developing a total marketing program to satisfy these wants and desires is becoming increasingly obvious. American Airline's success in promoting air freight is an excellent example. Airplanes carry people all day long and into the night. But from midnight until 6:00 a.m., many of these expensive assets sit idle. To more effectively utilize these assets, American approached Raytheon Corporation as a possible air cargo customer.

After considerable study of Raytheon's distribution operations, American proposed to eliminate five field warehouses from which Raytheon supplied transistors and vacuum tubes to distributors, who in turn resold to small radio and television repair shops throughout the nation. Instead, American proposed that it would supply the distributors directly by overnight air cargo—by picking up daily orders at the factory each night, and transporting them to fourteen break-bulk locations throughout the nation. From there common carrier truckers could deliver the orders immediately to distributors. In addition to these physical arrangements, American enlisted the help of the Friden Company

and Western Union. Together the companies designed an elaborate automatic data transmission system to control invoicing, shipping, inventories, and production. The resulting proposal was so complete that it was easy for Raytheon to make a decision to use air cargo.

The point is that the product in this case was not air cargo—it was a fully integrated, automated, and complete communications-distributions system. This system met Raytheon's need for more efficient distribution of its transistors and vacuum tubes.

Adapted from Theodore Levitt, "Improving Sales Through Product Augmentation," *European Business Review*, April 1969, pp. 5–12, with permission of the publisher.

Products are usually classified according to search or shopping effort and consumer loyalty. Effort, as we noted in Chapter 6 on buying behavior (recall Exhibit 6-7), can be thought of as a continuum running from very extensive effort in a given exchange to almost no effort at all. For ease of communication, the ends of this continuum are usually labeled *convenience good* and *shopping good*. Thus, a convenience good would be one for which the consumer would expend very little effort; conversely, a shopping good might generate considerable search effort on the part of the consumer. Loyalty refers generally to the consumer's insistence upon a given product brand or store in which to buy it. This dimension, too, can be viewed as a continuum, with end points labeled *unsought goods* and *specialty goods*. Relating these two dimensions results in a four-way classification of consumer goods. (Of course, the classification system is to some extent arbitrary, but it is useful in organizing thinking about product decisions in particular and marketing programs in general.)

Exhibit 9-18 illustrates this classification of consumer goods. Note that the vertical axis is the effort dimension: convenience/shopping; the horizontal axis is the loyalty dimension: unsought/specialty. Let us look at examples of products in each category.

Quadrant I represents convenience goods for which brand loyalty could develop. The classic example is Coca-Cola. Many people prefer Coke to other beverages, but will substitute a Pepsi or a beer if a Coke is

Exhibit 9-18 Classifications of Consumer Goods

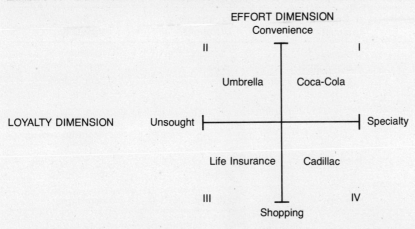

not readily available. In Quadrant II, the umbrella is perhaps the standard example of an unsought convenience good. Most people do not set out to satisfy a desire for protection from rain—until it rains. At that time, the desire for an umbrella is acute, and the consumer generally buys the first one available, regardless of brand. Note, however, that Knirps is currently trying to move the umbrella into the specialty category.

Quadrant III contains products which are usually unsought and which require considerable shopping effort on the part of the consumer. The usual example here is life insurance. Very few individuals exhibit shopping behavior for life insurance. The buying process (recall Chapter 6) is generally triggered by marketing effort on the part of life insurance vendors. Even after recognizing the desire for insurance coverage, the consumer must exert effort to explain his or her situation to the agent, evaluate various policy alternatives, and sometimes take a medical examination. It is possible to develop loyalty to a particular brand of life insurance. But in this case, brand loyalty generally develops through a particular insurance agent as a result of a long-time relationship with a given client.

Finally, in Quadrant IV are products for which the consumer will spend considerable effort to obtain a particular type or brand. Automobile buying, especially for prestige brands like Cadillac, illustrates buying behavior for this type of product.

Obviously, these categories can aid a marketing manager developing market programs for products. Exhibit 9-19 relates our four product examples to other marketing program decisions.

For the convenience/specialty product, in this case, Coca-Cola, the most important product decisions are brand identification and packaging. Coke now comes in individual bottles or cans, or in resealable large

Exhibit 9-19   Classification-of-Goods Guidelines for Marketing Program Formulation

	I. Convenience/ Specialty	II. Convenience/ Unsought	III. Shopping/ Unsought	IV. Shopping/ Specialty
Product	Coca-Cola: branding, packaging	Umbrella: quality control	Life Insurance: options	Cadillac: design, performance, service
Promotion	mass advertising	point of purchase	personal selling	personal selling image advertising
Distribution	saturation	intensive	personal or mail delivery	location
Pricing	competitive	markup	bundled	negotiable

bottles, or dispensed from the soda fountain. Mass advertising and saturation distribution can be used to make Coke widely available to consumers. Pricing for such a product is generally competitive, i.e., marketers of various brands of convenience/specialty goods generally price them similarly within a given market.

For the unsought convenience good, perhaps the most important product decision is quality control. The consumer wants the umbrella to operate properly and not leak; this is not a time for a product malfunction. Since this product is not sought by the consumer and generally is not bought by brand, promotion would in most cases be limited to point-of-purchase information so that the consumer could find the umbrella easily when needed. Distribution would be intensive, i.e., the product would have to be available in many places, but perhaps not everywhere, as is the case with Coke. Price would probably be set on a markup-over-cost basis.

For life insurance, the shopping/unsought good, product decisions would generally involve designing a number of different options so that the agent could put together a package of life insurance protection tailored to the desires of a given customer. Promotion is perhaps the most important aspect of the marketing program of shopping/unsought goods. While some advertising might be done, the major promotional effort is personal selling. Product distribution would probably be handled by the agent on a personal basis or through the mails. Pricing is generally "bundled," i.e., one total premium is generally quoted for the insurance protection, advice and service provided by the agent, and provisions for taking loans against the cash value of the policy.

In the shopping/specialty category, product decisions would emphasize design, performance, and service. The promotion mix would include some advertising and considerable personal selling. In terms of distribution, the key factor would be a convenient location from which to serve customers. The price of shopping/specialty goods is generally negotiable.

We shall have considerably more to say about promotion, distribution, and pricing decisions in succeeding chapters. Our purpose at this point is to demonstrate the necessity for coordinating various decisions into a total marketing program. Classifications-of-goods theories do provide some guidance for this integration. To date, however, the usefulness of such classification schemes is quite limited because the categories are not precise. If we had to select one category for soft drinks, it would be in Quadrant II, unsought/convenience goods, but we noted that Coca-Cola is a specialty good for many consumers.

In addition, some marketing students desire a different classification scheme for industrial goods (those products used by organizations rather than for final consumption). Any such distinction would be arbitrary. Great quantities of Coca-Cola are purchased by various types of organizations. And many other products, such as pencils, typewriters, life insurance, even some foodstuffs, can be either industrial or consumer goods depending on the purpose for which they are bought. The point is that while there is obvious merit to the concept of classification of goods, the present state of knowledge is such that only rather general guidelines can be given. Clearly, a better theory would be a real advance in marketing knowledge. Exhibit 9-20 presents one rather imaginative attempt here, but much remains to be done in this area.

CONCLUDING NOTE

In product decisions, the two key words are *specificity* and *integration*. Product strategy must be developed for the specific situation which the manager faces. Strategy must derive from a careful analysis of the market, and matching of market wants and desires with the objectives, resources, and functions of the organization. By the same token, product decisions must be integrated with pricing, promotion, and distribution decisions. The entire marketing program must be a coordinated effort to maximize the payoff from relationships with customers, the rest of the organization, and society in general.

Of course, this is easy to say, but it is not always easy to do. Generalized frameworks for thinking about marketing decisions are useful. But they are guides—not substitutes—for hard thinking about a particular situation. The marketing models used in this book, for example, can be quite helpful in structuring thinking and highlighting points that should be investigated, but they must be adapted to each situation.

Development of this type of skill takes practice. While you cannot expect to become a proficient marketing manager from studying this (or any) text—however diligently you do so—you can develop habits of thinking and analysis that can be very useful in actual marketing management situations.

Exhibit 9-20 Aspinwall's Characteristics of Goods Theory

The characteristics of goods theory attempts to arrange all marketable products in systematic and useful fashion. The theory sets up a continuous scale rather than discrete classes of products, and defines the criteria by which any product can be assigned to an appropriate place on the scale. The product scale is described in terms of a color spectrum ranging from red to yellow. Although the spectrum suggests an infinite gradation of different colors, Aspinwall groups them broadly into three categories: red, orange, and yellow goods. The table lists the five criteria by which goods are judged, and the characteristic value of each of the three types of goods for each criterion. For example, pencils have a high replacement rate, high adjustment, low searching time—so pencils could be classified in this scheme as red goods.

These marketing characteristics of a product determine the most appropriate and economical method for promoting and distributing it, according to Aspinwall. If the existing promotion and distribution patterns of a product differ significantly from these color-plot indications, Aspinwall claims that this indicates a need for possible change and improvement in promotion and distribution methods. The figure summarizes these relationships.

Characteristics of Goods Theory

| | Color Classification | | |
Characteristics	Red Goods	Orange Goods	Yellow Goods
Replacement Rate	High	Medium	Low
Gross Margin	Low	Medium	High
Adjustment	Low	Medium	High
Time of Consumption	Low	Medium	High
Searching Time	Low	Medium	High

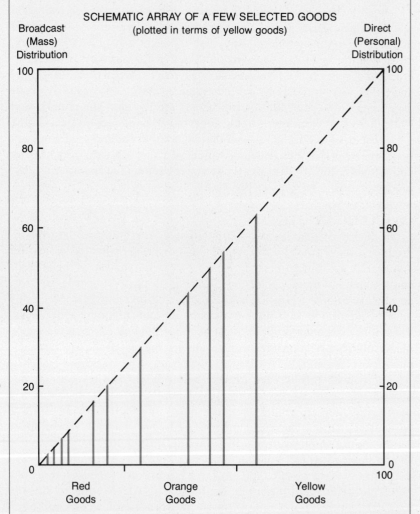

SCHEMATIC ARRAY OF A FEW SELECTED GOODS
(plotted in terms of yellow goods)

Broadcast (Mass) Distribution

Direct (Personal) Distribution

Red Goods Orange Goods Yellow Goods

Adapted from Leo V. Aspinwall, "The Marketing Characteristics of Goods," and "Parallel Systems of Promotion and Distribution," in *Four Marketing Theories* (University of Colorado, 1961), with permission of the author and the publisher.

KEY TERMS AND CONCEPTS

Product from the Consumer's Viewpoint
   bundle of utilities
   vehicle for want satisfaction
Product to the Producer
   primary output
   result of processing resources
Product Life Cycle
   introduction
   growth
   maturity
   decline
Product Type
   form
   class
   brand
New Product Development
   idea generation
   screening
   economic analysis
   development
   testing
   commercialization
Product Maturity
   market penetration
   product differentiation
   recycling
Product Decline
   re-entry
   phase out
   modification
   elimination
Matching Product to Consumer's Wants
   product extensions
   other marketing mix decisions
Product Level
   mix
   line
   item
Branding
   physical identification
   legal protection
   basis for marketing effort

Branding Strategy
  individual item
  family
  single brand
"Battle of the Brands"
  manufacturer vs. middleman
Product Extensions
  design
  packaging
  service
Classifications-of-Goods Theories
  effort
  loyalty

QUESTIONS FOR DISCUSSION

1. What "bundles of utilities" are offered by the following products: a Cadillac, a Volkswagen, a World Series or Super Bowl ticket, a set of false teeth, a life insurance policy, the United Fund, a .22 caliber pistol, a toupee, a "joint" of marijuana? How could market segments be defined for these products?

2. What stage in the product life cycle would you place each of the above products in? Why?

3. Consider an unknown politician running for office as a new product. Trace his/her progress through the six stages of new product development. What factors determine whether he/she reaches the introduction stage? the growth stage? maturity? decline?

4. Suppose that you have the responsibility for marketing decisions for the following "mature-stage" products: the internal combustion engine, major league baseball, network television, beer, home radios, religion (whatever religion you are most interested in), and the volunteer army. Discuss possible market penetration, product differentiation, and recycling strategies for these products. If you consider one or more of these products in the decline stage (rather than maturity), would you recommend phase out, modification or elimination? Why? Defend your reasoning.

5. What differences, if any, are there in two television sets manufactured by the same well-known company, one sold under that company's brand, the other by Sears? Would your answer differ if the product were a can of peas, and the retailer were A & P? Why?

6. Your company has developed a new type of liquid detergent. Researchers believe it offers significant advantages over liquid detergents now on the market. Assuming that they are correct, how much attention, if

any, should be paid to packaging? Why? What type of packaging would you recommend? Defend your reasoning.

7. How would you categorize the products in question 1 in terms of classification-of-goods? (You may find Exhibit 9-20 helpful here.)

SUGGESTED READING

1. Ralph S. Alexander.
"The Death and Burial of Sick Products." *Journal of Marketing*, April 1964, pp. 1–7. Classic exposition of the human as well as technical problems of product elimination; reprinted in Gabriel M. Gelb and Betsy D. Gelb. *Insights for Marketing Management*. 2nd ed. Goodyear, 1977.

2. Thomas L. Berg.
Mismarketing: Case Histories of Marketing Misfires. Garden City, N.Y.: Doubleday and Company, 1970. A well-researched and entertainingly written account of a number of marketing failures; also contains a summary chapter on how to profit from mistakes, and how to do research on marketing failures.

3. John Brooks.
The Fate of the Edsel and Other Business Adventures. New York: Harper and Row, 1963. Another well-researched glimpse into the actual world of product decisions; written in journalistic style; valuable background reading for the marketing manager.

4. Peter F. Drucker.
Managing for Results: Economic Tasks and Risk-Taking Decisions. New York: Harper and Row, 1964. A short, brilliant analysis of managerial tasks; emphasizes the need to relate organization products to customer wants and desires.

5. Theodore Levitt.
Marketing for Business Growth. McGraw-Hill, 1974. Brilliant exposition addressed to top managers; many insights into the marketing orientation, product development and innovation, product life cycle, etc.

6. Cornelius S. Muije.
"How Decisions Are Made to Stop Developing or Testing New Products." *1973 Conference Proceedings*. American Marketing Association, 1974. Muije was Marketing Research Director for Brown & Williamson Tobacco Co. when this paper was written; he examines critically and names names; reprinted in Gelb and Gelb, *Insights for Marketing Management*.

7. Robert R. Rothberg, editor.
Corporate Strategy and Product Innovation. Free Press, 1976. Comprehensive anthology of papers in this area.

10 / PROMOTION DECISIONS

In addition to producing a product, the organization must let potential customers know of its existence and of the benefits it provides. This chapter is devoted to decisions related to this element of the marketing program. Major points include:

1. Promotion is persuasive communication about an organization and its products. The communication process (communicator, message, media, audience, feedback) is the foundation of promotion.

2. The four channels of promotion are personal selling, advertising, publicity, and sales promotion.

3. Personal selling—oral communication with prospective purchasers—is the most frequently performed marketing activity. Management of this activity is challenging, and is excellent training for middle and upper marketing management positions.

4. Advertising—paid, nonpersonal promotional effort by an identified sponsor—is marketing's most visible activity. The scope and diversity of advertising is vast, and its effectiveness is difficult to measure. Advertising management, therefore, is interesting—and complex.

5. Publicity is nonpaid mass communication about an organization or its products. Publicity management is similar in concept, but often separated in fact, from advertising management.

6. Sales promotion is a catchall term describing promotional activities other than personal selling, advertising, or publicity. This amorphous area cries out for better management as its importance in the total promotional mix increases.

7. The promotion program seeks to coordinate all of the organization's promotional efforts in a given situation.

Ralph Waldo Emerson said:

> If a man can write a better book, preach a better sermon, or make a better mousetrap than his neighbors, though he builds his house in the woods, the world will make a beaten path to his door.

Emerson was wrong. The book will remain unread, the sermon unheeded, and the mousetrap will sit on the shelf and rot—unless the world (1) knows about those products, and (2) believes that they possess want-satisfying capabilities.

Promotion decisions focus upon accomplishing these two purposes. We look first at the nature of promotion; next we examine its major components—personal selling, advertising, and sales promotion—in more detail. The chapter closes with a discussion of factors involved in formulating the product mix and integrating promotion decisions into the marketing program.

THE NATURE OF PROMOTION

We pointed out in Chapter 1 that communication is a prerequisite to exchange activity. Now we wish to focus upon improving the effectiveness and/or efficiency of an organization's communications about exchange. This involves adding an element of persuasion to the organization's communications, and managing them carefully. More precisely, this book defines *promotion* as:

> communications that inform potential customers of the existence of products, and persuade them that those products have want-satisfying capabilities.

To explain this definition, let us look at the process of communication as it is used in marketing and at the four types of promotional tools.

The Communications Process in Marketing

The communications process is outlined in Exhibit 10-1. The process contains five elements—the communicator, the message, the channel, the audience, and feedback—and can be summarized as: Who . . . says what . . . in what way . . . to whom . . . with what effect?

In marketing management, the communicator is the manager who desires to promote a product. The audience is the target market segment. Feedback is the flow of information from the consumer to the marketer. These elements of the communication process in marketing have been discussed in some detail in this book. In this section of the chapter, we examine the message content and channels through which the message flows.

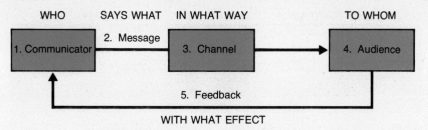

Exhibit 10-1   The Communications Process

WHO   SAYS WHAT   IN WHAT WAY   TO WHOM

1. Communicator   2. Message   3. Channel   4. Audience

5. Feedback

WITH WHAT EFFECT

Based upon the discussion in H.D. Lasswell, *Power and Personality* (New York: W. W. Norton, 1948), pp. 37–51.

Promotion Messages

A promotion message is the symbolization of product features in terms of customers' wants and desires. We noted in the product chapter that consumers do not buy physical goods, expert services, or abstract ideas—they buy expectations of benefits. The promotion message, therefore, is the communication of these benefits to consumers.

Communication, semanticists tell us, is the result of common understanding of symbols by communicator and audience. Exhibit 10-2 illustrates the way communications works. The communicator who desires to get a certain point across to an audience first encodes that message. That is, he/she translates ideas into symbols—words, pictures, numbers—that represent the ideas. The encoded symbols, the message, is transmitted (through some channel) to the audience. The audience then decodes the message, i.e, translates the symbols into ideas that it understands. For communications to take place, therefore, the audience and the communicator must share certain experiences, i.e., must be able to symbolize certain ideas and events in a fashion understandable to each other. This is shown in the diagram by the overlapping fields of experience of communicator and audience. Semanticists sometimes refer to this area as the *extensional bargain.* Unless their fields of experience do overlap, communicator and audience will have no extensional bargain and will be unable to communicate.

The most obvious example of such a failure occurs when communicator and audience do not speak the same language. Product benefits described in English may not be communicated to a Frenchman, a Japanese, or a Bantu. As we noted in Chapter 6, translations from language to language often result in miscommunication. Even individuals who share the same culture may be from different social classes and/or have different reference groups—and, therefore, have had different experiences. In such cases, communications may be less than perfect. As we pointed out in the buyer behavior chapter, for example, most marketing decision makers are from the upper-middle social class, and are above average in intelligence, while the bulk of the audiences they are trying to

**Exhibit 10-2 How Communication
Works**

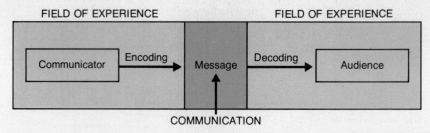

FIELD OF EXPERIENCE · FIELD OF EXPERIENCE

Communicator → Encoding → Message → Decoding → Audience

COMMUNICATION

Adapted from Wilbur Schramm, "How Communication Works," in *The Process and Effect of Mass
Communications,* ed. Wilbur Schramm (Ill.: University of Illinois Press, 1954).

reach are lower-middle or upper-lower classes, and are of average
intelligence. Or, the communicator may simply not be stressing the
benefits that the audience is interested in. Technical data on product
performance, for example, must be translated into consumer convenience,
comfort, or safety.

Promotion, by definition, is persuasive communication. That is, the
communicator deliberately arranges the message so as to affect the mental
sets and behavior of the audience in specified ways. Recall from our
discussion of the buying process in Chapter 6 that consumers obtain
information from many sources, including promotional material from
various organizations. One very significant aspect of the buying process is
the evaluation of that information, e.g., its usefulness, its immediacy, and
the perceived credibility of its source.

Of course, promotion, like all marketing activities, must be regulated
by society (regulation, as we discussed in Chapter 4, means defining the
legal limits of marketing activities). Fraudulent, deceitful promotion is
clearly outside these limits. Classic examples include television commercials in which the shaving cream that "softens beards as tough as
sandpaper" was actually applied to a sheet of plexiglass, and a new type of
automobile windshield that would supposedly reduce distortion was
actually photographed without any glass at all. Moreover, almost every
consumer has at one time or another been involved in a situation in which
used merchandise was represented as new, product performance claims
were exaggerated, the advertised bargain model was unavailable but a
better model could be obtained at a slightly higher price, and so on. As we
stressed in the public policy chapter, such practices should be vigorously
attacked with all legal means available.

Within the limits of legality, however, creativity and imagination
must be liberally applied to promotional activities used to symbolize
product values. It is neither effective nor efficient for promotion to "tell the
whole truth"—promotional messages must be designed to influence the
attitudes and/or behavior of the audience with which the marketer is
trying to communicate. Promotion, by definition, must persuade. Exhibit

Levitt argues clearly and forcefully that embellishment and distortion are among the legitimate and socially desirable purposes of promotion. He offers several examples of the universality of man's desires for illusions, symbols, and implications of more than pure functionality:

1. Consider poetry. Keats does not offer a truthful engineering description of his Grecian urn. He offers, instead—with exquisite attention to meter, rhyme, allusion, illusion, metaphor, and sound—a lyrical, exaggerated, distorted, and palpably false description.
2. All the Popes in history have countenanced the costly architecture of St. Peter's Basilica and its extravagant interior decoration. "All around the globe, nothing typifies man's materialism so much as the temples in which he preaches asceticism."
3. Women modify, embellish, and amplify themselves with colored paste for the lips and powders and lotions for the face; men as well as women use devices to take hair off the face and others to put it on the head. "Like the inhabitants of isolated African regions, where not a single whiff of advertising has ever intruded, we all encrust ourselves with rings, pendants, bracelets, neckties, clips, chains, and snaps."

In short, Levitt argues that ". . . man seeks to transcend nature in the raw everywhere . . . he obviously wants and needs the promises, the imagery, and the symbols of the poet and the priest. He refuses to live a life of primitive barbarism or sterile functionalism." Promotion—the symbolization of product attributes—fulfills a necessary function in human behavior. While falsehood and duplicity should be condemned and outlawed, promotion should communicate more than factual information.

Adapted from Theodore Levitt, "The Morality (?) of Advertising." *Harvard Business Review,* July-August 1970, pp. 84–92, with permission of the publisher.

10-3 presents Levitt's vigorous and well-reasoned rationale for the purpose of promotion activities.

The Promotion Mix

The final step in the communications process is the delivery of the communicator's message through some channel to the audience. There are basically four promotion channels: personal selling, advertising, sales promotion and publicity.

Personal Selling. When the term marketing is mentioned, most people usually think in terms of personal selling activities. The American Marketing Association (*Marketing Definitions,* 1960, p. 9) defines personal selling as:

> Oral presentation in a conversation with one or more prospective purchasers for the purpose of making sales.

The hallmark of personal selling is interaction between marketer and customer. As the parties converse by telephone or face-to-face, they interact—noting each other's personal characteristics, motivations, likes and dislikes, behavior patterns, and reasons for participating in the conversation. Each party can help or hinder the other by the way in which he/she participates in the interaction.

A combination of several factors makes personal selling especially effective. The sales person can observe the potential customer's behavior, and change the sales talk to more closely match the customer's wants and desires. The salesperson can point out the specific advantages of the product, probe objections and answer them, and ask directly for the sale. But this effectiveness is often purchased at high cost in efficiency. One-to-one relationships are relatively expensive. Personal selling, therefore, may not be the best promotion medium.

Advertising. Advertising is nonpersonal or mass promotion. Specifically, the American Marketing Association (*Marketing Definitions*, p. 18) definition is:

> Any paid form of nonpersonal presentation and promotion of ideas, goods, or services by an identified sponsor.

Thus, advertising lacks the interaction between marketer and consumer that characterizes personal selling. It is one-way communication—from the marketer to a mass of potential customers. The means of mass communication can be many and varied, e.g., magazine and newspaper space, motion pictures, outdoor posters, signs, skywriting, direct mail, novelties (calendars, blotters), radio and television, cards (car, bus, etc.), catalogs, directories and references, programs and menus, and circulars. Consequently, advertising sacrifices the effectiveness which is generated by the feedback in personal selling—no tailor-made adjustments in this sales pitch, no probing for objections, etc. On the other hand, advertising is more efficient; it can reach large numbers of potential customers at relatively low cost. To some extent, therefore, personal selling and advertising are complementary, rather than alternative, promotion channels.

Publicity. The definition of advertising stressed that it was paid promotional activity. Publicity, in contrast, is promotional material not paid for by an identified sponsor. Specifically, the American Marketing Association definition (*Marketing Definitions*, p. 19) is:

> Nonpersonal stimulation of demand for a product, service or business unit by planting commercially significant news about it in a published medium or obtaining favorable presentation of it on radio, television, or stage that is not paid for by the sponsor.

Despite this conceptual contrast, publicity decisions are quite similar to those of advertising. Consequently, we have more to say about publicity in the section on advertising.

Sales Promotion. Numerous other types of promotional activities augment personal selling, advertising and publicity. The usual practice in marketing literature is simply to lump these activities into one additional category, called *sales promotion,* defined by the American Marketing Association (*Marketing Definitions,* p. 20) as:

> Those marketing activities, other than personal selling, advertising and publicity, that stimulate consumer purchasing and dealer effectiveness, such as display, shows and exhibitions, demonstrations, and various nonrecurring selling efforts not in the ordinary routine.

The term sales promotion is a catchall for a wide variety of promotional activities, but this category is important. Sales promotion expenditures in organizations in an industrial economy have been variously estimated at between 20 and 35 percent of the total promotional budget. Sales promotions often supplement advertising and personal selling, capitalizing on the consumer interest and product knowledge generated by these media. For example, product samples complement advertising in new product introductions. Therefore, sales promotion plays an integral role in the total promotional program of an organization.

In summary, promotion is the process of persuasive communication from marketer to potential customer. The content of the promotion message and the media through which it is transmitted constitute the heart of the promotion program of an organization. Personal selling, advertising, and sales promotion are the major channels through which messages are designed and transmitted. Let us examine them in some detail and then integrate all promotional decisions into the marketing program.

PERSONAL SELLING

As noted above, personal selling involves direct interaction between marketer and customer. Consequently, personal selling activities in an industrial economy require many people—in excess of five and a half million (of a total work force of eighty-three million) in 1974. An activity of such significance to individuals, organizations, and the economy as a whole should be carefully studied. More specifically, we develop this topic at some length because there are so many job opportunities in the sales field.

The Personal Selling Function

From the view of the organization, the salesman or saleswoman is just one part of the total marketing function. Personal selling—oral communication between salesperson and prospect—is one channel for promotional activities. Promotion, in turn, is one element of the marketing program, which is derived from the wants and desires of the target market.

From the customer's perspective, the salesperson represents the entire organization. Even the most sophisticated of customers does not always bear in mind those necessary, but unseen, elements of the marketing program with which he has no contact. He tends, instead, to view the salesperson as the personification of the entire marketing function. The customer is likely to blame the salesperson for product failures, billing errors, misdeliveries, or anything else that goes wrong with the transaction. Conversely, the customer may also credit the salesperson for satisfying his wants and desires, though this satisfaction has actually been achieved through numerous marketing activities.

Consequently, the salesperson fills a complex role. In addition to all of the usual influences which two people exert upon each other in the ordinary course of their contact, the salesperson is attempting to communicate product benefits and persuade the customer that those benefits will satisfy his wants and desires. Although this generalization applies to all personal selling activities, there are vast differences in specific selling situations. Consequently, selling situations are often classified in various ways. I prefer to classify selling situations into five categories:

1. *Responsive selling*—in which the salesperson is expected to react to the customer's demands. The two major types here are route-driving and retailing. Drivers who deliver soft drinks, milk, bread, and fuel oil; and clerks in department stores, clothing stores, appliance stores, and specialty shops are examples of this type of selling. Responsive selling focuses on the purchase-decision stage of the buying process. Most customers have already recognized their desires, and have largely completed the search stage. Good service and a pleasant personality may produce a few sales, but this type of salesperson does not originate many sales.

2. *Trade selling*—here the salesperson is primarily an order taker as in responsive selling, but there is more emphasis upon service. That is, the trade salesperson focuses upon the use and evaluation stage of the buying process. Trade selling predominates in the food, textiles, apparel, and household products industries. Most sales personnel of wholesalers also fall into this category. Trade selling primarily involves order-taking, expediting deliveries, setting up displays, and rotating stock. In their contacts with buyers, trade salespeople may actually be discouraged from hard selling.

3. *Missionary selling*—here the objective is to influence the decider who is different from the purchaser/user of the product. The classic example is the drug "detail man" whose job is to explain the products of pharmaceutical manufacturers to medical doctors. The missionary salesperson does not close the sale. The doctor does not use the drugs, but because the doctor decides which drug to prescribe, he/she becomes the missionary salesperson's target market. Missionary selling is also common in food

manufacturing, distilling, and brewing; transportation and warehousing; and the utilities.

4. *Technical selling*—in which the salesperson solves customers' problems through expertise and experience. Technical selling is common in industrial goods, e.g., chemicals, machinery, and heavy equipment. The emphasis here is upon the search stage of the buying process. The salesperson's ability to identify, analyze, and solve customers' problems is essential; in a sense technical selling resembles professional consulting.

5. *"Creative" selling*—in which the salesperson "creates" demand for products. There are two categories here: tangibles (vacuum cleaners, automobiles, encyclopedias, real estate) and intangibles (insurance, investments, education). This type of selling focuses on the entire buying process from want recognition through search and purchase to product use and evaluation. The quote marks indicate my dissatisfaction with the traditional label of creative selling. While it is true that this type of selling generally requires more creativity than do the other types discussed, creativity is necessary to some degree in performing all types of personal selling.

Performing the Personal Selling Function

In performing personal selling activities, the salesperson becomes closely involved with customers, with other elements of the marketing mix, with other organizational functions, and with environmental factors. In short, the individual salesperson performing his/her duties often participates, to a greater degree than in any other single marketing job, in all phases of the marketing plan (seeking, matching, programming, consummating). These activities can be broadly classified as selling duties and supporting duties.

Selling duties closely parallel the buying process discussed in Chapter 6: want recognition, search, purchase, and use and evaluation. To move the customer through these stages in the buying process, the salesperson engages in prospecting, preparation, presentation, and postsale activities. We look at each in turn.

Prospecting. Just as an organization seeks target market segments for its products, an individual salesperson seeks potential customers. That is, he/she attempts to identify MAD individuals (Money, Authority, Desire). In the less creative selling situations, e.g., responsive and trade, prospecting is a rather cut-and-dried activity. The customers are already identified, or they identify themselves. In the more creative selling situations, however, prospecting is quite important. It reduces the time that the salesperson might spend in making presentations to individuals who are not viable potential customers for the product he/she is selling.

There are a number of sources of potential customers. Appropriate sources vary by type of product to be sold. A life insurance salesperson, for example, might examine birth and graduation announcements in the newspapers, become active in a church or civic organization, use present customers for referrals, or depend upon leads generated by company advertising. A salesperson of plumbing fixtures, by contrast, might find more pertinent information in reports of new construction published by F.W. Dodge Corp., building permits, and records of utility connections. An oil-tool equipment salesperson might do his/her prospecting at industry trade shows, or in membership directories of trade associations, records of past customers, and news and notes in trade magazines.

Preparation. Just as prospecting is analogous to the seeking function for total marketing activities, preparation is analogous to the matching function. That is, the salesperson must be knowledgeable about both the customer's wants and desires, and the products that the organization can offer to satisfy the customer. On the customer's side of the match, the object is to find out as much as possible about the customer's wants and desires so that the product can be tailored to those specific requirements. This activity, often termed *qualifying* the prospect, might involve determining what products or brands the prospect is now using, and his/her evaluation of them; also useful would be an estimate of the amount of product that the customer might use, some understanding of the customer's personal likes and dislikes, and his/her company's policies with respect to purchases.

To achieve the best match between the product and the customer's wants and desires, the salesperson must also have a thorough knowledge of product features, performance, capabilities, limitations, and so forth. He/she should also be aware of competitor's products, environmental conditions, and organizational policies and procedures concerning such factors as availability, return allowances, services and warranties, etc.

Presentation. Once the salesperson has sought and found potential customers and has matched their wants with his/her products, the next step is to present that product to the customer. The sales presentation should be closely related to the consumers' buying process. An alternative formulation of this process, more familiar to sales people and sales managers, is AIDA—Attention, Interest, Desire, and Action.

The first step in the sales presentation is to focus the prospect's attention on the product as a means of satisfying a want or desire. In some cases, the prospect may be aware of the product through various means, such as the organization's advertising, the prospect's personal experience, the experiences of others, and so forth. The prospect may already recognize a desire, and the salesperson's attention-getting task is merely to show that his product might satisfy that want. In more creative selling situations, on the other hand, the salesperson may cause the prospect to recognize a want or desire. The salesperson might, for example, ask a leading question: Would you be interested in cutting your costs by 20 percent? In the event of your death, would your family be provided for? Or the salesperson might offer some premium in return for the opportunity to make the sales presentation.

Upon obtaining the prospect's attention, the salesperson's next step is to arouse and increase interest in his product. The prospect is now searching for a way of satisfying a want or desire, so the key for the salesperson is to focus upon those product attributes that are meaningful for the particular customer addressed. For example, a typewriter salesperson might stress low cost to a student, trouble-free operation to the housewife, and durability and reliability to the organization buyer.

For many types of products, a demonstration is very helpful. When presenting technical products, the salesperson may call in engineers and specialists to supplement and extend the sales presentation. Some companies employ *canned* sales talks—they require sales people to repeat verbatim or with only minor changes the presentation prepared by the organization. Canned sales talks have the advantage of thorough coverage of the points that the organization has found useful in previous sales. Canned sales talks are most effective when the salesperson knows them so well that they sound natural.

If the salesperson judges that the customer is interested in his/her product, the *trial close* will be used to test the prospect's desire to purchase it. That is, the salesperson will ask such questions as: Do you prefer the pink model or the blue one? Or, will you take it with you, or can we deliver it? If the salesperson has not created sufficient customer desire for the product, the trial close may pinpoint at least some of the customer's objections. Of course, the customer may not know, or may not care to divulge, all of his/her reservations about the product. The salesperson may have to probe gently but firmly to uncover possible resistances.

Postsale Activities.   Unfortunately, not every sales presentation results in a sale. The salesperson may call several times and make several different presentations before moving the customer to the action stage— the purchase decision. Nor does reaching this stage necessarily complete the task. The salesperson must write the order, possibly arrange for shipment and delivery, facilitate granting of credit to the customer, reassure him on the wisdom of his decision, and contact the customer from time to time to maintain good will and to smooth over any problems that arise.

Supporting Duties.   The salesperson has responsibilities in addition to selling. First, some part of his/her time must be spent in studying to keep up with changes in the organization's products and policies, competitors' activities, and environmental conditions. Of course, this responsibility is shared by every marketing manager, but it is particularly important that the salesperson be well informed, since he/she represents the organization to its customers. Second, the salesperson must manage his/her own activities. In even the least creative of sales jobs, the salesperson and no one else determines how much time will be spent with a given prospect, what route will be followed in moving from customer to customer, what appeals will be used, what demonstrations will be made and so forth. In short, the salesperson is a manager in every sense of that term. And sometimes managerial responsibilities conflict with selling duties. My favorite story here is the young salesman who was told that he should make twelve calls each day (on the assumption that the law of averages would produce a sale for a given number of calls). On his eleventh call, the salesman had succeeded in reaching the interest stage—"tell me more, young man," the prospect invited. But the day was nearly over, and the salesman responded, "I would like to, Sir, but I must leave to make my twelfth call of the day."

The third non-selling responsibility of the salesperson is to complete a certain amount of paper work related to his activities. As we discussed in Chapter 8 on marketing information, the organization needs data on number of sales, type of product sold, customer characteristics, and so on. Moreover, some organizations want more than routine paper work, asking that their salespeople be "eyes and ears," i.e., gather marketing intelligence. To the organization, both types of information generating activities are necessary. But from the salesperson's point of view, such activities are boring and distracting. Consequently, the organization should assist the salesperson in performing these duties by providing standardized, easily completed forms, clear lines of communication, and feedback assuring that the information is used.

Finally, the salesperson is expected to generate good will toward the organization. This may sometimes conflict with the salesperson's desire to obtain a particular order or it may require more time than necessary simply to complete an order.

This brief overview has hardly done justice to the function of personal selling. The stages in the selling process do not always proceed as logically and clearly as we have described, and problems arise at each stage. Moreover, most sales people are working with more than one customer at any given moment, and there never seems to be enough time to perform the nonselling duties. Personal selling is a marketing activity that requires particular skills and abilities.

Selling Skills and Abilities

Sales people play many roles—persuaders, information gatherers, service technicians, customer ego-builders, expediters, coordinators, problem definers, travelers, display arrangers. They represent their organizations to customers, and customers to their organization. Sales people often operate independently of direct supervision, so they must handle the ambiguities and role conflicts of their positions with relatively little help and guidance from their superiors. Sales people generally are rather well paid, have considerable freedom of action, and may be responsible for spending significant organizational funds in pursuit of sales. On the other hand, they do not have the power and authority to compel either customers or other organizational units to do their bidding, selling often is perceived as a low-status occupation, and some sales jobs require that the salesperson spend considerable time away from home and family.

The inevitable management question is: What kind of individual is capable of performing successfully in such situations? The obvious approach is to list the qualifications that a good salesperson should have, and then devise testing and training procedures to identify individuals who have these qualifications.

Given the focus on personal characteristics, many organizations have tried to use psychological tests in selecting their sales people. In general, however, the testing approach has not been notably successful. There are basically two reasons for this. The first relates to the design of tests of this type. To be valid and reliable in a statistical sense, the tests must measure a number of different traits, and must do so in standardized fashion. The result, therefore, is that the tests tend to screen out creative, individualistic personalities and to produce average scores on a number of psychological traits. The tests tend to downplay creativity and, originality to lose sight of the composite trait *sales ability* in a sea of specific psychological attributes.

Second, the test must focus upon measurable qualities. This has two consequences. In the first place, tests tend to measure surrogates of ability, e.g., interests, experience, intelligence, personality traits. While these factors may correlate with sales ability, they are not necessarily components of that ability. The second consequence is that what the tests are measuring is usually apparent to anyone of average intelligence. It is, therefore, relatively easy to respond to the test in ways that will be considered favorable. If, for example, the respondent is asked whether he/she would prefer to be addressing a P.T.A. group, reading a good book alone, or riding a horse in the country, he/she would not have much difficulty in choosing the P.T.A. response—provided that the interview was for a sales job.

In light of these difficulties with generalized tests, progress in this area would seem to come from boiling down the capabilities and qualifications of successful salesmanship to their barest essentials. My own preference is the following four categories of qualities and capabilities:

1. *energy*—the physical and mental stamina to cope with long hours,

Evans studied the interpersonal relationship (dyad) between life insurance salesmen and their prospects. He examined successful and unsuccessful sales calls of certain salesmen, and concluded that the successful dyads are more alike than the unsuccessful ones. The table provides specific examples. Note that the successful percentage is consistently higher for dyads with the same characteristics than for dyads that differ on a particular characteristic. In short, the more alike the salesman and his prospect, the greater the likelihood for a sale—according to this research.

Characteristic of Dyad	Meaning of "Same"	Percentage Sold When Characteristic is:	
		Same	Different
Physical:			
height	similar or salesman taller	32	28
age	less than 9 years difference	33	25
Demographic:			
income	similar or salesman's greater	33	20
education	similar or salesman's greater	35	23
religion	membership in same creed	32	28
Preference:			
politics	membership in same party	35	27
smoking habits	both smoke or neither does	32	28

Adapted from Franklin B. Evans, "Selling as a Dyadic Relationship—A New Approach," *The American Behavioral Scientist,* May 1963, p. 70.

traveling, transporting of sample cases, and unfamiliar surroundings;

2. *enthusiasm*—the ability to motivate oneself, to continue on in the face of failure, to remain optimistic about future opportunities;

3. *empathy*—an understanding of customers' wants, likes, and dislikes, and motivating factors;

4. *drive*—the persistence to close the sale, the need for dominating the selling situation, and the will to win.

Of course, this list is merely illustrative of the factors that have been identified as important to successful salesmanship, but it is, I think, fairly typical.

But these abilities are only prerequisites to successful sales performance. Each sales situation is different. Consequently, basic abilities must be supplemented by specific knowledge (of products, company policies, customer requirements, and competitive actions) and by successful behavioral interactions with the customer. In fact, a classic study by Evans contends that it is the interaction of salesperson and customer, the *dyad*, that determines whether or not a sale is made in a given case. Evans' work is presented in Exhibit 10-4. Subsequent studies have verified its basic point: other factors being equal, people tend to buy from people who are like themselves.

In summary, we have said that personal selling is a complex marketing activity that requires particular kinds of abilities. But personal selling must also be integrated with other aspects of promotion, other elements of the marketing program, and other organizational functions and objectives. For this reason, personal selling must be carefully managed.

Management of Personal Selling

Management of the personal selling function involves basically six activities: recruiting, training, motivating, and controlling individual sales people, and organizing and supporting the work of a group of salespeople. We look at each of these six activities in turn.

Recruiting. Obviously, the first task of sales management is to secure a sufficient number of qualified sales people. Most organizations that employ personal selling as a part of their marketing program have some salespeople on their payrolls. Rarely is the task one of recruiting an entire sales force at any given time. Recruiting should be an ongoing activity of sales management, because of the turnover of existing sales people, and organizational growth and development. The first step in recruiting sales people is to determine what qualifications and abilities are needed. Ideally, the recruiter should know what to look for. This determination should derive logically from the hierarchy of objectives: corporate, marketing, promotion, and down to selling. Perhaps the most efficient way of determining these qualifications is to prepare an explicit and comprehensive job description, such as that shown in Exhibit 10-5.

The next step is to generate applicants for the position to be filled. This is very much a marketing activity—in which the organization seeks customers who are willing to exchange their time, energy, and talents for the rewards offered by the position. In short, the task is one of seeking applicants who have the required qualifications, and matching them to the duties required.

There are a number of potential sources of sales personnel. These can be classified into three categories: internal, sales people with other organizations, and other institutions. Many applicants for sales jobs are generated internally. For example, a particular applicant may be referred by the company's sales people or other employees, or may be employed in some other department and wish to transfer to sales.

Second, some organizations advertise (in newspapers, trade magazines, and/or school publications) for sales people. Another important source of applicants for sales jobs is sales people with other organizations. A competitor's salesperson may wish to change jobs, for example, or a

As a P&G salesman or sales manager, you have two types of responsibilities:

Volume Responsibility
You accept personal sales responsibility for 2-5 important chain and wholesale accounts in your area. You work with their entire management group: the advertising and merchandising managers, buyers, store operations manager, warehousing and data processing personnel, and the top executives such as General Manager, Vice President and President. You know their needs from firsthand, personal sales contact. You work to solve day-to-day problems and develop long-range plans for growth. Your sales responsibilities include analyzing your accounts' business to enable you to make sound recommendations involving purchasing, product handling, merchandising ideas, advertising, display and all other aspects of promotional activity. It is your responsibility to introduce new brands and sizes, to administer merchandising funds, and solve shipping and other operational problems as they occur.

You create and test new merchandising plans and techniques that can increase product volume. Sometimes the plans are local in nature and involve product characteristics that tie in with civic, sports or other events. Other merchandising plans can be national in scope and include price-packs, coupons, or premiums. You test your own ideas as well as those created by staff groups in Cincinnati or by other line managers. Sales themes, advertising layouts, and point-of-purchase materials are valuable business builders, and welcomed by your customers.

You provide the company with business analyses: sales volume forecasts, market trends, competitive activity information and other data which enable the company to follow marketing activities nationally. Frequently you take action on the spot on your own initiative. In other cases, you recommend the course of action the company should take in your area. A national marketing program incorporates variations suggested by Sales Management for regional differences. Corporate marketing strategy is a composite of the thinking of the Advertising and the Sales Departments.

People Responsibility
You lead and motivate the people who report to you. The pace for your organization is set by your sales efforts with your accounts. You increase your organization's effectiveness with good leadership practices. You provide the operational direction for your organization, and plan the immediate and long-range goals. *You are responsible for developing the people in your organization.* You develop and direct training programs that are personalized to each individual's needs and goals. You promote those who are ready for additional responsibility.

You staff your organization's manpower needs. You recruit sources (college, employment agency, newspaper, etc.) for salesmen based on your needs. The key to our recruiting is to select the person whose career/job goals can be realized at P&G.

You are a responsible member of your community. An extension of your business leadership can be your voluntary participation in activities and events in your civic, social and business community. Because P&G Sales Managers are leaders and doers, they are frequently in the forefront of local efforts to improve the quality of living.

salesperson in a different industry may wish to move into the organization's field. Moreover, the organization's purchasing agents interview many sales people from various suppliers each day—it may be that some of them might wish to join the organization.

Applicants for sales jobs are also generated by several types of other institutions. Schools are one major source—universities, junior colleges, and high schools often have placement facilities that the organization can make use of in finding applicants for sales jobs. Employment agencies constitute another institution with a vested interest in placing its clients. Finally, many professional organizations maintain placement services for their members, e.g., Sales and Marketing Executives Club, Advertising Association, and the professional associations of many trade groups.

The third phase of recruiting is the selection of sales people from applicants. As noted above, selection is essentially a process of matching the applicant's qualifications to the duties and rewards of the position. The first step is completion of the application blank, which provides information about the applicant's education, work experiences, personal and family characteristics, and so forth. Second, references are often requested. Appraisals by responsible people familiar with the applicant's background are useful in eliminating obviously unsuitable candidates. Since the applicant has supplied the names of references, favorable information is to be expected, and unfavorable comments are, therefore, particularly significant. Moreover, even generally favorable appraisals sometimes provide useful insights into particular facets of the candidate's character or abilities.

The third selection tool employed by almost all organizations is the interview. Since selling involves personal interaction, most sales managers place particular emphasis upon an applicant's performance in an interview situation. Attention is paid to the applicant's dress, manners, bearing, facial expressions, gestures, and poise—as well as to what he/she has to say, and how well it is said. In addition to these standard tools, some organizations, as noted above, use psychological tests of one type or another. The value of such tests can be overemphasized, but they can provide useful information on such factors as intelligence level, career preferences and interests, verbal and quantitative skills, etc.

Some organizations attempt to formalize the selection procedure. Decision rules for selecting or rejecting a given applicant are formulated on the basis of past experience and the performance of current successful salesmen. These rules are then translated into a formalized rating system and applied to each applicant. As with other formalized decision aids, a system of this type can be useful in guiding selection procedures, but should not be allowed to take the place of executive judgment.

Training. Whatever his/her background and abilities, the newly-hired applicant is seldom ready to become a productive salesperson immediately. A period of training is needed to gain the necessary knowledge and experience. The knowledge required is of two types: *substantive*— knowledge of product characteristics and performance, company policies, major competitors, applicable legislation, and so on; and *procedural*—how to fill out forms, who in the organization to turn to for various kinds of information, industry jargon and customs, and so on. Experience means being involved in various selling situations and exposure to other responsibilities that the salesperson is expected to meet.

Training programs vary from organization to organization. In smaller organizations, the program may be an informal apprenticeship to a more experienced salesperson who shows the new man or woman the ropes. But some organizations have formal and elaborate training programs, perhaps lasting many months, and involving the latest teaching techniques and equipment.

Motivating. We pointed out above that selling, perhaps more than any other type of marketing activity, requires a high level of motivation. In its selection procedures, the organization looks for individuals who innately have strong self-motivation. But the organization can help here, too. Motivating factors can be both financial and psychic.

Perhaps the major motivating factor in selling is the compensation that the salesperson receives. Generally, the financial rewards of selling compare quite favorably with other lines of work. The particulars of the compensation plan vary widely, however. This is because sales management must consider several competing factors in designing the plan. From the salesperson's point of view, the plan should provide a basic level of income that can be counted on when things are not going too well. At the same time, he/she would like above-average earnings when times are good. Management would like the compensation plan to be related to the salesperson's productivity, and to be relatively simple and easy to operate. Customary industry practices, competitors' sales plans, and environmental conditions must also be taken into account.

In designing the compensation plan, management can work with four elements: salary, commission based on productivity, expenses (e.g., reimbursement for travel, meals, and lodging), and fringe benefits (e.g., paid vacation, hospitalization insurance). The mix of these elements employed in a given organization should result from the marketing and personal selling objectives established for the marketing program. A straight-salary plan, for example, provides maximum security and minimum incentive for above average performance; it is simple to operate, and sales people are willing to devote time to nonselling duties, such as record keeping and customer service. Responsive, trade, and missionary selling tend to be compensated in this manner.

A plan that emphasizes commission based on productivity, on the other hand, might be appropriate in situations which require aggressive selling and relatively little time for nonselling duties, e.g., insurance and securities, real estate, and door-to-door selling. In practice, most organizations employ some combination of salary and commission. The treatment of expenses also is generally geared rather closely to prevailing practice in the given industry.

But man does not live by bread alone—sales people are not motivated strictly by financial reward. They, like everyone else, desire job satisfaction. It is particularly important to provide this motivation to sales personnel since they represent the organization.

Many alternatives are available. First, the salesperson should believe that his/her work is useful and important to customers, the organization, and society in general. This suggests that the company should have a regular program of informing salespersonnel of organizational activities and accomplishments, and showing specifically how their work fits into the overall organization. Good performance should be recognized—through contests, salesperson-of-the-month designations, awards banquets, and so on. Finally, a very important part of the sales management task is simply to be available to listen to and advise the salesperson. After dealing with customers all day, many sales people simply want to blow off steam; the sales manager can listen and may be able to offer helpful advice. Whatever the methods employed, the organization should recognize the importance of motivating its sales personnel. And most organizations do; that is why sales motivation itself is a big business—many books, articles, and programs have been developed to aid in motivating sales personnel.

Controlling. The salesperson often works without direct supervision, and yet his/her performance is vital to organizational success—*nothing moves until the sale is made.* Consequently, the most significant and challenging task of sales management is to insure that the salesperson's performance is up to standard. As we noted in Chapter 5, the process of control involves establishing performance standards, measuring actual performance, and taking corrective action as needed. We devote much of Chapter 13 to a comprehensive examination of the control process in marketing. At this point, we look briefly at some dimensions of the control task as it relates to sales management.

First, a number of different indicators of sales performance could be employed. Among the most commonly used are total volume, revenue, gross margin contribution (revenue minus cost of goods sold), net margin contribution (gross margin minus direct selling expenses), and net profit (net margin contribution minus allocated costs). All of these indicators relate more or less directly to products sold. But the organization might also wish to note the number of calls a salesman makes, new accounts opened (and accounts lost); the accuracy and timeliness of paper work; and the quantity, accuracy and timeliness of intelligence reports filed. In addition, customers sometimes write letters or otherwise provide feedback on sales people and some organizations formalize this feedback in the form of a questionnaire to customers.

Each of these indicators can be measured in a number of different ways: raw numbers (dollars, units, cases, pounds, feet, carloads), percentages, ranking, various statistics (mean, median, mode, range, standard deviation). In addition to the quantitative measures, most sales managers make some sort of qualitative appraisal of their sales personnel, including general appearance, product knowledge, relations with customers, and efficiency in performing nonselling duties. Finally, any of the information discussed above may be broken down on the basis of product lines, individual customers, or territories.

Thus, performance measurement for controlling sales personnel is no easy task. After performance has been measured and checked against standards, corrective action may be required. This, too, is a complex task, which we discuss in some detail in Chapter 13.

The four aspects of sales management discussed to this point can be viewed in terms of individual salespersons. The sales manager also must perform two additional tasks that are less easily related to any individual salesperson: organizing and supporting.

Organizing. The organizing function of sales management is simply an application of the principle of division of labor. The sales manager almost always has more than one salesperson reporting to him/her. The task, therefore, is to organize the work of all sales people so that the group produces at its best. Two issues of major importance here are sales force specialization, and routing and scheduling.

Sales people basically cover a territory—whether a department or area in a store, a delivery route, an area of a city or other geographic unit. One question inevitably arises: within this territory, should the salesperson represent all products to all customers in the territory, or should some degree of specialization be employed? For example, it may be that because of product differences, efficiency in sales performance could be gained by assigning different sales people to different products. An appliance store, for example, may have its washing machine expert, and its stereo expert; IBM Corporation has one sales force for its computers and another for its typewriters and office machines. Alternatively, an organization may find itself marketing to different types of customers, and designate different sales people to serve these different customers. For example, a grocery products wholesaler may have different sales people calling on retail grocery stores and on institutions such as hospitals and schools.

In principle, the advantages and disadvantages of specialization are relatively clear: increased specialization means greater expertise in dealing with particular products and/or customers, but the company may find that it needs more sales people to represent its various products to different customers in the same territory. An alternative approach is to make the territories small enough so that one salesperson can cover all customers and all products in that territory. The proper amount and degree of specialization will vary in each case, depending upon such factors as organizational resources, product complexity, number of customers, industry custom, competitors' activities, general economic conditions, and so forth. And the most carefully designed sales force structure becomes outdated as these factors change over time.

Another major issue in organizing work loads is the matter of assigning sales people to territories, and routing and scheduling their work. Determining the best size and shape of each salesperson's territory can be a thorny problem. The major considerations are territory potential and territory work load. As discussed in Chapter 7, sales potential refers to potential product demand in a given area. Ideally, one might want to equalize the potential available to each salesperson by drawing territorial boundaries in accordance with estimated potential. However, the amount of work necessary to achieve a given level of potential should also be considered—the ideal here would be an equal work load for each salesperson.

Unfortunately, these two considerations often conflict, necessitating tradeoffs. For example, a person selling oil drilling equipment may have more than he/she can do to cover the potential in metropolitan Houston, while an equal potential in the mountain regions of the U.S. might involve traveling in seven or eight states. Clearly, the Houston salesperson stands a much better chance of realizing his/her potential than does the Western salesperson. But if their work loads are equalized (in terms of expected sales quota and number of sales calls), the Houston salesperson is likely to be more productive. Or to put it another way, the cost of each sale in the western region is likely to be greater. In practice, therefore, before organizations draw territorial boundaries, both factors must be considered. This type of problem is amenable, at least in principle, to mathematical analysis, e.g., linear programming and routing algorithms.

Supporting. The sales manager must support the efforts of his/her sales personnel. Many possibilities are available. First, the sales manager or supervisor ordinarily has sales experience, and can offer advice. Second, the salesperson needs several types of information: customer characteristics and past purchasing patterns, descriptions and appraisals of competitors' products, production and delivery schedules for the product, credit policies, and so forth. Third, sales people's activities can be facilitated by such organizational resources as expense accounts, company cars, product samples, brochures, and so forth. And fourth, the salesperson is supported by other elements of the marketing mix—advertising, sales promotion, pricing decisions, product features—and other organizational characteristics and activities (reputation, financial strength, product design and engineering, and so forth). Since the number of possibilities for sales

In these days of shortages, one might suppose that salesmen could take life a little easier, letting customers come to them for badly needed goods and materials. In fact, though, salesmen have to work harder than ever. They are, in effect, required to administer complex rationing programs for many vital materials, including steel, aluminum, plastics, and synthetic fibers.

But while salesmen of scarce goods have become allocators of their products, they are aware that their markets could again become highly competitive. So they have to look to the future and deal graciously with purchasing agents—even the one who, upon being informed of a new rationing move, Telexed the salesman: "F - - - YOU. STRONG LETTER TO FOLLOW."

An easygoing fellow with an affable grin, Charles E. Wright is no stranger to selling.

Now thirty-four, Wright is based in Houston, Texas, where most of Armco's market is energy related: companies that make everything from tankers to drilling rigs to electric-utility poles to nuclear-reactor pressure vessels. Steel has been tight in Texas since late last summer, and for the first time in his career as a salesman, Chuck Wright has been in the position of rationing steel among his customers.

Before the steel shortage hit Wright's territory, his job was in most respects like that of any other industrial salesman. His primary objectives, he says, were to "get orders from anybody who could put a carload together," and to "do a lot of survey work—find out who was buying what kind of tons from whom."

Wright says that "cold calls" on new sales prospects were the most interesting. "I'd try to find out as much as I could about a prospect's company, the products he made, what problems he had in selling them. And then I'd say, 'Let me have a chance to quote on your steel requirements. Let me have a trial order.'"

The steel shortage has practically put an end to Wright's calls on new customers, and his relations with old ones have become strained. Nowadays, he can sell steel only to those customers who have a buying "history" with his company. Armco has established a strict allocation program, based upon a customer's record of past purchases.

Wright tells those customers who bought a lot of foreign steel when it was cheap that they don't have enough "history" with Armco to get all the steel they need. And he leaves them with the thought that when steel again becomes more plentiful, it would be wise for them to establish a more stable relationship with a U.S. supplier —for instance, Armco.

While good-naturedly warning loyal customers against falling into bad habits in the future, Wright does everything he can to keep them supplied now. If he hears that one of his competitors has stock that he lacks, he'll pass the good news along to his customers. He'll also help his customers by telling one of them when another has usable leftovers from its manufacturing process.

Relations between Wright and his own company have also undergone a sometimes trying change.

One of Wright's altercations with the production department came after it began to book orders for other accounts from inventory being held in reserve for a customer of his. "That customer did $4 million last year, a lot of money for one account," he says. "You don't screw people like that for long and still remain friends."

Source: Excerpted from Michael B. Rothfeld, "A New Kind of Challenge for Salesmen," *Fortune* (April, 1974), p. 156–8.

support are many and varied, and since different salespeople require different kinds of support, the sales manager must be constantly alert to the particular needs of the different salespeople that report to him/her.

In short, management of the personal selling function is a mainstay of many marketing programs. Sales management is in fact the most pervasive, and perhaps the most significant, of all managerial activities in marketing. This brief discussion has done little more than overview this important area, but it should provide a framework for understanding and evaluating sales management.

Personal Selling Today

Career opportunities in personal selling today (and every day) are tremendous. Many young people, however, do not wish to consider a career in selling or in sales management. Selling conjures up such stereotypes as Harold Hill, the musical con man in "The Music Man"; Willy Loman, the tragic failure in Arthur Miller's "Death of a Salesman"; the glib, intensive door-to-door peddler, or the underpaid retail clerk. But selling to manufacturers, wholesalers, retailers, and consumers is much more varied and sophisticated than these stereotypes indicate. Increasingly, the role of the salesperson is changing from the old *hard sell* (although such people will always exist) to a more professional, consulting approach to the satisfaction of the customer's wants and desires. As noted above, selling and sales management are not easy careers, but the potential rewards are great.

Many organizations found out just how important their sales personnel really were during a time when organizations were beginning to think sales people were superfluous—the period of severe supply shortages in the early 1970s. Exhibit 10-6 illustrates this fundamental point.

Moreover, personal selling is excellent training for higher marketing management positions, for two reasons. First, as noted above, there are many, many sales jobs. Thus, in a given organization, an individual often has a higher probability of obtaining a sales position than a job in any other department. Second, personal selling is a microcosm of the entire marketing function. The salesperson learns to relate effectively to customers, other aspects of the organization, and society in general. He/she experiences many different types of problems, and is involved in different situations. And the results of his/her work are clearly visible to superiors. Consequently, if successful, he/she develops attributes of self-reliance, sound judgment, high motivation, and effective human relations that are essential in higher management positions. In terms of both appropriateness of background and simple probabilities, therefore, an individual interested in a middle- or upper-level marketing management position would be well-advised to consider beginning his/her career as a salesperson.

ADVERTISING AND PUBLICITY

As important as personal selling is to the marketing function, it is by no means the only necessary activity. Exhibit 10-7 presents the classic portrayal of the interdependence of personal selling and other elements of the marketing mix. We examine first the nature of advertising in an industrial society, then the major dimensions of advertising management, and finally the process of developing an advertising campaign.

Exhibit 10-7   The Customer Meets the Salesman

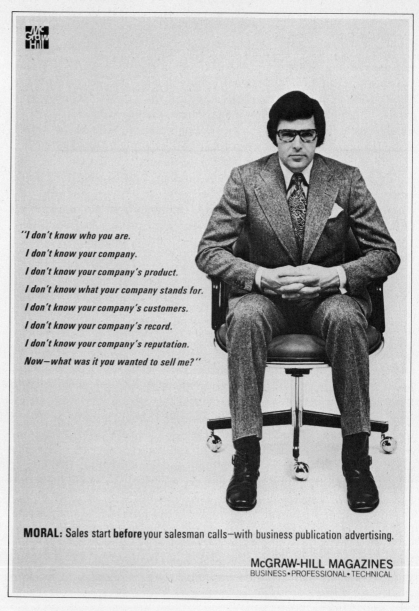

"I don't know who you are.

I don't know your company.

I don't know your company's product.

I don't know what your company stands for.

I don't know your company's customers.

I don't know your company's record.

I don't know your company's reputation.

Now—what was it you wanted to sell me?"

MORAL: Sales start **before** your salesman calls—with business publication advertising.

McGRAW-HILL MAGAZINES
BUSINESS•PROFESSIONAL•TECHNICAL

Reprinted by permission of McGraw-Hill Magazines, Business/Professional/Technical.

Nature of Advertising

As we noted earlier in the chapter, advertising is any paid form of nonpersonal presentation and promotion of products by an identified sponsor. This brief definition encompasses marketing activities of signif-

Exhibit 10-8 Economic Dimensions of U.S. Advertising

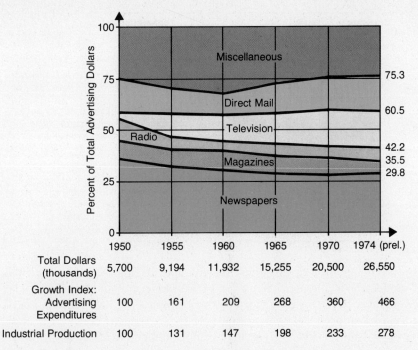

	1950	1955	1960	1965	1970	1974 (prel.)
Total Dollars (thousands)	5,700	9,194	11,932	15,255	20,500	26,550
Growth Index: Advertising Expenditures	100	161	209	268	360	466
Industrial Production	100	131	147	198	233	278

Data from *1975 Statistical Abstract of the U.S.* (Washington, D.C.: U.S. Government Printing Office, 1976), pp. 731, 791.

icant scope and wide diversity. The scope of advertising activities is summarized in Exhibit 10-8. In the United States, for example, total expenditures on advertising during the past twenty years have increased almost fourfold—from $5.7 billion to more than $20 billion. This rate of growth is considerably greater than the growth in industrial production during a comparable period.

The figure also indicates that the way these advertising dollars are spent has changed with the times. The most dramatic shift has been the rapid rise in the use of television—largely at the expense of radio, but also reducing the proportion spent in magazines and newspapers. And these figures do not even hint at the vast diversity of advertising activities—from handbills announcing sales at the local shopping center to television commercials costing $25,000 to produce and upwards of $200,000 per minute to place on the air—from classified ads by the thousand to full page spreads in glossy magazines—from computer-prepared personalized letters to large outdoor billboards.

In order to understand and manage activities of such scope and diversity, students of advertising often categorize them. The major categories, as shown in Exhibit 10-9, correspond to the communication process model: who. . . says what . . . in what way . . . to whom?

Exhibit 10-9   Ways of Categorizing Advertising

Category	Explanation
Sponsor [who]:	
Manufacturer	Paid by manufacturer
Middleman	Paid by middleman
Individual	Classified advertisement
Content [says what]:	
Product	Market a particular product or brand
"Institutional"	Enhance organizational image
Advertorial	Present organization's position
Channel [in what way]:	
Print	Newspapers, magazines
Broadcast	Television, radio
Direct	Mail, billboards, and handbills
Audience: [to whom]:	
Consumer (national, regional, local)	Aimed at final consumer
Trade (national, regional, local)	Aimed at organizational buyer

The sponsor of an advertisement may be the manufacturer of a product, a wholesaler or retailer of a product, or an individual. The content of the advertising message may be product-related—promotion of a particular product to build brand loyalty, to explain product usage and/ or new features. The purpose may be institutional—to enhance the image of the organization. For example, a firm might stress its good citizenship and contributions to its community, a trade association might promote the role of its industry in the economic system, and even states and nations advertise for tourists and industry locations. A third type of message that is becoming increasingly prominent today is the *advertorial* which presents the organization's position on a social issue. Exhibit 10-10 is an example of this type of message content.

In general, there are three channels through which the message reaches the audience: print, principally newspapers and magazines; broadcast, radio and television; and direct advertising, mail and/or billboards. Choice of channel is particularly important since the channel used will determine, to a large extent, the type of audience to be reached. Customers, the target audience, can also be subdivided in many ways. The major categories are final consumers and intermediate customers (organizational buyers).

Publicity

In contrast to paid advertising, information about an organization can be disseminated without organizational sponsorship. When such communications affect demand for the organization's product, they are called publicity. The distinction between advertising and publicity is that the former is paid for by an identified sponsor and the latter is not.

This distinction is clear in concept, but becomes a bit blurred in fact.

Exhibit 10-10   Advertorial Advertising

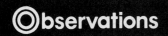

Shark-bait. The terrifying motion picture "Jaws" probably caused millions of Americans to scan the oceans apprehensively before venturing into the water last summer. But the truth is that even death by bee sting is more likely than being eaten by a shark. An

estimated 120 Americans were killed last year by lightning, yet worldwide there were no more than 50 recorded attacks by sharks, and less than a third of these attacks were fatal.

As oil people, we sympathize with the owners of beach cottages, hotels and water-ski shops who suffered from the "Jaws" exaggerations. We know from experience how quickly movies, TV and the press can establish fiction as fact—and how hard it is to correct the damage to one's reputation from untruths. A sample of the problem:

We were "Jawed" by Jack Anderson. Oil company profits, said this columnist recently, are "more fabulous than the pirate treasures of the Blackbeard era." He said that Mobil made "$3.6 billion net profit" last year. He was not only wrong; he overstated our actual net income by more than $2.5 billion.

Chewed out by Senator Jackson. We've grown accustomed to distortion. Remember Senator Jackson's charge, during the gasoline-line months of early 1974, that oil companies were making "obscene profits"? Sure you do, because the words were catchy, and the media gave this unsupported assertion wide coverage. But who recalls the facts which eventually emerged? Mobil last year earned a profit of roughly 2¢ per gallon of product sold. In first-half 1975, profit ran about 1.4¢ per gallon. Our annualized rate of return on average assets during this period was about 5.3 percent, the lowest in 15 years. Profit must go up to attract the hundreds of billions of investment dollars the industry will need to find new U.S. oil and gas and reduce dependence on imported petroleum.

"I HOOKED HIM WITH MY LAST COLUMN"

And now, dismemberment?

A bill introduced by a group of Senators would break up an estimated 22 oil companies on the charge that a few large firms now control the industry. Since when is 22 a "few"? Sure, the industry has large companies, but no one company has more than eight percent of the gasoline market. The industry is much less concentrated than such others as steel, autos or network TV. At last count, there were some 8,000 petroleum producers, about 135 refining companies, and more than 3,000 marketing companies and wholesalers.

Besides, in an age when energy investments have to be enormous (one offshore producing platform recently cost more than $300 million), America is *lucky* to have companies big enough to invest big, so the oil will be there when consumers need it. It takes companies of such great size to find, produce and process the 47 million barrels of oil that are needed each day by the U.S. and the rest of the non-communist world.

It's been a bellyfull. Our battle to get the facts straight has been frustrating at times . . . Remember, for example, those pictures in *Life* of the 1969 Santa Barbara, California, oil spill? Actually, there have been only four serious spills out of some 19,000 U.S. offshore wells drilled, and none resulted in permanent damage to the environment. But the publicity made government stall on authorizing new offshore drilling, helping to create today's overdependence on foreign oil . . . And what about those sensational TV and newspaper charges, during the oil embargo, that the oil companies were holding tankers of oil offshore, waiting for prices to go up. Investigation by the Coast Guard and Federal Energy Administration showed this to be *totally false*. Yet many people never heard that—and the story still haunts us.

Most critics aren't sharks, of course. We know that. And no- body's perfect, including oil companies. But while we recognize our critics' right to chew us out when we're wrong, we do wish they'd stick to facts. Because facts are what people need to make rational decisions on energy. And few things are more important to America than that.

This column appeared in *The New York Times* and other newspapers on Sunday, October 26, 1975. © 1975 Mobil Oil Corporation. Courtesy Mobil Oil Corporation.

It is possible, for example, for information about an organization to be disseminated because it is news. Examples here are numerous: the Justice Department's antitrust suit against International Business Machines (IBM) Corporation, and the actions of the Great Atlantic and Pacific Tea Company in recent years in lowering prices. An organization may be newsworthy because it has contributed a substantial sum to an educational institution or charity, or because it has suffered a disaster, or because it has invented a new product or process, or because its advertising has been questioned by the Federal Trade Commission, or it has announced the building of a new plant, or because consumers have boycotted it, etc. Such information is not necessarily promotion (persuasive communication), but it may affect the opinions and attitudes of potential customers.

For this reason, more and more organizations are realizing that information about the organization can interact with other promotional activities, and, therefore, should be carefully managed. Information favorable to the organization or its product may be more readily accepted by the potential consumer if it is presented as news rather than advertising—the consumer is more likely to regard it as objective information, rather than as persuasive communication. Many organizations have publicists who write news stories and submit them to newspapers, magazines, radio and television stations, in hopes that they will be published or broadcast. Public relations people also represent the organization when unfavorable events occur, e.g., disaster, and/or accusations of wrongdoing.

Publicity is not costless advertising, but a type of promotional activity that must be managed. While activities associated with publicity are not typically considered to be within the marketing function, they logically could be. Most of the decisions associated with publicity management are quite similar to decisions concerning advertising campaign strategy and management. The preceding discussion provides background for a brief look at the development of an advertising campaign.

The Advertising Campaign

The basic purpose of any advertising campaign is to advance the customer through stages in the buying process. Advertising campaign decisions can be divided into two major categories—message and media—for purpose of discussion, but in an actual situation both types of decisions must be considered more or less simultaneously.

The Message. What the advertisement says is perhaps the crucial determinant of the success of the campaign. The advertising message is promotion and, therefore, should be designed to persuade the reader or viewer to formulate the attitudes and/or take the action advocated in the advertisement. Creating effective advertising messages is an art, a job for professionals. The tasks, including writing advertising copy, designing page layouts for print advertisement, and visual and aural backgrounds for broadcast advertisements, require specialized abilities and experience. A discussion of these tasks is beyond the scope of this book, but the interested reader is referred to a text on advertising, such as Sandage and Fryburger.

From the managerial point of view, this creative work must complement the theme and advance the objectives of the campaign. A controversy on this point in advertising circles today is whether the creativity of the theme or its position with respect to competitive advertising is the determinant of a successful campaign. The argument of the positionists is overviewed in Exhibit 10-11. Predictably, *positioning* has been attacked as a fad, and Messrs. Trout and Ries have been accused of using the positioning concept to promote their own advertising agency. The most significant criticism of the positioning concept seems to be that it substitutes consumer share-of-mind for creative copy writing. As illustrated in Exhibit 10-12, for example, Greenland contends that even the best positioned ads would have little impact upon the consumer's mind if they were not creatively phrased.

The creativity versus positioning argument has stirred considerable controversy in advertising trade journals. Clearly, however, the most successful advertisements have both. And advertising is supported by other promotional tools when appropriate, and by other types of marketing effort. In short, stripped of its verbiage and elements of faddism, the positioning controversy is essentially an affirmation of the concept of market segmentation—a concept which we noted in Chapter 7 is becoming increasingly fundamental to successful marketing management.

Media. After the message decision, the decision maker faces media choices. As noted above, these choices are print (newspapers, magazines), broadcast (radio, television), and direct (mail, billboards, etc.). In light of the advertising objectives and message, therefore, the media decision is twofold: choice of type of media in which to insert the advertisement, and the timing of the insertion.

Each of the types of media have certain characteristics, which may be either advantages or limitations for a particular advertisement. Exhibit 10-

Theme	Creative copy
7-Up is not a Cola.	"The UnCola"
Let us drive you in our bus instead of driving your car.	"Take the bus, and leave the driving to us."
Shop by turning the pages of the telephone directory.	"Let your fingers do the walking."
If you drink a lot of beer, Schaefer is a good beer to drink	"The beer to have when you're having more than one."
We don't rent as many cars, so we have to do more for our customers.	"We try harder."

Exhibit 10-12   Examples of Advertising Creativity

Adapted from Leo Greenland, "Is This the Era of Positioning?" *Advertising Age*, 29 May 1972.

13 briefly reviews these characteristics of the major types of media. In choosing the medium which best serves the advertising objectives and budget already specified, the decision maker must evaluate the characteristics of the different media types. One basic criterion for this evaluation is cost per exposure—the total cost of the advertisement divided by the number of people who are exposed to it. Newspaper advertising, for example, is quoted on the basis of the *mill line rate,* i.e., the cost per line per one million circulation; television advertisements are evaluated on the basis of cost per thousand viewers. The cost-per-exposure criterion is crude, but easily measured. Many media choices are based on this criterion alone.

Improvements in the cost-per-exposure criterion can take two forms: effectiveness and efficiency. Effectiveness essentially involves improving the impact of the advertisement upon the target audience. One method is to select the medium which best presents the message. For example, deliciously prepared foods can be best presented on television, while products requiring lengthy explanations need print media. Color reproduction is better in magazines than in newspapers, and television is superior to radio in terms of involving the listener or viewer in the commercial. The second method of improving the effectiveness of media selection is to use the medium which best reaches the target audience. For example, direct mail can be sent to precisely the desired consumers, provided that a list of their addresses is known. Advertisements for products used primarily by males, e.g., beer, shaving articles and automobiles, are often featured on sports programs on radio and television.

On the other hand, the efficiency of media selection might be improved by considering the total production cost. While the cost per thousand of a television commercial might be low, organizations with limited funds for advertising expenditures may be forced to rule out television. Another consideration of efficiency is production lead time. Advertisements for magazines must be prepared several months in

Exhibit 10-13 Characteristics of Major Advertising Media

Print

Newspapers—local coverage; short production time; low cost per exposure; permits relatively long messages; can use some color; mass appeal.

Magazines—audience can be general or specialized; require relatively long lead time; cost varies with type of magazine; permits lengthy messages; effective use of color photographs; appeals can be tailored.

Broadcast

Radio—local coverage; relatively short production time; relatively low cost per exposure; generally mass appeal; message must be short; no permanent message.

Television—national or local coverage; relatively long (and expensive) production; relatively expensive (although exposure is high); permits dramatic messages; messages short and nonpermanent.

Direct

Mail—Selective coverage with mailing lists; short production time; relatively expensive to pinpoint prospects; appeals can be tailored; difficult to hold prospect's attention.

Billboards—national or local coverage; relatively long production time; relatively inexpensive; message must be very brief.

advance, and the production of television advertisements is quite time consuming. Newspaper ads, on the other hand, can be prepared rather quickly and cheaply, and inserted and taken out again relatively easily.

The second type of media decision relates to the timing of the advertisement. Grocery advertisements, for example, are often inserted in newspapers on Thursdays to provide information that consumers need for their weekly shopping trips. And billboards often advertise nearby gasoline service stations or restaurants. Some products are seasonal in nature: lawn care equipment in the spring, and camping and hunting equipment in the fall. Beyond these rather obvious examples, there is considerable difference of opinion among advertising professionals as to the timing of a series of advertisements. If four advertisements are to be placed during a given month, should they be spaced one per week, or concentrated at the beginning or end of the month, or should some more complex pattern be employed? This type of question cannot usually be answered in general terms; the objective to be achieved by the advertising campaign must be considered. For example, brand awareness might best be achieved with a concentrated burst at the beginning of the period, while reminder advertising might be most effective if spaced evenly throughout the period.

Campaign Implementation: The Advertising Agency. Implementation of the campaign involves such mundane but necessary tasks as producing the message (writing, recording, and filming), and planning and scheduling

Exhibit 10-14   A Brief Profile of Advertising Agencies

An advertising agency is an organization that performs various promotion activities for client firms. These activities are usually classified as *research* (analysis of audience characteristics and desires), *creative* (development of the message), *media* (selection of media, placement and timing of messages), and *services* (public relations, sales promotion, management advice). The agency is generally organized according to these functions, plus sales (agency salesmen are generally called account executives).

The phrase "Madison Avenue" generally refers to the work of advertising agencies, particularly those in New York and Chicago. Despite its pervasive influence upon American life, the world of Madison Avenue is rather small. In 1971, there were only 6,000 agencies in the U. S. They handled 45 percent of total U. S. advertising expenditures—approximately $9 billion. And the ten largest agencies (J. Walter Thompson; McCann-Erickson; Young and Rubicam; Ted Bates; Leo Burnett; Batton, Barton, Durstine, and Osborne; Ogilvy and Mather; Doyle Dane Bernbach; Grey Advertising; and Foote, Cone and Belding) accounted for 30 percent of this total. These ten agencies employed only 13,600 people in 1971.

Moreover, agencies are under attack from several quarters. Some companies have formed their own *in-house* agencies, and many clients are seeking to dismantle the traditional 15 percent commission system—basis of most agency compensation. Furthermore, the agencies' concentration and visibility make them a natural target for the Federal Trade Commission and other public policy makers.

Consequently, there will be changes in advertising agencies. But they are not likely to disappear, because they can provide expertise and support for an organization's promotion activities. These services are products for which a market will continue to exist.

Compiled by the author from various sources, including Carol J. Loomis, "Those Throbbing Headaches on Madison Avenue," *Fortune,* February, 1972, p. 103ff.

the media advertising. The fundamental implementation decision is *make-or-buy*, that is, whether to do a task internally, or to have someone outside the organization do it. Examples outside the promotion area include such questions as: Shall we commit corporate resources to a research and development program or shall we lease patent rights? And shall we manufacture a certain machine part or shall we subcontract the manufacture of that part to another firm?

For the campaign, the make-or-buy decision involves the use of organizational personnel versus engaging an advertising agency. Exhibit 10-14 overviews the activities of such agencies. Basically, the agencies offer professional expertise—specialized training, broad knowledge, and in-depth experience with advertising problems. A second benefit of outside agencies derives from the agency's lack of involvement of the day-to-day affairs of the organization—it can bring to the campaign a problem-solving approach not distorted by routine tasks, and relatively uninfluenced by prior approaches, personality differences, or organization politics. Third, agencies permit division-of-labor economies—the agency is hired when needed, and is not on the payroll when its services are not required.

On the other hand, agencies have certain limitations. First, their employment may be detrimental to the morale of people inside the organization who feel that they can handle the promotional program.

Moreover, the agency has other interests. These interests may at times conflict with the interests of the particular organization, or they may simply leave insufficient time to devote to the organization's program. Finally, the agency costs are out-of-pocket costs. While it is true that division-of-labor economies accrue from the use of outside specialists, they are hired with actual dollars. If the organization allows internal personnel to handle the project, additional expenses may not necessarily be of the hard-cash variety.

Advertising Management

According to economic theory, the purpose of advertising, indeed all promotion, is to shift the demand curve to the right, i.e., to increase demand for the product at all price levels, ceteris paribus. The problem is that other factors are not equal. Other marketing mix decisions (product quality, packaging, branding, channel selection, shipping and delivery), supplier factors (raw materials deliveries, manufacturing quality control, credit policies), and societal factors (competitors' actions, decisions by government regulatory bodies, general economic conditions, and so forth), influence consumer demand. Consequently, management of advertising activities is particularly difficult because it is so hard to measure the results of advertising decisions. The crux of the matter is summarized in a statement attributed to department store mogul John Wanamaker and others:

> I know that half of what I spend on advertising is wasted, but I do not know which half.

In practice, advertising is a particularly creative and intuitive field. Advertising management sets two basic parameters within which creativity and intuition are allowed to operate: advertising objectives and the budget. The effectiveness of advertising is measured with respect to these parameters.

Objectives. In making advertising decisions, the marketing manager may have any number of objectives in mind. For example, the purpose of a particular advertisement or advertising campaign may range from the introduction of a new product or brand to reminders that a popular brand is still available, from general corporate image building to the sale of a particular product, from information to assist the salesperson in getting in to see a prospect to accomplishing the actual sale itself through return mail. Advertisements, therefore, must be related specifically to particular objectives. In general, objectives can be discussed in terms of relationships with customers, the organization, and society.

One factor governing the objective of an advertisement or an advertising campaign is the stage in the buying process of the customer or the target market. In the first stage—recognition of want or desire—the purpose of the advertisement might be simply to make the customer aware of a particular problem or desire. Texas Instruments, a calculator manufacturer, might sponsor an advertisement demonstrating the frustrations of preparing a tax return by hand, and Palmolive dishwashing detergent ads might emphasize that dishwashing can result in red and roughened hands. In the search stage, the advertising objective is to show that the product can satisfy the want or desire perceived in the first stage: *a calculator is efficient* and *Palmolive is mild.* Advertising objectives for other stages of the buying process are similarly interpreted. (You might test your understanding of this discussion by identifying the objectives of other advertisements with respect to the buying process.) It is particularly instructive to compare the advertisements for different brands of a particular product. For example, advertisements for the soft drink Dr. Pepper urge viewers to try it (the purchase stage), apparently on the assumption that consumers who try the product will like it. Coca-Cola, on the other hand, emphasizes the favorable evaluation of its product by consumers (". . . it's the real thing").

In addition to relating advertising objectives to customer considerations, advertising must also complement the objectives of other marketing managers, and managers of other functions in the organization. A graphic example is provided here by the turnabout in advertising by the major oil companies. Until the early 1970s, petroleum advertising stressed increased product usage as well as brand loyalty. But the energy shortage forced the companies to change their basic objectives, and consequently their marketing objectives—including advertising. Current oil company advertisements are more of the institutional, image-building nature—stressing the companies' determination to overcome the energy shortage, and suggesting ways in which consumers could use petroleum products most efficiently.

Similarly, advertising objectives must be coordinated with other marketing mix elements. The advertisement that exhorts consumers to *rush right out to your store and buy this new item* will not be very effective if sufficient supplies of that item have not yet been delivered to the store. In addition, advertising claims of product reliability and high performance can be contradicted by inferior workmanship and poor quality control.

Advertising objectives must also conform substantially to the desires of society. As we noted in Chapter 4 on public policy, society's interest in the truthfulness of information content of advertising has risen rapidly in recent years. Various citizens groups, including Nader's Raiders and the Boston-based Action for Children's Television (ACT), have been highly critical of some advertising. And the Federal Trade Commission has focused its activities in the area of regulation of advertising. Moreover, several industry groups have established standards for their advertising, and are paying particular attention to these standards today. The trade journal *Advertising Age,* for example, regularly features a column entitled, "Ads We Can Do Without," those with questionable taste or ethics.

In short, decisions implementing advertising objectives can be quite involved. A first step, however, is to formulate the objectives that are stated in operational terms. If, for example, brand awareness is the objective, a statement such as, "Achieve brand recognition by 20 percent of the viewers of *The Johnny Carson Show* by the end of the year," provides specific guidelines for the development of the advertising campaign to meet these objectives.

Advertising Budget. The second parameter of advertising management is the total budget allocated to the particular advertising campaign. Exhibit 10-15 shows the advertising budgets for selected leading advertisers in the United States in 1975. This table indicates that advertising is of primary importance to consumer products companies—the larger budgets, in dollars and percentages, are allocated by companies marketing products to final consumers, and most have rather lengthy channels of distribution. Some important facts, however, are not shown in this table. For example, Sears, Roebuck and Company spends considerably more on advertising than does Procter & Gamble Company. Exhibit 10-15 shows only expenditures on national advertising; Sears' local advertising is not included in the total. Second, the United States government is in tenth place in total advertising expenditures. Of course, the government is the recipient of large amounts of free public service advertising ("Mail Early" and "Register in January if you are an alien."), but advertising campaigns to support such marketing efforts as the all-volunteer army have caused the government's advertising expenditures to rise rapidly.

Budgeting of advertising is a very important decision for marketing management—four methods are commonly used: percentage-of-sales, follow competition, use all available funds, and match objectives and tasks.

Perhaps the most commonly used method of determining the advertising budget is to allocate a percentage of sales to advertising. This method is widely accepted, because it is extremely easy to implement. But it is logically indefensible—it says that advertising is a result, not a cause, of sales. As we noted in our discussion of forecasting in Chapter 7, levels of marketing effort (including advertising) should logically be determined before sales forecasts are made. Moreover, the percentage-of-sales method says nothing about how the total advertising appropriation is to be allocated among territories or products.

The second budgeting method—following competitors' budgeting decisions—has essentially the same strengths and weaknesses. It is easy to

Exhibit 10-15 1975 Budgets of
Selected Leading Advertisers

Rank and Company	Advertising	Sales	Advertising as Percent of Sales
Cars			
2 General Motors Corp.	$225,000,000	$35,724,911,215	0.6
15 Chrysler Corp.	98,200,000	7,589,404,581	1.3
18 Ford Motor Co.	91,000,000	24,099,100,000	0.4
63 Volkswagen of America	37,750,000	7,450,762,143	0.5
71 American Motors Corp.	32,915,200	2,282,199,000	1.4
Soaps, cleansers (and allied)			
1 Procter & Gamble Co.	360,000,000	4,550,000,000	7.9
11 Colgate-Palmolive Co.	108,000,000	1,100,000,000	9.8
21 Lever Bros.	85,000,000	747,500,000	11.0
65 S. C. Johnson & Son	36,000,000	287,000,000	12.5
83 Clorox Co.	26,675,000	721,505,000	3.7
Tobacco			
9 R. J. Reynolds Industries Inc.	113,600,000	4,837,643,000	2.3
14 Philip Morris Inc.	99,500,000	3,642,414,000	2.7
27 American Brands	74,000,000	4,055,300,000	1.8
43 Brown & Williamson Tobacco Co.	57,000,000	1,523,100,000	3.7
48 Liggett Group Inc.	53,000,000	812,974,000	6.5
Drugs and cosmetics			
5 Bristol-Myers Co.	170,000,000	1,827,669,000	9.3
6 Warner-Lambert Co.	169,000,000	1,218,134,000	13.9
7 American Home Products	138,000,000	2,408,919,000	5.7
16 Richardson-Merrell	94,472,000	658,691,000	14.3
22 Gillette Co.	84,000,000	1,406,906,000	6.0
Retail chains			
2 Sears, Roebuck & Co.†	225,000,000	11,555,947,000	1.9
34 J. C. Penney Co.	68,000,000	7,678,600,000	0.9
Chemicals			
27 American Cyanamid Co.	74,000,000	1,157,066,000	6.4
68 Union Carbide Corp.	35,468,000	3,738,900,000	0.9
Photographic equipment			
46 Eastman Kodak Co.	55,200,000	4,958,536,000	1.1
76 Polaroid Corp.	30,500,000	812,703,000	3.8
Oil			
8 Mobil Oil Corp.	135,900,000	27,178,955,000	0.5
78 Exxon Corp.	30,170,000	48,761,000,000	0.1
99 Shell Oil Co.	18,500,000	8,244,466,000	0.2

†Does not include local advertising

Reprinted from *Advertising Age*, 23 August, 1976, p. 28, with permission of the publisher.

implement, and it does tend to minimize competition via advertising. But it also has no logical foundation. In the first place, the competitor being followed may have no better idea of the ultimate advertising appropriation. Second, it is not likely that the organization's objectives will be exactly the same as those of the competitor copied.

The third decision rule is to allocate all available funds to advertising. The argument advanced in support of this method is essentially that returns from advertising are vast (potentially infinite) whereas returns from allocating organizational funds to any other activities, e.g., reducing manufacturing or distribution costs, are limited. This is true in concept, but this method does not relate advertising expenditures to organizational objectives. If, for example, funds are "tight" in a given period, the advertising budget will be cut. This may be the very time, however, when advertising can be most helpful in augmenting revenues. Moreover, it is not possible under this method to do any long-range planning about advertising decision making.

The fourth commonly used method of setting the advertising budget is to define the objectives that advertising should accomplish, and then appropriate the budget needed to achieve these objectives. This method, therefore, essentially "builds up" the total advertising budget, rather than determining the total and then dividing it among possible objectives, as the other three methods do. This method is certainly more logical than the first three, but it may result in a total appropriation larger than the company can afford. This method may also produce an advertising budget that costs more than the revenues it produces. And since it requires specification of objectives, it is more difficult and, therefore, expensive to implement than the other methods mentioned.

Measuring Advertising Effectiveness. All of these commonly accepted methods for appropriating advertising have defects. The defects derive principally from the difficulty in measuring the effectiveness of advertising. Ideally, most organizations would like to assess the effectiveness of advertising relative to their basic objective—profits or sales in the case of economic organizations. The problem, however, is that many factors other than advertising contribute to sales and profit levels. If, therefore, a new advertising campaign is implemented and sales rise, there is some question that the rise in sales can be attributed to the new campaign. At the other extreme, those aspects of advertising which are most subject to measurement, e.g., respondent recall of advertising copy, recognition of brand names, and identification of advertising slogans—are pretty far removed from sales and profits. The fact that a consumer can repeat an advertising jingle word-for-word may say nothing at all about the consumer's desire for the product mentioned in the jingle.

To be sure, some successes in measuring the effectiveness of advertis-

Exhibit 10-16 Measuring the Effectiveness of Advertising

General Motors used the following buying process model to measure the effectiveness of an advertising campaign for the Watusi automobile:

Unawareness
↓
Awareness
↓
Buying Class
↓
Consideration Class
↓
First Choice

Unawareness—respondent does not remember the name of the automobile.
Awareness—respondent remembers the name of the automobile.
Buying Class—all brands that the respondent considers to be competitive, whether he regards them favorably or unfavorably.
Consideration Class—brands to which the respondent will give favorable consideration next time he enters the market.
First Choice—respondent will consider the Watusi his first choice next time he enters the market.

A panel of consumers was interviewed at several points in time; this panel provided a basis for determining changes in consumer preferences and tracing these to actual sales behavior.

The table shows the results.

The study indicates that five percent of the people in the panel considered Watusi their "first choice," and that 56 percent of these people (First choice preference level) actually purchased a Watusi within the following six-month period of time. This study enabled GM to estimate the economic value of moving a person through the stages of the buying process.

Adapted from Gail Smith, "How GM Measures Ad Effectiveness," *Printer's Ink*, 14 May 1965, pp. 19–29.

Preference Level	Actual Preference	Sales Behavior for Each Preference Level (for next six months)
Watusi first choice	5%	56% of 5%
Watusi in consideration class	7%	22% of 7%
Watusi in buying class	8%	9% of 8%
Aware of Watusi	14%	5% of 14%
Not aware of Watusi	66%	4% of 66%
	100%	

ing, and, therefore, in providing guidelines for advertising budget-setting, have been reported. One of the best known is the General Motors research on the Watusi automobile, which is presented in Exhibit 10-16. In general, these successes have employed relatively sophisticated decision-making procedures, e.g., linear programming, decision theory and simulation. Moreover, they are generally relatively expensive, and are limited specifically to the situation for which they were developed. They treat advertising expenditures as investment—quite logical, as Dean points out in Exhibit 10-17—but contrary to prevailing income tax laws.

SALES PROMOTION

As we noted at the beginning of the chapter, the term *sales promotion* is a catchall—any promotion effort not classed as personal selling, advertising, or publicity, is sales promotion. Thus, sales promotion is a difficult area to describe, but it is one that cannot be ignored. It is a part of the total promotional mix of most organizations, and may account for more than half of total promotional expenditures in some organizations. We look first at the nature, and then at the management, of sales promotion.

The Nature of Sales Promotion

Since sales promotion is traditionally defined in terms of what it is not, discussions of what it is usually begin with examples. Exhibit 10-18 presents a fairly comprehensive list.

Sales promotions to consumers are many and varied. Almost everyone has at one time or another received a free sample of a product, generally through the mail. Considerable evidence indicates that new soaps, detergents, toothpastes, and other packaged goods are tried and subsequently purchased much more often if product samples supplement national advertising. Coupons in newspapers and magazines have a similar, if less dramatic, effect. A new wrinkle here is the sending of coupon sets for various products through the mail. Magazine order-form inserts, which can be torn out and sent to the magazine as subscription requests or to order other merchandise, are also increasing in popularity.

In the supermarket, "three cents off" moves a lot of soap and

Consumer Promotions	Channel Promotions
Product samples: giving away product to induce trial	Bonus: extra cash payment for sales
Coupon: certificate that reduces price	PM (Premium or Push Money): bonus on certain brand
Magazine tear-out order forms	Consignment: manufacturer finances distributor inventories
Cents-off promotion: reduction in regular price	Contests: prizes to best sales effort in a given period
Premium: small extra "gift" with product	Cooperative advertising: manufacturer and distributor share advertising costs
Competition: sweepstakes, contests, etc.	Dealer-listed promotion: manufacturer's ad that lists distributor
Demonstrations: showing of product in use	Point-of-purchase displays: counter-top racks, posters, mechanized signs
Brochures and leaflets Trading stamps	Trade shows and conventions

Exhibit 10-18 Examples of Sales Promotion Activities

Adapted by the author from various sources, including John F. Luick and William L. Ziegler, *Sales Promotion and Modern Merchandising* (New York: McGraw-Hill, 1968); Philip Kotler, *Marketing Management: Analysis, Planning and Control,* 2nd ed., (Englewood Cliffs, N.J.: Prentice Hall, 1972), pp. 649–52; and Roger A. Strang, "Sales Promotion—Fast Growth, Faulty Management," Harvard Business Review, (July-August, 1976), p. 123. Copyright © 1976 by the President and Fellows of Harvard College; all rights reserved.

detergent. So do the little paring knives and other premiums attached to the box. And the consumer can register for a chance to win a Hawaiian vacation or a new car. In-store demonstrations of new types of food products or of appliances in operation have proved effective, as have brochures and leaflets announcing special sales or inviting credit applications. At the cash register, many consumers do not feel that their shopping trip is complete if they do not receive their green stamps—which they assiduously paste into books to redeem for merchandise.

Sales promotions to intermediate customers are equally diverse, but they fall basically into two categories: price reductions and customer-promotion aids. Price reductions may be in the form of bonuses, premiums for sales of certain products, inventory financing through consignment, and prizes for sales above quota. Consumer-promotion aids may take the form of cooperative advertising, in which the manufacturer shares the cost of advertising with the middleman; or in some cases pays the total cost. Manufacturers provide many types of point-of-purchase materials. A third type of sales promotion to channel members is the trade show or convention in which manufacturers display their wares at gatherings of middlemen.

This diverse assortment of promotional tools is playing an increasingly large role in the total promotional programs in many organizations. Although differences in definitions make comparisons difficult, sales promotion activity in the United States appears to be both larger than advertising expenditures and rising at a faster rate. The vice president of one packaged goods manufacturer reported that the ratio of the sales promotion budget to the advertising budget in the early 1970s was two to one. Clearly, sales promotion activities should be carefully managed.

Management of Sales Promotion
The increasing importance of sales promotion in the total promotion mix may pass unnoticed in many organizations because sales promotion expenditures are not recorded separately. In some organizations these expenditures are included in the advertising budget; in others, they are part of sales force expenses. In other cases, the extra product required for a bonus pack may be recorded as a manufacturing expense, or the cost of special labels may be charged to packaging. The loss of revenue from a temporary price reduction may not be noted at all.

As with advertising, the problems with managing sales promotion relate to diverse objectives and unsophisticated budgeting procedures. For example, Strang's research ("Sales Promotion—Fast Growth, Faulty Management") indicates that advertising and promotion interact to produce higher sales than an equivalent investment in either alone. Yet, "synergy" is seldom a stated objective, advertising and promotion budgets may be prepared independently, and the budgeting procedure is seldom carefully considered. As one of Strang's respondents described it, the usual approach is likely to be, "How much did we have to spend last year? How much have we got to spend this year? How will we cut it up?"

This cavalier approach to so important an activity can lead to serious problems, such as the trade war described in Exhibit 10-19. Strang suggests, and other authorities concur, that sales promotion deserves at least as much managerial attention as advertising. The managerial concerns appear to be similar: setting objectives, budgeting to achieve those objectives, testing various sales promotions alternatives beforehand, and measuring their effectiveness afterward. In fact, all elements of the promotional mix need to be coordinated and integrated into the marketing program.

PROMOTION DECISIONS AND PROGRAM INTEGRATION
Promotion decisions, like others in the marketing program, derive ideally from target market selection and organizational and marketing plans to satisfy that market. These decisions focus upon designing an appropriate

Exhibit 10-19   No One Wins a Sales Promotion War

Strang reports that an experienced marketing executive documented the history of a trade promotion war that cut profits for the major competitors. He did not identify the market, but Strang thought it was that of a frequently purchased consumer good.

In 1969 the market was growing at twice the population rate and three brands accounted for 55% of total sales. In the following year, a new brand manager for the smallest of these brands decided to try to increase sales by reducing advertising and offering higher trade allowances. This tactic led to an initial increase in sales, but it also led to a response from competitors.

Over the next two years, cycles of response and counter response saw promotion increase by 450% and advertising decrease by 38%. The net result for all three brands together was: a 3% increase in total sales, a 1.4% drop in market share, and a 35% decline in profits, as the figure shows.

Source: Roger A. Strang, "Sales Promotion—Fast Growth, Faulty Management." *Harvard Business Review,* (July–August, 1976), pp. 115–124.

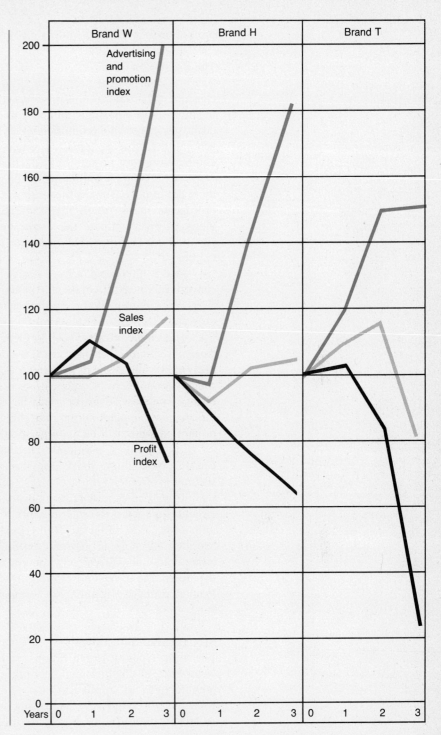

promotion mix and then integrating that mix into the marketing program.

The Promotion Mix

The basic purpose of promotion is ultimately to persuade customers to consume the organization's products. The customer, therefore, is perhaps the most important single influence upon the promotion mix. Exhibit 10-20 illustrates possible promotion mixes for different types of customers. In general, the more potential customers there are, the greater will be the emphasis on mass promotion—advertising and publicity—and the less the emphasis upon personal selling. If the product is widely consumed, i.e., if there are almost as many customers in the purchase stage of the buying process as there are in the want recognition stage, mass promotion methods will dominate the entire promotion mix. This describes the situation for a household products manufacturer such as Procter & Gamble.

On the other hand, a Ford dealer has many potential customers, but converts relatively few of these to actual purchasers of the product. In such a case, the nature of the promotion mix will change as the customer progresses through the stages in the buying process.

A defense contractor such as General Dynamics faces yet a different customer situation. It has very few customers, and these customers are likely to become aware of the need for new equipment through publicity— congressional hearings, publications of economic growth statistics and so forth. Some mass advertising may be useful in the search stage, primarily for corporate image-building, but the major emphasis in the contractors' promotional mix will be upon personal selling, and service after the sale.

For a political candidate (President Carter is surely one of this decade's outstanding marketing success stories), the customer's *buying decision* is of crucial importance, so the timing of promotional efforts is significant. The candidate relies primarily upon publicity at first, but as election time nears, he may rely upon mass advertising, direct mail and billboards, and publicity. Right before election day, he may spend considerable time in personal selling—handshaking, speaking before groups, etc., and will also rely upon broadcast media to some extent. After the "sale," the usage and evaluation stage of the buying process will be handled primarily by publicity, perhaps with some direct mail to constituents.

Mix/Program Integration

For some types of organizations, promotion decisions must also take cognizance of channel members other than customers. For example, a manufacturer of appliances may grant advertising allowances to or participate in cooperative advertising with his middlemen. Manufacturers of grocery products often employ missionary salespersons—whose per-

Exhibit 10-20   Promotion Alternatives at Various Stages of the Buying Process for Different Products

Stages in Buying Process	Household Products Manufacturer (P&G)	Automobile Dealer (Ford)	Defense Contractor (General Dynamics)	Political Candidate (Jimmy Carter)
1. Want Recognition	mass advertising coupons, samples	mass advertising	publicity (congressional hearings)	publicity
2. Search	mass advertising, packaging, branding	mass advertising, personal selling	publicity, personal selling	mass advertising, direct mail and billboards, publicity
3. Purchase Decision	mass advertising, price promotions	personal selling, price promotions	personal selling	personal selling, mass advertising
4. Use and Evaluation	mass advertising	personal selling, service, publicity	personal selling, service, publicity	publicity, direct mail

sonal selling job is not to take orders, but to maintain smooth and cordial relations with channel members. The promotion program may also have an effect upon other types of intermediaries, e.g., banks that provide working capital, and potential company investors.

The promotion mix must be coordinated with other elements of the marketing program. Product features, performance record, warranties, stage of product life cycle, and so forth, must be carefully studied to develop promotional appeals that communicate product strengths. Similarly, price quotes must be accurate, and promotion must be coordinated with distribution. Nothing is more frustrating to a salesperson than to promise delivery by a certain date, and then find that the shipping department will be unable to meet that commitment.

Internal and external supply constraints must also be considered. An organization that desires rapid growth must invest heavily in promotion, particularly if it tries to compete on a national scale. Moreover, the firm's image is to a large extent shaped by its promotional program, and the promotion program is certainly affected by other functions of the organization. The energy shortage, primarily a production problem, caused oil companies and power companies to change the theme of their advertising from use more to use it wisely.

Promotion decisions should take into account the promotional activities of competitors. For example, it used to be considered bad form in an ethical sense, as well as bad strategy, to mention a competitor by name, but as we noted in the discussion of product positioning earlier in the chapter, many companies have developed what they consider to be successful promotional programs on the basis of direct comparisons with competitors. Avis tries harder than Hertz, Arrid Extra-Dry is better than Ban Roll-on, and the Continental rides better than the Cadillac. Even when competitors are not attacked head-on, their promotion campaigns provide clues that can be used to strengthen the organization's promotional program. (Listerine tastes bad, so use Scope).

Promotion decisions must also take cognizance of societal factors. We noted in Chapter 4 that the Federal Trade Commission and other government agencies are closely scrutinizing advertising these days. In fact, a new word has entered the advertising lexicon. It is *legaled.* Chuck Blore, a leading advertising executive, noted (*Business Week*, July 10,-1972, p. 50), "We used to get a client's O.K. before a commercial went on the air. Now, it gets on only after each part has been legaled. The script is legaled, the tapes are legaled, and so on . . . no one questions anything. If legal says change it, you change it." Exhibit 10-21 overviews public policy affecting promotion decisions.

Finally, the Supreme Court of the United States may have heralded a fundamental change in the legal aspects of promotion decisions. In May, 1976, it struck down a Virginia law that barred advertising of prescription drug prices. The decision gave "commercial speech" (promotion) a large measure of protection under the First Amendment to the Constitution. This ruling seems to reverse a 1942 ruling in which the Court held that the Constitution places no restraint on the right of the government to proscribe "purely commercial advertising."

Apparently, this decision means that similar restrictions in the laws of more than half the states will be unenforceable. These laws generally forbid advertising prices of such products as eyeglasses, funeral services, and prescription drugs. We may soon witness local price wars over competing brands of such products. And the Court decision may also mean that restrictions against advertising such commodities as cigarettes and liquor may be struck down.

In an area of perhaps larger import, this decision may portend a more definitive ruling on whether free speech applies to the promotion of professional services, e.g., doctors and lawyers. Medical societies and bar associations have for years restricted their members from promoting their services on the grounds that price competition would "lower professional standards in fields where high levels of professionalism are required." If any group of professionals had privately agreed to promote their services, they would have been in violation of the Sherman Antitrust Act. A 1943 Supreme Court decision which still stands, however, immunizes such agreements when they are promulgated by state authorities in the name of the public welfare. Marketing managers will certainly be interested in finding out whether the doctrine of the "consumer's right to know" is sufficient to pierce the professional's shield of antitrust immunity. Promotion decisions are likely to be greatly affected by the marketing opportunities opened up by the Supreme Court in this case.

In short, promotion strategy formulation requires consideration of all

Exhibit 10-21 Public Policy Affecting Promotion Decisions

Promotion is probably the most visible of all marketing mix elements. The impact of public policy upon promotion decisions has increased in recent years. The three major areas are:

1. *Advertising Content*—The Federal Trade Commission Act of 1914 and the Wheeler-Lea amendment of 1938 are the principal vehicles by which public policy regulates advertising content. There are three major categories of such regulation:

(a) *False advertising*—Public policy should prohibit advertising that is simply untrue. The FTC has become much more vigorous in its prosecution of false advertising claims in the 1960s and 1970s. Gone are the shaving cream commercials that used plexiglass instead of sandpaper, the ice cream commercials featuring mashed potatoes, and the marbles in the vegetable soup to cause the vegetables to rise to the top. The advertiser can expect increasingly vigorous enforcement of prohibitions against false advertising.

(b) *Deception*—Advertising that is not necessarily untrue, but which may tend to deceive the consumer, is more difficult to regulate. Here, too, enforcement in the 1960s and 1970s has become more vigorous. The FTC has, for example, ruled that "diet bread" cannot be advertised as having fewer calories simply because the loaf is sliced thinner, or that "Six-month floor wax" is not appropriate unless the wax does last for six months under *typical* conditions. Deception in advertising is a very unsettled area in public policy at the present time. But the general principle appears to be that standards of deception are based upon what would be "deceiving to the public, which includes the ignorant, the unthinking, and the credulous."

(c) *Bait and Switch Advertising*— This is the tactic of advertising an unusually good buy ("three full rooms of furniture for $199"), and then switching the consumer attracted to the store by this advertisement to a more expensive product. This type of advertising is illegal in some states, but the practice is widespread. Recently, the FTC has taken action against advertisers who misrepresent the true nature of their offer, and has issued guidelines designed to curb the use of bait advertising.

2. *Promotional Allowances and Services*—Under Sections 2(d) and 2(e) of the Robinson-Patman Act, sellers must make promotional allowances and services available to all customers on proportionately equal terms. As noted when discussing this act, it is exceedingly complex and difficult to interpret these provisions. Specifically, public policy has not established the meaning of "proportionately equal terms," particularly where large and small customers are involved. Again, the FTC has issued guidelines, and subsequent litigation may clarify the meaning of these sections of the Robinson-Patman Act.

3. *Activities of sales representatives*—Selling activities such as the following are deemed illegal or are often regulated: discriminating against buyers on the basis of race, sex, or creed; bribing buyers, purchasing agents, or other employees of customers; procuring technical or trade secrets of competitors by espionage, bribery, or similar illicit means; disparaging competitors; selling used items as new; offering fake buying advantages; failing to inform buyers of their rights, e.g., the seventy-two hour "cooling off" period; and employing any other "false or misleading representation which deceives or has the capacity to deceive or mislead."

This summary has merely outlined some of the major areas of public policy regulation upon promotion decisions. As we noted earlier in the chapter, the marketing decision maker is well advised to have his promotion decisions *legaled*.

Source: Compiled by the author from various sources, including Gaylord A. Jentz, "Federal Regulation of Advertising," *American Business Law Journal*, January 1968, pp. 409–27; Louis W. Stern and John R. Grabner, Jr., *Competition in the Market Place*, (Chicago: Scott, Foresman and Company, 1970), pp. 126–30, and Ovid Riso, editor, *The Dartnell Sales Manager's Handbook*, 11th edition (The Dartnell Corporation: 1968), p. 320–22.

the factors that affect the entire marketing program, and the integration of promotion decisions with these factors in mind at three levels: among promotion elements (personal selling, advertising, publicity, and sales promotion), with other marketing mix elements (product, price and distribution), and with other organizational objectives and functions. We have reviewed the basic principles here, but promotion mix design and integration must be carefully tailored to each specific situation.

CONCLUDING NOTE

Promotion, from the point of view of most laymen and many marketing students, is the most interesting of all marketing activities. It probably produces the most severe managerial problems. At the macro level, the problem is that promotion, by its very nature, must be visible to the public. The argument that promotion is unnecessary—a view that stems largely from the pure competition model—is not difficult to refute: promotion is a source of product information in the imperfectly competitive markets of the real world. Promotion is also criticized for being wasteful, in that more resources than necessary are devoted to promotional activities. In addition, promotional activities are accused of being misleading, if not in the sense of out-and-out fraud, then in the sense of embellishment and hyperbole. There is some validity to these criticisms, but the fact remains that promotion activities are necessary in an industrial society, and grow increasingly important as society becomes larger and more impersonal.

At the micro or individual firm level, the problems arise from difficulties in obtaining answers to criticisms raised at the macro level. Promotion managers must stop the abuses of the few who engage in illegal activities, and must exercise care and self-restraint in the design and implementation of promotion programs. At the same time, promotional activities must be defended as important and necessary in our industrial society.

The problem, however, is that we know relatively little about how promotion works. We are not entirely sure why one person is a good salesperson and another a poor one, why one advertisement seems to lead to increased sales and another equally entertaining or provocative advertisement does not. In view of its importance at both macro and micro levels, we can expect continued efforts at solving these problems.

For these reasons, promotion is perhaps the most interesting and challenging area for marketing students. Most of the beginning marketing jobs are in personal selling, and a great deal of the glamour attributed to marketing is associated with advertising. Promotional activities represent only one part of total marketing activities, but they may be the most significant part.

KEY TERMS AND CONCEPTS

Definition of Promotion
  persuasive communication
Communication Process
  communicator
  message
  medium
  audience
  feedback
Promotion Message
Promotion Mix
  personal selling
  advertising
  publicity
  sales promotion
The Personal Selling Function
  prospecting
  preparation
  presentation
  post-sale
  supporting duties
Selling Skills
Management of Personal Selling
  recruiting
  training
  motivating
  controlling
  organizing
  supporting

Nature of Advertising
  sponsor
  content
  channels
  audience
Advertising Campaign
  objectives
  message
  media
Advertising Objectives
  hierarchy
  operational statements
Advertising Budget
  percent-of-sales
  follow competition
  available funds
  objective-and-task
Advertising Effectiveness
  sales vs. communication
  hierarchy-of-effects
Publicity
Sales Promotion
  consumer promotions
  channel promotions
  management
Promotion Decisions
  mix
  marketing program
  supplier considerations
  public policy constraints

QUESTIONS FOR DISCUSSION

1. One minute of prime time television advertising costs approximately $50,000. Many a company could compensate and support a salesman handsomely for an entire year for this amount. The sales manager would surely argue that the salesman, working the entire year, could sell more than a single one-minute exposure of one ad. Evaluate this argument.

2. Evaluate the effect of "advertorials," e.g., those offered by the oil companies in opposition to possible divestiture legislation. To whom are such messages aimed? How would you determine their effectiveness?

3. The public library in your town is interested in increasing circulation

and readership of its products. Design a promotion mix to accomplish this objective. Be sure to comment upon possible roles to be played by personal selling, advertising, publicity, and sales promotion.

4. Contrast promotional mixes for consumer goods with those of industrial goods. What is the role of each of the four channels in each case?

5. Contrast the responsibilities of personal selling with those of sales management. How are they alike? How are they different? How is sales management different from management of other types of activities?

6. Most major publishers of college textbooks employ salespersons. Describe such a position. What are its responsibilities? What background (abilities, education, experience) is needed? How does such a salesperson spend his/her time?

7. Design an advertising campaign (objectives, audience, message, media) for such products as a new calorie-free beer, a men's facial depilatory, a professional basketball team, and a proposed vehicle tax to support an urban mass transit system.

8. Some attention has been given in the marketing literature to the concept of a vice-president for promotion. Basically, this position would be responsible for all promotional activities of an organization. Discuss strengths and weaknesses for this idea. What background should such a person possess for this position?

SUGGESTED READING

The Communications Process:
 1. Edgar Crane.
Marketing Communications: Decision-Making as a Process of Interaction Between Buyer and Seller, 2nd ed. John Wiley and Sons, 1972. Review of principles of social psychology and communications and their application to marketing situations; research, as opposed to management, oriented; good book for reference purposes.

 2. Anatol Rapoport.
Operational Philosophy; Integrating Thought and Action. New York, Harper and Row, 1953; reissued by the Institute for General Semantics, 1969. Brilliant review and synthesis of the field of general semantics; emphasizes the role of language and communication in all human actions; not easy reading, but worth the effort.

 3. Wilbur Schramm, editor.
The Process and Effects of Mass Communication. University of Illinois Press, 1954. The classic anthology of the concepts and methods of communication.

Personal Selling:

4. *Napoleon Hill.*

Think and Grow Rich. This book is one of the most successful of the motivate-yourself-to-success books on personal selling; emphasizes the art of salesmanship; contains useful insights, but should be examined critically.

5. C. A. Pederson and M. D. Wright.

Salesmanship: Principles and Methods. 6th ed. Homewood, Ill.: Richard D. Irwin, 1975. Standard textbook on salesmanship; emphasizes the *science* of personal selling; in effect, the converse of the Hill book.

6. Richard R. Still and Edward W. Cundiff.

Sales Management: Decisions, Policies, and Cases, 3rd ed., Englewood Cliffs, N. J.: Prentice-Hall, 1974. Standard textbook on sales management.

Advertising:

7. Andrew S. C. Ehrenberg.

"Repetitive Advertising and the Consumer," *Journal of Advertising Research*, April 1974 , pp. 25–34. Lucid and insightful comments on the actual effects of advertising by one of the world's great management scholars; argues that advertising's major role is to reinforce attitudes and behavior patterns, rather than to create or change them. This article is reprinted in Gabriel M. and Betsy D. Gelb, *Insights for Marketing Management.* 2nd edition, Goodyear, 1977.

8. George Lois.

George, Be Careful. Saturday Review Press, 1973. Insider's view of Madison Avenue; contains numerous anecdotes and insights into the real world of advertising; entertaining.

9. Charles H. Sandage and Vernon Fryburger.

Advertising Theory and Practice. 9th ed. Richard D. Irwin, 1975. Standard textbook on advertising.

10. Jack Trout and Al Ries.

"Positioning Cuts Through Chaos in Market Place." *Advertising Age,* May 1, 1972. Basic statement of the concept of positioning advertisements; contains many examples of contemporary advertising strategy. This article is reprinted in Gelb and Gelb, *Insights for Marketing Management.*

Promotion Strategy:

11. James F. Engel, Hugh G. Wales, and Martin R. Warshaw.

Promotional Strategy. Richard D. Irwin, 3rd ed. 1975. Standard textbook on promotional strategy.

12. John A. Howard and James Hulbert.

Advertising and the Public Interest; A Staff Report to the Federal Trade Commission. Crain Communications, 1973. A careful review, analysis and evaluation of theories presented to the Federal Trade Commission in

1971; also contains conclusions and recommendations by Professors Howard and Hulbert that may significantly influence promotional decision making.

13. "The New Supersalesman: Wired for Success," *Business Week*, Jan. 6, 1973, p. 58-62. Informative review of the role of the salesperson in the 1970s; provides examples in such areas as sales productivity, women in the sales force, lessons of failure, and contemporary sales training. This article is reprinted in Gelb and Gelb, *Insights for Marketing Management*.

14. Theodore Levitt.
"Communications and Industrial Selling." *Journal of Marketing*, April 1967. A report of careful and scholarly research into the role of various elements of the promotion mix in an industrial setting; provides empirical support for many of the points made in this chapter. This article is reprinted in Gelb and Gelb, *Insights for Marketing Management*.

"Of course I'm enjoying myself, dear—I just
wondered if there were any shopping centers nearby."

11/DISTRIBUTION DECISIONS

This chapter focuses upon distribution. Decisions in this area are significant in their own right, and also bear major responsibility for coordinating and integrating the marketing mix. Key points include:

1. The marketing channel is a sequential linkage of institutions and relationships through which products, use rights, payments and information flow from originator to buyer. In an industrial economy, almost all channels involve middlemen.

2. Distribution management involves the coordination of vertical relationships among institutions that comprise the channel. The basic objectives guiding distribution decisions are based upon economic considerations and power considerations.

3. Vertical channel relationships are those that concern different levels (originator, wholesaler, retailer) of a given channel. Vertical channel decisions involve basic questions of conflict and cooperation among channel members.

4. Horizontal relationships are those that concern different organizations on the same channel level. Wholesalers and retailers face particular kinds of decisions in each area of the marketing mix.

5. Physical distribution is the movement of tangible goods through the channel. The focus of physical distribution management is shifting from cost minimization through technological advances to channel-length profit maximization through interorganizational coordination.

6. Integration of distribution decisions with the rest of the marketing mix ultimately involves issues of channel length. These issues are often poorly understood by society, and are heavily regulated.

Most product originators in a modern economy do not market directly to ultimate consumers. Consequently, distribution activities are a significant aspect of economic life. Decisions about distribution are important to organizations and to society. We begin, as usual, with a look at the nature of such decisions.

NATURE OF DISTRIBUTION DECISIONS

This section of the chapter provides the necessary background and foundation for our examination of distribution decisions. We review channel concepts and examine objectives for channel management.

Review of the Channel Concept

When we discussed the channel concept in Chapter 4, we described the channel as a link or conduit (a carrier of flows) between originator and consumer. More precisely, the American Marketing Association (*Marketing Definitions*, 1960, p. 10) defines a channel of distribution as "the structure of intracompany organization units and extracompany agents and dealers, wholesale and retail, through which a commodity, product, or service is marketed." The definition employed in this book captures the essence of AMA definition, but is phrased in the terminology of our definition of marketing:

> a marketing channel is the sequential linkage of institutions and relationships through which a product flows from originator to buyer.

To provide a foundation for our discussion of channel management decisions in this chapter, let us review the salient points about distribution channels that we covered in earlier chapters. Five ideas are of prime importance:

1. Exchange involves negotiation of terms of trade between parties. Generally, the more parties, the more negotiations; the more negotiations, the less efficient the economic system.

2. Middlemen interposed between originator and ultimate consumer can improve the efficiency of the economic system.

3. In an industrial economy, originator and ultimate consumer seldom confront each other directly. Most products are handled by one or more middlemen.

4. In addition to products themselves, channels accommodate flows of use rights, payment, and information.

5. The flows between originator and buyer must occur if exchange transactions are to be consummated. Channel length and complexity, therefore, depend upon the effectiveness and/or efficiency of the middlemen who manage the various flows.

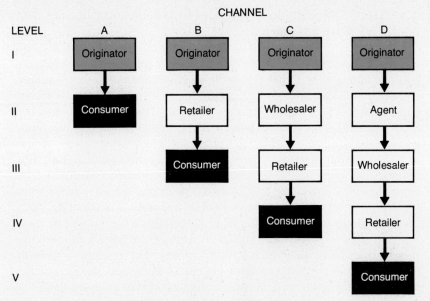

CHANNEL

Exhibit 11-1 Examples of Marketing Channels

Exhibit 11-1 completes our review of the basic channel concept by depicting essential terms and relationships. Note first the lengths of the different channels, labeled A, B, C, and D. In channel A, the products move directly from originator to consumer. This channel is not typical of an industrial society, but it might represent such products as military weapon systems, or electric power generating equipment. Most products are marketed to ultimate consumers through retailers—middlemen who specialize in dealing with ultimate consumers. In some cases, e.g., Sears and A & P, the retailers are large enough to deal directly with product originators. In other cases, one or more wholesalers might span the part of the channel linking originators to retailers. Let us again emphasize the point that the consumer may be an organization or a household.

Second, it is important when discussing channels of distribution to distinguish between vertical and horizontal relationships. Vertical relationships occur as a product flows within one channel from originator to consumer. Horizontal relationships, on the other hand, refer to events that occur across channels at a given level of the distribution system. For example, vertical integration would occur in channel D if the retailer merged with the second wholesaler. Horizontal integration would occur if the retailers in channels C and D were to merge.

Organizational Objectives for Channel Management

Channel decisions, like all marketing decisions, are governed by the objectives and resources of the organization. In managing channel activities, two broad categories of objectives—economic payoffs and power—are usually considered.

Economic Objectives. Perhaps the most fundamental economic objective is cost minimization. Other factors being equal, the marketing manager will strive to deliver flows of physical product, use rights, information, and payment to the buyer at the least possible cost. This criterion is often the basic channel decision guide, particularly in not-for-profit organizations, e.g., hospitals, school districts, and political parties.

Cost minimization, however, should not become an end in itself. It is an efficiency criterion; the effectiveness of performance should also be considered. Profit-seeking organizations, therefore, consider the margin (contribution to profit) of various channel activities. For example, costs might be minimized by shipping all products from a central warehouse—but customers might be more effectively served from branch warehouses, thereby increasing sales and possibly profits. The analytical tools of accounting and marketing research, e.g., break-even analysis, and surveys and experimentation, can be employed to evaluate channel decisions according to cost and profit criteria.

In addition to the basic cost and profit criteria, other economic factors might also be considered in channel decision making. For example, an organization might want to stabilize the flows of cost and/or profits over time. An organization marketing seasonal products, for example, might devise storage and distribution patterns so as to equalize the manufacturing workload throughout the year. This is why manufacturers of air conditioning and heating equipment have off-season special sales. Or the fixed costs of operation may be so high that excess production is marketed on a marginal-cost basis. Until the recent energy shortage, for example, the major petroleum manufacturing companies sold excess gasoline to independent operators at prices that allowed the independents to retail gasoline at a price several cents-per-gallon below the prices charged by the major companies. As demand began to outpace supply in the 1970s, however, the majors no longer had to sell excess gasoline to independents to achieve production stability.

Another economic factor in channel decision making is the total investment required in the channel system. Even General Motors, one of the world's largest organizations, could not afford the investment required to own all of its automobile dealers. And even if an organization could afford such an investment, it might conclude that its financial leverage could be improved by investing those funds in organizational activities other than channel management. If, for example, a firm could achieve a 20 percent return on more modern production facilities or an improved advertising campaign, and only a 10 percent return on its channel investment, it would obviously not commit those funds to channel activities. Consequently, economic analysis—dollars-and-cents realities—play a significant role in channel decisions.

Channel Power Objectives. But channel decisions are not made entirely on the basis of rational economic analysis. Most channel decisions are influenced to some degree by factors that do not translate easily into economic terms. In general, these considerations relate to the ability of the individual channel member to influence his own actions and those of other channel members, i.e., power considerations.

Perhaps the most fundamental power consideration is channel control. Channel control consists of influencing other channel members to conform to the objectives of the controlling organization. But this is no easy task. We discussed (Chapter 5) the difficulties faced by marketing managers in influencing managers of other functions within the organization to conform to marketing objectives. In channel management, these difficulties are magnified because channel members may be completely different organizations.

In essence, channel control derives from bargaining strength. A manufacturer such as Coca-Cola or Magnavox may have a superior product that middlemen desire to handle. Or the promotion strength of companies like Procter & Gamble and Campbell's Soups may compel middlemen to carry these products. The wholesaler may have bargaining strength in a given channel by virtue of knowledge of market conditions or local contacts. Wholesalers often control channel arrangements in developing economies. In Japan, for example, grocery retailing is so fragmented and so oriented to traditional ways of accomplishing marketing activities that several levels of wholesalers are required to move goods through the channel. Exhibit 11-2 illustrates this system. And the retailer may also be able to control the channel; usually it is the largest retailer with sufficient buying power, e.g., A & P, and Safeway stores.

Control is not the only power criterion in channel management. Many wholesaling and retailing organizations, even in industrialized societies, are basically one-man operations—founded and managed by one man and perhaps members of his family. Quite often the dominant criterion of channel decisions in such organizations is independence. These people have developed organizations of a certain size and profitability, and are content with that attainment. They are more interested in the rewards associated with being their own bosses than they are in increased profits, growth, or other possible objectives.

A related criterion is organizational stability—the attitude of management toward decisions that call for organizational change. For example, an independent wholesaler or retailer may desire to grow, but at the same time may fear the organizational problems that would result from such growth, e.g., having his son-in-law manage the new branch warehouse. On

Exhibit 11-2   Japanese Distribution Channel for Food Products

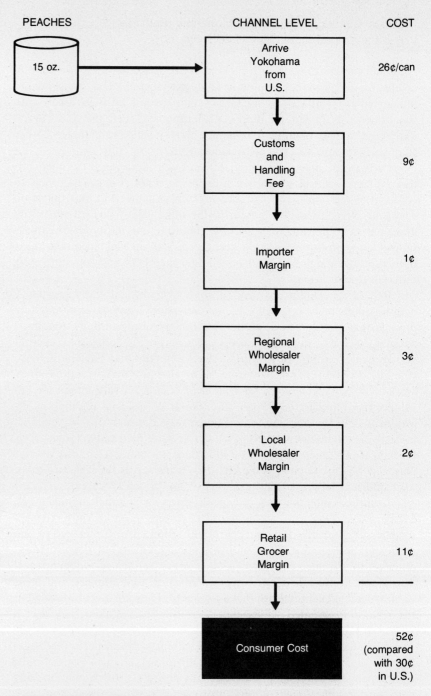

	CHANNEL LEVEL	COST
PEACHES 15 oz.	Arrive Yokohama from U.S.	26¢/can
	Customs and Handling Fee	9¢
	Importer Margin	1¢
	Regional Wholesaler Margin	3¢
	Local Wholesaler Margin	2¢
	Retail Grocer Margin	11¢
	Consumer Cost	52¢ (compared with 30¢ in U.S.)

Adapted from William D. Hartley, "How Not to Do It: Cumbersome Japanese Distribution System Stumps U. S. Concerns," *Wall Street Journal,* 2 March 1972, pp. 1, 8.

the other hand, many channel members are very definitely interested in growth and market coverage. They may be quite willing to sacrifice short-term profits and other economic objectives, as well as a certain degree of control, to increase total sales and expand market coverage.

The organization's image is of concern in many marketing decisions, particularly those related to channel activities. Manufacturers who have striven for a reputation of product excellence, for example, might fight hard to keep their products out of discount stores. Or a retailer desiring to present an image of quality might invest considerable sums in a prestigious location and expensive store fixtures. Another store may attempt to establish a reputation for low prices, and might, therefore, advertise that it will meet any competitive price.

In short, channel decisions are governed basically by the objectives and resources of the total organization. The factors that influence these decisions may be primarily economic, or primarily power-oriented. Let us look now at channel design and management.

CHANNEL DESIGN AND MANAGEMENT
The purpose of channel management is to coordinate flows of product, use rights, payment, and information from product originator or distributor to buyer. The decisions which comprise these management activities are termed *vertical decisions*. There are two major types: design decisions and management decisions.

Channel Design Decisions
In concept, a channel is a conduit—a sequential linkage of institutions and relationships—through which flows of products, use rights, payment, and information move between originator and buyer. Ideally, therefore, channel design should begin with the characteristics of the target market. As we discussed in Chapter 7, marketing-mix decisions, including channel design, should derive from the wants and desires, buying power, and environmental conditions that characterize a target market. The target market's wants and desires are then matched with organizational objectives and resources to provide a basis for developing a marketing program. Decisions about other marketing-mix elements plus consideration of channel objectives as discussed above, provide guidelines for designing the best channel arrangement to serve the needs of the target market.

The channel-customer relationship can be conceived as a continuum with extremes of one outlet for the product and many outlets for the product. Exhibit 11-3 illustrates this continuum. Channel designs that result in few outlets are termed *exclusive* distribution. For example, there may be only one Rolls Royce dealer in a given city, or a distributor of industrial machinery may have an exclusive franchise for a given geographic area. At the other extreme, products like cigarettes and chewing

Exhibit 11-3 Continuum of Possible Channel-Target Market Relationships

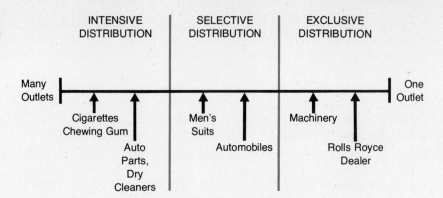

gum are available to potential consumers at many, many outlets—*intensive* distribution. Similarly, auto-parts houses and dry cleaning establishments are usually numerous in a given market. Between these extremes, an organization might follow a policy of *selective* distribution, i.e., making the product available to consumers in several, but not all, available outlets. Automobiles, for example, are often available from more than one dealer in a given market, and a given brand of men's suits is also offered in several stores. Ideally, the intensity of product distribution is a direct result of, and is complementary to, other marketing-mix decisions. Thus, the objective of channel design is to produce the best channel network for a particular organization.

The foregoing represents a simplified treatment of channel design decisions. This treatment points out the major elements in channel decisions, and their interrelationships. It is, therefore, useful to begin a discussion of vertical channel decisions in this way. An organization, however, rarely has an opportunity to build a channel network from scratch; most organizations, even new companies, find that they must deal with existing markets and channel relationships.

Existing channel relationships are dynamic, for two reasons. First, there is continuous evolution in all aspects of any economic system, particularly channel relationships. Over time, markets expand and contract; middlemen prosper and go bankrupt; economic conditions, competitors' activities, and governmental actions fluctuate. At any given time, therefore, the existing channel structure of any market is likely to appear rather complex and irrational—precisely because it was not the result of some coordinated marketing plan. Second, the evolutionary pattern may be disrupted by the actions of a distribution innovator. We saw in Chapter 3, for example, how such organizations as Sears, A & P, Holiday Inns, and McDonald's changed distribution patterns in various markets. In short, vertical channel decisions are rarely decisions involving the design of ideal channel relationships. Usually the task is the more difficult one of managing existing channels.

Channel Management

The effective, efficient delivery of channel flows involves administration of managerial cooperation and conflict among the organizations which comprise a given channel. The need for cooperation is obvious: the ultimate purpose of the channel is to consummate exchange transactions by delivering flows of product, use rights and information to consumers, and returning flows of payment and information. Clearly, it is in the interest of all channel members to satisfy consumers' wants and desires. The need for channel cooperation is merely an extension of the *marketing concept:* determining consumer wants and desires, and then providing the products that satisfy them.

The concept of channel conflict, too, is merely an extension of internal organizational conflicts (discussed in Chapter 5). However, the fact that many channels are composed of more than one organization means that it is more difficult to reconcile differing organizational objectives. In terms of economic efficiency, for example, a retailer might decrease costs by getting other channel members to perform certain marketing activities, e.g., warehousing, credit, or promotion. But they then would bear the costs of these activities. And there may be different power objectives. As discussed above, many wholesalers and retailers are essentially one-man operations—and they may not desire to grow. Conversely, a growth-oriented retailer like Sears or Penney's might like to contract for the total production of a given manufacturer, but that manufacturer might prefer to maintain a degree of independence by selling to more than one retailer, even if that preference resulted in some loss of total revenue. Moreover, the manufacturer is interested in building customer loyalty to his/her brand. The object is to get the customer to purchase the manufacturer's brand wherever the customer shops. The wholesaler and retailer, on the other hand, are interested in developing customer loyalty to their organizations (store loyalty), no matter what product the consumer might desire to purchase. In addition to these general possibilities for channel conflict, the various channel members stress different aspects of the marketing mix in their marketing programs.

Exhibit 11-4 provides illustrative examples. It shows, for example, that many manufacturers expect some degree of product knowledge on the part of wholesalers and retailers; that wholesalers are expected not to carry competing lines, but that retailers are realistically expected only to provide adequate shelf space for the manufacturer's brand. Similarly, the wholesaler would like the manufacturer to produce quality products, and not to sell them directly to retailers (e.g., for the purpose of private branding, or because the retailer buys in large quantities). The wholesaler

	Manufacturer Expects of:	
	Wholesaler	Retailer
Product	Know manufacturer's products	Know manufacturer's products
	Do not carry competing brands	Honor warranties
	Relay customer ideas, complaints	Provide adequate shelf space
	Carry complementary lines	Do not develop private brands
		Relay ideas, complaints
		Offer services (delivery, installation, etc.)
Promotion	Aggressively push manufacturer's products	Advertise manufacturer's products
	Grant credit to retailers	Maintain quality image
		Employ knowledgeable sales personnel
Distribution	Serve many retailers	Serve many customers
	Meet shipping schedules	Maintain adequate stocks
	Maintain adequate inventories	
		Keep convenient hours
		Open branch locations, deliver, etc.
Price	Sell at low margins	Keep prices low
	Pass on discounts	Pass on discounts
	Pay promptly	

expects the retailer to accept the wholesaler's offerings and to provide adequate shelf space for the product. The retailer expects the manufacturer to produce quality products and to honor warranty commitments; from the wholesaler, the retailer expects a wide assortment of products, and knowledgeable assistance in making his selections. Differences in the marketing programs of different channel members for the other marketing mix elements are similarly interpreted.

Because channel members are different organizations, they may experience conflicts of objectives and operating methods. Clearly, customer satisfaction requires that channel cooperation be maximized and conflicts minimized. There are basically two approaches here: the channel captain and integrated channel systems.

The Channel Captain. This approach to channel management assumes that one channel member must lead the others to achieve the degree of cooperation required for customer satisfaction. The question thus boils down to: Who is best qualified to lead in a given situation? Of course, specific factors influence each case, but marketing students usually recognize the following generalizations:

Wholesaler Expects of:		Retailer Expects of:	
Manufacturer	Retailer	Manufacturer	Wholesaler
Offer quality products	Accept wholesaler's assortment	Produce quality products	Offer wide assortment
Provide sturdy packaging	Provide adequate shelf space	Carry wide, deep line	Have product knowledge
Offer wide, deep line		Offers new products	
Do not sell to retailers		Honor warranties	
		Use attractive packaging	
Do extensive consumer advertising	Promote wholesaler's lines	Do missionary work—displays, product, advice, etc.	Employ helpful, not aggressive sales personnel
Offer liberal credit terms		Do extensive customer advertising	Provide cooperative advertising
Have liberal returns policy	Have stable ordering pattern	Keep adequate supplies of popular items	Make fast deliveries in small lots
Have exclusive distribution rights	Order in large lots	Provide fast on-time shipments	Maintain liberal returns policy
Offer low prices	Keep prices low	Suggest prices that permit large margins	Offer low prices and price concessions
Make price concessions	Pass on discounts		
	Make prompt payments		

1. Manufacturer—the manufacturer's claim to channel captaincy is essentially production oriented (as opposed to marketing oriented), but it is strong. The argument for channel leadership by the manufacturer stems from two bases. First, the manufacturer knows the product: he/she researched and developed the product, understands its features, warranties, servicing, etc. The manufacturer can train and direct salespersons, advertise to final consumers, and greatly influence final product price. For these reasons, he/she is in the best position, some authorities say, to design and manage channel relationships.

The second argument for the manufacturer as channel captain is more pragmatic: manufacturers generally have more economic power than do middlemen or retailers. This is not always true, of course, but manufacturing generally requires more capital and a larger minimum scale of operations. Consequently, particularly in the United States, manufacturers dominate many channel relationships. Examples here include the automobile companies, the petroleum companies, and to a lesser but still significant extent, home products firms like Procter & Gamble, Lever Brothers, American Home Products, and Bristol-Myers. Moreover, the manufacturer generally has the legal right to sell his product to whomever he pleases. For these reasons, it can be argued rather strongly that channel-coordination decisions and other aspects of channel management should be led by the manufacturer.

2. Retailer—the retailer's claim to channel captaincy derives basically from the marketing concept. Ideally, the retailer stands the best chance of knowing the wants and desires of final consumers. Since the marketing concept dictates that consumers' wants and desires should be the focal point for all marketing activities, logically it should follow that the retailer is in the best position to implement that concept.

As logical as this argument is, it usually wins out only when the retailer has sufficient economic clout. For example, Sears, Penney's, A & P, and other retailing giants often provide channel leadership—perhaps to some degree because they are practicing the marketing concept, but probably because they have the economic power to seriously influence, if not compel, cooperation from wholesalers and manufacturers.

3. Wholesaler—few marketing scholars champion, on logical grounds, the cause of the wholesaler as channel captain. Wholesalers do provide channel leadership, however, when they control access to certain markets, i.e., in small towns, there may be one or two wholesale drug or grocery distributors. By virtue of their near-monopoly positions, such organizations may come to dominate channel relationships within those areas.

In reality, channel dominance and structures vary. For one thing, innovative entrepreneurs seek to establish new types of channel relationships. Second, a manufacturer may find that the best channel of distribution to large customers may not be the most efficient one for smaller accounts. That is, while the majority of business may be conducted through regular wholesalers, the manufacturer may serve certain large retailers directly and may service small outlying accounts through mail order or by the use of an agent. Similarly, a retailer may obtain the bulk of his stock from wholesalers, but have an exclusive arrangement with certain manufacturers for specific product lines. And, as we discuss in more detail in a subsequent section, marketing activities at each level in the channel may become fairly complex. Scrambled merchandising at the retail level is more and more prevalent (for example, drug items are increasingly found in supermarkets and discount stores).

In short, while the channel-captain concept has a logical foundation— and a great deal of basis in fact—it essentially advocates the management, rather than the minimization, of channel conflict. Of course, conflict is not necessarily bad. The coordination of differing objectives and marketing programs, however, is a complex and never-ending task.

Vertical Channel Systems. The second approach to obtaining channel cooperation is really an extension of the concept of the organization as a system. The reasoning is simple: if channel conflict results from differing organizational objectives, integrating the channel into one organization should tend to alleviate the differences.

The advantages of vertical channel systems over conventional channels are summarized in Exhibit 11-5. For example, detailed planning might replace bargaining and negotiation as means of achieving organizational objectives. Also, there are obvious economies of scale in reducing total direct costs and in supporting the work of such specialists as operations researchers, computer programmers, and behavioral scientists. While there are some disadvantages to vertical integration (initial investment, disruptions of day-to-day activities while the integration is taking place, and certain legal restrictions discussed below), vertical systems are increasing rapidly in the United States and in other advanced economic systems.

There are basically three types of vertical systems: corporate, administered, and contractual. Exhibit 11-6 provides examples to guide our discussion.

1. Corporate Systems. Obviously, the most definite way of achieving vertical integration is for one organization to control, through ownership, the entire channel. Singer Corporation, for example, both manufactures and retails sewing machines and associated goods (thread) and services (sewing lessons). Similarly, Sherwin-Williams paints, Firestone Tires, and Hart, Schaffner and Marx men's clothing are vertically integrated from production to retail sale. The corporate vertical marketing system essentially reduces problems of channel decision making to intraorganizational problems. This is not to say that such problems thereby disappear, but that the corporate system, ostensibly at least, has one set of objectives for which it is striving.

2. Administered Systems. The administered vertical channel system is simply a formalization of the channel captain principle. If an organization has the economic clout to dominate a channel, a likely next step is that that organization will begin to plan and implement marketing programs for the channel as a whole. The difference between the administered vertical system and the channel captain approach to channel coordination and control is, therefore, essentially one of formalizing and making explicit comprehensive programs for product promotion and merchandising. Magnavox Corporation, for example, carefully nurtures via advertising a consumer reputation for quality and excellence, rigorously screens its dealers for integrity and reliability, and eschews any form of price competition. Similarly, Kraftco extensively promotes its products to consumers, packages them attractively, and provides display assistance and merchandising advice to retail grocers.

Exhibit 11-5   Salient Characteristics of Competing Distribution Networks

Network Characteristics	Conventional Marketing Channel	Integrated Marketing System
Composition of network	Network composed of isolated and autonomous units, each of which performs a conventionally defined set of marketing functions. Coordination primarily achieved through bargaining and negotiation.	Network composed of interconnected units, each of which performs an optimum combination of marketing functions. Coordination achieved through the use of detailed plans and comprehensive programs.
Economic capability of member units	Operating units frequently unable to achieve systemic economies.	Operating units *programmed* to achieve systemic economies.
Organizational stability	Open network with low index of member loyalty and relative ease of entry. Network therefore tends to be unstable.	Open network but entry rigorously controlled by the system's requirements and by market conditions. Membership loyalty assured through the use of owner-ship or contractual agreements. As a result, network tends to be relatively stable.
Number and composition of decision makers	Large number of strategists supported by a slightly larger number of operating executives.	Limited number of strategists supported by a *significantly* larger number of staff and operating executives.
Analytical focus of strategic decision makers	Strategists preoccupied with cost, volume, and investment relationships at a *single* stage of the marketing process.	Strategists preoccupied with cost, volume, and investment relationships at *all* stages of the marketing process. Corresponding emphasis on the "total cost" concept accompanied by a continuous search for favorable economic trade-offs.
Underlying decision-making process	Heavy reliance on judgmental decisions made by generalists.	Heavy reliance on "scientific" decisions made by specialists or committees of specialists.
Institutional loyalties of decision makers	Decision makers emotionally committed to traditional forms of distribution.	Decision makers *analytically* committed to marketing concept and viable institutions.

Excerpted from "Perspectives for Distribution Programming," by Bert C. McCammon, Jr., from *Vertical Marketing Systems,* edited by Louis P. Bucklin. Copyright © 1970 by Scott, Foresman and Company. Reprinted by permission of the publisher.

Clearly, the management of channel relationships in an administrative system is potentially more complex than management of a corporate vertical system. However, many organizations, even organizations as large as General Electric and Campbell's Soups, could not realistically generate the capital required to own all outlets for their products. To the extent, therefore, that the channel can be administered to develop potentially successful market plans for their products, and carry out these plans, many of the advantages of vertically integrated systems can be achieved.

3. Contractual Vertical Systems. While corporate and administered vertical channel systems have been increasing rapidly, the greatest growth has

Exhibit 11-6   Examples of Vertical Marketing Systems

1. Corporate	2. Administered
Singer Corp. (sewing machines)	Magnavox (home entertainment)
Sherwin-Williams (paint)	Campbell (soups)
Firestone (tires)	Village (women's apparel)
Hart, Schaffner & Marx (men's clothing)	Kraftco (foods)
Eagle Stores (discount)	O. M. Scott & Sons (lawn products)
Sears (department stores)	General Electric (appliances)
Holiday Inns (motels)	
A & P (groceries)	

3. Contractual

Franchise	*Voluntaries*
(manufacturer-sponsored)	*(wholesaler-sponsored)*
Retailers:	Independent Grocers' Alliance
Hertz Car Rentals	McKesson and Robbins (drugs)
Ford dealers	Southland ("7-11" convenience groceries)
Kentucky Fried Chicken	
McDonald's	*Cooperatives*
Ramada Inn	*(retailer sponsored)*
Midas Muffler	Associated Grocers
Hallmark Card Shops	MARTA (Metropolitan Appliance Radio
Wholesalers	Television Association)
Coca-Cola bottlers	

Adapted from Bert C. McCammon, Jr., "Perspectives for Distribution Programming," from *Vertical Marketing Systems*, ed. Louis P. Bucklin (Chicago: Scott, Foresman and Company, 1970), pp. 43–6; and David T. Kottat, Roger D. Blackwell and James F. Robeson, *Strategic Marketing* (New York: Holt, Rinehart and Winston, 1972), pp. 287–94.

been in the area of contractual vertical systems. The contractual arrangement is essentially a compromise between the efficient but expensive corporate system, and the more feasible but less controllable administered system. The compromise is a legal agreement between independent organizations to pursue common channel objectives. The number of potential examples of contractual vertical systems is so large that it is useful to categorize them—on the basis of the initiator or sponsor of the system. Manufacturers, wholesalers, and retailers sponsor vertical marketing systems. Perhaps the most common type of vertical channel system is the manufacturer-sponsored retailing franchise. The classic example here is the automobile dealership. An automobile dealer is an independent businessperson, but is almost always affiliated with a particular automobile manufacturer. Dealer and manufacturer sign an extensive franchising agreement, covering such factors as location, service facilities, financing arrangements, and advertising policies. As we noted in Chapter 3, the franchising concept expanded rapidly during the 1960s. Successful franchises include Hertz Car Rentals, Kentucky Fried Chicken, McDonald's hamburgers and Midas Muffler shops.

A manufacturer might also sponsor franchises at the wholesale level. The classic example here is Coca-Cola; other beer and soft drink manufacturers often have similar arrangements. Sometimes, the driving force behind the development of the contractual vertical system is the wholesaler. Independent Grocers Alliance, for example, has for years coordinated manufacturer, branding, and distribution of grocery products to its member IGA stores. The drug wholesaler McKesson and Robbins performs the same function for its members in the ethical drug and pharmaceuticals industry, and Southland Corporation has recently emerged as a leader in the field of convenience grocery stores by using the wholesaler sponsored voluntary vertical channel system. Less frequently, retailers organize and integrate backward through the channel. Examples of this type of vertical system include Associated Grocers, Inc., and MARTA (Metropolitan Appliance Radio Television Association).

The rapid growth of contractual vertical systems attests to their success. The vertical system does not solve all marketing problems, as many fast-food franchisees found to their great sorrow in the 1960s, but the potential for increasing both the effectiveness and the efficiency of marketing programs—particularly channel decisions—is evident.

In summary, the advantages of systematizing vertical channel decisions are becoming increasingly apparent in industrialized economies. The vertical marketing system can achieve economies in purchasing, management training, mass advertising, and even facilities design and construction. In short, vertical channel decision making is increasingly a process of rationalizing and formalizing strategies for the total channel. Organizations—particularly wholesaling and retailing organizations—not affiliated with a vertical system will find it increasingly difficult to meet organizational objectives. In more homely words, the "mom and pop" grocery store or motel is dying—or is being absorbed by a vertical system.

DECISIONS OF WHOLESALERS AND RETAILERS

Wholesalers and retailers are, of course, organizations—and, therefore, must make marketing decisions. While their decision making is conceptually similar to decisions faced by any type of organization, wholesalers and retailers must emphasize certain types of marketing activities. This section briefly examines such decisions, within the framework of the four P's—product, promotion, place (distribution), and price.

Product Decisions of Wholesalers and Retailers

As we discussed in Chapter 9, product decisions are the heart of any marketing program. For wholesalers and retailers who do not originate products (i.e., do not usually add form utility), product decisions are of three types: assortment policies, buying policies, and product extensions.

Exhibit 11-7 Examples of Middlemen Classified by Assortment Policy

	Narrow	Wide
Shallow	**Retailers** "Mom-and-pop" grocery store Independent appliance dealer Small lunch counter **Wholesalers** Rack jobber Broker Truck wholesaler	**Retailers** Convenience food store Discount house Cafeteria **Wholesalers** Mail-order house Manufacturer's agent
Deep	**Retailers** Delicatessen Franchised appliance store Ethnic restaurant **Wholesalers** Drop shipper Selling agent	**Retailers** Supermarket Department store Major restaurant **Wholesalers** Full-line wholesaler Commission merchant

Assortment Policies. Product assortment policy—the width and depth of the product line (recall Exhibit 9-10)—is a fundamental marketing decision for any organization. For wholesalers and retailers, the product assortment policy is particularly important since the type of products purchased for resale determines to a large extent the structure and function of the middleman's organization. Exhibit 11-7 provides examples of middlemen with different types of product assortments.

The major constraint upon assortment policy is the organization's capital structure—many middlemen desire wider or deeper assortments, provided that they can secure the capital to support the increased size. Organizations that have shallow and/or narrow product assortments, in other words, generally do so because they are small in size and scope of operations. In the retailing field, there are mom-and-pop grocery stores, independent merchants (e.g., an appliance dealer), and small lunch counters. Wholesalers in this category might include the rack jobber or truck wholesaler, and the independent broker whose product is information of value to a buyer or seller.

If capital requirements permit, most middlemen will expand their product assortments. Whether this expansion is in terms of wider product lines or more depth within a few lines is primarily a matter of organizational objectives, i.e., the preferences of the owners of the organization.

Wide product lines generally serve the wants and desires of a number of different customers, thereby imparting some degree of stability to the operations of the organization. Examples of retailers with wide product assortments include convenience food stores, discount houses, and cafeterias. The mail-order house and the manufacturer's agent are wholesaling examples of middlemen who have wide product assortments.

On the other hand, depth in a few product lines gives the middleman an advantage in terms of knowledge and expertise in these lines. He/she, therefore, becomes better able to serve the wants and desires of certain customers. Examples of retailers that have deep but narrow product lines include delicatessens, franchised appliance or clothing stores, and ethnic restaurants that specialize in serving the dishes of a particular country or culture. An example of a wholesaler with deep but narrow lines is the drop shipper, who takes title but not physical possession of products, particularly bulky products requiring simple, low-cost transportation (e.g., shipments of coal, lumber, chemical products). Another example is the selling agent, who represents several manufacturers of competing products, but does not take title to them.

If the product line is both wide and deep, the organization can serve many customers thoroughly. Retailing examples include supermarkets, department stores, and major restaurants. At the wholesale level, the full-line wholesaler takes title to and markets an extensive product assignment, while the commission merchant handles many marketing activities on a wide variety of products, but does not take title to them.

Purchasing. Since the product assortment is the fundamental basis of the middleman's business, he takes particular care in performing the purchasing function. For example, many products are purchased on the basis of detailed specifications and are examined carefully to be sure that quality standards are met. Competitive bidding is encouraged on a number of types of products. Many organizations pursue a deliberate policy of purchasing similar products from more than one supplier—to avoid dependence upon any one source of supply. In some cases, fixed percentages of total purchases are allocated to the various suppliers. Finally, buying decisions in many organizations are made by committee. Exhibit 11-8 presents a classic example of committee purchasing.

Product Extensions. Product extensions play an important role in differentiating the offerings of a given middleman from those of competitors. For many industrial wholesalers, perhaps the most important product extensions are those that relate to installation and servicing of complex equipment. Fast, competent work in bringing new installations to operational readiness and in trouble-shooting problems for products already in operation often spell the difference between profit and loss for contractors,

Exhibit 11-8 Deliberations of a Chain Grocery Buying Committee

Few items gain admission to the nation's supermarkets without the express consent of a buying committee. The authors tape recorded deliberations of such a committee at one of its regular meetings. These deliberations were based upon factual presentation about all facets of the product under consideration—price, markup, and competitive products. The table below provides an outline of most of the factors considered pertinent to the committee.

The authors summarized the significant implications from their study of this committee's deliberations:

1. Advertising is the catalyst for much of the committee's discussion—committee members displayed sophisticated knowledge of advertising, and felt that its influence created demand for the product.

2. Once on the shelf, the product is expected to perform—neither advertising nor personal selling will save a product that has performed poorly; shelf space is at a premium, so products are judged in terms of sales. Shelf space, however, is not the ultimate determinant—although shelf space is limited, new products are continually accepted for display, often without dropping equivalent products from the shelves.

3. Profit is not necessarily the predominant factor—customer satisfaction and demand can override strict profit considerations.

4. Company and brand image are also important factors—products of known organizations and carrying established brands are favorably regarded; image is not the deciding criterion, but it can be a major influence.

Adapted from Donald G. Hileman and Leonard A. Rosenstein, "Deliberations of a Chain Grocery Buying Committee," *Journal of Marketing*, January 1961, pp. 52–55, with permission of the publisher, the American Marketing Association.

Factors Considered by the Buying Committee

Product Characteristics
Newness
Differentness or uniqueness
Taste appeal
Quality aspects
Mass appeal vs. limited appeal
Shelf life
Evaluation of personal sampling
Convenience aspects

Packaging
Size of container
Shelf stacking properties
Number of items to case
Novelty aspects of package or container
Similarity of size to existing competition
Consumer demand and acceptance of size

Profit Area
Cost
Anticipated profit (in percent)
Prepricing
Inventory costs
Competitive pricing of same item
Markup in relation to product group
Markup in relation to store averages
Guaranteed sale
Fair traded

Miscellaneous Factors
Difference in store size
Test market results
Warehousing considerations
Transportation considerations
Diet fad
Shelf space and back-room inventory
Company image
Brand image
Season of year
Integrity of supplier
Experience
Consumer demand
Variation in demand between areas of company
National vs. private label
Length of time product on market
Branch unwillingness to pioneer

Competitive Aspects
Completeness of competitive lines now stocked
Competitive stores carrying new product

Merchandising
Store demonstrations
Merchandising allowances
Distribution allowances
Point-of-purchase materials
Special displays
Uniqueness of merchandising
Free goods
Consumer allowance
General office merchandising recommendations
Special promotional allowances

Advertising
Length of campaign
Frequency of campaign
Media selection and impact
Advertising allowances
Copy:
  Use of product
  Tie-in with other products
National vs. localized advertising
Cooperative advertising
Complete line vs. product advertising

machine shops, stores, and other businesses. The wholesaler who can provide these services becomes a valued supplier, even if the basic product offered is quite similar to those of other suppliers. Final household consumers also are more likely to patronize retailers that provide such services.

Perhaps the major product extension issue facing middlemen who sell to final consumers, however, is the "battle of the brands." As we discussed in Chapter 9, wholesalers and retailers of many types of products have begun to offer these products under their own brand names—in addition to, or instead of, brands identified with a manufacturer. The middleman with sufficient marketing resources and expertise to build consumer loyalty to his organization might seriously consider private branding, because this practice generally permits higher profit margins, and/or lower prices to the consumer. There are difficulties with private branding, however. The middleman often must also handle manufacturers' brands of the same product. The manufacturers' brands are often promoted extensively through broadcast media to final consumers and are pushed through the channel by missionary salespersons.

Promotion Decisions of Wholesalers and Retailers

Promotion—persuasive communication about the ways products can satisfy customers' wants and desires—poses somewhat different problems for wholesalers than for retailers. We look at each in turn.

Wholesaler Promotion Policies. The wholesaler can use promotion in two ways to facilitate the flow of products through the channel. First, promotional activities—primarily advertising—to final consumers can be used to *pull* products through the channel. On the other hand, various promotional tools—primarily personal selling—can be directed to other channel members to *push* products through the channel.

In implementing a pull strategy, the wholesaler relies heavily upon cooperative advertising. A wholesaler of heating and air conditioning supplies, for example, might advertise the types and brands of products carried (perhaps sharing costs with the manufacturer of those products) and include in the advertising the names of local retailers from whom these products can be purchased. The pull of such advertising may be augmented with such promotional devices as off-season price discounts, premium merchandise (e.g., a free coffee pot), or a lottery for a grand prize.

A push promotional strategy, on the other hand, generally involves the wholesaler's salespersons or sales agents, who call on retailers to promote the wholesaler's products. The personal selling effort may be augmented by advertisements in trade publications and sales promotional devices like calendars or pen and pencil sets.

Exhibit 11-9 Atmospherics as a Marketing Tool

Kotler defines the term *atmospherics* to be the conscious designing of space to create certain effects in buyers. The management of atmospherics can be a particularly important promotional tool for retailers. For example, a restaurant may have a *good, busy,* or *depressing* atmosphere.

The atmosphere of an organization is apprehended through four of the five senses shown here.

For example, the typical atmosphere of a funeral parlor is subdued, quiet, orderly. The typical atmosphere of a discotheque is bright, noisy, loud, rough.

Other examples of successful atmospheres include Brass Boot stores, operated by Nunn-Bush company, which recreate the atmosphere of a Victorian English club; the untidy, dusty appearance of most antique shops, carefully arranged so that the buyer might think he/she can, by skillful and persistent browsing, uncover a valuable antique amid all the junk; and the bright, arty look of some of the *hot, creative* advertising agencies.

Kotler stresses that atmospherics should be carefully managed to reflect the tastes and desires of the target market segment.

Adapted from Philip Kotler, "Atmospherics as a Marketing Tool," *Journal of Retailing*, Winter, 1973–74, pp. 48–64.

Visual	Aural	Olfactory	Tactile
Color	Volume	Scent	Softness
Brightness	Pitch	Freshness	Smoothness
Size			Temperature
Shape			

Retailer Promotional Policies. At the retail level, promotional activity is focused upon the final household consumer. Retail advertising generally stresses the prices and types of merchandise available for the next few days. It is fast and informative. This advertising may be augmented with direct mail pieces, hand delivered circulars, in-store personal selling efforts (which range from extremely helpful to downright distracting), and sales promotional devices such as end-of-season sales, trading stamps, and lotteries.

A less immediately obvious, but no less important, purpose of retail promotion is the development of the image of the organization in the customer's mind. As we discussed in Chapter 10 on promotion, customer impressions and opinions of the organization are formed and influenced by advertising messages, the media through which these messages are transmitted, the behavior of salesclerks, and the types of sales promotion devices employed. Moreover, Kotler suggests in Exhibit 11-9 that the atmosphere of the establishment itself can be a promotional tool.

Distribution Decisions of Wholesalers and Retailers

As we noted at the beginning of this chapter, successful distribution decisions for any organization result from integration of distribution strategies with those of other mix elements. We discussed the importance of establishing and maintaining viable channel relationships in the section on vertical channel decisions. At this point we look briefly at the decisions required to move the product through the channel at each level.

The basic decisions for product movement, and, therefore, perhaps the most fundamental of distribution decisions, are those that deal with location of facilities. For most organizations, the addition or relocation of facilities is infrequent and location decisions tend to be made on a case-by-case basis. Many such decisions are made intuitively by the manager responsible, or are the result of factors specific to a given situation, e.g., the new warehouse is located on land already owned by the organization. Organizations that make location decisions more frequently, e.g., department store chains, major oil companies seeking retail outlets, and franchisers like McDonald's and Kentucky Fried Chicken, have more formalized methods of site selection. These range from careful analysis of successful locations through checklists of relevant factors to rather complex mathematical analyses.

For some types of retailing, location is absolutely vital. There is, for example, a tiny shop located adjacent to the main entrance of the Fairmont Hotel in New Orleans. This shop sells exotic lingerie, and its main customers are traveling businessmen. Most women would not buy such apparel for themselves, and most men would not be caught dead in such a shop in their home towns. However, these risqué items are appropriate returning-home gifts for the traveling businessman or conventioneer.

Distribution strategy at the retailing level is changing rapidly today—primarily to offer the customer greater convenience. Manifestations of this trend include stores open late at night and on weekends, encouragement of shopping by telephone and through catalogs, and the growth of the superstore or *hypermarche*. The superstore, perhaps more common in major European cities than in the U.S. at present, is designed to serve at one time all of the routine wants of the typical middle income household. Such a list would include virtually all foods prepared at home, personal care products, alcoholic beverages and tobacco, leisure time books, magazines, records, some hobby and craft items, and most household services such as laundry, dry cleaning, and shoe repair.

Pricing Policies of Wholesalers and Retailers
Because the middleman, by definition, is buying products for resale, his pricing decisions are particularly significant. This significance follows from the basic accounting relationship:

$$\text{price} - \text{cost of goods sold} = \text{gross margin}.$$

We noted above that most middlemen pay particular attention to purchasing activities—to minimize costs of goods sold. Pricing is the other side of the gross margin relationship. As illustrated in Exhibit 11-10, gross

Type of Middleman	Cost of Goods Sold	Gross Margin	Expenses	Profit Before Taxes
		(percent)		
Wholesalers:				
Appliances	80.0	20.0	16.8	3.2
Automobile Parts	72.0	28.0	23.8	4.2
Building Materials	77.9	22.1	19.1	3.1
Coal and Coke	88.9	11.1	2.6	8.5
Drugs	80.9	19.1	15.9	3.3
General Merchandise	76.5	23.5	19.9	3.6
Groceries	90.0	10.0	8.8	1.2
Industrial Chemicals	78.6	21.4	16.1	5.3
Petroleum Products	78.4	21.6	14.8	6.8
Grain	93.6	6.4	3.9	2.5
Fuel Oil	83.8	16.2	10.1	6.1
Retailers:				
Appliances	66.7	33.3	30.9	2.4
Automobiles	83.7	16.3	14.9	1.3
Building Materials	72.1	27.9	24.3	3.6
Department Stores	68.5	31.5	29.1	2.5
Drugs	75.1	24.9	21.8	3.0
Gasoline	79.4	20.6	15.0	5.6
Groceries	81.0	19.0	17.5	1.6
Liquor	78.4	21.6	18.9	2.7
Restaurants	51.9	48.1	42.5	5.6
Fuel Oil	79.0	21.0	16.2	4.8
Automobile Accessories	84.8	15.2	13.1	2.1
Automobile Repairs	69.8	30.2	27.8	2.4

Exhibit 11-10   Margins of Selected Middlemen

Abstracted by the author from *Annual Statement Studies*, 1975 ed. (Robert Morris Associates, 1975).

margins of wholesalers average about 20 percent. Retailers' gross margins fluctuate more widely, but average 35 to 40 percent. Expenses consume most of the gross margin, leaving middlemen with net profits generally below those of other types of profit-seeking organizations. Exhibit 11-11

This summary focuses on the used-book market. Let's trace a textbook from origination through the distribution system to a student consumer—and beyond.

The book is written by a professor who supplies a manuscript to a publisher. The publisher designs, edits, prints, and binds the book. The publisher promotes the book to professors teaching courses in that field. The professor selects a book and informs campus bookstores. The bookstore manager orders books, marks up the publisher's price 25 percent and sells the book to students, i.e., conveys both the physical book and the use rights in return for payment.

The student "consumes" the knowledge in the text, but in most cases does not use up the physical book. At the end of the semester or quarter, the student sells the book back to the bookstore for 50 percent of the retail price paid. The bookstore manager then marks the book up 50 percent, i.e., to 75 percent of the original retail price, and sells the book to another student.

If the book is not to be used at the school in the future, the bookstore buys the book from the student for a nominal sum (typically $1.00) and then sells the book for 25 percent of the original retail price to a used-book dealer. Used-book dealers maintain nationwide contacts with all college bookstores, and sell to them for 50 percent of the original retail price of the book. So when a professor adopts a book at a school for the first time, the bookstore may be able to offer used books to students at 75 percent of the new book price.

Thus, students buy used books at reduced prices and the bookstore profit margin is higher on used books than on new ones. Some books are sold three or four times. The average is around 2.5 times. But the publisher is paid only once.

The publisher understands this system. So the original price of the book must be set high enough to cover costs and contribute to profits. The author is encouraged to revise the book, so that used copies of old editions rapidly become obsolete.

discusses markups of middlemen of special interest to students—and to textbook authors.

As we note in Chapter 12, the middleman usually relies on rapid inventory turnover to achieve an acceptable Return on Investment (ROI). Pricing decisions, therefore, must take cognizance of both margin and turnover considerations.

In summary of this section, all organizations make distribution decisions, but the channel decisions which wholesalers and retailers face are particularly significant. The fundamental objective of such "horizontal" channel decision making is to coordinate all channel flows and to integrate channel decisions with other marketing-mix decisions. Perhaps the most important component of both horizontal and vertical decision making is the management of physical product flows.

PHYSICAL DISTRIBUTION

To this point, we have been examining distribution decisions in terms of the four flows: product, use rights, payment, and information. In this section, we look specifically at physical product flows. Organizations concerned with the marketing of goods, as distinct from services or ideas, must devote significant managerial attention to physical product flows. We review the principles of physical distribution management, looking

Exhibit 11-12 Physical Distribution Objectives

Service Factor	Objectives
Order-cycle time	To develop a physical distribution system capable of effecting delivery of the product within 8 days from the initiation of a customer order: transmission of order—1 day order processing (order entry, credit verification, picking and packing)—3 days delivery—4 days.
Dependability of delivery	To insure that 95 percent of all deliveries will be made within the 8-day standard and that under no circumstances will deliveries be made earlier than 6 days nor later than 9 days from the initiation of an order.
Inventory levels	To maintain inventories of finished goods at levels which will permit: 97 percent of all incoming orders for class A items to be filled 85 percent of all incoming orders for class B items to be filled 70 percent of all incoming orders for class C items to be filled.
Accuracy in order filling	To be capable of filling customer orders with 99 percent accuracy.
Damage in transit	To insure that damage to merchandise in transit does not exceed 1 percent.
Communications	To maintain a communication system which permits salespersons to transmit orders on a daily basis and which is capable of accurately responding to customer inquiries on order status within four hours.

From David T. Kollat, Roger D. Blackwell, and James F. Robeson, *Strategic Marketing* (Holt, Rinehart and Winston, 1972), p. 316. Copyright ©1972 by Holt, Rinehart and Winston, Inc. Reprinted by permission of Holt, Rinehart and Winston, Inc.

first at physical distribution from a systems point of view. Then we examine the two major classes of physical distribution decisions—storage and shipping—and finally discuss the need for integrated physical distribution management.

Integrated Approach to Physical Distribution

Axiomatically, the objective of physical distribution is to "deliver the right goods to the right customer at the right time and place." This axiom was most poetically phrased by Robert Woodruff, former president of Coca-Cola; he said, "Our policy is to put Coke within an armslength of desire." The manager's task is to translate this truism into meaningful guidelines for administering the physical product flow from the organization to the customer.

Physical distribution objectives can be more precisely analyzed when they are phrased in terms of effectiveness and efficiency. The effectiveness of the physical distribution function is indicated by the level of service provided to the organization's customers. Exhibit 11-12 presents examples

Exhibit 11-13 Relationships among Physical Distribution Activities

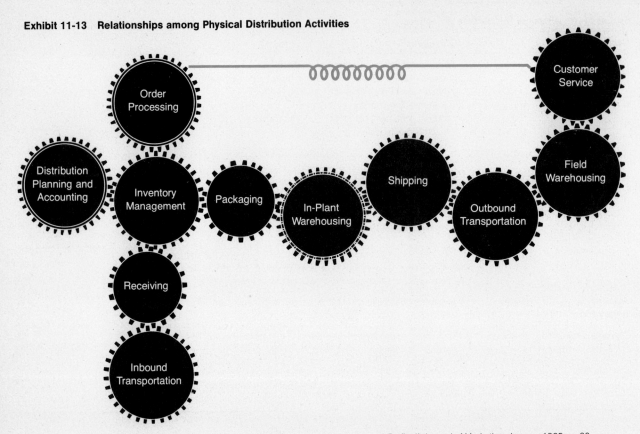

Adapted from Wendell M. Stewart, "Physical Distribution: A Key to Improved Volume and Profits," *Journal of Marketing,* January 1965, p. 66.

of various service components and possible levels of service for each of these components. For example, one service objective might be to complete the order-cycle in eight working days; another objective might be to insure that delivery times do not vary more than two days from this standard, and so on. But as in other areas of management, efficiency considerations must be balanced against the effectiveness objectives. Specifically, the achievement of service levels such as those illustrated in Exhibit 11-12 requires performance of a number of interrelating organizational activities. Exhibit 11-13 depicts the major activities and their relationships.

Note that the diagram stresses distribution planning and control (accounting). Goods arriving on inbound transportation must be received and held in inventory. Orders must be processed and matched against inventory. Products must be packaged, stored, and shipped—often to field warehouses. Thus, the service objective of delivery within eight working days may conflict with the objective of minimizing transportation costs.

Many other effectiveness/efficiency tradeoffs could also be cited, e.g., fast (air) versus cheap (water) transportation modes, maintaining high inventory levels for rapid customer service versus lower inventory costs at the risk of possible stockouts.

Thus, physical distribution management essentially involves various types of effectiveness and/or efficiency tradeoffs. At present, the basic decision rule for most organizations is to minimize total distribution costs subject to the maintenance of a satisfactory level of customer service. Satisfactory service levels are difficult to define—but most physical distribution managers develop over a period of time an intuitive feel for a satisfactory level of customer service in their specific situations. Costs, on the other hand, are rather more easily quantified and controlled. Therefore, many of the improvements in contemporary physical distribution management have resulted from the application of improved technologies to the minimization of distribution costs. Exhibit 11-14 summarizes the basic relationships among distribution costs: the trade-off between decreasing shipping costs and rising storage costs as the number of units involved increases. We examine each of these components of the basic physical distribution trade-off in succeeding sections.

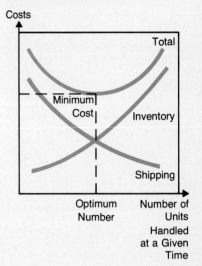

Exhibit 11-14   Basic Physical Distribution Trade-off

Inventory Policies

If the organization were concerned solely with effectively serving customer wants and desires, its inventory policy would be to maintain sufficient stock to fill all customer orders. However, such a service level might be cost-inefficient. Studies of inventory policy generally agree that the investment required to support a given level of service increases at an increasing rate. Exhibit 11-15 illustrates this point.

This hypothetical but not untypical relationship shows that an organization would require an inventory investment of $400,000 to serve 85 percent of its customers from existing stock. To increase that service standard to 90 percent would require another $100,000 investment in inventory—and a further 5 percent increase in the service standard would require a $200,000 increase in inventory investment. Clearly, there is a trade-off between effective customer service and efficient utilization of organizational resources. Determining the optimum trade-off point thus becomes the objective of inventory policy. The two major factors to be considered in pursuing this objective are the order quantity and the timing of inventory purchases.

Inventory Quantity Decisions. Perhaps the most fundamental inventory decision is how much to order at a given time. This decision involves balancing the types of costs associated with holding small inventory stocks against those associated with larger levels of inventory. The classic conceptual approach to this problem is to find the minimum point on the

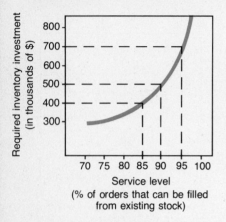
total cost curve of Exhibit 11-14, by using calculus. In actual decisions, many factors influence this basic trade-off.

The factors associated with keeping inventory levels small include the cost of frequent order processing and the high costs of handling small orders (less than carload freight rates, less certain delivery times, and so on). Also, ordering in small quantities reduces the availability of quantity discounts on prices. In addition, small inventory levels increase the probability that stockouts will occur—with resulting customer dissatisfaction. And in markets where prices are rising (the condition for most products these days), buying in small lots means that subsequent purchases of the same product will be more expensive.

On the other hand, different kinds of costs are associated with maintaining large inventory levels. The most obvious is high storage costs. In addition to the direct storage charges, high inventories mean capital tied up in the inventories, and higher taxes and insurance rates. Moreover, products stored in a warehouse are subject to possible damage, deterioration, and obsolescence. And if prices for the product do subsequently decline, the opportunity to purchase the product at lower prices will be foreclosed by the existing inventories.

Of course, the value placed upon each of these types of costs will differ for different organizations, environmental circumstances, times, and managerial preferences. While these factors are numerous and complex, inventory management is one of the areas of marketing that lends itself most readily to formalized decision analysis. A number of quantitative tools have been developed to aid the marketing manager in making inventory quantity decisions.

Timing of Inventory Purchases. Closely related to the quantity of purchase is the timing of that purchase. Specifically, inventory purchases should be timed to maintain the quantity of inventory determined to be optimum. Given the desired inventory level, the purchase decision is basically a function of two factors: the rate of inventory depletion and the lead time required to place and receive an order. If these factors are known in a given situation, then the inventory timing decision can be represented as shown in Exhibit 11-16(a).

Suppose, for example, that the inventory depletion rate is two units per day and that order lead time is ten days. If this were the case, then the organization could maintain a 100 percent service level by reordering when inventory fell to twenty units. Since, as we discussed in previous paragraphs, a 100 percent service level may be inefficient, the organization could achieve any desired service level by adjusting the reorder point accordingly. The inventory level required to meet the service standard under conditions of known depletion rate and order lead time is called the *basic stock.*

(a) No variability in expectations

Exhibit 11-16   Inventory Timing Decisions

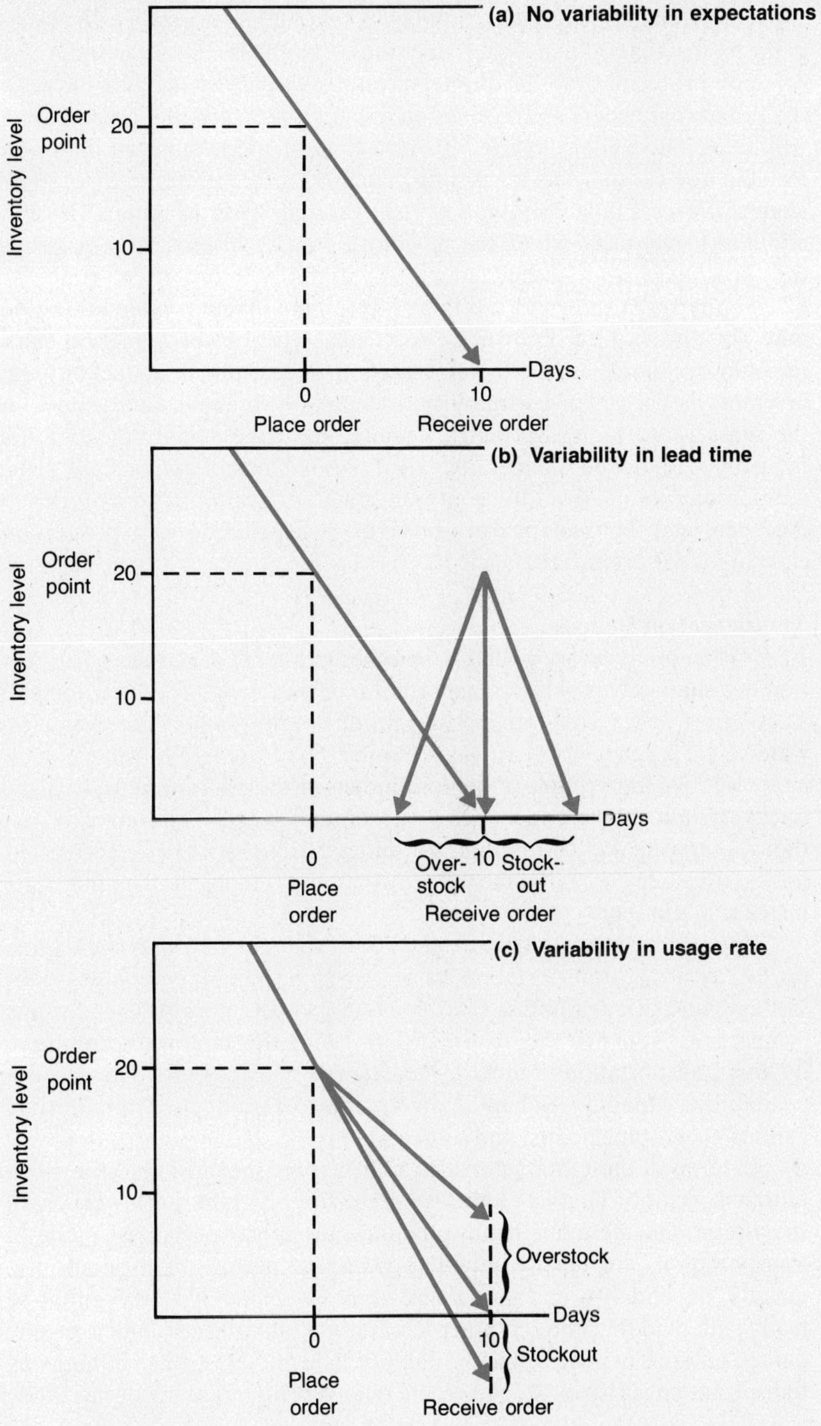

(b) Variability in lead time

(c) Variability in usage rate

Adapted from Philip Kotler, *Marketing Management: Analysis, Planning and Control,* 2nd ed., ©1972, Prentice-Hall, Inc., p. 608, by permission of Prentice-Hall, Inc.

Unfortunately, marketing managers seldom have certain knowledge of the factors that influence their decisions. Exhibit 11-16(b) illustrates one common problem: order lead time may not always be exactly ten days. To the extent that orders are received in less than ten days, the organization will be overstocked; conversely, a lead time of more than ten days will result in a stockout. Most marketing managers would prefer to carry some degree of excess inventory than to risk customer dissatisfaction. Thus, in addition to the basic stock, the inventory policies of most organizations call for a *safety stock*—a hedge against variability in order lead time.

Similarly, as shown in Exhibit 11-16(c), the inventory depletion rate may not always be a known constant quantity. Lower depletion rates result in overstock, and a higher depletion rate results in a stockout. An inventory hedge against variability in depletion rates is a safety stock in the same sense as is the hedge against lead time variability, but the depletion-rate hedge is generally called *seasonal* or *promotion stock*. This terminology results from the common practice of building inventories to meet seasonal demands for products, or to coordinate with promotion campaigns for the product.

Transportation Policies

In addition to inventory policies, the other major set of physical distribution decisions involves the transportation of that inventory to customers. There are five ways of transporting products: railroads, motor vehicles, waterways, pipelines, and airways. Exhibit 11-17 provides a general look at the relative importance of the four modes of transportation for U.S. intercity freight traffic which carry substantial freight. The airways, although carrying 175,000 million ton-miles of freight in 1973, accounted for less than one percent of the total. But this may change as the jumbo jets increase in number.

The underlying rationale for the above statistics becomes clear when the five modes of transportation are analyzed in terms of comparative advantages and disadvantages. Exhibit 11-18 provides a framework for this comparison. Note first the six dimensions generally employed to compare the five transportation modes: speed, frequency of possible delivery, dependability, capability to handle diverse types of products, availability to various geographic points, and total cost.

In terms of these characteristics, railroads are the most versatile mode of transportation. That is, railroads rank neither highest nor lowest on all six criteria. On the other hand, pipelines, the most specialized mode of transportation, are ideally suited to transport petroleum products frequently, dependably, and at low cost—but are relatively slow, cannot be readily adapted for products other than petroleum products, and are quite limited in terms of geographic availability. The relative growth of highway transportation is also explained by the relatively high ranking of this mode

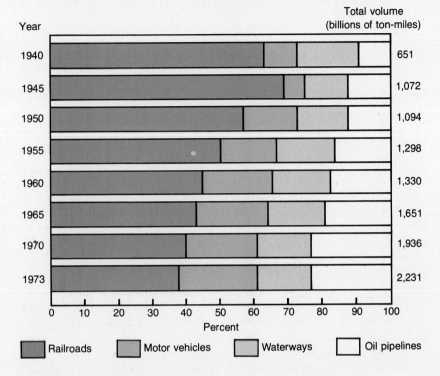

PERCENT DISTRIBUTION OF TON-MILES OF DOMESTIC INTERCITY
FREIGHT TRAFFIC, BY TYPE OF TRANSPORTATION: 1940 TO 1973

Total volume
(billions of ton-miles)

Year		Total volume (billions of ton-miles)
1940		651
1945		1,072
1950		1,094
1955		1,298
1960		1,330
1965		1,651
1970		1,936
1973		2,231

Percent

■ Railroads   ■ Motor vehicles   ■ Waterways   □ Oil pipelines

Exhibit 11-17   Percent Distribution of Ton-Miles of Domestic Intercity Freight Traffic, by Type of Transportation: 1940 to 1973

Adapted from Table 936, 1975 *Statistical Abstract of the U. S.* (Washington, D. C.: U. S. Government Printing Office, 1975), p. 561.

of transportation on all six criteria. Similarly, although the airways are extremely fast, they rank lowest in terms of dependability and cost, and are limited in the types of products that they can transport. Of course, these are very general rankings; they should be considered guidelines for transportation decision making in specific areas.

Transportation costs require a few additional comments. First, the determination of actual transportation costs for the various modes of transport is a very involved process. Freight charges are based upon a detailed system of commodity and geographic classifications and rate schedules. These rates are regulated for each of the five transportation methods by various state and federal agencies. A detailed examination of actual freight rates, therefore, is outside of the scope of this book. However, Exhibit 11-19 summarizes some of the basic factors underlying differences in freight rates for various commodities and geographic locations.

Second, the way to compare transportation costs is total portal-to-

Exhibit 11-18   General Comparison of Transportation Modes

Characteristic	Ranking				
	1	2	3	4	5
Speed (portal-to-portal time)	Air	Highway	Rail	Water	Pipeline
Frequency (scheduled shipments per day)	Pipeline	Highway	Air	Rail	Water
Dependability (meeting schedules)	Pipeline	Highway	Rail	Water	Air
Capability (ability to handle various products)	Water	Rail	Highway	Air	Pipeline
Availability (number of geographic points served)	Highway	Rail	Air	Water	Pipeline
Cost (total transportation costs)	Water	Pipeline	Rail	Highway	Air

Adapted from James L. Heskett, Robert J. Ivie, and Nicholas A. Glaskowsky, *Business Logistics* (New York: Ronald Press, 1964), pp. 71 ff.

portal cost. For example, the capacity of the proposed C5A transport plane to lower air freight costs is great. However, unless airport ground freight-handling facilities and surface transportation to final destination are significantly upgraded, the total cost of air freight will not decline significantly when the C5A is introduced.

Third, all transportation modes except pipelines can be classified as private, contract, or common carriers. A *private carrier* is a truck, airplane, railcar or ship operated by an individual organization. A *contract carrier* is an independent organization that agrees to transport products according to a contractual arrangement. A *common carrier* operates transportation facilities on a schedule basis between predetermined points. Anyone wishing to ship products conforming to the carrier's regulations between those two points according to the carrier's schedule may do so.

Thus, transportation costs typify the make-or-buy alternative: the common carrier provides maximum flexibility in that it can be *bought* only when needed; on the other hand, the private carrier represents the *make* option—it is available when needed, but must be paid for regardless of usage. The contract carrier represents a compromise between the make or buy extremes in transportation cost alternatives.

Physical Distribution Management
Our discussion of physical distribution decisions to this point has been principally concerned with the objective of minimizing physical distribution costs. Cost minimization has occupied the attention of physical distribution managers for the past decade or so, and great strides have been made. Exhibit 11-20 presents examples of factors contributing to

Exhibit 11-19 Factors Affecting
Freight-Rate Differences

Commodity Differences	Geographic Differences
1. Loading characteristics (compare wheat, milk, pharmaceuticals)	1. Distance (costs increase with distance, though less than proportionately)
2. Risk of loss or damage (compare cement, dynamite, orchids)	2. Conditions (adverse weather, mountains, etc. increase costs)
3. Liability assumed by carrier (complete or limited)	3. Transfers (handling, rerouting, etc. increase costs)
4. Customary volume (larger volume means lower costs)	4. Density of traffic (costs are generally lower in areas handling considerable traffic)
5. Regularity of traffic (greater regularity means lower costs)	5. Balance (when more traffic flows one way than returns, rates to the return point are lower)
6. Equipment required (refrigerated cars for beef; flat cars for lumber)	

Adapted from D. P. Locklin, *Economics of Transportation*, 6th ed. (Homewood, Ill.: Richard D. Irwin, 1966), pp. 410–17; 34–41.

these advances. In the future, however, advances are more likely to result from changes in the organizational structure and the responsibilities of managers associated with physical distribution activities.

Changing Nature of Physical Distribution Management. Physical distribution decisions often involve trade-offs at various levels. Consider these examples:

1. Transportation: shipment by air versus shipment by rail.

2. Physical distribution management: carload rail shipments and inventory storage versus truck shipments as needed.

3. The marketing function: improved distribution service level versus lower prices to the consumer.

4. The organization: long production runs and storage of inventory for seasonal needs versus short production runs as needed.

Notable progress has been made in methods used to transport products. These advances can be grouped in five categories:

1. Increased size—Since the end of World War II, the maximum capacity of an ocean tanker has increased from 15,600 tons to 300,000 tons; the DC-3 airplane has been supplanted by the 747, DC-8-63F, and C5A aircraft; *Big John* hopper cars are carrying grain and ore, and trucks are considerably longer and wider.

2. Improved facilities—With a big boost from federal subsidies, airports grow larger and more sophisticated, the interstate highway system nears completion, improved tracks permit higher speed train operation, and navigable waterways increase (e.g., a nine-foot channel connecting Tulsa, Oklahoma with the Mississippi River); even larger airports and superports for ocean tankers are on the drawing boards.

3. Combinations of methods—*Piggybacking* the shipment of loaded truck trailers by rail flat car has proved to be the forerunner of a number of ways of combining transportation methods, e.g., *fishybacking* (shipping truck trailers by barge), containerization of ocean cargo, unit trains, and converting passenger aircraft to freighters at night.

4. Scientific decision making—Computers have provided the major push here, not only in terms of improved paperwork flow, but in providing better data for mathematical decision making techniques such as linear programming, simulation, and critical path scheduling.

5. Systems approaches—Systems analysts have combined all of the above advances with traditional transportation decision making procedures, such as discounted cash flows, to solve specific transportation problems for various organizations.

Compiled by the author from various sources, including "New Strategies to Move Goods," *Business Week,* 24 September 1966, p. 112ff; and James L. Heskett, "Sweeping Changes in Distribution," *Harvard Business Review,* March–April 1973, pp. 123–32.

5. The channel of distribution: negotiation as to whether organization or customer will bear freight charges.

6. The environment: improved pollution control equipment on diesel trucks versus improved profits for the organization.

The point is that each one of these examples involves managerial considerations beyond the relatively simple objective of minimizing the cost of physical distribution. The basic thrust of this view of the development of physical distribution is summarized by Heskett in three stages.

Stage 1 is the thrust of physical distribution policies as discussed in previous paragraphs: emphasis upon minimizing the cost of physical distribution activities, subject to maintenance of some level of customer satisfaction. Although there are organizations that have yet to reach this stage, the majority of organizations that have significant physical distribution activities recognize the potential benefits of formalized efforts to minimize physical distribution costs.

Now, however, progressive organizations are realizing that minimization of physical distribution cost does not necessarily lead to maximization of organizational profits (or whatever ultimate objective the organization aspires to). They are finding that if they state the objective in terms of profit maximization subject to a cost constraint, they may make different physical distribution decisions. Thus, *Stage 2* represents a shift from cost minimization to profit maximization, perhaps by holding smaller inventories and relying more on high speed transport. This situation might be typical of a restaurant serving fresh seafood, a small retailer relying upon rapid delivery from his wholesaler, or a boutique specializing in high fashion merchandise. Of course, the change from cost minimization to profit maximization might in other situations cause a shift to lower speed transportation and higher inventories.

In *Stage 3*, the profit maximization objective is extended from the single organization to the entire channel. In terms of physical distribution management, the Stage 2 orientation requires coordinated management of physical distribution activities within the organization. Stage 3 requires interinstitutional cooperation.

The importance of balancing various physical distribution costs to achieve the least cost alternative has been emphasized. And this section presented examples of possible trade-offs between physical distribution activities and other activities both within and outside of the organization. It is clear, in concept at least, that the management of such activities could be improved if they were the responsibility of a single manager for physical distribution.

The Physical Distribution Manager. The physical distribution manager concept is just beginning to receive serious attention in marketing literature. Such a manager could function at two different levels. First, he/she could coordinate physical distribution activities within the area of marketing, and, therefore, report to the chief marketing officer. Organizationally, the PDM would then be on a level with the advertising manager, general sales manager, director of marketing research, and others reporting directly to the chief marketing officer. In terms of responsibilities, the physical distribution manager at this level would be responsible for managing physical distribution activities of shipping, storage, order processing, and so forth. His/her main coordinating activities would involve relationships with the other marketing managers.

An alternative concept is to include physical distribution activities with inbound materials handling activities—under the direction of a vice president for logistics. Organizationally, the logistics manager would be on a level with the chief marketing officer, chief production officer, and chief financial officer. In this view, the job would entail management of all physical flows into and out of the organization, and coordination of physical flows with production, finance, and marketing.

Despite its conceptual appeal, the concept of a physical distribution manager at either level implies a substantial change in the managerial structure of most organizations. Organization politics, sheer inertia, and substantial start up costs make such changes painful. Consequently, there have been few reported experiences with the physical distribution manager concept. But its potential is great. For example, in organizations that need close contact with consumers, placing the physical distribution manager within the marketing function provides a mechanism for coordinating inventories with national promotional campaigns, cents-off deals, and so forth. On the other hand, organizations whose products are bulky, perishable, delicate, or otherwise require extensive and careful handling and storage might find a vice president for logistics helpful. Organizations that recognize the value of a physical distribution manager, but are unwilling to concentrate such responsibility in one individual, may find that some of the advantages of this arrangement can be attained through a physical distribution committee—which meets periodically to discuss problems and iron out difficulties.

Interorganizational Management of Physical Distribution. Even more complex organizational changes would be required to implement successful physical distribution management between organizations. As we discussed earlier in this chapter, the distribution channel as an integrated network holds great promise—and significant problems. In terms of the physical distribution aspects of such an integration, James Heskett sees four stages of organizational development:

1. *Channel member coordination*—the coordination of policies and practices to enable channel members to perform existing functions more effectively, e.g., the unitized handling of products by means of such devices as pallets.
2. *Shifting responsibilities*—the shift of functions and responsibilities from one institution to another in the channel, e.g., the trend among small retailers to hold minimum inventory stocks and rely upon wholesalers to supply their needs quickly.
3. *Third-party arrangements*—the creation of joint-venture or third-party institutions to eliminate duplication of performance of channel functions, e.g., a separate joint-venture company to handle all distribution activities for several firms, consolidated regional warehouses, and/or consolidated regional receiving depots.
4. *Vertical integration*—integration of physical distribution operations in the channel by means of merger or acquisition, contract, or administrative clout, e.g., Sears, Kraftco, and other organizations mentioned in the previous discussion of vertical integration.

In summary of this section, we have said that organizations have begun to realize significant savings from viewing physical distribution costs from a total systems perspective. Although many organizations can still attain significant savings in this way, future changes in physical distribution management are likely to be focused upon profit maximization rather than cost minimization, and will be achieved through organizational change rather than technological advances or formalized decision procedures.

DISTRIBUTION DECISIONS AND MARKETING PROGRAM INTEGRATION

We have looked separately at distribution channel objectives, channel design and management decision areas of wholesalers and retailers, and decisions related to physical distribution. In practice, however, these decisions are interrelated, and must be integrated with decisions about other elements of the marketing program. At the risk of oversimplifying some aspects of distribution decisions, we discuss this integration in terms of channel length. We close with a brief review of the regulation of distribution activities and resentment toward marketers.

Distribution Channel Length

Distribution decisions in a given organization ultimately manifest themselves in the length of the distribution channel. Any number of factors might influence the selection and operation of channels used by a given organization. The marketing management model can be used to organize thinking about these factors and provide a consistent framework for their analysis. Following this model, we look at customer factors, organizational (supplier) factors, and societal factors. Exhibit 11-21 guides the discussion.

Customer Factors. In accordance with the marketing concept, the most important extraorganizational factors influencing channel decisions are consumer characteristics and desires. Obviously, the fewer customers an organization has, the more likely it is to market directly to them, i.e., a *short* channel. Similarly, the larger an individual customer is, the more likely the organization is to market directly to that customer. Conversely, the more customers an organization has, particularly if these customers individually are small, the more likely the organization is to use a long channel—one consisting of several middlemen. Similarly, it becomes less feasible to market directly to customers as their geographic dispersion increases.

The length of the channel also depends upon the various kinds of specialized demands that customers might place upon the organization. In general, the greater the demand for nonstandard product features, unusual credit arrangements, product installation and service that the customer requires, the more likely it is that the channel of distribution to that customer will be relatively short. Generally, the greater the significance of each individual customer to the organization, the more likely it is that the customer will be served by a short, direct channel.

Exhibit 11-21 Examples of Factors Influencing Channel Decisions

	Factors That Tend to Produce: A Short Channel	A Long Channel
Customer factors	few large-volume customers	many small-volume customers
	customers with specialized demands	customers who buy standardized products
	new territory, no established middlemen	strong, established middlemen
Organizational factors	exclusive distribution objective	intensive distribution objective
	heavy economic clout	little economic clout
	extensive knowledge of market	limited knowledge of market
	bulky, perishable or highly technical product	small, hardy, unsophisticated product
	push-type promotion	pull-type promotion
Societal factors	few, weak competitors	many strong competitors
	dynamic economic conditions and practices	stable or recessionary conditions
	loose, informal regulation	tight, formalized regulation

These generalizations may be modified by the characteristics and desires of middlemen in the customary channels through which the organization operates. For example, a middleman in a given channel may have the financial and managerial capability to be of considerable service to the organization. In such a case, he would be included in the channel. Even if his capabilities were not great, many middlemen have established relationships with retailers and ultimate consumers in a given market, which insure their presence in the channel. Often these relationships are based upon long standing tradition and mutual trust, and, therefore, are particularly difficult to overcome, as in Japan.

Organizational Factors. Given the channel economic and power objectives discussed at the beginning of the chapter, perhaps the most important set of factors influencing channel decisions are other marketing-mix decisions—particularly product decisions. Obviously, the larger the physical bulk of the product, the greater its perishability, or the higher its unit value, the more necessary a short and direct channel becomes. Examples might include bulky products like coal and iron ore, perishables such as bread and fresh vegetables, and goods of high unit value, e.g., aircraft or buildings. Similarly, products like computer systems, which require extensive installation, training of customers, employees, and maintenance often require direct contact between manufacturer and consumer.

Channel decisions are also related to promotion decisions. A firm whose promotional strategy is basically one of appealing to the ultimate consumer and then relying upon consumer demand to *pull* products through the channel can afford a more lengthy channel than an organization which *pushes* its product by concentrating its marketing effort upon other channel members.

Societal Factors. The societal situation within which a channel exists must also be considered. Perhaps the most direct environmental influence upon channel decision making is the marketing strategies of competitors. It is generally difficult and expensive to meet firmly entrenched competitors directly. In markets where competitors dominate customary channels, therefore, a firm may elect to distribute its products in a different way. For example, Hanes Corporation introduced its L'eggs panty hose line in supermarkets rather than in department stores; several firms market life insurance by mail, rather than through the typical agency arrangement. On the other hand, customer buying patterns may be so definite that a manufacturer or distributor is forced to use the same channel that his competitors use. This situation is typical, for example, of food products—consumers shopping for food desire to compare brands, prices, etc. Food producers and distributors, therefore, want their products to be displayed in retail stores near those of competitors.

Economic conditions also influence channel decisions. For example, management may have a wider choice of channel alternatives in times of prosperity. Moreover, in a dynamic economic environment, as opposed to one in which economic customs and traditions are relatively stable, producers and distributors can more easily experiment with various channel arrangements. Discount operations, for example, often encounter great difficulties in less developed countries, and even in rural sections of America. (And as we pointed out in Chapter 4 on public policy, these traditions are sometimes formalized into laws and regulations: Sunday closing laws, chain store taxes, prohibitions against door-to-door selling, and so on.)

The risk of presenting a list such as Exhibit 11-21 is that it will be accepted by the reader as fact rather than as a framework for analyzing a particular situation. This table is useful for the latter purpose, but should not be considered a definitive statement. It is an oversimplification to reduce the impact of these factors to a statement of their probable effect upon channel length, and it should be remembered that these factors are interrelated. That is, an organization's objectives, resources, and product policies; the characteristics of its channel members and customers; the behavior of its competitors; the general level of economic activity; and the type and degree of governmental activity are all related. Consequently, assessments of the probable impact of any one of these factors are of necessity incomplete. The factors can be separated to be studied, but must be considered in concert by the marketing decision maker in a given situation.

Resentment and Regulation of Distribution Activities

As discussed earlier (Chapter 4) the development of economic society, with its resulting separation of product origination and product consumption, requires marketing activity—channels of distribution and institutions within that channel (middlemen). These middlemen exist because they perform essential channel activities effectively and efficiently. And yet, the creation of time, place, and possession utilities is not a tangible set of activities like the creation of form utility through origination. Consequently, the marketer is often resented. He has been called a huckster, a hidden persuader, a parasite.

Resentment of the marketer is not new. From Plato to the French physiocrats to Karl Marx, philosophers have considered marketing nonproductive. Cox notes (*Distribution in a High Level Economy*, p. 20):

> . . . whereas bulky goods such as grain, could be moved economically only down rivers or before prevailing winds, trade upriver, cross-country, and against the wind has to be confined to small, easily transported goods of high unit value—what some students have called a trade in "trinkets."

> Here we find the dim prototype of the huckster and the hidden persuader, perhaps another root source of hostility to marketing. The city man bargained with the farmer at a disadvantage. He bought necessities but often had to sell goods people could well do without. He was thus forced to use his wits as a salesman and no doubt early gained a reputation for persuading unsophisticated country people to part with goods of substantial worth in return for gimcracks and gewgaws that had, perhaps, much glitter but very little gold.

> Such feelings exist today. They are exacerbated by inflation and the rhetoric of some politicians, and by the actions of marketers themselves. Examples are easy to find: shoddy products, poor service, high prices. The result is that distribution activities are among the most heavily regulated of all social activities. Thus, distribution decisions are complex and difficult. Exhibit 11-22 is a review of major areas.

CONCLUDING NOTE

A clear grasp of the channel concept is fundamental to understanding

Exhibit 11-22 Public Policy and Distribution Decisions

Many types of distribution decisions are subject to particular public policy scrutiny. Perhaps the six most often mentioned areas are:

1. Mergers. Vertical and horizontal integration is particularly significant in channel management. A merger is one means of achieving such integration. Mergers are not illegal per se; they are subject to the Clayton Act (Section 7) and its Celler-Kefauver amendment provisions relating to the "probably injurious effect upon competition" or "tendency to create a monopoly." The courts and enforcement agencies tend to concentrate upon merger activities of firms with large market shares.

2. Dealer Selection. In general, a manufacturer has the right to select the middlemen with whom he will deal. This right was enunciated in the Colgate case, and formalized in Section 2 (a) of the Robinson-Patman Act. But the Colgate doctrine has been modified, e.g., in cases where the refusal-to-deal could be inter-preted as restraining trade or fixing prices.

3. Exclusive Dealing. Agreements by middlemen that they will not handle the products of a manufacturer's competitor are not illegal per se. They are, however, subject to the provisions of the Clayton Act (Section 3) and the Federal Trade Commission Act (Section 5, i.e., the arrangement must not substantially lessen competition or tend to create a monopoly, and both parties must enter voluntarily into the agreement). Recent FTC activity in this area, e.g., charging major oil companies with forcing dealers to carry the companies' tires, batteries, and accessories, indicate possible changes in the legal status of this type of channel activity.

4. Exclusive Territories. Again, agreements between manufacturer and middleman giving the middleman the exclusive right to sell the manufacturer's product within a defined territory are not illegal per se. The key to legality appears to be a bilateral vertical agreement between the manufacturer and each individual middleman. Of course, horizontal market divisions are expressly prohibited by the Sherman Act. Exclusive territorial arrangements tend to produce the same effect, but so far have been considered legal so long as there is no collusion among channel members at a given level.

5. Tying Arrangements. A tying arrangement allows a middleman to buy one product only if he buys others. This activity is illegal under Section 3 of the Clayton Act, provided that there is evidence of injury to competition resulting from the arrangement.

6. Transportation Regulation. All transportation modes are carefully regulated by various federal, state and local authorities, e.g., the Civil Aeronautics Board, Interstate Commerce Commission, and U. S. Maritime Commission. Regulations pertain to such areas as rate-making, safety standards, weight and speed restrictions, and many others.

Of course, many other distribution decisions are also subject to various types of public policy provisions. The marketing manager is well advised to seek legal advice when these types of decisions are involved.

Compiled by the author from various sources, including Marshall C. Howard, *Legal Aspects of Marketing* (New York: McGraw-Hill, 1964); Louis W. Stern and John R. Grabner, Jr., *Competition in the Market Place* (Chicago: Scott, Foresman and Company, 1970); and Earl W. Kintner, *An Anti-Trust Primer,* 2nd ed. (McGraw-Hill, 1973).

marketing processes in an industrial economy. A distribution system is a complex and sophisticated network of channel relationships. And the nature of these relationships is changing. The general pattern of dominance by a manufacturer as channel captain no longer holds for many types of products. There is increasing vertical integration, often initiated by the retailer or wholesaler, and many resulting legal complexities. In addition, concentration at each level is increasing. At the same time, there are many new types of products, vigorous competition between types of middlemen, and increasingly rapid environmental change. Consequently, channel management must become more sophisticated.

We have made great strides in formalizing management of physical distribution flows (although these problems are by no means solved). There is considerable room, however, for development in the more fundamental areas of managing the intra- and inter-organizational aspects of channel relationships and product distribution. There are questions here of goal-setting, of power and authority allocations, of negotiation and compromise, for the channel as a whole.

Channel management may appear to be less glamorous than promotion management, and perhaps less dynamic than new product development, but integrating channel decisions into the marketing program of the organization may prove to have been the most challenging area of marketing management in the 1970s.

KEY TERMS AND CONCEPTS

Channel Concept
Channel Flows
  product
  use rights
  payment
  information
Channel Objectives
  economic
  power
Channel Design
  exclusive distribution
  selective distribution
  intensive distribution
Channel Management
  cooperation
  conflict
Channel Captain
  manufacturer
  retailer
  wholesaler
Vertical Channel Systems
  corporate
  administrative
  contractual

Decisions of Wholesalers and Retailers
  product
  promotion
  distribution
  price
Physical Distribution Axiom
Basic Physical Distributive
Tradeoff
  shipping costs
  storage costs
Inventory Decisions
  quantity
  timing
Transportation Modes
  airways
  pipelines
  highways
  railroads
  waterways
Physical Distribution Management
  changing nature
  P D manager concept
  interorganizational management
Factors Affecting Channel Length
  customer
  organization
  societal

QUESTIONS FOR DISCUSSION

1. The perennial cry is: Eliminate the middleman and save his costs. What does this statement mean? Is it valid? Why or why not? How is the concept of vertical channel structures related to this statement?

2. List products that probably would be marketed using an intensive distribution strategy; a selective strategy; an exclusive strategy. Defend your list. What strategies of other mix elements (product, price, promotion) would likely be associated with each of these distribution strategies? Why?

3. Your organization is a wholesaler of meats, or furniture and fixtures, or janitorial supplies. Part of your sales are to restaurants. How would marketing to McDonald's or Howard Johnson's differ from marketing to independent restaurants? Would you solicit the accounts of chains or franchises? Why or why not?

4. Test your innovative thinking powers: devise alternative distribution channels for automobiles, gasoline, life insurance, or haircuts. What problems would your ideas encounter? How would you handle these problems?

5. What methods of physical distribution (shipping *and* storage) would you recommend for such products as beef cattle, wheat, natural gas, spare parts for industrial machinery, first class mail, and women's fashions? Defend your choices.

6. Examine the physical distribution manager concept. What would be the responsibilities of such a post? What background (education, abilities experience) should such an individual possess? Where in the organization should he/she be located? Discuss the strengths and weaknesses of such a position.

7. Use Exhibit 11-21 to examine possible channels for such products as fresh fruit, ready mix concrete, beer, mutual funds, college-level courses in marketing, and marijuana.

SUGGESTED READING

Readings on channel management are divided into three categories: classic material, anthologies, and articles of particular significance.

Classic material:
1. Reavis Cox.
Distribution in a High-Level Economy. Englewood Cliffs, N. J.: Prentice-Hall, 1965. Comprehensive, readable review and synthesis of empirical work in channels.

Anthologies:
2. Louis P. Bucklin, editor.
Vertical Marketing Systems. Glenview Ill.: Scott, Foresman and Com-

pany, 1970. Collection of original papers on the more abstract conceptual issues in channel management, contributed by some of the discipline's leading scholars.

3. Bruce E. Mallen, editor.
The Marketing Channel: A Conceptual Viewpoint. John Wiley and Sons, 1967. Well-chosen collection of readings emphasizing channel structures and the behavioral relationships among channel components.

4. Bruce J. Walker and Joel D. Haynes, editors.
Marketing Channels and Institutions: Readings on Distribution Concepts and Practices. Grid, 1973. Recent collection of basic articles in various areas related to channel management.

Articles:
5. James L. Heskett.
"Sweeping Changes in Distribution," *Harvard Business Review,* March/April, 1973, pp. 123–32. Readable comprehensive review and synthesis of the area of physical distribution management. Reprinted in Gabriel M. Gelb and Betsy D. Gelb, *Insights for Marketing Management,* 2nd ed., Goodyear, 1977.

6. Claude R. Martin, Jr.
"The Contribution of the Professional Buyer to a Store's Success or Failure," *Journal of Retailing,* Summer 1973, pp. 69–80. Scholarly comparison of decision marketing by two retail managers; many jobs for marketing students are in the retail sector. Reprinted in Gelb and Gelb, *Insights for Marketing Management.*

7. M. S. Moyer.
"Toward More Responsive Marketing Channels," *Journal of Retailing,* Spring 1975, pp. 7ff. Thorough literature review of the area of information needs for effective distribution decisions; insightful, and suggests possible future developments. Reprinted in Gelb and Gelb, *Insights for Marketing Management.*

DUNEGAN'S PEOPLE by Ralph Dunegan; Courtesy of Field Newspaper Syndicate.

"MRS. ALBERTSON WAS GIVING A $100 REBATE WITH EACH $100 KITTEN, MOM! THEY DIDN'T COST US A CENT!"

12/PRICING DECISIONS

This chapter is the last of the four on the marketing program. Pricing decisions generally complement decisions in other areas to complete the exchange transaction. Major points include:

1. Prices communicate the terms under which an individual or organization is willing to engage in exchange. Consumers, society, and other managers in the organization, therefore, scrutinize pricing decisions particularly closely.

2. The economist's theory of price provides a useful foundation for a general understanding of the area of pricing, but is an inadequate framework for actual pricing decisions.

3. In practice, most organization pricing decisions are based primarily upon one of four orientations: demand-oriented, cost-oriented, competition-oriented, or regulation-oriented. Analysis underlying pricing decisions is very meaningful to the organization, but is often not sophisticated.

4. Pricing decisions are guided by overall organizational objectives. A base price is usually established, and adjustment from that base is made to more closely match the organization's product and consumers' wants and desires.

Everything has its price. More precisely, the value of products that are candidates for potential exchange must be communicated to other parties to an exchange potential transaction. Pricing decisions, therefore, are fundamental to marketing management—since they communicate the terms under which an organization is willing to engage in exchange. In this chapter, we briefly review the nature of pricing—consumer, societal, and organizational perspectives on pricing decisions, and the concepts and limitations of price theory. Second, the bases for pricing decisions are examined. Then pricing decisions are integrated into the marketing program.

THE NATURE OF PRICE

Pricing is an aspect of marketing that has received considerable scholarly attention. We look briefly at the theoretical role played by pricing in the exchange process—and at the limitations of this theory—after we have examined pricing from the perspective of the three participants in an exchange.

Pricing Perspectives

Recall that exchange requires interrelationships among consumer, society, and the organization. To each of these participants, price has a very definite meaning.

Consumer's View of Price. The consumer, as we may have said once or twice before, does not buy products; he/she buys expectations of benefits. That is, the goal is satisfaction—which is obtained by extracting utility from the product. To obtain the utility, the consumer must pay for the product: the price of the product represents the utility he/she must forego to obtain the product. Price, from the consumer's point of view, represents a sacrifice of purchasing power required to obtain the given product. Since the consumer has alternative ways of allocating purchasing power, the essential question for any given product becomes: is it worth it?

The consumer answers this question in terms of the familiar equation:

$$\text{satisfaction} = \text{benefit} - \text{cost}.$$

The product price presents the cost part of the equation, from the consumer's perspective. To be sure, benefits as well as cost will be considered, but most consumers develop fairly definite notions of what the price of a product should be. This notion is generally thought of in terms of some reasonable range. A reasonable price range for a new automobile, for example, would probably be between $4000 and $6000 for most people. Only a small proportion of consumers would seriously consider purchasing an automobile costing $10,000 or more, and a new car priced at less than $1000 would generate considerable skepticism. From the consumer's point of view, therefore, price is always a consideration in an exchange. It may not be the determining factor, but it is influential.

The Role of Price in Society. As we discussed in the chapter on the economic system and public policy, price plays a very important role in an industrial society. Market prices indicate the average valuation placed upon particular products by members of the society, and the market mechanism uses product prices to adjust supply and demand—and therefore, allocate resources among potential uses. Moreover, prices are relatively unambiguous and easily understood product characteristics. It is much easier, for example, to demonstrate that industrial societies have generally rising price levels than it is to demonstrate a generally rising level of product quality, improvements in product distribution, or better advertising.

The Organization's View of Pricing. Pricing decisions are extremely important to the organization, because they directly govern revenues: Revenue = Price × Quantity. For this reason, nonmarketing executives are familiar with and concerned about product prices, perhaps to a greater extent than other marketing mix elements.

Thus the marketing manager must understand how price is viewed by the consumer, society, and other decision makers within the organization. Moreover, he/she must integrate pricing decisions with product, promotion, and distribution decisions. In summary, the impact of the pricing decision is likely to be significant—perhaps more significant than other types of marketing decisions—and, therefore, a marketing manager feels considerable pressure to make correct price decisions. Given these perspectives upon price, a sound, useful theoretical framework for pricing decisions would be welcomed by marketing managers.

Price Theory
Economists have emphasized—indeed continue to emphasize—the central role of pricing decisions in organizational behavior. They have developed an elaborate theoretical structure for pricing decisions based upon three assumptions: profit maximization, marginality, and elasticity.

As shown in Exhibit 12-1, the essential relationships are as follows. As a consequence of the principle of diminishing marginal utility (Chapter 6), the slope of the demand or average revenue curve falls as the number of units demanded increases. Marginal revenue, the increment of revenue derived from the last unit demanded, falls more rapidly than does average revenue (twice as fast if average revenue is a linear function). On the cost side, average cost falls as output increases (economies of scale) up to a

Exhibit 12-1 Marginal Approach to
Pricing

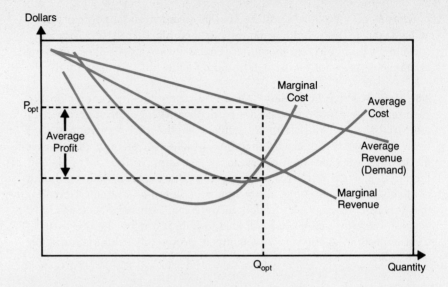

point, and then begins to increase again—because of the diseconomies of large-scale production. Marginal cost falls more rapidly than does average cost, then rises more rapidly as average cost begins to rise. The optimum quantity for production is indicated by the point at which marginal cost equals marginal revenue, Q_{opt}.

Now we can see the central role played by price in this theory. Given the profit maximization assumption, the marketing manager should set the price that generates the amount of demand which will equate revenue and cost. In Exhibit 12-1, P_{opt} will generate a demand for Q_{opt} (the quantity which exactly equates marginal revenue and marginal cost). In short, if the marketing manager knows the demand and cost functions, he can set the price for all products which maximizes the organization's profit.

**Exhibit 12-2 Demand Elasticity
Guides Pricing Decisions**

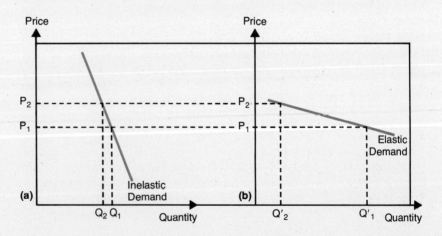

This theory is precise—even elegant. But what happens when the demand and/or cost functions are not known? Perhaps, for example, the marketing manager is attempting to set the price of a new product, or perhaps raw material costs, competitors' actions, or consumers' tastes have changed. According to economists, the shape of the demand curve is all-important. Demand curves for *elastic* products require different pricing decisions than do the demand curves of *inelastic* products. Exhibit 12-2 illustrates these differences: (a) depicts inelastic demand, and (b) shows elastic demand.

Elasticity is defined to be the amount of change in quantity produced by a change in price. More precisely, elasticity is measured by the formula:

$$E = \frac{\dfrac{\text{change in quantity}}{\text{initial quantity}}}{\dfrac{\text{change in price}}{\text{initial price}}}$$

Consider, for example, an increase in price from P_1 to P_2—as shown in part (a) of Exhibit 12-2. Note that that price increase produced a decrease in quantity demanded from Q_1 to Q_2. But note that the decrease in quantity is less than proportional to the increase in price. Conversely, if demand is elastic as shown in the (b) part of the figure, an increase in price from P_1 to P_2 will produce a greater than proportional decrease in quantity demanded—from Q'_1 to Q'_2. In the case of a price decrease, the opposite analysis would occur: a price reduction to P_1 would increase demand on the inelastic curve from Q_2 to Q_1—a less than proportional increase. On the other hand, on the elastic curve, a price decrease from P_2 to P_1 would produce the greater than proportional increase in demand Q'_2 to Q'_1. [Pedantic aside: it is not possible to estimate elasticity from the shape of a demand curve, since E differs at different points on the curve.]

Clearly, therefore, a marketing manager should determine if possible whether product demand is elastic or inelastic. In general, elasticity of demand increases as a function of three factors: product substitutes, product uses, and percentage of total purchasing power required to buy the product. The price elasticity of demand for a product with many substitutes—e.g., steel, aluminum, major appliances—will be greater than demand for a product such as gasoline or salt, which has few substitutes. Secondly, demand for products with many uses, e.g., wood, petroleum, plastics, will be more elastic—sensitive to price changes—than will demand for products such as foodstuffs—which have one primary use. And demand for a product such as a major appliance or an automobile will be more elastic than demand for a product like cigarettes or chewing gum, since the price of the former products would represent a significantly greater proportion of the consumer's total budget.

According to economic theory, therefore, pricing decisions arc relatively simple: the marketing manager simply determines the elasticity of his product and adjusts prices upward or downward on that basis. Unfortunately, this theory has significant limitations.

Limitations of Price Theory

Price theory limitations can be grouped into two basic categories: theoretical constraints, and data availability.

Theoretical Constraints. The economist's favorite phrase, ceteris paribus, neatly removes from consideration the influence of factors other than the price of the product. But let us examine the "all other things being equal" assumption in light of the marketing management model. First, as we noted in Chapter 2, the organization has objectives in addition to—and perhaps even instead of—profit maximization. Moreover, it may not have the resources necessary to build a plant large enough to achieve economies of scale. Second, as we discussed in Chapter 4, the theory completely ignores channels of distribution—buyers and sellers are thought to exchange products and payment directly. But channels do exist for most products in an industrial society, and the objectives of middlemen may differ from those of the organization. Moreover, consumers' tastes may change.

The society and environmental forces constitute a third area in which all other things may not be equal. The major factor, of course, is actions of competitors. Also, government regulations and general economic conditions may not square with the assumptions of the purely competitive model, e.g., price freezes and controls. And finally, the organization will strive to influence consumers in ways other than changing the price of the product: by advertising, personal selling, product design, and distribution strategies. The theory ignores these nonprice influences.

Data Availability. In addition to these omissions from the theory itself, the marketing manager faces problems in obtaining the data needed to make decisions on the basis of marginality and elasticity. As we discussed in Chapter 8, many times the data are simply unavailable. And when they are available, the research process may take too long or cost too much.

Does this mean that the economic theory of pricing should be dismissed? Emphatically not—for two reasons. First, the theoretical tenets and implications of price theory are deeply imbedded into our social structure—consumers are supposed to behave "rationally," many public-policy makers draft and enforce legislation and regulations designed to

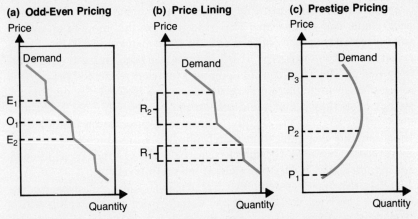

(a) Odd-Even Pricing

Price

Demand

E_1
O_1
E_2

Quantity

(b) Price Lining

Price

Demand

R_2

R_1

Quantity

(c) Prestige Pricing

Price

Demand

P_3

P_2

P_1

Quantity

Adapted from Edward R. Hawkins, "Price Policies and Theory," *Journal of Marketing*, January 1954, pp. 233–40, with permission of the publisher, the American Marketing Association.

Exhibit 12-3 Psychological Impact of Pricing Decisions

foster the pure competition ideal, and almost all organizational decision makers pay some attention to the goal of profit maximization. Second, the model is extremely useful in providing a general foundation for an understanding of actual pricing practices.

BASES FOR PRICING DECISIONS

Pricing decisions are a bit more complex than economic theory might indicate. On the revenue side of the profit equation, demand and market factors do play an important role in pricing decisions. On the other hand, costs are a major consideration in nearly every pricing decision. Many organizations, therefore, give some consideration to both demand and cost factors—their decisions are essentially profit oriented. In certain types of situations, competition is a major consideration. And governmental pricing regulations are increasingly important. We look at each in turn.

Demand-Oriented Pricing

Product demand is, of course, an important factor in pricing decisions, but the concept of demand is not as simple as economists portray it. Let us examine three types of variations on the traditional demand curve discussed in the previous section: psychological impact of prices on demand, differing intensities of demand, and demand for inferior goods.

Psychological Pricing. Perhaps the most significant factor not included in the standard economic treatment of demand analysis is the psychological effect of prices upon consumers. That is, prices may be perceived differently by different consumers, because of varying tastes, knowledge about the product, buying power, and so on. Exhibit 12-3 presents several examples of the psychological impact of prices.

The (a) part of the figure depicts the type of demand curve that might occur under *odd-even* pricing. This concept states that more of a product will be demanded at the old price of $5.95 than at an even $6.00, or at $595 rather than $600. This type of pricing practice was probably originally instituted as a financial control upon the sales clerk—it forced the clerk to make change and, therefore, record the sale. However, a number of studies have shown that some consumers, particularly final household consumers, perceive the slightly reduced odd price to be considerably lower than the even price immediately above it. Consequently, demand is more elastic between E_1 and O_1 than between O_1 and E_2. Odd-even pricing, therefore, is very prevalent at the retail level.

Part (b) depicts essentially an extension of the odd-even pricing concept. This idea is that there are certain price ranges within which demand is relatively inelastic, e.g., R_1 and R_2; between ranges, however, demand is thought to be sensitive to price. Thus, there are automobiles in the $4000 price range, the $6000 price range, and the $7000 to $10,000 price range. If this type of demand characterizes his product, the marketer can maximize his revenue by pricing at the top of the range—a compact car for $3999, or an intermediate sedan at $5995.

Exhibit 12-3 (c) depicts a third type of psychological impact of pricing—the tendency to equate quality with price. "That price is so low that the product must not be any good." Conversely, a product priced higher than others in its product class may be perceived as having greater quality or prestige. Thus, as price is increased from P_1 to P_2, demand increases. Of course, there must be a limit to this psychological perception of product quality—if the price is raised to P_3, demand will decrease. Products like Bayer aspirin, Cadillacs, and furs and jewelry are often cited as examples of prestige products.

Price Discrimination. We have stressed the concept of market segmentation—grouping customers with homogeneous wants and desires. Since different market segments have differing wants and desires, the intensity of their demand for a given product may differ. An organization could take advantage of this difference by varying the product offered to the different segments. Unfortunately, economists call this practice "price discrimination," which sounds immoral if not illegal. On the contrary, the intent of such a pricing practice is beneficial to the consumer. It attempts to match product values precisely to the desires of different market segments.

Exhibit 12-4 illustrates this point. What may appear to an economist to be one demand curve, indicated by the heavy line D, may in fact be portions of demand curves D_1, D_2, and D_3 of three different market segments. If demand for a given product does follow such a pattern, a decision to discriminate on a price basis—offer the same product at different prices to different segments—may be worthwhile to both the consumer and the organization. For example, suppose that the product in Exhibit 12-4 is automobiles. Segment one has relatively inelastic demand; this type of demand would be characteristic of a very loyal purchaser. Segment three, on the other hand, is very sensitive to price; perhaps this is the fleet buying segment. Segment two might represent the hardnosed individual car buyer. One means of distinguishing among different intensities of demand is the amount of negotiation involved in the purchase: the more the customer is sensitive to price, the more likely he/she is to negotiate.

Another basis for price discrimination is marketing channel position. Recall from Chapter 4 our discussion of the Robinson-Patman Act—price discrimination is forbidden among buyers of *like quality and grade,* but this law does not apply when the same product is sold to both wholesalers and retailers, since they are assumed to perform different functions in the distribution channel.

Demand intensity can also vary for certain products on the basis of location. Examples here include theater and stadium seats, hotel and motel accommodations, and travel classes. In each case, some locations are better than others—front row or 50-yard-line seats, rooms on the top floor or facing the ocean, and first class seats or staterooms. Some customers are willing to pay premium prices for the better locations, while others are not. Since an unoccupied location is a dead loss for the marketer, it makes sense to offer the different locations at different prices to satisfy different intensities of demand. Similarly, demand intensity may vary according to time. For example, resort hotels have slack seasons, and rental automobiles are in relatively light demand on weekends. Consequently, the marketer may improve total revenue by charging a lower price to customer segments willing to use the product at off-peak times.

Note that for price discrimination to be effective, two conditions must exist. First, the intensities of demand—reflected by demand elasticities—must be different in the different segments. Second, buyers in the lower-priced segment must not be able to resell the product to buyers in the higher-priced segment. For example, as we discussed in Chapter 4, legal regulations upon wholesaling and retailing activities preclude such a possibility. And of course, it is difficult to sell a ticket on a plane that has departed, or to a play that has been performed. Ticket scalping (reselling at higher than the printed price) however, is not unknown; most municipalities have laws against this practice.

Inferior Goods. In concept, the orthodox demand curve slopes downward and to the right (ceteris paribus): as price is decreased, more of the product will be demanded, and vice versa. Demand for certain types of products, however, may tend to increase as prices rise. In general, these products are

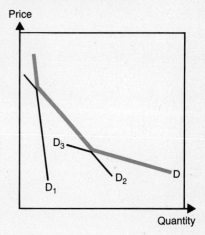

Exhibit 12-4   Demand Curves in Different Market Segments

less expensive substitutes for products that consumers prefer—hence the term *inferior goods*. The classic example is the substitution of ground meat for steak as the price of meat rises. This seeming contradiction of the economist's law of demand results from the fact that the demand for meat is relatively inelastic. Consequently, when prices rise, consumers tend to substitute lower-priced cuts of meat for the higher-priced cuts, so as to consume relatively the same amount of meat.

Consequently, in setting price, the marketing manager should consider the prices of products which can be substituted for his product. Even if demand for the inferior product does not actually increase, shifts in demand for various products do occur as a result of pricing decisions for substitute products. Examples here would include paper containers for glass, plastics for steel, gasified coal for fuel oil or natural gas, compact cars for luxury sedans, and so on.

In short, there is no question that product demand affects pricing decisions. The marketer must consider demand in setting price—and demand in the real world is a bit more complex than that described in most textbooks on economic theory. But demand analysis alone is inadequate for pricing decisions for two reasons. First, as we discussed in Chapter 7, it is difficult to obtain accurate estimates of demand relationships. Second, the marketer must consider costs as well as demand.

Cost-Oriented Pricing

In contrast to demand pricing—in which prices are set by market forces—cost-oriented pricing is based essentially on considerations within the organization. Thus, cost-based pricing decisions are said to be *administered*. Some organizations rely almost exclusively on administered prices, and all organizations pay considerable attention to the costs of producing and marketing their products.

The basic approach to cost-oriented pricing is to add a certain percentage to the cost of the product. This percentage is called the *markup;* Exhibit 12-5 illustrates this approach. The table indicates that a manufacturing firm has determined that the cost of producing a certain product is $20. In order to recover marketing costs, other expenses, and make some profit, the firm's marketing manager adds $4 to the cost of the product and sells it to a wholesaler for $24. Thus the cost of the product to the wholesaler is $24; he adds his markup ($6) to the $24 to arrive at a selling price to the retailer of $30. The retailer adds her markup, $20, to the $30 she paid for the product to arrive at a price to the consumer of $50.

Markups are often discussed in terms of percentages. This can be confusing—because percentages can be calculated on two different bases. As shown in the table, the markup percentage can use either cost or selling price as a base. Of course, the percentage obtained in a given case will differ depending on which base is used. In discussing markups, therefore,

Exhibit 12-5 Markup Relationships in Cost-Oriented Pricing

Relationship	Manufacturer	Wholesaler	Retailer
Cost	$20	$24	$30
Markup	4	6	20
Selling Price	$24	$30	$50
Markup on Cost	4/20 = 20%	6/24 = 25%	20/30 = 67%
Markup on Selling Price	4/24 = 17%	6/30 = 20%	20/50 = 40%

the base—cost or selling price—should be clearly communicated.

Markup pricing is quite prevalent—particularly among retailers and wholesalers. It has the important virtues of (1) simplicity of operation, and (2) ease of understanding. Moreover, when this approach to pricing is followed by most organizations in a given industry, prices tend to be similar. Price competition, therefore, is less severe than might otherwise be the case. And, perhaps through long usage, customers have come to understand and accept the idea of markup pricing. Thus the concept of a "fair markup" prevails and enjoys social sanction in many industries.

But markup pricing is a naive approach to pricing decisions because it ignores both cost variations and the influence of demand factors upon a particular product. If the manager attempts to find some rationale for the markup percentage used, these factors will have to be examined—unless he or she simply is going along with established pricing practices in an industry.

The break-even concept discussed in most business school courses is the basic tool for the analysis of cost-based pricing decisions. Exhibit 12-6 (a) restates the basic relationships of the break-even concept. The (b) part of the figure illustrates the effect of markup percentages upon revenue—the higher the markup, the steeper the slope of the revenue line, and, therefore, the lower the break-even quantity. For example, R_1 has the highest percentage markup and correspondingly the lowest break-even point—Q_{be1}. R_2 and R_3, representing lesser markups, have higher break-even points. Thus the break-even concept clarifies the relationships between cost, markup, and revenue, but it does not help the marketing manager decide what price to set.

For many organizations, that decision is made by top management in the form of a desired return on investment. Exhibit 12-6 (c) illustrates the effect of a target rate of return upon the break-even analysis. The amount of the desired return is, in effect, an additional fixed commitment. Therefore, it can simply be added to the total cost associated with the product. It raises the break-even point accordingly. Thus the underlying rationale for cost-oriented pricing is to set a price that will generate the desired return on investment. But that may be easier said than done.

Return on Investment (ROI) is, by definition, a ratio—the ratio of

Exhibit 12-6 Using the Break-Even Concept in Cost-Oriented Pricing

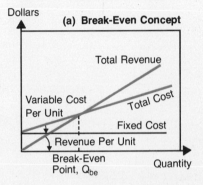

(a) Break-Even Concept

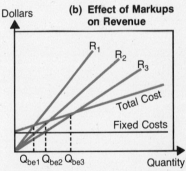

(b) Effect of Markups on Revenue

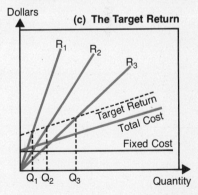

(c) The Target Return

Exhibit 12-7   Adding a Demand Estimate to Break-Even Analysis

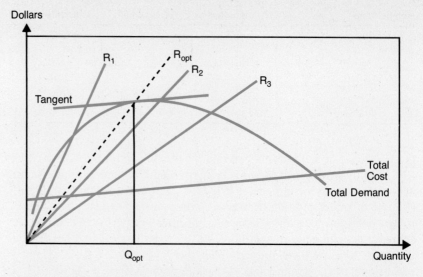

Adapted from Edward R. Hawkins, "Price Policies and Theory," *Journal of Marketing*, January 1954, pp. 233–40, with permission of the publisher, the American Marketing Association.

profit to equity. To see the role played by price in Return on Investment, the basic ROI ratio can be decomposed as follows:

$$\text{ROI} = \underbrace{\frac{\text{revenues}}{\text{assets}}}_{\text{turnover}} \times \underbrace{\frac{\text{profits}}{\text{revenues}}}_{\text{earnings}} \times \underbrace{\frac{\text{assets}}{\text{equity}}}_{\text{leverage}}$$

Thus the three components of return on investment are themselves ratios: turnover, earnings, and financial leverage. Pricing decisions are an integral component of two of these ratios, since revenues are obtained by multiplying price per unit times the number of units demanded. Thus ROI can be improved through pricing decisions that increase turnover while maintaining earnings. Grocery stores, for example, operate on a thin earnings ratio; they do it by relatively rapid turnover. Conversely, if turnover can be maintained, ROI can be improved by increasing the earnings ratio. And, of course, any marketing manager would be pleased with increases in both ratios.

But this approach to pricing is incomplete, for two related reasons. First, the target return on investment assumes a given level of revenues, i.e., a certain sales volume. At the same time, however, revenue depends upon the price charged; thus, there is circular reasoning involved in this approach to pricing. In addition, other marketing mix factors—product design, promotion, distribution decisions—also affect revenues. Despite these conceptual flaws, target-return pricing is a relatively common practice, particularly in manufacturing industries. Consequently, as we noted in Chapter 5, decisions on programming marketing effort are on a firmer conceptual basis if estimates of potential demand as well as product cost are included in the deliberations.

Profit-Based Pricing

The revenue relationships shown in the usual break-even analysis are simply projections of price times quantity for various quantities of the product. This projection discloses only what total revenue will be if various amounts of the product are sold. It does not say whether or not these amounts can be sold. Before making the pricing decision, therefore, a marketing manager will consider at least intuitively the effect of price upon the quantity demanded. Intuition may be aided by experience in pricing, competitors' actions, and assessments of the possible effect of other environmental factors, particularly governmental regulation.

If the marketer has some estimate of potential demand for his/her product (perhaps using the concepts and techniques we discussed in Chapter 8), this estimate can be incorporated into the break-even analysis. Given the total demand and total costs for a given product, the manager could—in concept at least—find the profit maximizing price. Exhibit 12-7 illustrates this type of analysis.

Note that in this figure *total demand*—rather than the usual average demand curve—which slopes downward and to the right—is presented. Various revenues represented by different markups are shown. Note that revenues will be maximized where the difference between total demand and total cost is greatest. Graphically, this point occurs where the tangent to the total demand curve is parallel to the total cost line. Thus, maximum revenue (R_{opt}) can be obtained by setting a price that results in a revenue line with a slope through the tangent point, as shown in the figure by the dashed line. Note, also, that adding a target return to the total cost will not change the optimum price. Since the target return is a fixed amount, it does not change the slope of either the total demand curve or the total cost line.

This extension of break-even analysis can be useful in making pricing decisions, but it too is subject to several limitations. First, the circular reasoning discussed above is not eliminated: the demand curve must be estimated in order to find the optimum price, but demand is influenced by that price. Second, the numbers used in the break-even analysis are assumed to be precise. For the most part, however, these numbers are estimates, particularly on the demand side. Consequently, uncertainty is always present in break-even analysis. Darden has suggested an extension of the break-even analysis to account for uncertainty. His concept is that total demand estimates should be expressed in terms of pessimistic, most likely, and optimistic terms. Exhibit 12-8 illustrates this extension.

Exhibit 12-8 Demand Uncertainty in Break-Even Analysis

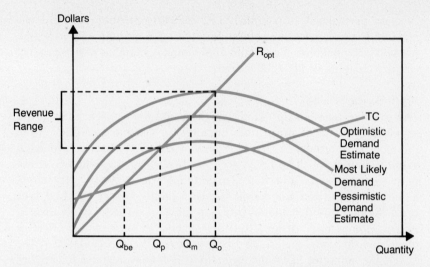

Adapted from Bill R. Darden, "An Operational Approach to Product Pricing," *Journal of Marketing,* April 1968, pp. 29–33, with permission of the publisher, the American Marketing Association.

Note that once the three demand estimates have been added to the break-even chart, the profit maximizing price can be plotted and the range of revenues can be determined. The effect of different prices on the revenue range can also be explored. Darden further suggests that this approach can be operationalized by using the beta probability distribution to obtain the expected demand curve.

One final point about break-even analysis is worth emphasizing. The break-even chart as presented seems to imply that the price of the product should be selected to cover all of the fixed and variable costs associated with the product. However, there is a fundamental difference between fixed costs and variable costs. Variable costs occur unit-by-unit as the product is produced. But fixed costs are incurred for a given period of time, no matter how many units are produced during that period. Thus, the decision maker can avoid incurring variable costs by not producing the product, but fixed costs cannot be avoided in this manner. Fixed costs continue to mount even when no products are being produced.

Now suppose that an organization has an opportunity to produce and sell some of its output at a price less than necessary to break even. Should it do so? The answer may very well be yes—on two conditions. First, the price must be sufficient to cover all of the variable costs of producing the product, and make some contribution to the fixed costs. Second, it must not be possible to save the fixed cost by not producing. The point is that in the long run and over all products, the organization must at least break-even, and would hope to make some return on its investment. In the short run and for particular products, however, pricing which permits some contribution to fixed costs, even though not covering all of them, may be worthwhile. Consider the following example.

Problem: Shall Trans Global Airlines run an extra daily flight from City X to City Y?

The facts:

Fully-allocated costs of this flight	$4,500
Out-of-pocket costs of this flight	$2,000
Flight should gross	$3,100

Decision: Run the flight. It will add $1,100 to net profit, because it will add $3,100 to revenues and only $2,000 to costs. Overhead and other costs, totaling $2,500 ($4,500 minus $2,000), would be incurred whether the flight is run or not. Therefore, fully-allocated or "average" costs of $4,500 are not relevant to this business decision. It's the out-of-pocket or "marginal" costs that count.

The contribution-to-margin approach maintains that an organization should undertake any activity that adds more to revenue than it does to variable costs—in the short run. Suppose, for example, that TGA adds an extra flight at an off-peak time—probably late at night. That flight is charged only with the variable or out-of-pocket costs—the actual dollars that TGA has to pay out to run a flight. If a ground crew already on duty can service the plane, the flight is not charged a penny of their salary expense. There may even be some costs eliminated in running the flight—men will not be needed to roll the plane to a hangar if it flies on to another stop.

Competition-Oriented Pricing

So far, we have stressed the importance of cost factors and product demand in setting prices. In some situations, a third factor—competition—must also be included. For instance, some products are so similar and competition is so entrenched that a given organization must follow industry pricing practices closely. Pricing decisions in bidding situations also require a careful assessment of competitors' pricing practices.

Meeting Competition. When products are relatively homogeneous, the market will tend to cause similar prices—although the structure of the market may range from almost pure competition to oligopoly. If the market tends toward pure competition, no individual seller can influence the price of the product. Such products as raw foodstuffs, iron ore, chemicals, textiles, chewing gum, cigarettes, and gasoline tend to be relatively similar in price within a particular market for this reason. A given organization in such a situation cannot charge more for its product, and need not charge less.

In an oligopoly situation, on the other hand, each organization knows the price is set by its competitors—and they in turn know its prices. As we discussed in Chapter 4, the *kinked-demand curve* hypothesis is widely used to explain oligopoly pricing practices. Thus, any individual oligopolist has little incentive to set a price different from that charged by others in the same industry. This is not to say that prices never change. Shifts in demand, changes in availability of raw materials, economic conditions, and so on require price changes from time to time. The usual procedure, as we discussed in Chapter 4, is for the industry to tacitly recognize a price leader—one organization in the industry which sets the pattern for prevailing prices. In the automobile industry, for example, General Motors is usually considered the price leader; in steel, it is United States Steel; and in aluminum, it is Aluminum Company of America (Alcoa).

Thus, when products are homogeneous, prices tend to be similar—in spite of disparities in market structures and/or differences in cost of production. Organizations in these types of situations, therefore, place relatively little emphasis on price. Other (nonprice) elements of the marketing mix—promotion, product differentiation, service, distribution patterns, and warranties—are emphasized. Moreover, effective control of the costs of production is extremely important in such a situation.

Bidding. In some cases, prices are set by bidding. Here the buyer solicits price offers from various organizations. The organization's bid is its price offer, and the buyer selects from among the various bids. This pricing practice is common in industrial marketing—particularly in bidding for large shipments of homogeneous products, or for custom-tailored products, such as original equipment manufacture and defense contract work. As we noted in Chapter 6, many of the products purchased by government agencies are purchased on a bid basis.

From the point of view of the individual organization, therefore, it is essential that attention be paid to possible bids of competitors. This is an area in which considerable mathematical development has taken place at the conceptual level—in the area called *game theory*. The concepts here become sophisticated and complex (the interested reader is referred to the Alpert discussion, pp. 63–73), but the basic problem remains one of securing the data to perform the analysis.

As we noted in the promotion chapter, a good deal of the time of salesmen in industries that use sealed bid pricing is spent in probing buyers for clues to appropriate bids. And some of this intelligence can also be obtained by covert means. Exhibit 12-9 presents an interesting, if somewhat dated, example of the important role that price bidding can play in an organization.

Regulation-oriented Pricing.
In contrast to the other bases for pricing decisions discussed in this section of the chapter, regulation is not generally recognized as the primary

I n 1960, the National Collegiate Athletic Association (NCAA) was accepting bids for television rights to Saturday afternoon college football games. The National Broadcasting Company (NBC) had telecast the games for the past four years, and everyone in the industry assumed that NBC would again bid for the games. The Columbia Broadcasting System (CBS) had the National Football League games, so it was not expected to bid. The American Broadcasting Company (ABC) was at that time considered to be somewhat less than equal to NBC and CBS in sports coverage. ABC had only bowling and a filmed golf show; the American Football League had not yet been founded. Consequently, it was assumed in the industry that ABC did not have the financial where-withal to bid for the college football telecast.

But ABC had a secret weapon—an agreement with Gillette Company to begin telecasting the razor-blade manufacturer's beloved Friday Night at the Fights—which NBC had dropped, on the grounds that it was a dying, dirty sport with a dwindling audience. Gillette agreed to underwrite ABC's bid for NCAA football. The bidding procedure called for all interested parties to assemble at a suite at the Royal Manhattan Hotel. At noon, NCAA representative Asa Bushnell would call for bids for the games. ABC management knew that NBC's strategy would be to carry two envelopes—a high bid and a low bid for the games. The NBC representative, Tom Gallery, would hesitate as bids were called for—to see if other bids were forthcoming. If they were, he would submit the high bid; if not, NBC would get the games for a lower bid. ABC felt that it could better NBC's low bid—assumed to be around $5.5 million, but not the high bid—assumed to be in the neighborhood of $10 million. The problem, therefore, was to get the bid envelope into the hands of NCAA officials without someone from NBC noticing ABC's presence. ABC's decision was to send Stanton Frankle—described as a "tall, thin, balding fellow with the gentle, forgettable appearance of a small-town depot agent"—to submit its bid. Frankle arrived carrying the sealed bid, wearing a plain business suit, and slipped unobtrusively into a corner chair. Secrecy was so complete that the bid was typed by ABC officials—not even a secretary was involved.

At the appointed hour, Mr. Bushnell called for bids, and Mr. Gallery hesitated perceptibly. Mr. Frankle did not stir. Mr. Gallery rose and put his envelope before Bushnell—presumably the lower bid. Then and only then did Frankle introduce himself and present ABC's bid to Bushnell. "Tom Gallery could only gulp, for there was no opportunity for a counter-bid that day." ABC's man in the corner had won rights to televise college football for 1960–61, a product that ABC continues to market to this day.

Adapted from William O. Johnson, Jr., "The Biggest TV Game of Them All," *The Houston Post,* 7 March 1971, magazine section, pp. 4–13, an excerpt from Johnson's *Super Spectator and the Electric Lilliputians* (New York: Little, Brown & Company, 1971).

tions. I think that it should be. Both the number of regulations and the impact of their authority upon decision-making are increasing rapidly. Consequently, regulation is now a factor in almost all pricing decisions, and may become the dominant pricing concern for some organizations.

Generally, the influence of regulation upon prices is upward pressure. Many organizations find that they must raise prices to cover the cost of complying with the policies of various government agencies. When the Consumer Product Safety Commission decrees that the fabric in children's clothes must be flame-resistant, the costs of producing non-inflammable clothes are reflected in higher prices. Even when the object of the regulation is not to protect consumers, costs of compliance are more easily recovered through price increases than by lowering wages or dividends. For example, costs of complying with the provisions of the Occupational Safety and Health Act, or with edicts issued by the Equal Employment Opportunity Commission or the Environmental Protection Agency, may be passed along to consumers in terms of price increases.

Regulation has traditionally been the basis for pricing in industries served by "natural monopolies." Rates for products such as electricity, gas, water, and telephone service are generally calculated by a formula based on the organization's asset base. These formulas can become quite complex, but fundamentally reflect society's conception of a "fair" return on investment—generally in the six to eight percent range. This pricing orientation at least partially explains the utility's penchant for capitalizing assets and depreciating them as slowly as tax law allows: the larger the asset base, given the fixed percentage of return, the larger the dollar amount earned will be. Other traditional regulation-based prices include interest rate ceilings on savings deposits and installment loans. The minimum markup laws which wholesalers and retailers of milk and other dairy products must adhere to in some states, and transportation rates (air fares, railroad, trucking, and ship and barge rates) are also regulated by various government agencies.

The 1970s witnessed the resurrection of a venerable type of regulation upon prices: price controls. On August 15, 1971, President Nixon instituted a price freeze for 90 days. To administer the price control system after the 90-day freeze, he appointed C. Jackson Grayson to head a group of lawyers, economists, and accountants who, together with representatives of business and labor, would constitute the Federal Price Commission. The Commission interpreted its Congressional mandate to be to bring down the rate of inflation to a level of two to three percent by the end of 1972, to sustain or at least not impede the economic recovery, and to do this in a way that would not result in an explosion of prices when controls were lifted.

These objectives are admirable, and not new. On October 20, 1774, the Continental Congress decreed that "all manufactures of this country be sold at reasonable prices" and that "vendors of goods or merchandise will not take advantage of scarcity of goods . . . but will sell the same at rates we have been respectively accustomed to for twelve months last past." Price controls were also instituted in this country during World War II.

Controls are not solely an American experience. Fifteen months after his election on a platform opposing price controls, Prime Minister Pierre Trudeau imposed price controls in Canada in 1975. During the same year, the Shah of Iran ordered not just a price freeze, but a fifteen percent across-the-board cutback in prices. History records many other price control decrees.

Controls inevitably generate questions. For example: Are previously negotiated contracts calling for future delivery at higher prices valid? How is seasonality to be accounted for; may resort hotels charge more over Labor Day than at other times? Is Halloween candy a seasonal product? In addition to seasonality, questions engendered by the cyclical nature of demand for many products had to be considered. Steel manufacturing in the United States, caught in a cyclical trough of low prices when the freeze was imposed in 1971, simply had to live with the lower prices. On the other hand, raw farm products are so numerous and so diverse that they had to be exempted entirely from price controls. But is honey a raw product, or a processed food? What about fish and other seafood when shelled, shucked, skinned, or scaled? And how about the effects of such uncontrollable factors as changes in the weather, or the disappearance in 1972 of the anchovy crop off Peru, which dramatically increased the price of fish on the world market? Exhibit 12-10 describes how pricers react to such questions.

Means of enforcing control regulations vary with the government in question. In 1774, the Continental Congress tried jawboning—"dirty hawkers and forestallers" were denounced. The Shah of Iran jailed violators on the spot. The U.S. Price Commission had the authority to levy fines, although it rarely did so. But nothing seems to work. The phrase "not worth a Continental" remains a part of the American lexicon. Grayson's opinion, which I share, is that price controls ultimately do more harm than good. I would be more comfortable with less regulation of prices and more emphasis on the market mechanism. Exhibit 12-11 indicates that it might meet social objectives more effectively, too.

The pricing decision maker, however, must take public policy regulations into account. For the near future, developed economies are likely to experience more price regulation rather than less. In addition, as we have discussed in this section, consumer expectations are rising, costs are increasing, and competition is more keen. I believe that price will play a more important role in marketing strategy than it did in the 1960s and early 1970s. Therefore, pricing decisions must be carefully and systematically integrated into the marketing program.

PRICING DECISIONS AND MARKETING PROGRAM INTEGRATION

We have reviewed the basic economic theory of pricing, and we have discussed the major pricing practices of organizations. Now we are ready to look at the process of pricing decision making. In Exhibit 12-12 the pricing process is related to the marketing plan. Pricing objectives should be related to the hierarchy of overall organizational objectives. Then the marketing functions of seeking and matching are performed. As a beginning point for marketing programming, a reference, or base, price is

Exhibit 12-10   How Pricers React to Price Controls

Executives of profit-seeking firms attempt to maintain their profits even in the face of price controls. The methods used are many and varied. Here are some typical examples:

1. *Withdraw the product*—when rising costs squeeze profits against price ceilings, withdraw the product from the market. The product may be dropped entirely. In Iran, a young price-adjuster checking a coffee shop menu in 1975 saw that a banana split cost 90 dinars (about $1.30). "I know the market price of bananas—10 dinars is the most I will allow," he said. Unable to explain that a banana split is much more than a banana cut in half, the coffee shop manager simply stopped selling banana splits. Alternatively, the product may be offered to an uncontrolled market at a higher price. During 1973, for example, the world pricing of bailing wire used by farmers to bundle crops was above the U.S.-controlled price. Japanese producers sold their wire in Europe; bailing wire in the United States was in short supply.

2. *Manipulate costs*—efficient companies generating profits in excess of the control-specified margin would be ordered to reduce prices to bring margins into line. Rather than do that, many companies pad expenses to keep margins in line. In a multiproduct firm, pricing controls are set on the total line. This means that price increases for some products could be steep, while the price might hold firm on other items in the line.

3. *Introduce new products*—price controls based upon previous experience do not apply to new products. In many cases, firms offer genuinely new products to the market. In other cases, however, products are repackaged or trivial services are added to them. For example, some U.S. com-panies cut an eighth of an inch off plywood sheets, describe the cut as a service, and then increase the price.

4. *Ask for exceptions*—another approach is to petition the Price Commission for exceptions to the price guidelines. During the first nine months of 1973, 1500 companies filed 4,741 requests for price increases with the Commission. Ninety-three percent of these requests were granted.

5. *Cheat*—controls can also be evaded by illegal means. As we discussed in Chapter 4, a "black market" inevitably springs up when the market price of a product is above the controlled price. Profits from black market activities are often substantial. And bribes or kickbacks can be paid, records can be forged, etc. Of course we offer no concrete examples of illegal activities.

Source: Compiled by the author from various sources including Grayson, *Confessions of a Price Controller;* and Walter Guzzardi, Jr., "What We Should Have Learned About Controls," *Fortune* (March 1975), pp. 102ff.

Exhibit 12-11   The Market Mechanism and Social Objectives

Moonshine whiskey is a time-honored staple of the Appalachian Mountains. The black market for bootleg moonshine has existed as long as there has been a government tax upon legitimate whiskey.

Today, however, the price sys-tem appears to be doing what regulation has not accomplished: eliminating moonshine. This is because in recent years the price of sugar, an essential ingredient in moonshine, has tripled. It takes at least 10 pounds of sugar to make a gallon of moonshine whiskey. With other inflationary factors added, the moonshine that had sold a few years ago for $6 a gallon reached $15 a gallon in mid 1975.

At that price, plus retail markup, a customer can buy "government whiskey"—tax and all. Unlike the process used for hastily made moonshine, legitimate whiskey making slowly draws natural sugars from the grains being distilled, so distillers do not need large amounts of sugar.

Source: Jonathan Kwitny, "Moonshiners in South Find Sales are Down as Costs Go Up," *The Wall Street Journal* (July 30, 1975), pp. 1, 16.

Exhibit 12-12   The Pricing Process

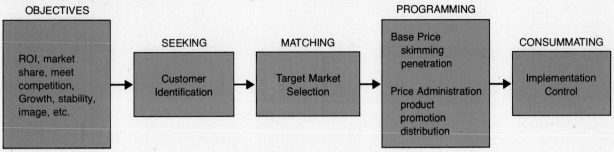

determined. This price may tend to be high (skimming) or low (penetration). After considering other marketing-mix decisions, specific prices are administered by adjusting the base price.

Pricing Objectives

Pricing decisions, like all decisions, must be based upon objectives. In the classic study of pricing objectives in major U.S. corporations, published in 1958, Kaplan and his colleagues found that the most commonly cited pricing objectives were target return on investment, maintenance of market share, meeting competition, and stabilizing industry prices.

Of course, this was a study of twenty of the largest corporations in America, and it is somewhat dated. Younger and/or smaller organizations may have different pricing objectives. A more comprehensive and up-to-date list of possible pricing objectives is suggested in Exhibit 12-13.

Pricing objectives for a particular organization, therefore, are related to that organization's overall objectives and marketing programs. Thus, pricing decisons can become exceedingly complex. Obviously, a framework for translating these considerations into specific prices for various product lines is needed. The planning model—objectives, seeking, matching, programming, and consummating (implementation and control)—can guide actual decision making. Pricing decisions in this process begin with a base price.

The Base Price

As we have noted, there is, inevitably, circular reasoning involved in pricing decisons. Revenue is generated by price per unit times quantity of units demanded, but demand is influenced by price. Moreover, price is the most easily adjustable element of the marketing mix. As the marketing program is implemented, prices can be changed quickly to match more closely the product offering of the organization to consumer wants and desires. But the pricing process must begin somewhere. Specifically, a base price must be established as the marketing program is being formulated—

Exhibit 12-13 Potential Pricing Objectives

1. Maximum long-run profits
2. Maximum short-run profits
3. Growth
4. Stabilize market
5. Desensitize customers to price
6. Maintain price-leadership arrangement
7. Discourage entrants
8. Speed exit of marginal firms
9. Avoid government investigation and control
10. Maintain loyalty of middlemen and get their sales support
11. Avoid demands for "more" from suppliers—labor in particular
12. Enhance image of firm and its offerings
13. Be regarded as "fair" by customers (ultimate)
14. Create interest and excitement about the item
15. Be considered trustworthy and reliable by rivals
16. Help in the sale of weak items in the line
17. Discourage others from cutting prices
18. Make a product "visible"
19. "Spoil market" to obtain high price for sale of business
20. Build traffic

Excerpted from Alfred R. Oxenfeldt, "A Decision Making Structure for Price Decisions," *Journal of Marketing,* January 1973, pp. 48–53, with permission of the publisher, the American Marketing Association.

to provide a starting point for formulation of the program, and a basis for price administration.

The marketing manager has any number of choices in setting the base price. A continuum of possibilities ranging from highest price to lowest price can clarify these alternatives. The top of the continuum is a price that generates no demand; at the other extreme, the price is so low that no amount of demand will generate sufficient revenues to cover costs. Exhibit 12-14 presents the continuum of base price alternatives.

Pricing rather high in the range of possible prices is called *skimming.* This term was originally used by Joel Dean to describe the strategy of entering the market with a new product priced so as to generate the most profitable sales, to "skim the cream" of the market as rapidly as possible. In terms of new products, demand is likely to be more inelastic in the early stages of the product life cycle; the high price provides a large margin which generates cash flow quickly, and if the price is too high it can be lowered more easily than a low price can be raised.

On the other hand, a low price *penetrates* the market most thoroughly—providing maximum product exposure and sales growth potential. In general, then, the base price decision involves selecting a level somewhere between skimming and penetration for each product line. Some of the factors which might influence this decision are also shown in the figure. Such factors as unique product features, for example, rising

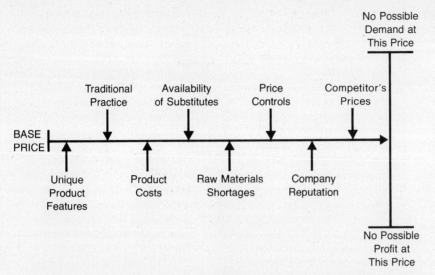

Exhibit 12-14 Factors in Determining
the Base Price Level

Adapted and drawn by the author from Joel Dean, "Pricing Policies for New Products," *Harvard
Business Review,* November–December 1950, pp. 28–36, with permission of the publisher.

costs, shortages, or a company reputation for quality, will influence the
base price in an upward direction. Conversely, traditional practices, the
availability of substitutes, federal price controls, intense price competition, tend to result in a lower base price. Of course, the exhibit presents
only a few examples of the many factors that might influence the base
price. The marketing management model can be used to structure a
systematic examination of the possible influence of various factors.
Exhibit 12-15 highlights legal considerations. Moreover, the information/
decision model discussed in Chapter 8 could be used to formally structure
and analyze the various alternative base price decisions. But even after the
base price is selected, the marketing manager's pricing decisions are not
completed. The base price must be administered.

Price Administration

For many products, a price is fixed. This is particularly true at the retail
level in mature economies—prices of groceries, clothing, books, gardening
tools, gasoline, and many other products are clearly marked on the
merchandise. Any consumer wishing to purchase the product pays that
price. In terms of total marketing transactions, however, the fixed price is
the exception rather than the rule; most prices are negotiated. Most
industrial purchasing, most government contracts, most retail transactions
in less developed economies, and even a proportion of retail sales in
mature economies involve variable pricing. The final price depends on the
bargaining strength and abilities of buyer and seller.

Exhibit 12-15   Public Policy Regulation of Pricing Decisions

Primarily because of the influence of price theory, pricing decisions are perhaps the most closely scrutinized of all marketing decisions. In fact, it has been suggested not entirely in jest that pricing below the market is *predatory;* pricing above the market is *exploitive;* and pricing at the market price is *collusive.* In addition, the pricer must be concerned with discrimination and deception in pricing.

1. *Predatory Pricing*—In times past, a firm might sell its products for less than their cost for a period of time, in hopes of driving a competitor out of business. Such practices are regulated at the national level by antitrust legislation (Sherman and Clayton Acts), and several states have *unfair trade practices acts.* The latter acts require minimum mark-ups—generally 2 percent at wholesale and 6 percent at retail—on most products. Predatory pricing is not particularly prevalent in a mature economy, although gasoline price wars (which, given the energy shortage, are perhaps a thing of the past), and the recent actions of the Great Atlantic and Pacific Tea Company, are sometimes alleged to be predatory.

2. *Exploitive Pricing*—Price increases are of major concern to consumers. In 1971 and again in 1973, President Nixon imposed price controls upon many types of products. Although each President has repeatedly disavowed price controls as other than emergency measures, it is likely that pricers will need to watch federal price guidelines carefully during the decade of the 70s.

3. *Price Collusion*—Agreements among competitors to charge an identical price are generally held to be illegal per se under the Sherman and Clayton Acts. However, agreements under the supervision of government agencies, e.g., transportation rates and local milk industry agreements, are legal. Collusion on prices is difficult to prove, because identical or very similar prices may indicate one of three dissimilar conditions: (1) the market may be very competitive, with consumers possessing sufficient knowledge to equalize prices throughout the market—retail prices of a product like gasoline, beer, and cigarettes are probably similar for this reason; (2) the industry follows the pricing decisions of a price leader, e.g., General Motors or United States Steel; and (3) there is a collusive agreement to fix prices, e.g., the gypsum industry case (Exhibit 4-19).

4. *Price Discrimination*—Selling a product of *like grade and quality* to different consumers for different prices is illegal under the Robinson-Patman Act, "where the effect of such discrimination may be to substantially lessen competition or may tend to create a monopoly in any line of commerce . . . " Price discrimination litigation under the Robinson-Patman Act is perhaps the most complex and time consuming of all marketing litigation. In general, price differentials may be justified on a cost basis, or as the good-faith attempt to meet a competitor's equally low price, or that the differential is not harmful to competition.

5. *Price Deception*—Posted prices for some products, particularly consumer goods, sometimes bear little relationship to the actual price of the product. A classic example is new car pricing—almost everyone receives some discount from the *list* price. Similarly, there are "Buy one, get one free" sales, "Going out of business" sales, and so forth. Such acts as the Automobile Information Disclosure Act, Truth in Lending Act, and unit pricing statutes, have been enacted to combat deceptive advertising. In addition, the FTC issued its *Guides Against Deceptive Pricing.*

6. *Unit Price Information*—Prices of retail products must be clearly displayed. Packaged goods must have the Universal Product Code on the labels. In addition, price control regulations, when in effect, specify that base price information must be available.

Since pricing practices are so closely scrutinized, it behooves the pricer to obtain competent legal advice on pricing decisions, particularly in these six areas.

Adapted from Marshall C. Howard, *Legal Aspects of Marketing* (McGraw-Hill Book Company, 1964); Louis W. Stern and John R. Grabner, Jr., *Competition in the Market Place* (Scott, Foresman and Company, 1970); and Earl W. Kintner, *An Anti-Trust Primer*, 2nd ed. (Macmillan, 1973), and other sources.

Exhibit 12-16 Factors in Price Administration

Product-Related	Promotion-Related	Channel-Related
Product extensions	Discount from list price	Trade discount
Trade-in	Cash discount	Brokerage discount
Returns	Credit	Quantity discount
	Cumulative quantity discount	
Leasing		Freight charges
Changes in specifications	Advertising allowance	Currency exchange rates
	Trading stamps	Seasonal discounts

For example, as we discussed in Chapter 6, most organizations have purchasing agents—who spend the majority of their time negotiating prices and terms for the products they buy; most government purchases are on a bid basis, and identical automobiles or homes may be sold at different prices to different buyers. The emphasis of pricing practices varies with cultural differences—in some countries the negotiations seem to be the end rather than the means to the end. Buying a beer in a Middle Eastern bazaar can involve an hour's discussion.

Price negotiation takes many forms. In effect, these negotiations and resulting adjustments in prices are really ways of fine-tuning the other marketing mix elements to most closely meet the wants and desires of specific customers. Consequently, one means of improving understanding of the numerous different ways that prices can be adjusted is to group them according to their relationships with other marketing mix elements. Exhibit 12-16 provides examples of the major types of price adjustments grouped in this way to guide our further discussion.

Product-Related Price Adjustments. As we discussed in the previous chapters, the basic product may be extended in a number of ways: delivery, installation, service, warranty, branding, or packaging. In many cases, these product extensions are subject to negotiation between buyer and seller. The customer may request return privileges if the merchandise cannot be resold as expected, or if it is damaged or does not perform according to expectations. In the case of consumer durable goods and industrial installations and machinery, the customer often owns an older version of the product. The price of the new product in such a case frequently involves a trade-in on the old product. Automobiles, office machines, furniture and appliances, aircraft, and industrial machinery are among products whose price often involves a trade-in.

The negotiation may involve the leasing of use rights to the product, rather than its outright purchase. Leasing may be advantageous to a customer who has insufficient capital to purchase the product, who does not wish to provide maintenance and service on the product, or who feels that the product may soon become obsolete. From the seller's point of view, leasing may be attractive because the seller can depreciate the product for tax purposes, can control its performance through service and maintenance, and can achieve economies of scale in purchasing and maintaining products in a certain class. Leasing has grown rapidly as a pricing practice in recent years—these days almost every product imaginable can be leased as well as purchased.

A final product-related pricing adjustment is to change the specifications of the product. In order to maintain the traditional 15-cent price for candy bars, for example, many manufacturers decrease the size and weight of the bar. Another example is automobile manufacturers, who have done product-related price adjusting by making accessories that used to be standard equipment optional.

Promotion-Related Price Adjustments. Perhaps the most popular form of price adjustment is a simple discount from the base or list price. In industrial buying situations, adjustments in the discount applied to various products can be made more easily than changing the base prices of the products as conditions of supply, competition, and demand vary. The industrial salesperson has merely to replace one page in the catalog with the latest discount rates, rather than replacing the entire catalog. And at the retail level, sales of merchandise at reduced prices are an increasingly common phenomenon.

Automobile manufacturers instituted another form of cash discount during the recession in 1975. They did not reduce the list price (possibly fearing a return of price controls), but offered cash rebates of $200–$500 for a car purchased during the specified time. The rebate programs did succeed in boosting sales during the rebate period, but sales fell off again when the rebates were terminated.

Another very common price adjustment is the cash discount. For example, a supplier may offer credit terms of *2/10 net 30,* which means that a discount of 2 percent from the list price will be allowed for payments made within 10 days, and the net amount (list price less returns and allowances) is due in 30 days. Thus, the 2 percent discount is a promotional device—and a very attractive one. By paying the invoice just 20 days sooner than it is due, the organization is in effect borrowing money at the rate of 36 percent per year ($360 \div 20 = 18$ periods in which a 2 percent discount could be earned; $18 \times 2 = 36$ percent). Similar reasoning applies to those consumer credit card arrangements: paying the total amount within 30 days avoids a finance charge of $1\frac{1}{2}$ percent per month, or 18 percent per year.

A third type of product-related adjustment is the extension of credit. Credit is very much a promotional tool; taking advantage of credit terms, in effect, lowers the price of the product. Credit availability is particularly important for the purchase of homes, automobiles, and other durable goods. In 1976, the payment period for automobile loans was extended from 3 years to 5 years—actually increasing the price of the automobile when interest charges are considered, but making that payment easier to meet on a monthly basis. Two-thirds of automobiles purchased in the United States are financed on credit. Another promotion-related price adjustment is the cumulative quantity discount which lowers the total price of an order purchased during a given period by some specified percentage. This is clearly a promotional device to increase total order size. Similarly, some manufacturers give retailers an advertising allowance—sometimes based upon size of purchase. This allowance is to be used for advertising the products to final consumers, and is, therefore, a reduction in the price of the product. Finally, trading stamps, given by many retail establishments, are a controversial promotional tool. There is some evidence to show that trading stamps actually increase the prices of products with which they are associated, but many consumers consider trading stamps to be a price reduction.

Channel-Related Price Adjustment. The greatest majority of adjustments to list price occur in channel relationships. Perhaps the most common is the trade discount. A manufacturer, for example, may quote trade discounts of 40 and 10 percent. The wholesaler is charged the retail price less discounts of 40 and 10 percent; he is expected to keep the 10 percent to cover the costs of his wholesaling activities, and to pass the product along to the retailer at a 40 percent discount. For example, if a manufacturer expects the retail price to be $400, the retailer would pay $240 ($400 less 40 percent) to the wholesaler, who in turn would pay $216 ($240 less 10 percent) to the manufacturer. Note that the 40 and 10 percent discounts do not add up to a 50 percent reduction in price; each discount is computed on the basis of the amount remaining after the previous percentage has been deducted.

Trade discounts originated in traditional channels, in which the activities of wholesalers and retailers were clearly different and relatively easy to define. In such cases, the discounts roughly reflected the costs of marketing effort by each middleman in the channel. Now, however, channel relationships are more complex, and it is more difficult to determine an appropriate trade discount structure. In addition, some distribution channels make use of the services of brokers—middlemen who do not take title to the goods, but who do perform facilitating activities. Brokers normally are allowed what amounts to a trade discount for their services. However, as channel relationships have become more complex, many channel members have assumed brokerage functions and have requested brokerage allowances for these functions. Under the Robinson-Patman Act, such allowances are illegal—but the marketing manager in a highly competitive channel may be forced to grant an advertising allowance or discount from list price which may be construed as a brokerage discount.

The noncumulative quantity discount is another important channel-related price adjustment. In contrast to the cumulative quantity discount, which is essentially a promotional device, the noncumulative quantity discount applies to purchases taken in large lots. It essentially is a price reduction to compensate the buyer for assuming shipping and/or storage charges. For example, many firms charge a higher price for *less than carload* (l.c.l.) lots than they do for carload lots. (In this case, a car is a railroad boxcar.) This is simply because shipping costs in carload lots are considerably lower than the rates for l.c.l. lots.

Product prices can also reflect freight charges directly. The pricing of products for which the freight charge is significant can be extremely complex. The simplest system is one in which the selling price is quoted f.o.b. mill or factory. The term *f.o.b.* means *free on board;* f.o.b. mill or factory means that the seller pays the cost of loading the shipment aboard a carrier—the buyer is responsible for the product and all freight charges beyond that point. On the other hand, an organization might establish a uniform pricing policy, one price to all buyers regardless of location. This policy is in effect *f.o.b. buyer's location.* The f.o.b. *factory price* is, in effect, price discrimination in favor of buyers located close to the seller; conversely, f.o.b. *buyer's location* pricing discriminates against those located close to the seller. Compromise pricing policies have included *zone-delivered* pricing—in which the manufacturer designates zones within which delivery charges will be identical; *basing-point* pricing—in which the seller quotes the price plus freight charges from a given base point to the buyer's location (raw steel products, for example, used to be quoted on a basis of freight charges from Pittsburgh, no matter where the steel was actually produced); and *freight absorption* pricing—in which the seller agrees to absorb some portion of freight charges. This is a complex area because price discrimination is illegal. Consequently, whatever adjustment the seller makes with respect to freight charges can be challenged on some grounds.

A different type of price adjustment is required in international marketing, because the value of one currency relative to another fluctuates from time to time. If a list price is quoted in American dollars, for example, the price of the product in Japan or in Canada may vary from day to day depending on the exchange rates of Japanese yen and Canadian dollars for American dollars. Managing pricing decisions in international markets, therefore, involves complex questions of arbitrage, which are beyond the scope of this book. However, marketing managers should be aware that this problem does arise in international marketing.

A final type of channel-related price adjustment is the seasonal allowance. At the retail level, vacations at ski resorts are cheaper in the spring, and swimming pool construction is cheaper in the fall, because these periods represent slack seasons for the seller. (This is an application of contribution to margin pricing that we discussed earlier in the chapter). Similarly, seasonal discounts may be granted within channels. Such discounts shift the storage function from the seller to the buyer, and help to smooth out the seller's production activities throughout the year. Seasonal discounts may be offered in cash, or they may involve forward-dating. The latter practice simply involves dating an invoice several months in advance. The buyer is not expected to pay the invoice until the due date—thus the seller has, in effect, extended credit to the buyer. Seasonal discounts may also take the form of guarantees against price declines.

In summary, pricing objectives must be related to the overall objectives of the organization. Once this is done, a base price will be set. Then adjustments to the base price can be made as the marketing program is implemented, to improve the match between product utility and consumer wants and desires. The possible pricing objectives, base price decisions, and means of adjusting the base price are literally infinite.

CONCLUDING NOTE

Pricing decisions are important to any organization. First, price directly affects revenue obtained per unit, and it interacts with other marketing mix elements to affect the number of units demanded. Second, price is the easiest marketing mix element for the layman to understand. Consumers and public policy makers can more readily comprehend changes in product prices than they can differences in product quality, promotional strategies, or distribution decisions. Consequently, pricing decisions are closely scrutinized by the society in which the organization functions.

Pricing decisions are neither so all-encompassing nor so simple as economic theory suggests. Pricing decisions are more closely intertwined with overall managerial objectives and strategies than are other marketing mix elements. For example, the advertising manager is generally given a budget and told to create advertisements with maximum impact for that amount of resources. In pricing, however, production personnel control costs, and financial managers are concerned with rates of return, liquidity, and risk—all of which are directly affected by the prices charged for a given product. As a result, authority and responsibility for pricing decisions is much less clear-cut than product, promotion, and distribution decisions. Many different people within the organization are likely to have some influence over the pricing decision.

Marketing scholars and economists really have not developed particularly useful theoretical bases for actual pricing decisions. The economic decision rule of pure competition is clearly inadequate, and recent evidence shows that it is not as easy for an organization—even a giant corporation—to "administer" prices as some economists have suggested, e.g., John Kenneth Galbraith (*The New Industrial State*), and Gardiner Means (*The Modern Corporation and Private Propety*). Consequently, pricing decisions in most organizations today are based on intuition, past experience, and industry rules-of-thumb. Considerable research into pricing activities is underway, but at present, textbooks can offer little beyond generalizations and descriptions of industry practice to pricing decision makers.

KEY TERMS AND CONCEPTS

Price Perspectives
  consumer
  society
  organization
Price Theory
  profit maximization
  marginality
  elasticity
Limitations of Price Theory
  theoretical constraints
  data availability
Pricing Policies
  demand-oriented
  cost-oriented
  competition-oriented
  regulation-oriented
Demand Considerations
  psychological pricing
  price discrimination
  inferior goods
Cost Considerations
  markups
  break-even concept
  return on investment (ROI)
Profit Considerations
  demand uncertainty
  marginal pricing

Competition Considerations
  leader pricing
  bidding
Price Objectives
  target return on
    investment
  market share
  meeting competition
  industry stabilization
Base Price
  skimming
  penetration
Price Administration
  (see Exhibit 12-16)

QUESTIONS FOR DISCUSSION

1. From your own experience, indicate prices or price ranges that you consider fair for the following products: a motel room, two professional football tickets, a good restaurant meal, an apartment, and a new suit or dress. What is the basis for your answer in each case?

2. Suppose that the fixed costs of producing a certain product were $250,000, the variable cost per unit was $10, and top management desired a target return of 20 percent. Find:

a. The quantity that must be sold at $15 per unit to obtain the target.

b. The price necessary to achieve the target at a volume of 50,000 units. Evaluate the strengths and weaknesses of this information.

c. Suppose the company were offered a contract to purchase 100,000 units at $12.00. Should it accept? Why or why not?

3. Categorize the price elasticities of the following products: gasoline, football tickets, automobiles, salt, candy bars, jet aircraft. Identify influential factors in each case.

4. How would you go about pricing such products as: a new type of pump for oil well operations, a new flavor cake mix, and a copying machine that reproduces colors?

5. What types of price adjustments would be most effective for such products as:

a. structural steel
b. fashion dresses
c. automobiles
d. the services of a CPA?

SUGGESTED READING

1. Mark I. Alpert.
Pricing Decisions. Glenview, Ill.: Scott, Foresman and Company, 1971. A short paperback discussion of pricing; very informative and well-referenced, but written at a somewhat advanced level.

2. Gilbert Burck.
"The Myths and Realities of Corporate Pricing." *Fortune*, April 1972, pp. 84–9, 125–26. Comprehensive, well-written survey of current thinking and research on pricing practices; this article is reprinted in Betsy D. and Gabriel M. Gelb, *Insights for Marketing Management.*

3. Jackson Grayson, Jr. with Louis Neeb.
Confessions of a Price Controller. Dow Jones-Irwin, 1974. An account of Grayson's tenure as chairman of the Price Commission under President Nixon; written for the intelligent laymen rather than the lawyer or economist; engrossing anecdotes of day-to-day operations; Grayson's

experiences result in a firm commitment to market forces as opposed to government regulations of prices.

4. Joseph P. Guiltinan.

"Risks-Adversive Pricing Policies: Problems and Alternatives," *Journal of Marketing*. January 1976, pp. 10–15. Overview of problems and procedures for setting and administering prices during periods of "stagflation"; well-researched and carefully written. Reprinted in Gelb and Gelb.

5. D. H. Kaplan and others.

Pricing in Big Business. The Brookings Institute,1958. Classic study of the pricing activities of America's largest corporations.

6. Earl W. Kintner.

An Anti-trust Primer, 2nd ed. Macmillan, 1973. The standard layman's guide to this area; written by the former chairman of the Federal Trade Commission.

7. Donald F. Mulvihill and Steven Paranka, eds.

Price Policies and Practices: A Source Book of Readings. New York: John Wiley and Sons, 1967. Collections of articles and talks about pricing activities and decisions.

8. Alfred R. Oxenfeldt.

Pricing Strategies Amacon, 1975. Relatively short overview; written for the pricing executive by perhaps the leading academic authority on pricing; this book is a summary and synthesis of Oxenfeldt's work over the years; no startling insights, but much practical information.

13/IMPLEMENTATION AND CONTROL OF THE MARKETING PROGRAM

This chapter completes and summarizes our examination of the marketing program. The previous four chapters were devoted to *planning to do;* this chapter focuses on what the marketing manager *does.* Major points include:

1. Implementation of the marketing program involves the managerial functions of organizing, coordinating, and motivating.

2. Marketing control is the process of adjusting the marketing program's actual performance to the objectives of the marketing plan. Marketing control involves translating objectives to performance standards, measurement of actual performance, and taking corrective action if necessary.

3. In accordance with the basic exchange model, marketing performance should be measured in terms of three sets of objectives: those of the organization, of customers, and of society in general. Volume/cost/profit measures for the first set are rather well-developed. There is increasing need for better techniques for the measurement of performance at the customer and societal levels.

4. The marketing audit concept—the systematic appraisal of marketing functions in light of the marketing plan of an organization— has much to recommend it. Few organizations today, however, employ this concept on a regular basis.

Legend has it that, as they were preparing for their historic flight at Kitty Hawk, Wilbur Wright turned to his brother and said, "Yes, Orville, but will it fly?"

Much of the material in a textbook on marketing management must be devoted to marketing planning—setting objectives, analyzing the environment for opportunities, and designing programs to take advantage of the opportunities. In actual situations, managers devote much of their time to assessing results of their programs.

There are relatively few general guidelines that a textbook can offer on the implementation and control of marketing programs. The fundamental guidelines we examine in this chapter constitute our discussion of the marketing function of consummating exchange transactions. We begin with an overview of marketing performance assessment.

IMPLEMENTATION OF THE MARKETING PROGRAM
Students of management list various managerial functions, e.g., planning, staffing, organizing, coordinating, motivating, and controlling. In previous chapters, we have devoted considerable attention to marketing planning, and later in the chapter we discuss marketing control. We discussed sales personnel staffing in Chapter 10, and, in Chapter 2, qualifications for marketing management positions. At this point, we briefly review marketing planning and organization, and then comment upon coordinating the program and motivating marketing personnel.

A Brief Review of Marketing Planning
The basic marketing planning process model was presented in Exhibit 5-8. It is recast in performance terms as Exhibit 13-1. The planning phases—objective-setting, seeking, matching and marketing programming—have been extensively discussed in the intervening chapters. Briefly, the fundamentals include:

1. *Objectives*—First, organizational objectives are hierarchical. For example, a basic organizational objective of profit maximization may require a marketing strategy of maximum sales volume, which in turn requires extensive advertising campaigns, which results in an attempt to maximize audience exposure through a mass medium such as network television. Second, to measure and control performance, the objectives should be operational—stated in terms that can be communicated and measured. An operational statement of the maximum-sales-volume objective, for example, might be to sell 200,000 units before the end of the fiscal year.

2. *Seeking*—This phase of planning involves (1) identifying potential customers, and (2) assessing their wants and desires in light of organizational objectives and capabilities. A basic example is that, while everyone has to eat, no restaurant can expect to satisfy everyone. The management

Exhibit 13-1   Assessing Marketing Performance

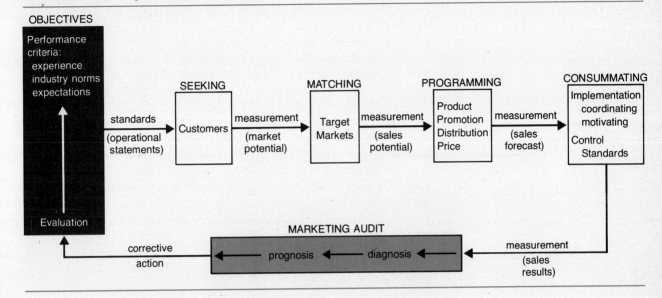

of a given restaurant, therefore, might attempt to predict the demand for different types of dishes prepared in various ways. One segment of the population might like Italian dishes, another might prefer fast-service American food, and a third might desire an extensive variety of dishes.

3. Matching—This phase involves selecting the target market from the various market segments that have been identified and assessed. Target market selection is based upon the matching of customer desires and product benefits to meet organizational objectives in light of supplier and societal constraints.

4. Programming—After the target market has been selected, decisions about various aspects of the marketing mix (product, promotion, distribution, and price) will be made. If the restaurant's management decides to serve the segment desiring a variety of foods, it might feature a wide product line, fast service, low prices, and convenient mealtime hours—a cafeteria.

Finally, the marketing program must be integrated. Program integration involves the synchronization of various mix elements to serve the wants and desires of the target market effectively and efficiently. For example, a cafeteria, which presumably has a profit-seeking objective, would pursue purchasing and food preparation policies that offered a varied selection at competitive prices to customers. In addition, it would promote these policies on television and in newspapers, and perhaps would feature special dishes on different days; it would also endeavor to provide adequate seating space for customers during peak hours.

Program integration can be considerably more complex than the cafeteria example illustrates. Recall from Chapter 9 that the products of an organization must be managed at three levels: the individual product item, the product portfolio, and the marketing program. We illustrate program integration at the product item level, and use the issues raised to demonstrate the need for careful organization for marketing programming.

At the individual product level, the product life-cycle concept (Exhibit 9-1) is expanded in Exhibit 13-2 to provide one type of framework for evaluating integration efforts. In the introductory phase of a life cycle of a given product, the organizational objectives might be to wean the product in the marketplace, i.e., to move it from the category of an experimental new product to an established position in the organization's product line. During the growth stage that objective might change to maximization of market share—which in turn might give way to profit maximization during maturity and to the minimization of effort required to maintain market share in the decline stage.

Decisions in analysis and programming might change over the life cycle of the product. (You might trace through several additional rows or columns of this figure in order to better understand issues involved in program integration.) With this brief review of market planning as background, let us look now at organizing for marketing programming.

Organizing for Marketing Programming
Organizing marketing activities involves both a permanent structure for the marketing function, and a rationale by which this structure can be adjusted to accommodate various marketing programs. As we discussed in Chapter 5, in most contemporary organizations, the basic structure involves separation of marketing operations and marketing services. Adjustments to this basic structure are based primarily upon geography, products, or customers (Exhibit 5-5). Now that we have examined marketing strategy and the separate decision areas of the marketing program, we can see how the basic structure of the marketing function is organized to cope with the dynamics of market program implementation. Exhibit 13-3 guides the discussion. Each individual product is guided through its life cycle by a product manager in some large and diversified organizations, or by the sales manager in charge of a particular line, geographic district, or type of customer.

Responsibility for the product portfolio is divided. In most organizations it is the top ranking sales force officer—often called the General Sales Manager—who bears responsibility for marketing the present product mix. At the same time, product identification (branding) is the respon-

Exhibit 13-2 Example of Program Integration in Various Stages of Product Life Cycle

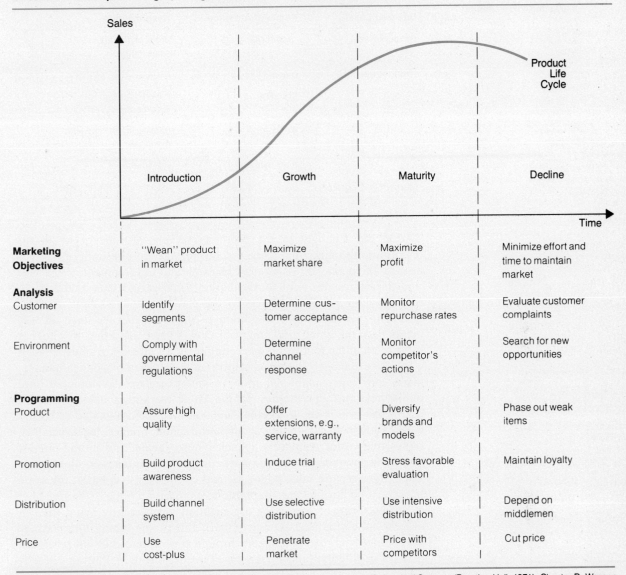

	Introduction	Growth	Maturity	Decline
Marketing Objectives	"Wean" product in market	Maximize market share	Maximize profit	Minimize effort and time to maintain market
Analysis				
Customer	Identify segments	Determine customer acceptance	Monitor repurchase rates	Evaluate customer complaints
Environment	Comply with governmental regulations	Determine channel response	Monitor competitor's actions	Search for new opportunities
Programming				
Product	Assure high quality	Offer extensions, e.g., service, warranty	Diversify brands and models	Phase out weak items
Promotion	Build product awareness	Induce trial	Stress favorable evaluation	Maintain loyalty
Distribution	Build channel system	Use selective distribution	Use intensive distribution	Depend on middlemen
Price	Use cost-plus	Penetrate market	Price with competitors	Cut price

Source: Adapted by the author from various sources, including David J. Luck, *Product Policy and Strategy* (Prentice-Hall, 1971); Chester R. Wasson, *Product Management* (Challenge Books, 1971); and Nariman K. Dhalla and Sonia Yuspeh, "Forget the Product Life Cycle Concept," *Harvard Business Review* (January–February 1976), pp. 102–111. I am indebted to Professors Arthur Prell and Raymond LaGarce for illuminating discussions on the PLC.

sibility of the advertising manager, with increasing input and sometimes veto power by the organization's legal counsel. Responsibility for product extensions may be held by the advertising manager, or in a larger organization may devolve upon managers of packaging, installation,

Exhibit 13-3 Organizing for Marketing Programming

Decision Level	Focus of Attention	Organizational Responsibility
Product Item	product life cycle	product manager sales manager
Product Portfolio	present mix	general sales manager
	branding	advertising manager legal counsel
	extensions	packaging, service, etc. managers
	mix changes	R&D manager
Marketing Program	planning process	marketing vice-president

service, etc. Changes in the product mix are of concern to all the organization's marketing managers, but primary responsibility usually is held by the manager in charge of research and development.

Overall responsibility for the marketing program is exercised through the marketing planning process by the chief marketing officer, the vice president of marketing. In addition to the managers we have already mentioned, the chief marketing officer will have reporting to him/her some or all of the following: marketing research director, traffic manager, warehouse manager. In some organizations, people in personnel management, long-range planning, training and executive development, and public relations may report to the chief marketing officer. Finally, individuals within the marketing function must be designated as liaison with middlemen, facilitating agents, production, finance, legal, vendors, representatives of regulatory agencies, news media, and public interest groups. In short, organizing for marketing programming is no simple task. The basic structure must be logical and comprehensive, but at the same time must be flexible and adaptable to change.

New forms of marketing organization are currently being tried in order to cope with the dynamics of marketing programming. One strategy here is simply to rotate managers through various line and staff positions, perhaps in different functional areas of the organization. Putting a district sales manager in a marketing planning spot, for example, can be a real eye-opener for him, and his perspective can frequently improve marketing planning. A second structural development is the *matrix organization*, i.e., structuring authority/responsibility patterns that cut across traditional organizational lines. Exhibit 13-4 presents one example of the use of the matrix organization, the venture team, which can be employed in new product development, and in setting up a marketing or management information system.

Exhibit 13-4 The Venture Team—Example of Matrix Organization

The efforts of most organizations to take advantage of the dual rewards of operating efficiency and maximum impact in the marketplace result in an organization structured along bureaucratic lines. Bureaucracy, with its well-established patterns of communication, fully defined jobs, and lines of authority is ideally suited to managing the ongoing functions of the organization.

But the future of many enterprises is more dependent upon the successful launching of new products than on the day-to-day conduct of established affairs. The venture team is an organizational innovation designed to fit structure to the task of new product development. As shown in the figure, a venture team is a separate organizational entity with the participants drawn from various units of the organization, predominantly technical areas such as design engineering, application engineering, production, market research, and finance. These teams operate within the broad outlines of the marketing plan almost as separate entrepreneurships, with top management linkage and support, the broad mission of successful new product development, and flexible life span and membership.

Despite some problems in achieving technical and marketing balance on the teams, and in appraising the contribution of individual team members to organizational objectives, the venture team concept seems ideally suited to nonroutine tasks such as new product development, appraising mergers and acquisitions, and implementing information systems.

Adapted from Richard M. Hill and James D. Hlavacek, "The Venture Team: A New Concept in Marketing Organization," *Journal of Marketing,* July 1972, pp. 44–50, with permission of the publisher, the American Marketing Association.

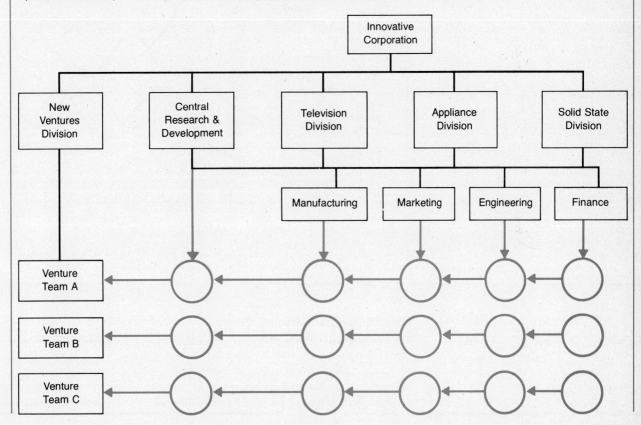

Exhibit 13-5 Consequences of Marketing Program Interactions

(a) Interactions

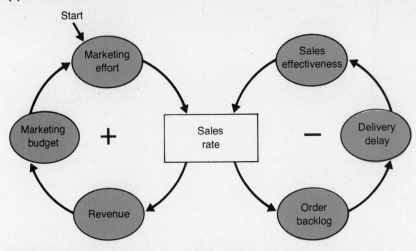

(b) Consequences

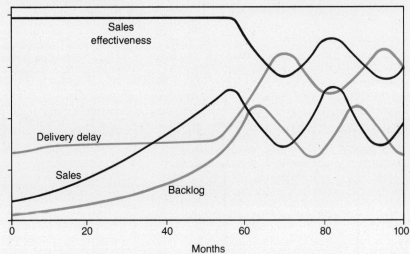

Adapted from Jay W. Forrester, "Market Growth As Influenced by Capital Investment," *Collected Papers of Jay W. Forrester,* © Copyright Wright-Allen Press, Cambridge, Mass., 1974. Reprinted by permission of the publisher.

Coordinating the Marketing Program

Throughout this book, we have stressed the interrelationships among marketing activities. Exhibit 13-5 presents one simplified but very clear illustration of such interrelationships. The (a) part shows that marketing effort has a positive effect upon the sales rate, which in turn increases revenue, which leads to a larger marketing budget which can be used to

Exhibit 13-6   Examples of Factors that the Marketing Program Should Coordinate

Customer	Supplier	Society	Marketing Program
Consumer:	*Production:*	*Regulators:*	*Product:*
Order size and frequency; complaints and adjustments; payment.	Raw materials shipments; plant output rates; quality control.	Reports to Internal Revenue Service; Federal Price Control Commission; Equal Employment Opportunity Commission; Federal Trade Commission.	Sizes and colors; special customer requirements; installation.
Middlemen:	*Finance:*		*Price:*
Delivery schedules; service to customers; cooperative advertising.	Working capital requirements (for inventories, credit and marketing expense; capital budgeting of marketing investments).	*Competitors:*	Price list; price adjustment procedures; price marking.
Facilitating Agents:		Intelligence; counter strategy; new products.	*Promotion:*
Marketing research reports; advertising campaign planning; railroad strikes.	*Personnel:*	*Influencers:*	Dissemination of product information to salesmen; media schedules; "legaling" of campaigns.
	Hiring of salesmen; union demands; employee training.	Environmentalists' suit; minority group boycott.	*Distribution:*
			Store hours; order form completion; delivery schedules; order expediting.

improve marketing effort. But this positive effect also influences other organizational activities. For example, the increased sales rate will eventually cause an order backlog as production facilities reach capacity. The order backlog results in a delivery delay which reduces sales effectiveness and, therefore, results in a lower sales rate. The consequences of these interrelationships are shown more clearly in part (b). Sales effectiveness is high—sales rise rapidly during the sixty-month period before production capacity is reached. At this point, the order backlog rises and delivery delays increase; these decrease sales effectiveness and subsequently sales. As sales decline, the order backlog lessens, delivery delay decreases, and sales effectiveness increases—thus causing the cycle to occur again. The point, so graphically demonstrated by Forrester's computer, is that even relatively simple systems interact in complex ways. In more homely words, real-life management is always messy.

Many other variables could be added to this example. Exhibit 13-6 presents examples of types of factors which influence the marketing effort, and, therefore, should be carefully coordinated. Of course, both exhibits cover only a few of the many possible interrelationships among marketing program activities. These activities must be carefully coordinated if the program is to succeed.

Coordination. Program coordination addresses the questions: *who, where, when,* and *how* (marketing strategy formulation presumably has already

Exhibit 13-7   Critical Path Scheduling in Program Implementation

Suppose that an organization desiring to introduce a new product must coordinate the eight activities listed in the table below (estimated completion times are also included):

Activity	Completion Time (months)
1. Program start	6
2. Consumer testing	3
3. Production planning	2
4. Marketing budget	1
5. Sampling	2
6. Channel commitments	3
7. Product distribution	1
8. Advertising campaign	4
Total Time	22

Note that if each of these activities is performed in sequence, the total time to implement the program is 22 months. This time can be reduced by Critical Path Scheduling procedures. The first step is to lay out a network showing activities in this program that can be completed simultaneously:

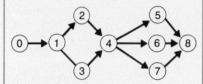

There are several (six, to be exact) different paths from program start (1) to introducing the advertising campaign (8). The path which takes the longest number of months to complete is: 0-1-2-4-6-8; this path requires 17 months. First note that the project can be completed in 17 months as opposed to 22 months. Second, note that this path is the *critical path:* activities located on this path must be completed on schedule if the program is to be implemented in 17 months. On the other hand, activities not on the critical path, e.g., production planning, can be delayed without delaying the total program completion time.

This simplified example can be extended in many ways. First, modern computers can handle many activities and reduce computation times. Second, the computer can be used to calculate new critical path schedules if activities can be reprogrammed for completion in less time. Third, the cost of activity completion can be added to the network. Fourth, since the time estimates are uncertain, probability distributions can be attached to them, and used to calculate expected times and probabilities of completing the program by a given date.

For a more complete discussion at an elementary level and further references, see Richard I. Levin and Charles A. Kirkpatrick, *Planning and Control with PERT/CPM* (New York: McGraw-Hill, 1966).

---

answered the questions *what* and *why*). Numerous methods are employed to answer these questions and to synchronize marketing program implementation. Perhaps the most commonly employed are schedules, budgets, and checklists. For example, a program to bring a new food product to market will include the scheduling of a number of different activities over various periods of time, budgets of resources to accomplish these activities, and checklists to be sure that significant details are not overlooked. Program coordination decision making can be aided by various mathematical procedures: Exhibit 13-7 illustrates the application of Critical Path Scheduling to program implementation.

Communication. Information necessary for program implementation must be communicated. Communication, as we discussed in Chapter 10, involves common understanding between communicator and audience. Managerial communication depends principally upon two factors: a clearly structured organization (well-defined communication channels) and managerial receptivity to communications (relatively noiseless mes-

1. Information Dissemination	2. Instruction	3. Interaction
Up-to-date organization charts and telephone directories	Training programs	Executive lunchrooms
An organization newsletter	Formal performance appraisals	Interdepartmental committees
Computer time-sharing	Supervisor coaching	Role playing and sensitivity training
An organization library, competently staffed		

Exhibit 13-8 Some Methods of Improving Intraorganizational Communications

sage flow). More specifically, managerial communication is enhanced when information flows freely up and down the organization's structure, as well as laterally. This two-way flow of communication requires an attitude of openness to the communication of ideas, criticism, and other information.

This ideal is not always easy to attain. For one thing, any information channel is subject to *noise*—errors and interruptions in information transmission. Recall, for example, the experiment performed in basic psychology in which one individual is given a paragraph or two of information and told to whisper that information as accurately as possible to the individual sitting next to him. After several individuals have been communicated to and in turn have communicated this information, the last individual is asked to repeat the story aloud. Inevitably, many unintended errors and subtle changes have been introduced. Secondly, information may be deliberately distorted. No one likes to give the boss bad news. Consequently, the information may be compressed and edited to make the subordinate appear in a more favorable light. (Some writers call this phenomenon *uncertainty absorption*.)

Organizations generally, and marketing management in particular, should attempt to foster complete and open information flows. Exhibit 13-8 presents examples of several different kinds of ways of improving organizational communications. Information dissemination and instructions are an integral part of the communications activities in any organization. Similarly, most organizations today recognize the value of executive interaction, both informally (perhaps in the executive dining room) or more formally on various interdepartmental committees. In addition, some organizations are beginning to experiment with some of the more sophisticated techniques of the behavioral sciences, e.g., role playing, sensitivity training, and transactional analysis groups.

Motivation. In Chapter 6, we discussed motivation—inducing people to act in a desired manner—with respect to buying behavior. Similar principles apply to the motivation of organizational subordinates. Much has been written about motivation; all authorities agree that two principles are paramount. First, people join organizations to fulfill their individual objectives. The manager seeking to motivate people, therefore, must recognize these individual goals. Second, the manager must show that attainment of organizational objectives will lead to the accomplishment of individual objectives. (Note that this, in essence, is no different from recognizing customer wants and desires and matching organizational products to them.) As we noted in Chapter 6, it is considerably easier to enunciate these two principles than it is to carry them out in a given situation. Of all the expert advice given about managerial motivation, the classic is Douglas McGregor's *Theory Y* approach. Exhibit 13-9 reviews these principles.

An extension of Theory Y is Management by Objectives (MBO). Essentially, the MBO approach marries McGregor's Theory Y with Drucker's emphasis on the managerial importance of balancing needs and goals to get results (see *Managing for Results*). The MBO process generally consists of three steps:

1. Development of organizational objectives by top management (Recall Chapter 5).

2. At each level in the objective hierarchy, superiors and subordinates jointly develop objectives for the subordinate that are consistent with overall organizational objectives set by top management.

3. At the end of the planning period, superior and subordinate evaluate the subordinate's performance in light of the agreed upon objectives.

The MBO approach capitalizes on Theory Y commitment to clear operationally stated objectives that the individual participates in specifying. Thus, MBO is a motivational process, since individual commitments and achievement of results can lead to a high level of intrinsic job satisfaction. Exhibit 13-10 presents an example.

We do not mean to imply that motivating marketing personnel is easy. In particular, MBO is not a panacea for marketing management's motivational problems. There have been failures in applying the approach—basically in not recognizing that a systematic, comprehensive, long-term investment by the organization's managers is required. There have also been successes. MBO is more than participative management. Moreover, further refinements are on the horizon. One promising approach is called BARS (Behaviorally Anchored Rating Scales). The extension here is that the objectives at each level are set through an empirical process of psychologically scaling dimensions of job performance, and behavior appropriate to that performance for each organizational level.

CONTROL OF MARKETING PROGRAMS
Once the marketing program has been implemented, the manager begins to see whether the actual results of the program conform to its objectives.

Robert Townsend has trenchantly summarized McGregor's approach to motivation. He noted first the incorrect assumptions (McGregor called them Theory X assumptions) under which many managers operate:

1. People hate work.
2. They have to be driven and threatened with punishment to get them to work toward organizational objectives.
3. They like security, aren't ambitious, want to be told what to do, dislike responsibility.

Townsend maintains that these assumptions lead to such directing practices as the following:

1. Office hours 9–5 for everybody except the fattest cats at the top. Just a giant, cheap time clock. (Are we buying brains or hours?)
2. Unilateral promotions. For more money and a bigger title I'm expected to jump at the chance of moving my family to New York City. I run away from the friends and a lifestyle in Denver that have made me effective and my family happy. (Organization comes first; individuals must sacrifice themselves to its demands.)
3. Hundreds of millions of dollars are spent annually communicating with the employees. The message always boils down to: "Work hard, obey orders. We'll take care of you." (That message is obsolete by fifty years and wasn't very promising then either.)

In contrast to these assumptions, Townsend summarizes McGregor's Theory Y assumptions as follows:

1. Man is a wanting animal.
2. His behavior is determined by unsatisfied needs that he wants to satisfy.
3. His needs form a value hierarchy [Recall Maslow from Chapter 6] that is internal, not external:

   (a) Body (I can't breathe.)
   (b) Safety (How can I protect myself from . . .?)
   (c) Social (I want to belong.)
   (d) Ego (1. Gee, I'm terrific. 2. Aren't I? Yes.)
   (e) Development (Gee, I'm better than I was last year.)

This theory of human motivation leads to the following conclusions about the way managers should direct subordinates:

1. People don't hate work. It's as natural as rest or play.
2. They don't have to be forced or threatened. If they commit themselves to mutual objectives, they'll drive themselves more effectively than you can drive them.
3. But they'll commit themselves only to the extent they can see ways of satisfying their ego and development needs. (Remember the others are pretty well satisfied [in modern industrial societies] and are no longer prime drives.)

Townsend concludes this masterful summary of McGregor's work with the statement that Theory Y is the explanation for Ho Chi Minh's unbelievable 25-year survival against the mighty blasts of Theory X monsters of three nations:

"There is nothing to distinguish their generals from their private soldiers except the star they wear on their collars. Their uniform is cut out of the same material, they wear the same boots, their cork helmets are identical, and their colonels go on foot like privates. They live on the rice they carry on them, on the tubers that they pull out of the forest earth, on the fish they catch and on the water of the mountain streams. No beautiful secretaries, no prepackaged rations, no cars or fluttering pennants . . . no military bands. But victory, damn it, victory!"

Summarization based on Robert Townsend, *Up the Organization* (New York: Alfred A. Knopf, 1970), pp. 139–43, with permission of Alfred A. Knopf; Ho Chi Minh quote taken by Townsend from Jules Roy, *The Battle of Dienbienphu* (New York: Harper and Row, 1965) p. 304 with permission of Harper and Row. For a more complete discussion, see Douglas McGregor, *The Human Side of Enterprise* (New York: McGraw-Hill, 1960), especially pp. 33–57.

Generally, they do not—at least, not in all respects. Perhaps the most fundamental maxim of management is a dictum known as *Murphy's Law:*

    If anything can go wrong, it will;

and its corollary:

    If nothing can go wrong, something will go wrong anyway.

Exhibit 13-10 MBO Planning and Performance Evaluation Form

Performance and Action Plan for John Smith—Divisional Sales Manager

Objective Statement	3 months		Plan	6 months		Plan	9 months		Plan	1 year	
	Pro-jected	Actual		Pro-jected	Actual		Pro-jected	Actual		Pro-jected	Actual
1. Expand in S.W. region and achieve 10% market penetration	1%	.5%	Temporary transfer of salesmen to S.W. terri-tory	4%	3.5%	Increase advertising expenditure 10%	7%	5.5%	Develop sales promotion to counter competition	10%	——
2. Increase profit on product line A by 7% over 2 years	.25%	.25%	Continue rate & type of promotion, continue expense reduction	.5%	.6%	Watch other product lines for losses at the expense of this increase	1.5%	2.1%	Consider readjusting goal if performance continues	3%	——
3. Select 2 salesmen for territorial sales management positions out of 20 initial candidates	2	20	Rotate candidates with most potential in district mgr.'s office	2	11	Allow each candidate to participate in significant ''people'' decisions	2	5	Allow each candidate to participate in significant ''strategy'' decisions	2	——

Source: Michael J. Etzel and John M. Ivancevich, ''Management by Objectives in Marketing. Philosophy, Process, and Problems,'' *Journal of Marketing* (October 1974), p. 51.

As regards marketing problems, Murphy was an optimist. The marketing manager has to be concerned not only with the planning and implementation of marketing programs, but with their control. Control is the process by which the results of marketing efforts are brought into closer harmony with marketing objectives. This section provides an overview of the control process: standards, measurement, and corrective actions.

Standards for Marketing Control

The first step in marketing control is to translate organizational objectives into standards against which performance can be measured. In general, there are three bases for performance standards—industry norms, past performance, and managerial expectations. Exhibit 13-11 provides examples of types and sources of marketing performance standards for various aspects of marketing operations.

Many organizations operate in established industries. These organizations can usually secure information about the performance of other members of the industry for use in guiding their own performance. For

Exhibit 13-11   Examples of Types and Sources of Marketing Performance

| Aspect of Marketing Operations | Types of Standards | | |
	Industry Norms	Past Performance	Managerial Expectations
Sales	Annual reports Trade publications	Marketing department	Sales forecast
Market Share	Trade publications	Marketing department	Market share forecast
Prices	Observation of competitors Customers	Marketing department	Pricing policy decision
Expenditures (advertising, sales, shipping)	Trade publications	Accounting department	Budgets
Profits	Annual reports Trade publications	Accounting department	Pro forma statements
Return on Investment	Annual reports Trade publications	Comptroller's office	Pro forma statements
Number of Employees	Trade publications	Personnel department	Policy decision
Corporate Image	Special Studies	Special Studies	Policy decision

Keith K. Cox and Ben M. Enis, *The Marketing Research Process* (Pacific Palisades, Calif.: Goodyear Publishing Company, 1972), p. 491, with permission of the publisher.

example, competitors' sales, pricing policies, and advertising strategies are usually obtainable from annual reports, and by observing competitors' activities. Industry norms can be quite useful as general guidelines for marketing performance standards. The underlying assumption of this type of standard is that if organizational performance is comparable to that of others in the industry, things cannot be too bad. This, of course, is not necessarily true. For example, an organization's market share may hold steady while the total market declines, or its share may fall as the total market expands. In essence, industry norms provide comparisons with average performance.

A second basis for performance standards is past performance—how do this month's or year's sales compare to those of last month or year? This information should be available from sources within the organization—marketing department records, accounting data, personnel files, and so forth. Frequently, however, such information is not available in useful form. A Marketing Information System, if operational, can help here. Past performance measures provide at least a minimum standard, a benchmark by which to measure subsequent efforts. Also, trends of performance over time can be analyzed. However, the use of past information assumes that historical patterns have relevance for future decisions. It may be misleading to measure current performance on the basis of these results.

The third basis for performance standards is "what the boss thinks." Forecasts, budgets, schedules, and policy decisions become standards against which actual performance is measured. These standards may involve both industry norms and past performance, but they also take estimates of future conditions into account. To the extent that managerial expectations are realistic, they probably provide the most useful standards for measuring performance. Assessments of future conditions—based on the decision maker's intuition and experience, plus information—perhaps provide the most feasible standards for the situation which the decision maker will face. Of course, as compared with industry norms or past performance, managerial expectations are more subjective and uncertain. Consequently, they are more open to criticism.

The guiding principles of performance standards for marketing control are that they are derived from organizational objectives, and they are to be stated in operational terms. The next step is to measure actual performance against the objectives represented by the standards.

Measurement for Marketing Control

As we noted in outlining the marketing planning process in Chapter 5, marketing program performance should be measured in terms of both effectiveness (degree of objective attainment) and efficiency (degree of effectiveness per unit of resource input expended). In terms of the equation,

$$\text{Payoff} = \text{Benefit} - \text{Cost},$$

effectiveness relates to the benefit side of the equation, and efficiency to the cost component. Exhibit 13-12 illustrates this relationship.

We noted in Chapter 3 that society participates with the organization and the customer in every exchange transaction. For this reason, measurement of the benefit-effectiveness and cost-efficiency of a marketing program should take cognizance of benefits and costs to each of the three participants. In terms of marketing control, this leads to three levels of measurement of marketing performance: performance relative to marketing standards (which presumably reflect organizational objectives, including supply constraints), relative to customer satisfaction, and relative to the satisfaction of society. Exhibit 13-13 provides examples of possible measurements at each level.

The most common level for measuring marketing program performance is internal operations. Internal measures of effectiveness generally include sales volume, market share, growth rates of sales and market share, as well as more specific measures such as number of sales calls and

Exhibit 13-12   Effectiveness and Efficiency in Objective Attainment

	Benefit	
Cost	Effective	Not Effective
Efficient	Baking ten cakes in the morning and having exactly ten cakes demanded that day	Producing only black automobiles
Not Efficient	Killing a fly with a sledge hammer	Spending many dollars on bidding for a contract but not getting it

advertising recall rates. The efficiency with which these benefits are attained is usually measured in terms of salesperson's expenses as a percent of sales, sales per sales call, advertising cost per thousand exposures, percentage of deliveries made within the time allowed, inventory turnover, sales per square foot of floor space, and so on. Crude measures of these internal factors date from the beginning of commerce, and relatively sophisticated approaches to such measures stem from the scientific management studies of the early twentieth century.

In line with the marketing concept, organizations began in the late 1950s and early 1960s to measure customer (channel member or ultimate consumer) satisfaction. Effectively satisfying customers can be measured basically by purchase amounts, and also by repurchase rates, product quality perception, degree of loyalty to store brand, and organizational image held by the customer. Efficiency, from the customer's point of view, can be measured basically in terms of product prices, and also in terms of the number of different organizations that a customer patronizes for a given product, the time expended per purchase, number and severity of customer complaints and so on. Some of the methods used to measure customer satisfaction (surveys, experiments, behavioral observations, purchase panels, etc.) were discussed in Chapter 8.

Some of marketing's critics suggest that the consumerism (Exhibit 2-7) movement indicates both the need for performance measures, and the relatively little progress in providing performance measures at the customer level. On the effectiveness side, measures of additional product benefits or convenience need to be developed. Efficiency might be measured in terms of customer complaints or cost of lost sales. The Better Business Bureau, certain congressmen (e.g., Senators Hart, Magnusson, Moss, and Representative Eckhart), and various federal, state, and local consumer-oriented agencies receive numerous complaints. And the cost to a firm of a sale it fails to make—a factor included in most theoretical models of inventory control—is rarely measured with any precision.

The picture at the societal level is similar. Examples of improvements in marketing effectiveness at the societal level might include promotion of racial tolerance by integrated advertising and improvements in the quality of life (gains in GNP are an inadequate measure of improvements in living quality). But the issues at this level tend to be complex. Electric utility companies are frequently criticized for advertising their services in this period of scarce energy. Their rebuttal is that optimum operating efficiencies—and therefore maximum social efficiency—require steady operations (no peaks and valleys in demand for electricity) which advertising helps produce. Similarly, one regional brewer in Texas switched to all-aluminum cans, which are recyclable. This would seem to be a type of marketing effort that improves social efficiency, but aluminum is very expensive to produce (production consumes great amounts of electric power). Perhaps the social efficiency of glass containers, or even cardboard ones, would be superior to that of aluminum.

Many effectiveness measures at the societal level are standards enacted through public policy: product quality (e.g., pure food and drug standards), safety (automobiles, flammable fabrics), occupational licenses for doctors, beauticians, and real estate agents. In addition, the government has recently moved into affirmative action in the marketing of houses, e.g., requiring a subdivision developer accused of racial discrimination to place 10 percent of its total advertising budget in black-oriented newspapers and radio stations. The issue of advertising truthfulness discussed in Chapter 10 can also be viewed as a social-effectiveness indicator. In general, however, organizational responsibilities to society are difficult to measure. Exhibit 13-14 describes one attempt to provide a framework for measurement at all three levels.

This outline of the levels of marketing performance measurement suggests three pertinent conclusions:

1. Marketing managers must be concerned about effectiveness and efficiency at all three levels. Automobile manufacturers, for example, may be able to profitably build large, gas-guzzling automobiles that individual consumers want very much to own, but find them prohibited or heavily taxed to increase social satisfaction. On the other hand, social standards for emission control have led to prices that many customers consider exorbitant. And the car that is satisfactory to society in general and to consumers as individuals may be unprofitable to the organization.

2. While these levels are conceptually distinct, there are interactions among them. Moreover, both benefits and costs can be either direct or indirect. The automobile manufacturer who promotes a high performance car to fulfill the direct desires of one market segment may be indirectly damaging his image with consumers who are economy- or ecologically-oriented.

3. The present state of knowledge and skills for performance measurement decreases as we move from internal operations to customer satisfaction to

Level of Standard	Effectiveness (Benefit)	Efficiency (Cost)
Internal Marketing Operations	Sales volume Market share Growth rate Number of sales calls Advertising recall rates	Salesmen's expenses (% of sales) Sales per call Ad cost per thousand exposures On-time delivery percentage Inventory turnover Sales per square foot of space
Customer Satisfaction	Purchase amounts Repurchase rate Product quality perception Loyalty to store and brand Organizational image	Product price Number of organizations patronized Time expended per purchase Complaint ratio
Satisfaction of Society	Product quality standards Product safety standards Occupational licenses Customer mix Advertising truthfulness	Product life Material requirements Energy consumption

Exhibit 13-13 Levels of Measurement of Marketing Performance

societal satisfaction. We know most about how to measure effectiveness and efficiency at the internal operations level, relatively less about customer satisfaction, and almost nothing about precise measurement of societal satisfaction.

The following section is devoted to techniques that can be employed to measure marketing performance at these three levels. We conclude this discussion of the control process in marketing with a look at the corrective action stage.

Corrective Action in Marketing Control

All efforts at marketing control will be to no avail if the actions necessary to bring actual performance into line with standards are not taken. But change is painful—remember the fellow who got a new boomerang and then killed himself trying to throw the old one away? Corrective action is particularly painful in marketing. There are no hard-and-fast rules to guide managers in this area, but the fundamental problems associated with corrective action fall basically into two categories: technical problems and human problems.

Technical Problems. The first (and perhaps most complex) technical problem that a manager contemplating corrective action faces is identi-

Exhibit 13-14 Framework for Evaluation of a Television Advertisement

	Benefits		Costs
		Direct	
Producer	Product exposure, company image enhancement, specific information		Production costs of the advertisement, media time
		Indirect	
	Carryover effect to other products, goodwill derived from sponsoring a popular program, prestige of national name		Opportunity costs of a different campaign, damage to image from sponsoring unpopular program
		Direct	
Consumer	Product information, new or better uses for the product		Opportunity cost of time expended viewing the commerical
		Indirect	
	Entertainment or knowledge derived from the program		Advertising costs borne by products purchased, irritation with commercials and programs, misleading information
		Direct	
Society	Generation of jobs, incomes, taxes		Resources expended to produce and air commercial, time and energy consumed viewing
		Indirect	
	Increased expectations contributing to rising standards of living, entertainment, knowledge dissemination, contribution to social change		Inefficient allocation of resources, legal and economic consequences of deception, excess power over program content

Source: Richard E. Homans and Ben M. Enis, "A Guide for Appraising Marketing Activities," *Business Horizons* (Oct. 1973), pp. 20–30.

fication of specific causes of the particular deviation from standard. One common standard, as noted above, is sales effectiveness. When sales are not as high as the manager believes they should be, he/she will try to determine why this is so. But many factors influence sales. It may be difficult to isolate the particular factor or factors responsible for the deviation in a given case. For this reason, marketing decision makers sometimes turn to other measures of effectiveness, e.g., advertising recall, number of sales calls, and so on. The difficulty is that such measures have to be related to the type of benefit the organization ultimately is striving for; in many cases, such relationships are tenuous at best.

The second technical difficulty is one of time lags associated with the desired corrective action. There are four types of such lags. First, it takes a certain amount of time to identify the causes of the measured deviation. Second, it takes time to decide what action should be taken. Third, implementing that action requires time; and fourth, additional time is needed to measure the impact of the implemented action upon results. Often a manager finds that after allowing for each of these four types of lags, the problem that he/she set out to correct has changed in the meantime. Perhaps a salesperson's poor performance in a given period, for example, was the result of certain personal difficulties. The sales manager must notice the lackluster performance, trace the problem to the particular salesperson, decide to spend some time traveling with that individual, and then actually accompany him/her. By this time, the salesperson may have straightened out the personal difficulties, be again performing at normal level, and consequently resent the undue interference of the sales manager.

The third type of technical problem in taking corrective action is budget constraints. The fundamental question here is deceptively simple: is the contemplated action worth more than it costs? In principle, one should not pay more than 99 cents to get a dollar's worth of control. The classic example here is product quality control inspection. Assume, for instance, that the production process for a particular product results in 10 percent defectives. Defective products mean dissatisfied customers. One hundred percent inspection of the products will reveal 90 percent of the defects. One inspection of the production run will reduce the defectives to 1 percent, as follows: 90 percent nondefectives, plus $.90 (.10) = .09$ defectives identified by inspection. A second inspection, while presumably costing the same as the first, will reduce the defective rate only $.9(.01) = .009$, or less than 1 percent. It may well be that, in terms of increased customer satisfaction, the second inspection is not worthwhile.

Human Problems. Even if these technical difficulties can be overcome in a given situation, corrective action almost always involves people, and this means potential behavioral problems stemming from resistance to change. In the first place, people become committed to certain ideas or ways of doing things. Too often, for example, the marketing executive who helped develop a new product is unwilling to accept the fact that the marketplace does not want that product. Or a salesperson may enjoy calling on customers who are no longer profitable to the organization. Corrective action to eliminate these problems may be damaging to the egos of those individuals. Moreover, this action may be detrimental to the morale of other members of the organization—"If they sacked old Jane, will I be next?"

In view of such potential difficulties, marketing executives sometimes do not act quickly enough—organizational inertia prevents proper corrective action. Organizational tradition is also a powerful source of such inertia. "We can't drop that product. The founder of the company developed it." Or "Son, we don't do it that way in this organization." On the other hand, there are risks associated with acting too precipitantly. The marketing manager must evaluate each of these types of problems before taking corrective action. The next section explores techniques of analysis to aid in measuring performance and the taking of corrective action when needed.

VOLUME/COST/PROFIT MEASUREMENT

For any organization, marketing performance at any level must ultimately be measured, at least in part, in dollars-and-cents terms. This section explores fundamentals of marketing productivity measurement. After a brief examination of basic measurement concepts, we concentrate on measurement at the internal operations level.

Measurement Concepts

The measurement of marketing performance in a given organization involves a set of activities specific to that organization, because marketing effort derives from the particular marketing plan developed by that organization. Performance measurement should adhere to four fundamental principles.

First, the standards for measuring performance should be clear and explicitly communicated before the marketing effort to be measured is undertaken. Clear standards prevent misunderstandings about the nature of the expected effort, communication assures that the standard is known to those who will be measured by it, and advance notice precludes changing the rules in the middle of the game. For example, a 20 percent increase over last year's sales volume is clearly preferable to "We want you to do a better job this year, Joe," which may lead to "Gee, boss, I thought you wanted 10 percent; I had no idea you expected 30 percent."

To communicate unambiguous standards in advance means that the unit of analysis must be carefully defined. The standard must specify who, what, how much, where, and when. For example, a sale may be recorded when the salesperson writes the order, when the invoice is prepared, when the product is shipped, or when the bill is collected. Does a salesperson get credit for a sales call if he/she talks with the prospect on the telephone, or briefly shakes hands, or only if the prospect allows sufficient time for the salesperson to complete a call report? The basic unit of analysis will vary for different organizations, and possibly within a given organization at different times. But the standard should be specified clearly for a particular organization at a given time.

The second principle is that measurement should encompass a total systems perspective. Ideally, therefore, the impact of all factors upon organizational objectives should be measured. For example, the return to an airline from investment in faster aircraft and an emphasis on on-time flight performance will be diminished if passengers must wait 30 minutes for their luggage. A high sales volume generally is good, but not if it is accompanied by high salespersons' expense accounts or bad debt losses. And marketing objectives might be satisfied by providing the customer unusual product modifications at the expense of overtime work in the machine shop. In short, the organization should be viewed as a system striving to achieve an ultimate objective. Performance should be measured in light of contribution to that overall objective.

While the systems perspective should pervade performance measurement, it often happens that a few factors are critical to the attainment of organizational objectives. The third principle of performance measurement, therefore, is to focus upon significant performance factors. This phenomenon, which is very pervasive in human affairs, is sometimes called the principle of concentration. For example, a few salespeople produce most of the orders in many companies, a few customers are the heaviest volume purchasers, eight of ten new products ultimately fail, mature markets tend to be dominated by a few competitors, and so on.

Finally, one of the fundamental theorems of management is that an individual should be accountable only for factors that he/she can control. The corollary for measurement is that the results of each individual's area of responsibility should be measured. But this is easier to say than to do. For instance, how much of the sales volume in a given territory can be attributed to the efforts of salespeople and sales managers in that territory, and how much to national advertising, product design, or manufacturing excellence? The concept, however, is clear: results should be traceable to the individual responsible for the performance that generated those results. Now let us see how these principles can be applied to marketing performance measurement, beginning with volume analysis.

Volume Analysis

As the term is used in this context, volume refers to the benefit portion of the payoff equation—the effectiveness with which organizational objectives are pursued. In marketing, volume is generally measured in terms of sales. We discuss sales analysis first, and then briefly review some other ways to measure volume.

For purposes of illustration, let us suppose that a company, rather unimaginatively named Hypothetical Products Corporation, had annual sales of $10,000,000 in its most recent year. In accordance with the control concepts discussed in the previous section, HPC has carefully defined its control standards, e.g., when a sale actually takes place, and measures sales performance according to two standards: last year's performance and quotas for the current year. The company's products are sold in four sales territories. Exhibit 13-15 presents the basic sales analysis of HPC.

Exhibit 13-15 HPC Sales Analysis by Territories

Territory	Actual Sales ($000)	Performance Last Year	Budget This Year	Performance Index (Actual ÷ Standard) Last Year	Quota
A	$4,000	$3,500	$4,500	1.14	89
B	2,000	2,500	3,000	.80	.67
C	3,000	2,500	2,500	1.20	1.20
D	1,000	1,200	900	.83	1.11
Total	$10,000	$9,700	$10,900	1.03	.92

Note: Data are hypothetical

Note first that actual sales for the most recent reporting period were not evenly distributed among the four territories. Territory A generated the most sales, and Territory D generated the smallest amount. But this simple comparison of absolute magnitudes is not particularly meaningful. Many factors influence sales, and some of these (e.g., competitors' actions, general economic conditions, governmental regulations, and production schedules) are essentially beyond the control of the marketing manager. More meaningful results are obtained when sales are compared against standards. As compared with the previous year's performance, Territory C has done well and Territory A also improved; Territories B and D did worse this year than last. Performance relative to this year's quota expectations is even more pertinent. Territory C did well by this criteria also. Territory A, however, did not do as well as expected, and Territory D, despite some slippage from the previous year's performance, did better than management expected. Finally, Territory B looks even worse on the quota criterion than it did relative to last year's performance.

This initial breakdown of HPC's total sales by sales territories provides some information for marketing management. A more detailed analysis of sales, particularly in Territories A and B, would provide additional information. Exhibit 13-16 presents breakdowns of sales in these territories by sales representative.

The patterns revealed by the sales representatives' performance in the two territories are very different. In Territory A, the failure of the territory as a whole to meet its quota is attributable entirely to salesman Adams. His performance is considerably worse than his previous year's performance, and even further below his quota for the present year. In contrast, Berrera and Ms. Cole performed adequately, and the new man Dulski exceeded management's expectations. In Territory D, on the other hand, the poor performance seems to be about equally the fault of all three salesmen.

Thus, HPC's general sales manager might contemplate different types of corrective action for the poor performance of the two territories.

Exhibit 13-16   HPC Sales Analysis by Sales Representative

(a) Sales Breakdown for Territory A

Salesman	Actual Sales ($000)	Standards ($000) Performance Last Year	Standards ($000) Budget (Sales Quota)	Performance Index (Actual ÷ Standard) Last Year	Performance Index (Actual ÷ Standard) Quota
Adams	$ 700	$1,200	$1,500	.58	.47
Berrera	1,300	1,100	1,300	1.18	1.00
Cole	1,100	800	1,000	1.38	1.10
Dulski	900	[a]	700		1.29
Territory Total	$4,000	$3,100	$4,500	1.29	.89

[a] Dulski was not with HPC last year; the sales representative he replaced sold $400,000.

(b) Sales Breakdown for Territory B

Salesman	Sales ($000)	Standards ($000) Performance Last Year	Standards ($000) Budget Quota	Performance Index (Actual ÷ Standard) Last Year	Performance Index (Actual ÷ Standard) Quota
Egbert	$ 750	$ 950	$1,050	.79	.71
Fontaine	650	800	1,000	.81	.65
Glotz	600	750	950	.80	.63
Territory Total	$2,000	$2,500	$3,000	.80	.67

Note: Data are hypothetical.

He certainly would want to have a talk with Mr. Adams—improvement in that individual's performance might bring the entire territory up to standard. The uniformly lackluster performances in Territory B, on the other hand, suggest either that there are three people having trouble (rather unlikely) or that some other factor is influencing sales in that territory. Perhaps the district sales manager is not doing his job, or perhaps a competitor is doing particularly well in that area.

In short, it is often useful to break down aggregate sales figures. It may be necessary to examine several successively finer breakdowns to identify causes of problems. And then the analyst may find that the problem is beyond the control of the manager directly responsible for volume performance. The influence of external factors on volume performance may cause an adjustment in volume standards.

Sales are not the only basis upon which volume performance can be measured. Physical unit measurement is useful in some cases, e.g., a political organization seeking votes or a church seeking converts. Second, many organizations are as interested in the rate of growth in sales or physical units as they are in the absolute magnitude. Third, many companies, particularly those in well-defined industries, measure market share. Market share is generally defined to be the proportion of an organization's sales to total sales in that industry. Finally, as noted above, the marketing manager may be unable to control certain factors that influence sales. Some organizations take cognizance of this possibility by measuring not raw sales, but gross margins or even net profit. These volume measures require an understanding of marketing costs.

Cost Analysis

Marketing cost measurement is relative; costs can almost always be reduced. But will efficiency thereby be improved? For example, an increase in advertising expenditures may result in a more than proportionate increase in sales or a decrease in the amount of personal selling effort required to attain a given level of sales. Therefore, marketing costs should always be measured relative to standards of performance.

Cost Measurement Fundamentals. Since almost all cost information in an organization is compiled by the accounting department, the place to begin marketing-cost analysis is with traditional accounting statements. Exhibit 13-17 (a) presents a highly simplified version of the accountant's traditional or "natural" income statement for HPC, Inc. Note that the usual format is

$$
\begin{aligned}
&\text{Sales} \\
-\ &\text{Cost of Goods Sold} \\
\hline
=\ &\text{Gross Margin} \\
-\ &\text{Expenses} \\
\hline
=\ &\text{Net Profit}
\end{aligned}
$$

[Pedantic aside: income taxes are ignored to simplify the discussion.] This format is suitable for reporting financial results to outside parties, but is generally of little value for marketing planning and control. A rearrangement of this information in functional form would improve its value for marketing decision making.

Part (b) of Exhibit 13-17 presents this rearrangement. In accordance with our earlier discussion of the organization's structure of marketing activities, marketing activities are divided into operations (sales, advertising, and physical distribution) and marketing services. Expenses incurred by each area of marketing operations, marketing services, and nonmarketing activities are as shown in part (b). This tabulation indicates, for example, that the most important costs by function are respectively: salaries of sales representatives and sales managers for the selling operation, rent (primarily warehouse space) for physical distribution, and accounts payable (perhaps for an agency's services) for advertising. This

Exhibit 13-17 Analysis of HPC Marketing Costs

(a) "Natural" Income Statement ($000)

Sales	$10,000
Cost of Goods Sold	6,000
Gross Margin	4,000

Expenses

Salaries	$1,500,000	
Rent	300,000	
Accounts Payable	400,000	
Depreciation	1,000,000	3,200
Net Profit		$800

(b) Functional Accounts

Expenses ($000)	Sales	Advertising	Physical Distribution	Marketing Services	Nonmarketing	Total
			Marketing Operations		Nonmarketing	Total
Salaries	$400	50	100	60	890	1,500
Rent	50	20	80	25	125	300
Accounts Payable	10	60	20	15	295	400
Depreciation	15	—	35	—	950	1,000
Total	$475	130	235	100	2,260	$3,200

(c) Functional Breakdown of Sales Account by Territories

Sales Expenses ($000)	A	B	C	D	Total
		Sales Territory			Total
Salaries	$150	100	90	60	400
Rent	20	12	10	8	50
Accounts Payable	3	4	2	1	10
Depreciation	4	2	7	2	15
Total	$177	118	109	71	$475

Note: Data are hypothetical

rearrangement of expenses by function gives the marketing manager a better idea of the nature of marketing costs.

Further improvement could be made by decomposing the functional costs, perhaps by geographic sales territory. The (c) part of Exhibit 13-17 presents this breakdown. It shows, for example, that expenses are highest in Territory A and lowest in Territory D. This is due primarily to sales salaries of $150,000 in Territory A. On the other hand, accounts payable expense is highest in Territory B, while depreciation expenses are greatest in Territory C. In probing for reasons underlying these figures, management might find, for example, that the sales manager for the district comprised of these territories has her office in Territory A; therefore, her entire salary is charged to Territory A. The high accounts payable in Territory B may reflect unusual sales expenses—perhaps the sales representatives are still ordering steaks for their customers despite the directive from headquarters to trim entertainment expenses. And the high depreciation charge in Territory C may be the result of greater wear-and-tear on automobiles in a mountainous area.

Additional information might be provided by a further breakdown. For example, an examination of expense accounts of sales representatives might disclose that one has become careless, extravagant, or possibly even dishonest. Other breakdowns of marketing costs by product line or by customer might also prove useful.

Cost Allocation. Functional decomposition of marketing costs assumes that the costs can be traced to the particular function under investigation. This assumption is not always valid. In the above example, for instance, the district sales manager's salary was placed in Territory A. Presumably, however, the district manager is responsible for sales in all four territories. Some part of her salary, therefore, is applicable to each of the four territories. But it is simply not possible in most cases to determine precisely what proportion of that salary should in fact be charged to each of the four territories.

An accountant's reaction to this difficulty is to allocate the salary to the territories. As a basis for the allocation, he/she might simply divide the salary into four equal parts and allocate one part to each territory. This is certainly the simplest allocation method, but it may not be entirely fair. The supervisor in Territory D might argue that his territory is only half the size of Territory A, and, therefore, should receive only half the salary allocation. Another commonly employed procedure is to allocate the administrative salary overhead on the basis of total sales—if Territory B accounts for 30 percent of sales in the district, then it should be allocated 30 percent of the sales salary overhead. But the district manager may in fact be spending most of her time in Territory C, trying to strengthen the company's weak position in that territory. Ideally, her salary should be allocated in proportion to her effort in each territory, but proportion of effort is not always easy to determine. (For example, the manager could keep track of time spent on each territory's affairs. But that would be a nuisance.)

The above discussion illustrates the basic dilemma faced by accountants. For reporting purposes, the books must balance. Every penny must be accounted for. For marketing decision making, however, the allocation of costs to balance the books may obscure relevant information. For decision-making purposes, therefore, direct costing procedures may be more appropriate than traditional accounting methods (called absorption costing).

Direct Costing. The basic difference between absorption and direct costing lies in the treatment of those costs which cannot be traced directly to a given decision unit. For example, the general sales manager of HPC is responsible for sales quotas in all four sales territories. He must, therefore, devote some of his effort to each territory. It would be very difficult, however, to determine precisely how much of his salary was related specifically to his efforts in a given territory. Thus, in most organizations, the sales manager's salary is allocated under the absorption-costing method to the various territories.

The two most commonly used allocation methods, as noted above, are equal division and in proportion to total sales in the territory. These two allocation methods produce vastly different results. Suppose that the manager's salary and expenses for the current period totalled $50,000. An equal allocation would assign $12,500 ($50,000 ÷ 4) to each of the four territories. Allocation on the basis of percentage of sales (Exhibit 13-15) would require that Territory A absorb 40 percent of the $50,000 or $20,000 as contrasted with a $5,000 absorption of the sales manager's salary in Territory D. Which method is most correct, or most fair? This is an extremely difficult question to answer. No matter how the common costs are allocated, some managers will feel that they are being held responsible for costs over which they have no control.

Direct costing avoids possible controversies of this nature by not assigning to a decision unit costs that cannot be traced directly to that unit. The advantages of this method for specific decision situations are illustrated in the following section on profit analysis.

Profit Analysis

We have looked at volume measurement (effectiveness) and cost measurement (efficiency). Clearly, a more comprehensive analysis of marketing performance could be obtained by measuring the net payoff (effectiveness — efficiency). Payoffs, as noted above, are usually stated in terms of profit. We look first at profit analysis, continuing to use the HPC example, and then look at ways of improving profit performance.

Exhibit 13-18 summarizes the relevant figures for our analysis. The (a) part presents an income statement in traditional accounting form, i.e., employing absorption costing. The direct and allocated costs, however, are separated to facilitate subsequent analysis. Note that Territory A appears to be most profitable, that Territory D is only marginally profitable, and that Territory B actually shows a loss. (The precision of these observations

Exhibit 13-18　HPC Contribution to Profit Analysis by Territories

(a) Income Statement in Traditional Form

| | Sales Territory | | | | |
	A	B	C	D	Total
Sales	$4,000	$2,000	$3,000	$1,000	$10,000
—Cost of Goods Sold	2,200	1,400	1,750	650	6,000
Gross Margin	1,800	600	1,250	350	4,000
Expenses					
Direct	300	400	250	80	1,030
Allocated	600	900	500	170	2,170
Total	900	1,300	750	250	3,200
Net Profit	$ 900	$ <700>	$ 500	$ 100	$ 800

(b) Income Statement Assuming Territory B Eliminated

	A	C	D	Total
Sales	$4,000	$3,000	$1,000	$8,000
—Cost of Goods Sold	2,200	1,750	650	5,600
Gross Margin	1,800	1,250	350	3,400
Expenses	1,200	1,050	550	2,800
Net Profit	$ 600	$ 200	$ <200>	$ 600

(c) Income Statement in Contribution to Profit Form

	A	B	C	D	Total
Sales	$4,000	$2,000	$3,000	$1,000	$10,000
—Direct Costs					
Cost of Goods					
Sold	2,200	1,400	1,750	650	6,000
Expenses	300	400	250	80	1,030
Total	2,500	1,800	2,000	730	7,030
Contribution Margin	1,500	200	1,000	270	2,970
Allocated Costs					2,170
Net Profit					$800

Note: Data are hypothetical.

could be increased by presenting the data in part (a) in percentage form; a percentage of sales for each type of cost would provide a clearer comparison of performance among territories.)

Suppose that additional analysis indicates that Territory B, the unprofitable territory, should be eliminated. Part (b) shows the effect upon the income statement of eliminating Territory B. First, sales in Territory B would be lost (in an actual case, other territories would probably pick up some sales from customers in Territory B, but this factor is ignored to simplify the analysis). Second, the direct expenses of operating Territory B would be eliminated. But the expenses *allocated* to Territory B, e.g., salary of the general sales manager, rent on buildings, and depreciation on equipment formerly used in Territory B (unless disposed of), would not be eliminated. These expenses have been reallocated, perhaps on an equal basis, to Territories A, C, and D.

Note that the result of the proposed elimination of Territory B would be to reduce not only total revenues, but the profits of all three remaining territories. Territory D, in fact, would become unprofitable (assuming that equal allocation of common costs was employed). A different allocation pattern, for example, assigning all of the costs formerly allocated to Territory B to Territory A, would produce a different pattern of profitability among the territories.

This simplified example illustrates the point that allocation of common costs can significantly affect the profitability of decision units. Since the allocation must depend upon the judgment of the accountant, it is to some extent arbitrary and open to question. For this reason, a clearer picture of performance in each of the territories can be obtained by recasting the income statement in contribution to profit form. Part (c) presents the pertinent data.

Note that the only change from the traditional income statement is to separate the direct costs from the allocated costs, resulting in a contribution margin figure for each territory. This analysis shows that all four territories are contributing something to allocated costs and profits. Of course, Territories B and D are still not performing as well as Territories A and C; performances in B and D should be examined more closely. But the basic tenet of direct-costing is that the activities of a particular decision unit should not be discontinued as long as those activities are meeting direct costs and contributing something to allocated costs and profit. This decision rule is extremely useful in measuring managerial performance and guiding corrective action among units within the organization.

Over the planning horizon, of course, the organization as a whole must cover all costs, whether direct or allocated. Much of the opposition of accountants to direct costing results from their belief that managers will not make the distinction between short-run, intraorganizational decision making and long-run, total organization decisions. (An organization cannot lose money on every unit and make it up on volume.) With this caveat in mind, however, profit performance of units within the organization can be very usefully measured with the direct costing approach.

In addition, direct costing focuses on *margins,* as opposed to averages or other summary measures of marketing performance. Recall that the

Exhibit 13-19   Marginal Analysis Should Guide Decision Making

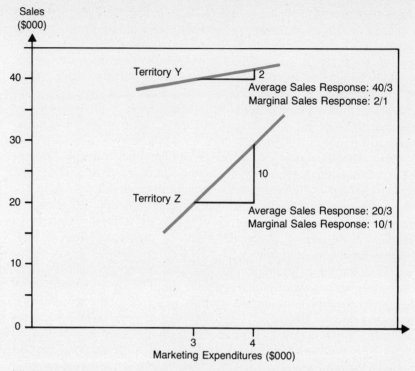

Adapted from Philip Kotler, *Marketing Management: Analysis, Planning and Control,* 2nd ed. © Prentice-Hall, 1972, p. 381, with permission of Prentice-Hall.

fundamental tenet of economic theory is that performance is optimized when marginal cost equals marginal revenue. Consequently, marginal analysis provides useful guidelines for corrective action. Exhibit 13-19 provides an example.

This figure shows that an expenditure of $3,000 of marketing effort returns sales of $40,000 in Territory Y and $20,000 in Territory Z. If additional marketing effort is to be expended in one of these territories, Territory Y might at first glance appear to be the preferable one. However, an increase of expenditure of $1,000 in Territory Y would increase sales only $2,000, while that same $1,000 spent in Territory Z would produce a $10,000 increase. This is because the marginal response to sales in Territory Z is considerably higher than the marginal response in Territory Y.

Of course, an organization usually does not have the information necessary to determine the marginal response rates of volume to effort. Even without this information, however, profit performance can be improved in two ways: by increasing the margin or by increasing the turnover. Exhibit 13-20 presents examples. The marginal return from each unit can be improved (i.e., the break-even point can be lowered) by

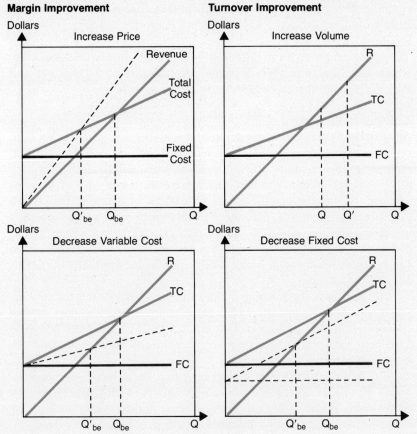

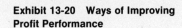

Exhibit 13-20   Ways of Improving Profit Performance

increasing price or decreasing variable costs. The turnover of assets used to produce sales can be improved by decreasing the fixed costs of assets employed, or by increasing the volume of sales with a given level of assets.

Our discussion of marketing performance measurement has employed economic sales, costs, and profit figures, because performance measurement concepts and techniques are more fully developed and, therefore, most clearly illustrated with figures of this nature. Our earlier discussion of the customer and societal level of performance indicates, however, that measurement techniques need to be developed for these levels also. Further improvement in the process of marketing control could be attained by instituting the marketing audit.

INSTITUTING A MARKETING AUDIT

We made a strong plea in Chapter 5 for the concept of the marketing audit. This concept can be a very useful foundation for marketing planning. If marketing management desired to use it operationally, the audit would be instituted as part of the control process, as shown in Exhibit 13-1.

Audit institution by an organization would raise four questions: what, when, how, and who. We examine the activities to be audited and their timing, and the procedures personnel required.

Activities to Be Audited

Any marketing activity can be audited. It is useful to distinguish between two types of marketing audits: the individual operation audit and the total marketing function audit. The former focuses on an individual marketing activity—development of a new product, performance in a given sales territory, relationships with specific customers, or requests for certain marketing information. This view of the marketing audit is simply marketing control—standards, measurement, and corrective action—as discussed in the previous section, but systematically administered. Exhibit 13-21 presents an interesting and rather sophisticated approach to marketing activity auditing.

A total marketing function audit, by contrast, is a systematic evaluation of all marketing operations in a given organization. Regular, systematic audits of the marketing function would appear to have great potential for effective and efficient marketing control, but this idea has not yet been adopted by many organizations.

Too often, interest in auditing marketing activities is a response to crisis—"For God's sake, find out what happened, will you?" But crises may be the worst possible times to do systematic and objective analyses of marketing activities. Ideally, the auditing of marketing activities should be a planned part of continuous marketing control activities.

Audit Procedure and Personnel

The marketing audit is accomplished by systematically evaluating the activity or function in terms of the planning process: objectives, seeking, matching, programming, and consummating. Evaluation of these steps should encompass both effectiveness and efficiency dimensions: can this activity be accomplished in some better fashion and/or can it be accomplished with less expenditure of resources?

Different types of people can be used to conduct the marketing audit. Four arrangements are possible. First, the executive in charge of a given marketing operation could audit that operation. No doubt he/she knows most about it. A serious limitation of the self-audit, however, is the lack of independent appraisal. The executive is likely to suppress unfavorable information generated by the audit, and such work would take time from other duties. Second, a task force of personnel from other organizational units could be assigned to audit a marketing activity. Again, objectivity

Adapted from C. Merle Crawford, "The Trajectory Theory of Goal Setting for New Products," *Journal of Marketing Research,* May 1966, pp. 117–125. Reprinted from *Journal of Marketing Research,* published by the American Marketing Association.

Exhibit 13-21   Trajectory Concept of New Product Auditing

Crawford suggests an auditing procedure for new product performance. His concept, as shown in the figure, is that the desired objective—sales (or brand awareness, product trial, retailer stocking, or market share)—be plotted as a *trajectory* over time. For example, to achieve sales level s_4 at time period $t + 10$, sales must be s_2 at time t. (This is the performance standard). If, however, actual sales at time t are s_1, then projected actual sales at time $t + 10$ will be s_3. Corrective action, therefore, can be taken at time t, in time to reach the sales objective (s_4) by time $t + 10$.

The trajectory concept has obvious implications for managing the product life cycle. A Marketing Information System could incorporate this model and generate the required data.

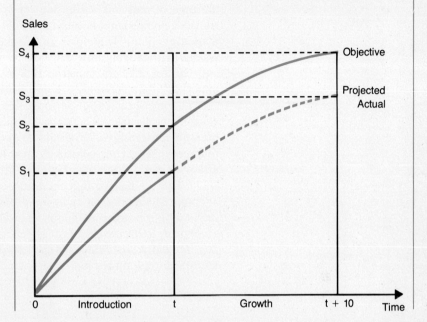

could suffer from the personal relationships involved; moreover, these people are taken away from their own responsibilities.

Third, the task could be given to a full-time internal staff group, perhaps under the direction of a *marketing controller.* The marketing controller and his/her staff might be sufficiently detached from the marketing department so that an independent audit could be conducted. Another advantage is that the internal audit staff would become specialists in conducting marketing audits in that particular organizational situation. However, this procedure would be expensive, and personal relationships which could detract from the objectivity of the groups could develop.

Fourth, an outside consultant with broad experience could be engaged. A consultant is likely to be more objective than inside auditors, and has the time to execute such an audit. Disadvantages include the cost of outside consulting and perhaps reluctance to give the consultant information needed to conduct the audit.

In summary, the marketing audit—a systematic appraisal of marketing operation for control purposes—would seem to be a significant step forward for marketing management. Of course, an audit must be tailored to the requirements of specific organization situations.

CONCLUDING NOTE

Most of this book focuses on marketing planning: objectives, seeking, matching, and programming. Marketing implementation and control receive less attention—not because they are less significant (a majority of the time of most marketing managers is spent on implementation and control activities), but because these activities should be derived from the marketing plan. Therefore, they relate rather specifically to certain situations; relatively little can be said in general about implementation and control. Do not construe this to mean that these stages are not important; they definitely are part of the marketing planning process.

The measurement of performance at customer and societal levels is worth reemphasizing. There are significant issues here, and such issues are becoming increasingly important. We can look for research on techniques to improve marketing control at these levels and also new organizational arrangements, e.g., the marketing-controller concept discussed above.

Finally, I believe that the audit concept will ultimately be widely adopted. The marketing audit can provide a framework for systematizing the planning process. Although marketing is a field less amenable than accounting to the development of generally accepted principles, a systematic, regularly scheduled audit of marketing operations would provide useful information for marketing planning and control.

KEY TERMS AND CONCEPTS

Management Functions
  planning
  staffing
  organizing
  coordinating
  motivating
  controlling
Marketing Planning Process
  objectives
  seeking
  matching
  programming
  implementation
  measurement
    (effectiveness,
    efficiency)
  corrective action
The Product Manager
Program Coordination
  who
  where
  when
  how
Critical Path Scheduling
Motivation
  theory X, theory Y
  management by objectives
Murphy's Law
Marketing Control Standards
  industry norms
  past performance
  managerial expectations
Measuring Marketing Performance
  organizational level
  customer level
  societal level
  effectiveness and
    efficiency

Corrective Action
  technical problems
  human problems
Volume/Cost/Profit Measurement
  payoff = benefits − costs
Measurement Concepts
  explicit communication
  systems perspective
  concentration
  responsibility/accountability
Volume (Sales) Analysis
  functional breakdown
  territorial breakdown
Cost Analysis
  natural accounts
  functional accounts
  territorial breakdown
Cost Allocation
  direct vs. absorption
    costing
Profit Analysis
  contribution to profit
  marginal analysis
  improvement
    (margin increase,
    turnover increase)
Marketing Audit Institution
  activity
  total function
  marketing controller concept

QUESTIONS FOR DISCUSSION

1. Choose an organization, e.g., Procter & Gamble, IBM, a political party, your university, a one-person sales agency. Discuss implementation of the marketing program of the organization. Be sure to include organization of the marketing function, coordination of the program, and motivation of marketing personnel.

2. Apply marketing control concepts and techniques to the organizations of question 1. What standards of performance do you think appropriate? How would performance be measured for these standards? What corrective actions might be necessary? Defend your answers to each question.

3. Suppose that a company produces several different products, and that its salespeople are expected to sell all of these products on each sales call. For purposes of determining the profitability of each product line, how would you suggest that the salesperson's costs (salary, commission, expenses) be allocated among product lines? Mention several different possibilities, and then choose the one you think most appropriate. Defend your choice.

4. After conducting a study of its distribution costs, a company's marketing controller recommends that the company not accept orders below a certain minimum size. Before accepting this recommendation, what factors should the marketing vice president consider? Why?

5. An increasingly serious aspect of marketing control for many organizations is the recall of defective products. Automobile manufacturers seem especially plagued. How would you apply the material in this chapter to managing the product recall?

6. What problem might an outside auditor encounter on his initial visit to an organization he has been engaged to audit?

7. One of the most effective forms of promotion is product sampling. In the spring of 1972, for example, Procter & Gamble Company mailed to a national sample of households a trial-size (2-oz.) aerosol spray can of *Sure* deodorant. This mailing had to be coordinated with a national advertising campaign for this new product. The trial-size can was manufactured specifically for this promotion, and would not be used in regular production of this product. Discuss possible marketing/production problems that might arise in the course of this promotion. What should the marketing manager do to solve these problems?

SUGGESTED READING

1. *Analyzing and Improving Marketing Performance.*
Report No. 32. American Marketing Association, 1959. A series of short essays by leading marketing scholars and practitioners; papers by Abraham Shuchman, Richard D. Crisp, and Alfred R. Oxenfeldt on the marketing audit concept are particularly worthwhile.

2. Keith K. Cox and Ben M. Enis.
The Marketing Research Process. Pacific Palisades, Calif.: Goodyear Publishing Company, 1972. Again, material in this book has been abstracted and condensed from the author's earlier work, particularly Chapter 13, pp. 463–509; a more in-depth treatment of the author's approach to marketing planning and control is presented.

3. Peter F. Drucker.
Managing for Results. New York: Harper and Row, 1964. A concise, readable statement of the role and scope of the manager's tasks, emphasizing the importance of marketing planning and control.

4. Richard I. Levin and Charles A. Kirkpatrick.
Planning and Control with PERT/CPM. McGraw-Hill, 1966. A brief, easy-to-read introduction to Critical Path Scheduling Methods.

5. Douglas McGregor.
The Human Side of Enterprise. McGraw-Hill, 1960. The classic treatment of human problems and their effect upon organizational planning and control; must reading for the serious student of management; easy reading.

6. Charles H. Sevin.
Marketing Productivity Analysis. McGraw-Hill, 1965. A short treatment of issues in marketing control; contains many examples; recommended for reference by marketing students and marketing managers.

7. Robert Townsend.
Up the Organization. New York: Alfred A. Knopf, 1970. Witty, tongue-in-cheek—but often incisive—advice on how to manage an organization; a profitable evening's reading.

Three articles in the Gelb and Gelb reading book, *Insights for Marketing Management,* 2nd ed. Goodyear, 1977, are applicable to the material in this chapter:

8. Lee Adler.
"Systems Approach to Marketing," *Harvard Business Review,* May–June 1967, pp. 105–18. Classic application of systems concepts to marketing programming.

9. James H. Myers and A. C. Samli.
"Management Control of Marketing Research," *Journal of Marketing Research,* August 1969, pp. 267–77. Readable overview of various approaches to information assembly for performance measurement.

10. Leland L. Beik and Stephen L. Buzby.
"Profitability Analysis by Market Segments," *Journal of Marketing,* July 1973, pp. 30–39. Skillfully connects volume/cost/profit measurement to market segmentation strategy.

CASE 10 / LOVE AND WAR IN THE TEXAS SKIES

How does a new, unknown company tackle an established competitor in the airline industry? And when the competitor fights back, how does the newcomer survive?

Southwest Airlines, a Dallas firm which began operations in 1971, pinned its hopes on a marketing plan that combined lower fares, a superior on-time record, pioneering at a close-to-downtown airport, the role of an underdog, and both advertising and stewardesses who assured its passengers, "We love you."

The airline was born in the courts. Incorporated in Texas in 1967, the company received its required Certificate of Public Convenience and Necessity from the state in 1968. Immediately, however, three airlines already serving its proposed Houston-Dallas-San Antonio triangle route began legal proceedings to prevent Southwest from operating. After a series of appeals, the Texas Supreme Court ruled in favor of Southwest, but the three competitors asked the U.S. Supreme Court for a hearing. In December 1970, the nation's highest court declined to reverse the state court decision, and Southwest was—belatedly—in business.

The new airline set out to serve what a *Houston Business Journal* analysis described as one of the most heavily traveled intrastate commuter markets of the 1970s. Noting that only California, Florida, and Texas have major metropolitan areas far enough apart to economically justify the use of intrastate air traffic, a securities analyst pointed to the success of Pacific Southwest Airlines between Los Angeles and San Francisco as a model of the potential available to Southwest.

Getting Off The Ground

Right in the middle of what Southwest executives describe as the 1971 "airline depression," the new airline began operation. Those planning its entry into a market dominated by Braniff, but also served by Texas International and Continental, described their situation this way:

1. We have an unknown airline.

2. It's a shuttle service—a triangle including Houston, Dallas, and San Antonio.

3. Our competition is entrenched.

Southwest's planners decided to "explode on the scene," to look "big-time," and to communicate the benefits of trying the new airline once. They believed that better on-time performance than competition would generate repeat business if the commuters who made up the market could be induced to try just one flight.

They began with teaser ads, displaying provocative headlines and no clue as to who had placed them. "Call this number and be physically elevated," suggested one. When the caller dialed the number, a young lady with a sexy voice informed the caller that a new airline would begin service next week. She purred that it would fly Boeing 737 jet aircraft and would feature stewardesses in hot pants, who would offer "a lot of attention . . ."

Huge four-color ads the Sunday before startup echoed the same theme: Southwest would fly not planes, but "love birds;" would issue tickets in ten seconds from a "love machine;" would serve not just drinks, but "love potions." The ads featured Southwest's slogan: *There's somebody else up there who loves you.*

Significantly, the new airline also advertised a lovely price: a $20 fare, $8 less than that charged by its competition. The decision to compete on a price basis was possible because Southwest, an intrastate airline, is not subject to regulation by the Civil Aeronautics Board.

Inaugurating service June 18, 1971 (from Dallas's Love Field, of course), Southwest found, as expected, that in only a matter of days Braniff had met its $20 fare. In fact, company executives claim to have anticipated Braniff's move so surely that they had already authorized ads reading "The other airline may have met our price, but you can't buy love." This campaign ran in newspapers and on television in the three cities served by Southwest. The ads provided a preview of what would become a favorite Southwest tactic: showing Braniff as a corporate bully outwitted by tiny Southwest.

The First Year

Executives at Southwest knew, however, that clever advertising was not enough to change the entrenched habit-patterns of businessmen used to making reservations on Braniff. During the first year, company execu-

From Betsy D. Gelb and Ben M. Enis, *Marketing Is Everybody's Business*, Goodyear Publishing Company.

tives attacked this major segment of their market on three fronts: direct mail, ticketing, and finding a more convenient airport.

The direct mail brochure went out to 36,000 businessmen; spreading the "love" theme and pointing out that instead of the bother of a bought-in-advance ticket, Southwest offered ten-second ticketing at the airport. To make the service credible, Southwest added—and promoted—a related benefit: if any plane was full when the traveler arrived, he'd be flown free on the next plane.

A more spectacular move came in May of 1972. Southwest bought a fourth Boeing 737 and introduced flights to and from Houston's Hobby Airport, the airport which had served as the city's main field until 1970, but which then had been supplanted by Houston Intercontinental Airport, considerably farther from downtown.

The move embellished Southwest's underdog image, because Braniff reacted almost immediately by moving some of its flights to Hobby. "Unfair!" cried the Southwest spokesmen who testified before the Houston City Council in an effort to have Braniff denied the right to fly from Hobby. "They're only moving to Hobby to try to put us out of business," asserted press releases. "They don't worry about public convenience or they would have stayed at Hobby in the first place. They're just trying to get us out of the picture, and then they'll move all their flights back to Intercontinental," Southwest complained. Braniff was allowed to operate from Hobby, however, and Southwest responded by moving all of its Houston flights there, permitting the sale of the newly purchased fourth plane.

For May and June 1972, Southwest averaged 32 passengers per flight, nearly covering what its annual report called "cash costs;" a figure which included interest on borrowed funds. At that time, an average of 43 passengers would have been required to cover all costs.

About this time, Southwest began experimenting with a $10 nightly flight after 9 P.M. The reasoning was that the business (daytime) market was fairly inelastic as far as price was concerned; if business people had to travel, they would fly, and not enough business people were driving 300 miles or taking the bus to cut costs to make much difference. At night, however, a different market segment would be involved: travelers visiting cousins or returning to college, and these potential customers could be lured from bus or car to plane only by a fare that would be truly competitive with those of other means of transportation.

The night flights, aimed at nonbusiness travelers, were promoted on country-and Western and Top 40 radio stations; a contrast to the television promotions aimed at businessmen. The radio spot announcements talked about "frivolity flights" and were thoroughly frivolous in format: one bit of dialogue featured a prospective traveler asking "Can I get there cheaper than Southwest?" and receiving the cheerful answer, "Sure—strap 5000 pigeons to your arms!"

The combination of the Southwest move to a more convenient airport and its inauguration of economical night flights provided an excuse for the airline to implement its strategy of looking "big-time." Ads appeared in both Houston newspapers near the end of May that were unsigned by an advertiser, but asked, "Who's Number 1 at Hobby?"

A chart in the ad compared Southwest's schedule of flights from Hobby Airport to Dallas with Braniff's schedule from Hobby to Dallas and made it obvious that Southwest had many more such flights; ignoring the fact that Braniff was also flying out of Intercontinental Airport. It compared fares: Southwest's "$20 one-class" and $10 at night with Braniff's $28 first class, $20 for coach. It compared aircraft; describing the Southwest Boeing 737 as "the most modern short-haul aircraft flying today," and Braniff's Boeing 720 as "a 12-year-old aircraft from the pre-fan-jet era." It noted that Southwest boasted a 96 percent on-time record versus 75 percent for Braniff. Finally, it compared cocktail prices: $1 on Southwest versus $1.50 on Braniff, and closed the ad with a coupon offering a free drink if the traveler handed the coupon to "the airline you think is Number 1."

Southwest stewardesses handed out "quite a few" free drinks to travelers who got the message, reported SW executives.

All's Fare in the Love War

Southwest's $20 fare was fine for promotion, but no help to an airline struggling to get out of the red. July is traditionally a bad month for a commuter airline; with total demand down anyway, Southwest decided the time was ripe for another change—a fare increase.

Newspaper ads July 13 proclaimed, "From now on, we fly only one way: Executive Class." A picture of a balding traveler surrounded by three smiling hostesses illustrated the message: free drinks, plane interiors redesigned to provide more legroom—and a $6 increase to $26 for a one-way flight.

Lamar Muse, Southwest's president, blamed the price increase on "destructive actions by competitive carriers which have inhibited our projected rate of growth toward profitability." Specifically, he said, Braniff had added flights at Hobby even though it was averaging less than 20 passengers per flight, a "deliberate overscheduling of flights . . . to dilute the market temporarily and . . . deny Southwest sufficient traffic to cover its costs."

Neither Braniff nor Texas International, Southwest's competitors on the Dallas-Houston route, duplicated the Southwest price increase immediately. But within two weeks of the Southwest increase, both Braniff and TI matched the $6 boost. Braniff also matched the free drinks, and in a move which provoked howls of protest from Southwest, Braniff offered a $10 fare on what it called "late-evening flights"—starting at 7:30 P.M.

In a statement before the Texas Aeronautics Commission, a Southwest spokesman claimed that Braniff's $10 fare at 7:30 was just an attempt "to divert . . . traffic from our 6:30 P.M. flights." He also took to the commission Southwest's plea to use Dallas' Love Field even after the opening of a new Dallas-Fort Worth airport, scheduled to begin operations in late 1973. Airlines serving Dallas had agreed to move to the new airport when plans to develop it were announced, but

Southwest claimed not to be bound by an agreement it had not signed. Furthermore, Southwest was delighted with the publicity from the hearings, and proclaimed that travelers would be served in both Houston and Dallas at convenient airports *only* because Southwest had the public's interests at heart.

As the summer dip in total air traffic gave way to more robust statistics for fall, Southwest found its load factor rising again, in spite of the intense competition. By November of 1972, the average number of passengers per flight reached 37, covering all cash costs and about half the noncash costs. After a December setback, the load factor rose again in January, and reached 38 passengers per flight by the middle of the month.

Escalation of the War

As Southwest stated in its annual report, however, the largest single remaining problem was "the very substantial losses being incurred" in the Dallas-San Antonio market. The report put the problem this way:

Unlike the Dallas-Houston market, where the company's hourly schedule pattern is fully competitive, Southwest operates only four trips in each direction each weekday in this market, versus seventeen trips by our principal competitor. Therefore, if the businessman uses Southwest regularly, he must plan his business appointments around our schedules, which is the reverse of what most businessmen normally do.

Case Exhibit 10-1   Statistical Summary Since Inception

| | Year Ended December 31, | | | 6/18/71 (date started) |
	1974	1973	1972	12/31/71
Number of flights	12,382	10,619	10,576	6,051
Number of passengers	759,721	543,407	308,999	108,554
Average passengers per flight	61.4	51.2	29.2	17.9
Average revenue per flight	$1,199.50	$867.20	$566.80	$351.93
Average cost per flight	$1,026.62	$850.75	$767.61	$800.28
Average revenue per passenger	$19.55	$16.95	$19.40	$19.62
Average cost per passenger	$16.73	$16.62	$26.27	$44.61
Average gallons fuel per trip	745	791	772	816
Average cost of fuel per trip	$165.86	$90.67	$86.42	$86.16
Average number of employees	284	215	187	182
Number of employees at end of year	323	238	183	195

Southwest tackled the problem in late January 1973, with a "60-day half-price sale" on every flight from Dallas to San Antonio or San Antonio to Houston. The company believed, its annual report said, that businessmen would be persuaded to try the airline once, and would become regulars because they would find better service (faster ticketing, better on-time performance, more "loving" hostesses) than they had previously found on competitive airlines.

By February 1, 1973, the overall Southwest load factor had benefited enough from increases in the Dallas-San Antonio market to reach 40 passengers. Southwest executives admit, however, that they were flabbergasted when Dallas and Houston papers Thursday morning, February 1, carried fullpage Braniff ads offering a 60-day half-price sale on flights between Dallas and Hobby airport in Houston—the route that had been keeping Southwest alive.

"Braniff's 'Get acquainted Sale,'" trumpeted the ad's headline. The schedules between Hobby and Dallas were printed below, with no mention of Braniff's other flights between Dallas and Houston, terminating at Houston's Intercontinental Airport.

By Monday, February 5, Southwest had prepared its counterattack. Readers of Houston papers that morning saw a repeat of the Braniff full-page ad offering its half-price sale but also saw a two-page spread by Southwest headlined, "Nobody's going to shoot Southwest Airlines out of the sky for a lousy $13. If they'll fly you for $13, we'll fly you for $13."

What Southwest offered was a two-price system. Travelers who wanted to fly for $13 were told that they wouldn't have to fly Braniff to obtain the lower fare; Southwest would meet it. But travelers were also offered a "special gift" if they would fly Southwest at the regular $26 fare, obviously in the hope that expense-account travelers would be happy to let their companies pay the extra $13 and thereby earn as a gift a fifth of whiskey.

The ads cost Southwest $22,000, a figure that included not only production costs and newspaper space, but also the mailing of printed brochure versions of the ad to businessmen in Dallas and Houston, and the distribution of the brochures on street corners downtown the same day the ad appeared. If any traveler was unaware that Southwest had a case to make, it wasn't for lack of effort on the airline's part.

The ad said that Braniff was trying to bankrupt Southwest. "Why is Braniff's reduced fare good only at Hobby?", insinuated one line. Furthermore, the copy pointed out, if Braniff succeeded in its efforts the real losers would be the traveling public. "Remember what it was like before Southwest Airlines?" became the new slogan. With Southwest out of the competitive picture, its ad proclaimed, fares would rise, Braniff would retreat from Hobby, and no airline would stay at Dallas' Love Field once the new and less accessible airport opened. The ad concluded:

If you again want to be the hostage of Braniff and pay whatever they demand with service only through Houston's Intercontinental Airport and the new Dallas-Fort Worth Regional Airport, then your choice is Braniff. If this seems like a poor choice, then you're getting our point!

In statements to the press, Braniff denied an intention to run anybody out of business, and simply said that the half-price sale was designed to call attention to its service to Hobby. Braniff also denied that a price war was in progress, noting that "We have 87 flights where we are in direct competition with Southwest and we offer a special fare on only 15."

From Red to Black

Both airlines agreed that, measured in terms of volume, business was better then ever. In fact, for 1973, the number of flights operated by Southwest stayed almost constant. Passenger traffic increased 76 percent; over half a million Texans flew Southwest in 1973. Even though passengers paid 13 percent less for their tickets in '73 than in '72, Southwest experienced a 54 percent increase in operating revenues. The net effect was a slight profit in 1973. This was the year in which Southwest Airlines turned the corner from red to black.

Southwest president Lamar Muse attributed the increase to (1) his airline's ability to continue to operate from Dallas' close-in Love Field and (2) the diversion of highway travel to air as a result of the energy shortage which created higher prices for gasoline and lower speed limits. Even a 25 percent increase in the price of jet fuel increased Southwest's overall operating costs less than three percent.

In 1973, a Senate subcommittee began looking into federal regulations of airfares. Senator Edward M. Kennedy of Massachusetts cited Southwest and its prototype, Pacific Southwest Airlines of California, as evidence that intrastate airlines provide "efficient, low-cost air service tailored to the marketplace under the harsh eye of consumer demand rather than the price formulas of market-protective rules of the Civil Aeronautics Board." At the time of the study, the 248 mile trip between Dallas and San Antonio cost $23.15. A coach passenger flying 190 miles from Boston to New York City paid $28.70. Kennedy estimated that the direct and indirect costs of federal regulation of the airlines range from $1 billion to $3.5 billion annually. Airfares were said to be 30 to 100 percent higher than they might be in a freely competitive system.

Southwest Takes Off

Southwest's performance in 1974 continued to support Kennedy's contentions. As Case Exhibit 10-1 indicates, Southwest grew rapidly in 1974. Revenues increased as a result of a forty percent gain in passengers carried, and the inauguration of a package express business. Expenses also increased, but the rate was less than one percent per passenger carried.

Given these results, Southwest undertook expansion plans. It took delivery of a fourth Boeing 737 jet and ordered a fifth to be delivered in fall '75. Permission was granted by the Texas Aeronautical Commission to begin service from Dallas and Houston to the Rio Grande Valley in 1975.

A significant milestone was passed when appeals by the city of Dallas were denied all the way to the Supreme Court level, enabling Southwest to continue to operate from Love Field in Dallas and Hobby Airport in Houston. A Dallas *Times Herald* study showed that in 1974 air service through the two close-in airports saved Texans $24 million and 368,000 travel hours.

In the first part of 1975, prospects continued to look good for Southwest Airlines. The volume of traffic and passenger load factors continued to grow. So Mr. Muse and his managers began to formulate plans to provide service to other Texas cities. They contemplated service to Austin, the state capital, located in the center of the state between San Antonio and Dallas. And they planned to expand westward to Lubbock and El Paso, and to Amarillo in the northern Panhandle. Mr. Muse indicated that Southwest would also be interested in serving cities outside of Texas, such as Tulsa and Oklahoma City, Kansas City and Shreveport, Louisiana. But Muse indicated that the latter possibility hinged upon federal legislation, such as that proposed by Senator Kennedy, "that would lessen the power of the Civil Aeronautics Board to set fares, restrict entry into markets and approve anti-competitive airline agreements."

CASE 11 / L'EGGS PRODUCTS, INC.

"Up with mini skirts" was the fashion cry of the late 1960s. As skirts got shorter, a number of products were affected. One of the "mini" effects was explosive growth in sales of pantyhose. Introduced in the early 1960s, U.S. production of pantyhose reached 4.5 million dozen in 1967; the figure was 14 million dozen in 1968, and in excess of 80 million dozen by 1972. Sales for 1967 represented less than one percent of total sales of ladies' hosiery, but pantyhose accounted for more than 80 percent of hosiery sales by 1972.

THE HOSIERY MARKET

Hosiery is big business. In 1971, total sales of ladies' hosiery was $1.84 billion. This market was incredibly fragmented. There were literally hundreds of small-, medium-, and large-sized companies selling as many as 600 different brands of stockings and pantyhose. The top three manufacturers were Burlington Industries, Kayser-Roth, and Hanes. Each had well known brand names, but no single manufacturer's brand accounted for as much as 10 percent of the market. Although industry data were sparse, insiders guessed that the largest sales were racked up by retailers such as J.C. Penney and Sears rather than by manufacturers. In addition, there was significant private labeling by department stores, discount operations, supermarkets, and drugstores.

In fact, the rapid rise in market shares of supermarkets and drugstores relative to department stores, the traditional outlet for pantyhose, startled the industry. In 1967, department stores accounted for 36 percent of all sales, while supermarkets and drugstores sold 4 percent. By 1970, the department store share had fallen to 20 percent while the supermarket and drugstore share had risen to 22 percent. As a result, brand identification was almost nonexistent. One discount store representative commented, "One of our most popular lines has no brand name at all. The package just says pantyhose. We have sold nearly 2.5 million pairs in the past two and a half years." Competition was fierce, primarily on a price basis. In some supermarkets, pantyhose were selling for as low as 39¢ a pair.

HANES MARKET RESEARCH

Until 1969, Hanes had marketed its brand of hosiery only through department stores and specialty shops. Hanes also marketed a variety of other products including boys' and girls' underwear, sweaters and sport shirts, men's hosiery, and brassieres, girdles and ladies' swimwear. Both of its major competitors, Burlington Industries and Kayser-Roth, were considerably larger in terms of both sales and financial resources. Giant retailers such as Sears and J.C. Penney's were also very interested in this burgeoning market.

Hanes hired 33-year-old David E. Harrold, a former marketing manager at General Foods Corporation, to research this market. Hanes paid $400,000 for market research—a very high price in the normally conservative hosiery industry. Two different types of studies were conducted. A mail questionnaire sent to 883 women provided statistically reliable data. At the same time, in-depth interviews of 150 women were used to gauge women's attitudes toward pantyhose. The findings of the two studies were very consistent. The number one problem was *fit*. Women complained that hosiery of the same size varied widely in terms of quality. One woman said, "One week they sagged and bagged, the next week they were so tight that I could hardly sit down."

The studies also indicated that women were not particularly impressed by strong price promotion of hosiery in supermarkets and drugstores. They would be willing to pay more for pantyhose that were of consistent quality and had some degree of durability. Many women commented that a small snag in one leg ruined an entire pair of pantyhose. In addition, a study indicated that the total market was very large, conservatively estimated at 80 million women. Even 5 percent of this market, though it may look small, represents 4 million women.

THE PRODUCT

The marketing concept notwithstanding, the impetus for the consumer research was a significant technological breakthrough by Hanes fabric technicians. An R&D

Source: Written by the author from various news sources, including Glenn H. Snyder, "Supers turn fashion line into hot commodity," *Progressive Grocer* (November, 1971); "Our L'eggs fit your legs," *Business Week*, (March 25, 1972); David E. Harrold, Speech before the New York Chapter of the American Marketing Association, November, 1972; "L'eggs Products Inc.," a case in W. Wayne Talarzyk, *Contemporary Cases in Marketing* (Dryden, 1974); and "The Sag in Pantyhose," *Business Week* (January 15, 1975).

team had developed a one-sized, stretch pantyhose that would fit about 75 percent of all women. The product had no shape at all until donned for the first time; then it shaped itself to the legs of the wearer. Thus, the basic product seemed to solve the consumers' most serious complant about pantyhose. With the new product, fit could be practically guaranteed.

In order to build brand identity, Hanes commissioned the design firm of Lubalin, Smith and Carnase to develop a packaging concept which would uniquely identify the product. The package developed was the now familiar white plastic egg—about 4 inches high, sitting on end in a round paper collar, the color of which designates the style and color of the hose inside. The brand name L'eggs followed naturally.

PROMOTION

This situation was a promotion manager's dream. Into a market in which consumer brand identification was almost nonexistent, the unique name and packaging of a technically superior product could be introduced. The first objective was to build brand awareness in the consumer. and also in wholesalers and retailers.

The introductory advertising budget for L'eggs in 1970 was $10 million. This amount represented almost twice that spent by the total hosiery industry in 1969. Newspaper and television advertisements complemented point-of-purchase displays featuring the slogan, "Our L'eggs fit your legs." An additional $5 million was invested in direct mail coupons offering 35 cents off on the purchase of L'eggs pantyhose.

DISTRIBUTION

L'eggs distribution methods were also unique to the industry. Rather than relying on wholesalers, Hanes developed a cadre of 450 route girls. These driver-sales people delivered L'eggs in distinctive white vans directly to local supermarkets and drugstores. Their red, white, and blue hot-pants uniforms further distinguished the L'eggs image from that of other pantyhose.

The route girls set up and serviced within the supermarkets and drugstores the "L'eggs Boutique." This was a freestanding display unit two feet in diameter, which carried twenty-four dozen pantyhose. This display unit occupied only two and one-half square feet of floor space. And the L'eggs girls did all of the restocking and cleaning.

To overcome the out-of-stock and service problems that haunted other hosiery manufacturers, Hanes commissioned Executive Control Systems of Atlanta to develop an information and control system. The ECS system integrated all activities from manufacturing to placement of the product in the store. After the first product assortment provided on consignment, resupplies were based upon sales in individual display units. The computerized system coordinated manufacturing, warehouse distribution, retail inventory balance, sales and market analysis, and billings.

PRICE

Price was the clincher: L'eggs were sold on consignment. Retailers had no investment in inventory, and no employee time devoted to the product.

L'eggs pantyhose were fair traded at $1.39, which at that time was at least 30 cents more per pair than most pantyhose sold in supermarkets and drugstores. This price, however, was less than the average price of pantyhose, including Hanes' own brand, sold in department stores and specialty shops. This price provided the retailer with a 35 percent margin and approximately $1,300 per year in profits on each display—not bad for no investment, two and one-half square feet of floor space, and no stocking and servicing requirements.

THE FUTURE

During 1970 and 1971, Hanes continued market-by-market rollout of its L'eggs brand. During 1972, distribution encompassed 75 percent of the United States. L'eggs thus became, in only the third year of its existence, the largest selling brand of manufacturer's hosiery. The 450 route girls were stocking and servicing 50,000 "L'eggs Boutiques" in supermarkets and drugstores.

Both Kayser-Roth (No Nonsense) and Burlington Industries (Activ) developed one-sized pantyhose to compete with L'eggs. In addition, private brands were price-promoted aggressively. An even more ominous trend was the increasing acceptance of women's pants. Women turned from the mini, not to the maxi, but to tailored slacks and jeans.

In response to these trends, Hanes manager Harrold began plans to market several new products. These included L'eggs Sheer-from-Tummy-to-Toes; a "Queen-size" pantyhose designed to fit those 25 percent of women who are too large for L'eggs regular size; a support-hose in pantyhose style called "Sheer Energy"; a 99¢ brand of regular pantyhose called "1st to Last"; and, finally, L'eggs "Knee Highs."

CASE 12 / TEXAS SAFE WATER, INC.

Water used to be considered a "free good." All one had to do was turn the tap and out came a limitless supply of clean water for drinking, bathing, waste disposal, industrial usage, etc. But no longer. Water is more and more seen as a valuable commodity with various potential uses and benefits. The Texas Safe Water Company, Inc. is marketing a product designed to enhance one of water's fundamental uses.

The Environment

There is no question that water purity is an issue of increasing concern today. There are rumors of possible epidemics of such dread diseases as cholera and typhoid. More than one city has recently experienced near-panic buying of bottled water. And the cost of water supply and sewage treatment is a political issue in many cities. There is also no doubt that, by and large, the water supply today is more susceptible to pollution than it has been in the past. In the last ten years, more than 500 new chemical compounds, ranging from insecticides to industrial chemicals to commercial cleaning agents, have been put into use each year. Much of the residue from chemicals eventually enters water supply sources.

Consequently, municipal water systems generally add chlorine and other chemicals to improve water quality. A few years ago, the Environmental Protection Agency began to test methods of water treatment. EPA approval of water treatment devices is not easy to obtain; requirements are strict. The Food and Drug Administration is moving in Congress to have water declared a food. If Congress approves this measure, the FDA will assume responsibility for purity of water ingested into the body, i.e., used for drinking, cooking preparing beverages, etc. Consequently, there does seem to be a potential market for products that improve quality of water for ingestion.

The Product

Texas Safe Water Company, Inc. is marketing a water purification system manufactured by Pollution Control Products, Inc. This product, termed the MARK II Naturalizer Water Unit, is designed to purify drinking water. It consists of three connecting polyvinylchloride canisters of chemicals through which tap water flows. The device is certified by the Environmental Protection Agency to remove foreign substances such as insecticides, pesticides, algae, rust, sediment, chlorine, chloroform, carbon tetrachloride, bacteria, mercury and arsenic. The system is installed under a kitchen or a wet bar sink by attaching it to the cold water intake line, drilling a hole in the sink, and attaching a special faucet. The unit is compact, requiring only 16" x 8" x 8".

The system has no movable parts or electrical connections and it has no internal metal parts to corrode or rust. Its construction is certified by the International Association of Plumbing and Mechanical Officials and by Southern Building Codes International. The system provides water at a cost of approximately 5¢ per gallon for the average family. After two years, one of the filter units must be replaced. The replacement cost is $75. The unit retails for $275.

The MARK II can be installed by a salesperson in approximately 35 minutes. Product units are shipped C.O.D. Houston. The units are small enough to inventory in the sales office and can be transported by private automobile.

Potential Markets

The system purifies water intended for ingestion into the body. Consequently, the potential market is vast. Residences, both single family and apartment, are one obvious target. The unit is also suitable for boats and recreational vehicles. (The MARK II is standard equipment on GM's Explorer line of RV's.) And it can be used in commercial establishments like taverns and restaurants, in institutions such as schools and hospitals, and in commercial and industrial buildings.

Two major types of benefits are apparent. First, water treated by this system tastes better. Blind taste tests have shown that potential customers can tell the difference between water treated with the MARK II and ordinary tapwater. Consequently, the unit improves the taste of coffee, tea, frozen juices, ice cubes, mixed drinks, soup, and all vegetables cooked in water. The ability to remove potentially harmful foreign matter makes the product of interest to anyone concerned about health and safety.

Competition

From the customer's view, there are several ways to

Permission to adapt, courtesy Texas Safe Water Company.

solving the problem of obtaining pure water for ingestion. The first is to purchase bottled water. Companies such as Ozarka deliver water monthly for an average price of $.50 per gallon. The best type of bottled water is distilled water, which is produced by the process of evaporation. It is absolutely pure, so pure that needed elements such as calcium and phosphate are removed from it. There is evidence that removal of such trace elements can contribute to heart disease. For example, *Consumers Bulletin* recommends that distilled water not be drunk.

The second way of obtaining pure water is to treat the water in some way. The MARK II is one such system. Another system uses an ion exchange process, replacing ions of harmful substances (iron, mercury) with ions of sodium. This process is somewhat less expensive than the MARK II, but it has not received EPA certification because it filters chlorine from the water in the early stages of the process, allowing the possibility of bacteria buildup before the water is delivered for ingestion. In addition, there are any number of other filtering and softening systems. In general, these are less expensive and less reliable than the MARK II or the ion exchange system. Water softeners remove minerals, but do not remove bacteria or germs.

Another process—reverse osmosis—is possible. In fact, this was the method used by the astronauts in space. But it does have some technical limitations, and has had few commercial applications as yet.

The Company

Texas Safe Water Company, Inc. is a distributor for the MARK II in the 13-county Gulf Coast region of Texas. The manufacturer, Pollution Control Products, Inc., cannot grant an exclusive distributorship, because of the Robinson-Patman Act. But Texas Safe Water Company, Inc. is the only distributor currently marketing the MARK II in this region. In addition, Texas Safe Water Company, Inc. has the right of first refusal over distributorships in other areas of Texas. And it can set up dealers to whom it would sell the product for $175 for resale to consumers.

At the moment, Texas Safe Water Company, Inc. is a rather small but growing concern. Initial capitalization was $15,000; the monthly operating budget is $3,000. It is operated by Mr. John Davis, his secretary and six full-time salespersons. In addition, John has recently hired two women to make telephone calls to set up appointments for the salesperson to demonstrate the unit in people's homes. John and his salespersons also contact potential commercial and institutional users, and residential builders.

Texas Safe Water Company, Inc. is in the process of recruiting additional salespersons. Salespersons are paid on commission according to the following scale:

$65 on sales generated from office
$75 on prospected sale

Mr. Davis believes that an average salesperson can easily sell 20 units per month. The telephone contact persons are paid $2 per appointment set up and $5 per unit sold from an appointment.

The company receives considerable support from the parent company of Pollution Control Products, which is Consolidated Foods, Inc., producers and marketers of such products as Sara Lee pastries, Gant shirts, and perhaps most importantly, Electrolux vacuum cleaners. Thus, the parent company has had considerable experience in presenting reasonably complex products to consumers.

Consolidated Foods supplies sales training manuals, demonstration flip charts (which reflect a considerable amount of research, including newspaper stories on impurities in water, pertinent statistics, etc.). The company also supplies print copy for magazine and newspaper advertising, and tapes of commercials for radio and television. Thus, Texas Safe Water Company, Inc. has only to buy space or time. In addition, each salesperson is furnished a demonstration unit, and the company recently gave Texas Safe Water Company, Inc. three units to be placed in models of condominium apartments.

QUESTIONS FOR ANALYSIS OF CASES

1. Outline the marketing strategy for the company to follow in marketing its products. Use Exhibit 7-13 as a guide (but not a substitute) for your thinking, and sketch the broad outlines of your strategy. Pay particular attention to target market characteristics and the organizational situation.

2. Now focus attention upon the four elements of the marketing program:

   a. *product*—benefits (from the customers' viewpoint), key decisions as the product is developed, possible strategies for the various line cycle stages, impact of this product upon the company's line, and useful product extensions.

   b. *promotion*—role to be played by advertising, personal selling, sales promotion, and publicity—at each stage in the buying process.

   c. *distribution*—channel(s) for this product; types of middlemen involved, physical distribution considerations, if any.

   d. *price*—demand, cost and competitive factors; pricing objectives, base price strategy, and useful price adjustments.

For each market mix element, make specific recommendations. Defend your recommendations, paying particular attention to mix interrelationships.

3. Discuss problems of implementation that might arise with the program you have outlined. Be sure to consider difficulties in coordinating marketing mix variables, and in motivating organizational personnel to accomplish the tasks you envision for them.

4. Outline the control procedures you deem appropriate for this marketing program. Pay particular attention to operational standards, potential measurement problems, and difficulties in taking corrective actions that might be required.

PART 5 MARKETING MANAGEMENT IN PERSPECTIVE

After studying this final part of the book, you should be able to:

1. Understand the basic functions and tasks for which marketing managers are responsible.

2. Identify the major supply, customer, and societal factors that influence and constrain the marketing manager.

3. Imagine yourself as a marketing manager, and evaluate your capabilities for an interest in holding such a position.

Ralston Purina

"Ecology programs! . . Pollution programs! . . Public relations programs! . . Remember when we could admit we were in business just to make money?"

14 / MANAGEMENT MARKETING ACTIVITIES TODAY

This is the final chapter of the book. The two purposes of the chapter are to recapitulate briefly the basic points stressed in the text, and to emphasize the role of the individual manager in marketing activities. Major points include:

1. The marketing management model is useful for structuring the tasks of marketing management. The basic features of the model are the organization and external suppliers, the channel of distribution (middlemen, facilitating agencies, customers), the environment (sociocultural, economic, governmental, and ecological systems), and the marketing function (seeking, matching, programming, and consummating).

2. The management of marketing activities basically involves relationships with three areas: customers, suppliers and society. Trends and developments in each of these areas require that the marketing manager have both breadth and depth of knowledge to foresee potential opportunities and threats.

3. Marketing myopia persists, and in more dimensions, but the marketing manager can overcome marketing myopia by applying the marketing concept generically to relationships with customers, suppliers, and society.

4. Marketing management is complex, difficult, and frustrating; but it is also stimulating, rewarding and enjoyable.

The cartoon on the previous page underscores clearly the contemporary complexities of management. This is particularly true of marketing management. It is marketing that generates payoffs—sales, votes, converts to an idea, or whatever. Other organizational functions certainly play important roles, but in the last analysis, "Nothing moves until the sale is made."

The fundamental perspective of this book, therefore, is that marketing management is a significant determinant of organizational success. It is the individual marketing manager who largely makes success—or failure—happen. Let's review briefly the marketing management task.

A BRIEF REVIEW OF MARKETING MANAGEMENT

Throughout the book, we have returned again and again to two basic frameworks for understanding the four functions of marketing management: (1) marketing management's three relationships, and (2) the planning process which energizes coordination of the functions with respect to the relationships. I hope these frameworks are old friends to you now. Perhaps you do not need to review them, but just to be sure that we enter this final lap together, let us hit the highlights of these fundamentals one more time. We begin by looking at basic definitions.

Fundamental Definitions

Recall from Chapter 1 that we defined marketing to be:

> Exchange activities conducted by individuals and organizations for the purpose of satisfying human wants.

We argued that the exchange process could be broadly construed to encompass not only the purchase of economic goods and services, but any exchange of things of value entered into voluntarily with the expectation of increasing net satisfaction.

When an individual or organization desires to improve the performance of marketing activities, then it should focus on the management of those activities. Thus our definition of marketing management is:

> the process of increasing the effectiveness and/or efficiency by which marketing activities are performed by individuals or organizations.

Management of marketing activities involves an integrated, comprehensive approach to the performance of four functions with respect to three types of constituents.

Marketing's Three Relationships with Constituents

Exhibit 2-5 has been reproduced as Exhibit 14-1 to guide the discussion.

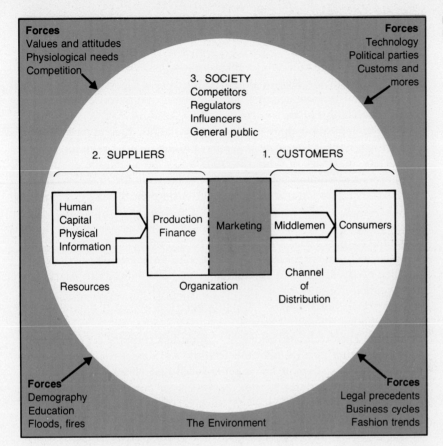

Exhibit 14-1   The Marketing Management Model

Forces
Values and attitudes
Physiological needs
Competition

Forces
Technology
Political parties
Customs and
  mores

3. SOCIETY
Competitors
Regulators
Influencers
General public

2. SUPPLIERS   1. CUSTOMERS

| Human Capital Physical Information | Production Finance | Marketing | Middlemen | Consumers |

Resources

Organization

Channel
of
Distribution

Forces
Demography
Education
Floods, fires

The Environment

Forces
Legal precedents
Business cycles
Fashion trends

At the center of the diagram, attention is focused upon the marketing function in an organization. In accordance with the marketing concept, the first relationship that marketing has is with customers. Marketing manages flows of physical products, use rights, information and payment in the channel of distribution between organization and ultimate consumer. In the channel for the given product, there may be one or more middlemen (wholesalers or retailers). In relationship with customers, marketing managers might also make use of facilitating agents such as marketing research firms, banks and other lending institutions, and shipping and warehousing concerns.

Customer relationships imply that marketing management has a product or products to offer. Thus, the second relationship is between marketing management and suppliers of products. Products are the output of a system transforming resources (human, capital, physical, and information) into products. These resources may be procured from vendors external to the organization, or generated internally. Similarly, the processing of products may have both external and internal aspects. In addition to the production function within the organization, other functions such as finance, personnel management, accounting and control, etc. are performed. The marketing function takes place within the organization. It is useful to view an organization as a total system processing resource inputs to produce product outputs for the purpose of attaining organizational objectives.

The organization does not exist in isolation. It is a part of, and interacts with, the larger society. We have found it convenient to categorize society in terms of four different types: competitors, regulators, influencers and opinion leaders, and the general public.

The dynamic nature of these relationships is represented by the circular shape of the total environment within which the marketing manager functions. In addition, environmental forces push upon it and cause it to change. There are many such forces; their magnitude, direction and relevance depend upon specific situations, but the exhibit does show a number of environmental forces likely to be significant in marketing management decisions in the future.

The Marketing Planning Process

To operate effectively and efficiently within this complex set of relationships, marketing management must follow a systematic, comprehensive planning process. Exhibit 5-8 is reproduced as Exhibit 14-2 for convenience in structuring this part of our review of marketing management fundamentals.

The marketing planning process begins with the setting of organizational objectives by top management. Ideally, these objectives are structured in hierarchical fashion and stated in operational terms. If these two conditions are met, then objectives can be translated into performance standards to guide the marketing functions of seeking, matching, programming, and consummating. Briefly, *seeking* involves the delineation of market segments—the identification of wants and desires of particular customer groups, and the estimates of the potential contribution of each segment to organizational objectives. The *matching* phase involves selection of the target market from the market segments identified in the seeking function. Matching is accomplished by bringing together segment characteristics (wants and desires, buying power, competition and other environmental conditions) with the organizational situation (objectives, constraints, and alternatives).

Once the target market has been identified, the marketing manager can develop a *program* to satisfy wants and desires of the target market. The program consists of the integration of elements of the marketing mix: product, promotion, distribution, and price. The last step in programming is forecasting sales which will result from the implementation of the

Exhibit 14-2 The Marketing Management Process

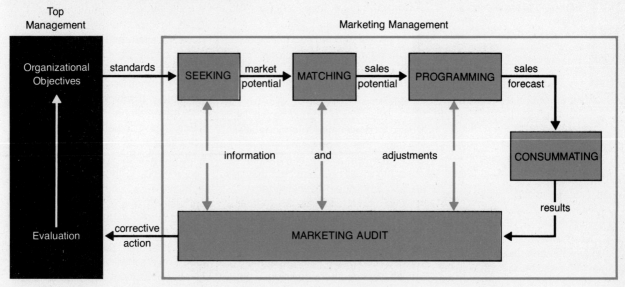

program. The final marketing function, *consummating,* involves the myriad details of actually putting the marketing program into effect, monitoring its performance, and taking corrective action if necessary.

The preceding paragraphs provide only the barest outline of the functions of marketing management. These functions have been discussed throughout the book so, hopefully, this brief review of basic fundamentals is sufficient. The point that we wish to emphasize in this chapter is that the *marketing manager* is responsible for performing these functions. After the academicians have developed their theories, the social critics have made their comments, the public policy makers have promulgated regulations, and consumers have indicated their desires—the marketing manager bears the responsibility for action. His/her decisions must guide marketing activities so as to satisfy organizational objectives, consumers, and society in general. Exhibit 14-3 presents Drucker's masterful statement of this point. In the next section, we look at future trends and developments in these three areas of the marketing manager's responsibility.

CHANGING NATURE OF MARKETING MANAGEMENT RELATIONSHIPS

The marketing management model reviewed in the previous section provides a framework for managerial planning and decision making. Now we look at some major trends in the three areas that the marketing manager must relate to, and how he or she might respond to such trends. This discussion of marketing's future relationships presents examples to stimulate your thinking about the scope and nature of future activities of marketing managers. We begin with customer relationships.

Changing Customer Relationships

Following the marketing management model, we group customers into the three categories of consumers, middlemen, and facilitating agents, as in Exhibit 14-4. We examine trends in each category and discuss forces that underlie these trends.

Consumers. There will be new markets. We discussed in Chapter 3 the growth of groups not generally considered in the family life-cycle concept: singles (those who have never married—or who are widowed or divorced), and the expansion of that part of the population that we refer to as senior citizens. In addition, governmental units at all levels are consuming

Exhibit 14-4   The Changing Customer

Types of Customers		
Category: Consumers	Middleman	Facilitating Agents
new markets:	rise of repair, reuse,	broader services
singles	and recycling	more use of marketing
senior citizens	vertical integration	
governmental units	more concentration	
international	polarization: super-	
better shoppers	store vs. specialty shop	
Forces: changing demographics	economic growth	
changing life styles	more competition	
rising expectations	public policy change	
trend of public policy	structural change	
fluctuating fashion trends		
"stagflation"		

increasing quantities of products of every type and description. International markets are increasingly a factor in the planning of American corporations. Rising standards of living in much of the world indicate that there will be many opportunities in international marketing.

These new consumers will be better shoppers. Housewives now carry hand calculators to monitor grocery purchases, government specifications become more detailed and more sophisticated, and the international consumer brings new ideas and customs to the marketplace. In their grain purchasing in 1972 and 1975, for example, Russian traders proved themselves to be very adroit shoppers. The newly oil-rich nations have enormous buying power which they are using shrewdly and conservatively to advance national goals.

Some of the forces underlying changing consumer patterns have already been mentioned: changing demographics and lifestyles. In addition, the 1970s are a time of rising expectations. We have landed men on the moon, produced electronic calculators which retail for less than $10, and made great strides in such areas as civil rights, health care, and reducing pollution. Of course, some will say that not enough progress has been made in these areas, but the point is that progress and change are visible today. In their role as consumers, people see no reason why similar progress cannot be made in such areas as providing safer products, improving durability and efficiency of operation, and handling complaints. We have noted throughout the text that such expectations constitute one of the dominant themes which public policy addresses.

Fashion trends continue to fluctuate. America has not lost its taste for newness. In European countries, by contrast, consumers are said to be more "mature," in that they are generally less addicted to swings in fashion. If Americans experience much more "stagflation"—that combination of inflation and recession that characterized the middle 1970s—they too might begin to mature in the European tradition.

Middlemen. If consumers mature, we may see the rise of middlemen who specialize in repair, reuse, and recycling services. The automobile seems a likely candidate here. If buyers keep their automobiles longer (lengthening credit terms encourage this), then new car sales will suffer at the expense of automobile service firms.

As we discussed in the distribution chapter, I think we can safely predict more vertical integration of distribution channels, and more concentration: fewer firms doing a greater proportion of the total business. Another interesting trend at the retail level is polarization. That is, at the same time the superstore is rising to prominence—selling everything from auto parts to groceries to appliances—the number of specialties shops is also increasing. And I think that we will see many facilitating agents offering a broader range of services and making greater use of marketing concepts and techniques. Banks are trying to be friendlier these days, and advertising agencies are increasingly modifying the traditional 15 percent fee system to better serve client demands.

Underlying forces for change in both middleman and facilitating agent relate primarily to continued economic growth. Despite the recent recession, there are generally more people with more money to spend. At the same time, there is more competition and increasing pressure from public policy. In consequence, there is need to change the structure of many distribution channels—more manufacturers are selling directly to large retailers, traditional wholesalers are assuming new responsibilities, and so on. Of course, these changes in customer relationships lead to modifications in supplier relationships.

Changes in Supplier Relationships

We approach these changes in terms of each of the four resource inputs, as shown in Exhibit 14-5. Sometimes the changes affect organizational buyers differently from external suppliers. The forces underlying these changes are also interesting.

Human Resources. Top management and personnel experts are increasingly worried about the phenomenon of employee alienation. Briefly, there is evidence to suggest that many employees consider themselves to be unimportant cogs in vast impersonal production machines. The person, for example, who spends eight hours a day tightening 72 bolts per hour on automobile engines sweeping past on an assembly line derives very little satisfaction from the work. This is a concern of all management, and is particularly important to marketing managers when it results in defective

Exhibit 14-5   Changes in Supplier Relationships

	Types of Supplier			
Category	Human	Physical	Capital	Information
Organizational:	employee alienation employee interest	more intermittent shortages higher prices longer production times	more expensive require more documentation	more needed more costly to procure more emphasis on management
External:	more contract services	more intermittent shortages higher prices longer delivery times	more expensive "crowding out"	integrated systems
Forces:	rising expectations self-actualization	Third World cartels inflation price controls rising world-wide demand national policies	governmental monetary and fiscal policy political uncertainties	costs of decision making closer governmental scrutiny

or dangerous products. At the same time, some employees are becoming more interested in their work. In a few cases, assembly lines are redesigned to give workers a greater sense of participation in the production of the total product. In other cases, members of labor unions have preserved their jobs by cooperating with management, even, in one instance, taking over some selling responsibilities rather than accepting layoffs from production jobs. Heightened employee interest in organizational management may be attributable at least partly, as Drucker points out, to the fact that employees either directly or through their pension plans now own some 40 percent of all outstanding common stock in public profit-seeking corporations. It also appears likely that more talents and abilities of people will be available from external suppliers on a contract basis.

The underlying forces here are similar to ones we discussed in the consumer section: changing life styles and rising expectations. Perhaps the culmination is the widening of the quest for self-actualization (recall Maslow's hierarchy of needs from Chapter 6). As "lower order" needs are increasingly satisfied in industrial societies, individuals in those societies turn their attention to fuller development of their inner potentials.

Physical Resources. In contrast to the flowering of human potential, the picture is less sanguine for physical resources. Suppliers, both organizational and external, can expect increasing intermittent bouts of shortages of various raw materials and components. I doubt that we shall soon again experience the complete reversal from buyers' to sellers' markets that we saw in 1973–74, but there will be spot shortages. These shortages will result in higher prices and longer delivery and/or production times. Increasing managerial attention will be focused upon coping with supply shortages. These soon become marketing problems. Marketers are the ones who must face the organization's customers and tell them that orders will be delayed, or that prices will have to be renegotiated.

The forces underlying these shortages are economic and political. It is a simple economic fact that demand for many products is rising world-wide. More and more of the world's population are becoming "MAD" consumers. The political aspects are a bit more complex. Inflation is a chronic problem worldwide. Many governments are experimenting with or at least talking about price controls and other economic policies such as export quotas, import duties, and so on. In addition, many Third World countries, seeing the success that the OPEC countries have had with their petroleum cartel, are attempting to do the same for such raw materials as coffee, tin, bauxite, and sugar. To the extent that these cartels are successful, prices will rise and/or shortages will develop. Finally, raw materials and component supplies are affected by national policies that are not economic in character. For example, if the United States sticks to its pledge to Black African nations not to trade with Rhodesia, an important source of chromium will be cut off. The world's only other significant exporter of chromium is the U.S.S.R.

Capital Resources. The situation for capital is similar. Whether procured internally, i.e., from earnings retained from profits, or externally, either by borrowing or issuing new stock, capital is likely to be more expensive. Internal capital commitments will thus probably require more extensive documentation, i.e., more careful calculations of costs and benefits of organizational projects.

In the capital markets, some experts are worried about a phe-nomenon they call "crowding out." They fear that greatly expanded governmental activities which require procurement of capital will leave insufficient funds for the private sector. The underlying forces here are largely governmental in nature. First, monetary and fiscal policy is both a major determinant of the rate of inflation and the primary cause of crowding out. In addition, difficulties of capital procurement are increased by uncertainty regarding possible political action. We discussed in Chap-ter 4 the antitrust suit pending against American Telephone and Tele-graph Company. And there is talk in the halls of Congress of breaking up the petroleum companies. These governmental actions have many poten-tial ramifications, both good and bad. One of them is that investors and lenders are wary of committing capital to organizations subject to possible governmental action.

Exhibit 14-6   The Dynamic Society

	Societal Members			
Category:	Competitors	Regulators	Influencers	General Public
	more intertype more multinational more concentration more use of political process	more business/govern- ment interface more and tighter restric- tions on marketing continuing struggle between regulation and market incentives some emphasis on costs and benefits	more attempts more use of "mar- keting" more use of advocacy	increasing education and sophistication less blind faith in knowledge more secular, humanistic and rational values less traditional, religious and mystic more open and social structure "one world," i.e., increasingly common sociocultural patterns more varied subcultures and life styles
Forces:	economic growth international development rapid technological progress more emphasis on nontechnical impli- cations	pressure to "do something" naive view, in some cases, of economics	rising expectations rising distrust of market system	ecological concerns

Information as a Resource. We argued in Chapter 8 that information should be considered an organizational resource, because it is expensive to procure and therefore should be managed carefully. These internal concerns are complemented by the need, particularly in vertically integrated systems, to permit information flow throughout the system. This involves linking data banks from different organizations into the same information system. The underlying forces here include the rising cost of making decisions, and increasing governmental demands for information for policy making and regulatory purposes.

The Dynamic Society

Changes in customer and supplier relationships are reflected in the larger social dynamics. Exhibit 14-6 provides structure for this part of the discussion, again in terms of the categories of societal members presented in the marketing management model.

Competitors. There is no question in my mind that there will be more intertype competition. That is, organizations must be concerned with the actions not only of organizations that offer similar products, but those that offer different products to serve the same desires. While it is true, for example, that there is more concentration in the beer industry (market shares of Anheuser-Busch, Schlitz, Pabst, and Coors are increasing), fruit wines, soft drinks, and light whiskeys are increasingly serving the beverage demands of beer drinkers. This is especially true at the international level. Not only are American concerns developing markets abroad, but "foreign" corporations are making inroads into American markets: Japanese automobiles and television sets, Russian shipping and vodka, Swedish steel and motion pictures. Even America's long time free-world dominance in aircraft manufacture is being challenged by a French firm, Airbus Industrie.

Competitors are also increasingly turning to the political process to resolve economic conflicts. Dominant firms are particularly vulnerable to private antitrust suits. Landmarks here include Control Data Corporation's suit against IBM, and Carterfone Corporation's victory over American Telephone and Telegraph. The underlying forces here are some of the same ones that we have mentioned earlier. The major one is economic growth, particularly in terms of international development. Perhaps of greater long-run import, however, is the rapid pace of technological progress. The slide rule and the pin-lever watch are obsolete, massive computer installations are increasingly giving way to small desk-type computers, and a massive search is underway to improve or replace the reciprocating piston automobile engine.

Regulators. Competition between fewer large organizations means that the invisible hand of many small economic institutions is increasingly replaced by the very visible activities of corporate giants. Inevitably, this trend will lead to closer interfaces between large organizations and various governmental agencies. We can expect more and tighter restrictions on marketing and a continuing struggle between regulation and market incentives. There will be increasing emphasis upon calculation of cost and benefits of public policy proposals. At the same time, I think that we will experience more public policy development by the advocacy process.

Driving forces here include unrelenting pressure upon public servants to "do something." This is another manifestation of rising expectations; "why can't our government solve these problems?" In addition, my own personal opinion is that some public policy makers seem to have a rather naive view of economic reality. For example, elementary economics textbooks extol the virtues of pure competition. Many public policy makers argue for breaking up IBM, AT&T, or the oil companies for this reason. But they forget the assumptions underlying pure competition, especially the one about instantaneous and costless transactions. While it might be true that great benefits might ultimately accrue to consumers from such action, the corporations will fight divestiture. Since these corporate giants are capable of sustaining legal battles for some years, it is difficult to see how public policy makers can really believe that divestiture will result in a net saving of resources to society in the foreseeable future.

Influencers. The pressure to do something comes largely from influencers—academicians and social critics who shape public opinion. There appear to be more such individuals and groups today, and they are becoming more adept at using both the tools of marketing and those of advocacy. Again the driving force is rising social expectations. Moreover, the influencers seem to have a profound distrust of the market mechanism. Thus, there is increasing pressure on government agencies to intervene in the operations of the economic system.

General Public. In broad terms, all of the potential changes discussed above are manifestations of such general trends as increasing education and sophistication, and lessening of blind faith in the value of scientific knowledge and material progress. Values and attitudes are becoming more attuned to conditions and problems of this world, and to rational approaches to solving these problems, rather than to reliance upon religion, superstition, or tradition. In addition, the social structures of modern societies tend to become more similar, whether the society is American, Western European, Russian, Japanese, or even Chinese. These social structures are becoming relatively more open, e.g., there is more freedom of movement from one social class to another. There are more varied subcultures and life styles within the basic cultural pattern of a mature society.

Perhaps the overall driving force behind changes in the attitudes and actions of the general public is increasing concern for ecology. That is, the way living things (including human beings) interrelate and the way they relate to the earth, air, and water of this planet will play an increasingly important role in the future environment of marketing. Thus, the marketing manager needs to be aware of several basic trends in the ecosystem.

First, although population growth is beginning to taper off in mature industrial economies, the population of the world as a whole is increasing explosively. Exhibit 14-7 shows this trend in dramatic form. It took millions of years for the total population of the earth to reach one billion; that population doubled to two billion in eighty years, and is expected to double again to four billion by 1975. These data present one example of exponential growth, a phenomenon of mounting concern to ecologists.

Ever increasing growth is dangerous to the ecosystem because the resources of the earth, enormous as they are, are finite. Until quite

Exhibit 14-7   World Population

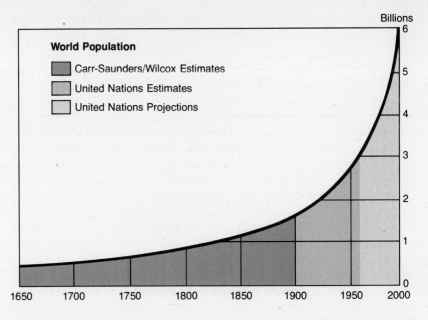

Billions

World Population

☐ Carr-Saunders/Wilcox Estimates

☐ United Nations Estimates

☐ United Nations Projections

Adapted from Donald J. Bogue, *Principles of Demography* (New York: John Wiley and Sons, 1969) with permission of the publisher.

recently, resources were so plentiful, relative to man's use of them, that it was not necessary to consider using resources efficiently. We had, in the words of economist Kenneth Boulding, a *cowboy* economy—resources were a limitless frontier for man to exploit. However, as both the number of people and their average level of resource use increase, it is rather suddenly becoming clear that man must shift from a cowboy economy to a *spaceship* economy. While the cowboy economy seeks to maximize want satisfaction, the spaceship economy seeks to minimize resource expenditures necessary to maintain some given level of want satisfaction.

While such comments are important in that they raise significant questions, their basically pessimistic conclusions should not go unchallenged. It may be, for example, that the exponential growth pattern shown in Exhibit 14-7 really tells only half the story. An alternative is shown in Exhibit 14-8. Kahn argues that viewing population growth from the perspective of a longer baseline indicates that the present sharp increase is a rather temporary aberration of the long-term rate of population growth.

Man must also recognize the interdependence of different components of the ecosystem. The energy crisis provides a graphic example here. Increased energy use by developed economies, particularly in the Western world, generates demand for machinery that uses energy, and increases pollution of the atmosphere. This increased demand also heightens

Exhibit 14-8   Population Growth Rate in Long-Term Historical Perspective

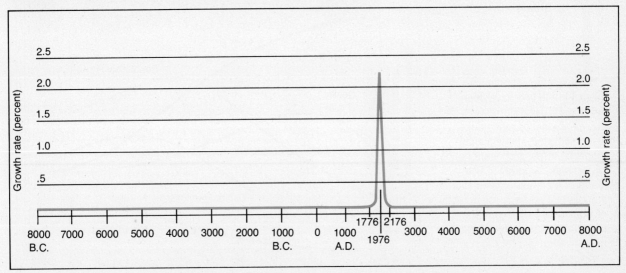

political tensions in South America and the Middle East—since these at present are major petroleum producing areas of the world. The shortage spawns political activity designed to alleviate hardships resulting from the shortage, and also spurs research and development for new technologies. In short, the ecosystem illustrates on a grand scale the basic maxim of systems analysis: everything depends on everything else.

The exponential growth in population and living standards together with the finite resources and the interdependence of ecosystem components require that man adapt to the environment. As we noted in Chapter 3, one of the basic values held by members of an industrial society is that nature can be adapted to man's needs. This is true, up to a point. Many ecologists are now saying that this point is rapidly being approached. The mature industrial economy must make the transition from abundance to scarcity, from wasteful consumption to careful husbanding of resources. Exhibit 14-9 briefly reviews a celebrated study in this area.

To repeat for emphasis, it is essential that the marketing manager be cognizant of environmental influences upon plans, decisions, and actions. The marketing environment is diverse, complex, and dynamic. In the future there will be more rapidly changing opportunities for and threats to marketing management. There will be new markets and new competitors for these markets; there will be new customers—more affluent, better educated, and more sophisticated buyers. There will be new materials, methods, and processes for producing products, but also new governmen-

Exhibit 14-9 The Limits to Growth

The ecological principles discussed in the text have been developed (using Forrester's *industrial dynamics* techniques) into a sophisticated mathematical model by a research team headed by Dennis L. Meadows. The model is a computer simulation of the interrelated behavior patterns of significant variables in the ecosystem. For example, the basic relationship for the population variable is as follows:

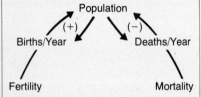

The model is complex. It is the result of a large-scale research project sponsored by the prestigious Club of Rome, a loose federation of eminent people from some 25 nations, including scientists, industrialists, economists, sociologists, and educators. Results of this simulation are expressed in terms of five significant ecological variables. The standard run, or basic conclusion, of the simulation is shown in the top figure at right.

This model assumes no major changes in the physical, economic, or social relationships that have governed the development of the world system in the past. The variables follow historical values from 1900 to 1970. Food,

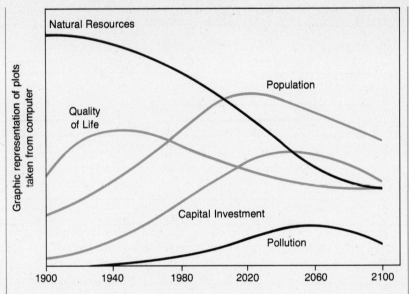

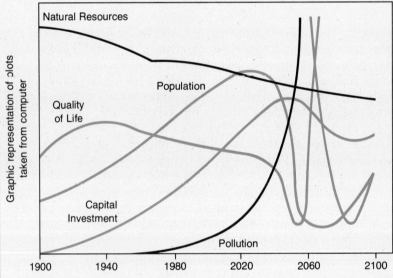

industrial output, and population grow exponentially until the rapidly diminishing resource base forces a slowdown in economic growth. Because of natural delays in a system, both population and pollution continue to increase for some time after the increase of industrialization. Population growth is finally halted by a rise in the death rate due to decreased food and medical services.

But surely man will act to divert such a crisis; historical patterns will be changed. The bottom figure shows that even if extremely optimistic changes are assumed, catastrophe is delayed but not averted. Assumptions include fully exploited resources, 75 percent recycled. Also, pollution generation is reduced to one-fourth of its 1970 value. Land yields are doubled, and effective methods of birth control are made available to the world population. The result is temporary achievement of a constant population with a world average income per capita that reaches nearly the present U.S. level. Finally, though, industrial growth is halted, and the death rate rises as resources are depleted, pollution accumulated, and food production declines.

Clark and Fulmer note the major criticism of the model: It rules out the possibility of exponential growth in technological progress. (The exponential growth of other factors will surely swamp any factor not granted exponential form.) The Meadows team made this assumption because technological progress is very difficult to predict. We may, for example, harness the unlimited energy of the sun or find other inhabitable planets.

Kahn points out that *The Limits to Growth* team employed some questionable calculations. For example, Meadows predicts that the world's aluminum will be used up in, at most, 49 years. Since the earth's crust contains about 8 percent aluminum, or roughly two million trillion tons, a discrepancy is evident. It is that Meadows counted only known reserves of bauxite, the ore from which aluminum is now refined. But U.S. Bureau of Mines reports show that the world has virtually inexhaustible potential resources of aluminous materials other than bauxite. For example, one U.S. deposit of oil shale contains 19 billion tons of the mineral dawsonite, which is about 1/5 pure aluminum. This mineral would be available as a by-product of extracting shale oil. Similarly, although known reserves of iron ore will last only 154 years at Meadows' projected usage rate, no one has made any attempt to estimate the quantities of iron ore resources not presently identified. But they must be enormous since iron constitutes fully 6 percent of the earth's crust.

The point is that rising prices, which *The Limits to Growth* model ignored, change both the supply and the demand of resources.

Assume, Kahn says, that the price of copper rises to $10/lb. The U.S. has ''consumed'' about 90 million tons of copper, but most of it still exists in various forms within structures or equipment. The rise in price would cause a rush to locate old brass beds, brass handles, copper pots, lamps, locks and other copper scrap—including 65 billion pennies worth a nickel each. Copper is not consumed; rather, it is a renewable resource. Mining and smelting just change it from a low-grade ore below ground to a very high-grade ore above ground.

Despite these faults, *The Limits to Growth* study is significant; it has focused attention on ecology. Marketing managers need to be aware of ecology. Since marketing is a major influence in the allocation of the world's resources, it, therefore, has a major impact upon the ecosystem.

Source: Based upon various sources, including Jay W. Forrester, *World Dynamics* (Cambridge, Mass., Wright-Allen-Press, 1971); D. H. Meadows, D. L. Meadows, Jorgen Randers and W. W. Behrens III, *The Limits of Growth* (New York, Universe Books, 1972); and Thomas B. Clark and Robert M. Fulmer, "the Limits to *The Limits of Growth,*" *Business Horizons,* June 1973, pp. 88–96, with the permission of the publishers; and Herman Kahn, William Browne and William Martel, *The Next 200 Years: A Scenario for America and the World.* (William Morrow and Co. 1976), adapted from pp. 88–96. Copyright © 1976 William Morrow & Company, Inc.

tal regulations, new shortages of critical components, and new types and scales of costs and prices.

And therein lies the crux of the problem for marketing managers. It is easy to speculate about the future. As Theodore Levitt sardonically notes (*Marketing for Business Growth*, pp. 226-9), all a futurist requires is "a lively imagination and a facile command of the active verb." Contradictions abound. Alive today in the Western world are more scientists than have lived in all of man's history. At the same time, there is enormous interest in mysticism, astrology, tarot cards, and witchcraft. Televised baseball has not curtailed live attendance at games. Nor has television killed the movies—though it killed some of the old movie companies which refused to make the relatively minor adaptations which the situation called for. It is the marketing manager who must see the specific opportunities and threats in the myriad changes of the modern world. This is the challenge to marketing management.

THE CHALLENGE TO MARKETING MANAGEMENT

In 1960, Levitt wrote perhaps the marketing discipline's single most influential article, "Marketing Myopia." We have quoted it repeatedly and offered numerous examples of its basic thesis, which is that marketing managers should not take a near-sighted view of their products, but should see them through the customer's eyes: "find a desire and then fill it." As we approach 1980, Levitt's admonition still has relevance, but the challenges to the marketing manager are more complex today. With apologies to Levitt for corrupting his title, I think that marketing managers today may suffer from myopia in three dimensions. If so, we should suggest methods of vision correction.

Marketing Myopia Matrix

In extending his classic article, Levitt developed the marketing matrix shown in Exhibit 14-10. The horizontal scale measures the marketing manager's concern for customers: one for low and nine for high. Henry Ford would get a 1 for his insistence that customers could have any color they wanted, as long as it was black. A sales representative might get a 9 for telling a customer without qualification, "any size price cut a competitor can make, we can make a better one." The vertical scale measures the marketing manager's company concern. A score of 9 might be achieved by introducing an effective cost-reduction program that lessens customer service. Lowest concern for the company rates a 1—the posture that any sum of money should be spent to get the desired results. Any attitude or action of the marketing manager can be located on the matrix. Here are examples:

(0,9)—max customers, min company: The marketing manager never charges a lease customer for damages to equipment, regardless of cost to the company.

(9,0)—min customer, max company: the manager always looks for ways to justify the status quo—always insisting that a customer take a new product as is; never trying to tailor the product to the customer's needs.

Exhibit 14-10   The Marketing Matrix

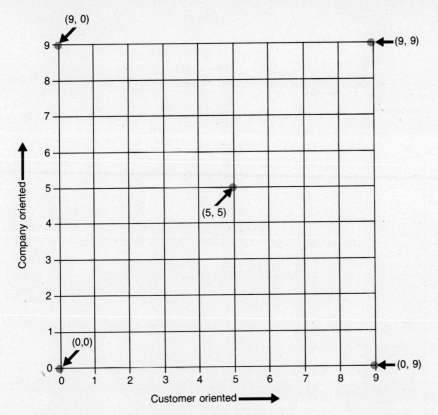

Source: Adapted from Theodore Levitt, *Marketing for Business Growth* (McGraw-Hill, 1974).

(0,0)—min customer, min company: This marketing manager will not last long.

(5,5)—medium customer, medium company: This is the middle-of-the-road situation; meeting competition is the planning guide.

(9,9)—max customer, max company: the marketing company concept argues that a company cannot be effectively marketing-oriented unless the marketing viewpoint infuses every aspect of the organization. The 9,9 location indicates genuine identification of the customer's problems and desires—and a high degree of competence in satisfying the customer.

The marketing matrix is a framework for structuring thinking about marketing management's relationships with customers and with the rest of the organization. As Levitt points out, "In a large company, specialization is inescapable. There will be need-finders and need-fillers. These will not

Exhibit 14-11 Marketing Myopia in Three Dimensions

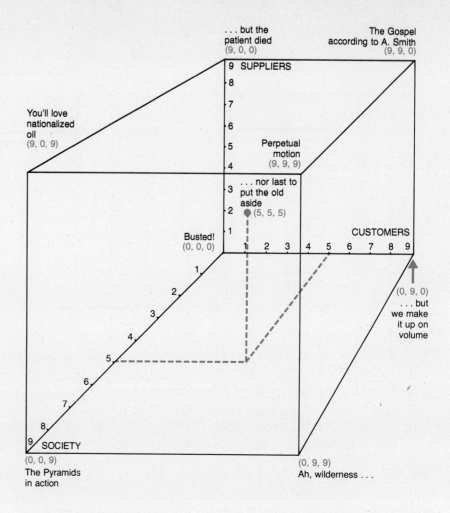

be the same person. Corporate cupids must exist to make matches between them." This lyrical passage is a good description of some of the tasks of marketing management. But I think that an additional dimension is needed.

Marketing Myopia in Three Dimensions

In keeping with the marketing management model used in this book, I would change the vertical axis to include suppliers as well as other managers of the organization. As we discussed in the last chapter, the marketing manager must attempt to measure the societal consequences of marketing decisions. Using the marketing matrix in this way would result in a three-dimensional matrix, or cube. Exhibit 14-11 presents this three-dimensional matrix, with comments upon significant locations:

(0,9,0)—min supplier, max customer, min society: We lose money on every sale . . . but we make it up on volume. New York City's rent-control program is a good example here.

(9,0,0)—max supplier, min customer, min society: The operation was a success . . . but the patient died. This happens too often when engineering or manufacturing excellence is not based upon customer's desires or social needs.

(0,0,9)—min supplier, min customer, max society: Here we have the pyramids in action. I think that perhaps the Humphrey-Hawkins full employment bill is today's best example of this position.

(9,9,0)—max supplier, max customer, min society: Given a societal dimension, the 9,9 position no longer looks so good. This is the gospel according to Adam Smith, and complete disregard for social responsibility is not in vogue these days.

(0,9,9)—min supplier, max customer, max society: Ahh, wilderness . . . this is the position of the diehard environmentalist. No amount of oil from Alaska's North Slope is worth disturbing the caribou herds.

(9,0,9)—max supplier, min customer, max society: A popular bumper-sticker in Houston these days is, "If you like the Post Office . . . You'll love nationalized oil." Nationalization rarely leads to customer satisfaction, as the patron of any telephone system outside the United States can attest.

(0,0,0)—min supplier, min customer, min society: No marketer likes to think that his/her organization will become bankrupt. But it could happen; ask the managers of W.T. Grant Co.

(5,5,5)—medium supplier, medium customer, medium society: Be not the first by whom the new is tried . . . nor last to put the old aside. As Levitt noted, this is the middle-of-the-road position. Examples here are left as an exercise for the reader.

(9,9,9)—max supplier, max customer, max society: Perpetual motion, the ideal position. I would think that an organization marketing solar energy at competitive prices or the medical research laboratory that perfected a cancer cure might approach this position. But staying there would require marketing effort of great magnitude and capabilities—perpetual motion.

Again, the three-dimensional marketing matrix is no more than a framework for formulating thought. This late in our labors, I thought we might have a little fun with the names of the positions without, I hope, detracting from the importance of the basic point.

Toward 20/20 Vision

Near-sightedness by marketing managers can take more forms today. A good optometrist can correct visual myopia. Correction of marketing myopia, by contrast, requires first recognizing that one is near-sighted, and then taking appropriate action. Levitt's admonition, "Find a need and fill it," still holds, but it must be applied to all three dimensions.

Customer Dimension. Despite all that has been said and done since 1960, marketing myopia in the traditional form still exists. American Telephone and Telegraph Company, for example, elevated a marketing vice-president to the same level as the other corporate vice-presidents only in 1973—after Federal Communications Commissions rulings gave competitors the right to attach non–Bell equipment to telephone company lines, and approved transmission of long distance telephone communications by microwave relay as well as by telephone wire. And there was the case of the metropolitan transit official in a city that shall remain nameless who rerouted buses around the crowded downtown area because the drivers were falling behind schedule. Now the buses run on time because they make fewer stops downtown to pick up passengers. Peter Drucker wrote in 1968 that the rise of the consumerism movement is "the shame of the marketing concept"; consumerism lives, indicating that traditional myopia still exists.

Marketing myopia attained a new form during the period of supply shortages in the early 1970s. There is no question that the problems marketing managers face change when demand exceeds supply. The term "demarketing" has been applied to the management of this set of problems. This term is unfortunate because it seems to suggest de-emphasis upon marketing functions when product supplies are tight. But reducing marketing effort at such a time can have disastrous consequences. To keep a customer's goodwill when his/her order can be only partially filled may require more time and ingenuity on the part of the sales representative than was spent landing the account in the first place. Similarly, a company may find itself doing more advertising to encourage wise use and conservation of the product than it did when it was reminding potential customers that supplies were ample. In short, the marketer attempts to *manage* demand, rather than just to enlarge or stimulate it. The tasks involved are certainly different, but surely no easier, when demand exceeds supply.

Supplier Dimension. When supplies are short, managerial attention naturally focuses upon suppliers. In the early 1970s, for example, we found purchasing agents taking salespeople to lunch, the exact converse of the usual selling situation. Note that we said selling and not marketing. Just as organizations found, in the 1950s, that they could make more profits by marketing rather than selling to customers, so purchasing agents found that sweet-talking the sales representative did little good if the rep had no product to deliver. This is marketing myopia in reverse.

As we discussed in Chapter 2, the marketing concept can be applied generically. In this case, the purchasing agent could strive to understand the seller's situation, and thereby perhaps meet his/her own needs. For example, a buyer of $1500 valves found a shipment delayed because a $40 control wheel was unavailable. He had the valves shipped without the control wheel, then had his own machine shop fashion control wheels from $6 worth of bar stock. The American Motors Pacer provides another example of the generic marketing concept. The Pacer is a well-designed small car: it gets good gas mileage, has excellent visibility and good road-handling characteristics. American Motors customers seem to like it. The real story here is that the Pacer was designed to be manufactured from existing American Motors parts. Therefore, relatively little retooling and few expensive new dies were required.

In some cases, marketing myopia may not be a perceptual problem (lack of marketing vision), but a physiological one, i.e., the organization may be unable to respond to customers' desires as seen by the marketing department. Remember that the marketing concept emphasizes not only identifying customer desires, but also integrating total organizational effort toward the satisfaction of those desires. In a large organization, this may be difficult to do.

Perhaps it is a simple communication problem: the production people may not understand a marketing request. Or perhaps those reductions in the product line that cause sales representatives so much anguish were ordered by the financial vice president in order to maintain profit margins in the face of rising costs. Or it may be, as we discussed in the product chapter, that management's attitude toward risk and innovation is becoming more conservative. Research priorities may be reallocated away from basic innovation and toward refinements and new applications of existing products.

To address such problems, some organizations have been experimenting with the position of *integrator,* i.e., a person who is charged specifically with the task of coordinating supply and demand. The product manager (Exhibit 5-6) is one type of integrator. A different example is provided by managers of venture teams (Exhibit 13-4). Research into this type of position indicates that integrators need to be seen as contributing to important marketing and production decisions on the basis of their general management competence and specific product knowledge; that they must be able to balance competing viewpoints, e.g., production and sales, short-range and long-range considerations; and that they must have interpersonal skills for resolving interdepartmental conflicts and disputes.

Societal Dimension. I think that it can be fairly said that marketing as well as other types of managers are most myopic with respect to this dimension. Organizations are a part of the larger society, and they do have social responsibilities. Kotler (Exhibit 2-7) has called for revising the marketing concept to take long-run social welfare into account. He quotes the great British statesman Disraeli, "we serve the people's interests, not their desires." This is easier said than done. As we discussed in Chapter 13, students and practitioners of management know relatively little about how to measure social responsibility.

Marketing thinking can help in at least two ways. First, there is a time period between the initial public perception of a social problem and the development of public policies to alleviate it. A case in point is the ozone controversy. We know that the fluorocarbons in aerosol spraycans rise to the upper atmosphere after they are released. The upper atmosphere contains molecules of ozone which screen harmful ultraviolet radiation from sunlight before it reaches the earth. There is some evidence that the escaped fluorocarbons are decomposing a part of the ozone layer. If true, of course, this is a serious threat to life; but the data so far are inconclusive. Some manufacturers of aerosol sprays maintain that until the danger is confirmed, they should be allowed to continue to sell their products, providing jobs, paying taxes, etc. Other firms have turned this environmental threat into an opportunity. Manufacturers of deodorant applied in stick form, by roll-on, or with a manual pressure sprayer are touting the environmental advantages of their product. One manufacturer's advertising theme is "get off the can and on the stick."

A second way in which marketing vision can be focused upon the societal dimension is in the marketing—not the selling—of the market system itself. We noted earlier in the chapter that quite a few influential members of society seem basically to distrust the market system. It may be that they can be persuaded, or at least their influence can be offset, by careful programs of marketing the market system. Some of the oil companies, for example, are publishing "advertorials" explaining their views on the divestiture controversy. We will not comment on the efficacy of some of these efforts.

As difficult as the three-dimensional marketing tasks appear to be when considered in isolation, the difficulties multiply when one considers possible conflicts among the dimensions. Actions taken to approve the safety of the working environment (which please suppliers) may result in higher costs for consumers. Similarly, the catalytic converters on 1975 and later automobiles do reduce exhaust pollution, but are expensive and sometimes difficult to maintain. A crucial supplier/society conflict today is the issue of pollution vs. jobs. In more than one town, executives of an industry ordered to modernize production facilities to meet pollution requirements have opted to close the plant down rather than make the required expenditures. So the environment is improved, but jobs are lost. Certainly these are not easy issues to resolve, but I think that applying the marketing concept generically might suggest opportunities in these environmental threats. For instance, it might be possible to attract a new tenant to the shutdown plant, one whose production does not pollute the environment. And there are certainly marketing opportunities in these conflicts. Compliance with the Occupational Safety and Health Act has caused problems for many organizations, but OSHA has been a real boon to marketers of safety equipment.

In short, marketing management is responsible for a delicate integration and balancing of competing customer, supplier, and societal objectives. And these responsibilities must be performed in an environment which is complex, dynamic, largely uncontrollable, and sometimes poorly understood. So marketing is not easy to study, research, or to practice. But then neither is it dull.

Any product—good, service, or idea—must be marketed. If that product is to be marketed successfully, it must be managed effectively and efficiently. The personal satisfaction associated with competent marketing management and its contribution to whatever overall objective an organization may have can be as deep and as sweet as that resulting from any activity engaged in by man.

CONCLUDING NOTE

We have come a long way together in our study of marketing management. (You might look briefly back at the photographs in the front of the book to see just how far we have come, and how much you have learned about marketing.) Marketing activities are a part of any human society, and marketing management, therefore, is a significant determinant of the human condition. You have learned some of the fundamentals of marketing management in this book, but the learning process never stops. To guide your further study and thought about marketing, I offer the following closing comments:

> *axiom:* The underlying concept or framework necessary to understand a given situation is usually relatively simple. To understand a situation, reduce it to a fairly basic model. *corollary:* Implementing that concept, however, is without exception more difficult than it appears to be. Murphy's Law and Parkinson's Law apply to the application of abstract concepts to particular situations. Simplification is required for understanding, but a comprehensive consideration of pertinent factors is necessary for successful action. I have found principles of systems theory to be useful in this regard.

> *axiom:* In any management endeavor, people usually cause more of the problems than all of the other resources, processes, and environ-

mental factors combined. *corollary:* This truism is particularly valid in marketing. The marketing manager must deal with people in all three areas of responsibility—customers, suppliers, and society.

axiom: The pace of technological and physical change is swift, but the pace of social and cultural change is usually slower. *corollary:* This means for any organization, environmental change contains potential opportunities for achieving organizational objectives, and threats to these objectives. The marketing manager must continually monitor the processes of change, and be alert to organizational adaptations to change that might result in the attainment of organization objectives.

axiom: No one ever learned to be a manager from a textbook or in a classroom; management is learned by experience. *corollary:* If an individual has a sufficient supply of the necessary qualities, however, textbook and classroom can considerably shorten the time and effort required to achieve managerial competence. The trick is to be able to take academic material and apply it to actual situations.

Marketing is a fascinating field to study. Marketing management is a crucial determinant of organizational success and societal development. I have tried to capture in this book the essential fundamentals—the achievements and the absurdities, the uses and the misuses, the problems and the promise—of the marketing management process. I sincerely hope that you found the book worthwhile.

KEY TERMS AND CONCEPTS

Marketing Management Model
  customers
  suppliers
  society
  environment and forces
  marketing function
Functions of Marketing
  seeking
  matching
  programming
  consummating
Environmental Trends
  customer
  supplier
  societal
  ecological

Marketing Myopia
  matrix
  three dimensions
Marketing Concept
  selling
  demarketing
  generic

QUESTIONS FOR DISCUSSION

1. The customer, supplier, and societal trends shown in Exhibits 14-3, -4, and -5 are illustrative but not inclusive. Select one of these exhibits and research other trends and underlying environmental sources. Identify specific opportunities and threats for marketers of certain types of products.

2. One of the most exciting articles I've seen recently is Gene Bylinsky's "Science Is on the Trail of the Fountain of Youth," *Fortune* (July 1976), pp. 134–40. The chart below captures the article's major theme.

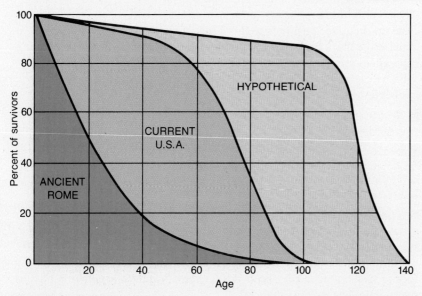

Exhibit 14-12   On the Trail of the Fountain of Youth

George Nicholson for *Fortune* Magazine. Adapted from Gene Bylinsky, "Science Is on the Trail of the Fountain of Youth."

The intrinsic life span of the human species has remained unchanged since the Biblical "three score and ten," but a far greater proportion of people now live out that full life span. Roy Walford of U.C.L.A., who designed the chart above, thinks that the new discoveries about aging herald the day when this intrinsic life span can be stretched by pushing diseases of old age into the final stage of a longer life.

If scientists are successful in prolonging life, and especially extending the healthy middle years, what implications might arise for marketing?

3. Consider such activities as the following:

   A financial vice president seeks a loan from a bank
   A merchant bribes a government official
   A graduate student seeks a fellowship
   A man endeavors to win a woman's heart
   An evangelist holds a revival
   An insurance agent is active in his church or synagogue

   Are these examples of marketing activities? Consider both positive and negative arguments here. If such activities can be considered marketing, how is the manager in each case performing each of the marketing functions of seeking, matching, programming, and consummating?

4. Consider the following quotes about marketing:

"With the supermarket as our temple and the singing commercial our litany, are we likely to fire the world with an irresistible vision of America's exalted purposes and inspiring way of life?" (Adlai Stevenson)

"Marketing occupies a critical role in respect to [economic] development . . . indeed marketing is the most important multiplier of such effort." (Peter Drucker)

"Television is the candy the child molester [advertiser] gives your kids." (Nicholas Johnson)

"The marketplace responds to the tastes of consumers . . . it is unfair to criticize the market place for fulfilling these desires . . . it is like blaming the waiters in restaurants for obesity." (George Stigler)

What is each of these gentlemen saying about marketing? What are the implications of these remarks for the marketing manager?

5. What opportunities for and/or threats to marketing management do you see in such environmental trends as Zero Population Growth, the energy shortage, the expanding technology in plastics, the desire for security, rapidly increasing disposable income, the apparent detente with communist countries, and the mounting evidence linking lung cancer with cigarette smoking? Explore these possibilities in some detail.

6. The chapter discusses qualities that a competent marketing manager should possess. Competence in other professions is sometimes certified, e.g., lawyers and accountants, and sometimes licensed, e.g., physicians. Should competence in marketing management be recognized in such a formal fashion? Consider both positive and negative arguments on this question. What is your opinion?

7. In view of all that we have said about marketing management, would you want to be a marketing manager? Consider both positive and negative aspects of a career in marketing management from your personal point of view.

SUGGESTED READING

For this last chapter, I have selected several books that could extend your knowledge of marketing, five scholars whose works are central to marketing management, and several books that present theses of interest to marketing managers.

Marketing Books:

1. Philip Kotler.
Marketing Management, 3rd edition. Prentice-Hall, 1976. Perhaps the standard advanced text on marketing management.

2. David W. Cravens, Gerald E. Hills, and Robert B. Woodruff.
Marketing Decision Making. Irwin, 1976. A new, comprehensive and well-researched advanced text on marketing management.

3. Gabriel M. Gelb and Betsy D. Gelb, editors.
Insights for Marketing Management. 2nd edition Goodyear Publishing Company, 1977. Designed as a companion volume to the present text. Contains two articles of particular interest to this chapter:

4. Raymond A. Bauer and Stephen A. Greyser.
"The Dialogue That Never Happens." *Harvard Business Review.* November–December, 1967, pp. 2 ff. Insightful discussion of differences in the perceptions of marketers and social critics of the nature, uses, and abuses of marketing activities; offers concrete proposals for improving communications between these two groups.

5. Herman Kahn and William Browne, "A World Turning Point: And a Better Prospect For the Future," *Futurist.* December 1975, pp. 284 ff. Condensation of *The Next 200 Years.*

6. Ben M. Enis and Keith K. Cox, editors.
Marketing Classics, 3rd edition. Allyn & Bacon, 1977. Articles chosen for their enduring value to marketing scholarship and management.

Important Management Books:
7. Wroe Alderson.

Marketing Behavior and Executive Action. Irwin, 1957. Classic theoretical treatment of marketing management.

8. Peter Drucker.
Managing for Results: Economic Tasks and Risk-Take Decisions. New York: Harper and Row, 1964, and *Management: Tasks, Responsibilities, Practices.* Harper & Row, 1973. Best works, in my opinion, by perhaps the world's greatest living management scholar.

9. Jay W. Forrester.
Industrial Dynamics. Wright-Allen Press, 1961. Standard work in systems analysis; basis for the work of Meadows, *et al.*

10. John Kenneth Galbraith.
Economics and the Public Purpose. Houghton Mifflin, 1973. Synthesis of his earlier works, and recommendations for reform of the economic systems of mature societies; brilliant, insightful questions, but less valuable answers.

11. Theodore Levitt.
Marketing for Business Growth. McGraw-Hill, 1974. Concise statement of basics of marketing management; written for the executive.

Provocative Reading:
12. Donella Meadows, and others.
The Limits to Growth. Universe Books, 1972. As noted in Exhibit 14-9, this

easy-to-read book raises serious question about the ecological impact of industrial society; this one should be carefully read and considered.

13. Mihajlo Mesarovic and Eduard Pestel.
Mankind at the Turning Point. E. P. Dutton & Co., 1974. Followup report to the Club of Rome; addresses some of the flaws in *The Limits to Growth.*

14. Herman Kahn, William Browne and Leon Martel.
The Next 200 Years: A Scenario for America and the World. William Morrow and Company, 1976. Searching, and I think persuasive, rebuttal to *The Limits to Growth* and *Mankind at the Turning Point;* Kahn heads the Hudson Institute, a private think tank which focuses upon the future.

15. Alvin Toffler.
Future Shock. New York: Random House, 1970. You have probably heard about this one, and with good reason; Toffler's thesis—that society is changing so rapidly that individuals become disoriented and confused—is a must for marketing students; easy reading, but a bit verbose; already a bit dated—which perhaps proves Toffler's point.

16. Robert Heinlein.
I Will Fear No Evil. New York: G. P. Putnam's Sons, 1970. Science fiction novel by my favorite author; incredibly entertaining and provocative extrapolation of the impact of technology upon society—concerns the economic, legal, moral, and societal ramifications of a successful brain transplant; ranges widely over contemporary morals and customs. I also recommend in this regard Heinlein's *Stranger in a Strange Land.* G. P. Putnam's Sons, 1961.

CASE 13 / MASSACHUSETTS STATE LOTTERY

In early June, 1972, Mr. Louis J. Totino, Deputy Director of Marketing of the Massachusetts State Lottery, was asked by the Lottery Director to review the marketing program for the State Lottery and to recommend any changes based on the past two months during which the lottery had been operational. Lottery tickets had first gone on sale in Massachusetts on March 22, 1972.

The Massachusetts State Lottery had been established by legislation enacted by the Senate and the House of Representatives of the Commonwealth of Massachusetts on September 27, 1971. The main purpose of the State Lottery was to provide additional revenue for the Commonwealth—these revenues to be used for state assistance to cities and towns, with distribution based on a predetermined formula. Legislative leaders hoped that the new State Lottery would serve the additional purpose of reducing illegal organized gambling in the state.

The law specified, among other things, that prizes should amount to no less than 45 percent of total revenues; that costs for the operation and administration of the lottery should not exceed 15 percent; and that a minimum of 40 percent was to go to the State Treasury for disbursement to the cities and towns of Massachusetts. In addition, the legislature designated the bill as an "emergency law" which was to be implemented as soon as possible. As a result of this mandate for the early initiation of the lottery, the Commission had decided against collecting primary market data; instead they had adopted a marketing program which was similar in many respects to the successful New Jersey lottery. In formulating their marketing approach, staff members had relied heavily on the experiences of officials in other states operating lotteries.

Early predictions for ticket sales had ranged from 75 million dollars to 150 million dollars in annual gross revenue. The Lottery staff had estimated that, based on per capita sales for the first week of operation of other state lotteries, Massachusetts' annual gross revenue could range from 25 million dollars to 90 million dollars. In a press release of January 27, 1972, the Lottery Director, Dr. William E. Perrault, forecasted, "Based on New Jersey's current rate of anticipated annual sales of $110 million, Massachusetts' sales could reach as high as $75 million annually. This would result in a return to the cities and towns of up to $30 million."

The enthusiastic initial reception in the first week resulted in sales of about 4.8 million tickets at a price of 50¢ each. However, ticket sales for the second week dropped by 50 percent to 2.4 million before picking up during the third week, when 3.5 million tickets were sold. Since then ticket sales had leveled off at a rate of 3 million tickets per week. Lottery management's goal was to give Massachusetts the highest potential per capita ticket sales of any state lottery.

At a staff meeting held in late May, several possibilities were suggested to stimulate ticket sales. These included: (1) having tickets available to the public up to the day before the weekly drawing, (2) having subscription sales in which a player could reserve the same number for a specific duration, and (3) increasing the number of winners of smaller prizes. Further, members thought that some incentive should be provided to the individuals who actually sold the lottery tickets at the outlets.

As a consequence of this meeting, Mr. Totino was reviewing the marketing approach adopted for the lottery with the hope of recommending to the Director changes which might increase the sale of lottery tickets substantially. At the same time he had available research data which had been provided to him by a group of marketing research students at Northeastern University in Boston. Since these data were collected six weeks prior to the first drawing date, Mr. Totino wondered if and how he could use the data, and whether or not he should collect more recent information to aid him in his analysis.

MARKETING PROGRAM

Price, Prizes, Drawings

The price for each ticket was set by the Commission at 50¢ and weekly drawings were held each Thursday in various cities and towns in Massachusetts. In addition, "Millionaire" drawings were periodically held, with the

"Massachusetts State Lottery," developed by Dharmendra T. Verma and Frederick Wiseman. Copyright © 1972 by Dharmendra T. Verma, Bentley College, and Frederick Wiseman, Northeastern University, College of Business Administration.

exact frequency being determined by the number of tickets sold. For example, if ticket sales averaged 3.2 million per week, millionaire drawings would be held on a monthly basis.

The top prize in the Weekly Drawing was, as in New Jersey, $50,000. Both states had identical prize structures for the millionaire drawings. The difference in the prize structures was that Massachusetts was able to hold more frequent Millionaire Drawings by offering weekly prizes of $2500, $250, and $25 in place of New Jersey's $4,000, $400, and $40 prizes. The value of the various prizes won and the number of such winners for each million tickets sold were as follows:

	Number of Winners	Prize
	1	$ 50,000
	9	2,500
	90	250
	900	25
TOTAL:	1,000	$117,500

This prize distribution left $107,500 undistributed which was used to finance the "Millionaire" drawing. This enabled Massachusetts to have more frequent bonus drawings than New Jersey. It was anticipated that such drawings would substantially increase interest and, as a result, raise ticket sales during the weeks directly preceding and following a Millionaire drawing. No other state held millionaire drawings as frequently.

Promotional Efforts

After reviewing proposals from a number of locally based advertising agencies, State Lottery officials finally selected Humphrey, Browning and MacDougall, Inc., of Boston to act as the lottery's advertising agency. Before the final selection, two additional advertising agencies were invited to present their themes. One of these, Ingalls Associates, Inc., had submitted a campaign based on a four leaf clover with a dollar sign superimposed on it. The message: "Good fortune and cash." A second unsuccessful finalist, Harold Cabot, Inc., had a design which consisted of a rainbow and the proverbial pot of gold.

Humphrey, Browning and MacDougall, Inc.'s promotion revolved around the idea of calling the lottery "The Game." In a *Boston Globe* interview (March 28, 1972), company executives explained their reasoning: "We wanted to get across the idea that it was fun . . .

The idea is that the words lottery and sweepstakes immediately connote gambling and have over the years developed a negative connotation. . . . The only way the lottery is going to be successful is not to have only gamblers playing it, but to have everyone playing it" (Malcolm MacDougall, Creative Director). Tom McCarthy, the agency's art director, explained, "We decided it was just too good to mess up with a symbol. . . . The letters of 'The Game' presented on the lottery tickets are green (for money) with shadings of yellow (for levity) and minute black lines (for authenticity)." McCarthy added that he had etched an intricate pattern for the tickets to pose a greater challenge for counterfeiters.

In addition to the basic name, "The Game," the agency had developed a variety of informational advertisements explaining the workings of the lottery. Slogans were also designed to reinforce the basic theme. For example: "It's not how you play THE GAME, it's whether you win or lose"; "Why marry a millionaire when for 50¢ you could be one? Play THE GAME"; "Money can't make you happy. But it can make you rich"; "Want to trade your Kennedy half-dollar for $50,000? Play THE GAME."

Consumer advertising was restricted to print advertising in local newspapers, on billboards and on transit vehicles. Federal Communications Commission regulations against broadcasting advertising or promotional messages on the lottery prevented the use of television or radio. In addition, postal regulations prohibit the mailing of newspapers with lottery information. A variety of point-of-purchase displays were made available to sales agents.

The advertising program adopted by the Lottery Commission called for an annual expenditure of approximately one million dollars—with half of this being planned for the March through June period.[1] The reason for the relatively large initial expenditures was the desire to make people aware of the new lottery and its workings. Tentative allocation of the budget among the various media consisted of: newspapers (40 percent); billboards (20 percent); point-of-purchase displays (16 percent); transit advertisements (6.6 percent); taxicab displays (3 percent); production costs (7 percent); and other special promotional and publicity items (7.4 percent).

Winners Advisory Panel. In addition to the promotional efforts adopted, the Commission set up a Winners

Advisory Panel to advise on tax and other problems winners might encounter. This panel included representatives from the Boston Bar Association, the Massachusetts Society of Certified Public Accountants and the Boston Safe Deposit and Trust Company, a leading Boston investment advising company.

Organization and Distribution

The Marketing Staff of the Lottery Commission was composed of three district managers reporting directly to the Deputy Director of Marketing. These district managers dealt with problems encountered by the sales agents (outlets selling lottery tickets) and coordinated the activities of the 18 field representatives, who each serviced approximately 200 agents. All employees of the Lottery Commission were salaried.

Number and Types of Agents. About 3,800 business establishments throughout the state were selected to become ticket agents. The types of outlets chosen included supermarkets, newsstands, tobacco shops, package stores, bars, restaurants, hotels and department stores. Heavy emphasis was placed on supermarkets, which had proved to be so successful in New Jersey. By selecting so many different types of outlets, the Commission hoped to reach a cross section of the population, and to make it convenient for people to purchase tickets. In addition, the Commission wanted to have tickets sold in many different types of "atmospheres" in order to appeal to all potential buyers. The decision as to how many agents to allow in each area was based on the published retail sales statistics and the number of retail establishments per town, as well as the size of the population served. The character of potential sales agents' clientele was also considered in that applicants whose customers were mostly under 18 were not granted licenses.

Criteria for Selection of Agents. Lottery Commission officials indicated that individual agents were selected on the basis of the traffic count in each outlet, its proximity to a major center of shopping, the number of tickets it was thought could be sold in a given outlet, how actively the owner and/or manager would promote sales of tickets and the agent's ability to pass security and credit checks, and the insuring that the convenience of the public would be served by having tickets

easily and readily available. A major concern, according to officials, was to select "reputable" and "respectable" outlets.

Incentives for Agents. Each agent received a 5% commission on each ticket sold in his establishment. In addition, he received a 1% bonus on a winning ticket (for $2,500 or larger prizes) sold in his establishment, so that, for example, an agent selling a million-dollar winning ticket would receive a $10,000 bonus. The bonuses and commissions were taken out of the 15% of revenue allocated for administrative expenses, not from the prize money pool.

In the case of chain stores, the corporation received the commissions and the bonuses. However, several plans were being considered whereby a corporation would give all or part of its lottery revenue to the store selling winning tickets, and whereby individual employees selling winning tickets would receive all or part of the 1% bonus. So far, one chain store had given their $10,000 bonus to the store where the winning ticket was sold, to be shared by all of that store's employees; while a second store gave its $200 bonus to the cashier who sold the winning ticket.

Procedure for the Distribution of Tickets. About 70 banks having a total of about 700 branches throughout the Commonwealth were chosen to distribute lottery tickets to retail outlets. The selection of these banks was based upon their ability to service the agents. Factors considered included the bank's hours of operation, its size and location. The function of banks was to act as financial depositories for the Lottery Commission, as well as to serve as convenient distribution points for the agents.

When the Lottery was first begun, agents went to a participating bank on a Wednesday, 15 days before the drawing date, to pick up tickets. These tickets would be sold until the following Wednesday (8 days prior to the drawing date), at which time all unsold tickets would be returned to the bank. At this time, all tickets sold would be paid for by the agent and tickets for the next drawing (to be held in 15 days) then would be picked up. The tickets distributed to the agents were sealed in packages of 100; all unsealed packages had to be kept by the agent, regardless of whether or not they were sold. As a result, agents were reluctant to open new packages for customers late on Tuesday. In addition, agents were not allowed to sell tickets on Sunday because of state laws.

It was felt that initially the best possible way to maximize sales within the shortest time frame was through the use of enthusiastic sales clerks together with point-of-purchase displays. Once the lottery had been in operation for some time, a decision would be made concerning the additional use of vending machines. By early May, twelve machines were being test marketed at airports, subway stations, bus terminals and restaurants. The selection of these locations was based on how inconvenient it would be for a person to sell tickets at that location. The preference still was to have people, rather than machines, sell tickets whenever and wherever possible. This policy differed from New Jersey's, which placed a much heavier emphasis on machines, with the availability of late ticket purchases, in their distribution network.

Consulting. During the same time that the administrative positions were being filled in January of 1972, the Lottery Commission had entered into a $300,000 contract with the well-known consulting firm of Arthur D. Little, Inc. (ADL) of Cambridge, Massachusetts. Their function was to set up the structure of the lottery, and to assist the Director in any way necessary in the operation of the lottery.

The Arthur D. Little consultants, working in conjunction with the lottery staff, aided in the establishment of and providing of recommendations for the prize structure, ticket design, determination of the number of agents (total and per district), agent selection, training and supervision of the field force, allotment and revisions of territories, setting up the schedule of events in each weekly cycle and handling the distribution of point-of-sale materials and information brochures. ADL also made comparative analyses and recommendations for the selection of the computer hardware and software, handling operations, packaging, the drawing equipment to be used in selecting winners, and made up a PERT chart to help assure that everything else would go according to schedule.

Sales Results

Tickets for "The Game" went on sale in Massachusetts on March 22, 1972 and the first drawing was held Thursday, April 6, 1972. Sales for the first week totalled $2,391,500 (4,783,000 tickets). This figure was 20 percent higher than the "optimistic prediction" of 4 million tickets made by Dr. William Perrault, Lottery Director, two weeks prior to the first sale. He termed the results of the initial sales "most satisfying." Dr. Perrault said, "The people of Massachusetts responded overwhelmingly to The Game and made it the success we at the lottery knew it would be. . . ." (*Boston Globe*, April 2, 1972, p. 22). In proportion to the State's population of 5.7 million, the sale of the 4.8 million tickets represented 0.84 tickets per person in Massachusetts. Among the eligible (over 18 years of age) purchasers, 1.3 tickets were sold per person. Interestingly, while Massachusetts officials were pleased with the lottery results, New Hampshire officials disclosed that during the first week of the Massachusetts State Lottery sales of New Hampshire's 50¢ "Sweepstakes" tickets had declined 11 per cent. The same situation prevailed in New York, where lottery ticket sales declined by approximately 10 per cent.

Sales for the second drawing (April 13, 1972) totaled $1,187,594.50 (2,375,189 tickets), and the third week (April 20, 1972) showed sales of $1,737,456 (3,474,912 tickets). Dr. Perrault explained that the main reason for the drop in ticket sales for the second week was that the first drawing on April 6 had not been held by the date sales agents had to settle their accounts for the April 13th drawing. "Tickets for the first drawing were on sale from March 22, 1972 through March 29, 1972. Tickets for the second drawing were on sale from March 29, 1972 through April 5, 1972. Many of the purchasers of tickets the first week were waiting to see the results of the first drawing on April 6 prior to making further ticket purchases." Recent ticket sales have stabilized at a rate of 3 million tickets per week.

While reviewing a list of the major prize-winning ticket holders, the Director had noted that the first "Millionaire" winner was a 47-year-old automobile assembly worker who had two children; the second "Millionaire" was a newly married 25-year-old telephone repair man.[2] Some of the other $50,000 and over winners included the following:

47-year-old laborer, married with two children
40-year-old housewife, married with two children
31-year-old shipper, married with one child
55-year-old meat packer, married with no children
36-year-old foreman, married with five children

[1] The expectation of $800,000 to $1,000,000 in advertising billings over the year made Humphrey, Browning and MacDougall the largest locally based advertising agency in Boston. Coincidentally, the agency also handled the accounts of Parker Brothers, Inc., the manufacturers of the "Monopoly" game.

[2] The first millionaire drawing was held in Boston on May 8, 1972. The second millionaire drawing was held on May 30, 1972.

CASE 14 / NEW YORK EMERGENCY NUMBER

The calls were pouring in at an unusually high rate at Police Headquarters yesterday about how hot it was, how the water wasn't running, how a big dog was after a cat again, and, occasionally, about a shooting or a suicide.

It was the fifth anniversary of the 911 system, the consolidation of the police, fire department and ambulance services through a single phone number, and it appeared that city residents, by the thousands, were ignoring Mayor Lindsay's appeal last week not to dial 911 except in a true emergency.[1]

So began a story in *The New York Times* in July 1973 describing some of the problems surrounding New York City's 911 emergency telephone number. Flooded with calls which were often quite inconsequential, the Police Department found itself unable to respond promptly to genuine emergencies.

Rising public criticism of such delayed responses had convinced Mayor John V. Lindsay and his advisers that a public education campaign should be developed to discourage use of 911 for non-emergency calls. The problem was how to devise a campaign which would differentiate emergencies from non-emergencies without reducing citizen confidence in the 911 system. As the Mayor stated, "We're suffering from success."

Development of the 911 Concept
In March 1967, the President's Commission on Law Enforcement and Administration of Justice recommended that, "Wherever practical a single [emergency] number should be established, at least within a metropolitan area and preferably over the entire United States." By dialing a simple, easily-remembered series of digits, any citizen would be able to summon a quick response to an emergency.[2]

At that time, most American cities had innumerable different numbers for fire, police and ambulance service. The St. Louis telephone directory listed 161 emergency numbers on a single page, Washington, D.C. had at least 45 emergency numbers and Los Angeles County had 50 numbers for police alone. The existing numbers were hard to memorize and rarely duplicated in other cities.

Hence the suggestion for a simple, universal, emergency number. The concept was not new, having already been implemented in a number of other countries. Great Britain had used the number 999 ever since 1937 to call police, fire or ambulance service. Although skeptics argued that the services desired could be reached just as simply by dialing 0 for the operator, studies showed that going through the operator took longer and that every second counted in achieving an effective response to emergency situations.

The rising crime rate and civil unrest of the late sixties lent urgency to the Presidential Commission's recommendation. After some prodding, the American Telephone and Telegraph Company announced in January 1968 that it would make the digits 911 available as the single emergency telephone number throughout the nation.[3] However, the decision on whether or not to use this facility was left up to individual local governments.

Implementation in New York
In New York City, which was often regarded as a magnification of the good and bad points of American city life, the 911 concept seemed ideal to the city administration and the police department. Mayor Lindsay's promise of a "Fun City" depended to a great degree on removing the fear of crime which affected both resident and visitor alike. Although New York had had a single emergency police number since November 1964, the seven digits (440-1234) were less easily remembered than 911 and took longer to dial.

The idea of easy access to police protection and emergency help was viewed not only as a solution to lawlessness, but also as a cure for citizen alienation. Anyone could "dial 911" and, because there would be no back-door to police help, all citizens would receive equal protection. Inspector Anthony Bouza (later Assistant Chief and Commander of the Police Communications Division) pointed out that 911 was to be " . . . a police-extended offer to participate in the solution of a citizen's problems . . . to overcome cultural and psychological barriers to these contacts [between citizen and policeman]."[4]

As the largest municipal police force in the nation, this reduction in citizen alienation was especially important to the New York City Police Department. With 32,000 well-paid officers protecting eight million New Yorkers in five boroughs, the department provided one of the highest police-to-citizen ratios in the world. However, New York City continued to be regarded as a crime center. The organization of the force was divided along both functional and geographical lines. Functionally, there were detective, public affairs, communications and other divisions, while geographically the department split into 75 precincts and seven field service area commands (the five boroughs plus Manhattan and Brooklyn divided north/south). Over the years the NYCPD had been responsible for a number of innovations in police methods and technology, and their initiation of the 911 system in the summer of 1968 would be the first of any major city and only the third in the nation.

From the Police Department viewpoint, the major benefit desired was a reduction in crime, with more criminals being apprehended and hopefully many crimes deterred. An important secondary benefit sought was greater community support of the police, through citizen participation in crime detection and a resultant increased confidence in the force. In fact, the same President's Commission report which advocated 911 also included a Task Force Report which showed a significant relationship between police response time to a crime and the probability of an arrest. The initiation of a "911" system was therefore expected to yield a double bonus: technologically speeding the emergency response by police from the time of notification, and at the same time improving the probability that the police would be rapidly notified of emergencies through citizen initiative.

The Emergency Communications Center

A centralized communications system had been recommended several years earlier, but it was only after several "hot" summers and AT&T's announcement of 911 availability that the Mayor's Office gave the go-ahead for the multi-million dollar project.

Technologically the project was almost totally handled by the New York Telephone Company in coordination with the police. Previously there had been five geographically separate "communications centers" in each of the city's five boroughs. Each answered calls to the "old" police emergency number, 400-1234, dialed from its portion of the city, and each had its own method for dispatching officers to the scene. Now there was to be one communications center handling all emergency calls via "automatic call distributors" (ACDs) which would continuously and evenly feed incoming calls to 48 switchboard positions.[5] These positions would in turn be linked by a 12-channel color-coded conveyer belt to the radio dispatch consoles for each borough. An ACD operator would receive a call, fill out the appropriately colored dispatch form, and place it on the belt where it would be whisked to the appropriate dispatcher.[6]

The dispatchers were linked to more than 500 radio motor patrol (RMP) cars and to an increasing number of walkie-talkie-equipped foot patrol officers through VHF radio antennas located atop the Empire State Building in midtown Manhattan. Additional back-ups were located at Police Headquarters downtown. Each dispatcher covered about a dozen precincts with a separate radio frequency for that area.

Later this entire system was to be augmented by the department's IBM 306 computer which, by providing automatic dispatch assistance, would further speed the process. While complex and expensive, the system would provide a far simpler and more efficient means of handling emergency calls than previous approaches.

Planning the Communications Campaign

No less complex was the problem of getting the message of 911 to the citizens of and visitors to New York City. It would do no good to have a highly efficient system ready to answer emergencies if the populace did not know of or care to make use of the system. The Mayor's Office, telephone company, and police department were to coordinate the "marketing" of 911. The Mayor would be in overall charge, as well as specifically initiating press releases at timed intervals. The police would furnish some material from their printing office, as well as specifically applying the message on all department forms and stationery and the large mobile "billboards" provided by the doors and trunks of their radio cars. The New York Telephone Company would, in coordination with their advertising agency, develop the marketing message and generally provide for its dissemination.

In view of the Mayor's desire for this effort to be a highly visible symbol of his administration's efforts on behalf of "law and order," and because the system was to be used by a citizenry which was highly diverse and of which many were poorly educated or of non-English-speaking backgrounds, the message had to be both bold and simple. After some discussion the campaign slogan became: "DIAL 911." This message, with the number written large inside a square logo, was to be endlessly repeated throughout the city, often in conjunction with an additional message.

Most critical was the timing of the campaign. To create the maximum awareness desired, it was felt that the campaign had to "hit" all at once, but if it was premature and people began using the system too early—before it was ready—then they might quickly condemn it as simply another publicity flop. And so, on the week of June 24, 1968, after the last of a series of publicity releases on the forthcoming project had been reprinted in the *Times, News* and *Post,* the city received a publicity blitz. All telephone booths[7] received a bright red decal, police cars sported the symbol, subways and billboards urged the message too. Newspapers carried advertising and end-of-the-month telephone bills displayed the logo. It was a saturation campaign.

Inauguration of the System

The following Monday, on July 1, 1968, Mayor Lindsay made the first "official" call inaugurating the system. After several false starts, caused by dialing 911 on an inside line, the Mayor finally got through, identified himself, and suggested that a squad car be sent to lock up the City Council. In his dedication speech, Mr. Lindsay said:

> This is, perhaps, the most important event of my administration as Mayor. The miraculous new electronic communications system we inaugurate this morning will affect the life of every New Yorker in every part of our city, every hour of the day. No longer will a citizen in distress risk injury to life or property because of an archaic communications system.[8]

After less than four weeks of operation, the Police Department reported that emergency telephone calls had risen from 12,000 daily under the old 440-1234 number to 18,000 (including 2000 for ambulances and 200–300 for fire emergencies) for 911. "The big thing we're doing is building up the public's access to us," commented Deputy Chief Inspector William J. Kanz of the Communications Division. Officials claimed that police cars typically arrived at the scene of a complaint within two minutes of a telephone call, more than a minute faster than under the previous system.[9]

Despite several complaints of slow response, the initial reaction was generally one of jubilation and acclamation. The police officer was indeed the New Yorker's friend; after all, wasn't he being turned to in ever increasing numbers? It was felt that 911 by its success was bringing about a better community relationship between citizen and government by overcoming the reluctance of many people to call the police. As Inspector Bouza later pointed out:

> The implication of . . . [overcoming inhibitions] is tremendous because it reveals that the police are not dealing with a known volume of work, but rather with a flexible volume, the size of which depends on the accessibility and efficiency of the police.[10]

Concern Over Delayed Responses

Yet this "accessibility and efficiency" were the very points which, after the initial successful reaction, began to trouble both citizen and policeman alike, not to mention Mayor John Lindsay. The original criteria for 911 operations had involved a heavy emphasis on speed of answering. An efficient system required that over 90% of all calls be answered within 15 seconds of the first ring and 95% within 30 seconds. These figures were indeed not only met but exceeded. However, with 18,000 calls a day this still meant that almost a thousand calls took longer than half a minute for response; time during which a person hung up, became antagonized, or more simply lost confidence in the system.

As always, it was the bad news which gained the publicity. Articles began appearing in the city's three dailies questioning the efficacy of the 911 system, or more pointedly, the efficiency of the New York City Police Department itself. 911 became the butt of some of the more typical "New York City life" jokes, drawing guffaws from local TV and radio personalities as they called the emergency number on the air for the amusement of their viewers and listeners.

In keeping with the complex technology of the system, the Police Department with the aid of telephone company consultants turned to improving the mechanics of the system. Operations analysis dictated that there no longer be a "secondary" pool of operators awaiting overflow calls, but that all operators be thrown into the breech to answer primary demand. Since there was an unexpectedly large number of Spanish-speaking callers, more bilingual operators were put on the line for transfers. Yet while the answering speed goals continued to be exceeded and improved, the criticism of police response continued.

Part of the problem resulted from the system centralization. Much of the souring of public response to 911 was due to the fact that people perceived the success or failure of the police in terms of *overall* response, which meant prompt arrival "on the scene." But the ever-increasing volume of calls at peak times (such as Saturday nights) meant an ever-increasing volume of "radio runs" in which cars were dispatched to callers; in many cases callers who did not require a squad car and its two officers to solve their problem. Previously, for example, kindly Precinct Sergeant O'Reilly knew that Mrs. Smith called the precinct whenever her husband stayed out a little late for a snort with the boys, whereupon the sergeant managed to calm the situation over the phone. Now Mrs. Smith called 911 which, answering her call within 15 seconds, immediately dispatched a radio motor patrol car to her door.

Facing this type of problem, the Department first requested additional patrol cars from the Mayor. Communications also initiated a "screening" process which identified those calls which, in the operator's judgment, did not require a dispatch. Still another response to the need for improved service was the introduction in October 1969 of the SPRINT system, real-time computer direction of the entire call reception and car dispatching system by two IBM 360 computers. All these system improvements resulted in reductions in call-answering time and overall response time.

Yet as crime in the country at large—and in New York City in particular—continued to rise, people continued to make use of 911 in growing numbers. In 1972 the Department, having made continuous use of technology to keep up with demand, now began to wonder if

perhaps another approach was needed. In particular, many involved with 911 felt that there should be some way of cutting down on the non-emergency calls which were entering the system; not only the "Mrs. Smith's husband" type of calls which ought by rights to still go to the precinct, but also those which the police had never handled and were not equipped to handle.

How to Eliminate Non-Emergency Calls?

The situation finally came to a head in the summer of 1973, when hot weather sometimes helped push the total number of calls to well over 20,000 a day. Many of these calls were relatively inconsequential, such as requests for policemen to fix a malfunctioning airconditioner. "What may be an emergency for a lot of people," said Sergeant Albert Lucci, a Supervisor in the Communications Center, "isn't necessarily an emergency for the police. A lot of people just don't realize this."[11]

As a result, the 48 emergency phone circuits were often jammed with non-emergencies. "Sometimes," added Sergeant Lucci, "it takes a while for people with real emergencies to get through to us." Out of a daily average of 18,000 calls, studies had shown that only 7,100 were real emergencies to which police cars were dispatched. Other calls concerned such diverse problems as Medicaid information, marriage licenses, open hydrants, street potholes and even VD information.

To an amazing degree, 911 had apparently won both the respect and disregard of the typical New Yorker who took city services for granted. The communications system had in many respects become similar to the all-night talk shows on the popular city radio stations, but better yet, 911 was free. Every pay telephone displayed the invitation to "dial 911," including the prominent notation that it was a free, "dimeless" call. Police cars, while perhaps not as omnipresent, still urged the citizens to dial 911. The emergency phone system was perhaps the only real city-wide "freebie" left in New York.

The rising volume of complaints about slow police response to the initial 911 call (delays of 5 to 45 minutes were cited) and subsequent tardy follow-up were a matter of serious concern to both the police and the city administration. The problem was particularly acute on weekends and on weekday evenings.[12]

The question was, what to do? An appeal by Mayor Lindsay in early July not to dial 911 except in a genuine emergency had no apparent impact. In an editorial, *The*

New York Times argued that "it is too easy for New Yorkers to make use of the emergency system, it costs too little in time and trouble, and therefore the temptation to dial '911' for trivial reasons has apparently become more irresistible." The editorial thereupon suggested that dialing 911 be "made a little more bothersome"—perhaps by turning it into a seven digit number like 911-1000.[13] Others argued that the problem could be resolved by charging for 911 calls from pay phones.

After discussions between the Police Department, the Telephone Company, and the Mayor's Office, it was eventually decided that some form of educational campaign was needed. At issue was the form the campaign should take. What organization(s) should sponsor it? At whom should it be directed? What media should it use? And what should the messages say?

Watching the situation in New York City with some interest was adjacent Nassau County on Long Island, which was about to introduce its own 911 service. The Nassau County Police Department was very anxious to avoid a repetition of the problems which had plagued New York City and wondered what strategy to employ.

[1]"Calls to 911 Show that One Man's Vexation is Another Man's Dire Emergency," by Pranay Gupte, *New York Times,* July 10, 1973, pp. 43, 83.

[2]"911—A Hot Line for Emergencies," by J. Edward Roush, *Readers' Digest,* December 1968, pp. 211–219.

[3]"AT&T Units Plan '911' Emergency Number Nationwide: Cost Will Exceed $50 Million," *Wall Street Journal,* January 15, 1968, p. 3.

[4]"911 = Panacea or Nostrum?" by Anthony V. Bouza, *Bulletin* (Associated Public Safety Communications Officers), March 1972, pp. 8 + .

[5]"Electronics in Law Enforcement," by Marce Eleccion, *IEEE Spectrum,* February 1973, pp. 33–40.

[6]"Police Emergency Center Dedicated by Mayor," by David Burnham, *New York Times,* July 2, 1968, p. 43.

[7]Pay telephone booths were converted to make it possible to dial 911 without first inserting a dime.

[8]"Police Emergency Center Dedicated by Mayor," by David Burnham, *New York Times,* July 2, 1968, p. 43.

[9]"911 Busy Number, Police Here Find," *New York Times,* July 27, 1968, p. 25.

[10]"911 = Panacea or Nostrum?" by Anthony V. Bouza, *Bulletin* (Associated Public Safety Communications Officers), March 1972, pp. 8 + .

[11]"Calls to 911 Show that One Man's Vexation is Another Man's Dire Emergency," by Pranay Gupte, *New York Times,* July 10, 1973, pp. 43, 83.

[12]"Delays are Cited on Calls to 911" by Pranay Gupte, *New York Times,* July 23, 1973, p. 1.

[13]"Emergency Calls . . ." New York Times, August 14, 1973, p. 32.

CASE 15 / PEOPLE'S ELECTRIC COMPANY, INCORPORATED

Benton Hughes' buzzer rang. It was Louise, his secretary. "It's Bob Adams calling from the state capital. He says it's reasonably urgent, but he'll be glad to call later if you're tied up now." Hughes thought a moment. He was trying to outline a speech to be given at the noon luncheon meeting of the State Association of Municipal Officials, and here it was 10:30 a.m. already. But Bob Adams was an important figure at the State Assembly and was a good friend who didn't bother you unless there was ample justification. And if he didn't talk to Bob, he would probably spend too much time wondering what the call was about to do justice to the speech. "O.K. Louise, put him on, but after that tell anyone who calls that I'm out of the office." That would be true, but of course he would only be hiding in the small room in the basement where he went when he absolutely could not afford to be disturbed except in a real crisis, and Louise knew very well what a real crisis was.

"Ben, it's Bob Adams calling. I know you're very busy, but I wasn't sure you knew that Friday afternoon at 2:00 p.m. the Natural Resources Committee will be holding its first meeting on Lou Tomasi's bill to forbid all advertising by electric utilities. I'd be glad to see if you can have half an hour for a presentation. I really think you ought to appear." Friday afternoon! Why hadn't Frank Foley, the company lobbyist, told him about that? "Bob, I'm most grateful indeed for your call. If you feel it's important, of course I'll rearrange some commitments and appear. You know the situation up there better than I do. Let's talk tomorrow when I've had time to put a few ideas on paper. O.K.?" There was a satisfied grunt from the other end of the line. "That's great, Ben. I guarantee you won't be wasting your time. The bill is written in terms of social objectives no one can protest, but I feel it has very dangerous implications. I'll wait for a call from you tomorrow. See you!" The phone was hung up at the other end. "Good old Bob! He tried hard to make life easier for a fellow. The world needs more of this type," thought Benton Hughes, as he disappeared down the back stairway to his hiding place.

Background

The People's Electric Company is located in one of the smaller, less populous states in the eastern United States. It was formed in the middle 1930s when five small electric companies with adjacent areas of service had been unable to cope with the financial hardships of the "great depression" and had been relieved to have Benton Hughes' predecessor devise a plan to merge them. The company has grown through the intervening years to the point where it has roughly $250 million in assets and annual sales of nearly $65 million. The company has about 200,000 customers and 1200 employees. Sales are divided approximately 50% to residential customers, 40% industrial and commercial, 5% governmental agencies, and 5% wholesale. The wholesale customers are very small municipal electric systems which generate little or none of their needs.

The company purchases about 50% of the power it sells from sources outside the state. Its own generation capacity is divided equally between small hydro stations and oil-burning gas turbines. The outside sources provide the great bulk of the "base" power that is needed on a 24-hour per day basis, while company units take care of "peaking" needs, i.e. the surge in additional usage coming when many people are cooking, washing, drying, or using electricity in other ways simultaneously during waking hours. This arrangement has worked well for many years, although more recently, peaking needs have been growing much more rapidly than base requirements and the company's "load factor," the relationship between average usage and peak usage, has been declining. The company is working on this problem, since capacity unused except at peak times increases costs dramatically.

In addition to generation and purchase of power, People's Electric operates high-voltage transmission

Written by David K. Smith, Professor of Economics, Middlebury College, and Gordon E. Miracle, Professor of Advertising, Michigan State University. Although the name of the company has been disguised, the case is based on factual material. Some of the facts have been modified to protect the identity of the company, but the essential realism of the case has been preserved in order that it may serve as an appropriate basis for classroom discussion of issues faced by "People's" executives. The case is not intended to illustrate correct or incorrect handling of administrative problems.

lines to carry its power to the local "on-the-street" distribution lines. It also owns stock in certain generating and transmission companies along with other electric companies of similar nature in that part of the nation. It operates a group of twenty-two retail stores in its largest communities. These were started many years ago when the company was trying hard to increase electricity usage in order to realize the substantial economies of scale possible when very large capital investments in generating and transmission equipment are made. The company's figures show an average of about $1200 invested in plant and equipment for each customer. If each customer uses more power, once the transmission and distribution system is established, the per-unit cost will obviously fall rapidly. People's has always prided itself on maintaining its plant and equipment in excellent operating condition. Its line losses (loss of electricity during transmission) of about 9% indicate that it has succeeded.

The company is regulated by a number of state and national agencies, as is traditional with natural monopolies in the United States. The State Public Utilities Commission is the agency with which People's Electric has the most contact. This commission's approval is necessary for all security issues, rate changes and conditions of service changes, and for construction of generating and transmission facilities. Relationships between the Commission and People's Electric have been good through the years, although the Commission is recognized as strongly oriented toward protecting the consumer and has been supported emphatically in this attitude by recent governors of the state. The utilities are required to provide explicit evidence that any requests they file are justifiable. People's Electric is proud of the rapport and respect mutually evidenced in dealings with its regulatory bodies, and especially with the Commission. The company feels that it has tried hard to live up to the legal specifications of the state law that the power wanted by the people should be supplied and at lowest possible cost. And the Commission in its attitudes and statements implicitly has agreed that these legal requirements have been met. Recently, however, certain conservationists have questioned both the propriety of trying to supply all the power the public wants and supplying it at lowest costs when higher costs might preserve the environment. The Commission has not been visibly influenced by this argument yet.

People's Electric has been operating under sub-stantial financial pressures for one and one-half years, as national inflation has finally had a pronounced effect on utility cost structures. The company had not asked for a rate increase for nearly 20 years prior to 1971, as increased usage and economies of scale had more than offset price increases for labor and materials.

The financial pressures began to develop as early as 1969, when earnings per share of common stock had slipped from $3.70 to $3.60. 1970 earnings had slipped still further to $3.45, and 1971 had shown a disastrous $3.25. This last figure was later corrected to $3.50 when the Public Utilities Commission approved a rate increase retroactive to 1971. The company had not changed its dividend of $3.00 per share during this period of declining earnings, although the dividend payout ratio had changed dramatically and annual inflation of approximately 6% had diminished the purchasing power of the dividend. The investment bankers who advised People's Electric counseled that holders of utility stocks viewed the dividend as equal to that of a bond in regularity of receipt, and decreasing the dividend would have led to a sharp decrease in the price of company stock, which was barely equal to book value already.

Another important factor in the financial picture is the bond indenture requirement in the Series M issue that if earnings before income taxes are *not* equal to or in excess of twice the interest requirement on all bonds, *no* new bonds can be sold. This requirement has been a factor since 1970, when short-term bank loans have risen to the level of $15,000,000, at which time it would have been normal to pay them off either through a bond or stock issue. Electric utilities traditionally finance 50% of their assets by bond issues and the balance by equity securities. Now, in the middle of 1972, People's Electric is in the awkward position of being unable to issue bonds and unwilling to sell common or preferred stock because market prices for the stock are so low. While the company's banks have been cooperative in lending beyond levels they would actually prefer, it is clear that the banks hoped that People's will be able to convince the Public Utility Commission that substantial rate increases are badly needed. People's had, in fact, asked for an increase in rates of nearly 25% in the middle of 1971, but after extended hearings the Commission had awarded only 15%, early in 1972. A new request for further rate increases of about 15% is nearly ready for filing with the Commission. This request is based on disappointing earnings projections for 1972 and thereafter as cost increases, especially for purchased power, continue to plague the company. In 1972, projections show earnings after taxes below the annual dividend, and an operating *loss* will be experienced under existing rates in 1973 and henceforth. Informal discussions with the staff of the Commission on the proposed second rate increase have been entirely satisfactory, and People's Electric feels that the Commission realizes that the present financial arrangements are intolerable. It is also clear that the Commission recognizes the burden of high interest rates for long- and short-term borrowing when company earnings on its rate base have been about 6.1% in recent years. The last bond issue sold by People's Electric, late in 1970, carried an interest rate of 8.5%.

The rate of increase in usage of electricity in the area served by People's Electric has been very high for the past few years. It has been slightly in excess of 9% in both total kilowatt hours used and in peak usage, i.e. maximum amount of power used at any one point in time. That rate of increase amounts roughly to a 100% increase in usage every eight years. Looking ahead, there is reason to believe the increase will continue at about the same rate, at least for the near future. The population of the state has increased about 11.5% in the last decade, with 60% of the increase coming in the last three years. Further increases in population at about the same rate are projected. The vacation home industry has become a very large factor in the company's market area, and most of these are ''all-electric,'' i.e., space heating, hot water, cooking, and lights are all based on electricity. A substantial share of the new non-vacation homes are also all-electric, even though heating costs for oil are significantly cheaper.

From the company viewpoint, the all-electric homes are wonderful. Annual kilowatt hour usage in an all-electric home is about 32,000 kilowatt hours on the average while it is only about 6000 kilowatt hours in a home which has space heating and hot water through oil or gas. Of course the all-electric homes intensify the firm's peaking problem, which is already a matter of great concern, but research projects[1] exploring the effect of cutting off electric space heating units and electric hot water during peak periods are expected to have productive results insofar as the magnitude of the peak is concerned.

While the company anticipates the necessity of building a major generating station (400,000- to 500,-000-kilowatt capacity) every two to three years after 1980 if the rate of increased usage persists, it tends to accept this challenge as an obligation rather than to seek ways to minimize usage. People's Electric is acutely conscious of the public resistance to new generating stations after preliminary explorations for possible sites in 1971 and 1972 aroused storms of protests from a wide spectrum of interests in the geographic area under consideration. It is hoped that less opposition might develop in certain less affluent sections of the state.

Benton Hughes, the Chairman of the Board and Chief Executive Officer, has been with People's Electric since 1950. He brought with him an excellent background in finance and insurance and is a director of several other large enterprises. His contacts with banks are so well established through years of personal acquaintance that he can get on the telephone in the morning and have oral commitments for $20,000,000 of bank loans by the end of the day. He is the only one at People's with this type of capability, although there is a competent supporting staff in finance. He has brought a very broad point of view and substantial intellectual curiosity to his job. He did graduate work in economics and finance and has taught for a time in a university. On several occasions through the years, governors of the state (frequently well-known to him) have sought his advice and participation on a wide variety of matters. He finds himself mildly amused by the contemporary surge of interest in the environment, since he served on several special commissions at the state level to call attention to pollution problems and urge measures to protect the natural beauty of the area long before such activities had become ''popular.'' While he insists on a high degree of financial responsibility in government, he regards himself as a liberal in attitude toward proposals for improving society. He feels that the position of stature his company holds throughout the state directly reflects the stature of its most-senior executives. Now, as he approaches retirement in one and one-half years, he wonders more and more frequently about the degree of confidence he should place in his own judgment and evaluations, especially when they differ from those of his closest associate within the company, John Stevens, the President.

As is so often the case in electric utilities, the two most senior executives at People's are an expert in finance and an expert in engineering. John Stevens is a man in his early fifties who has been an engineer with the firm ever since graduating from engineering school. Stevens knows the company's system in amazing detail, and he also knows its people. He is a relaxed and kindly man whose work has brought him into close touch with even those employees furthest from the home office. The employees, largely men, respect him as a person and for his knowledge. He has conducted labor negotiations for the company for many years and with conspicuous success. It has been said that the company has *always* lived up to the spirit and letter of what he has agreed to—without exception. John Stevens is not concerned with finance; he accepts Benton Hughes' judgment as to the limits by which engineering projects so dear to his heart have to be constrained. Neither is he concerned with public relations or public affairs. He views his job as that of making certain the necessary wheels turn so that there will be electric power wherever and whenever needed in the company's area of service. After all, someone has to "keep the fire going." As far as he is concerned, others can work to embellish a public image which Stevens feels depends strongly on the quality of service provided. As he often says, "There has to be a cake to frost." He has already indicated to Hughes that he feels his particular talents are best used in dealing with his present responsibilities; he does not wish to become Board Chairman or Chief Executive Officer when Hughes retires. The two men work very well together, each with a high degree of respect for the other.

The Friday Hearing

Hughes' speech at the luncheon meeting of the State Association of Municipal Employees drew a surprisingly enthusiastic response considering the time Benton Hughes had been able to give to its preparation. He then returned to his office to contemplate what to say to Bob Adams the next morning.

"The Tomasi bill to forbid electric companies to do any advertising comes up in committee day after tomorrow, Louise. I've got to give it some thought. If you have any ideas that might be useful, from the standpoint of the housewife, I'd welcome them." Benton Hughes wants his people to be completely frank with him, and they are. Louise responded: "My son in high school came home from a meeting of the Environmental Quality Club last night and asked me why People's Electric was advertising electric appliances in the same newspapers which reported voltage reductions[2] three times in the last ten days. I told him it was too complicated for me to understand and let it go at that. But shouldn't I have had an answer for him?" That was just like Louise. Every now and then she would say something that really made one think. "Be sure I have my tape recorder when I go to the capital Friday, Louise, so you can listen to what I say. There might be an answer for Eddie."

"If you're thinking about Friday afternoon, Mr. Hughes," remarked Louise, "you might want to listen to the tape of Lou Tomasi's address at the high school graduation last night. Larry Green left it here while you were out." Now that *was* a good idea! Benton Hughes had heard that the focus of the address was on the failure of the electric utility industry to assume a level of social responsibility consistent with the environmental crisis. Fortunately, Larry Green, his public relations man, had been alert enough to discover the nature of the talk in advance and tape it. It might be that Tomasi's argument would duplicate the logic behind his bill to prohibit advertising by the utilities. "O.K. Louise, let's have it. I have to know what the people around town are talking about anyhow. Do we have a file of newspaper clippings on Tomasi?"

Hughes knew that Lou Tomasi had grown up in the family contracting business which had been very successful over the years. Shortly after the death of the patriarch father, the founder, there had been an argument within the family over how things should be run, and the two brothers who agreed had bought out the remaining brother's (Lou's) share. With no financial pressures facing him henceforth, Lou became interested in studying the problems of the state and, as he became more and more concerned, he turned to political action. Now, he was Chairman of the State Environmental Quality Committee, a group which believed in diligent study of an issue and then appropriate political action. He had recently run successfully for the State Assembly, and shortly after taking office had introduced a bill to prohibit advertising by utilities. Hughes knew him slightly and felt that he was one of the more responsible of the environmentalists making the headlines so frequently these days.

"Superintendent Jones, Principal Brown, School Directors, Parents, Friends, and Students," the address began, in typical style. "It is clear to me that I was asked to give the graduation address tonight because I am Chairman of the State Environmental Quality Committee, and in this capacity can provide you with certain useful information about the environmental crisis that now exists. It is appropriate that this message be directed particularly toward the generation you students represent. You and your children and grandchildren will more likely be the victims of the environmental crisis than my generation; you and your children and grandchildren will certainly have to be more effective in taking appropriate action than my generation has been or is likely to be. I am absolutely delighted that many of you are legal voters this year since the voting age has been lowered to 18, for I know that you will more likely support progressive legislation than will older voters.

"Yes, there certainly is an environmental crisis! On some occasions in recent years the air in certain regions has been so badly polluted that human beings simply could not live. The most acute case of this was in fact, several years ago, in a small community in Pennsylvania, Donora, where a substantial number of people simply drowned to death in a sea of polluted air. But to come closer to home, you may recall that for four days last summer, a crisis in air pollution existed just a few hours' drive from here, in Connecticut. The air was so bad that state officials *begged* workers at all levels to leave their cars at home and take public transportation to work. At the same time, all those with heart trouble and respiratory diseases were warned to stay inside and remain as quiet as possible. But the crisis is not limited to air pollution! Remember that several of our beaches and rivers were closed for swimming in the middle of last summer because the water was so dangerously polluted. And you know that swordfish and certain other fish cannot be sold in our markets because concentrations of mercury and radioactive materials are above the danger point.

"But perhaps the most amazing thing about the crisis is the lack of concern shown by the public! The public doesn't seem to realize that it subsidizes business every time it allows pollution to take place rather than requiring expenditures on pollution control equipment! The *real* cost of production properly includes the *social costs*—the burden the public absorbs when it accepts pollution, and mark my words, very shortly *all* business will have to pay the social costs as well as accounting costs. Many firms with progressive managements have already accepted the concept of including social costs in their cost calculations. But much still remains to be done.

"As you know, I ran for the state legislative body on a program of commitment to introduce legislation designed to help us save ourselves and future generations before it is too late—if it is not already. Your action in electing me to replace a veteran of 20 years' service conveys a mandate I must exercise as best I can in your behalf. I have recently acted on that mandate by introducing a bill which would prohibit all advertising by electric utilities selling power in this state, as many of you know. This bill will come up for committee hearing on Friday afternoon, the 24th.

"In my opinion, it is immoral, unethical, and even dishonest to advertise, i.e., to encourage, the use of more electricity. That is a very strong statement, I realize, but you are as conscious as I of the number of voltage reductions the electric companies have been forced to make during the past summer. How can advertising be viewed as anything but irrational and possibly dishonest, if there is insufficient power to supply those needs already in existence? But it is not the short-run situation toward which the bill is largely directed. You must realize that the usage of electricity in this state has been increasing at the rate of slightly more than 9% annually for at least a half a dozen years, and industry forecasts predict this rate will continue. This level of increase means that we will have increased usage by 100% every eight years! Let me repeat that. We have been told to expect a 100% increase in the use of electric power every eight years! That means additional generation, with its particulate, SO_2, nitrous oxide and radioactive emissions. That means the sacrificing of our field and forest vistas for necessary transmission lines and substations. That means more air, water, scenery, and noise pollution in very large doses! We simply cannot permit the use of electrical energy to increase that rapidly even if we had the energy sources to generate the power, and we do not—at least we do not without grave hazard to our own lives.

"I am absolutely dumbfounded by the fact that key utility executives permit or even encourage advertising! In effect, they are encouraging us to act in such a way as to speed up the process by which we drown ourselves in our self-created pollution, as the Club of Rome Report outlines. How can it be anything but immoral, unethical, and insane to urge people to shorten their own lives? Advertising by the electric utilities seems to me to be the most socially irresponsible practice I know of in contemporary society. I hope that we may end by law what should have been terminated voluntarily by enlightened business leaders, and I do want you to know that I know many of them and that I respect them very much for many things that they do and have done. But on matters of such obvious moral and ethical importance, there simply can be no compromise.

"Your State Public Service Board is required to ascertain that actions taken by electric companies are 'in the public good.' This is a very broad guideline, and I submit to you that what is proposed in my bill is most definitely 'in the public good.' My only reason for submitting the proposal was the promotion of the interest of the public!

"I hope that you will support me in my bill to prohibit advertising. Letters or phone calls to the appropriate state officials and to your own representatives carry more weight than you can imagine. In this situation, the stakes are so high that we too can hardly avoid being called immoral and unethical if we do not undertake at least this small measure. Thank you, and good night."

"Well," thought Benton Hughes, "that gives me something to work on! Tomasi did present a lucid and attractive argument. Wish I knew what I was going to say on Friday afternoon!"

In the quiet of his office, Hughes found himself pondering not only *what* was the answer but *which* of *several* answers would best serve the many interests he would have to represent in his comments on Friday. Of course, it didn't make sense to advertise if People's didn't have anything to sell. It didn't take high school students to realize that! But it wasn't the company's fault that the biggest generating unit at Consolidated Electric had broken down and the entire "eastern grid"

had had to reduce voltage in order to provide the "Big City" with enough power to keep going with voltages set at the lowest level possible. With the reduced voltage the computer at General Accessories had malfunctioned and paychecks for 10,000 workers had not been printed. What a ruckus that had caused! And if only the Committee for Environmental Sanity hadn't gone to court to prevent Urban Edison from starting up its new atomic power plant, the Atomic Energy Commission would certainly have given the operating permit and the 100,000 kilowatts People's Electric was scraping along without would have been there. Boy, was he glad he wasn't Don Anderson, Board Chairman at Urban Edison, with a $400 million atomic power plant entirely finished and costing $100,000 every day it wasn't permitted to operate! Sometimes "the people" don't seem to realize that the cost of all this sort of thing must be paid by no one but themselves ultimately. If the rainfall during the summer had been anywhere near normal, the company could have used its own hydro rather than reduce voltage. No one seems to remember that there was not one single voltage reduction in the first thirty-five years of People's operations, and now, only the second year in which *any* had occurred, everyone was upset. But this kind of thinking was obviously not the orderly, logical basis for working toward his call to Bob Adams in the morning or to his Friday afternoon presentation. It was time to sit down and list the fundamental questions involved and sketch the most promising answers to them.

Hughes took a pad of paper and wrote "Why Advertise?" at the top. Then he took another pad and wrote "Why Prohibit Advertising?" at its top. Under "Why Advertise?" he noted several points:

1. Public needs to know and has the right to know of devices which will improve standard of living. Public health and safety are directly involved here.

2. Electrically heated homes with power generated efficiently at central stations are environmentally better than equivalent homes each with oil burner.

3. Cost of electric heating installation is less than oil installation.

4. Company stores cannot compete with furniture and appliance dealers without support of company advertising.

5. Philosophy of regulated monopolies involves free-

dom of management within rates set as long as management is responsible.

6. Increased customer usage permits larger generating units and transmission lines and sub-stations of higher capacity, resulting in considerable economies of scale which everyone benefits from, and increased off-peak usage contributes substantially to attainment of economies.

7. Public image of electric companies should be promoted continually through institutional advertising; prime role of utilities is providing best possible service at lowest possible cost to customers.

8. Expansion of municipals and co-operatives[3] most effectively prevented through high-quality institutional advertising, leading to appreciation of all that private utilities accomplish.

Yes, there were really good reasons for the advertising done by utilities!

In approaching the "Why Prohibit Advertising" listing Hughes insisted that he be as honest as possible with himself. There were certainly some important factors which should be admitted, and arguments against less valid points should be detailed after the points were noted.

1. Public should not be asked to pay for advertising when supplies of electricity cannot supply existing needs. (Answer: Supply problem is of short-term nature and is based on under-estimates of needs several years ago and construction delays caused by inflationary factors and environmentalists. Short-term problem does not call for solution of unlimited time span. Furthermore, it is to the advantage of consumers to level out the valleys in the load curve by increased off-peak usage.)

2. Since People's Electric is preparing another request for rate increases, cannot the public be spared part of this increase through elimination of advertising? (Answer: Public thinks very large sums are spent on advertising! This is simply not so. Radio and newspaper advertising by People's covering the past twelve months totals only $50,000 after rebates from equipment manufacturers are included, i.e. 25¢ per year per customer. Equipment and appliance manufacturers do most of the advertising the public sees.)

3. Energy resources are in short supply throughout the entire nation, hence we should not encourage more intensive use of them. (Answer: Yes, natural gas is in very short supply and low-sulphur-content oil is also in short supply. There is much more high-sulphur-content oil. All sources of hydro power have been developed, at least in the eastern United States with which we are concerned. There is *no* shortage of atomic fuel for atomic power plants, and we expect technological progress to bring us the "breeder" reactor which creates more fuel than it uses by the mid-1980s.)

4. Generation of electricity creates vast pollution problems, and any increase in usage only brings closer the day we are drowned in pollution, as the Club of Rome Report suggests. (Answer: Pollution control devices presently available can remove over 95% of the particulate pollution in the smoke from coal-fueled steam plants. Natural gas and oil furnaces do not involve significant particulate emissions, at least if reasonable quality oil is used. There are no known devices to adequately control SO_2 and nitrous oxide emissions, although vigorous efforts are being made to develop them. Thermal pollution can be taken care of through canals and/or cooling towers with technology already in use. Radioactive air emissions from atomic power plants will be so small as to not be measurable with scientific instruments at the site. Fog will be a problem at certain seasons of the year when cooling towers are running. Disposition of "spent" or used-up atomic fuel is a problem, and this problem is the sole responsibility of the Atomic Energy Commission which has reserved jurisdiction. The people should know that we are talking about radioactive materials with dangerous characteristics in excess of 10,000 years in some instances. Isn't the real question here whether or not eliminating advertising will achieve solutions when advertising involves such small sums?)

5. The rate of increase in electricity usage is so high that when one examines the volume of plants and equipment which would be required it is clear that we simply cannot allow such an increase in usage to continue. (Answer: The electric utilities provide electricity—a *service*. They do not invent the devices which use electricity. If devices using electricity were not invented, promoted, and sold, the usage of electricity would not go up as rapidly. No one is being *forced* to use more electricity! The utilities in this state are required by law to provide the power the people want. The Public Utility Commission is responsible for seeing that

this is done. Yes, the consequences of continuing the rate of increase in usage of the past several years are truly awesome! And if we could be sure that the rate of growth would moderate, we would certainly not build the necessary plant and equipment. Note that it would be much easier for the utilities if the growth rate were lower! Perhaps the laws should be amended to remove the requirement that the companies provide the power wanted—but who would support such legislation?)

6. It is immoral and unethical to urge people to take actions which will probably be to their detriment and even their death, even if they do not realize this today. (Answer: Evidence is not good as to the probability of such drastic results. Many electrically operated devices *promote* longevity rather than diminish it. What is moral and what is ethical are matters of opinion and not of fact.)

7. You agree that there are certain very unfortunate consequences which will occur if rates of increase in usage of electricity continue and if energy sources are squandered as profligately as in the past, but you do not accept the prohibition of advertising as a reasonable way to prevent these things from happening. What suggestions would *you* have for preventing the events we fear from happening? (Answer: Since advertising is not closely tied to increases or decreases in the usage of electricity, the logical way to secure change is to take direct action to get what is desired. Some form of rationing is implicit here, and not indirect and uncertain influences such as advertising. If a customer knows that he had only so many kilowatt hours to be used on all the various uses he would have at hand, he can select that combination of uses which maximizes his well-being. Advertising is still legitimate within the array of uses the customer should have the freedom to consider.)

On the way home, Hughes thought to himself: "There are really two central matters to be worked on. First, what to say on Friday must be attended to. But after that, what about the future? There are some very large and important questions here.

"What strategy should I base Friday's remarks on? Tomasi's arguments are highly emotional, and perhaps deliberately so. Does one deal with emotion through use of additional emotion? Or does one trust rational arguments to remove emotion and lead to an intelligent decision? Should I simply tear Tomasi apart—discredit him? He really doesn't know what he's talking about, yet tearing him apart would only make him an enemy for life. And he's not a stupid man. Can I take the offensive? I always liked the idea that the best defense is a strong offense. And we haven't done anything which needs defending! If only Tomasi and the other legislators knew what we've been through to protect the public in recent years! And industry in the United States will spend $205 billion between now and 1980 on pollution abatement equipment and cost of operation!

"I still think that what is moral and what is not is entirely a personal matter. There just aren't any universal criteria which can be used! Perhaps we *are* going through a transition in social thinking, as that article in the Edison Electric monthly bulletin argued, but when management is judged largely on the basis of short-run performance, how can anyone who wants to keep his job and the confidence of his Board act on the basis of long-run considerations? On the other hand, perhaps fellows as close to retirement as I am are the ones best able to do so! That could be very interesting indeed, but there's too much going on already to permit such departures. There is still the question of how any responsible company keeps in line with major transitions in social thinking. That's a good item for the Executive Committee meeting Monday.

"What would be involved in a long-run program of action? Should People's attempt to educate the public on these matters, and if so, how—a public relations program? Corporate advertising of institutional nature? What other educational techniques are there? We don't know much about that area. And, should we try to do something to educate the legislature? What can we give people who already can't read all they're supposed to? Should I take them to lunch in small groups? But can I afford that kind of time? Do we have anyone else who could be trusted to do this? What do legislators think when the 'second team' is sent up to talk to them?" Benton Hughes thought as he drove on: "Perhaps we need some outside help on these problems—but who *really* knows enough about our industry? Most of the consultants I've dealt with aren't very useful when intimate knowledge of the individual company situation and the environment in which it operates is required. And consultants are so terribly expensive when you don't know what you'll get from them. I've never seen a consultant yet who didn't recommend an action program well beyond the financial capacities of the company, or at least what I thought was beyond! But some people think I'm a "penny pincher." In any event why am I thinking about such bits and pieces when we haven't even been able to agree on what fundamental objectives the company has? What *are* we accomplishing? What do we *want* to accomplish? Is it realistic to want to accomplish these things? That meeting of the Planning Committee yesterday didn't get anywhere. Could it have been because we didn't have any goals clearly in mind? If I let myself think about a range of things *that* fundamental, I'll *never* be able to retire! But can I leave People's before we get the answers to questions like these?"

[1]The electric utilities in the U.S. have been criticized frequently and vehemently by conservation groups for not spending more time and money on research and development. The percent of the sales dollar spent on R & D by the utilities is admittedly low, relative to the representative industrial company, but the utilities point out that they are in the business of *supplying* electricity, and not making appliances or equipment which uses electricity. The bulk of the meaningful R & D would therefore be carried on by the equipment manufacturers. One experiment which has been conducted, however, does show promise. In an effort to reduce the rate at which peak usage has been growing, a substantial number of owners of "all-electric" houses have participated in an experiment through which radio-controlled switches at the electric company may be used to cut off the flow of power to heating panels and hot water tanks in individual homes. If a substantial usage of power may be cut off by this means just before the peak-usage period is reached, then the peak will be reduced and additional generation equipment will not be needed. The research has attempted to discover both how much power can be saved through this procedure and how long it will be before the customer realizes that he has had no power coming to his heating panels and hot water unit. There is little indication that customers notice anything has happened when the power is cut off for periods up to one-half hour in length.

[2]During the past three summers, when electric power has been so scarce in the eastern United States, a substantial number of "voltage reductions" have taken place. This means that instead of supplying electricity to customers at the normal 110 volts, regulating devices are adjusted to send a lesser voltage to the customers, thus saving power and spreading what is available among all users rather than cutting off electricity to some and supplying it to others. A voltage reduction of 5% is most frequent, and would be put into effect over a rather wide area; for example, if Consolidated Edison, in New York, has supply problems, a voltage reduction of 5% might be put into effect through all of the six New England states so that power could be released to New York City. A voltage reduction of 8% is the maximum which can be put into effect without being conspicuous to the customer and damaging to appliances and equipment. If an 8% voltage reduction were made, the customer might notice his TV picture shrinking slightly in size, his

electric stove taking longer to heat up, or electric motors taking longer to reach normal operating speed and with more heating up in the process. Normally, the public does not know that a voltage reduction occurred until it reads about it in the newspaper after the fact.

[3]Electricity is sold to retail customers by three types of utility: privately owned (investor-owned) companies, municipally owned and operated units, and co-operatives.

The co-operatives are owned by those to whom the electricity is sold, and each user of the power has one vote in meetings of the co-operative. The "co-ops" date from the 1930s, when a national agency, the Rural Electrification Administration (REA), was established to assist people (mostly farmers) living in areas of low population density in obtaining electric service they lacked. The forming of co-operatives was encouraged by the REA, and money was lent at 2% for constructing the facilities needed. This interest rate has not changed in the interim.

A substantial number of municipalities—mostly small—have chosen to own and operate their own facilities for electricity distribution. They can obtain funds for the facilities at lower cost than companies run on the basis of private capital. In addition, they do not have the burden of property taxes, although many make a contribution to the municipality in lieu of tax payments to remove this criticism. More than 75% of all electricity retailed in the United States is sold by the private companies, and the proportion of the power generated is substantially larger—90% approximately. The municipals and co-ops most frequently buy their power in part or whole from the private companies, which are large enough to build the very large and expensive plants needed for low-cost power.

QUESTIONS FOR ANALYSIS OF CASES

1. Using Exhibit 5–9, prepare a careful and thorough marketing audit for this situation. Be sure to cover both prognosis and diagnosis. Use the marketing relationships framework to identify key marketing elements in this situation.

2. On the basis of the marketing audit you have performed, specify organizational objectives in operational terms. Identify possible marketing objectives that must be accomplished if the basic organizational objective is to be met. Now develop a marketing plan, in terms of seeking, matching, programming, and consummating for this situation. Defend your recommendations.

Name Index

A

A & P (Great Atlantic & Pacific Tea Co.), 125, 343, 386, 415, 417, 420, 424, 427

Ackoff, Russell L., 182

Action for Children's Television (ACT), 393

Adler, Lee, 273, 306, 531

Advertising Age, 394, 395

Advertising Association, 375

Albaum, Gerald, 298

Alcoa (Aluminum Co. of America), 474

Alderson, Wroe, 29, 55, 573

Alexander, Ralph S., 82, 357

Alpert, Mark I, 474, 489

American Brands, 395

American Broadcasting Company (ABC), 475

American Cyanamid Co., 395

American Home Products, 395, 423

American Marketing Association, 18, 38, 41, 341, 342, 364, 365, 414, 431, 530

American Motors Corp., 395

American Telephone & Telegraph (AT&T), 184–86

Anheuser-Busch, Inc., 556

Armco Steel, 191–193, 380

Aspinwall, Leo V., 354

Associated Grocers, 427, 428

Avis Rent-a-Car, 403

B

Ballachey, Egerton L., 237

Barthol, Richard T., 217

Batten, Barton, Durstine, Osborn (BBDO), 215, 391

Bauer, P. T., 107

Bauer, Raymond A., 573

Behrens, W. W. III, 561

Beik, Leland, 531

Bell, Martin L., 41

Bell Laboratories, 340

Bennett, Peter D., 210, 237

Bentham, Jeremy, 199

Berelson, Bernard, 559

Berg, Thomas L., 329, 357

Better Business Bureau, 509

Better Homes and Gardens, 250

Bishop, James J., 136, 140

Blackwell, Roger D., 237, 427, 437

Blore, Chuck, 404

Bogue, Donald J., 558

Booz, Allen & Hamilton, Inc., 327

Borden, Neil H., 261–62

Boulding, Kenneth, 558

Boyd, Harper, Jr., 306

Brand Rating Research Corp., 253

Brien, Richard H., 300

Bristol Myers Co., 395, 423

Britton, Francis M., 57

Brooks, John, 357

Brooks Brothers, 260

Brown & Williamson Tobacco Co., 395

Browne, William, 561, 573, 574

Bucklin, Louis T., 426, 455

Burck, Gilbert, 158, 489

Burnett, Leo, 391

Burton, John, 278

Business Week, 50, 138, 146, 174, 184, 211, 255, 295, 329, 348, 404, 410, 446

Buzby, Stephen L., 531

C

Campbell, Donald, 306

Campbell's Soups, 417, 427

Carter, Jimmy, 402, 403

Caves, Richard, 158

Cayley, Murray A., 266

Choate, Robert, 40

Chrysler Corp., 395

City of the Future, 61–63

Clark, Thomas B., 561

Clausi, A. S., 328

Clorox Co., 395

Coca-Cola, 217, 258–59, 350, 393, 417, 427, 428

Colgate-Palmolive, 393, 395

Colley, Russell H., 203

Colliers Weekly, 134

Columbia Broadcasting Company (CBS), 475

Common Cause, 35

Consolidated Edison, 145

Consumer Reports, 204

Consumer Product Safety Commission, 475

Control Data Corp., 146, 556

Cottonwood Village, 315–17

Subject Index

normal distribution
  of human intelligence, 209E
processes
  learning, 216–18
  motivation, 212–16
  perception, 216
Inventory decisions, 439
  cost at service levels, 440E
  quantity
    economic order formula, 439–40
  timing of purchases, 440–42, 441E

J

Judgment sampling, 291

K

Kinked demand curve, 110E, 474

L

Learning
  concepts
    reinforcement, 217
    repetition, 217
  Howard-Sheth model of, 217
  Pavlov's experiments, 216–17
Leasing, 6
Leisure time newspaper, 307–09
Life cycle
  and buying behavior, 73
Lockheed loan guarantee, 132
Loyalty patterns, 230–31

M

Mail order houses, 119–20
Marginality
  and price, 461–62, 462E
Market
  development of, 7–8
Market chains, 125
Market concentration, 112
Market entry, barriers to, 112
  cost,
    absolute cost, 115
    economies of scale, 115
  marketing effort, 112–13
    product differentiation, 112
    promotion, 112
Market mechanism
  controls on the, 132–33
    legislature, 132

rationing, 134
    wage and price, 132
  devices
    exemptions, 139–43
    subsidies and loans, 131–32
    taxes and tariffs, 131
Market penetration
  through pricing, 480–81
Market potential, 257–8
Market programming
  systems approach to, 350E
Market segmentation
  concept of, 242
  criteria for
    accessibility, 243
    identity, 245
    responsiveness, 245
    significance, 245–46
  definition of, 242
  nature of, 242–43
Market segmentation demand
  concepts, 257–60
  measurement of, 257–58
Market segmentation strategies
  benefits
    customer focus, 243
    program formulation, 244
    target market selection, 244,
      258–60
      characteristics of 258–60
      and organizational situation,
        259–60
    view, 243E
  costs
    market coverage, 244–45
  hierarchy of bases, 246E
    customer state-of-being, 246
    customer state-of-mind, 249–52
    product benefit, 253–55
    product usage, 252–53
  and the marketing mix 260–62
  philosophies, 256–57, 257E
    concentrated marketing, 256
    differentiated marketing, 256
  process of formulation, 261E
    and the marketing management
      model, 35–37, 36E
  and the sales forecasting
    interpretations of, 263–64
Market structure continuum, 109E
  competition/monopoly continuum
    monopolistic (atomistic)
      competition, 109

About the Author

Ben M. Enis (Ph.D., Louisiana State University, 1967) is Professor of Marketing at the University of Houston. His teaching abilities have been recognized in awards presented by The College of Business Administration Alumni Association and by The Faculty Senate of the University of Houston. His teaching experience ranges from calculus to business policy and includes virtually every type of marketing course offered in a modern curriculum. He has taught freshmen, seniors, MBA students, Ph.D. candidates, and business executives.

Dr. Enis has written four previous books: *The Marketing Research Process* (with Keith K. Cox), *Marketing Classics* (Cox, co-editor), *Marketing Decisions: A Bayesian Approach* (with Charles L. Broome) and *Experimentation for Marketing Decisions* (with Cox). In addition, Enis has contributed a number of scholarly articles to such publications as *Journal of Marketing, Journal of Marketing Research, Journal of Advertising Research, Journal of Retailing, California Management Review, Business Horizons, Business and Society Review* and several issues of *American Marketing Association Conference Proceedings*. He is a member of the Editorial Board of the *Journal of Marketing*.

He is committed to marketing education. More than a dozen of his professional papers have been devoted to topics in this area. He has chaired both of the major education-oriented functions of the American Marketing Association: the Fall Educator's Conference and the Doctoral Consortium. In 1977, he was elected Vice-President for Education of the AMA.

Dr. Enis has also served as a consultant to firms in banking, retailing, building materials distribution, health care, consumer goods manufacturing, and publishing. He is a past president of the Houston Chapter of the American Marketing Association, and a member of the Houston Junior Chamber of Commerce.

Exhibit 2-5   The Marketing Management Model

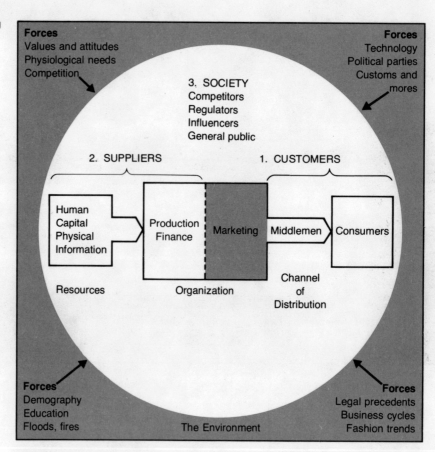

Forces
Values and attitudes
Physiological needs
Competition

Forces
Technology
Political parties
Customs and
mores

3. SOCIETY
Competitors
Regulators
Influencers
General public

2. SUPPLIERS   1. CUSTOMERS

Human
Capital
Physical
Information

Production
Finance

Marketing

Middlemen

Consumers

Resources   Organization

Channel
of
Distribution

Forces
Demography
Education
Floods, fires

The Environment

Forces
Legal precedents
Business cycles
Fashion trends